Business Insights	Companies in Assig...
Warren Buffet on MD&A Warren Buffet on Management Talk Warren Buffet on Audit Committees	Abercrombie & Fitch, Briggs & Stratton, Cisco, ...olive, Dell, DuPont, Ford, Intel, JetBlue, Kraft , Nordstrom, General Mills, General Motors, Hewlett-Packard, Kimberly-Clark, McDonald's, Merck, Motorola, Nokia, Procter & Gamble, Wal-Mart, Walt Disney, Winn-Dixie
Disney Abandons GO.Com Disney's Film and Television Costs How Much Disney Debt is Reasonable? Disney's Unrecognized Liabilities Disney's Book and Market Values	Abercrombie & Fitch, Albertsons, Briggs & Stratton, Harley-Davidson, Kimberly-Clark, Microsoft, Nike, Nordstrom, Procter & Gamble, Starbuck's, Target, 3M, World Wrestling Entertainment
3M's Return on Equity Breakdown The 3M Margin Turnover at 3M	Abercrombie & Fitch, Albertsons, Alcoa, Caterpillar, Coca-Cola, Colgate-Palmolive, CVS, The Gap, Harley-Davidson, Home Depot, Kroger, McDonald's, Merck, Nike , PepsiCo, Proctor & Gamble, Reebok, SBC Communications, Southwest Airlines, Target, Toys "R"Us, Verizon Communications, Viacom, Wal-Mart, Walt Disney, Walgreen
Ratio Equilibrium Cisco's Revenue Recognition Disney's Revenue Recognition Cisco's R&D Cisco's Restructuring Pro Forma Income and Managerial Motives	Abbott Laboratories, Abercrombie & Fitch, Agilent Technologies, Altria, Amazon.Com, AOL Time Warner, Bank of America, Banner Ad Corporation, Bristol-Myers Squibb, CVS, Dell, Dow Chemical, eBay, FedEx, The Gap, General Electric, Hewlett-Packard, Honeywell International, Intuit, Johnson Controls, Miller Brewing, Merck, Oracle, Pfizer, Real Money.Com, The Street.Com, 3M, Viacom, Walgreen, Xerox
Sears' Cookie Jar WorldCom and Improper Cost Capitalization	Abbott Laboratories, AOL Time Warner, Best Buy, Carnival, Caterpillar, Colgate-Palmolive, Deere & Company, General Electric, Harley-Davidson, Hewlett-Packard, Intel, Kaiser Aluminum, Kmart, Kraft Foods, Microsoft, Oracle, Procter & Gamble, Rohm and Haas, Sears, Sharper Image, Stride Rite, 3M, Texas Instruments, WW Grainger
Pitfalls of Acquired Growth HP's Post-Acquisition Accounting Under Fire	Abbott Laboratories, Amgen, Berkshire Hathaway, Caterpillar, CNA Financial, DuPont, General Mills, Hewlett-Packard, MetLife, Merck, Pfizer, Shin Caterpillar Mitsubishi
Verizon's Zero Coupon Debt	Abbott Laboratories, AT&T, Boston Scientific, Bristol-Myers Squibb, Comcast, CVS, Fitch Ratings, General Mills, International Paper, Lockheed Martin, Southwest Airlines
2004's Top 10 Global Stock Issuances 2004's Top 10 Global Underwriters of Equity Issuances	Abercrombie & Fitch, Altria, AT&T, Bristol-Myers Squibb, Caterpillar, Fortune Brands, IMS Health, JetBlue Airlines
Imputed Discount Rate for Leases How Pensions Confound Income Analysis	Abercrombie & Fitch, American Express, Best Buy, Dow Chemical, FedEx, Fortune Brands, General Motors, Reebok, Southwest Airlines, Staples
What is eBay's Income? What is eBay's Operating Cash Flow? Tyco Buys Operating Cash Flow	Abercrombie & Fitch, Best Buy, Bristol-Myers Squibb, Black & Decker, Cingular Wireless, The Gap, General Mills, Harley-Davidson, Merck, Midwest Airlines, Nike, SBC Communications
Analysts' Earnings Forecasts	Abbott Laboratories, Abercrombie & Fitch, Albertsons, FedEx, Harley-Davidson, PepsiCo, 3M, Starbucks
Comprehensive Case	Comprehensive Case

Second Edition

Financial Accounting for MBAs

PETER D. EASTON

JOHN J. WILD

ROBERT F. HALSEY

Cambridge
BUSINESS PUBLISHERS

To my daughters, Joanne and Stacey
    —PDE

To my wife Gail and children, Kimberly, Jonathan, Stephanie, and Trevor;
and my parents, Leonard and Mary
    —JJW

To my wife Ellie and children, Grace and Christian
    —RFH

Cambridge Business Publishers

FINANCIAL ACCOUNTING FOR MBAs, Second Edition, by Peter D. Easton,
John J. Wild, and Robert F. Halsey.

ISBN 0-9759701-1-9

To order this book, contact the company via email **customerservice@cambridgepub.com** or call
800-619-6473.

For permission to use material from this text, contact the company via email
permissions@cambridgepub.com.

Printed in the United States of America.
10 9 8 7 6 5 4 3 2 1

ABOUT THE AUTHORS

The combined skills and expertise of Easton, Wild, and Halsey create the ideal team to author the first new financial accounting textbook for MBAs in more than a generation. Their collective experience in award-winning teaching, consulting, and research in the area of financial accounting and analysis provides a powerful foundation for this innovative textbook.

Peter D. Easton is an expert in accounting and valuation and holds the Notre Dame Alumni Chair in Accountancy in the Mendoza College of Business. Professor Easton's expertise is widely recognized by the academic research community and by the legal community. Professor Easton has been qualified as an expert witness in the Delaware Chancery Court and he has consulted on valuation issues for investment firms and accounting firms in Australia, the UK, and the USA.

Professor Easton holds undergraduate degrees from the University of Adelaide and the University of South Australia. He holds a graduate degree from the University of New England and a PhD in Business Administration (majoring in accounting and finance) from the University of California, Berkeley.

Professor Easton's research on corporate valuation has been published in the *Journal of Accounting and Economics, Journal of Accounting Research, The Accounting Review, Contemporary Accounting Research, Review of Accounting Studies,* and *Journal of Business Finance and Accounting.* Professor Easton has served as an associate editor for 11 leading accounting journals and he is currently an associate editor for the *Journal of Accounting Research, Contemporary Accounting Research, Journal of Business Finance and Accounting,* and *Journal of Accounting, Auditing, and Finance.* He is an editor of the *Review of Accounting Studies.*

Professor Easton has held appointments at the University of Chicago, the University of California at Berkeley, Ohio State University, Macquarie University, the Australian Graduate School of Management, the University of Melbourne, and Nyenrode University. He is the recipient of numerous awards for excellence in teaching and in research. Professor Easton regularly teaches accounting analysis and security valuation to MBAs. In addition, Professor Easton has taught managerial accounting at the graduate level.

John J. Wild is professor of accounting and the Robert and Monica Beyer Distinguished Professor at the University of Wisconsin at Madison. He previously held appointments at Michigan State University and the University of Manchester in England. He received his BBA, MS, and PhD from the University of Wisconsin.

Professor Wild teaches courses in accounting and analysis at both the undergraduate and graduate levels. He has received the Mabel W. Chipman Excellence-in-Teaching Award, the departmental Excellence-in-Teaching Award, and the MBA Teaching Excellence Award from the 2003 graduation class at the University of Wisconsin. He also received the Beta Alpha Psi and Salmonson Excellence-in-Teaching Award from Michigan State University. Professor Wild is a past KPMG Peat Marwick National Fellow and is a prior recipient of fellowships from the American Accounting Association and the Ernst & Young Foundation.

Professor Wild is an active member of the American Accounting Association and its sections. He has served on several committees of these organizations, including the Outstanding Accounting Educator Award, Wildman Award, National Program Advisory, Publications, and Research Committees. Professor Wild is author of several best-selling books. His research articles on financial accounting and analysis appear in *The Accounting Review, Journal of Accounting Research, Journal of Accounting and Economics, Contemporary Accounting Research, Journal of Accounting, Auditing & Finance, Journal of Accounting and Public Policy, Journal of Business Finance and Accounting, Auditing: A Journal of Theory and Practice,* and other accounting and business journals. He is past associate editor of *Contemporary Accounting Research* and has served on editorial boards of several respected journals, including *The Accounting Review* and the *Journal of Accounting and Public Policy.*

Robert F. Halsey is an associate professor at Babson College. He received his MBA and PhD from the University of Wisconsin. Prior to obtaining his PhD he worked as the chief financial officer (CFO) of a privately held retailing and manufacturing company and as the vice president and manager of the commercial lending division of a large bank.

Professor Halsey teaches courses in financial and managerial accounting at both the graduate and undergraduate levels, including a popular course in financial statement analysis for second year MBA students. He has also taught numerous executive education courses for large multinational companies through Babson's School of Executive Education as well as for a number of stock brokerage firms in the Boston area. He is regarded as an innovative teacher and has been recognized for outstanding teaching at both the University of Wisconsin and Babson College. He is the recipient of an Ernst & Young Fellowship and is a member of the Beta Gamma Sigma and Phi Eta Sigma honor societies.

Professor Halsey's research interests are in the area of financial reporting, including firm valuation, financial statement analysis, and disclosure issues. He is the coauthor of *Financial Statement Analysis,* published by McGraw-Hill/Irwin, and has publications in *Advances in Quantitative Analysis of Finance and Accounting, The Journal of the American Taxation Association, Issues in Accounting Education, The Portable MBA in Finance and Accounting* (3rd ed.), the *CPA Journal, AICPA Professor/Practitioner Case Development Program,* and in other accounting and analysis journals. He has also developed exam preparation materials for the CFA examination and administers numerous CFA review courses in the Northeast.

PREFACE

Welcome to *Financial Accounting for MBAs, Second Edition.* Our main goal in writing this book was to satisfy the needs of today's business manager by providing the most contemporary, engaging, and user-oriented textbook available. This book is the product of extensive market research including focus groups, market surveys, class tests, manuscript reviews, and interviews with faculty from across the country. We are grateful to students and faculty who used the First Edition and whose feedback greatly benefited this Second Edition.

> "This is a fantastic book. It strikes the right balance between accounting details and user-oriented analysis. The students are going to love it."
> —Xiao-Jun Zhang, *University of California–Berkeley*

■ TARGET AUDIENCE

Financial Accounting for MBAs is intended for use in full-time, part-time, executive, and evening MBA programs that include a financial accounting course as part of the curriculum, and one in which managerial decision making and analysis are emphasized. This book easily accommodates mini-courses lasting only several days as well as extended courses lasting a full semester.

> "The authors have accomplished their goal of writing a book that is appropriate for MBA and Executive courses."
> —Greg Miller, *Harvard Business School*

■ INNOVATIVE APPROACH

Financial Accounting for MBAs is managerially oriented and focuses on the most salient aspects of accounting. It teaches MBA students how to read, analyze, and interpret financial accounting data to make informed business decisions. This textbook makes financial accounting **engaging**, **relevant**, and **contemporary**. To that end, it consistently incorporates **real company data**, both in the body of each module and throughout assignment material.

> "A very refreshing way of presenting the materials and up-to-date on the topics."
> —Sri Sridharan, *Northwestern University*

■ FLEXIBLE STRUCTURE

The MBA curricula, instructor preferences, and course lengths vary across schools. Accordingly and to the extent possible, the 12 **modules** that make up *Financial Accounting for MBAs* were designed independently of one another. This modular presentation enables each school and instructor to "customize" the book to best fit the needs of their students. Our introduction and discussion of financial statements constitute Modules 1 and 2. Module 3 presents the analysis of financial statements with an emphasis on profitability analysis. Modules 4 through 9 highlight major financial accounting topics including assets, liabilities, equity, and off-balance-sheet financing. Module 10 explains adjusting and forecasting financial statements. Module 11 introduces simple valuation models. Module 12 concludes with a comprehensive case on Kimberly-Clark and acts as a capstone for the course.

Flexibility for Courses of Varying Lengths

Many instructors have approached us to ask about suggested class structures based on courses of varying length. To that end, we provide the following table of possible course designs:

	15 Week Semester Course	10 Week Quarter Course	6 Week Mini Course	1 Week Intensive Course
Module 1 Introducing Financial Accounting for MBAs	Week 1	Week 1	Week 1	Day 1
Module 2 Constructing and Reporting Financial Statements	Week 2	Week 2	Week 2	
Module 3 Analyzing and Interpreting Financial Statements	Weeks 3 and 4	Week 3	Week 3	Day 2
Module 4 Reporting and Analyzing Operating Income	Week 5	Week 4	Skim	Skim
Module 5 Reporting and Analyzing Operating Assets	Week 6	Week 5	Week 4	Day 3
Module 6 Reporting and Analyzing Intercorporate Investments	Week 7	Optional	Optional	Optional
Module 7 Reporting and Analyzing Nonowner Financing	Week 8	Week 6	Week 5	Day 4
Module 8 Reporting and Analyzing Owner Financing	Week 9	Week 7	Week 6	Day 5
Module 9 Reporting and Analyzing Off-Balance-Sheet Financing	Weeks 10 and 11	Week 8	Optional	Optional
Module 10 Adjusting and Forecasting Financial Statements	Week 12	Week 9	Optional	Optional
Module 11 Analyzing and Valuing Equity Securities	Week 13	Week 10	Optional	Optional
Module 12 Constructing and Illustrating a Comprehensive Case	Week 14	Optional	Optional	Optional

> "A breath of fresh air—it is a text with a format and structure that breaks, a bit, from the traditional path followed by other financial accounting textbooks."
> —**Charles Wasley,** *University of Rochester*

Flexibility for Courses of Varying Emphases

Faculty feedback identifies a wide range of instructional approaches to the MBA core course. Anchoring the two ends of this spectrum are a core "financial accounting" focus and a core "accounting, analysis, and valuation" focus. The following alternative course structures represent these two approaches. Based on personal preference, your course might mirror one of these approaches or represent a blend of the two.

Core Financial Accounting	Core Accounting, Analysis and Valuation
Module 1 Introducing Financial Accounting for MBAs	Module 1 Introducing Financial Accounting for MBAs
Module 2 Constructing and Reporting Financial Statements	Module 2 Constructing and Reporting Financial Statements
Module 4 Reporting and Analyzing Operating Income	Module 3 Analyzing and Interpreting Financial Statements
Module 5 Reporting and Analyzing Operating Assets	Module 4 Reporting and Analyzing Operating Income
Module 6 Reporting and Analyzing Intercorporate Investments	Module 9 Reporting and Analyzing Off-Balance-Sheet Financing (optional)
Module 7 Reporting and Analyzing Nonowner Financing	Module 10 Adjusting and Forecasting Financial Statements
Module 8 Reporting and Analyzing Owner Financing	Module 11 Analyzing and Valuing Company Securities
Module 9 Reporting and Analyzing Off-Balance-Sheet Financing (optional)	Module 12 Constructing and Illustrating a Comprehensive Case (optional)

■ MANAGERIAL EMPHASIS

As MBA instructors we recognize that the core MBA financial accounting course is not directed toward accounting majors. *Financial Accounting for MBAs* embraces this reality. This book highlights **financial reporting**, **analysis**, **interpretation**, and **decision making**, and downplays accounting mechanics such as detailed journal entries and ledger preparation. We do, however, incorporate the following **financial statement effects template** when relevant to train MBA students in understanding the economic ramifications of transactions and their impacts on all key financial statements. This analytical tool is a great resource for MBA students in learning accounting and applying it to their future courses and careers.

Transaction	Balance Sheet					Income Statement	
	Cash Asset	+ Noncash Assets	= Liabil- ities	+ Contrib. Capital	+ Retained Earnings	Revenues	− Expenses

Tomorrow's MBA graduates must be skilled in using financial statements to make business decisions. These skills often require application of ratio analyses, benchmarking, forecasting, valuation, and other aspects of financial statement analysis to decision making. Furthermore, tomorrow's MBA graduates must have the skills to go beyond basic financial statements and to interpret and apply nonfinancial statement disclosures, such as footnotes and supplementary reports.

This book, therefore, emphasizes real company data, including detailed footnote and other management disclosures, and shows how to use this information to make managerial inferences and decisions. This approach makes financial accounting interesting and relevant for all MBA students.

"There is a strong and consistent emphasis on managerial decision making. The use of actual financial statement data and detailed company profiles allows students to think concretely about the concepts being presented."
—**Court Huber,** *University of Texas–Austin*

■ INNOVATIVE PEDAGOGY

Financial Accounting for MBAs includes special features specifically designed for the MBA student.

Focus Companies for Each Module

Each module's content is explained through the accounting and reporting activities of real companies. To that end, each module incorporates a "focus company" for special emphasis and demonstration. The enhanced instructional value of focus companies comes from the way they engage MBA students in real analysis and interpretation. Focus companies were selected based on the industries that MBA students typically enter upon graduation.

Focus Company by Module

MODULE 1	Berkshire Hathaway	MODULE 7	Verizon Communications
MODULE 2	Walt Disney Company	MODULE 8	Pfizer
MODULE 3	3M	MODULE 9	Midwest Airlines
MODULE 4	Cisco Systems	MODULE 10	Procter & Gamble
MODULE 5	Gillette Company	MODULE 11	Johnson & Johnson
MODULE 6	Hewlett-Packard	MODULE 12	Kimberly-Clark

"This book uses real world examples to illustrate major accounting concepts; the illustration is concise yet comprhensive."
    —Agnes Cheng, *University of Houston*

Real Company Data Throughout

Market research and reviewer feedback tell us that one of instructors' greatest frustrations with other MBA textbooks is their lack of real company data. We have gone to great lengths to incorporate real company data throughout each module to reinforce important concepts and engage MBA students. We engage nonaccounting MBA students specializing in finance, marketing, management, real estate, operations, and so forth, with companies and scenarios that are relevant to them. For representative examples, **SEE PAGES 3-6; 4-5; 5-10.**

"A book that includes more real-company material in the text and problems than do other books, and a book that includes financial statement analysis in a more central way."
    —Sanjay Kallapur, *Purdue University*

Managerial and Decision Making Orientation

One primary goal of an MBA financial accounting course is to teach students the skills needed to apply their accounting knowledge to solving real business problems and making informed business decisions. With that goal in mind, Managerial Decision boxes in each module encourage students to apply the material presented to solving actual business scenarios. For representative examples, **SEE PAGES 4-22; 5-31; 7-22.**

"I like the managerial decision boxes. I think these are great for MBAs because they illustrate and motivate why accounting is important for managers."
    —Michelle Yetman, *University of California–Davis*

Research Insights for MBAs

Academic research plays an important role in the way business is conducted, accounting is performed, and students are taught. It is important for students to recognize how modern research and modern business practice interact. Therefore, we periodically incorporate relevant research to help students understand the important relation between research and modern business. For representative examples, **SEE PAGES 3-9; 4-25; 10-7.**

Mid-Module and Module-End Reviews

Financial accounting can be challenging—especially for MBA students lacking business experience or previous exposure to business courses. To reinforce concepts presented in each module and to ensure student comprehension, we include mid-module and module-end reviews that require students to recall and apply the financial accounting techniques and concepts described in each module. For representative examples, **SEE PAGES 3-11; 10-9; 10-20.**

> "The mid-module reviews are a very good idea . . . The quicker and more often real company data is used in textbook chapters, the easier I think it is to motivate student interest in financial accounting and why it will be important to them once they graduate."
> —**Charles Wasley,** *University of Rochester*

Excellent, Class-Tested Assignment Materials

Excellent assignment material is a must-have component of any successful textbook (and class). We went to great lengths to create the best assignments possible. In keeping with the rest of the book, we used real company data extensively. We also ensured that assignments reflect our belief that MBA students should be trained in analyzing accounting information to make business decisions, as opposed to working on mechanical bookkeeping tasks. Assignments encourage students to analyze accounting information, interpret it, and apply the knowledge gained to a business decision. There are four categories of assignments: **Discussion Questions**, **Mini Exercises**, **Exercises**, and **Problems**. For representative examples, **SEE PAGES 3-34; 5-40; 9-32.**

> "The assignment materials require students to use actual financial statement information from a large numbr of companies, thus providing students with exposure to varying styles of presentation and disclosures in financial reporting."
> —**Jeff Williams,** *Ross School of Business, University of Michigan*

■ SECOND EDITION CHANGES

Based on classroom use and reviewer feedback, a number of substantive changes have been made in the second edition:

- Sophisticated four-color design to engage MBA students without distracting them.
- Greater use of real companies throughout the book and assignments, and business news and financial reports as recent as January 2005.
- Painstaking revision of each module to make each as self-contained as possible for maximum instructor flexibility.
- Revision of financial statement effects template (introduced in Module 2) to show the cash flow source by activity (operating, investing, or financing).
- Revision of financial statement effects template to include journal entries in the margin adjacent to each transaction analyzed. For faculty wishing to minimize accounting mechanics, the journal entries can be ignored without any loss of insight into or knowledge gained from the template.
- Appendix 2A on Transaction Analysis is expanded to cover additional transaction types and to include journal entries.
- Placement of Analyzing and Valuing Equity Securities (formerly Module 3) after Adjusting and Forecasting Financial Statements (Module 10) to ease students' transition into valuation.
- New focus companies for Module 10 on Adjusting and Forecasting Financial Statements (Proctor & Gamble) and for Module 11 on Analyzing and Valuing Equity Securities (Johnson & Johnson).
- Use of Proctor & Gamble for the Mid-Module and Module-End Reviews in Module 11 so students covering both Modules 10 and 11 can follow P&G from the adjusting and forecasting processes through the valuation process.

- Streamlined Module 11 on Analyzing and Valuing Equity Securities for easier classroom use.
- New comprehensive case featuring Kimberly-Clark (Module 12) to act as a capstone for the entire course by: reviewing financial statements (and related reports); recapping the analysis and forecasting of those statements; and valuing equity securities.
- A *Cash Effect Icon* is included in the book margin when we encounter and discuss important cash flow implications from a transaction. This icon (see margin) appears in each module and where appropriate.

$
Cash Effect

■ SUPPLEMENT PACKAGE

For Instructors

Electronic Solutions Manual: Created by the authors, the *Instructor's Manual with Solutions* contains teaching outlines and complete solutions to all the assignment material in the text.

PowerPoint: Created by the authors, the PowerPoint slides outline key elements of each module.

Electronic Test Bank: Written by the authors, the test bank includes multiple-choice items, matching questions, short essay questions, and problems.

Web Site: All instructor materials are accessible via the book's website (password protected) along with other useful links and information. www.cambridgepub.com

For Students

Student Solutions Manual: Created by the authors, the student solutions manual contains all solutions to the even-numbered assignment materials in the textbook. This is a restricted item that is only available to students after their instructor has authorized its purchase. **ISBN 0-9759701-2-7**

Web Site: Practice quizzes and other useful links are available to students free of charge on the book's website. www.cambridgepub.com

■ ACKNOWLEDGMENTS

The first and second editions of this book benefited greatly from the invaluable feedback of focus group attendees, reviewers, students, and colleagues. We are extremely grateful to them for their help in making this project a success.

Denny Beresford, *University of Georgia*
Mark Bradshaw, *Harvard University*
Lisa Bryant, *University of Oregon*
Agnes Cheng, *University of Houston*
Carol Dee, *Florida State University*
Elizabeth Demers, *University of Rochester*
Vicki Dickinson, *University of Wisconsin*
Jeffrey T. Doyle, *University of Utah*
Tom Dyckman, *Cornell University*
John Eichenseher, *University of Wisconsin*
Gerard Engeholm, *Pace University*
Mark Finn, *Northwestern University*
Richard Frankel, *Massachusetts Institute of Technology*
Marc Giullian, *Montana State University*
Jerry C.Y. Han, *University of Buffalo*
Carla Hayn, *University of California–Los Angeles*
Frank Heflin, *Northwestern University*
Clayton Hock, *Miami University*
Court Huber, *University of Texas*
Sanjay Kallapur, *Purdue University*
Ronald King, *Washington University*

Joshua Livnat, *New York University*
Barbara Lougee, *University of California–Irvine*
Gregory Miller, *Harvard University*
Dennis Murray, *University of Colorado–Denver*
Sandeep Nabar, *University of Oklahoma*
Kathy Petroni, *Michigan State University*
Kirk Philipich, *Ohio State University*
Morton Pincus, *University of Iowa*
Grace Pownall, *Emory University*
Susan Riffe, *Southern Methodist University*
Kenneth Shaw, *University of Missouri*
Pam Smith, *Northern Illinois University*
Sri Sridharan, *Northwestern University*
Charles Stanley, *Baylor University*
K.R. Subramanyam, *University of Southern California*
Gary Taylor, *University of Alabama*
Charles Wasley, *University of Rochester*
Greg Waymire, *Emory University*
Jeff Williams, *University of Michigan*
Michelle Yetman, *University of California–Davis*
Xiao-Jun Zhang, *University of California–Berkeley*

In addition, we are extremely grateful to George Werthman and the entire team at Cambridge Business Publishers for their encouragement, enthusiasm, and guidance. Their market research, editorial development, and promotional efforts surpassed our expectations. We have had a very positive textbook authoring experience thanks, in large part, to our publisher.

Peter D. Easton   John J. Wild   Robert F. Halsey

March 2005

COMPANIES USED IN ASSIGNMENTS

Module	Focus Company	Companies Featured in Assignments
Module 1 Introducing Financial Accounting for MBAs	Berkshire Hathaway	Abercrombie & Fitch; Briggs & Stratton; Cisco; Colgate-Palmolive; Dell; DuPont; Ford; Intel; JetBlue; Kraft; Nordstrom; General Mills; General Motors; Hewlett-Packard; Kimberly-Clark; McDonald's; Merck; Motorola; Nokia; Procter & Gamble; Wal-Mart; Walt Disney; Winn-Dixie
Module 2 Constructing and Reporting Financial Statements	The Walt Disney Company	Abercrombie & Fitch; Albertsons; Briggs & Stratton; Harley-Davidson; Kimberly-Clark; Microsoft; Nike; Nordstrom; Procter & Gamble; Starbuck's; Target; 3M; World Wrestling Entertainment
Module 3 Analyzing and Interpreting Financial Statements	3M	Abercrombie & Fitch; Albertsons; Alcoa; Caterpillar; Coca-Cola; Colgate-Palmolive; CVS; The Gap; Harley-Davidson; Home Depot; Kroger; McDonald's; Merck; Nike; PepsiCo; Proctor & Gamble; Reebok; SBC Communications; Southwest Airlines; Target; Toys-R-Us; Verizon Communications; Viacom; Wal-Mart; Walt Disney; Walgreen
Module 4 Reporting and Analyzing Operating Income	Cisco Systems	Abbott Laboratories; Abercrombie & Fitch; Agilent Technologies; Altria; Amazon; AOL Time Warner; Bank of America; Banner Ad Corporation; Bristol-Myers Squibb; CVS; Dell; Dow Chemical; eBay; FedEx; The Gap; General Electric; Hewlett-Packard; Honeywell International; Intuit; Johnson Controls; Miller Brewing; Merck; Oracle; Pfizer; Real Money.Com; The Street.Com; 3M; Viacom; Walgreen; Xerox
Module 5 Reporting and Analyzing Operating Assets	Gillette Company	Abbot Laboratories; AOL Time Warner; Best Buy; Carnival; Caterpillar; Colgate-Palmolive; Deere & Company; General Electric; Harley-Davidson; Hewlett-Packard; Intel; Kaiser Aluminum; Kmart; Kraft Foods; Microsoft; Oracle; Procter & Gamble; Rohm and Haas; Sears; Sharper Image; Stride Rite; 3M; Texas Instruments; WW Grainger
Module 6 Reporting and Analyzing Intercorporate Investments	Hewlett-Packard	Abbott Laboratories; Amgen; Berkshire Hathaway; Caterpillar; CNA Financial; DuPont; General Mills; Hewlett-Packard; MetLife; Merck; Pfizer; Shin Caterpillar Mitsubishi
Module 7 Reporting and Analyzing Nonowner Financing	Verizon Communications, Inc.	Abbott Laboratories; AT&T; Boston Scientific; Bristol-Myers Squibb; Comcast; CVS; Fitch Ratings, LTD; General Mills; International Paper; Lockheed Martin; Southwest Airlines
Module 8 Reporting and Analyzing Owner Financing	Pfizer	Abercrombie & Fitch; Altria; AT&T; Bristol-Myers Squibb; Caterpillar; Fortune Brands; IMS Health; JetBlue Airlines; Lucent Technologies; Merck; Proctor & Gamble; Viacom
Module 9 Reporting and Analyzing Off-Balance-Sheet Financing	Midwest Airlines	Abercrombie & Fitch; American Express; Best Buy; Dow Chemical; FedEx; Fortune Brands; General Motors; Reebok; Southwest Airlines; Staples; Target Corporation; Verizon Communications; Xerox; Yum Brands
Module 10 Adjusting and Forecasting Financial Statements	Procter & Gamble	Abercrombie & Fitch; Best Buy; Bristol-Myers Squibb; Black & Decker; Cingular Wireless; The Gap; General Mills; Harley-Davidson; Merck; Midwest Airlines; Nike; SBC Communications; Target; Toys-R-Us; Tyco International; Walgreens; Wal-Mart; Xerox
Module 11 Analyzing and Valuing Equity Securities	Johnson & Johnson	Abbott Laboratories; Abercrombie & Fitch; Albertson's; FedEx; Harley-Davidson; PepsiCo; 3M; Starbucks; Target
Module 12 Constructing and Illustrating a Comprehensive Case	Kimberly-Clark	Comprehensive Case

BRIEF CONTENTS

CONTENTS

MODULE 6

Reporting and Analyzing Intercorporate Investments   6-1

MODULE 7

Reporting and Analyzing Nonowner Financing   7-1

MODULE 8

Reporting and Analyzing Owner Financing   8-1

1

Introducing Financial Accounting for MBAs

SAGE OF OMAHA AND THE POWER OF ACCOUNTING

Berkshire Hathaway, Inc., is a holding company. It owns subsidiaries that pursue diverse business activities.[1] In 2003, Berkshire Hathaway reported total assets of $181 billion, stockholders' equity of $78 billion, sales of $64 billion, and 172,000 employees.

The legendary Warren Buffet, the 'Sage of Omaha,' who studied under the renowned Benjamin Graham (a founder of modern value-investing), manages Berkshire Hathaway. Buffet's investment philosophy is to acquire and hold businesses over the long run. His acquisition criteria, taken from his annual report, follow:

1. Large purchases (at least $50 million of before-tax earnings).
2. Demonstrated consistent earning power (future projections are of no interest to us, nor are 'turnaround' situations).
3. Businesses earning good returns on equity while employing little or no debt.
4. Management in place (we can't supply it).
5. Simple businesses (if there's lots of technology, we won't understand it).
6. An offering price (we don't want to waste our time or that of the seller by talking, even preliminarily, about a transaction when price is unknown).

At least three of Buffet's six criteria relate to financial performance. First, he seeks businesses with large and consistent earning power. Buffet is not only looking for solid historical earnings, but earnings that are measured according to accounting policies that closely mirror the underlying economic performance of the company. This will be a recurring theme as we discuss the differing character of operating and nonoperating sources of earnings as well as the impact that estimates and accounting policies have on numbers reported in the balance sheet and income statement.

Second, Buffet focuses on businesses earning good returns on equity, defined as net income divided by average equity: "Our preference would be to reach our goal by directly owning a diversified group of

---

[1]These include insurance (GEICO, General Re, and Berkshire Hathaway Reinsurance Division), manufacturing (Shaw Industries, Benjamin Moore, Johns Manville, and Fruit of the Loom), food distribution (McLane Company), flight training (FlightSafety International), aircraft leasing (NetJets®), home furnishing retailers (Nebraska Furniture Mart, RC Willey Home Furnishings, Star Furniture, and Jordan's Furniture), jewelry retailers (Borsheim's, Helzberg's Diamond Shops, and Ben Bridge Jeweler), financial products (BH Finance, Berkshire Hathaway Credit Corporation, XTRA, and CORT), publishing (Buffalo News), confectionary products (See's Candies), dairy treats (International Dairy Queen), and kitchen supplies (The Pampered Chef®).

businesses that generate cash and consistently earn above-average returns on capital" (Berkshire Hathaway 2002 annual report). Return on equity (capital) is a metric that many decision makers use to evaluate financial performance. It uses accounting information from both the income statement and the balance sheet. To achieve high-performance on this metric, managers must simultaneously focus on both of these financial statements. We describe a similar return in this module and again in our module on financial statement analysis.

Third, Buffet values companies based on their ability to generate consistent earnings and cash. He focuses on *intrinsic value*, which he defines in each annual report as follows:

> Intrinsic value is an all-important concept that offers the only logical approach to evaluating the relative attractiveness of investments and businesses. Intrinsic value can be defined simply: It is the discounted value of the cash that can be taken out of a business during its remaining life.

The discounted value Buffet describes is the present (today's) value of the cash flows the company expects to generate in the future. This concept of valuation is similar to the economists' notion of economic profit.

Cash is generated when companies operate profitably and efficiently. Like return on equity, positive cash flows result from good management of both the balance sheet and income statement. Over the long run, returns on equity are linked with cash flows.

Warren Buffet provides some especially useful investment guidance in his Chairman's letter from the Berkshire Hathaway 2002 annual report:

> Three suggestions for investors: First, beware of companies displaying weak accounting. If a company still does not expense options, or if its pension assumptions are fanciful, watch out. When managements take the low road in aspects that are visible, it is likely they are following a similar path behind the scenes. There is seldom just one cockroach in the kitchen.

> Second, unintelligible footnotes usually indicate untrustworthy management. If you can't understand a footnote or other managerial explanation, it's usually because the CEO doesn't want you to. Enron's descriptions of certain transactions still baffle me.

> Finally, be suspicious of companies that trumpet earnings projections and growth expectations. Businesses seldom operate in a tranquil, no-surprise environment, and earnings simply don't advance smoothly (except, of course, in the offering books of investment bankers).

(Continued on next page)

(Continued from previous page)

This book will explain Buffet's references to stock option accounting and pension assumptions as well as a whole host of other accounting issues that affect interpretation and valuation of company financial performance. We will analyze and interpret the footnotes, which Buffet views as crucial to successful analysis. Our philosophy is simple: we must understand the intricacies of financial reporting to become a critical reader and user of financial reports for company analysis and valuation. Financial statements tell a story, a business story. The task is to understand that story, analyze and interpret it in the context of competing stories, and apply the knowledge gleaned to business decisions.

Sources: *Berkshire Hathaway* 2003 10-K Report, *Berkshire Hathaway* 2003, 2002, and 2001 Annual Reports.

■ REPORTING ON BUSINESS ACTIVITIES

To effectively manage a company or infer whether it is well managed, we must understand business activities. The information system called *financial accounting* contributes to our understanding of these business activities. This system reports on a company's performance and financial condition, and conveys privileged information and insights of executive management.

Financial accounting information helps us, as managers, to evaluate potential future strategies and ascertain the effectiveness of present and past strategies. It improves the soundness of our investment decisions, such as how to allocate scarce resources across alternative investment projects and whether to invest additional resources in existing product lines or divisions. Financial accounting information is also used to prepare client proposals, analyze the effectiveness of production processes, and evaluate the performance of management teams.

Information that flows from the financial accounting system also helps us, as investors, to select the company whose common stock we purchase. Yet before it is used to make decisions, the financial accounting information must be scrutinized and sometimes adjusted. This is accomplished in part by analyzing information contained in footnotes to companies' financial reports so as to determine the quality of reported figures and any necessary adjustments.

More generally, financial accounting satisfies the needs of different groups of users. Within firms, the *functioning* of this information system involves application of accounting standards to produce financial reports. Effectively *using* this information system involves making judgments, assumptions, and estimates based on data contained in the financial reports. The greatest value we derive from this system as users of financial information is the insights we gain into business activities.

To effectively analyze and use accounting information, we must consider the business context in which it is created—see Exhibit 1.1. Without exception, all companies *plan* business activities, *finance*

EXHIBIT 1.1 ■ Business Activities

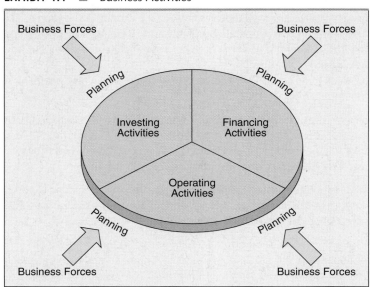

those activities, *invest* in those activities, and then engage in *operating* activities. Firms conduct all these activities while confronting *business forces,* including market constraints and competitive pressures. Examining each of these business activities helps us better understand the context of financial accounting and its proper application and interpretation.

Reporting of Planning Activities

The goals and objectives of a company are the outputs of its planning activities. Berkshire Hathaway, for example, strives to own a diversified set of businesses in a desire for a long-run return that exceeds the Standard & Poor's (S&P) index. As Warren Buffet comments in his annual report:

> Berkshire's long-term performance versus the S&P remains all-important. Our shareholders can buy the S&P through an index fund at very low cost. Unless we achieve gains in per-share intrinsic value in the future that outdo the S&P's performance, Charlie and I will be adding nothing to what you can accomplish on your own.

A company's *strategic* (or *business*) *plan* describes how it plans to achieve its goals and objectives. The plan's success depends on an effective review of market demand and supply. Specifically, the company must assess demand for its products and services, and assess the supply of its inputs (both labor and capital). The plan must also include competitive analyses, opportunity assessments, and consideration of business threats.

This type of strategic analysis is commonly called a S.W.O.T analysis (strengths, weaknesses, opportunities, and threats). The strategic plan is the output of such analysis. Such a plan specifies both broad management designs that generate company value and tactical actions that achieve those designs. Tactical actions involve production, marketing, human resources, operations, and supply-chain management.

Most information in a strategic plan is proprietary and guarded closely by management. However, outsiders can gain insight into planning activities through various channels. Less formal channels include newspapers, magazines, and company publications. More formal channels include management's Letter to Shareholders and its Management Discussion and Analysis (MD&A) report. DuPont, in its MD&A, describes its opportunities and plans as follows:

> The company expects . . . earnings per share to reflect increased sales volumes . . . [and] to benefit from continued efforts to control costs.

Understanding a company's planning activities helps focus accounting analysis and place it in context.

BUSINESS INSIGHT | **Warren Buffet on MD&A**

"When Charlie and I read reports, we have no interest in pictures of personnel, plants or products. References to EBITDA [earnings before interest, taxes, depreciation and amortization] make us shudder—does management think the tooth fairy pays for capital expenditures? We're very suspicious of accounting methodology that is vague or unclear, since too often that means management wishes to hide something. And we don't want to read messages that a public relations department or consultant has turned out. Instead, we expect a company's CEO to explain in his or her own words what's happening."
—Berkshire Hathaway annual report

Reporting of Financing Activities

A company's strategic plan guides management with its decisions on what resources to acquire. These resources include, for example, raw materials for product manufacturing, machinery to produce and support production, land and buildings to support operations, and sales outlets for products and services. Resource investments also include those in employees, marketing, and research and development.

Investments in resources require funding. **Financing activities** refer to methods that companies use to fund those resources. *Financial management* is the planning of resource needs, including the proper mix of different financing sources.

Companies obtain financing from two sources: equity (owner) financing and creditor (nonowner) financing. *Equity financing* is resources contributed to the company by its owners along with any income retained by the company. *Creditor* (or debt) *financing* is resources contributed from nonowners. We draw this distinction between financing sources for an important reason: creditor financing entails a legal obligation to repay amounts borrowed, usually with interest, and failure to repay amounts borrowed can yield severe consequences to the borrower. Equity financing entails no such legal obligation for repayment. All companies use both equity and creditor financing. An important goal is to employ these financing sources at the lowest possible cost and risk.

Berkshire Hathaway relies on both owner and nonowner financing. Its owners provide $78,341 million in financing (43%), while its nonowners provide $102,218 million (57%). Both groups provide financing in a desire for a return on their investment, after considering both expected return and risk. The following graph gives a sense of differences in financing proportions for several well-known companies.

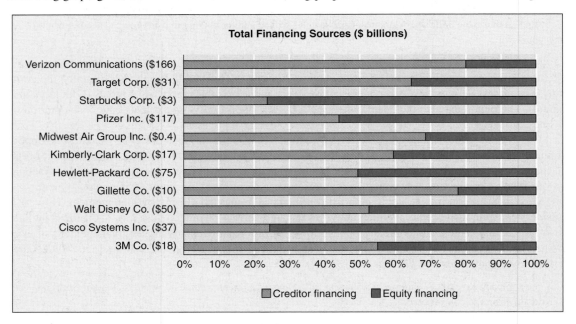

These companies are financed with different proportions of creditor and equity financing. Companies like Cisco Systems, Starbucks, and Pfizer utilize a greater proportion of equity financing than do Verizon, Gillette, and Midwest Air. This variation is not by chance. Each industry, over time, reaches its own optimum proportion of creditor and equity financing. We discuss this equilibrium concept later in the book.

We can further separate creditor (nonowner) financing into two sources:

1. Investing creditors—those who primarily finance investing activities (such as bank lenders).
2. Operating creditors—those who primarily finance operating activities (such as suppliers).

Investing creditors are lenders that are party to financing agreements that support investing activities. These agreements are often in the form of multiyear notes and bonds. Such agreements specify repayment terms, interest, and any mortgage and covenants. *Operating creditors* are lenders that are party to financing agreements that support operating activities. These agreements typically involve suppliers, employees, utilities, and government agencies.

The distinction between these two types of creditors is important. Obligations to investing creditors are generally interest bearing and are subject to legal agreements that can place constraints upon a company's operating activities. Obligations to operating creditors are generally non-interest bearing and represent an important source of funding for the company. Also, the ability of operating creditors to provide needed supplies of acceptable quality and at the appropriate time is crucial to company success.

Berkshire Hathaway reports total nonowner financing of $102,218 million, which consists of $26,145 million from investing creditors and $76,073 million from operating creditors. The following chart highlights differences in these sources of financing for the same set of companies described above.

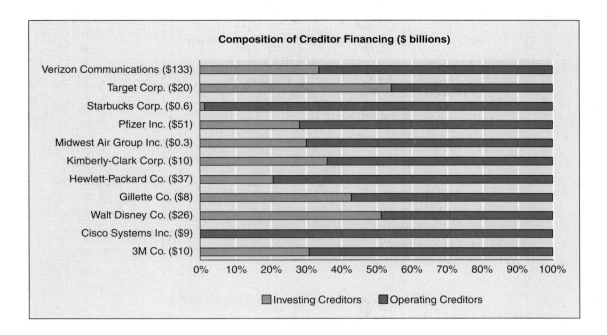

For most of these companies, operating creditors make up a larger proportion of creditor financing. This is a desired result as operating credit is typically interest-free and, therefore, costs less. Moreover, investing creditors usually require loan agreements or bond indentures that place restrictions on a company's activities and, thereby, limit its operating flexibility.

MANAGERIAL DECISION   You Are the Product Manager

There is often a friction between investor need for information and a company's desire to safeguard competitive advantages. Assume that you are the product manager for a key department at your company and you are asked for advice on the extent of information to disclose in the MD&A section of your annual report on a potentially very lucrative new product that your department has test marketed and plans to further finance. What advice do you provide and why? [Answer, p. 1-28]

Reporting of Investing Activities

Investing activities are the acquisition and disposition of resources, called *assets,* that a company uses to produce and sell its products and services. Companies differ on the amount and mix of investing resources. Some require buildings and inventories to operate. Others need only people. *Asset management* is the task of selecting the proper asset composition.

Investing resources are of two types:

1. Operating assets—resources devoted to operating activities
2. Nonoperating (financial) assets—resources devoted to nonoperating activities

Operating assets refer to resources devoted to executing a company's primary business activities. *Nonoperating* (or *financial*) *assets* consist of excess (nonoperating) resources such as those held for future expansion or unexpected needs. Such assets are often invested in other companies' stocks and in corporate or government bonds. The distinction between operating and nonoperating assets is important and impacts the analysis of financial performance described later in this and other modules. This is because companies concentrate most of their efforts in and create most of their market value from operating activities.

The following chart illustrates the breakdown between operating and nonoperating assets for several companies.

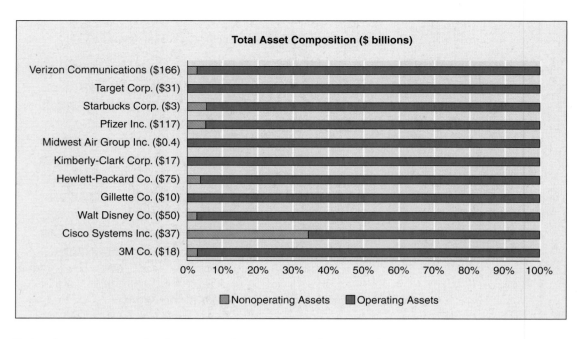

Total Asset Composition ($ billions)

Notice that most companies do not carry large amounts of nonoperating assets (such as investments). An exception is **Cisco Systems**, where its investments provide it with financial flexibility in a rapidly changing industry. Other companies such as **Microsoft**, however, have come under pressure from their owners (shareholders) to pay out a portion of such assets to their shareholders.

RESEARCH INSIGHT   Return and Risk

Return, also called *yield,* is the amount earned from an investment. Return is often expressed as the income from the investment divided by the amount invested. U.S. government bonds, for example, express return in the form of an interest rate such as 5%. **Risk** is the uncertainty of expected return. Each investment has risk, and some investments carry more risk than others. The trade-off between return and risk impacts investment decisions. The greater the investment risk, the greater is its expected return, and vice-versa. Government bonds earn a low return because they carry little risk of loss. We expect a greater return from a share of **Berkshire Hathaway**. Yet, that greater return carries greater risk, including risk of loss.

The following chart shows that return is higher for higher risk bonds and for bonds with more distant maturity dates. Specifically, return increases (shifts upward) as bond quality moves from U.S. treasury, which is the lowest risk bond, to BBB, which is a higher risk bond. This difference is substantial. For example, for a 10-year bond, the government bond yield is 4.71%, the AAA bond yield is 0.60% higher (at 5.31%), and the BBB bond yield is 1.41% higher (at 6.12%). Also, as maturity terms lengthen, uncertainty (risk) increases, and return increases.

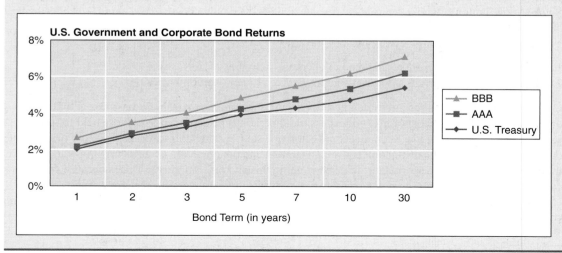

The total of a company's resources is referred to as its *assets*. Company financing, which consists of owner and nonowner financing, reflects claims on those assets. Owner claims on assets are referred to as *equity* and nonowner claims are referred to as *liabilities* (or debt). Since all financing must be invested in something, we obtain the following basic relation: *investing equals financing*. This equality is called the **accounting equation**, which is expressed as:

> **Investing = Nonowner Financing + Owner Financing, or**
> **Assets = Liabilities + Equity**

For a recent period, the accounting equation for Berkshire Hathaway follows ($ millions):

$$\$180,559 = \$102,218 + \$78,341$$

The accounting equation works for all companies at all times.

Reporting of Operating Activities

Operating activities are the use of company resources to produce, promote, and sell its products and services. These activities extend from input markets involving suppliers of materials and labor to a company's output markets involving customers of products and services. Input markets generate most *operating expenses* (or *costs*) such as inventory, salaries, materials, and logistics. Output markets generate *operating revenues* (or *sales*) to customers. Output markets also generate some operating expenses such as marketing and distributing products and services to customers. *Operating income,* also called *operating profit* or *operating earnings,* arises when operating revenues exceed operating expenses. An operating loss occurs when operating expenses exceed operating revenues. Selecting the proper mix of operating activities is known as *strategic management.*

Management performance with operating activities is assessed using various benchmarks. For example, Harley-Davidson earned $580 million in a recent year. This number by itself is not very meaningful. Instead, we can better assess income performance relative to the level of investment used to generate that income. Specifically, Harley's return on its average asset level of $3,490 million is 16.6%. The same $3,490 million invested in a savings account earning 2% would yield earnings of only $70 million.

Defining Company Value

Business activities are set within a mix of business forces. These forces include key stakeholders, which are individuals with vested interests in a company's performance and condition. Many of these stakeholders participate in **capital markets**, which refer to financing sources. Capital markets often involve a company's issuance of securities (stocks, bonds, and notes) that are traded on organized exchanges. They also include capital raised from family members, friends, venture capitalists, and local banks.

Most owners and nonowners formalize their claims on a company in the form of a *contract* or a *security.* A typical owner security is stock, and typical nonowner securities are bonds and notes. A security can often be traded in capital markets. For example, the original owners can sell those claims in capital markets if they wish to liquidate their securities. All subsequent owners are called *secondary holders* of such securities.

Company value is the value of all owner and nonowner claims.

> **Value of Company = Value of Nonowner Claims + Value of Owner Claims**

Owner value is referred to as *residual value,* which reflects its junior (subordinate) status to nonowner claims. Business activities are the *drivers* of company value.

■ CONSTRUCTING FINANCIAL STATEMENTS

Four financial statements are used to periodically report on a company's business activities. These statements are the: balance sheet, income statement, statement of equity, and statement of cash flows.

Exhibit 1.2 shows how these statements are linked across time. A balance sheet reports on a company's position at a *point in time.* The income statement, statement of equity, and the statement of cash flows report on performance over a *period of time.* The three statements in the middle of Exhibit 1.2 (period-of-time statements) link the balance sheet from the beginning to the end of a period.

EXHIBIT 1.2 ■ Financial Statement Links across Time

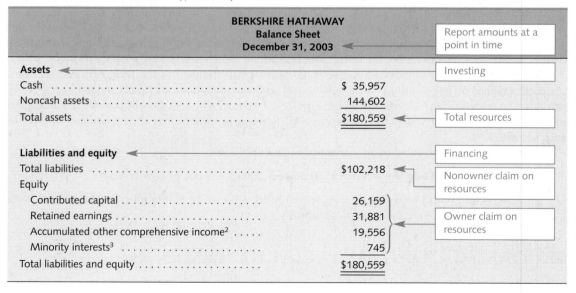

A one-year, or annual, reporting period is common, which is called the *accounting,* or *fiscal, year.* Semiannual, quarterly, and monthly reporting periods are also common. *Calendar-year* companies are those companies whose reporting period begins on January 1 and ends on December 31. **Berkshire Hathaway** is a calendar-year company. Some companies choose a fiscal year ending on a date other than December 31, such as when sales and inventory are low. For example, **J. Crew Group**'s fiscal year-end is always near February 1, after the busy holiday season.

Balance Sheet

A **balance sheet** reports on investing and financing activities. It lists amounts for assets, liabilities, and equity at a point in time. The accounting equation (also called the *balance sheet equation*) is the basis of the balance sheet: Assets = Liabilities + Equity.

The balance sheet for **Berkshire Hathaway** is in Exhibit 1.3. Refer to this balance sheet to verify the following amounts: assets = $180,559 million, liabilities = $102,218 million, and equity = $78,341 million. Assets equal liabilities plus equity, which reflects the equality of investing and financing totals.

EXHIBIT 1.3 ■ Balance Sheet ($ millions)

BERKSHIRE HATHAWAY Balance Sheet December 31, 2003		Report amounts at a point in time
Assets		Investing
Cash	$ 35,957	
Noncash assets	144,602	
Total assets	$180,559	Total resources
Liabilities and equity		Financing
Total liabilities	$102,218	Nonowner claim on resources
Equity		
Contributed capital	26,159	
Retained earnings	31,881	Owner claim on resources
Accumulated other comprehensive income[2]	19,556	
Minority interests[3]	745	
Total liabilities and equity	$180,559	

[2]*Other comprehensive income* refers to revenues and expenses that affect equity, but are not included in net income. The cumulative total of other comprehensive income is reported as *accumulated other comprehensive income,* which is reported on the balance sheet (see Module 2 for further explanation).

[3]*Minority interests* refer to claims of minority shareholders, which arise when Berkshire Hathaway acquires less than 100% of another company's stock. Minority shareholders have a claim on Berkshire's assets and earnings just like its common shareholders (see Module 6).

Income Statement

An **income statement** reports on operating activities. It lists amounts for revenues less expenses over a period of time. Revenues less expenses yield the bottom-line net income amount.

Berkshire Hathaway's income statement is in Exhibit 1.4. Refer to its income statement to verify the following: revenues = $63,859 million, expenses = $55,708 million, and net income = $8,151 million. Net income reflects the profit to owners for that specific period, while the line items of the statement detail how income is determined.

EXHIBIT 1.4 ■ Income Statement ($ millions)

BERKSHIRE HATHAWAY Income Statement For Year Ended December 31, 2003		Report amounts over a period of time
Revenues	$63,859	Inflows of net assets from revenues
Expenses	55,708	
Net income (loss)	$ 8,151	Outflows of net assets generating revenues

For manufacturing and merchandising companies, the cost of goods sold is an important measure and is also disclosed in the income statement. This measure is typically reported immediately following revenues. It is also common to report the gross profit subtotal, which is revenues less the cost of goods sold. The company's remaining expenses are then reported below gross profit. This income statement layout follows:

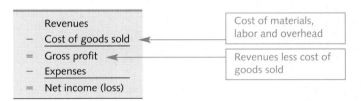

	Revenues	
−	Cost of goods sold	Cost of materials, labor and overhead
=	Gross profit	Revenues less cost of goods sold
−	Expenses	
=	Net income (loss)	

Statement of Equity

The **statement of stockholders' equity**, or simply *statement of equity,* reports on changes in key equity accounts over a period of time. Berkshire Hathaway's statement of stockholders' equity is in Exhibit 1.5. During the recent period, its equity changed due to share issuances and income reinvestment. Berkshire Hathaway details and classifies these changes into three categories:

- Contributed capital (includes preferred stock, common stock, and additional paid-in capital)
- Retained earnings (includes cumulative net income or loss, minus dividends)
- Accumulated other comprehensive income

EXHIBIT 1.5 ■ Statement of Equity ($ millions)

BERKSHIRE HATHAWAY Statement of Stockholders' Equity For Year Ended December 31, 2003				
	Contributed Capital	Retained Earnings	Accumulated Other Comprehensive Income	Report amounts over a period of time
December 31, 2002	$26,036	$23,730	$14,271	Beginning period amounts
Stock issuance	123			
Net income		8,151		Change in balances over a period
Dividends		0		
Other comprehensive income			5,285	
December 31, 2003	$26,159	$31,881	$19,556	Ending period amounts

Contributed capital represents the net amount contributed by shareholders (owners). Retained earnings (also called *earned capital*) represent the amount of income retained in the business and not distributed to shareholders in the form of dividends. The change in retained earnings links consecutive balance sheets via the income statement. For Berkshire Hathaway, its recent year's retained earnings increases from $23,730 million to $31,881 million. This increase of $8,151 million is explained by net income of $8,151 million and no payment of dividends. (Note: Ending retained earnings = Beginning retained earnings + Net income − Dividends. The combination of retained earnings and accumulated other comprehensive income is often referred to as *earned capital*.)

Statement of Cash Flows

$

Cash Effect

The **statement of cash flows** reports on net cash flows from operating, investing, and financing activities over a period of time. Berkshire Hathaway's statement of cash flows is in Exhibit 1.6. Its cash balance increased by $23,209 million in the recent period. Of this increase in cash, operating activities generated an $8,257 million cash inflow, investing activities generated a $16,113 million cash inflow, and financing activities yielded a cash outflow of $(1,161) million.

EXHIBIT 1.6 ■ Statement of Cash Flows ($ millions)

BERKSHIRE HATHAWAY Statement of Cash Flows For Year Ended December 31, 2003		
		Report amounts over a period of time
Operating cash flows	$ 8,257	Net cash flow from operating
Investing cash flows	16,113	Net cash flow from investing
Financing cash flows	(1,161)	Net cash flow from financing
Net increase (decrease) in cash	23,209	
Cash, December 31, 2002	12,748	Cash amounts per balance sheet
Cash, December 31, 2003	$35,957	

Berkshire Hathaway's $23,209 million net cash inflow does not equal its $8,151 million net income. Generally, a company's net cash flow for a period does *not* equal its net income. This is due to timing differences between when revenue and expense items are recognized and when cash is received and paid.

Both cash flow and net income numbers are important for business decisions. Each are used in security valuation models, and both help users of accounting reports understand and assess a company's past, present, and future business activities.

Financial Statement Linkages

Financial statements are not independent reports. They are linked. These links are shown in Exhibit 1.7 using Berkshire Hathaway's financial statements from Exhibits 1.3 through 1.6.

The left side of this exhibit shows Berkshire Hathaway's beginning-year balance sheet. Beginning-year assets equal $169,544 million, consisting of $12,748 million in cash and $156,796 million in noncash assets. These investments are financed with $104,116 million from nonowners and $65,428 million from owners. The owner portion consists of $26,036 million in contributed capital, $23,730 million in retained earnings, $14,271 million in accumulated other comprehensive income, and $1,391 million in minority interests (minority interests refer to outsider ownership of the company's subsidiaries).

Berkshire Hathaway's recent-period operating activities are reflected in the middle column of Exhibit 1.7. Its statement of cash flows explains how operating, financing, and investing activities increase the $12,748 million beginning-year cash balance to the $35,957 million year-end balance. This year-end cash balance is reported in the year-end balance sheet on the right side of the exhibit.

$

Cash Effect

Berkshire Hathaway's income statement reports $8,151 million net income, which explains the change in retained earnings reported in its statement of equity (Berkshire Hathaway did not pay any dividends to its shareholders during the year).

In summary, the balance sheet is a listing of investing and financing activities at a point in time. The three statements that report on (1) cash flows, (2) income, and (3) equity explain changes over a period of time for investing and financing activities. All transactions and events reflected in these three statements

EXHIBIT 1.7 ■ Articulation of Berkshire Hathaway Financial Statements ($ millions)

Statement of Cash Flows For Year Ended Dec. 31, 2003	
Operating cash flows	$ 8,257
Investing cash flows	16,113
Financing cash flows	(1,161)
Increase (decrease) in cash	23,209
Cash, Dec. 31, 2002	12,748
Cash, Dec. 31, 2003	$35,957

Balance Sheet Dec. 31, 2002	
Assets	
Cash	$ 12,748
Noncash assets	156,796
Total assets	$169,544
Liabilities and equity	
Total liabilities	$104,116
Equity	
Contributed capital	26,036
Retained earnings	23,730
Acc. other comp. inc.	14,271
Minority interests	1,391
Liabilities and equity	$169,544

Balance Sheet Dec. 31, 2003	
Assets	
Cash	$ 35,957
Noncash assets	144,602
Total assets	$180,559
Liabilities and equity	
Total liabilities	$102,218
Equity	
Contributed capital	26,159
Retained earnings	31,881
Acc. other comp. inc.	19,556
Minority interests	745
Liabilities and equity	$180,559

Income Statement For Year Ended Dec. 31, 2003	
Revenues	$63,859
Expenses	55,708
Net income (loss)	$ 8,151

Statement of Stockholders' Equity For Year Ended Dec. 31, 2003	
Contributed capital, Dec. 31, 2002	$26,036
Stock issuances and retirements	123
Contributed capital, Dec. 31, 2003	$26,159
Retained earnings, Dec. 31, 2002	$23,730
Net income	8,151
Less: dividends	0
Retained earnings, Dec. 31, 2003	$31,881
Accum. other comp. income, Dec. 31, 2002	$14,271
Other comprehensive income	5,285
Accum. other comp. income, Dec. 31, 2003	$19,556

Point in time   Period of time   Point in time

impact the balance sheet. That is, the income, cash flows, and equity statements explain changes in balance sheets. This linkage is known as the *articulation* of financial statements.

Information Beyond Financial Statements

Important information about a company is communicated to various decision makers through reports other than financial statements. These reports include the following:

- Management Discussion and Analysis (MD&A)
- Independent Auditor Report

- Financial statement footnotes
- Regulatory filings, including proxy statements and other SEC filings

We describe and explain the usefulness of these additional information sources throughout the book—some discussion is in Appendix 1A to this module.

■ MID-MODULE REVIEW ■

The following financial information is from Procter & Gamble, for the year ended June 30, 2004 ($ millions):

Cash asset, ending year	$5,469
Cash flows from operations	9,362
Sales	51,407
Stockholders' equity	17,278
Cost of goods sold	25,076
Cash flows from financing	(414)
Total liabilities	39,770
Expenses	19,850
Noncash assets	51,579
Cash flows from investing	(9,391)
Net income	6,481
Cash, beginning year	5,912

Required

Prepare an income statement, balance sheet, and statement of cash flows for Procter & Gamble at June 30, 2004.

Solution

PROCTER & GAMBLE
Income Statement
For Year Ended June 30, 2004

Sales	$51,407
Cost of goods sold	25,076
Gross profit	26,331
Expenses	19,850
Net income	$ 6,481

PROCTER & GAMBLE
Balance Sheet
June 30, 2004

Cash asset	$ 5,469	Total liabilities	$39,770
Noncash assets	51,579	Stockholders' equity	17,278
Total assets	$57,048	Total liabilities and equity	$57,048

PROCTER & GAMBLE
Statement of Cash Flows
For Year Ended June 30, 2004

Cash flows from operations	$9,362
Cash flows from investing	(9,391)
Cash flows from financing	(414)
Net increase (decrease) in cash	(443)
Cash, beginning year	5,912
Cash, ending year	$5,469

$
Cash Effect

■ DEMAND FOR AND SUPPLY OF INFORMATION

Financial accounting information facilitates economic transactions and promotes efficient resource allocations. Decision makers demand information on a company's past and prospective returns and risks. Companies are encouraged to supply such information to lower their costs of financing and some less obvious costs such as political, contracting, and labor costs.

As with all goods, the supply of information depends on companies weighing the costs of disclosure against the benefits of disclosure. Regulatory agencies intervene in this process with various disclosure requirements that establish a minimum supply of information.

Demand for Information

Demand for financial accounting information extends to numerous users that include:

- Managers and employees
- Creditors and suppliers
- Shareholders and directors
- Customers and sales staff
- Regulators and tax agencies
- Voters and their representatives

Managers and Employees

For their own well-being and future earnings potential, managers and employees demand accounting information on the financial condition, profitability, and prospects of their companies. Managers and employees also demand comparative financial information on competing companies and other business opportunities. This permits them to conduct comparative analyses to benchmark company performance and condition.

Managers and employees also demand financial accounting information for use in compensation and bonus contracts that are tied to such numbers. The popularity of employee profit sharing and stock ownership plans has further increased demand for financial information. Other sources of demand include union contracts that link wage negotiations to accounting numbers and for pension and benefit plans whose solvency depends on company performance.

Creditors and Suppliers

Creditors such as banks and other lenders demand financial accounting information to help determine loan terms, loan amounts, interest rates, and collateral. Creditors' loans often include contractual requirements, called **covenants**, for the loan recipient to maintain minimum levels of working capital, retained earnings, interest coverage, and so forth to safeguard lenders. Covenant violations can yield technical default, enabling the creditor to demand early payment or other compensation.

Suppliers similarly demand financial information to establish credit sales terms and to determine their long-term commitment to supply-chain relations. Both creditors and suppliers use financial information to monitor and adjust their contracts and commitments with a debtor company.

Shareholders and Directors

Shareholders and directors demand financial accounting information to assess the profitability and risks of companies. Shareholders and others (including investment analysts, brokers, potential investors, etc.) look for information useful in their investment decisions. **Fundamental analysis** uses financial information to estimate company value and, hence, buy-sell stock strategies. Even analysis based on *semistrong-form market efficiency* uses accounting numbers to estimate dividend yield and risk factors for portfolio selection.

Both directors and shareholders use accounting information to evaluate manager performance. Managers similarly use such information to request further compensation and managerial power from directors. Outside directors are crucial to determining who runs the company, and these directors use accounting information to help make this assessment.

RESEARCH INSIGHT   **Degrees of Market Efficiency**

Capital markets are efficient if, at any given time, current stock prices reflect information that determines those prices. That is, the market is efficient if disclosure of some information does not alter stock prices. This implies that excess stock returns cannot be earned from analysis of that information in predicting stock prices. Three degrees of market efficiency are defined with respect to the information set:

- Weak-form efficiency: The information set includes only the history of stock prices.
- Semistrong-form efficiency: The information set includes all information known to market participants, but is limited to public information.
- Strong-form efficiency: The information set includes all information known to market participants, including private information.

Strong-form efficiency is dismissed. Further, research has revealed stock pricing anomalies that cast doubt on semistrong-form efficiency. For example, investor over- and under-reaction to income announcements, the size effect (smaller firms yield higher returns), the book-to-market effect (firms with a higher book value-to-market value ratio earn higher returns), and others reject semistrong-form efficiency. There is also evidence that the degree of efficiency varies with the information environment such as the quality and quantity of disclosure, press coverage, and analyst following.

Customers and Sales Staff

Customers and sales staffs demand accounting information to assess the ability of a company to provide products or services as agreed and to assess the company's staying power and reliability. Customers and sales staffs also wish to estimate the company's profitability to assess fairness of returns on mutual transactions.

Regulators and Tax Agencies

Regulators and tax agencies demand accounting information for tax policies, antitrust assessments, public protection, price setting, import-export analyses, and various other uses. Timely and reliable information is crucial to effective regulatory policy. Moreover, accounting information is often central to social and economic policy. For example, governments often grant monopoly rights to electric and gas companies serving specific areas in exchange for regulation over prices charged to consumers. These prices are mainly determined from accounting measures of return.

Voters and their Representatives

Voters and their representatives to national, state, and local governments demand accounting information for policy decisions. The decisions can involve economic, social, taxation, and other initiatives. Voters and their representatives also use accounting information to monitor government spending. We have all heard of the $1,000 hammer type stories that are uncovered while sifting through accounting data. Contributors to nonprofit organizations also demand accounting information to assess the impact of their donations.

BUSINESS INSIGHT   **Warren Buffet on Management Talk**

"Bad terminology is the enemy of good thinking. When companies or investment professionals use terms such as 'EBITDA' and 'pro forma,' they want you to unthinkingly accept concepts that are dangerously flawed. (In golf, my score is frequently below par on a pro forma basis: I have firm plans to 'restructure' my putting stroke and therefore only count the swings I take before reaching the green.)"—Berkshire Hathaway annual report

---

Supply of Information

The supply of accounting information is determined by management's estimates of the benefits and costs of disclosure. That is, management would release information provided the benefits of disclosure outweigh the costs of disclosure.

Regulation and *bargaining power* also play roles in determining the supply of accounting information. Many areas of the world regulate the minimum levels of accounting disclosures. For example, regulators in the U.S. require financial statements, various note disclosures, and other reports on a regular basis. Moreover, some stakeholders possess ample bargaining power to obtain accounting information for themselves. These typically include private lenders and major suppliers and customers.

Recognize that the minimum, regulated supply of information is not the standard. We need only look at several annual reports to see considerable variance in the supply of accounting information. For example, differences abound on disclosures for segment operations, product performance reports, financing activities, and so forth. Both the quantity and quality of information differs across companies and over time.

Benefits of Disclosure

The benefits of supplying accounting information extend to a company's capital, labor, input, and output markets. Companies must compete in these markets. For example, capital markets provide the sources of financing; the better a company's prospects, the lower is its costs of capital (as reflected in lower interest rates or higher stock prices). The same holds for a company's recruiting efforts in labor markets and its ability to establish superior supplier-customer relations in the input and output markets.

A company's performance in these markets depends on success with its business activities *and* the market's awareness of that success. Companies reap the benefits of disclosure with good news information about their products, processes, management, and so forth. That is, there are real economic incentives for companies to disclose reliable (audited) accounting information enabling them to better compete in capital, labor, input, and output markets.

What inhibits companies from providing false or misleading good news? There are several constraints. An important constraint imposed by stakeholders is that of audit requirements and legal repercussions associated with inaccurate accounting information. Another relates to reputation effects from disclosures over time as events either support or refute earlier news.

Costs of Disclosure

The costs of supplying accounting information include its preparation and dissemination, competitive disadvantages, litigation potential, and political costs. Preparation and dissemination costs can be substantial, but much of this cost is already borne by inside managers for their own business decisions. The potential for information to yield competitive disadvantages is high. Companies are concerned that disclosures of their activities such as product or segment successes, strategic alliances or pursuits, technological or system innovations, and product or process quality improvements will harm their competitive advantages. Also, litigation costs can arise when disclosures yield expectations that are not met. Political costs also are usually linked to highly visible companies that must be careful to not generate excess profits; for example, government defense contractors and oil companies are often targets of public scrutiny.

■ PROFITABILITY ANALYSIS

There are many ways to measure company success. One crucial measure is profitability. Profitability reflects on whether or not a company is able to bring its product or service to the market in an efficient manner, and whether the market values that product or service. Companies that fail to perform on profitability are unlikely to succeed in the long run.

A key profitability metric for stakeholders and decision makers is company return on invested capital. This metric compares the level of net income with the amount of invested capital used to generate that income. Invested capital refers to total financing, which is the sum of both owner and nonowner financing. Since total financing equals total investing (assets), this return metric refers to the income generated by total assets. This section introduces the return on total assets metric and its corresponding disaggregation as a motivating and learning framework for much of our subsequent analyses in this book.

Measuring Return on Assets

Return on assets (ROA), also called return on invested capital, in its simplified form is computed as:

Return on Assets (ROA) = Net Income/Average Assets

For example, if we invest $100 in a savings account yielding $3 at year-end, the return on assets is 3%.

A company can be assessed from the perspective of its total financing base, which by definition equals total assets (or the total of liabilities and equity). The return on assets metric reflects the return from *all* assets (financing) entrusted to it, and does not distinguish return by its sources. Alternatively, analysis can concentrate on evaluating *operating* performance relative to operating assets. This is an important focus of Module 3.[4]

The income number in the numerator of the return measure reflects performance for a specific period. This implies that the asset measure used in the denominator should reflect the *average* asset level for that same period. Accordingly, we use the average asset level for ratio analysis in our examples and end-of-module assignments since it normally provides a better measure of capital utilization for a period and is the predominant method for analyst services, such as **S&P Compustat**. However, if circumstances dictate use of period-end amounts, then we will explicitly note the exception.

Disaggregating Return on Assets

Return on assets in its most simplified form is computed as net income divided by average total assets. This return can be disaggregated (separated) into meaningful components for profitability analysis as follows:

$$\frac{\text{Net Income}}{\text{Average Assets}} = \frac{\text{Net Income}}{\text{Sales}} \times \frac{\text{Sales}}{\text{Average Assets}}$$

The income to sales ratio is called **net profit margin**, or simply profit margin, which reflects the profitability of sales. The sales to average assets ratio is called **asset turnover**, or *total asset turnover,* which reflects effectiveness in generating sales from assets. The disaggregation of return on assets into profit margin and asset turnover is illustrated in Exhibit 1.8. (This disaggregation is sometimes called *DuPont analysis*; this is because DuPont's managers first developed and publicized this disaggregation analysis for business decisions by its managers.)

EXHIBIT 1.8 ■ Return on Assets Disaggregation

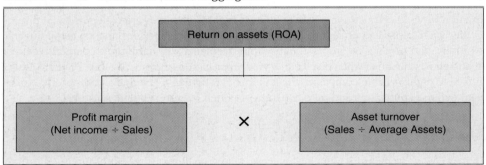

ROA can be further disaggregated to yield additional insights. For example, we can investigate profit margin (net income/sales) by analyzing its component ratios involving gross profit and individual expense items. Also, asset turnover (sales/average assets) can be broken down into turnover rates for each asset category such as receivables, inventories, and plant assets. These deeper levels of analyses yield insights into factors driving the higher-level results and can suggest areas that warrant management attention. Such analysis can lead to further efforts to enhance competitive advantages and to correct or discontinue those that are not.

There are an infinite number of combinations of profit margin and asset turnover that yield a target return on assets. To illustrate, Exhibit 1.9 graphs the 7% return on assets line for various combinations of these two profitability drivers. This exhibit also shows recent combinations of these drivers for several industries. Specifically, these points represent industry medians from over 55,000 observations over the decade and a half prior to 2005. Certain industries carry much higher profit margins with much lower asset turnovers, and vice-versa. This is basic economics at work.

---

[4]This module uses the generic, simplified form of return on assets (Net Income/Average Assets) for a simple introduction to ratio analysis. We discuss a more useful version called return on net operating assets (RNOA) in Module 3, which is measured as net operating profit after tax (NOPAT) divided by net operating assets (NOA).

EXHIBIT 1.9 ■ Profit Margin, Asset Turnover, and Return on Assets for Selected Industries

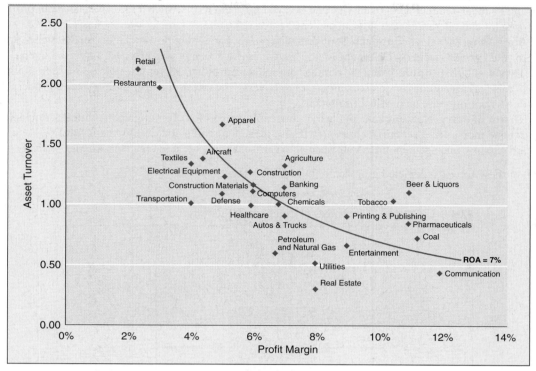

It is important to recognize that the key drivers of profitability are also key outputs of the financial accounting information system. Accordingly, good analysis demands that we understand accounting measurements, their limitations and strengths, and the potential for adjustments to further enrich our use of these numbers.

Berkshire Hathaway reported 2003 net income of $8.1 billion on average total assets of $175 billion, yielding a 4.6% return on assets, which is about average for all publicly traded companies. In his Chairman's report, Warren Buffet discusses the fact that he is finding it increasingly difficult to find undervalued investments of sufficient size to positively affect the performance of his company.

MANAGERIAL DECISION   You Are the Chief Financial Officer

You are reviewing your company's financial performance for the first six months of the year and are unsatisfied with the results. How can you use return on assets disaggregation to identify areas for improvement? [Answer, p. 1-28]

■ FINANCIAL ACCOUNTING AND BUSINESS ANALYSIS

Analysis and interpretation of financial statements must consider the broader business context in which a company operates. This section describes how to systematically consider those broader business forces to enhance our analytical and interpretive skills. We can then better extract the insights from financial statements and better estimate future performance and firm value.

Analyzing the Competitive Environment

Financial statements are influenced by five important forces that confront the company and determine its competitive intensity. One of these is **industry competitors**. Industry competition and rivalry raises the cost of doing business as companies must hire and train competitive workers, advertise products, research and develop products, and so forth. Beyond industry competitors are the four following forces that further add to the cost of doing business (adapted from Porter, 1980 and 1998):

- **Bargaining power of buyers.** Buyers with strong bargaining power can extract price concessions and demand a higher level of service and delayed payment terms. Such a force reduces both profits on sales and operating cash flows to sellers.
- **Bargaining power of suppliers.** Suppliers with strong bargaining power can demand a higher price for their goods and early payments, yielding adverse effects on profits and cash flows to buyers.
- **Threat of substitution.** When the number of product substitutes increases, sellers lose their ability to raise prices and/or pass on cost increases to buyers. The threat of substitution places considerable downward pressure on profits of sellers.
- **Threat of entry.** New entrants to a market increase competition. To mitigate that threat, companies expend monies to erect *barriers to entry*. These include research and development (R&D), advertising, management hires with special expertise, and mergers to create *economies of scale*.

Each of these forces is depicted graphically in Exhibit 1.10.

EXHIBIT 1.10 ■ Five Forces of Competitive Intensity

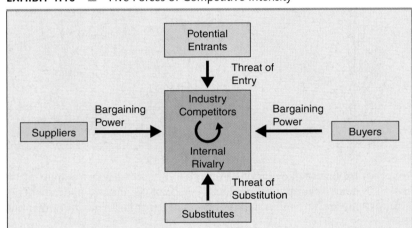

Reprinted with permission of The Free Press, a Division of Simon & Schuster Adult Publishing Group, from *COMPETITIVE STRATEGY: Techniques for Analyzing Industries and Competitors,* by Michael E. Porter. Copyright © 1980, 1998 by The Free Press. All rights reserved.

Applying Competitive Analysis for Financial Interpretations

We apply competitive analysis to help us interpret the financial results of McLane Company. McLane is a subsidiary of Berkshire Hathaway and was acquired in 2003 as explained in the following note to the Berkshire annual report:

> On May 23, 2003, Berkshire acquired McLane Company, Inc. from Wal-Mart Stores, Inc. Results of McLane's business operations are included in Berkshire's consolidated results beginning on that date. McLane's revenues were $13,743 million and pre-tax earnings totaled $150 million for the period from May 23 to December 31. Approximately 35% of McLane's revenues derived from sales to Wal-Mart Stores, Inc. McLane's business is marked by high sales volume and low profit margins. For its most recently completed fiscal year prior to the acquisition, McLane's sales and pre-tax earnings totaled approximately $21.9 billion and $220 million, respectively.

McLane is a wholesaler of food products in that it purchases food products in finished and semifinished form from agricultural and food-related businesses and resells them to grocery and convenience food stores. The extensive distribution network required in this business entails considerable investment.

A competitive analysis of McLane's financial results include the following observations:

- **Industry competitors.** McLane has many competitors with food products that are difficult to differentiate.
- **Bargaining power of buyers.** 35% of McLane's sales are to Wal-Mart. Wal-Mart has considerable buying power that limits seller profits. Further, the food industry is characterized by high turnover and low profit margins, which implies that cost control is key to success.
- **Bargaining power of suppliers.** McLane is large ($22 billion in annual sales), which implies its suppliers are unlikely to exert forces to increase its cost of sales.
- **Threat of substitution.** Grocery items are usually not well differentiated. This means the threat of substitution is high, which inhibits its ability to raise selling prices.
- **Threat of entry.** High investment costs (such as warehousing and logistics) are a barrier to entry in McLane's business. This means the threat of entry is relatively low.

Our analysis shows that McLane is a high-volume, low-margin company. Its ability to control costs is crucial to its financial performance, including its ability to fully utilize its assets. Evaluation of McLane's financial statements, therefore, should focus on these dimensions. In sum, a company's financial statements must be evaluated within the competitive environment.

Assessing the Broader Business Environment

A quality accounting analysis depends on an effective business analysis. Before we analyze a single accounting number, we must ask questions about the company's business environment such as the following:

- *Life cycle* At what stage in its life is this company? Is it a startup, experiencing growing pains? Is it strong and mature, reaping the benefits of competitive advantages? Is it nearing the end of its life, trying to milk what it can from stagnant product lines?
- *Outputs* What products does it sell? Are its products new, established, or dated? Do its products have substitutes? How complicated are its products to produce?
- *Buyers* Who are its buyers? Are buyers in good financial condition? Do buyers have substantial purchasing power? Can the seller dictate sales terms to buyers?
- *Inputs* Who are its suppliers? Are there many supply sources? Does the company depend on a few supply sources with potential for high input costs?
- *Competition* In what kind of markets does it operate? Are markets open and able to accept new investment? Is the market competitive? Does the company have competitive advantages? Can it protect itself from new entrants? At what cost? How must it compete to survive?
- *Capital* Must it seek capital from public markets? Is it going public? Is it seeking to use its stock to acquire another company? Is it in danger of defaulting on debt covenants? Are there incentives to tell an overly optimistic story to attract lower cost capital or to avoid default on debt?
- *Labor* Who are its managers? What are their backgrounds? Can they be trusted? Are they competent? What is the state of employee relations? Is labor unionized?
- *Governance* How effective is its corporate governance? Does its have a strong and independent board of directors? Does a strong audit committee of the board exist, and is it populated with outsiders? Does management have a large portion of its wealth tied to the company's stock?
- *Risk* Is it subject to lawsuits from competitors or shareholders? Is it under investigation by regulators? Has it changed auditors? If so, why? Are its auditors independent? Does it face environmental and/or political risks?

We must remember the broader business context in which a company operates as we read and interpret its financial statements. Exhibit 1.11 emphasizes that a review of financial statements, which reflect business activities, cannot be undertaken in a vacuum. It is contextual and can only be effectively undertaken within the framework of a thorough understanding of the broader forces that impact company performance.

EXHIBIT 1.11 ■ Business Context for Financial Statements

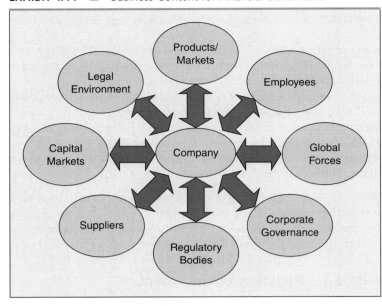

■ BOOK ORGANIZATION AND FLEXIBILITY

This book is aimed at those who use or will use financial accounting information to make better business decisions. As such, the book is focused on business decision makers both internal and external to companies. Profitability analysis is a guiding focus throughout, as it is a focus of attention by both internal and external decision makers. Accordingly, we use the return on assets disaggregation to help frame many discussions.

Our discussion of accounting emphasizes information, knowledge, and decision-making. These are the areas that provide the greatest value added. We focus on recording and compiling activities (the 'book-keeping' part of accounting) only to the extent necessary to pursue these more valuable management activities.

We begin the book with a focus on financial statements, including their preparation, analysis, and interpretation. Next, we introduce financial statement analysis objectives and techniques. This knowledge is useful background for other topics that focus on measuring, reporting, analyzing, and interpreting the core business activities of operating, investing, and financing. This includes off-balance-sheet financing and financial statement forecasting. We then show how accounting numbers are used in the valuation of securities, both debt and equity.

It is important to emphasize that each module, to the extent possible, is self-contained, with limited reference to any other module. This means that the instructor and reader can rearrange the ordering of modules or cover only a selected few. This is important as MBA programs and instructors offer diverse and valuable insights that complement the materials in this book.

Module 1 introduced the output of the financial reporting process: the balance sheet, the income statement, the statement of cash flows, and the statement of equity. Footnotes to each of those reports are an integral component of their usefulness. These financial reports and footnotes *reflect* the business activities of the company. We must keep this point in mind as we delve more deeply into principles that guide the preparation of financial reports. Financial statements are not reality; they merely reflect reality and provide us with clues concerning the degree to which the company is effectively managing its business activities. The more we understand the financial reporting process, the more skilled we will become in interpreting and acting on those clues.

■ MODULE-END REVIEW ■

Following are selected ratios of Procter & Gamble:

	Profit Margin	Asset Turnover
2003	12.0%	1.027
2004	12.6%	1.024

Required

a. Was the company profitable in 2004? What evidence supports your inference?
b. Do you interpret the change in the company's asset turnover rate as a positive development? Explain.
c. Compute the return on assets (ROA) for 2004 (show computations).

Solution

a. Procter & Gamble was profitable in 2004 as evidenced by its positive profit margin of 12.6%.
b. Asset turnover slightly decreased from 1.027 in 2003 to 1.024 in 2004. This is not a positive development as it indicates that assets are not generating the level of sales that they did in the prior year—however, this change is probably not material. Moreover, ROA increased in 2004; thus, the slight decline in turnover might be related to managerial initiatives to increase ROA.
c. Return on Assets (ROA) = Profit Margin × Asset Turnover = 12.6% × 1.024 = 12.9%

APPENDIX 1A

Accounting Principles and Governance Structures

■ FINANCIAL ACCOUNTING ENVIRONMENT

Information in financial statements is crucial to company valuation and, by extension, the valuation of its debt and equity securities. Financial statements affect prices paid for its equity securities and interest rates attached to its debt securities.

The importance of financial statements means that their reliability is of paramount importance. This includes the crucial role of *ethics*. To the extent that financial performance and condition are accurately communicated to business decision makers, debt and equity securities are more accurately priced. By extension, it is also important to recognize the crucial role of financial accounting in efficient resource allocation within and across economies. We must also recognize its importance to the effectiveness of securities markets—and other markets such as labor, input, and output markets.

To illustrate its importance, imagine the consequences of a breakdown in the integrity of financial accounting. Enron provides a case in point. Once it became clear to the markets that Enron had not faithfully and accurately reported its financial condition and performance, people became unwilling to purchase its securities. The value of its debt and equity securities dropped precipitously and the company was unable to obtain cash needed for operating activities. Within months of the disclosure of its financial accounting irregularities, Enron, with revenues of over $100 billion and total company value of over $60 billion, the fifth largest U.S. company, was bankrupt!

Further historical evidence of the importance of financial accounting is provided by the Great Depression of the 20th century. This depression was caused, in large part, by the failure of companies to faithfully report their financial condition and performance.

Oversight of Financial Accounting

The Great Depression led Congress to pass the 1933 Securities Act. This act had two main objectives: (1) to require disclosure of financial and other information about securities being offered for public sale; and (2) to prohibit deceit, misrepresentations, and other fraud in the sale of securities. This act also required that companies register all securities proposed for public sale and disclose information about the securities being offered, including information about company financial condition and performance. This act became and remains a foundation for contemporary financial accounting.

Congress also passed the 1934 Securities Act, which created the **Securities and Exchange Commission** (SEC) and gave it broad powers to regulate the issuance and trading of securities. The act also provided that companies with more than $10 million in assets and whose securities are held by more than 500 owners must file annual and other periodic reports, including financial statements that are available for download from the SEC's **EDGAR** database (www.sec.gov).

The SEC has ultimate authority over U.S. financial reporting, including setting accounting standards for preparing financial statements. The SEC has ceded the authority to set accounting standards to businesses themselves in the form of a nongovernmental body, the American Institute of Certified Public Accountants (AICPA). Over the years, the AICPA has sponsored three (nonoverlapping in time) standard-setting organizations, each of which was governed by representatives from private industry, including accountants, investment managers, securities analysts, academics, and corporate managers.

The current standard-setting organization is the **Financial Accounting Standards Board (FASB)**, which has published over 150 accounting standards governing the preparation of financial reports. This is in addition to over 40 standards that were written by predecessor organizations to the FASB and numerous bulletins and interpretations, all of which form the body of accounting standards governing financial statements, which are called **Generally Accepted Accounting Principles (GAAP)**.

The standard-setting process is arduous, often lasting a decade and involving extensive comment by the public, public officials, accountants, academics, investors, analysts, and corporate preparers of financial reports. The reason for this involved process is that amendments to existing standards or the creation of new standards affect the reported financial performance and condition of companies—that is, their reported profits and other measures of financial condition. Consequently, given the widespread impact of financial accounting, there are considerable **economic consequences** as a result of accounting changes.

Choices in Financial Accounting

Some people mistakenly assume that financial accounting is an exact discipline—that is, companies select the proper standard to account for a transaction and then follow the rules. The reality is that GAAP allows companies choices in preparing financial statements. The choice of methods often yields financial statements that are markedly different from one another in terms of reported income, assets, liabilities, and equity amounts.

People often are surprised that financial statements depend on numerous estimates. For example, companies must estimate the amounts owed from customers that will eventually be collected, the length of time that buildings and equipment will be productive, the value impairments of assets, the prediction of future costs such as warranties, the prediction of future pension costs, and so on.

Accounting standard setters walk a fine line regarding choice in accounting. On one hand, they are concerned that choice in preparing financial statements will lead to abuse by those seeking to gain by influencing decisions of those who rely on those statements. On the other hand, they are concerned that companies are too diverse for a 'one size fits all' financial accounting system.

For example, Enron exemplifies rigidity problems with accounting standards. A set of accounting standards relating to special purpose entities (SPEs) provided preparers with guidelines under which these entities are and are not aggregated with the companies that established them. Unfortunately, once guidelines are set, some people work diligently to structure these entities so as to just miss the requirements to aggregate them with the financial statements of the establishing company. This is one example of *off-balance-sheet financing*.

For most of its existence, the FASB has promulgated standards that were quite complicated and replete with guidelines. This invited abuse of the type embodied by the Enron scandal. Consequently, the pendulum has begun to swing away from such rigidity. Now, once financial statements are prepared, company management is required to step back from the details and make a judgment on whether the statements taken as a whole 'fairly present' the financial condition of the company.

Moreover, as a result of the 2002 **Sarbanes-Oxley Act**, the SEC requires the chief executive officer (CEO) of the company and its chief financial officer (CFO) to personally sign a statement attesting to the accuracy and completeness of financial statements. This requirement is an important step in restoring confidence in the integrity of financial accounting. The statements signed by both the CEO and CFO contain the following commitments:

- Both the CEO and CFO have personally reviewed the annual report
- There are no untrue statements of a material fact or the failure to state a material fact necessary to make the statements not misleading

- Financial statements fairly present in all material respects the financial condition of the company
- All material facts are disclosed to the company's auditors and board of directors
- No changes to its system of internal controls are made unless properly communicated

The prospect of personal losses is designed to make these managers more vigilant in monitoring the financial accounting system.

■ REGULATORY AND LEGAL ENVIRONMENT

Even though managers must personally attest to the completeness and accuracy of company financial statements, markets demand further assurances from outside parties to achieve the level of confidence necessary to warrant investment, credit, and other business decisions. The regulatory and legal environment provides further assurance that financial statements are complete and accurate.

Audit Committee

Law requires each publicly traded company to have a board of directors, where stockholders elect each director. This board represents the company owners and oversees management. The board also hires executive management and regularly reviews company operations.

The board of directors usually establishes several subcommittees to focus on particular governance tasks such as compensation, strategic plans, and financial management. Exhibit 1A.1 illustrates a typical organization of a company's governance structure. Corporate governance refers to the checks and balances that monitor company and manager activities. Governance committees are commonplace. One of these, the audit committee, oversees the financial accounting system.

EXHIBIT 1A.1

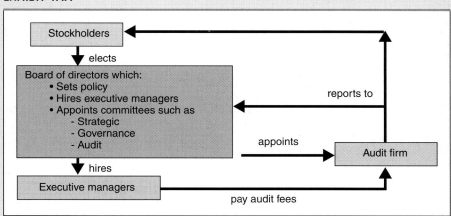

The audit committee preferably consists solely of outside directors, excluding the CEO. As part of its oversight of the financial accounting system, the audit committee focuses on **internal controls**, which refers to the policies and procedures used to protect assets, ensure reliable accounting, promote efficient operations, and urge adherence to company policies.

Statement of Management Responsibility

Financial statements for each publicly traded company must contain a **statement of responsibility** such as that for **DuPont** in Exhibit 1A.2.

EXHIBIT 1A.2 ▨ Responsibility for Financial Reporting

Responsibility for Financial Reporting Report of Independent Accountants

Management is responsible for the consolidated financial statements and the other financial information contained in this Annual Report on Form 10-K. The financial statements have been prepared in conformity with accounting principles generally accepted in the United States of America and are considered by management to present fairly the company's financial position, results of operations and cash flows. The financial statements include some amounts that are based on management's best estimates and judgments.

The company's system of internal controls is designed to provide reasonable assurance as to the protection of assets against loss from unauthorized use or disposition, and the reliability of financial records for preparing financial statements and maintaining accountability for assets. The company's business ethics policy is the cornerstone of our internal control system. This policy sets forth management's commitment to conduct business worldwide with the highest ethical standards and in conformity with applicable laws. The business ethics policy also requires that the documents supporting all transactions clearly describe their true nature and that all transactions be properly reported and classified in the financial records. The system is monitored by an extensive program of internal audit, and management believes that the system of internal controls at December 31, 2002, meets the objectives noted above.

The financial statements have been audited by the company's independent accountants, PricewaterhouseCoopers LLP. The purpose of their audit is to independently affirm the fairness of management's reporting of financial position, results of operations and cash flows. To express the opinion set forth in their report, they study and evaluate the internal controls to the extent they deem necessary. The adequacy of the company's internal controls and the accounting principles employed in financial reporting are under the general oversight of the Audit Committee of the Board of Directors. This committee also has responsibility for employing the independent accountants, subject to stockholder ratification. No member of this committee may be an officer or employee of the company or any subsidiary or affiliated company. The independent accountants and the internal auditors have direct access to the Audit Committee, and they meet with the committee from time to time, with and without management present, to discuss accounting, auditing and financial reporting matters.

The statement of responsibility contains several assertions by management:

1. Financial statements are prepared by management, which assumes responsibility for them
2. Financial statements are prepared in accordance with GAAP
3. Its system of internal controls provides *reasonable assurance* that assets are safeguarded and the information system is protected
4. Financial statements are audited by an outside auditing firm
5. Board of directors has an audit committee to oversee the financial accounting system and the system of internal controls

It is important to remember that management prepares financial statements—not the auditors that are hired to express an opinion on those statements. Moreover, remember that management's interests may or may not be aligned with those of other stakeholders.

Audit Report

Financial statements for each publicly traded company must be audited by an independent audit firm. There are four large, international auditing firms (and other smaller firms) that are authorized by the SEC to provide auditing services for companies that issue securities to the public:

1. **Deloitte & Touche LLP**
2. **Ernst & Young LLP**
3. **KPMG LLP**
4. **PricewaterhouseCoopers LLP**

These four firms provide opinions for the majority of financial statements filed by publicly traded U.S. companies. There also are a number of regional accounting firms that provide audit services for both publicly traded and non-traded private companies.

Auditors are hired by the company to review and express an opinion on its financial statements. The audit opinion expressed by Deloitte & Touche, LLP on the financial statements of Berkshire Hathaway is reproduced in Exhibit 1A.3.

EXHIBIT 1A.3   ■   Audit Report for Berkshire Hathaway

INDEPENDENT AUDITORS' REPORT

To the Board of Directors and Shareholders
Berkshire Hathaway Inc.

We have audited the accompanying consolidated balance sheets of Berkshire Hathaway Inc. and subsidiaries (the "Company") as of December 31, 2003 and 2002, and the related consolidated statements of earnings, cash flows and changes in shareholders' equity and comprehensive income for each of the three years in the period ended December 31, 2003. These financial statements are the responsibility of the Company's management. Our responsibility is to express an opinion on these financial statements based on our audits.

We conducted our audits in accordance with auditing standards generally accepted in the United States of America. Those standards require that we plan and perform the audit to obtain reasonable assurance about whether the financial statements are free of material misstatement. An audit includes examining, on a test basis, evidence supporting the amounts and disclosures in the financial statements. An audit also includes assessing the accounting principles used and significant estimates made by management, as well as evaluating the overall financial statement presentation. We believe that our audits provide a reasonable basis for our opinion.

In our opinion, such consolidated financial statements present fairly, in all material aspects, the financial position of Berkshire Hathaway Inc. and subsidiaries as of December 31, 2003 and 2002, and the results of their operations and their cash flows for each of the three years in the period ended December 31, 2003 in conformity with accounting principles generally accepted in the United States of America.

As described in Note 1 to the consolidated financial statements, the Company adopted Statement of Financial Accounting Standards No. 142 ("SFAS 142"), "Goodwill and Other Intangible Assets", effective January 1, 2002.

DELOITTE & TOUCHE LLP
March 4, 2004
Omaha, Nebraska

The basic structure of a 'clean' audit report is consistent across companies and includes these assertions:

- Financial statements *present fairly* and *in all material respects* a company's financial condition.
- Financial statements are prepared in conformity with GAAP.
- Financial statements are management's responsibility. Auditor responsibility is to express an opinion on those statements.
- Auditing involves a sampling of transactions, not investigation of each transaction.
- Audit opinion provides *reasonable assurance* that the statements are free of *material* misstatements, not a guarantee.
- Auditors review accounting policies used by management and the estimates used in preparing the statements.

The audit opinion is not based on a test of each transaction. Auditors usually develop statistical samples and infer test results to other transactions. The audit report is not a guarantee that no misstatements exist. Auditors only provide reasonable assurance that the statements are free of material misstatements. Their use of the word *reasonable* is deliberate, as they do not want to be held to an absolute standard should problems be subsequently uncovered. The word *material* is used in the sense that an item must be of sufficient magnitude to make a difference, that is, to change the perceptions or decisions of the user (such as a decision to purchase stock or extend credit).

The requirement of auditor independence is the cornerstone of effective auditing and is subject to debate as the company pays audit fees. Auditing firms often perform consulting services for the company it audits, such as tax planning, information system design and implementation, internal control evaluation, and benchmarking analyses.

Regulators have questioned the perceived lack of independence of auditing firms and the degree to which declining independence compromises the ability of auditing firms to challenge a client's dubious accounting. Auditing firms object to any assertion that their independence is compromised.

BUSINESS INSIGHT	Warren Buffet on Audit Committees

"Audit committees can't audit. Only a company's outside auditor can determine whether the earnings that a management purports to have made are suspect. Reforms that ignore this reality and that instead focus on the structure and charter of the audit committee will accomplish little.

As we've discussed, far too many managers have fudged their company's numbers in recent years, using both accounting and operational techniques that are typically legal but that nevertheless materially mislead investors. Frequently, auditors knew about these deceptions. Too often, however, they remained silent. The key job of the audit committee is simply to get the auditors to divulge what they know.

To do this job, the committee must make sure that the auditors worry more about misleading its members than about offending management. In recent years auditors have not felt that way. They have instead generally viewed the CEO, rather than the shareholders or directors, as their client. That has been a natural result of day-to-day working relationships and also of the auditors' understanding that, no matter what the book says, the CEO and CFO pay their fees and determine whether they are retained for both auditing and other work. The rules that have been recently instituted won't materially change this reality. What will break this cozy relationship is audit committees unequivocally putting auditors on the spot, making them understand they will become liable for major monetary penalties if they don't come forth with what they know or suspect."—Warren Buffet, Berkshire Hathaway annual report

■ SEC ENFORCEMENT ACTIONS

Companies whose securities are issued to the public must file reports with the SEC (see **www.sec.gov**). One of these reports is the 10-K, which includes the annual financial statements (quarterly statements are filed under report 10-Q). The 10-K report provides more information than the company's glossy annual report, which is partly a marketing document (although the basic financial statements are identical). You should use the 10-K because of its additional information.

The SEC has ultimate authority to accept or reject financial statements that companies submit. Should the SEC reject financial statements a company files, the company is then required to restate and refile them. Any restatement takes time and such companies usually incur a marked decline in its market value. For example, the following SEC press release is an example of SEC action against **Xerox** arising from its financial statements:

> *Washington, D.C., April 11, 2002*—The Securities and Exchange Commission today filed suit against **Xerox Corporation** in connection with a wide-ranging, four-year scheme to defraud investors. The SEC's complaint alleges that from at least 1997 through 2000, Xerox used a variety of what it called 'accounting actions' and 'accounting opportunities' to meet or exceed Wall Street expectations and disguise its true operating performance from investors. These actions, most of which violated generally accepted accounting principles (GAAP), accelerated the company's recognition of equipment revenue by over $3 billion and increased its pre-tax earnings by approximately $1.5 billion. Xerox agreed to settle the SEC's complaint by consenting to the entry of an injunction for violations of the antifraud and other provisions of the federal securities laws; restating its financials for the years 1997 to 2000; agreeing to a special review of its accounting controls; and paying an unprecedented $10 million penalty. (SEC Website, April 2002)

The SEC's power to require restatement, with its consequent damage to company reputation and company stock price, is a major deterrent to those desiring to bias their financial accounts to achieve a particular goal.

Courts

Courts provide remedies to individuals or companies that can show damages as a result of material misstatements in financial numbers. Typical court actions involve shareholders that sue the company and its auditors, alleging that the company disclosed, and auditors attested to, false and misleading financial statements. The number of such shareholder suits has increased dramatically according to Stanford Law School's Securities Class Action Clearinghouse, which commented that "an increasing percentage of the complaints filed allege financial misstatements and violations of GAAP, or generally accepted accounting principles."

Both the SEC and attorneys representing shareholders in a class action suit brought one such suit against **Rite Aid Corporation**, the large drug store chain. The SEC described Rite Aid's financial accounting as follows:

> Rite Aid's former senior management team engaged in a financial fraud that materially overstated the Company's net income for the fiscal years (FY) 1998, 1999, the intervening quarters and the first quarter of FY 2000. In addition, the

former senior management failed to disclose material information, including related party transactions, in Proxy and Registration Statements, as well as a Form 8-K filed in February 1999. Initially in July 2000 and later in October 2000, Rite Aid restated reported cumulative pre-tax income by a total of $2.3 billion and cumulative net income by $1.6 billion. Rite Aid's massive restatement was, and to this day is, the largest financial restatement of income by a public company. As a result of the improper acts and accounting practices described below, Rite Aid violated the reporting, books and records, and internal controls provisions of the Exchange Act.

Sections 13(a) and 13(b)(2)(A) of the Exchange Act and Rules 12b-20, 13a-1, and 13a-13 require issuers to make and keep accurate books, records, and accounts, to file annual and quarterly reports with the Commission, and to keep reported information current and not misleading. Section 13(b)(2)(B) of the Exchange Act requires issuers to devise and maintain a system of internal accounting controls sufficient to provide reasonable assurances that transactions are recorded as necessary to permit preparation of financial statements in conformity with generally accepted accounting principles and to maintain the accountability of assets.

Rite Aid's internal books, records, and accounts reflected numerous transactions that were invalid or without substantiation, had no legitimate business purpose, and were recorded in violation of GAAP. Moreover, from at least 1997 to July 11, 2000, all of the annual and quarterly reports that Rite Aid filed with the Commission contained misleading financial statements. As a result, Rite Aid violated Sections 13(a) and 13(b)(2)(A) of the Exchange Act and Rules 12b-20, 13a-1, and 13a-13 thereunder.

Rite Aid's system of internal accounting controls was not designed to provide reasonable assurances that transactions were recorded as necessary to permit preparation of financial statements in conformity with GAAP or to maintain the accountability of assets. Rite Aid's system of internal accounting controls failed to prevent, and indeed facilitated, the improper accounting practices described in detail above. As a result, Rite Aid violated Section 13(b) of the Exchange Act and Rule 13(b)(2)(B) thereunder. (Source: SEC Website, April 2003)

Rite Aid's settlement agreement with shareholders provided for the following payments:

1. Rite Aid agreed to pay $193 million in damages.
2. Rite Aid's auditors agreed to pay $125 million in damages.
3. Martin Grass, Rite Aid's former chair, agreed to pay $1.45 million in damages.
4. Timothy Noonan, Rite Aid's former COO, agreed to pay $130,000 in damages.

GUIDANCE ANSWERS

MANAGERIAL DECISION   You Are the Product Manager

There are at least two considerations that must be balanced—namely, the disclosure requirements and your company's need to protect its competitive advantages. You must comply with all minimum required disclosures. The extent to which you offer additional disclosures depends on the sensitivity of the information; that is, how beneficial it is to your existing and potential competitors. Another consideration is how the information disclosed will impact your existing and potential investors. Disclosures such as this can be beneficial in that they convey the positive investments that are available to your company. Still, there are many stakeholders impacted by your decision and each must be given due consideration.

MANAGERIAL DECISION   You Are the Chief Financial Officer

Financial performance is typically measured by return on assets, which can be disaggregated into the net profit margin (income/sales) and the asset turnover rate (sales/average assets). This disaggregation might lead you to a review of both the factors affecting profitability (gross margins and expense control) and how effectively your company is utilizing its assets (the turnover rates). Finding ways to increase profitability and reduce the amount of invested capital contributes to improved financial performance.

Superscript ^A denotes assignments based on Appendix 1A.

■ DISCUSSION QUESTIONS

Q1-1.   What are the three major business activities of a company that are motivated and shaped by planning activities? Explain each activity.

Q1-2. The accounting equation (Assets = Liabilities + Equity) is a fundamental business concept. Explain what this equation reveals about a company's sources and uses of funds and the claims on company resources.

Q1-3. Companies prepare four primary financial statements. What are those financial statements and what information is typically conveyed in each?

Q1-4. Does a balance sheet report on a period of time or at a point in time? Also, explain the information conveyed in that report.

Q1-5. Does an income statement report on a period of time or at a point in time? Also, explain the information conveyed in that report.

Q1-6. Does a statement of cash flows report on a period of time or at a point in time? Also, explain the information and activities conveyed in that report.

Q1-7. Explain what is meant by the articulation of financial statements.

Q1-8. The trade-off between risk and return is a fundamental business concept. Briefly describe both risk and return and their trade-off. Provide some examples that demonstrate investments of varying risk and the approximate returns that you might expect to earn on those investments.

Q1-9. Identify the five forces that influence competitive intensity and discuss the impact of each.

Q1-10. Financial statements are used by several interested stakeholders. Develop a listing of three or more potential external users of financial statements and their applications.

Q1-11. What ethical issues might managers face in dealing with confidential information?

Q1-12. Return on assets (ROA) is an important summary measure of financial performance. How is it computed? Describe what this metric reveals about company performance.

Q1-13. Refer to Exhibit 1.9 to answer (a) through (c).
- *a.* Discuss possible reasons for the difference in profit margin and asset turnover between the Retail and the Communication industries.
- *b.* Which industry is more profitable, Pharmaceuticals or Healthcare? Why do you believe this is the case?
- *c.* Which industry has the higher asset turnover, Restaurants or Agriculture? Why do you believe this is the case?

Procter & Gamble (PG)

Q1-14.[A] Access the 2004 10-K for Procter & Gamble at the SEC's EDGAR database of financial reports (www.sec.gov). Who is P&G's auditor? What specific language does its auditor use in expressing its opinion and what responsibilities does it assume?

Q1-15.[A] Business decision makers external to the company increasingly demand more financial information on business activities of companies. Discuss the reasons why companies have traditionally opposed the efforts of regulatory agencies like the SEC to require more disclosure.

Q1-16.[A] What are generally accepted accounting principles and what organization presently establishes them?

Enron (ENRNQ)

Q1-17.[A] Corporate governance has received considerable attention since the collapse of Enron and other accounting-related scandals. What is meant by corporate governance? What are the primary means by which sound corporate governance is achieved?

Q1-18.[A] What is the primary function of the auditor? To what does the auditor attest in its opinion?

■ MINI EXERCISES

Dell Computer Corporation (DELL)

M1-19. **Financing and Investing Relations, and Financing Sources**   Total assets of Dell Computer Corporation equal $15,470 million and its equity is $4,873 million. What is the amount of its liabilities? Does Dell receive more financing from its owners or nonowners, and what percentage of financing is provided by its owners?

Ford Motor Company (F)

M1-20. **Financing and Investing Relations, and Financing Sources**   Total assets of Ford Motor Company equal $315,920 million and its liabilities equal $304,269 million. What is the amount of its equity? Does Ford receive more financing from its owners or nonowners, and what percentage of financing is provided by its owners?

M1-21. **Applying the Accounting Equation and Computing Financing Proportions**   Use the accounting equation to compute the missing financial amounts (a), (b), and (c). Which of these companies is more owner-financed? Which of these companies is more nonowner-financed?

Hewlett-Packard (HPQ)

General Mills (GIS)

General Motors (GM)

($ millions)	Assets	=	Liabilities	+	Equity
Hewlett-Packard	$74,708		$ 36,962		$ (a)
General Mills	$18,227		$ (b)		$4,175
General Motors	$ (c)		$365,057		$6,814

M1-22. **Identifying Key Numbers from Financial Statements**   Access the 2004 10-K for Winn-Dixie Stores, Inc., at the SEC's EDGAR database for financial reports (www.sec.gov). What are Winn Dixie's dollar amounts for assets, liabilities, and equity at June 30, 2004? Confirm that the accounting equation holds in this case. What percent of Winn Dixie's assets is financed from nonowner financing sources?

Winn-Dixie
Stores, Inc.
(WIN)

M1-23. **Verifying Articulation of Financial Statements**   Access the 2002 10-K for DuPont at the SEC's EDGAR database of financial reports (www.sec.gov). Using its December 31, 2002, consolidated statement of stockholders' equity, prepare a table showing the articulation of its retained (reinvested) earnings for calendar-year 2002.

DuPont (DD)

M1-24. **Identifying Financial Statement Line Items and Accounts**   Several line items and account titles are listed below. For each, indicate in which of the following financial statement(s) you would likely find the item or account: income statement (IS), balance sheet (BS), statement of stockholders' equity (SE), or statement of cash flows (SCF).

a.	Cash asset	*d.*	Contributed capital	*g.*	Cash inflow for stock issued
b.	Expenses	*e.*	Cash outflow for land	*h.*	Cash outflow for dividends
c.	Noncash assets	*f.*	Retained earnings	*i.*	Net income

M1-25.[A] **Ethical Issues and Accounting Choices**   Assume that you are a technology services provider and you must decide on whether to record revenue from the installation of computer software for one of your clients. Your contract calls for acceptance of the software by the client within six months of installation before payment is due. Although you have not yet received formal acceptance, you are confident that it is forthcoming. Failure to record these revenues will cause your company to miss Wall Street's earnings estimates. What stakeholders will be affected by your decision and how might they be affected?

M1-26.[A] **Internal Controls and their Importance**   The Sarbanes-Oxley legislation requires companies to report on the effectiveness of their internal controls. What are internal controls and their purpose? Why do you think Congress felt it to be such an important area to monitor and report on?

■ EXERCISES

E1-27. **Applying the Accounting Equation and Assessing Financing Contributions**   Determine the missing amount from each of the separate situations (a), (b), and (c) below. Which of these companies is more owner-financed? Which of these companies is more nonowner-financed?

Motorola, Inc.
(MOT)

Kraft Foods
(KFT)

Merck & Co.
(MRK)

($ millions)	Assets	=	Liabilities	+	Equity
a. Motorola, Inc.	$31,152	=	$?		$11,239
b. Kraft Foods	$?	=	$31,268		$25,832
c. Merck & Co.	$47,561	=	$29,361		$?

E1-28. **Applying the Accounting Equation and Financial Statement Articulation**   Answer the following questions. (*Hint*: Apply the accounting equation.)

a. Intel had assets equal to $44,224 million and liabilities equal to $8,756 million for a recent year-end. What was the total equity for Intel's business at year-end?

b. At the beginning of a recent year, JetBlue's assets were $1,378 million and its equity was $415 million. During the year, assets increased $70 million and liabilities increased $30 million. What was its equity at the end of the year?

c. At the beginning of a recent year, The Walt Disney Company's liabilities equaled $26,197 million. During the year, assets increased by $400 million, and year-end assets equaled $50,388 million. Liabilities decreased $100 million during the year. What were its beginning and ending amounts for equity?

Intel (INTC)

JetBlue (JBLU)

The Walt
Disney
Company
(DIS)

E1-29. **Specifying Financial Information Users and Uses**   Financial statements have a wide audience of interested stakeholders. Identify two or more financial statement users that are external to the company. Specify two questions for each user identified that could be addressed or aided by use of financial statements.

E1-30. **Applying Financial Statement Relations to Compute Dividends**   Colgate-Palmolive reports the following dollar balances in its stockholders' equity.

Colgate-
Palmolive (CL)

($ millions)	2003	2002
Contributed capital, net	$ 45.8	$ 568.7
Retained earnings	7,433.0	6,518.5
Total equity	$7,478.8	$7,087.2

During 2003, Colgate-Palmolive reported net income of $1,421.3 million. What amount of dividends, if any, did Colgate-Palmolive pay to its shareholders in 2003? Assuming it paid dividends, this dividend amount constituted what percent of its net income?

**Briggs &
Stratton (BGG)**

E1-31. **Computing and Interpreting Financial Statement Ratios**   Following are selected ratios of **Briggs & Stratton** (manufacturer of engines).

	Net Profit Margin (Net Income/Sales)	Total Asset Turnover (Sales/Average Assets)
2000	8.58%	1.76
2001	3.66%	1.18

    a.   Was the company profitable in 2001? What evidence do you have of this?
    b.   Do you interpret the change in its total asset turnover rate as a positive development? Explain.
    c.   Compute the company's return on assets (ROA) for 2001 (show computations).

**Nordstrom,
Inc. (JWN)**

E1-32. **Computing Return on Assets and Applying the Accounting Equation**   **Nordstrom, Inc.**, reports net income of $242.8 million for its fiscal year ended January 2004. At the beginning of that year, Nordstrom had $4,096.4 million in total assets. By fiscal year-end 2004, total assets had grown to $4,465.7. What is Nordstrom's return on assets (ROA)? Does its ROA seem adequate? Explain.

E1-33.[A]   **Accounting in Society**   Financial accounting plays an important role in modern society and business.
    a.   Identify two or more external stakeholders that are interested in a company's financial statements and what their particular interests are.
    b.   What are *generally accepted accounting principles,* and what organization has primary responsibility for their formulation?
    c.   What role does financial accounting play in the allocation of society's financial resources?
    d.   What are three aspects of the accounting environment that can create ethical pressure on management?

■ PROBLEMS

**Procter &
Gamble (PG)**

P1-34. **Applying the Accounting Equation and Financial Statement Articulation**   The following table contains financial statement information for **Procter & Gamble** ($ millions):

Year	Assets	Liabilities	Equity	Net Income	Cash Dividends
2001	$?	$22,377	$12,010	$2,922	$1,943
2002	40,776	?	13,706	4,352	2,095
2003	43,706	27,520	?	5,186	2,246

Required
    a.   Compute the missing amounts for assets, liabilities, and equity for each year.
    b.   Compute return on assets for 2002 and 2003. The average ROA for all publicly traded companies is about 5.5%. How does P&G compare with this average?
    c.   What factors do you think might allow a company like P&G to reap above-average returns? (*Hint*: Consider the five forces of competitive intensity.)

**General Mills,
Inc. (GIS)**

P1-35. **Formulating Financial Statements from Raw Data**   Following is selected financial information from **General Mills, Inc.**, for its fiscal year ended May 30, 2004 ($ millions):

Cash asset	$ 751
Net cash from operations	1,461
Sales	11,070
Stockholders' equity	5,547
Cost of goods sold	6,584
Net cash from financing	(943)
Total liabilities	12,901
Total expenses	3,431
Noncash assets	17,697
Net cash from investing	(470)
Net income	1,055
Cash, beginning year	703

Required

Prepare an income statement, balance sheet, and statement of cash flows for General Mills, Inc.

P1-36. **Formulating Financial Statements from Raw Data** Following is selected financial information from Abercrombie & Fitch for its fiscal year ended January 31, 2004 ($ millions):

Abercrombie & Fitch (ANF)

Cash asset	$ 511
Cash flows from operations	282
Sales	1,708
Stockholders' equity	871
Cost of goods sold	991
Cash flows from financing	(92)
Total liabilities	328
Expenses	512
Noncash assets	688
Cash flows from investing	(99)
Net income	205
Cash, beginning year	420

Required

Prepare an income statement, balance sheet, and statement of cash flows for Abercrombie & Fitch.

P1-37. **Formulating Financial Statements from Raw Data** Following is selected financial information from Cisco Systems, Inc., for the year ended July 31, 2004 ($ millions):

Cisco Systems, Inc. (CSCO)

Cash asset	$ 3,722
Cash flows from operations	7,121
Sales	22,045
Stockholders' equity	25,916
Cost of goods sold	6,919
Cash flows from financing	(7,790)
Total liabilities	9,678
Expenses	10,725
Noncash assets	31,872
Cash flows from investing	466
Net income	4,401
Cash, beginning year	3,925

Required

Prepare an income statement, balance sheet, and statement of cash flows for Cisco Systems, Inc.

P1-38. **Formulating a Statement of Stockholders' Equity from Raw Data** Crocker Corporation began calendar-year 2005 with stockholders' equity of $100,000, consisting of contributed capital of $70,000 and retained earnings of $30,000. During 2005, it issued additional stock for total cash proceeds of $30,000. It also reported $50,000 of net income, of which $25,000 was paid as a cash dividend to shareholders.

Required

Prepare the 2005 statement of stockholders' equity for Crocker Corporation.

P1-39. Formulating a Statement of Stockholders' Equity from Raw Data   EA Systems, Inc., reports the following selected information at December 31, 2005 ($ millions):

Contributed capital, December 31, 2004 and 2005	$ 550
Retained earnings, December 31, 2004	2,437
Cash dividends, 2005	281
Net income, 2005	859

Required

Use this information to prepare its statement of stockholders' equity for 2005.

P1-40. Computing, Analyzing, and Interpreting Return on Assets   Following are summary financial statement data for both **Kimberly-Clark** and **Procter & Gamble** (industry competitors) for the years 2002 and 2003:

Kimberly-Clark Corporation (KMB)			
($ millions)	Total Assets	Net Sales	Net Income
2002	$15,586	$13,566	$1,675
2003	16,780	14,348	1,694

Procter & Gamble Company (PG)			
($ millions)	Total Assets	Net Sales	Net Income
2002	$40,776	$40,169	$4,352
2003	43,706	43,373	5,186

Required

a. Compute the return on assets (net income/average assets), the net profit margin (net income/sales), and the total asset turnover (sales/average assets) for both companies for 2003.

b. Verify that return on assets is equal to the product of net profit margin and total asset turnover for both companies. Show computations.

c. Which company reports a higher return on assets for 2003? Identify one or more reasons for this difference? (*Hint*: Consider the five forces of competitive intensity.)

P1-41. Computing, Analyzing, and Interpreting Return on Assets   Nokia manufactures, markets, and sells phones and other electronics. Total assets for Nokia are €23,920 in 2003 and €23,327 in 2002. In 2003, Nokia reported net income of €3,592 on sales of €29,455.

Required

a. What is Nokia's return on assets for 2003?

b. Does return on assets seem satisfactory for Nokia given that its competitors average a 12% return on assets? Explain.

c. What are total expenses for Nokia in 2003?

d. What is Nokia's average total amount of liabilities plus equity for 2003?

P1-42. Computing, Analyzing, and Interpreting Return on Assets and its Components   Abercrombie & Fitch (ANF) reported net income of $205 million on sales of $1,700 million for fiscal year ended January 31, 2004. The January 31, 2004, balance sheet of ANF reports the following ($ millions):

	2004	2003
Total assets	$1,199	$1,023

Required

a. What is ANF's return on assets? Given that the average ROA for all publicly traded firms is about 5.5%, how does ANF compare on ROA? Explain.

    b. Decompose ANF's ROA into its net profit margin and total asset turnover. Given that the average net profit margin and asset turnover rate for all publicly traded firms is about 4.3% and 1.2 times, respectively, how does ANF compare on these measures? Explain.

    c. Given the competitive nature of the retail clothing industry, can you identify any reasons why ANF should report an above-average level of financial performance? (*Hint*: Recall the five forces of competitive intensity)? Explain.

P1-43. **Computing, Analyzing, and Interpreting Return on Assets and its Components**   McDonald's Corporation (MCD) reported 2003 net income of $1,470 million on sales of $17,140 million. The December 31, 2003, balance sheet of MCD reports the following ($ millions):

McDonald's
Corporation
(MCD)

	2003	2002
Total assets	$25,525	$23,971

Required

    a. What is MCD's return on assets? Given that the average ROA for all publicly traded firms is about 5.5%, how does MCD compare on ROA? Explain.

    b. Decompose MCD's ROA into its net profit margin and total asset turnover. Given that the average net profit margin and asset turnover rate for all publicly traded firms is about 4.3% and 1.2 times, respectively, how does MCD compare on these measures? Explain.

    c. Given the competitive nature of the food service industry, can you identify any reasons why MCD should report this level of financial performance and any potential areas of concern? (*Hint*: Recall the five forces of competitive intensity.) Explain.

P1-44. **Computing, Analyzing, and Interpreting Return on Assets and its Components**   Wal-Mart (WMT) reported net income of $9,100 million on sales of $258,700 million for fiscal year ended January 31, 2004. The January 31, 2004, balance sheet of WMT reports the following ($ millions):

Wal-Mart
(WMT)

	2004	2003
Total assets	$104,912	$94,808

Required

    a. What is WMT's return on assets? Given that the average ROA for all publicly traded firms is about 5.5%, how does WMT compare on ROA? Explain.

    b. Decompose WMT's ROA into its net profit margin and total asset turnover. Given that the average net profit margin and asset turnover rate for all publicly traded firms is about 4.3% and 1.2 times, respectively, how does WMT compare on these measures? Explain.

    c. Given the competitive nature of the retailing industry, can you identify any reasons why WMT should report an above-average level of financial performance? (*Hint*: Recall the five forces of competitive intensity.) Explain.

P1-45. **Analysis and Explanation of Risk and Return**   The trade-off between risk and return is a fundamental business concept. It underlies all business activities and management decisions.

Required

    a. Identify three different types of investments and their approximate return to the investor.

    b. Drawing on your solutions to (a), do you see that the concept of higher expected risk yields higher expected return? Explain.

    c. Apply the risk and return trade-off to discuss an investment in Berkshire Hathaway stock vis-à-vis an investment in U.S. government bonds.

Berkshire
Hathaway
(BRKA)

2 Constructing and Reporting Financial Statements

WHERE'S THE PIXIE DUST?

The Walt Disney Company acquired the ABC Television Network and related media companies for $18.9 billion in 1996. To finance the purchase, it used $10.1 billion of its cash and issued 155 million shares of additional common stock. The stock issuance increased its stockholders' equity by $8.8 billion to $16.086 billion. This acquisition was pitched to investors as the ultimate business model for media conglomerates, providing increased distribution outlets for Disney's well-respected media content.

The reality, however, never matched the hype. ABC did not move up in the ratings game, continuing to lag behind NBC, CBS, and FOX. Six years later, *Barrons* wrote:

> Let us catalog the damage. Attendance at the Walt Disney Co.'s fabled theme parks is down about 5% this year; the company's ABC television network is running a distant third in the ratings race, and Disney's animation studios, while sporadically turning out hits, haven't produced a blockbuster since *The Lion King* in 1994. With earnings slipping each year since 1997, and the company's shares at 16–17—levels last seen in 1995—is it any wonder Disney chief executive Michael Eisner is guarding the keys to the corner office? It's enough to give Goofy the blues.

As of 2004, Disney's stockholders' equity had increased by $7.7 billion to $23.791 billion, approximately a 7% compound growth rate. More than $4.3 billion of that increase, however, occurred in the first three years after the ABC acquisition. After that, Eisner made a number of missteps:

- Eisner spent $5.2 billion for the Fox Family Channel in 2001, which has yet to bear fruit. According to one analyst, the price worked out to about 33 times operating earnings, well above industry norms of 15 to 20 times earnings. This purchase also boosted Disney's debt level, and contributed to a downgrading of Disney's bonds. (*Barrons*, 2002)
- Eisner boosted company revenues in large part by raising theme-park admission prices. A $28 ticket to Walt Disney World in 1987 now costs over $50, while a $21.50 ticket to Disneyland now costs over $40. Given that a family of four can't get through the gates for much under $200 a day, without special packages, some observers wonder whether Disney has lost its pricing power (*Barrons*, 2002). Critics also say the fabled Disney theme parks are suffering from deferred maintenance and off-the-shelf rides (*St. Petersburg Times*, March 2004).

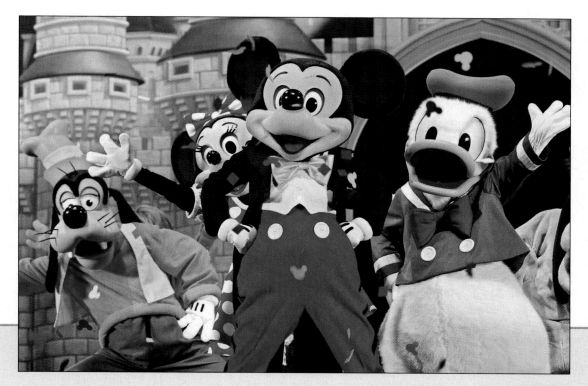

- Eisner handed the company's presidency to agent Michael Ovitz, who only lasted 14 months in the job, and subsequently, negotiated Ovitz's $140 million severance (dissenting shareholders say without board approval—*Washington Post,* 2004).
- Disney created the **Go.com** portal in 1999. However, Disney's attempt to compete with entrenched competitors in the portal and search-engine businesses never got off the ground. In 2001, it wrote off $820 million of intangible assets related to this venture as part of a restructuring program that reduced earnings by a total of $1.45 billion (Disney 2001 10-K).

Disney recognized $18.3 billion of goodwill when it acquired ABC. This meant that nearly the entire purchase price was allocated to goodwill (an intangible asset). Specifically, the fair market value of ABC's tangible assets (property, plant, and equipment) was $4.8 billion and the fair market value of its liabilities assumed was $4.2 billion. This means that Disney paid $18.9 billion for a company with net assets valued at $600 million ($4.8 billion − $4.2 billion) and recognized the difference as goodwill.

Disney's 2003 balance sheet also included a $494 million asset relating to its investment in Euro Disney, a separate company that operates its Paris theme park in which it has a 39% stake. This investment includes its ownership interest in the net equity of Euro Disney (approximately $27 million) as well as approximately $467 million in receivables from that entity. In 2003, Euro Disney reported a net loss of $56 million on $1.077 billion in revenues. Euro Disney's balance sheet reports $3.373 billion in assets, $3.304 billion in liabilities, and only $69 million in equity. Due to poor operating results, Euro Disney does not have sufficient cash flow to pay its debts and is now in default on its bonds.

This module expands our knowledge and analyses of all financial statements, including the balance sheet. The balance sheet reports the resources (assets) under control of management as well as the claims against those resources (liabilities and stockholders' equity). The balance sheet contains a wealth of information, including equity investments and intangible assets like goodwill.

Returning to Disney, during 2003 it earned $1.267 billion on sales of $27.061 billion. At first glance, this income appears on a par with that of the past few years. Upon closer scrutiny, the footnotes reveal that expenses were reduced by over $600 million due to nonamortization of the $18.3 billion of goodwill from the ABC acquisition per a recent accounting change (amortization was required in 2001 and prior years). Also, in

(Continued on next page)

(Continued from previous page)

2001, Disney wrote off $820 million of intangible assets as part of a $1.45 billion restructuring program. The write-off, coupled with the amortization of goodwill that was required under accounting standards at that date, resulted in a net *loss* for 2001 of $158 million.

This module also explains the preparation and analysis of the income statement. Income statements must be scrutinized for the information that they reveal about the viability of a company's products and services. One-time events, like nonoperating gains and losses and restructuring costs, provide insights into management's effectiveness in its role as steward of the capital that has been entrusted to it. We use those insights in projections of future performance. Our discussion in this module confronts these challenges and sets the stage for more in-depth discussions and analyses.

Again returning to Disney, in 2003 it reported $2.9 billion in cash from its operating activities, much more than the $1.267 billion in net income reported on the income statement. It also invested $1.034 billion of this operating cash flow into new attractions for its theme parks and other capital improvements, and paid out $1.523 billion cash to reduce its debt and to pay dividends to its shareholders.

Although Disney increased its cash balance by $344 million, we must look at the sources and uses of cash flows, and not necessarily the net increase (decrease) in cash. To do this, we analyze the statement of cash flows, which provides a wealth of cash flow information. This module shows how to use the statement of cash flows in conjunction with the balance sheet and income statement to provide a complete perspective on the financial condition and performance of a company.

In the final analysis, the largest asset of Disney is probably Mickey Mouse. This asset, however, is not reported on Disney's balance sheet because it cannot be reliably measured. Yet all of the income and cash flows it generates are very measurable and are reported in Disney's financial statements.

Without doubt, Disney is facing turbulent times. Says one employee, "I've been in the theme parks since they opened, and I can tell you there's no more pixie dust, especially among the workers" (*St. Petersburg Times,* 2004).

Sources: *St. Petersburg Times,* March 2004; *Washington Post,* 2004; *Barrons* 2002; *Walt Disney* 2004 and 2001 10-K Report.

■ INTRODUCTION

Prior to reviewing the four financial statements, we examine how costs flow through the financial accounting system. For this purpose, we look at the balance sheet (listing of what the company owns and what it owes at a point in time) and the income statement (listing of revenues, expenses, and income for a period of time).

The costs to acquire resources that a company intends to use in operations, such as inventories held for resale or equipment used in manufacturing, are recorded on the balance sheet as an asset. That cost remains on the company's balance sheet as an asset until it is used up or expires. Once used up, the cost is transferred from the balance sheet to the income statement and labeled as an expense. This is why assets are sometimes referred to as prepaid or deferred expenses. Exhibit 2.1 illustrates these cost flows.

EXHIBIT 2.1 ■ Flow of Costs

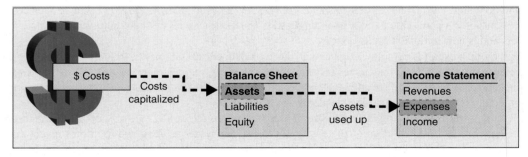

All costs are either held on the balance sheet or transferred to the income statement. If they are on the balance sheet, then assets are reported, expenses are deferred, and current income is higher. Once costs are transferred to the income statement, then assets are reduced, expenses are increased, and income is decreased.

Tracking costs is an important part of accounting. Most users of financial statements are concerned with cost flows. Many try to assess whether costs are properly transferred from the balance sheet to the income statement. If the cost transfer occurs more slowly than it should, current income is higher than it should be. If companies transfer costs too quickly, current income is lower than it should be. GAAP allows companies some flexibility in transferring costs. As such, there is potential for abuse, especially when managers confront pressures to achieve particular income targets. Recent scandals involving **WorldCom** and **Enron** regrettably illustrate improper recognition of costs to achieve income targets.

The transfer of costs impacts more than current period income. When costs are transferred too quickly, current period income is understated *and* future period income(s) is overstated because once costs are removed from the balance sheet they do not impact future period income. Conversely, if costs are removed too slowly from the balance sheet, current period income is overstated and future period income is understated. The improper transfer of costs, therefore, yields income shifting: increasing current period income and decreasing future period income, *or* depressing current period income and increasing future period income.

What does GAAP advise about the transfer of costs? Asset costs should transfer to the income statement when the asset is used in operating activities. For example, when inventories are purchased or manufactured, their cost is recorded on the balance sheet as an asset called *inventories*. When inventories are sold, they are considered used in operations and their cost is transferred to the income statement in an expense called *cost of goods sold.* Cost of good sold represents the cost of inventories sold for that period. This matches the cost of sales against the sales generated from the goods sold. Sales less cost of goods sold is gross profit.

As another example, consider equipment costs. When a company acquires equipment, the cost of the equipment is recorded on the balance sheet in an asset called *equipment* (often included in the general category of property, plant, and equipment, or PPE). When equipment is used in operations, a portion of the acquisition cost is transferred to the income statement to match against the sales it helped generate. To illustrate, if an asset costs $100,000, and 10% of it is used up this period in operating activities, then $10,000 of the asset's cost is transferred from the balance sheet to the income statement. This process is called *depreciation* and the expense related to this transfer of costs is called depreciation expense.

MANAGERIAL DECISION	**You Are the Securities Analyst**

You are analyzing the performance of a company that hired a new CEO during the current year. Several new charges relating to asset write-offs appear on the current year's income statement. How do you treat such charges? Are you especially concerned about the legitimacy of these charges? [Answer, p. 2-35]

■ BALANCE SHEET

The balance sheet is divided into three broad groups: assets, liabilities, and stockholders' equity. It provides us with information about the resources available to management and the claims against those resources by creditors and shareholders. The balance sheet is reported as of a point in time. Assets and liabilities are normally reported at their original purchase or issue price, not their current market value; exceptions are marketable securities and impaired assets. As a result, although assets that have permanently declined in value are written down, there can be unrealized gains associated with assets. Balance sheet accounts carry over from period to period; that is, the ending balance from one period becomes the beginning balance for the next.

Assets—Reflecting Investing Activities

Companies acquire assets to yield a return for their shareholders. Assets are expected to produce revenues, either directly such as with inventory that is sold or indirectly such as with a manufacturing plant that produces inventories for sale. To create shareholder value, assets must yield income that is in excess of the cost of the invested and borrowed funds utilized to acquire the assets.

The asset section of the **Walt Disney** balance sheet is shown in Exhibit 2.2. Disney reports $49,988 million of total assets as of September 30, its year-end. The amounts reported on the balance sheet are at a *point in time*—that is, the close of business on the day of the report.

EXHIBIT 2.2 ■ Asset Section of Walt Disney's Balance Sheet ($ millions)

THE WALT DISNEY COMPANY, INC.
Balance Sheet
September 30, 2003

Assets

Current Assets	Current assets	
Assets used up or converted to cash within one year	Cash and cash equivalents	$ 1,583
	Receivables	4,238
	Inventories	703
	Television costs	568
	Deferred income taxes	674
	Other current assets	548
	Total current assets	8,314
Long-Term Assets	Film and television costs	6,205
	Investments	1,849
	Parks, resorts and other property, at cost	
	Attractions, buildings and equipment	19,499
	Accumulated depreciation	(8,794)
		10,705
Assets not used up or converted to cash within one year	Projects in progress	1,076
	Land	897
		12,678
	Intangible assets, net	2,786
	Goodwill	16,966
	Other assets	1,190
	Total assets	$49,988

Walt Disney's business is not particularly seasonal. Other companies' balance sheets, such as those for retailers of children's toys, look quite different from one quarter to another. For example, **Toys 'R' Us** holds 50% more inventories during the winter quarter than it does during the summer period. Seasonality factors can result in large changes in the balance sheet at various points during the year and our analysis must consider these.

It is important to realize that managers only report on a balance sheet what they can reliably measure. This means that there is considerable information that is *not* reflected on a balance sheet. For example, the well-recognized image of Mickey Mouse is absent from Disney's balance sheet. This image is referred to as an unrecognized intangible asset. Like the Coke bottle silhouette, the Kleenex name, an excellent management team, or a well-designed supply-chain, intangible assets are only measured and reported on the balance sheet when they are purchased. As a result, *internally created* intangible assets, like the Mickey Mouse image, are not reported on a balance sheet. Many of these internally created intangible assets are of enormous value.

More generally, and in addition to being reliably measurable, an asset must possess two characteristics to be reported on the balance sheet:

1. It must be owned (or controlled) by the company.
2. It must possess expected future benefits.

The first requirement, owning or controlling an asset, implies that a company has legal title to the asset, such as the title to property, or has the unrestricted right to use the asset, such as a lease on the property. The second requirement implies that a company expects to realize a benefit from the asset. Benefits can be cash inflows from the sale of an asset or from sales of products produced by the asset. Benefits also can refer to the receipt of other assets such as with an account receivable from credit sales. Or, benefits can mean the reduction of a liability such as when assets are used to settle debts.

An asset's value can also be **impaired**—a situation where its market value is deemed to have permanently declined below its reported value. When such impairment occurs, the company removes the impaired amount from the asset value reported on the balance sheet and transfers that cost to the income statement. This process reduces current period income.

BUSINESS INSIGHT   **Disney Abandons Go.com**

The Wall Street Journal wrote in a 2001 article: GO.com has been a thorn in Disney's side almost since the moment it was created. The original idea was to create a general-interest portal that could compete with Yahoo! Inc. and others in attracting consumers to a Web gateway. But it quickly became clear that the incumbents were deeply entrenched and had a tremendous advantage.

Disney's decision to abandon GO.com prompted a reassessment of the investment value related to that business segment on its balance sheet. The value was deemed to be impaired, resulting in a charge of $1.45 billion on Disney's 2001 income statement for the write-off of intangible assets and the accrual of expected expenses with this restructuring as described in the following footnote to its 10-K:

> The company recorded restructuring and impairment charges totaling $1.45 billion. The GO.com charge is for the closure of the GO.com portal business and includes a non-cash write-off of intangible assets totaling $820 million. The investment impairment charge is for other-than-temporary declines in the fair value of certain Internet investments.

Asset write-off is a noncash charge. So to is the accrual of the expected restructuring expenses. However, there are cash outflows when the accrued liability is ultimately paid. Further, although a nonrecurring item, a write-off must not be ignored. It provides insight about the effectiveness, or lack thereof, of Disney's investment and management strategy.

The assets section of a balance sheet is presented in order of **liquidity**, which refers to the ease of converting noncash assets into cash. Cash is listed first as it is the most liquid asset. Next are usually marketable securities. These are short-term investments, such as stock holdings, that can be quickly sold to raise cash. Many companies invest excess cash (which generates no return) in marketable securities in a desire to yield a higher return. Accounts receivable often follow securities. These represent amounts due to the company from other companies (usually customers) and are commonly collected within 60 to 90 days. Inventories are often listed after receivables since their conversion into cash usually takes longer than the collection of receivables. Also, inventories are usually sold on credit and are not converted to cash until the resulting receivable is collected. Other assets such as prepaid expenses and taxes receivable are usually listed last. This collection of assets, from cash to prepaids, makes up what is often called *liquid assets*. Investment of cash into inventories that are subsequently sold, and then later result in cash when the receivables are collected, is the *cash cycle,* which is explained in Module 3.

Disney's liquid assets amount to $8,314 million, see Exhibit 2.2, which are more formally called **current assets**. Current assets are assets expected to be converted into cash or used in operations within the next year.[1]

$
Cash Effect

The amount of current assets is an important measure of liquidity. Companies require a degree of liquidity to effectively operate on a daily basis. However, current assets are expensive to hold—they must be insured, monitored, financed, and so forth—and they typically generate returns that are less than those from noncurrent assets. As a result, companies seek to maintain only just enough current assets to cover liquidity needs, but not so much so as to unnecessarily reduce income.

The second section of the balance sheet reports noncurrent (long-term) assets. Noncurrent assets consist of property, plant, and equipment (PPE), long-term investments, intangible assets (trademarks, franchises, goodwill, etc.). Noncurrent assets are not expected to be converted into cash for some time and are, therefore, listed after current assets.

---

[1]Technically, current assets include those assets expected to be converted into cash within the upcoming year or the company's operating cycle (the cash-to-cash cycle), whichever is longer. Fortune Brands (manufacturer of Jim Beam whiskey among other products) provides an example of the classification of inventories as a current asset with a cash conversion cycle of longer than one year. Its inventory footnote from a recent 10-K follows: "In accordance with generally recognized trade practices, bulk whiskey inventories are classified as current assets, although the majority of such inventories, due to the duration of aging processes, ordinarily will not be sold within one year."

| BUSINESS INSIGHT | Disney's Film and Television Costs |

Much of Disney's business (and market value) relates to development of media content, for both film and television. Motion picture costs often exceed $100 million. This is especially true for animated films with extensive graphic effects. How does Disney account for the costs of films like *Finding Nemo*? In footnotes to its 2003 10-K, Disney describes its accounting for film and television development costs as follows:

> Film and television production and participation costs are [capitalized and] expensed based on the ratio of the current period's gross revenues to estimated total gross revenues from all sources on an individual production basis . . . Television network series costs and multi-year sports rights are charged to expense based on the ratio of the current period's gross revenues to estimated total gross revenues from such programs. Estimates of total gross revenues can change significantly due to a variety of factors, including the level of market acceptance of film and television products, advertising rates and subscriber fees. Accordingly, revenue estimates are reviewed periodically and amortization is adjusted, if necessary.

Film and television costs are recorded on the balance sheet as assets. These assets are subsequently removed from the balance sheet and transferred to the income statement as expense based on the proportion of expected revenue earned in the current period. For example, if *Finding Nemo* is expected to earn total revenues of $500 million over its life, and it generates revenues of $200 million in the current year, then 2/5 of its development cost is removed from the balance sheet and recognized as expense in the year that those revenues are recorded. As Disney points out, the amount of cost recognized as expense depends on its estimates of total revenues for the film. These estimates are imprecise and prone to error— and even manager bias.

Assets are reported at their original acquisition prices, or **historical costs**, and not at their current market values (unless they are marketable investments or were recently deemed impaired and written down to market value). The concept of historical costs is not without controversy. The controversy arises because of the trade-off between the **relevance** of current market values for many business decisions and the **reliability** of historical cost measures.

To illustrate, when company valuation is the goal, then current market values of assets are arguably preferred (company value equals the value of its assets less amounts owed its creditors). What are the sources of market values? For some assets, like marketable securities, values are readily obtained from on-line quotes or from *The Wall Street Journal.* For other assets like property, plant, and equipment, we can only estimate their values until they are ultimately sold or used in operations. Allowing companies to report estimates of asset market values would introduce potential *bias* into financial reporting. Consequently, companies continue to report historical costs because the loss in reliability from introducing *subjectivity* with market values is considered greater than the loss in relevance from using historical costs.

Asset reporting is also limited in that companies only report what they can reliably measure. If a company cannot assign a monetary amount to an asset with relative certainty, it does not recognize it on the balance sheet. As a result, some assets are not reported on the balance sheet.

To illustrate, consider brand equity such as **Coca-Cola**'s ownership of its coke bottle silhouette and its logo. Notice that both basic requirements for an asset are met: Coke owns these brands and it expects to realize future benefits from them. The problem is reliably measuring expected future benefits. This means these assets are not reported on Coke's balance sheet. This is an omission of a sizable resource.

Some other intangible assets, which are usually nonphysical resources with uncertain benefits, are management quality and internally developed technology. Generally, such intangible assets confer a competitive advantage, yield above-normal income, but cannot be reliably measured.

It is as important to understand what is reported on the balance sheet and what *is not* reported on the balance sheet. The excluded assets often relate to knowledge-based assets, like people and technology. This is one reason that knowledge-based industries are so difficult to analyze. (The excluded assets are presumably reflected in company market values. This can yield a marked difference between company market values and their book values, or equity. This is illustrated in the following market value-to-book value ratios: Dell is 14.6; Harley-Davidson is 6.1, and Verizon is 2.8.)

Liabilities and Equity—Reflecting Financing Activities

Liabilities and equity represent the sources of capital to the company that are used to finance the acquisition of assets. Liabilities are borrowed funds such as accounts payable, accrued liabilities, and obligations to lenders or bond investors. They can be interest-bearing or non-interest-bearing. Equity represents capital that has been invested by the shareholders, either directly via the purchase of stock (net of any company repurchases of stock from its shareholders, called treasury stock) or indirectly in the form of retained earnings that reflect earnings that are reinvested in the business and not paid out as dividends. We discuss liabilities and equity in this section.

The liabilities and equity sections of the **Walt Disney** balance sheet are reproduced in Exhibit 2.3. Disney reports $25,769 million of total liabilities ($8,669 million + $10,643 million + $2,712 million + $3,745 million) and $24,219 million ($23,791 million + $428 million) of equity as of its 2003 year-end.

EXHIBIT 2.3 ■ Liabilities and Equity Sections of Walt Disney's Balance Sheet ($ millions)

	THE WALT DISNEY COMPANY, INC. Balance Sheet September 30, 2003	
	Liabilities and Shareholders' Equity	
Liabilities	Current liabilities	
	Accounts payable and other accrued liabilities	$ 5,044
	Current portion of borrowings	2,457
	Unearned royalties and other advances	1,168
	Total current liabilities	8,669
	Borrowings	10,643
	Deferred income taxes	2,712
	Other long-term liabilities	3,745
	Minority interests	428
Equity	Shareholders' equity	
	Preferred stock, $.01 par value	
	Authorized—100 million shares, Issued—none	—
	Common stock	
	Common stock—Disney, $.01 par value	
	Authorized—3.6 billion shares, Issued—2.1 billion shares	12,154
	Common stock—Internet Group, $.01 par value	
	Authorized—1.0 billion shares, Issued—none	—
	Retained earnings	13,817
	Accumulated other comprehensive loss	(653)
		25,318
	Treasury stock, at cost, 86.7 million and 81.4 million Disney shares	(1,527)
		23,791
	Total liabilities and shareholders' equity	$49,988

Callout annotations: Liabilities requiring payment within one year (pointing to Total current liabilities 8,669). Liabilities not requiring payment within one year (pointing to Borrowings 10,643, Deferred income taxes 2,712, Other long-term liabilities 3,745).

Why would Disney obtain capital from both borrowed funds and shareholders? Why not just one or the other? The answer lies in their relative costs and the contractual agreements that Disney has with each. Creditors have the first claim on the assets of the company. As a result, their position is not as risky and, accordingly, their expected return on investment is less than that required by shareholders (also, interest is tax deductible whereas dividends are not). So, then, why should a company not use all borrowed funds? The reason is that borrowed funds must be repaid and require periodic interest payments. If a company cannot pay these debts when they mature, creditors can force it into bankruptcy and potentially out of business. Shareholders, in contrast, cannot require repurchase of their stock, or even the payment of dividends. Thus, companies take on a level of debt that they can comfortably repay at reasonable interest costs. The remaining balance required to fund business activities is financed with higher cost equity capital.

| BUSINESS INSIGHT | How Much Disney Debt Is Reasonable? |

Disney reports total assets of $49,988 million, liabilities of $25,769 million, and equity of $24,219 million. This reveals that it finances 52% of its assets with borrowed funds and 48% with shareholder investment. This debt percentage is higher than that utilized by Viacom, but similar to other entertainment and media companies as shown below. Companies must monitor their financing sources and amounts. Too much reliance on equity capital is expensive. And, too much borrowing is risky. The level of debt that a company can effectively manage also depends on the stability and reliability of their operating cash flows.

Company ($ millions)	Assets	Liabilities	Liabilities as % of Total Assets	Equity	Equity as % of Total Assets
Walt Disney Company	$49,988	$25,769	52%	$24,219	48%
News Corp, Ltd	45,478	23,779	52%	21,699	48%
Six Flags, Inc	4,245	2,605	61%	1,640	39%
Viacom, Inc	89,754	27,266	30%	62,488	70%

Liabilities on the balance sheet are listed in order of maturity. Debts coming due first are listed first. For Disney, these are accounts payable, which are short-term payables due to other companies usually resulting from purchases of goods and services from suppliers, and loans payable during the upcoming year. Other short-term liabilities include unearned royalties, which are royalty payments received before they are actually earned, and accrued liabilities. For Disney, accrued liabilities include items such as wages payable to employees, retirement benefits payable, and income taxes payable.

Accounts payable arise when one company purchases goods or services from another company. Typically, sellers offer credit terms when selling to other companies, rather than expecting cash on delivery. The seller records an account receivable and the buyer records an account payable. Disney reports accounts payable of $4,095 million as of the balance sheet date. Liabilities that arise from transactions such as those making up its accounts payable are relatively uncomplicated. That is, a transaction occurs (inventory purchase), a bill is sent, and the amount owed is reported on the balance sheet as a liability. Disney also reports as part of its current liabilities the long-term debt that matures in the next year ($2,457 million).

Disney's accrued liabilities total $949 million. Accrued liabilities refer to incomplete transactions. For example, many companies provide a warranty on products sold. When the sale is recorded, companies must estimate the amount of warranty liability likely to be incurred and record that warranty cost in the same period that the sale is recorded. At the time of sale, companies can only estimate, or *accrue,* future warranty costs. Generally, companies must report such liabilities when both these conditions are met:

1. Occurrence of the obligation is *probable*
2. Amount of the obligation is *reasonably estimable*

Assuming these conditions are met, the company must record both the estimated liability on its balance sheet and the estimated warranty expense on its income statement. If only one condition is met, such liabilities are only described in the notes.

Disney's current liabilities total $8,669 million. **Current liabilities** are those obligations expected to require payment within one year or the operating cycle, whichever is longer. Analyses of companies commonly compare the level of current liabilities with that of current assets. We usually prefer more current assets than current liabilities to ensure that companies have sufficient liquidity to pay their short-term debts when they mature.

Net working capital, or simply working capital, reflects the difference between current assets and current liabilities and is defined as follows:

Net Working Capital = Current Assets − Current Liabilities

$
Cash Effect

The net working capital required to conduct business operations depends on the company's **operating cycle**, which is the time between paying cash for goods or employee services and receiving cash from customers—see Exhibit 2.4.

EXHIBIT 2.4 ■ Operating Cycle

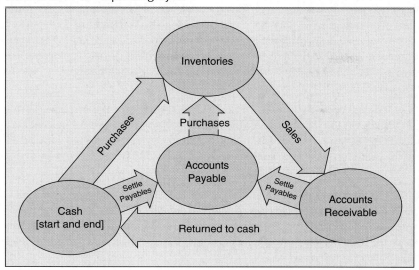

Manufacturing companies, for example, begin with cash that is used to purchase or manufacture inventories held for resale. Inventories are often purchased on credit (accounts payable) from other companies. This financing is called **trade credit**. When inventories are sold, they are often sold either on credit (accounts receivable) or for cash. When receivables are ultimately collected, a portion of the cash received is used to repay accounts payable and the remainder goes to the cash account for the next operating cycle.

When cash is invested in inventory, the inventory often remains with the company for 30 to 90 days. Once inventory is sold, the resulting accounts receivable often remains with the company for another 30 to 90 days. Assets such as inventory and receivables are not productive and, as such, companies strive to reduce operating cycles with various initiatives that aim to:

- Increase trade credit to minimize the cash invested in inventories
- Reduce inventory levels by improved production systems and management
- Decrease accounts receivable by better collection procedures

Noncurrent liabilities are obligations to be paid after one year or the operating cycle, whichever is longer. Disney reports $17,100 million ($10,643 million + $2,712 million + $3,745 million) of liabilities as noncurrent. Long-term debts that are scheduled to mature within the next year are classified as current liabilities called *current maturities of long-term debt*. Disney has $13,100 million of long-term debt, of which $2,457 million is scheduled to mature within 12 months of its balance sheet date, yielding $10,643 million in noncurrent liabilities.

Disney also reports $6,457 million of other long-term liabilities. Footnotes reveal that $2,712 million of this liability relates to deferred taxes owed to the IRS and other taxing authorities. Deferred taxes arise from differences between the taxable income Disney reports to taxing agencies and the pretax income it reports to shareholders. (Companies must normally maintain two sets of books—one per GAAP and the other per the tax code.) Disney's deferred taxes reflect future tax liabilities arising from this difference.

The remaining $3,745 million of other long-term liabilities relates to deferred revenues ($540 million), long-term lease obligations ($344 million), obligations for program licensing ($466 million), long-term employee benefit liability ($1,183 million), and other long-term obligations ($1,212 million). Deferred revenues, also called unearned revenues, arise when a company receives cash in advance of providing a good or service. This liability account reflects a company's obligation to provide this good or service in the future (see Appendix 2A for an example). Lease obligations represent payments that Disney must make under contracts for leased assets, and the employee benefit liability represents its obligations to employees under its pension and health plans.[2]

---

[2]We discuss deferred taxes, leases, and employee benefit obligations in other modules.

BUSINESS INSIGHT	Disney's Unrecognized Liabilities

Euro Disney has been unsuccessful since the day it opened. It also suffered a major blow to its cash flows when attendance dwindled from increased global terrorism. Under 2003 accounting standards, Disney reports its investment in Euro Disney on its balance sheet at its percent ownership interest. That is, at 39% of Euro Disney's equity of $69 million, or $27 million, plus accounts and notes receivable from that venture. However, a 2004 *New York Times* article reports that:

> Under new industry accounting rules Disney will be required for the first time in the second quarter to include on the balance sheet [the assets and liabilities of] its 39 percent stake in the debt-laden Euro Disney. . . . While the addition of Euro Disney's assets and liabilities is not expected to hurt earnings per share, analysts say . . . Euro Disney is saddled with $2.5 billion in debt.

Thus, behind the reported investment amount of $27 million are assets amounting to $3,373 million and liabilities of $3,304 million, much of which is currently in default. The new accounting rules referred to in the article were enacted following the Enron scandal and are designed to provide more disclosure on the balance sheet for off-balance-sheet investments. Disney's balance sheet now recognizes those previously unrecognized liabilities.

The equity section of a balance sheet consists of two basic components: contributed capital and earned capital. **Contributed capital** is the net funding that a company has received from issuing and acquiring its equity shares. That is, the funds received from issuing shares less any funds paid to repurchase such shares. Disney's equity section reports $24,219 million ($23,791 million + $428 million) in equity. Its contributed capital is $11,055 million, consisting of the following:

Account ($ millions)	
Preferred stock	$ 0
Common stock	12,154
Treasury stock (common shares repurchased)	(1,527)
Minority interests[3]	428
Total contributed capital	$11,055

Although account titles can vary across companies, it is important to understand that Disney received $12,154 million from issuing equity shares, paid out $1,527 million to repurchase some of its shares, and recognized $428 million as claims of minority shareholders from prior acquisitions of other companies. The common shares held in treasury can be resold in the future unless they are formally retired. Until resold, the cost of these treasury shares reduce total shareholders' equity.

Earned capital is the cumulative net income (and losses) that has been retained by the company (not paid out to shareholders as dividends). Earned capital typically includes retained earnings and accumulated other comprehensive income or loss.[4] Disney's earned capital consists of the following:

Account ($ millions)	
Retained earnings	$13,817
Accumulated other comprehensive income (loss)	(653)
Total earned capital	$13,164

---

[3]*Minority interests* represent claims of minority shareholders that arise when Disney acquires less than 100% of the stock of another company. Minority shareholders have a claim on the assets and earnings of the company just like other shareholders. We cover this topic further in Module 6 on investments.

[4]Accumulated other comprehensive income, AOCI, relates to items that affect equity, but do not flow through the income statement. We discuss this account later in the module.

There is an important relation for retained earnings that reconciles its beginning and ending balances as follows (sometimes formalized in a *retained earnings reconciliation*):

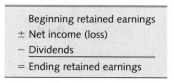

Beginning retained earnings
± Net income (loss)
− Dividends
= Ending retained earnings

This is a useful relation to remember, although there are other items that sometimes impact retained earnings. We revisit this relation after our discussion of the income statement and show how it links the balance sheet and income statement.

Reported stockholders' equity is company value as determined by GAAP, which is called company **book value**. This value is different from company **market value**, which is computed by multiplying the number of outstanding common shares by the per share market value. Book value and market value can differ for several reasons, and most relate to the timing and uncertainty for recognition of transactions and events in financial statements such as the following:

* GAAP generally reports assets and liabilities at historical costs; whereas the market attempts to estimate fair market values.
* GAAP excludes resources that cannot be reliably measured such as talented management, employee morale, recent innovations and successful marketing; whereas the market attempts to value these.
* GAAP does not consider market differences in which companies operate such as competitive conditions and expected changes; whereas the market attempts to factor in these differences in determining value.
* GAAP does not usually report expected future performance; whereas the market does attempt to predict and value future performance.

Presently for U.S. companies, book value is, on average, about two-thirds of market value. This means that the market has drawn on some different information or measurement processes in valuing equity shares. A major part of this information is in financial statement notes, but not all.

BUSINESS INSIGHT   Disney's Book and Market Values

Disney's market value has historically exceeded its book value of equity (see below). This is because much of Disney's market value results from intangible assets such as brand equity that are not fully reflected on its balance sheet. However, the difference between these two values has declined in recent years following abandonment of Go.com and poor performance in its television and film units as shown below. Conservative accounting depresses book value as R&D, advertising, wages, etc., are expensed rather than capitalized as assets. Intangible assets are capitalized only when purchased, and not when internally developed. Consequently, balance sheets of knowledge-based companies are, arguably, less informative.

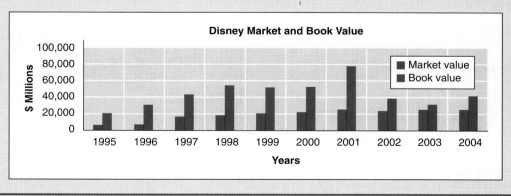

It is important to understand that, eventually, all factors determining company market value are reflected in financial statements and book value. Assets are eventually sold and liabilities are settled.

Moreover, talented management, employee morale, technological innovations, and successful marketing are all eventually recognized in profitability. The difference between book value and market value is timing. To the extent that market value is accurate, the change in stockholders' equity represents the change in company market value with a lag.

Financial Statement Effects Template

Disney reports total assets of $49,988 million, total liabilities of $25,769 million, and equity of $24,219 million (including minority interests in equity). There is an important equality that we use throughout the book for analysis of transactions and financial statements. Drawing on the **accounting equation**, Disney's relation is reflected as follows ($ million):

$$\textbf{Assets = Liabilities + Equity}$$
$$\$49,988 = \quad \$25,769 \quad + \$24,219$$

We often draw on this relation to assess the effects of transactions and events, different accounting methods, and choices that managers make in preparing financial statements. We are interested in knowing, for example, the effects of an asset write-off (removal of an impaired asset) on the balance sheet, income statement, and cash flow statement. Or, we might want to understand how the failure to recognize a liability would result in the understatement of liabilities, and the overstatement of profits and equity. To address these and a number of other financial reporting analyses, we employ the following *financial statement effects template*:

	Balance Sheet									Income Statement		
Transaction	Cash Asset	+	Noncash Assets	=	Liabil- ities	+	Contrib. Capital	+	Retained Earnings	Revenues	−	Expenses

The template captures the transaction and its financial statement effects on three of the major statements: balance sheet, income statement, and statement of cash flows. For the balance sheet, we differentiate between cash and noncash assets so as to identify the cash effects of transactions. Likewise, equity is separated into the contributed and earned capital components. Finally, income statement effects are separated into revenue and expense components. (By definition, any revenue or expense components impact retained earnings.) Use of this template is a convenient means to represent relatively complex financial accounting transactions and events in a simple, concise manner for both analysis and interpretation.

To illustrate the use of this template, let's examine the financial statement effects of a shareholder investing $1,000 cash in Disney (additional transactions and explanations are in Appendix 2A). Disney's cash would increase and Disney would issue stock to the shareholder, which increases equity (contributed capital). This transaction is reflected as follows:[5]

	Balance Sheet									Income Statement		
Transaction	Cash Asset	+	Noncash Assets	=	Liabil- ities	+	Contrib. Capital	+	Retained Earnings	Revenues	−	Expenses
Shareholder invests $1,000 cash	+1,000 Cash						+1,000 Common Stock					

Cash   1,000
   Common
   Stock   1,000

---

[5]Our focus throughout the book is on the financial statement effects of accounting transactions, as exemplified by this template grounded in the accounting equation (assets = liabilities + equity). In addition to showing the dollar effects of a transaction on the balance sheet, income statement, and statement of cash flows, we also include the accounting *journal entry* in the margin. For those of you unfamiliar with journal entries or those wishing to refresh this aspect of the language of accounting, we provide a brief introduction in Appendix 2A. This margin entry can be ignored without any loss of insight into or knowledge gained from the template.

Notice that both assets (cash) and equity (common stock) increase, and the accounting equation still applies (as it always must). Also notice that all major financial statements are reflected in this pedagogical tool. First, the balance sheet is reflected by assets (both cash and noncash), liabilities, and equity (contributed capital and retained earnings). Second, the income statement is reflected by revenues and expenses. Third, the statement of cash flows is reflected by changes in the cash balance. Finally, the statement of equity is reflected by changes in contributed capital and retained earnings. This tool can be expanded to include more detailed accounts if appropriate for your special analysis needs.

As an investing-related illustration, assume that Disney spends $5,000 for upgrading a ride. Cash would decrease and noncash (PPE) assets would increase as follows:

$ Cash Effect

Transaction	Balance Sheet						Income Statement		
	Cash Asset	+ Noncash Assets	= Liabil- ities	+ Contrib. Capital	+ Retained Earnings		Revenues	−	Expenses
Disney pays $5,000 cash to upgrade a ride	−5,000 Cash	+5,000 Park Rides							

Park Rides 5,000
Cash 5,000

Total assets remain unchanged. Disney exchanges one type of asset for another asset. Liabilities and equity are unaffected. Again, the accounting equation is maintained and remains in balance.

■ MID-MODULE REVIEW ■

Enter the letter of the balance sheet category in the space next to the balance sheet items numbered *1* through *20*. Enter an *x* in the space if the item is not reported on the balance sheet.

A. Current assets   C. Current liabilities   E. Equity
B. Long-term assets   D. Long-term liabilities

_____ 1. Accounts receivable
_____ 2. Goodwill
_____ 3. Resorts and property
_____ 4. Retained earnings
_____ 5. Intangible assets
_____ 6. Common stock
_____ 7. Repairs expense
_____ 8. Attractions and equipment
_____ 9. Treasury stock
_____ 10. Investments (noncurrent)

_____ 11. Depreciation expense
_____ 12. Cash equivalents
_____ 13. Parks and buildings
_____ 14. Accounts payable
_____ 15. Television costs (asset)
_____ 16. Borrowings (due in 25 years)
_____ 17. Income taxes payable
_____ 18. Inventories
_____ 19. Preferred stock
_____ 20. Unearned royalties (current)

Solution

1. A	6. E	11. X*	16. D
2. B	7. X*	12. A	17. C
3. B	8. B	13. B	18. A
4. E	9. E	14. C	19. E
5. B	10. B	15. B	20. C

*E is acceptable if viewed as expenses and revenues from the income statement being reflected in retained earnings.

■ INCOME STATEMENT

The income statement reports revenues earned during a period, the expenses incurred to generate those revenues, and the resulting net income or loss. The general structure of the income statement follows:

Total net sales (revenues)
− Total expenses (costs)
= Net income (loss)

Disney's income statement from its 2003 10-K is shown in Exhibit 2.5. Disney reported net income of $1,267 million on revenues of $27,061 million. As is typical of many large companies, less than $0.05 of each dollar of revenue is brought to the bottom line—for Disney, it is $0.047 of each dollar, computed as $1,267 million divided by $27,061 million. The remainder of that revenue dollar, $0.953 (computed as $1 minus $0.047) relates to costs incurred to generate its revenues, such as wages, advertising, interest, promotion, equipment costs, and film and television production expenses.

EXHIBIT 2.5 ■ Walt Disney's Income Statement ($ millions)

THE WALT DISNEY COMPANY, INC. Income Statement For Year Ended September 30, 2003	
Revenues	$ 27,061
Costs and expenses	(24,330)
Amortization of intangible assets	(18)
Gain on sale of businesses	16
Net interest expense	(793)
Equity in the income of investees	334
Restructuring and impairment charges	(16)
Income before income taxes, minority interests and the cumulative effect of accounting change	2,254
Income taxes	(789)
Minority interests share of income	(127)
Income before the cumulative effect of accounting change	1,338
Cumulative effect of accounting change	
Multiple element revenue accounting	(71)
Net income (loss)	$ 1,267

To analyze an income statement we need to understand some terminology. **Revenues** are increases in net assets (assets less liabilities) as a result of business activities. **Expenses** are the outflow or use of assets to generate revenues, including costs of products and services sold, operating costs like wages and advertising, and nonoperating costs like interest on debt. The difference between revenues and expenses is **net income** when revenues exceed expenses, or **net loss** when expenses exceed revenues. The terms income, profit, and earnings are used interchangeably (as are revenues and sales, and expenses and costs).

Operating expenses are the usual and customary costs that a company incurs to support its main business activities. These include cost of goods sold, selling expenses, depreciation expense, amortization expense,[6] and research and development expense. (Not all of these expenses require a cash outlay; for example, depreciation expense is a noncash expense, as are accruals of liabilities such as wages payable, that recognize the expense in advance of cash payment.) **Nonoperating expenses** relate to the company's financing and investing activities, and include interest revenue and interest expense. Business decision makers and analysts usually segregate operating and nonoperating activities as they offer different insights into company performance and condition.

In addition to categorizing costs as operating or nonoperating, it is also useful to categorize them by the extent to which they are likely to recur. One-time events are called **transitory items**.[7] One goal of analysis is to parse out transitory items so that one can better identify **core income** and use it to better forecast future income and cash flows to evaluate strategic alternatives and to value company securities. Core operating income focuses on operating activities that are likely to persist and, thus, are more relevant for company valuation (see Module 11).

---

[6]Amortization expense is like depreciation expense, except that it relates to intangible assets like patents and trademarks rather than tangible assets like equipment and buildings. Both involve the allocation of asset costs to the periods expected to benefit from the asset's use.

[7]Examples of transitory items include the gain or loss on the sale of an asset (the difference between the sale price and amount at which it is reported on the balance sheet), asset write-offs, and employee severance costs arising from restructuring activities. We discuss transitory items at length in Module 4.

To illustrate the effects of transactions and events—this time for revenue-related activities—assume that Disney (1) receives $2,000 cash from ticket sales and (2) pays $800 cash in wages expense. The effects of these transactions on its financial statements follow:

	Balance Sheet						Income Statement			
Transaction	Cash Asset	+	Noncash Assets	=	Liabil- ities	+	Contrib. Capital	+	Retained Earnings	Revenues − Expenses
Receives $2,000 cash from ticket sales	+2,000 Cash								+2,000 Retained Earnings	+2,000 Ticket Sales
Pays $800 cash for wages expense	−800 Cash								−800 Retained Earnings	− 800 Wages Expense

Cash 2,000
Ticket
Sales 2,000

Wages
Expense 800
Cash 800

Disney reports $2,000 of revenues, which increases income by $2,000. The retained earnings section of equity also increases by $2,000 to reflect the income earned (this reflects articulation of financial statements, an important concept that we again discuss later in this module). The $800 cash payment for wages is reported as an expense in Disney's income statement, which reduces both income and retained earnings.

Revenue Recognition

Revenue recognition is a principle prescribing that revenue is recognized when earned. Its application is crucial in income statement reporting. To illustrate, assume that a company purchases inventories for $100 on credit (also called *on account*), which it sells later in that same period for $150 cash.[8] Also assume this company pays $20 cash for sales employee wages during the period. Its income statement follows:

Sales	$ 150
Cost of goods sold	(100)
Gross profit	50
Wages expense	(20)
Net income	$ 30

Cost of goods sold is an expense item in the income statements of manufacturing and merchandising companies. It represents the cost of products that are sold during the period. The difference between sales (at selling prices) and cost of goods sold (at purchase price or manufacturing cost) is **gross profit**. Gross profit for manufacturers and merchandisers is an important number as it represents the remaining income available to cover all of the company's overhead and other expenses (selling, general, and administrative expenses).

Continuing with the above illustration, assume instead that the company sells its product on **credit terms** of 2/10, net 30 (credit terms 2/10 mean that the buyer can reduce its price by 2% if it pays within 10 days, and net 30 means that the buyer must pay its bill within 30 days). Does the seller still report $150 in sales? The answer is yes. Under GAAP, revenues are reported when a company has *earned* those sales. Earned means that the company has done everything required under the sales agreement—no major contingencies remain—and cash is realizable or realized. Notice that revenue can be recognized without cash collection. Also, the seller reports $150 in accounts receivable on its balance sheet.

$

Cash Effect

---

[8]Purchase of inventories on credit or on account means that the buyer does not pay the seller at the time of purchase. The buyer reports a liability (accounts payable) on its balance sheet that is later removed when payment is made. The seller reports an asset (accounts receivable) on its balance sheet until it is removed when the buyer pays.

Credit sales mean that companies can report substantial sales revenue and assets without receiving cash. This introduces additional risk when assessing the performance of such companies. When such receivables are ultimately collected, no further revenue is recorded because it was recorded earlier when the revenue recognition criteria were met. The collection of a receivable merely involves the decrease of one asset (accounts receivable) and the increase in another asset (cash).

Matching Principle

$

Cash Effect

The **matching principle** prescribes that all expenses incurred in generating revenues be recognized in the same period as the related revenues. The word *incurred* does not necessarily imply paid in cash, as the company can agree to a liability to pay these costs in the future.

Extending our above illustration, assume that the $20 of employee wages for the period is for work directed toward selling the $150 of goods, but that these wages are not paid until the first day of the *following* period. Should wages expense be recorded in the current or following period? Yes. Following the matching principle, the seller must record wages expense in the current period to match against the revenues it records, even though the wages are not yet paid in cash.

Notice that, unlike sales, no *external transaction or event* triggers the recording of wages expense. After $150 of sales and $100 in costs of goods sold are recorded, the financial statements are incomplete in failing to reflect employee wages necessary for their sale. They must be adjusted to reflect wages expense and the wages liability. More generally, managers must review financial statements before issuance to determine that all *internal transactions and events* such as this one are recorded.

These adjustments yield an **adjusting entry**, or **accrual**, which is a numerical alteration to the accounting records that is made in the absence of an external transaction or event to fairly present the financial condition and performance of a company. Adjusting entries for *accrued expenses* yield the following effects:

1. An *expense* reported in the income statement
2. A *liability* reported on the balance sheet.

Returning to our illustration, when wages are ultimately paid in the following period, both cash and the wages payable liability are reduced. No expense is recorded when cash is paid because it was recorded the prior period when wages were incurred.

To further extend this illustration, assume that inventories are purchased on credit terms of 1/15, net 60. Are costs of goods sold recorded even though they are not yet paid? Yes. The company has taken ownership of inventories and must match their costs against the sales generated.

Accounting adjustments also apply to revenues. *Accrued revenues* yield the following effects:

1. A *revenue* recorded in the income statement
2. A *receivable* recorded on the balance sheet

An example is the accrual of interest income from an investment, say, a bank account. (This commonly arises from investments of excess cash in short-term interest-bearing securities such as certificates of deposits and government and private bonds). When such a company reports its financial statements at period-end, it has earned interest revenue on these investments (interest is earned by the passage of time), but it may not yet have received payment. To fairly present its financial condition, it must accrue interest on the investment by recognizing interest revenue in its income statement and an interest receivable on its balance sheet.

MANAGERIAL DECISION   **You Are the Operations Manager**

You are the operations manager on a new consumer product that was launched this period with very successful sales. The Chief Financial Officer (CFO) asks you to prepare an estimate of warranty costs to charge against those sales. You question the CFO and the need for such an estimate and reply with confidence that you hope such charges are minimal. Why does the CFO desire a warranty cost estimate? What hurdles must you address in arriving at such an estimate? [Answer, p. 2-35]

Accrual Accounting

Accrual accounting refers to the recognition of revenue when earned (even if not received in cash) and the matching of expenses when incurred (even if not paid in cash).[9] Accrual accounting is required under U.S. GAAP and in most other countries as it is considered most useful for business decisions (information about cash flows is also important and is conveyed in the statement of cash flows discussed later in this module).

$ Cash Effect

To illustrate the financial statement effects of accrual accounting, let's return to the illustration above. Again, assume that sales are on credit, inventory purchases are on credit, and wages are not paid until the next period. The simplified income statement and balance sheet for the current period follow:

Income Statement	
Sales	$ 150
Cost of goods sold	(100)
Gross profit	50
Wages expense	(20)
Net income	$ 30

Balance Sheet	
Cash	$ 0
Accounts receivable	150
Total assets	$150
Accounts payable	$100
Wages payable	20
Retained earnings	30
Total liabilities and equity	$150

The income statement is identical to the earlier one. The balance sheet reflects a zero cash balance (no cash transaction has occurred to this point) and $150 of accounts receivable. Liabilities reflect the $100 accounts payable for the inventory purchase and the $20 wages payable to employees. Retained earnings reflect the $30 of net income, which is not paid out to shareholders as dividends. (In the next period, the receivable is collected and the payables are paid. These later cash transactions impact balance sheet accounts only and, consequently, have no effect on income statement accounts.)

The following table illustrates the effects of these transactions for the first period using the financial statement effects template (those for the second period are shown later in the module):

Transaction	Balance Sheet					Income Statement		
	Cash Asset	+ Noncash Assets	= Liabil- ities	+ Contrib. Capital	+ Retained Earnings	Revenues	− Expenses	

1. Purchase $100 of inventory on credit		+100 Inventory	+100 Accounts Payable					Inventory 100
								  Accounts
								    Payable 100

2. Sell inventory costing $100 at a selling price of $150 on credit		+150 Accounts Receivable −100 Inventory			+150 Retained Earnings −100 Retained Earnings	+150 Revenues	− 100 Cost of Goods Sold	Accounts
								  Receivable 150
								  Revenues 150
								Cost of
								  Goods Sold 100
								  Inventory 100

3. Employees earn $20 in wages that are not yet paid in cash			+ 20 Wages Payable		− 20 Retained Earnings		− 20 Wages Expense	Wages
								  Expense 20
								  Wages
								    Payable 20

Totals		+150	+120		+ 30	+150	− 120	

---

[9]**Cash accounting** recognizes revenues only when received in cash and expenses only when paid in cash. This is not acceptable accounting under GAAP.

The balance sheet reports $150 in noncash assets ($150 of accounts receivable), $120 of liabilities ($100 in accounts payable and $20 in wages payable), and stockholders' equity (retained earnings) of $30, which represents the income retained in the business and not paid out as dividends. The income statement reports $150 in sales (although not yet collected) and $120 in expenses ($100 of cost of goods sold and $20 of wage expense, both are not yet paid) for a net income of $30. (The accruals in this section are estimated with relative certainty. We know, for example, the wages earned by employees. However, many accruals must be estimated. We review the sources and effects of such estimation in other modules.)

Income from Continuing Operations and Transitory Items

To this point, we have only considered income from continuing operations and its components. A more comprehensive income statement format is in Exhibit 2.6. The most noticeable difference involves three additional components of net income located at the bottom of the statement.

EXHIBIT 2.6 ■ General Income Statement Format

Sales
− Cost of goods sold
Gross profit
− Operating expenses
− Nonoperating expenses
− Tax expenses ◄——— Tax expenses apply to items comprising income from continuing operations
Income from continuing operations
± Discontinued operations, net of tax
± Extraordinary items, net of tax   Transitory items are those not expected to recur
± Changes in accounting principles, net of tax
Net income

These three components are specifically segregated from the income from continuing operations and are defined as follows (these items are further described in Module 4):

1. **Discontinued operations**   Gains or losses (and net income or loss) from business segments that are being sold or have been sold in the current period.
2. **Extraordinary items**   Gains or losses from events that are both *unusual* and *infrequent* and are, therefore, excluded from income from continuing operations.
3. **Changes in accounting principles**   Cumulative income or loss from changes in accounting methods (such as depreciation costing methods).[10]

Companies must report the existence of these items when they occur.

These three components are segregated because they represent **transitory items**, which reflect transactions or events that are unlikely to recur. Many readers of financial statements are interested in *future* company performance. They analyze current year financial statements to gain clues to better *predict* future performance. (Stock prices, for example, are based on a company's expected cash flows.)

Transitory items, by definition, are unlikely to arise in future periods and, as a result, are largely irrelevant to predictions of future performance. This means that decision makers tend to focus on income from continuing operations because it is the level of profitability likely to **persist** (continue) into the future. As such, the financial press tends to focus on income from continuing operations when it discloses corporate earnings (often described as *earnings before one-time charges*).

---

[10]FASB has proposed a new standard that would no longer recognize the cumulative effect of changes in accounting principles. Under the new standard, a change would be applied retrospectively to all prior periods for which the effects of the change can be estimated. The new standard is proposed to take effect in 2005 or 2006.

■ STATEMENT OF EQUITY

The statement of stockholders' equity is a reconciliation of the beginning and ending balances of stockholders' equity accounts. Although equity accounts can vary across companies, they usually consist of the following:

- **Contributed capital** Contributed capital accounts often consist of common stock and any preferred stock and additional paid-in capital
- **Retained earnings** Retained (reinvested) earnings is typically reported along with accumulated other comprehensive income, which reflects changes in equity that are not recorded either in contributed capital accounts or net income
- **Treasury stock** Treasury stock refers to shares repurchased from shareholders by the company; this account reduces equity

The statement of stockholders' equity for Walt Disney is shown in Exhibit 2.7.

EXHIBIT 2.7 ■ Walt Disney's Statement of Stockholders' Equity

(in millions)	Common Stock	Retained Earnings	Accumulated Other Comprehensive Income (Loss)	Treasury Stock	Total Shareholders' Equity
THE WALT DISNEY COMPANY, INC. Statement of Stockholders' Equity For Year Ended September 30, 2003					
Balance at September 30, 2002	$12,107	$12,979	$ (85)	$(1,556)	$23,445
Exercise of stock options and restricted stock	47	—	—	29	76
Dividends ($0.21 per Disney share)	—	(429)	—	—	(429)
Other comprehensive loss (net of tax benefit of $334 million)	—	—	(568)	—	(568)
Net income	—	1,267	—	—	1,267
Balance at September 30, 2003	$12,154	$13,817	$(653)	$(1,527)	$23,791

Disney's first major equity component is that of contributed capital, which it titles common stock. The balance of its common stock at the beginning of the year is $12,107 million. During 2003, Disney issued $47 million of common stock to employees that exercised stock options. At the end of 2003, the common stock account reports a balance of $12,154 million.

Disney's second major component is retained earnings. It totals $12,979 million at the start of 2003. During the year, it is reduced by $429 million of dividend payments, but is increased by $1,267 million from net income. The balance of retained earnings at year-end is $13,817 million.

Its third major component is accumulated other comprehensive income, which decreased by $568 million during 2003—from $(85) million to $(653) million. Accumulated other comprehensive income relates to items that affect equity, but do not flow through the income statement. These mainly include unrealized gains and losses on certain marketable and derivative securities, foreign currency translation adjustments, and minimum pension liability adjustments. Each of these is explained in other modules.

Disney's fourth major component is treasury stock, which decreased by $29 million—from $(1,556) million to $(1,527) million. Treasury stock arises when a company repurchases stock from its shareholders. This has the opposite effect from the issuance of shares and, as a result, increases in treasury stock reduce stockholders' equity and vice versa.

In sum, total stockholders' equity begins the year at $23,445 million and ends 2003 with a balance of $23,791 million (excluding minority interest) for a net increase of $346 million.

To illustrate the financial statement effects of a simple equity transaction, assume that a company sells common stock for $9,000 cash. This transaction would effect financial statements as follows:

	Balance Sheet						Income Statement	
Transaction	Cash Asset	+ Noncash Assets	= Liabil- ities	+ Contrib. Capital	+ Retained Earnings		Revenues	– Expenses
Issue common stock for $9,000 cash	+9,000 Cash			+9,000 Common Stock				

Cash   9,000
  Common
    Stock   9,000

No revenue or income is recorded from a stock issuance. This is always the case. Companies cannot report income from capital transactions (transactions with its stockholders' relating to their investment in the company). That is, companies do not record revenue from stock issuances, they do not record expense from (treasury) stock repurchases, and they do not record expense from dividend payments to shareholders.

RESEARCH INSIGHT   Market-to-Book

The *market-to-book ratio,* also called *price-to-book,* refers to a company's market value divided by its book (equity) value—it is also computed as stock price per share divided by book value per share. Research shows that the market-to-book ratio exhibits considerable variability over time. Specifically, over the past few decades, the median (50th percentile) market-to-book ratio was less than 1.0 during the mid-1970s, over 2.0 during the mid-1990s, and often between 1.0 and 2.0 during the 1960s and 1980s. Research also explores the drivers of this variability in market-to-book. One purpose of fundamental analysis is to exploit such research to arrive at *intrinsic value,* which is the worth of a stock justified by all available information.

■ STATEMENT OF CASH FLOWS

$
Cash Effect

The balance sheet and income statement are prepared using accrual accounting, in which revenues are recognized when earned and expenses when incurred (matched). This means that companies can sometimes report income even though no cash is received. This adds an element of risk, as there are instances of companies that were profitable up to the time they declared bankruptcy. This can occur from cash shortages—such as when cash expectations do not materialize or when customers refuse to or cannot pay.

To assess cash flows, we must assess a company's cash management. Obligations to employees, creditors, and others are usually settled with cash. Also, stock prices are linked to the expected future cash generating ability of the company. Illiquid companies (those lacking cash) are at risk of failure and typically reflect poor investing activities. Given the importance of cash management, the SEC and FASB require disclosure of the statement of cash flows in addition to the balance sheet, income statement, and statement of equity.

The income statement provides information about the economic viability of the company's products and services. It tells us whether the market sufficiently values its products and services at prices that cover its costs and that also provide a reasonable return to the providers of capital (lenders and stockholders). On the other hand, the statement of cash flows provides information about the company's ability to generate cash from those same transactions. It tells us from what sources the company has generated its cash, so we can evaluate whether those sources are persistent or transitory, and what it has done with the cash generated.

The statement of cash flows is formatted to report cash inflows and outflows by the three primary business activities:

- *Cash flows from operating activities* Cash flows from the company's transactions and events that relate to its primary operations.
- *Cash flows from investing activities* Cash flows from acquisitions and divestitures of investments and long-term assets.
- *Cash flows from financing activities* Cash flows from issuances of and payments toward equity, borrowings, and long-term liabilities.

The net cash flows from these three sections yield the change in cash for the period.

In analyzing the statement of cash flows, you should not necessarily conclude that the company is better off if cash increases and worse off if cash decreases. It is not the cash change that is most important, but the sources for that change. For example, what are the sources of cash inflows? Are these sources transitory? Are these sources mainly from operating activities? To what uses have cash inflows been put? Such questions and answers are key to properly using the statement of cash flows.

Exhibit 2.8 shows Walt Disney's statement of cash flows. Disney reported $2,901 million in net cash inflows from operating activities in 2003. This is substantially in excess of its net income of $1,267 million. The difference is mainly due to $1,059 in depreciation, a noncash expense, on the income statement.

EXHIBIT 2.8 ■ Walt Disney's Statement of Cash Flows ($ millions)

THE WALT DISNEY COMPANY, INC. Statement of Cash Flows For Year Ended September 30, 2003	
Operating Activities	
Net Income (loss)	$ 1,267
Adjustments to reconcile income to cash flows	
Depreciation	1,059
Amortization of intangible assets	18
Deferred income taxes	441
Equity in the income of investees	(334)
Cash distributions received from equity investees	340
Minority interests share of income	127
Change in film and television costs	(369)
Gain on sale of businesses	(16)
Gain on sale of Knight-Ridder, Inc. shares	—
Restructuring and impairment charges	13
Write-off of aircraft leveraged lease	114
Cumulative effect of accounting changes	—
Other	(23)
Changes in working capital	
Receivables	(194)
Inventories	(6)
Other current assets	(28)
Accounts payable and other liabilities	275
Television costs	217
Cash provided by operations	2,901
Investing Activities	
Investments in parks, resorts and other property	(1,049)
Acquisitions (net of cash acquired)	(130)
Dispositions	166
Proceeds from sale of investments	40
Purchases of investments	(14)
Other	(47)
Cash used by investing activities	(1,034)
Financing Activities	
Borrowings	1,635
Reduction of borrowings	(2,059)
Commercial paper borrowings, net	(721)
Repurchases of common stock	—
Dividends	(429)
Exercise of stock options and other	51
Cash (used) provided by financing activities	(1,523)
Increase (decrease) in cash and cash equivalents	344
Cash and cash equivalents, beginning of year	1,239
Cash and cash equivalents, end of year	$ 1,583

Disney reported a net cash outflow of $1,034 million for investing activities, mainly for investments in its parks, resorts, and property ($1,049 million). Disney also used $1,523 million in financing activities, mainly for cash dividend payments ($429 million) and the settling/repayment of borrowings ($1,145 million cash outflow, computed as $1,635 million − $2,059 million − $721 million).

Overall, Disney's cash flow picture is adequate. It is generating positive operating cash flows, it is reinvesting cash in its infrastructure (parks and resorts) that benefits future performance, and it is retiring some debt.

Finally, we must remember that the difference between income and cash flow is important and warrants our attention. To understand this difference, let's briefly return to our earlier illustration. Following are period 1 transactions from that illustration along with additional transactions for period 2:

$
Cash Effect

Transaction Period 1	Balance Sheet					Income Statement	
	Cash Asset +	Noncash Assets =	Liabil-ities +	Contrib. Capital +	Retained Earnings	Revenues −	Expenses
1. Purchase $100 of inventory on credit		+100 Inventory	+100 Accounts Payable				
2. Sell inventory costing $100 for a selling price of $150 on credit		+150 Accounts Receivable −100 Inventory			+150 Retained Earnings −100 Retained Earnings	+150 Revenues	− 100 Cost of Goods Sold
3. Employees earn $20 in wages that are not yet paid in cash			+ 20 Wages Payable		− 20 Retained Earnings		− 20 Wages Expense
Total effects in period 1		+150	+120		+ 30	+150 −	120
Period 2							
4. Collect $150 cash from accounts receivable	+150 Cash	−150 Accounts Receivable					
5. Pay $100 cash toward accounts payable	−100 Cash		−100 Accounts Payable				
6. Pay $20 cash toward wages payable	− 20 Cash		− 20 Wages Payable				
Total balance sheet effects of periods 1 and 2	+ 30	0	0		+ 30		

Inventory 100
  Accounts Payable 100

Accounts Receivable 150
  Revenues 150
Cost of Goods Sold 100
  Inventory 100

Wages Expense 20
  Wages Payable 20

Cash 150
  Accounts Receivable 150

Accounts Payable 100
  Cash 100

Wages Payable 20
  Cash 20

At the end of period 1, this company reports $30 of income and no cash effects as the receivables are not yet collected and the accounts payable are not yet paid. In period 2, the receivables are collected and cash is paid to settle accounts payable and wages payable. However, the receipt and payment of cash in period 2 does *not* impact revenue, expense, and income. Revenue was recognized when earned and expense when incurred, which both occurred in period 1.

The company reports the following income and operating cash flows for each of these two periods:

	Net Income	Operating Cash Flows
Period 1	$30	$ 0
Period 2	0	30
Total of periods 1 and 2	$30	$30

Appendix 2B provides further details on the accounting mechanics of the statement of cash flows.

■ ARTICULATION OF FINANCIAL STATEMENTS

Financial statements are linked within and across time, which is called **articulation**. The balance sheet and income statement are mainly linked via retained earnings. Recall that retained earnings is updated each period as follows:

Beginning retained earnings
± Net income (loss)
− Dividends
= Ending retained earnings

Generally, retained earnings reflect cumulative income and loss not distributed to shareholders. Exhibit 2.9 shows **Walt Disney**'s change in retained earnings for 2003.

EXHIBIT 2.9 ■ Walt Disney's Retained Earnings Reconciliation

THE WALT DISNEY COMPANY, INC. Retained Earnings Reconciliation ($ millions) For Year Ended September 30, 2003
Retained earnings, September 30, 2002 . . . . $12,979
Add: Net income (loss) 1,267
14,246
Less: Dividends 429
Retained earnings, September 30, 2003 . . . . $13,817

This reconciliation of retained earnings provides the link between the balance sheet and income statement. Namely, the change in retained earnings is the amount by which shareholder value in the company changes for the period, as measured by GAAP. Stockholders' equity reflects that change, and the income statement details that change in value.

In the absence of owner equity transactions—such as stock issuances and purchases, and dividend payments—the change in stockholders' equity equals income or loss for the period. The income statement, thus, measures the change in company value per GAAP. This is not necessarily company value per the market. Of course, all value-relevant items eventually find their way into the income statement. So, from a macro-perspective, the income statement does measure change in company value. This is why stock prices react to income and why they react to guidance numbers (expected income) as reported by companies.

Articulation of the financial statements is shown in Exhibit 2.10. Disney begins 2003 with assets of $50,045 million, consisting of both cash for $1,239 million and noncash assets for $48,806 million. These investments are financed with $26,166 million from nonowners, or debt holders, and $23,879 million from shareholders (including claims of minority or noncontrolling shareholders). The owner financing consists of contributed capital for $12,107 million, total retained earnings of $12,979 million, accumulated other comprehensive loss of $(85) million, treasury stock of $1,556 million, and claims of minority, noncontrolling shareholders for $434 million.

EXHIBIT 2.10 ■ Articulation of Walt Disney Financial Statements ($ millions)

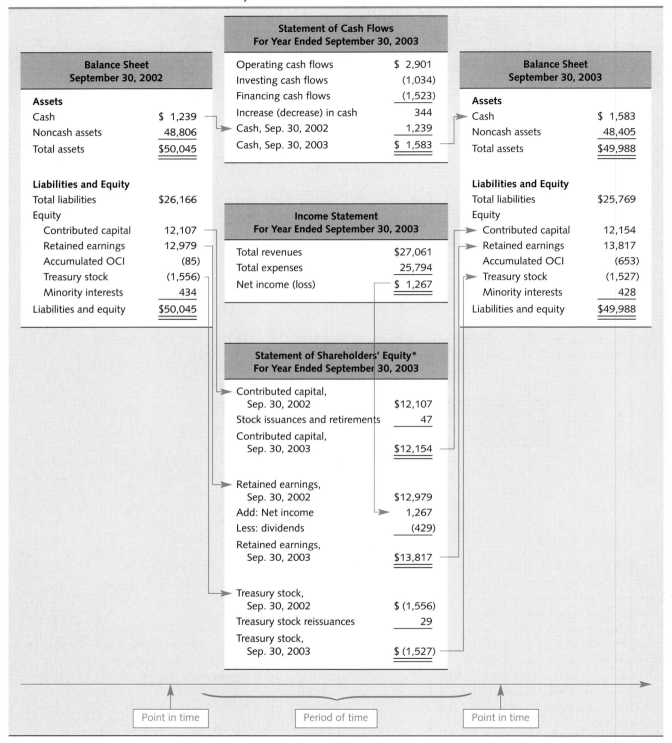

*For brevity, reconciliations for accumulated other comprehensive income and minority interests are not shown.

$

Cash Effect

Operating activities for 2003 are reflected in the middle column of Exhibit 2.10. The statement of cash flows explains how operating, investing, and financing activities increase the cash balance by $344 million from $1,239 million at the beginning of the year to $1,583 million at year-end. The year-end cash is reported in the year-end balance sheet on the right.

Disney's $1,267 million net income reported on the income statement is also carried over to the statement of shareholders' equity. The net income, less dividends paid of $429 million, helps explain the change in retained earnings reported in the statement of shareholders' equity.

■ ADDITIONAL INFORMATION DISCLOSURES

Companies with publicly traded securities must report a detailed discussion of their business activities as part of the 10-K report. This is called the **management discussion and analysis (MD&A)** section. For Disney, this discussion is available in its 10-K. The MD&A provides useful information. Exhibit 2.11 shows an outline listing the main topics of discussion from Walt Disney's MD&A.

EXHIBIT 2.11 ■ Outline of Disney's Management Discussion and Analysis

1. Analysis of operations
   - Sales
   - Earnings
   - Income taxes
   - Research and development
   - Restructuring activities
2. Accounting standards not yet adopted
3. Critical accounting estimates
4. Corporate outlook
5. Segment reviews (lengthy)
6. Liquidity and capital resources
   - Sources of liquidity
   - Uses of cash
   - Financial condition
   - Minority interest structures
   - Off-balance-sheet arrangements
   - Contractual obligations
7. Long-term employee benefits
8. Environmental matters
   - Remediation accruals
   - Remediation expenditures
9. Quantitative and qualitative disclosures about market risk
   - Derivatives and other hedging instruments
   - Foreign currency risk
   - Interest rate risk
   - Commodity price risk
   - Value at risk

The 10-K report also contains information related to: (1) any disagreements between the company and its auditor regarding financial statements or disclosures contained therein; (2) stock ownership by company officers, directors, and related parties; and (3) executive compensation. Also, the Letter to Shareholders in the annual report is another source of insight. Each of these reports is written by company management and, as a result, must be interpreted as part promotional.

Companies must disclose their significant accounting policies as reflected in financial statements. These are called **notes to financial statements**, or simply notes or footnotes. The notes discuss company accounting policies and estimates used in preparing its financial statements. We review and assess such notes as appropriate for analysis of company activities throughout this book.

MODULE-END REVIEW

Part 1

At December 31, 2005, the Waymire Corporation records show the following amounts. Use this information, as necessary, to prepare its 2005 income statement (ignore income taxes).

Cash	$ 3,000		Cash dividends	$ 1,000
Accounts receivable	12,000		Revenues	25,000
Office equipment	32,250		Rent expense	5,000
Land	36,000		Wages expense	8,000
Accounts payable	7,500		Utilities expense	2,000
Common stock	45,750		Other expenses	4,000

Solution

WAYMIRE CORPORATION
Income Statement
For Year Ended December 31, 2005

Revenues		$25,000
Expenses		
Wages expense	$8,000	
Rent expense	5,000	
Utilities expense	2,000	
Other expenses	4,000	
Total expenses		19,000
Net income		$ 6,000

Part 2

The following is selected financial information for Waymire Corporation for the year ended December 31, 2005:

Retained earnings, Dec. 31, 2005	$30,000		Dividends	$1,000
Net income	$6,000		Retained earnings, Dec. 31, 2004	$25,000

Prepare the 2005 calendar-year retained earnings reconciliation for this company.

Solution

WAYMIRE CORPORATION
Retained Earnings Reconciliation
For Year Ended December 31, 2005

Retained earnings, Dec. 31, 2004	$25,000
Add: Net income	6,000
Less: Dividends	(1,000)
Retained earnings, Dec. 31, 2005	$30,000

Part 3

Use the listing of accounts and figures reported in part 1 along with the ending retained earnings from part 2 to prepare the December 31, 2005 balance sheet for Waymire Corporation.

Solution

WAYMIRE CORPORATION Balance Sheet December 31, 2005			
Cash	$ 3,000	Accounts payable	$ 7,500
Accounts receivable	12,000		
Office equipment	32,250	Common stock	45,750
Land	36,000	Retained earnings	30,000
Total assets	$83,250	Total liabilities and equity	$83,250

APPENDIX 2A

Transaction Analysis and Accounting

Transaction analysis refers to the process of identifying the financial statement effects of transactions and events. For this purpose, we use the *financial statement effects* template:

	Balance Sheet					Income Statement	
Transaction	Cash Asset	+ Noncash Assets	= Liabil- ities	+ Contrib. Capital	+ Retained Earnings	Revenues	− Expenses

Each transaction or event is identified in the first column. Then, the financial statement effects are recorded with a + or − in the appropriate columns of the balance sheet (which includes the statement of cash flow effects) and income statement. Further, through contributed capital and retained earnings, this template also reflects the effects on the statement of equity via the effects on contributed capital and retained earnings.

This analysis is instructive as it reveals the financial impacts of transactions and events, and it provides insights into the effects of accounting choices. This appendix reviews several examples of common transactions and events to start you on the path of transaction analysis and interpretation.

Journal Entries

In addition to the financial statement effects template, we show the associated journal entry in the margin. A **journal entry** is an accounting entry in the financial records (journals) of a company. This is the *bookkeeping* aspect of accounting. Although most of you will never make a journal entry, many of you will interact with accounting and finance professionals in your companies who do, and you will find it useful to learn this language.

Accountants describe increases and decreases in accounts using the terms *debit* and *credit*. An easy way to remember what the words debit and credit reflect is to visualize a balance sheet with assets on the left and liabilities and equity on the right as follows.

Accounting Equation Layout	
Assets	Liabilities and Equity
Debit side Left side of balance sheet is debit side	Credit side Right side of balance sheet is credit side

The left side of the balance sheet is the debit side and the right side is the credit side. Assets, therefore, normally have a debit balance since they are on the left side. Liabilities and equity normally have a credit balance since they are on the right side. So, to reflect an increase in an asset, we debit the asset account, and to reflect an increase in a liability or equity account we credit the account. Conversely, to reflect a decrease in an asset account we credit it and to reflect a decrease in a liability or equity account we debit it. Of course, since the balance sheet must always balance (assets = liabilities + equity), so too, must total debits equal total credits in each journal entry (there can be more than one debit and credit in an entry).

The final piece relates to revenue and expense accounts. To remember these accounts, recall their effects on equity. As described above, anything that increases equity is a credit and anything that decreases equity is a debit. So, to reflect an increase in revenues (which increase equity), we credit the revenue account, and to reflect an increase in an expense account (which reduces equity), we debit it.

To summarize, the following table reflects use of the terms debit and credit to describe increases to balance sheet and income statement accounts:

		Debit	Credit
Balance sheet	Assets	Increase	Decrease
	Liabilities	Decrease	Increase
	Equity	Decrease	Increase
Income statement	Revenue	Decrease	Increase
	Expense	Increase	Decrease

To illustrate, the journal entries to record a credit sale of $150 for products costing $100 follow,

Accounts Receivable	150	
Revenues		150
Cost of Goods Sold	100	
Inventory		100

The journal entry to record the cash collection of the above receivable would be,

Cash	150	
Accounts Receivable		150

Debits are always recorded first followed by all of the credits, which are indented to identify them as credits. An alternative presentation is to utilize the symbols *dr* to denote debits and *cr* to denote credits that precede the account description. The remainder of this appendix considers several common transactions that we assess using both the financial statement effects template and the journal entry.

Credit Sales Transaction

Assume that a company sells products and services on credit to another party. The operating cycle for this transaction is reflected in the following template and is shown as a three-stage process.

Row 1 reflects the credit sale. The increase in accounts receivable is shown under noncash assets. Provided revenue is *earned,* it is recorded—even if cash is not yet collected. Accordingly, revenues increase, which also increase retained earnings via net income.

Row 2 reflects the cost of the goods (inventories) sold. Reduced inventory amounts are reflected as an expense (cost of goods sold), which reduces retained earnings via a decline in net income. If this sale is profitable, there is a net increase in assets as the receivable increase exceeds the inventories decrease *and* revenues exceed cost of goods sold.

Row 3 depicts collection of the account receivable. The increase in cash from collection is accompanied by a decrease in noncash assets (accounts receivable). No revenue is recorded when the receivable is collected because revenue was recorded when the sale occurred (when earned).

		Balance Sheet					Income Statement	
	Transaction	Cash Asset	+ Noncash Assets	= Liabil- ities	+ Contrib. Capital	+ Retained Earnings	Revenues	− Expenses
Accounts Receivable 150 Revenues 150	1. Products sold for $150 on credit		+150 Accounts Receivable			+150 Retained Earnings	+150 Revenues	
Cost of Goods Sold 100 Inventory 100	2. Cost of the inventory sold is $100		−100 Inventory			−100 Retained Earnings		− 100 Cost of Goods Sold

Transaction	Balance Sheet							Income Statement			
	Cash Asset	+	Noncash Assets	=	Liabil- ities	+	Contrib. Capital	+	Retained Earnings	Revenues	− Expenses
3. Collect $150 cash on accounts receivable	+150 Cash		−150 Accounts Receivable								

Cash 150
Accounts
Receivable 150

Expense Payment Transaction

Cash payment of expenses is reflected as transaction 4. This example uses the cash payment for wages. Cash is reduced and wages expense is reported in the income statement, the latter reduces income and retained earnings.

Transaction	Balance Sheet							Income Statement			
	Cash Asset	+	Noncash Assets	=	Liabil- ities	+	Contrib. Capital	+	Retained Earnings	Revenues	− Expenses
4. Employees paid $20 cash in wages	− 20 Cash								− 20 Retained Earnings		− 20 Wages Expense

Wages
Expense 20
Cash 20

Accrued Expense Transaction

To illustrate accrued expenses, assume that employees worked in one period, but are paid in the next period. Since wages expense must be recognized when *incurred,* regardless of when it is paid, the company must report wages expense as well as the liability for payment (wages payable) in the first period. The increase in expense reduces income and retained earnings.

When wages are paid in the next period, both cash and the wages payable liability are decreased. No expense is reported when cash is paid for wages earned in a prior period. The expense was recognized when it was incurred in the prior period. This is reflected as follows:

Transaction	Balance Sheet							Income Statement			
	Cash Asset	+	Noncash Assets	=	Liabil- ities	+	Contrib. Capital	+	Retained Earnings	Revenues	− Expenses
5. Employees earn $20 in wages that are not yet paid in cash					+ 20 Wages Payable				− 20 Retained Earnings		− 20 Wages Expense
6. Paid $20 cash toward wages payable	− 20 Cash				− 20 Wages Payable						

Wages
Expense 20
Wages
Payable 20

Wages
Payable 20
Cash 20

Accrual accounting is crucial for reporting the proper expense in the appropriate period's income statement. In the case of wages, the amount of the accrual is known with certainty. However, in some cases, accruals are estimated. Examples are estimating contingent liabilities such as warranty, litigation, environmental, and severance costs. These estimated accruals yield both liabilities and expenses. If these accruals are overestimated, reported income is too low, and if the accruals are underestimated, reported income is too high. We must be alert to the possibility of managers misreporting income through use of accruals, either unintentionally or intentionally.

Deferred Revenue Transaction

Deferred revenues, also called *unearned revenues,* arise when a company receives cash before revenues are earned. Examples are a magazine publisher that receives subscriptions in advance of publishing the magazine. When cash

$

Cash Effect

is received, the cash increase is recorded and so is a liability (titled *deferred,* or *unearned,* revenue). No revenues are recorded, and income is not increased because it is not yet earned. Later, when a company delivers its products or services, revenues are recognized. This occurs by reducing the deferred (unearned) revenue liability and increasing revenues, thus increasing income and retained earnings. This transaction process is reflected as follows:

Cash   500
  Deferred
    Revenues   500

Deferred
  Revenues   500
    Revenues   500

Transaction	Balance Sheet					Income Statement	
	Cash Asset +	Noncash Assets =	Liabil- ities +	Contrib. Capital +	Retained Earnings	Revenues −	Expenses
7. Receives $500 cash in advance of providing product or service	+500 Cash		+500 Deferred Revenues				
8. Provides product or service			−500 Deferred Revenues		+500 Retained Earnings	+500 Revenues	

Determination of when revenue is earned is not an exact science and is subject to discretion. If revenue is recognized prematurely, liabilities are underestimated and income is overstated. If revenue is incorrectly deferred, liabilities are overestimated and income is underestimated.

Asset Write-Down (Impairment) Transaction

Assets are recognized when they are estimated to possess future benefits, often in the form of expected cash inflows. When management determines that the expected benefits from an asset markedly decline, it must write down or write off the asset on the balance sheet. When this occurs, assets are reduced on the balance sheet, and this decline is reported on the income statement as an expense, thus reducing income and retained earnings. For depreciable and amortizable assets, the write-off represents an acceleration of depreciation or amortization. The impairment effects are illustrated as follows:

Write Off
  Expense   300
    Plant Assets   300

Transaction	Balance Sheet					Income Statement	
	Cash Asset +	Noncash Assets =	Liabil- ities +	Contrib. Capital +	Retained Earnings	Revenues −	Expenses
9. Write-down or write-off of $300 in plant assets		−300 Plant Assets			−300 Retained Earnings	−	300 Write Off Expense

A write-off depends on estimation of future asset benefits. Management determines when and to what extent an asset is impaired and, thus, the timing and amount of the write-off. Regarding timing, assets are often written down in concert with restructuring activities. The recognition of large write-offs and accruals is sometimes referred to as a *big bath.* The significance of big baths is evident when you consider the effect of the write-off on current and future income. Income is markedly reduced in the period of the write-off as costs are transferred from the balance sheet to the income statement. In future periods, income is not impacted by depreciation expense related to the write-off amount. If the write-off is larger than it should be, current income is too low and future income is too high. This shifts income from current periods to future periods. In contrast, if the write-off is improperly delayed, current period income is too high and future period income is too low.

APPENDIX 2B

Constructing the Statement of Cash Flows

Constructing the statement of cash flows, in the absence of transaction data, requires both the income statement and a comparative balance sheet for the current and prior period. The basic process is to adjust net income to get cash flows from operations, and then to review balance sheet changes to get cash flows from both investing and financing activities.

Net Income Adjustments to get Operating Cash Flows

The purpose of the statement of cash flows is to isolate and report the sources and uses of cash. There are two methods to compute the same operating cash flow measure. We illustrate the **indirect method** since it is, by far, the most widely used method in practice today (used by over 98% of public companies).[11] This method computes operating cash flow by adjusting net income.

$

Cash Effect

To illustrate, assume a company has one source of revenues (its services), one source of expenses (wages), and, currently, one asset (accounts receivable). It begins the period with $100,000 in accounts receivable that arise from last period's billings. During the current period, it generates service revenues of $300,000 cash and pays $200,000 cash in wages. Also during this period, it collects $50,000 of its beginning-period receivables. Thus, income for the period is $100,000 ($300,000 - $200,000), but its operating cash flow is $150,000 ($100,000 net income + $50,000 adjustment). The reduction in receivables accounts for the additional $50,000 of operating cash flow adjustment to net income.

More generally, under the indirect method, net cash flows from operations are computed as follows:

Net income	
± Operating items not impacting cash (e.g., depreciation and amortization addbacks)	①
± Nonoperating items not impacting cash (e.g., addback [remove] losses [gains] on asset sales)	②
± Changes in current assets and current liabilities	③
Net cash flows from operating activities	

Drawing on the simple example above, net income was $100,000 and the change in current assets (receivables) resulted in an additional $50,000 for a total net cash flow from operating activities of $150,000. Reductions in receivables (current assets) generate cash when they are collected. Conversely, reductions in liabilities (such as payment of accounts payable) use cash.

① The first adjustment to net income is for noncash operating items. Depreciation and amortization are common examples, which are added back to income. To understand this addback, note that the cash outflow usually occurs when the depreciable asset is acquired. The depreciation process allocates that cost over the assets' useful lives to match expense against the revenue generated by those assets. When depreciation expense is recorded, a portion of asset costs is removed from the balance sheet and transferred to the income statement as depreciation expense. Reduction of the asset's recorded amount is reflected as an increase in accumulated depreciation. The increase in accumulated depreciation reduces assets.

To illustrate, assume that $10 of depreciation is recorded on a new asset with an original cost of $100. The balance sheet reflects this as follows

Asset, at cost	$100
Less accumulated depreciation	(10)
Asset, net of accumulated depreciation	$ 90

For the first period, a $10 cost is allocated from the balance sheet asset to depreciation expense on the income statement. For the second period, another $10 is allocated to expense on the income statement. At the end of that second period, accumulated depreciation is $20 and the asset is shown (net of accumulated depreciation) on the balance sheet at $80. This process continues until the asset is fully depreciated, leaving only its salvage value. None of these allocations impacts cash. That is, the cash outflow occurs when the asset is acquired, and no cash is expended when recording depreciation expense.

Since the statement of cash flows focuses on cash flows only, we must eliminate noncash expenses (such as depreciation) from net income when adjusting it to get operating cash flows. Thus, we add back expenses such as

[11]The other method is the **direct method** which directly adjusts each category of the income statement. For example, sales are adjusted for the change in receivables, cost of goods sold is adjusted for the change in accounts payable and inventory, and SG&A is adjusted for changes in accrued liabilities. The resulting net cash flow from operations is identical to that computed by the indirect method. These two methods are identical in their computation of net cash flows from investing and financing activities.

depreciation and amortization, which are cost allocations (noncash expenses). This addback merely zeros out the expense from the computation of income as follows:

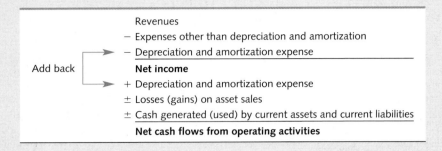

② The second income adjustment is for nonoperating gains and losses with no cash flow effects. One example is gains and losses from nonoperating asset sales (examples are gains and losses from sales of investments in securities and from discontinued operations); such gains and losses do not reflect any cash inflows or outflows. Instead, any cash inflows from asset sales, not their gains and losses, are reported under cash flows from investing activities.

③ Third, current asset and current liability adjustments are made to net income in computing operating cash flows as follows. This is a mechanical adjustment: examine the change in a current asset or current liability and record that change as a cash inflow or cash outflow per the decision rule in the table.

	Increases Reflect	Decreases Reflect
Current assets	Cash outflow	Cash inflow
Current liabilities	Cash inflow	Cash outflow

Illustrative Case

To illustrate the net income adjustments to get operating cash flow, we draw on the comparative balance sheets and income statement for Dye's PC Shop shown in Exhibit 2B.1.

EXHIBIT 2B.1 ■ PC Shop Comparative Balance Sheets and Income Statement

DYE'S PC SHOP Comparative Balance Sheets			
	Year-End 1	Year-End 2	Change from Prior Period
Assets			
Cash	$ 10,000	$ 15,000	$ 5,000
Accounts receivable	30,000	50,000	20,000
Inventories	100,000	125,000	25,000
Total current assets	140,000	190,000	50,000
Long-term assets, gross	200,000	250,000	50,000
Accumulated depreciation	(20,000)	(30,000)	10,000
Long-term assets, net	180,000	220,000	40,000
Total assets	$320,000	$410,000	90,000
Liabilities			
Accounts payable	$ 40,000	$ 60,000	$ 20,000
Bonds payable, long-term	200,000	180,000	(20,000)
Equity			
Common stock	50,000	100,000	50,000
Retained earnings	30,000	70,000	40,000
Total liabilities and equity	$320,000	$410,000	90,000

DYE'S PC SHOP Income Statement For Year Ended Year 2		
Sales		$300,000
Cost of goods sold	$190,000	
Expenses		
Salaries expense	50,000	
Depreciation expense	10,000	250,000
Net income*		$ 50,000

*Cash dividends declared and paid during Year 2 were $10,000.

The operating cash flows section begins with net income of $50,000 and then adjusts it for any noncash operating or nonoperating items not impacting cash, and then for changes in current assets and current liabilities. First, we identify one noncash operating item—depreciation expense of $10,000—which needs to be added back to income. No other operating or nonoperating items not impacting cash are identified in net income.

Second, the identified changes in current assets and current liabilities, as they reflect cash inflows and outflows, follow:

	Amount	As Reflected in Cash Flows
Increase in accounts receivable	$20,000	$(20,000)
Increase in inventories	25,000	(25,000)
Increase in accounts payable	20,000	20,000
Net change in working capital (excluding cash)	25,000	(25,000)

Consequently, the net cash flows from operations of Dye's PC Shop for Year 2—as computed from adjustments to net income—follows:

Net income	$50,000
Depreciation	10,000
Increase in accounts receivable	(20,000)
Increase in inventories	(25,000)
Increase in accounts payable	20,000
Net cash flow from operating activities	$35,000

Computing Cash Flows from Investing and Financing

The next step is to compute the cash flows from investing and financing activities. First, to compute net cash flows from investing activities, we recognize that these flows mainly arise from long-term asset purchases and sales. PC Shop's asset purchases were $50,000 for Year 2 (there were no asset sales); this is revealed by the balance sheet increase in long-term assets, which is reflected as a cash outflow from investing activities.

Second, to compute the net cash flows from financing activities, we recognize that these flows mainly arise from changes in long-term liability and the equity accounts. For Dye's PC Shop, the bond repayment ($20,000 outflow), stock issuance ($50,000 inflow), and dividend payment ($10,000 outflow) are relevant. The net cash flows from financing activities, therefore, yield a $20,000 net cash inflow.

The statement of cash flows shown in Exhibit 2B.2 reflects the discussions and computations for the illustrative case.[12]

---

[12]When looking at published 10-Ks, the amounts reported in the statement of cash flows do not always agree with what we would compute them to be using the reported income statement and changes in the reported balance sheet accounts. Reasons for this include:

1. The statement of cash flows includes only transactions involving cash receipt or payment. If an asset is acquired for noncash assets or seller financing, there is no cash involved and, therefore, it does not impact the statement of cash flows. Instead, such a purchase is described in a note as a *noncash investing and financing activity*. An example of this would be assets acquired under lease from the manufacturer.
2. When a company acquires another company in a stock transaction, the consolidated balance sheet reflects the increase in assets and liabilities, but no cash is paid. This acquisition is not reflected in the statement of cash flows but, instead, is described in a

(Continued on next page)

EXHIBIT 2B.2   ■   PC Shop Statement of Cash Flows

DYE'S PC SHOP Statement of Cash Flows For Year Ended Year 2	
Cash flows from operating activities	
Net income	$ 50,000
Adjustments to net income to get operating cash flows	
Depreciation expense	10,000
Accounts receivable increase	(20,000)
Inventories increase	(25,000)
Accounts payable increase	20,000
Net cash from operating activities	35,000
Cash flows from investing activities	
Purchase of long-term assets	(50,000)
Net cash flow from investing activities	(50,000)
Cash flows from financing activities	
Cash paid to retire bonds	(20,000)
Cash received from stock issuance	50,000
Cash paid for dividends	(10,000)
Net cash flow from financing activities	20,000
Net increase in cash	$ 5,000
Cash, beginning Year 2	10,000
Cash, ending Year 2	$ 15,000

GUIDANCE ANSWERS

MANAGERIAL DECISION   **You are the Securities Analyst**

Of special concern is the possibility that the new CEO is shifting costs to the current period in lieu of recording them in future periods. Evidence suggests that such behavior sometimes occurs when a new management team takes control. The reasoning is that the new management can blame current period performance on prior management and, at the same time, rid the balance sheet (and new management team) of costs that would normally be charged against future periods.

GUIDANCE ANSWERS

MANAGERIAL DECISION   **You are the Operations Manager**

The CFO desires a warranty cost estimate to match against the sales generated from the new product. To arrive at such an estimate, you must estimate the number and types of deficiencies in your product and the costs associated with each per the warranty provisions. This is often a difficult task for product engineers because it forces them to focus on the product failures and costs associated with them.

(Continued from previous page)

    note to the statement of cash flows as a *noncash investing and financing activity*. For example, in 2001 (the year of the ABC acquisition), Disney reports a cash outflow relating to acquisitions of $(8,432) million, which is the $10.1 billion cash portion of the purchase price less the cash acquired on ABC's balance sheet. The remainder of the purchase price ($8.8 billion) paid in stock is not reflected on its statement of cash flows.

3. Several items affect the balance sheet but do not affect the income statement. That is, they are charged to stockholders' equity accounts directly and do not run through the income statement. Examples are unrealized gains (losses) on available-for-sale securities, the recognition of minimum pension liability, foreign currency translation gains and losses, and gains and losses on some derivative (hedging) transactions. These topics are covered in later modules.

■ DISCUSSION QUESTIONS

Q2-1. The balance sheet consists of assets, liabilities, and equity. Define each category and provide two examples of accounts reported within each category.

Q2-2. Two important concepts that guide income statement reporting are the revenue recognition principle and the matching principle. Define and explain each of these two guiding principles.

Q2-3. GAAP is based on the concept of accrual accounting. Define and describe accrual accounting.

Q2-4. Analysts attempt to identify transitory items in an income statement. Define this term. What is the purpose of identifying transitory items?

Q2-5. What is the statement of stockholders' equity? What useful information is contained in that statement?

Q2-6. What is the statement of cash flows? What useful information is contained in that statement?

Q2-7. Define and explain the concept of financial statement articulation. What insight does knowledge of articulation provide us?

Q2-8. Describe the flow of costs for the purchase of a machine. At what point do such costs become expenses? Why is it necessary to match the expenses related to the machine in the same period with the revenues it produces?

Q2-9. What are the two essential characteristics of an asset?

Q2-10. What does the concept of liquidity refer to? Explain.

Q2-11. What does the term *current* denote when referring to assets?

Q2-12. Assets are recorded at historical costs even though current market values might, arguably, be more relevant to financial statement readers. Describe the reasoning behind historical cost usage.

Q2-13. Identify three intangible assets that are likely to be *excluded* from the balance sheet because they cannot be reliably measured.

Q2-14. What is an intangible asset? Provide three examples.

Q2-15. What are accrued liabilities? Provide an example.

Q2-16. What two conditions must be satisfied to require reporting of an accrued liability on the balance sheet?

Q2-17. Define net working capital. Explain how increasing the amount of trade credit can reduce the net working capital for a company.

Q2-18. What is the difference between company *book value* and *market value*? Explain why these two amounts can be different.

■ MINI EXERCISES

M2-19. Identifying and Classifying Financial Statement Items For each of the following items, identify whether they would be reported in the balance sheet (B) or income statement (I).

a.	Net income	*d.*	Accumulated depreciation	*g.*	Interest expense
b.	Retained earnings	*e.*	Wages expense	*h.*	Interest payable
c.	Depreciation expense	*f.*	Wages payable	*i.*	Unearned royalties

M2-20. Identifying and Classifying Financial Statement Items For each of the following items, identify whether they would be reported in the balance sheet (B) or income statement (I).

a.	Machinery	*e.*	Common stock	*i.*	Taxes expense
b.	Supplies expense	*f.*	Factory buildings	*j.*	Cost of goods sold
c.	Prepaid advertising	*g.*	Receivables	*k.*	Long-term debt
d.	Advertising expense	*h.*	Taxes payable	*l.*	Treasury stock

M2-21. Computation and Comparison of Income and Cash Flow Measures Healy Corporation recorded service revenues of $100,000 in 2005, of which $70,000 were for credit and $30,000 were for cash. Moreover, of the $70,000 credit sales for 2005, it collected $20,000 cash on those receivables before year-end 2005. The company also paid $25,000 cash for 2005 wages. Its employees also earned another $15,000 in wages for 2005, which were not yet paid at year-end 2005. (a) Compute the company's net income for 2005. (b) How much net cash inflow or outflow did the company generate in 2005? Explain.

M2-22. Assigning Accounts to Sections of the Balance Sheet Identify each of the following accounts as a component of assets (A), liabilities (L), or equity (E).

a.	Cash and cash equivalents	＿＿	*e.*	Accumulated depreciation	＿＿
b.	Wages payable	＿＿	*f.*	Retained earnings	＿＿
c.	Common stock	＿＿	*g.*	Additional paid-in capital	＿＿
d.	Equipment	＿＿	*h.*	Unearned revenues	＿＿

World
Wrestling
Entertainment
(WWE)

M2-23. **Computing Company Performance Using the Accounting Equation**   Use your knowledge of accounting relations to complete the following table for World Wrestling Entertainment, Inc.

	2003	2004
Beginning retained earnings	$89,089	$?
Net income (loss)	?	48,192
Dividends	0	15,060
Ending retained earnings	69,634	?

Johnson &
Johnson (JNJ)

M2-24. **Constructing a Retained Earnings Reconciliation from Financial Data**   Following is financial information from Johnson & Johnson for the year ended December 28, 2003. Prepare the 2003 calendar-year retained earnings reconciliation for Johnson & Johnson ($ millions).

Retained earnings, Dec. 29, 2002	$26,571	Dividends	$2,746
Net earnings	7,197	Retained earnings, Dec. 28, 2003	?
Other retained earnings changes	(519)		

M2-25. **Analyzing Transactions to Compute Net Income**   Guay Corp., a start-up company, provided services that were acceptable to its customers and billed those customers for $350,000 in 2004. However, Guay collected only $280,000 cash in 2004, and the remaining $70,000 of 2004 revenues were collected in 2005. Guay employees earned $200,000 in 2004 wages that were not paid until the first week of 2005. How much net income does Guay report for 2004? For 2005 (assuming no new transactions)?

M2-26. **Analyzing Transactions using the Financial Statement Effects Template**   Report the effects for each of the following independent transactions using the financial statement effects template provided.

	Balance Sheet					Income Statement	
Transaction	Cash Asset	+ Noncash Assets	= Liabil- ities	+ Contrib. Capital	+ Retained Earnings	Revenues	− Expenses
a. Issue stock for $1,000 cash							
b. Purchase inventory for $500 cash							
c. Sell inventory from b for $2,000 on credit							
d. Receive $2,000 cash on receivable from c							

■ EXERCISES

E2-27. **Constructing Financial Statements from Account Data**   Barth Company reports the following year-end account balances at December 31, 2005. Prepare the 2005 income statement and the balance sheet as of December 31, 2005.

Accounts payable	$ 16,000	Inventory	$ 36,000
Accounts receivable	30,000	Land	80,000
Bonds payable, long-term	200,000	Goodwill	8,000
Buildings	151,000	Retained earnings	60,000
Cash	48,000	Sales revenue	400,000
Common stock	150,000	Supplies	3,000
Cost of goods sold	180,000	Supplies expense	6,000
Equipment	70,000	Wages expense	40,000

E2-28. **Constructing Financial Statements from Transaction Data**   Baiman Corporation commences operations at the beginning of January. It provides its services on credit and bills its customers $30,000 for January sales. Its employees also earn January wages of $12,000 that are not paid until the first of February. Complete the following statements for the month-end of January.

Income Statement	
Sales	$
Wages expense	
Net income (loss)	$

Balance Sheet	
Cash	$
Accounts receivable	
Total assets	$
Wages payable	$
Retained earnings	
Total liabilities and equity	$

E2-29. **Analyzing and Reporting Financial Statement Effects of Transactions**   L. Demers launched a professional services firm on March 1. The firm will prepare financial statements at each month-end. In March (its first month), Demers executed the following transactions. Prepare an income statement for Demers Company for the month of March.

a. Demers (owner) invested $100,000 cash and additional assets that carried a $20,000 market value in the company in exchange for its common stock.
b. The company paid $3,200 cash for rent of office furnishings and facilities for March.
c. The company performed services for clients and immediately received $4,000 cash earned.
d. The company performed services for clients and sent a bill for $14,000 with payment due within 60 days.
e. Compensated an office employee $4,800 cash as salary for March.
f. Received $10,000 cash as partial payment on the amount owed from clients in transaction d.
g. The company paid $935 cash in dividends to Demers (owner).

E2-30. **Analyzing Transactions Using the Financial Statement Effects Template**   Enter the effects of each of the transactions a through g from Exercise 2-29 using the financial statement effects template shown in the module.

E2-31. **Identifying and Classifying Balance Sheet and Income Statement Accounts**   Following are selected accounts for Procter & Gamble. (a) Indicate the appropriate classification of each account as appearing in either its balance sheet (B) or its income statement (I). (b) Using the following data, compute its amounts for total assets and for total expenses. (c) Compute its net profit margin (net income/sales) and its debt-to-equity ratio (total liabilities/stockholders' equity).

Procter & Gamble (PG)

($ millions)	Amount	Classification
Sales	$43,373	
Accumulated depreciation	10,438	
Depreciation expense	1,703	
Retained earnings	11,686	
Net income	5,186	
Property, plant & equipment	13,104	
Selling, general & administrative expense	13,009	
Accounts receivable	3,038	
Total liabilities	27,520	
Stockholders' equity	16,186	

E2-32. **Identifying and Classifying Balance Sheet and Income Statement Accounts**   Following are selected accounts for Target Corporation. (a) Indicate the appropriate classification of each account as appearing in either its balance sheet (B) or its income statement (I). (b) Using the following data, compute its amounts for total assets and for total expenses. (c) Compute its net profit margin (net income/sales) and its debt-to-equity ratio (total liabilities/stockholders' equity).

Target Corporation (TGT)

($ millions)	Amount	Classification
Sales	$48,163	
Accumulated depreciation	6,178	
Depreciation expense	1,320	
Retained earnings	9,648	
Net income	1,841	
Property, plant & equipment	16,969	
Selling, general & administrative expense	11,534	
Accounts receivable	5,776	
Total liabilities	20,327	
Stockholders' equity	11,065	

Briggs & Stratton (BGG)

E2-33. Identifying and Classifying Balance Sheet and Income Statement Accounts Following are selected accounts for **Briggs & Stratton**. (*a*) Indicate the appropriate classification of each account as appearing in either its balance sheet (B) or its income statement (I). (*b*) Using the following data, compute its amounts for total assets and for total expenses. (*c*) Compute its net profit margin (net income/sales) and its debt-to-equity ratio (total liabilities/stockholders' equity).

($ millions)	Amount	Classification
Sales	$1,658	
Accumulated depreciation	506	
Depreciation expense	64	
Retained earnings	821	
Net income	81	
Property, plant & equipment	371	
Selling, general & administrative expense	178	
Accounts receivable	202	
Total liabilities	960	
Stockholders' equity	515	

Kimberly-Clark (KMB)

E2-34. Identifying and Classifying Balance Sheet and Income Statement Accounts Following are selected accounts for **Kimberly-Clark**. (*a*) Indicate the appropriate classification of each account as appearing in either its balance sheet (B) or its income statement (I). (*b*) Using the following data, compute its amounts for total assets and for total expenses. (*c*) Compute its net profit margin (net income/sales) and its debt-to-equity ratio (total liabilities/stockholders' equity).

($ millions)	Amount	Classification
Sales	$14,348	
Accumulated depreciation	6,916	
Depreciation expense	759	
Retained earnings	9,494	
Net income	1,694	
Property, plant & equipment	8,263	
Selling, general & administrative expense	2,376	
Accounts receivable	1,955	
Total liabilities	10,014	
Stockholders' equity	6,766	

YUM! Brands (YUM)

E2-35. Identifying and Classifying Balance Sheet and Income Statement Accounts Following are selected accounts for **YUM! Brands**. (*a*) Indicate the appropriate classification of each account as appearing in either its balance sheet (B) or its income statement (I). (*b*) Using the following data, compute its amounts for total assets and for total expenses. (*c*) Compute its net profit margin (net income/sales) and its debt-to-equity ratio (total liabilities/stockholders' equity).

($ millions)	Amount	Classification
Sales	$8,380	
Accumulated depreciation	2,326	
Depreciation expense	401	
Retained earnings	204	
Net income	617	
Property, plant & equipment	3,280	
Selling, general & administrative expense	973	
Accounts receivable	169	
Total liabilities	4,500	
Stockholders' equity	1,120	

E2-36.   Analyzing Transactions using the Financial Statement Effects Template   Record the effect of each of the following independent transactions using the financial statement effects template provided.

	Balance Sheet					Income Statement	
Transaction	Cash Asset	+ Noncash Assets	= Liabil- ities	+ Contrib. Capital	+ Retained Earnings	Revenues	− Expenses
a. $500 of wages are earned by employees but not yet paid							
b. $2,000 of inventory is purchased on credit							
c. The inventory purchase in b is sold for $3,000 on credit							
d. Collected $3,000 cash from the transaction c							
e. $5,000 of equipment is acquired for cash							
f. Record depreciation of $1,000 on equipment from transaction e							
g. Paid $10,000 on a note payable that came due							
h. Paid $2,000 cash interest on borrowings							

■ PROBLEMS

P2-37.   Analyzing and Interpreting the Financial Performance of Competitors   Abercrombie & Fitch (ANF) and Nordstrom (JWN) are major retailers that concentrate in the higher-end clothing lines. Following are selected data from their fiscal-year 2003 financial statements:

Abercrombie & Fitch (ANF)

Nordstrom (JWN)

($ millions)	ANF	JWN
Total liabilities and equity	$1,199	$4,466
Net income	195	205
Sales	1,596	1,708

Required

a.   What is the total amount of assets invested in (1) ANF and (2) JWN? What are the total expenses for each company (1) in dollars and (2) as a percentage of sales?

b.   What is the return on average assets for (1) ANF and (2) JWN? Note: ANF's total assets at the beginning of 2003 are $995 million and JWN's beginning 2003 assets are $4,096 million.

c.   Decompose each company's ROA into its net profit margin and asset turnover components. What do you conclude about the relative financial performance of these two companies from this disaggregation?

P2-38. Constructing and Analyzing Balance Sheet Numbers from Incomplete Data   Selected balance sheet amounts for **3M Company**, a manufacturer of consumer and business products, for five recent years follow:

3M Company (MMM)

($ millions)	Current Assets	Long-Term Assets	Total Assets	Current Liabilities	Long-Term Liabilities	Total Liabilities	Stockholders' Equity
1999	$6,066	$?	$13,896	$3,819	$?	$7,607	$6,289
2000	?	8,143	14,522	4,754	3,237	7,991	?
2001	6,296	8,310	?	?	4,011	8,520	6,086
2002	6,059	9,270	?	4,457	4,879	?	5,993
2003	?	9,880	17,600	5,082	4,633	9,715	?

Required

a.   Compute the missing balance sheet amounts for each of the five years shown.
b.   What types of accounts would you expect to be included in current assets? In long-term assets?

P2-39. Analyzing, Reconstructing and Interpreting Balance Sheet Data   Selected balance sheet amounts for **Abercrombie & Fitch**, a retailer of name-brand apparel at premium prices, for five recent fiscal-years follow ($ millions):

Abercrombie & Fitch (ANF)

	Current Assets	Long-Term Assets	Total Assets	Current Liabilities	Long-Term Liabilities	Total Liabilities	Stockholders' Equity
2000	$?	$158	$ 458	$138	$?	$147	$311
2001	304	284	?	155	10	165	?
2002	405	?	771	?	12	175	595
2003	601	394	?	211	?	245	750
2004	753	?	1,199	?	48	328	871

Required

a.   Compute the missing balance sheet amounts for each of the five years shown.
b.   What asset category would you expect to constitute the majority of its current assets?
c.   Has the proportion of current and long-term assets changed markedly over the past five years? Explain.
d.   Does the company appear to be conservatively financed; that is, financed by a greater proportion of equity than of debt? Explain

P2-40. Analyzing, Reconstructing and Interpreting Balance Sheet Data   Selected balance sheet amounts for **Albertsons Inc.**, a grocery company, for five recent fiscal-years follow ($ millions):

Albertsons Inc. (ABS)

	Current Assets	Long-Term Assets	Total Assets	Current Liabilities	Long-Term Liabilities	Total Liabilities	Stockholders' Equity
2000	$4,582	$?	$15,701	$4,055	$?	$ 9,999	$5,702
2001	4,300	11,778	?	3,395	6,989	?	5,694
2002	?	11,358	15,967	3,582	6,470	10,052	?
2003	4,268	10,943	?	3,448	?	10,014	5,197
2004	4,419	?	15,394	?	6,328	10,013	5,381

Required

a.   Compute the missing balance sheet amounts for each of the five years shown.
b.   What asset category would you expect to constitute the majority of its current assets? Of its long-term assets?

    c.   Is the company conservatively financed; that is, is it financed by a greater proportion of equity than of debt? Explain.

P2-41.   **Constructing and Analyzing Balance Sheet Numbers from Incomplete Data**   Selected balance sheet amounts for **Harley-Davidson, Inc.**, a motorcycle manufacturer, for five recent years follow ($ millions):

Harley-
Davidson, Inc.
(HDI)

	Current Assets	Long-Term Assets	Total Assets	Current Liabilities	Long-Term Liabilities	Total Liabilities	Stockholders' Equity
1999	$?	$1,163	$2,112	$518	$?	$ 951	$1,161
2000	1,297	1,139	?	498	533	1,031	?
2001	1,665	?	3,118	?	646	1,362	1,756
2002	2,067	?	3,861	990	?	1,628	2,233
2003	2,729	2,194	?	956	1,010	?	2,958

Required
    a.   Compute the missing amounts for each of the five years shown.
    b.   What asset categories would you expect to be included in its current assets? In its long-term assets?
    c.   Is the company conservatively financed; that is, is it financed by a greater proportion of equity than of debt? Explain.

P2-42.   **Analyzing, Reconstructing and Interpreting Balance Sheet Data**   Selected balance sheet amounts for **Microsoft, Inc.**, a software development company, for five recent fiscal years follow ($ millions):

Microsoft, Inc.
(MSFT)

	Current Assets	Long-Term Assets	Total Assets	Current Liabilities	Long-Term Liabilities	Total Liabilities	Stockholders' Equity
1999	$?	$16,923	$37,156	$ 8,718	$?	$ 8,718	$28,438
2000	30,308	21,842	?	9,755	?	10,782	41,368
2001	39,637	?	59,257	11,132	836	11,968	?
2002	48,576	19,070	?	12,744	2,722	?	52,180
2003	?	20,598	79,571	13,974	?	18,551	61,020

Required
    a.   Compute the missing amounts for each of the five years shown.
    b.   Microsoft is highly profitable and very liquid. What would you expect to be the major asset category constituting its current assets?
    c.   Is Microsoft conservatively financed, that is, financed by a greater proportion of equity than of debt? Explain.

P2-43.   **Analyzing, Reconstructing and Interpreting Income Statement Data**   Selected income statement information for **Nike, Inc.**, a manufacturer of athletic footwear, for five recent fiscal-years follows ($ millions):

Nike, Inc.
(NKE)

	Sales	Cost of Goods Sold	Gross Profit	Operating Expenses	Operating Income	Nonoperating Income	Net Income
1999	$?	$5,295	$3,482	$?	$ 837	$386	$451
2000	8,995	5,216	?	2,813	966	387	?
2001	9,489	?	3,901	2,903	999	?	590
2002	?	5,781	4,112	3,060	1,052	389	?
2003	10,697	6,074	?	?	1,246	772	474

Required
    a.   Compute the missing amounts for each of the five years shown.
    b.   Compute the gross profit margin (gross profit/sales) for each of the five years and comment on its level and any trends that are evident.
    c.   What would you expect to be the major cost categories constituting its operating expenses?

P2-44. **Constructing and Analyzing Income Statement Numbers from Incomplete Data**   Selected income statement information for **Starbucks Corporation**, a coffee-related restaurant chain, for five recent fiscal-years follows ($ millions):

Starbucks
Corporation
(SBUX)

	Sales	Cost of Goods Sold	Gross Profit	Operating Expenses	Operating Income	Nonoperating Income	Net Income
1999	$?	$1,336	$344	$187	$157	$ 55	$?
2000	2,169	1,737	?	240	192	?	95
2001	2,649	?	567	?	252	71	181
2002	?	2,598	691	390	301	86	?
2003	4,076	?	869	482	?	118	268

Required
a.   Compute the missing amounts for each of the five years shown.
b.   Compute the gross profit margin (gross profit/sales) for each of the five years and comment on its level and any trends that are evident.
c.   What would you expect to be the major cost categories constituting its operating expenses?

P2-45. **Analyzing, Reconstructing and Interpreting Income Statement Data**   Selected income statement information for **Target Corporation**, a department store chain, for five recent fiscal-years follows:

Target
Corporation
(TGT)

($ millions)	Sales	Cost of Goods Sold	Gross Profit	Operating Expenses	Operating Income	Nonoperating Income	Net Income
2000	$?	$23,029	$10,673	$ 8,344	$2,329	$1,185	$?
2001	36,903	25,295	?	9,130	2,478	?	1,264
2002	39,888	?	12,642	?	2,747	1,379	1,368
2003	?	29,260	14,657	11,393	3,264	1,610	?
2004	48,163	31,790	?	12,854	3,519	?	1,841

Required
a.   Compute the missing amounts for each of the five years shown.
b.   Compute the gross profit margin (gross profit/sales) for each of the five years and comment on its level and any trends that are evident.
c.   What would you expect to be the major cost categories constituting its operating expenses?

P2-46. **Analyzing Transactions using the Financial Statement Effects Template**   On March 1, S. Penman (owner) launched AniFoods, Inc., an organic foods retailing company. Following are the transactions for its first month of business.
a.   S. Penman (owner) contributed $100,000 cash to the company in return for common stock. Penman also lent the company $55,000. This $55,000 note is due one year hence.
b.   The company purchased equipment in the amount of $50,000, paying $10,000 cash and signing a note payable to the equipment manufacturer for the remaining balance.
c.   The company purchased inventory for $80,000 cash in March.
d.   The company had March sales of $100,000 of which $60,000 was for cash and $40,000 on credit. Total cost of goods sold for its March sales was $70,000.
e.   The company purchased advertising time from a local radio station for $10,000 cash.
f.   During March, $7,500 worth of radio spots purchased in e are aired. The remaining spots will be aired in April.
g.   Employee wages earned and paid during March total $15,000 cash.
h.   Prior to issuance of financial statements, the company recognized that employees had earned an additional $1,000 in wages that will be paid in the next period.
i.   The company recorded $2,000 of depreciation for March relating to its equipment.

Required
Record the effect of each of the transactions a through i using the financial statement effects template shown in the module.

P2-47. **Preparing an Income Statement and Balance Sheet from Transaction Data**   Use the information in Problem 2-46 to complete the following requirements.
Required
Prepare both a March income statement, and a balance sheet as of the end of March, for the company.

P2-48.[A] **Preparing Journal Entries for Business Transactions**   Use the information in Problem 2-46 to complete the following requirements.

Required

Prepare journal entries to record the business transactions *a* through *i* in Problem 2-46.

P2-49.[B] **Reconciling and Computing Operating Cash Flows from Net Income**   Petroni Company reports the following selected results for its calendar year 2005:

Net income	$135,000
Depreciation expense	25,000
Gain on sale of assets	5,000
Accounts receivable increase	10,000
Accounts payable increase	6,000
Prepaid expenses decrease	3,000
Wages payable decrease	4,000

Required

Prepare the operating section only of Petroni Company's statement of cash flows for 2005.

3 Analyzing and Interpreting Financial Statements

3M COMPANY

3M'S RACE TO THE TAPE

Jim McNerney is the Chairman and CEO of 3M. He is the first outsider to take the reins of 3M in its century-long history. McNerney joined 3M after losing a three-way race to succeed John F. Welch as chief executive of General Electric.

3M is a mini-GE in many respects. Both companies are industrial conglomerates that seek to balance slow-downs in one industry with upturns in others. Both companies also have strong traditions of discipline, quality, and a focus on measuring and rewarding performance. 3M has produced several world-famous brands such as Scotch® tape and Post-it® notes. Still, 3M is primarily a nuts-and-bolts type producer. It provides duct tape, turbines, and electronic gear that keep the industrial world humming.

The key to 3M's success is its research. Over the decades, 3M scientists and engineers have developed sandpaper, magnetic audiotape, molds and glues for orthodontia, lime-yellow traffic signs, respirators, floppy disks, and Scotchgard™. To this day, 3M draws its identity from its research success. 3M devotes more than $1 billion to research each year and has 1,000 scientists and engineers around the world searching for the next breakthrough.

Income has increased 35% since McNerney took control in 2001. 3M's income for 2003 topped off at $2.4 billion on sales of $18.23 billion, yielding a 13.2% net profit margin. Importantly, its return on equity (ROE), as shown below and defined as net income/average equity, has continued to climb since 2001, when restructuring costs cut into 3M's income as the new CEO refocused activities.

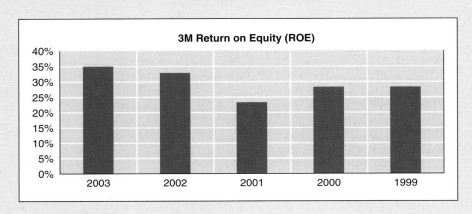

3M's increase in ROE has been accompanied by a steady increase in its stock price. By early 2005, 3M shares were valued at just over $82 per share, which is 35% higher than when McNerney took control. The Dow Jones Industrial Average, by contrast, shows no net (percent) increase for the same time period.

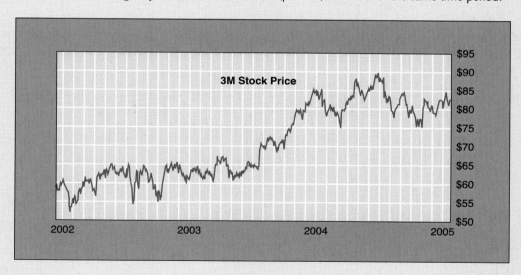

What is McNerney's secret? There is no doubt that one of McNerney's most urgent problems at 3M was its ballooning costs. Costs had grown at twice the rate of sales in the years prior to his arrival. McNerney's cost-control efforts generated an immediate savings of $500 million in 2001. That same year, he also streamlined purchasing, which generated another $100 million in savings.

One key to cost savings at 3M is its *Six Sigma* cost-cutting program, which was successfully applied at GE and a number of other companies now led by former GE executives. 3M is using Six Sigma for everything from focusing sales efforts to developing new kinds of duct tape.

McNerney's efforts are paying off. In 2003, sales rose in each of 3M's businesses except telecom, and income was up in all but the industrial division. Further, cash flows swelled by 29%, to $3.79 billion, and 3M's

(Continued on next page)

(Continued from previous page)

operating income margin widened by a full percentage point to nearly 21%. 3M also increased its inventory turnover, which contributed greatly to its increases in cash flows and profitability.

McNerney has also increased acquisitions by 3M. He hopes to use acquisitions to help grow sales 10% annually, nearly double the rate of the past decade. Fortunately for McNerney, 3M has the cash flows and the flexibility necessary to go shopping.

3M has funded its cash outflows for acquisitions in part with cash inflows from improved working capital management. For example, 3M's average collection period for its receivables has been reduced from 63 days in 1999 to 52 days in 2003. Increased production efficiencies and lower cost raw materials have boosted inventory turnover from 3.8 times per year to 5.0 times since McNerney took control. As a result, the working capital needed to run 3M has declined as a percent of sales, boosting both income and cash flows.

3M's management has brought operating discipline to the business, including a renewed focus on measures used to evaluate financial performance. This module focuses on such measures. A key to company success is ROE. This module explains ROE and focuses on *disaggregation of ROE,* also called DuPont analysis (after DuPont management that first successfully applied it). ROE disaggregation focuses on the drivers of ROE. This module also introduces liquidity and solvency analysis—another important aspect of company success. Specifically, we describe the factors relevant to credit analysis and its use in setting debt ratings and terms.

Sources: *BusinessWeek,* April 2004 and August 2002; *Financial Times,* July 2002; *Fortune Magazine,* August 2002; 3M 10-K report, 2004 and 2003.

■ INTRODUCTION

Effective financial statement analysis and interpretation begin with an understanding of the kinds of questions that are both important and can be aided by financial analysis. Then, determining which questions to ask is a function of the type of analysis we plan to conduct. Different stakeholders of a company have different analysis requirements. Consider the following:

Stakeholder	Types of Questions Guiding Analysis of Financial Statements
Creditor	Can the company pay the interest and principal on its debt? Does the company rely too much on nonowner financing?
Investor	Does the company earn an acceptable return on invested capital? Is the gross profit margin growing or shrinking? Does the company effectively use nonowner financing?
Manager	Are costs under control? Are company markets growing or shrinking? Do observed changes reflect opportunities or threats? Is the allocation of investment across different assets too high or too low?

A crucial aspect of analysis is identifying the business activities that drive company success. Namely, does company return on invested capital result from operating activities or nonoperating (often called *financial*) activities? The distinction between operating and nonoperating activities is important as it plays a key role in effective analysis.

Operating activities are the core activities of a company. They are the activities required to deliver a company's products or services to its customers. Operating activities include research and development of products, the establishment of supply chains, the assemblage of administrative and productive product support, the promotion and marketing of products, and after-sale customer services.

Operating activities are reflected on the balance sheet, for example, by receivables and inventories net of payables and accruals, and by long-term operating assets net of long-term operating liabilities. On the income statement, operating activities are reflected in revenues, costs of goods sold, and operating expenses such as selling, general, and administrative expenses. Operating activities have the most long-lasting (persistent) effects on the future profitability and cash flows of the company and, thus, are the primary value drivers for company stakeholders. It is for this reason that operating activities play such a prominent role in effective profitability analysis.

Nonoperating activities primarily relate to the investing and financing activities of a company. They are reflected on the balance sheet as nonoperating (financial) assets and liabilities, which expand and contract as a buffer to fluctuations in operating asset and liability levels. When operating assets grow faster than operating liabilities, nonoperating liabilities must increase to finance them (per the accounting equation). These liabilities contract when assets decline and can even turn negative, resulting in financial assets invested temporarily in marketable securities to provide some return until those funds are needed again for operations. On the income statement, nonoperating activities are reflected in expenses and revenues from those financial liabilities and assets. Although nonoperating activities are important and must be carefully managed, they are not the value drivers.

Module 1 introduced a simple measure of financial performance called *return on assets (ROA)*, defined as net income divided by average total assets. ROA is a widely quoted measure and, for that reason, it is one we should know. Net income in the ROA formula, however, is an aggregation of both operating and nonoperating components. Accordingly, it fails to distinguish between these two important activities and drivers of company performance. Likewise, total assets combine both operating and nonoperating assets and liabilities.[1] Effective analysis segregates operating and nonoperating activities and, consequently, we describe the *return on net operating assets* (RNOA) that is arguably more informative.

This module's explanation of financial statement analysis begins at the most aggregate level and works down to three levels of disaggregation. The most aggregate level is *return on equity* (ROE), which is generally regarded as the summary measure of financial performance. ROE is then disaggregated into key drivers of profitability and asset utilization. The framework of ROE disaggregation is depicted in Exhibit 3.1.

EXHIBIT 3.1 ■ Return on Equity (ROE) Disaggregation

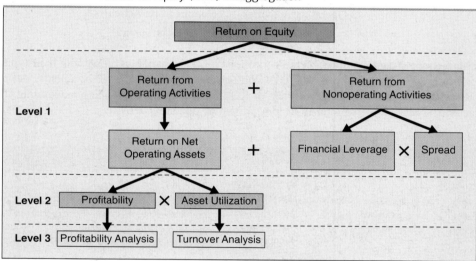

ROE disaggregation serves to answer several important questions in analyzing financial performance. Examples are:

* What is driving the company's financial performance?
  ○ Is it related solely to profitability?
  ○ What aspects of company profitability are important?
* Is the company effectively managing its balance sheet (investing and financing activities)?
* Is the company relying more on operating or nonoperating activities?
* Do its assets generate sufficient revenues?

These are but a sampling of questions that an analysis of ROE through its disaggregation can help answer.

The first level of disaggregation separates ROE into two basic drivers: return from operating activities and return from nonoperating activities. This identifies drivers by business activities. The second level of analysis examines the drivers of return on operating activities: profitability and asset utilization. A third level of disaggregation explores both of those components of return on operating activities for further insights into the drivers of company performance.

After a complete explanation of ROE disaggregation, we conclude the module with a discussion of credit analysis. A major part of credit analysis involves liquidity and solvency assessments. As part of that discussion, we identify the ratios typically used to determine bond investment ratings, a key determinant

---

[1]An alternate definition for return on assets is: ROA = (Net income + *After-tax interest expense*) / Average total assets. While the numerator in this formulation seeks to focus on operating income, the denominator (total assets) still includes nonoperating (financial) components.

of both bond prices and the cost of debt financing for many companies. In that spirit, we also introduce and describe bankruptcy prediction.

■ RETURN ON EQUITY (ROE)

Return on equity (ROE) is the ultimate measure of performance from the shareholders' perspective. It is computed as follows:

$$\text{ROE} = \text{Net Income/Average Equity}$$

Net income is the bottom line from the income statement. Net income includes revenues from all sources, both operating and nonoperating. It also includes expenses from all sources, including cost of goods sold, selling, general, and administrative expenses, and nonoperating (financial) expenses like interest.[2]

ROE is disaggregated into operating and nonoperating components as follows (see Appendix 3B for its derivation):

$$\text{ROE} = \boxed{\begin{array}{c}\text{Return from}\\ \text{Operating Activities}\end{array}} + \boxed{\begin{array}{c}\text{Return from}\\ \text{Nonoperating Activities}\end{array}}$$
$$= \quad\quad \text{RNOA} \quad\quad + \quad\quad (\text{FLEV} \times \text{Spread})$$

This is an important disaggregation, and the definitions for these variables along with their typical components are in Exhibit 3.2—this table includes additional variables that are subsequently defined. The above formula emphasizes the two key drivers of ROE: operating (RNOA) and nonoperating (FLEV × Spread) activities. Stakeholders prefer ROE to be driven by operating activities.

EXHIBIT 3.2 ■ Key Ratio Definitions

Ratio	Definition
ROE: return on equity	Net Income/Average Equity
RNOA: return on net operating assets	NOPAT/Average NOA
NOPAT: net operating profit after tax	Sales and other operating revenues less operating expenses such as cost of sales, taxes, selling, general, and administrative; it excludes nonoperating revenues and expenses such as those from financial assets and liabilities
NOA: net operating assets	Current and long-term operating assets less current and long-term operating liabilities; it excludes investments in securities, short- and long-term interest-bearing debt, and capitalized lease obligations
FLEV: financial leverage	Average NFO/Average Equity
NFO: net financial obligations	Financial (nonoperating) obligations less financial (nonoperating) assets
Spread	RNOA − NFR
NFR: net financial rate	NFE/Average NFO
NFE: net financial expense	NOPAT − Net income; it includes interest expense less revenues from nonoperating assets, net of tax

For a recent 34-year period, the median ROE achieved by all publicly traded U.S. companies was 12.2% (from Nissim and Penman, 2001). Most of this ROE is driven by RNOA as illustrated in the following table of median values for those companies and years:

ROE Disaggregation*	ROE	=	RNOA	+	(FLEV	×	Spread)
1st quartile (25th percentile)	6.3%		6.0%	+	0.05	×	−0.5%
Median (50th percentile)	12.2%	≈	10.3%	+	0.40	×	3.3%
3rd quartile (75th percentile)	17.6%		15.6%	+	0.93	×	10.3%

*Numbers in the table are medians (50th percentile) and quartiles (25th or 75th percentile); thus, the equation does not exactly equal ROE.

---

[2]Net income does not include dividend payments as they are not a deductible expense in the computation of GAAP income (instead, dividends are considered a distribution of income).

This table shows that companies are, on average, conservatively financed with a greater proportion of equity than net financial obligations (evident from FLEV < 1.0). Also, companies earn, on average, a positive spread on borrowed monies (3.3%). This is not always the case, however, as evidenced by the lowest 25% of companies. Most important, RNOA is, on average, approximately 84% of ROE (10.3%/12.2%).

BUSINESS INSIGHT   **3M's Return on Equity Breakdown**

The following graph shows that **3M**'s ROE and RNOA have increased steadily since 1999, with the exception of 2001, which was impacted by costs of its restructuring program.

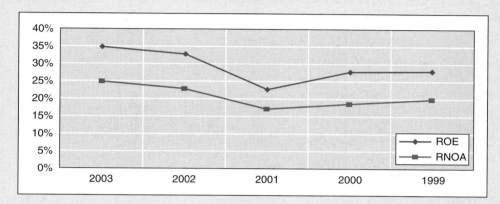

ROE exceeds RNOA in all years. The difference between ROE and RNOA lines is the return from nonoperating activities (FLEV × Spread). Since ROE exceeds RNOA for 3M, it shows that 3M is, on average, able to invest borrowed funds with a return exceeding its borrowing rate. The following data underlying this graph shows that 3M's financial leverage is only slightly higher than the 0.40 median for U.S. companies. Specifically, for 2003, and per the ROE disaggregation, 3M's ROE of 34.6% equals its RNOA of 24.7% plus its FLEV × Spread of 9.9%.

(in percents)	2003	2002	2001	2000	1999
ROE	34.6%	32.7%	22.7%	27.8%	28.0%
RNOA	24.7	22.5	16.8	18.4	19.6
FLEV	45.5	51.9	45.4	42.5	41.5
Spread	21.8	19.5	14.8	15.8	16.9

■ LEVEL 1 ANALYSIS—RNOA AND LEVERAGE

This section drills down one level in ROE disaggregation analysis to investigate the two main drivers of ROE: the return on net operating assets (RNOA) and the return from nonoperating activities (FLEV × Spread) as illustrated in Exhibit 3.3. We first discuss the return on net operating assets, followed by a discussion of the effects of financial leverage, including its advantages and disadvantages.

EXHIBIT 3.3 ■ Level 1 of ROE Disaggregation

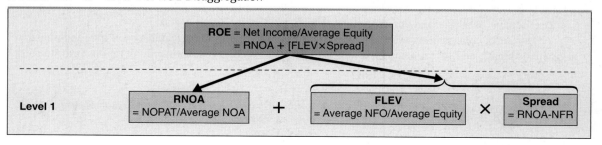

Return on Net Operating Assets (RNOA)

The return on net operating assets (RNOA) is normally the most important driver of ROE. It is computed as follows:

$$\text{RNOA} = \text{NOPAT/Average NOA}$$

where
>   NOPAT is net operating profit after tax
>   NOA is net operating assets

Both NOPAT and NOA are explained in detail below. RNOA reflects the operating side of the business (the other is the nonoperating, or financial, side). To appreciate the importance of RNOA, we must first understand the difference between the operating and nonoperating assets and liabilities (equity is always nonoperating).

Exhibit 3.4 presents a typical balance sheet with the nonoperating (financial) assets and liabilities highlighted. All other assets and liabilities are considered operating.

EXHIBIT 3.4 ■ Distinguishing Operating and Nonoperating Assets and Liabilities

Typical GAAP Balance Sheet [Nonoperating (Financial) Items Highlighted]	
Current assets	**Current liabilities**
Cash and cash equivalents	Short-term notes and interest payable
Short-term investments	Accounts payable
Accounts receivable	Accrued liabilities
Inventories	Deferred income tax liabilities
Prepaid expenses	Current maturities of long-term debt
Deferred income tax assets	
	Long-term liabilities
Long-term assets	Bonds and notes payable
Long-term investments in securities	Capitalized lease obligations
Property, plant & equipment, net	Pension and other postretirement liabilities
Natural resources	Deferred income tax liabilities
Equity method investments	
Intangible assets	**Minority interest**
Deferred income tax assets	
Capitalized lease assets	
Other long-term assets	**Total stockholders' equity**

Operating assets and liabilities are those necessary to conduct the company's business. These include current operating assets such as cash, accounts receivable, inventories, prepaid expenses, and short-term deferred tax assets. It also includes current operating liabilities such as accounts payable, accrued liabilities, and short-term deferred tax liabilities. **Net operating working capital (NOWC)** equals operating current assets less operating current liabilities.

The current nonoperating assets include short-term investments in marketable securities. The current nonoperating liabilities include short-term interest-bearing notes payable, interest payable, and current maturities of long-term interest-bearing liabilities (and capitalized lease obligations).

Long-term operating assets include property, plant, and equipment (PPE), long-term investments related to strategic acquisitions (equity method investments, goodwill, and acquired intangible assets), deferred tax assets, and capitalized lease assets. Long-term operating liabilities include pensions and other postretirement liabilities and deferred income tax liabilities.

Long-term nonoperating assets include long-term investments in marketable securities and nonstrategic investments, and investments in nonoperating assets (such as discontinued operations prior to sale).[3]

---

[3]Discontinued operations are, by definition, not part of the continuing operating activities of the company. Although not financial in nature, we classify them as nonoperating as they represent an investment in the process of disposition.

Long-term nonoperating liabilities include bonds and other long-term interest-bearing liabilities, and any noncurrent portion of capitalized leases. Stockholders' equity includes all of the components of contributed and earned capital, net of treasury stock and other comprehensive income, plus minority interest recognized from business combinations.

The distinction between operating and nonoperating activities is summarized in Exhibit 3.5. **Net operating assets (NOA)** of the company consist of current and long-term operating assets less current and long-term operating liabilities. Stated differently, net operating assets consist of net operating working capital plus long-term net operating assets.

EXHIBIT 3.5 ■ Simplified Operating and Nonoperating Balance Sheet

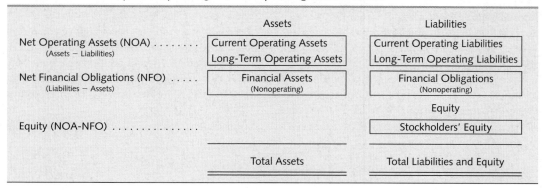

Nonoperating assets and liabilities are primarily financial in nature, and typically represent investments in marketable securities and discontinued operations, and borrowings in interest-bearing debt. **Net financial obligations (NFO)** are the net of financial (nonoperating) obligations less financial (nonoperating) assets. Net financial obligations are positive if financial obligations exceed financial assets and negative otherwise.

Since the accounting equation stipulates that Assets = Liabilities + Equity, we can also net this adjusted (reformulated) balance sheet to yield the following identity:

Net Operating Assets (NOA) = Net Financial Obligations (NFO) + Stockholders' Equity

The RNOA computation and analysis also require that we distinguish between operating and nonoperating profit. Net operating profit after tax (NOPAT), the numerator of RNOA, is the after-tax profit earned from net operating assets. It includes sales less: cost of goods sold (COGS), operating expenses (OE) such as selling, general, and administrative (SG&A) expenses, and taxes on pretax operating profit.[4] Items excluded from NOPAT include interest revenue and expense, dividend revenue, and income or loss from discontinued operations.[5] More generally, NOPAT is computed as follows:

NOPAT = (Sales − Operating Expenses) × [1 − (Tax Expense/Pretax Income)]

Sales less operating expense yields pretax operating profits. The expression (Tax Expense/Pretax Income) yields the effective tax rate for the period. Multiplying pretax operating profit by one minus the effective tax rate yields net operating profit after tax, or NOPAT.[6]

The operating versus nonoperating distinction is different from the core (also called permanent and persistent) versus transitory distinction for earnings components that was discussed in Module 2. Exhibit 3.6 lists typical income statement items categorized by operating versus nonoperating and by core versus transitory.[7]

---

[4]Earnings on equity method investments (covered in Module 6) are operating so long as the equity method investment is classified as a strategic acquisition.

[5]Net income or loss on discontinued operations, and the gain or loss on sale of its net assets, are treated as nonoperating items.

[6]In Module 2, we identified three categories of income statement items that are presented after income from continuing operations (called *below the line*), net of tax: discontinued operations, extraordinary items, and changes in accounting principles. Discontinued operations are generally viewed as nonoperating. Extraordinary items and changes in accounting principles are often related to operating activities and, if so, are included in NOPAT.

[7]The items listed are meant to give you a general idea of the composition of these categories and are not a complete listing.

EXHIBIT 3.6 ■ Distinguishing Operating, Nonoperating, Core, and Transitory Income

	Core	Transitory
Operating	Sales; cost of goods sold; selling, general, and administrative expenses; research and development; income taxes	Operating asset write-downs; nonrecurring restructuring accruals; gains and losses on sales of operating assets
Nonoperating	Dividends; interest revenues and expenses; hedging gains and losses	Debt retirement gains and losses; gains and losses on discontinued operations

RESEARCH INSIGHT   **Ratio Behavior over Time**

How do ROE, RNOA, and NFR ratios behave over time? Following is a graph of these ratios over a recent 34-year period (from graph B, p.134, of Nissim and Penman, 2001, *Review of Accounting Studies* 6 (1), pp. 109–154, with permission of Springer Science and Business Media). There is considerable variability in these ratios over time. Also, the proportion of RNOA to ROE is greater for some periods of time than for others. Yet, in all periods, RNOA exceeds the net financial rate, NFR. This is evidence of a positive effect, on average, for ROE from financial leverage.

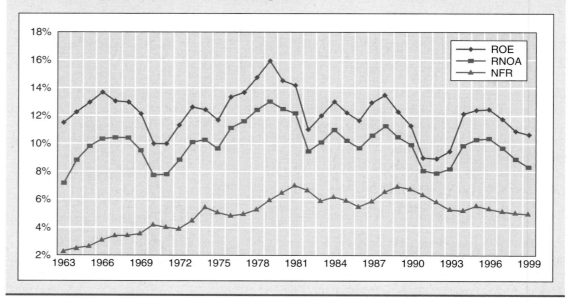

Financial Leverage and Risk

Management strives to increase ROE, and both RNOA and financial leverage (FLEV) are the drivers of ROE. Thus, one way to increase ROE is to increase RNOA through improved operating performance. The other way to increase ROE is with the successful use of financial leverage.

To illustrate the effect on ROE of increased financial leverage, assume that a company is financed solely with equity. This means that a $1,000 shareholder investment yields $1,000 in assets that earn a RNOA of, say, 10.3%. Alternatively, assume that this company is financed with $1,000 in shareholder equity and $500 in nonowner financing costing 6.1% after tax. In this case the ROE is 12.4%, computed as 10.3% + [($500/$1,000) × (10.3% − 6.1%)]. ROE is 10.3% without leverage, but 12.4% with leverage, a difference of 2.1%. The source of this difference is the $500 of debt-financed assets with a spread of 4.2% (10.3% − 6.1%); yielding a dollar increase of $21 or 2.1% of our $1,000 equity investment. This shows the beneficial effect on ROE from financial leverage *when a positive spread is achieved*.

If increases in financial leverage increase ROE, why are all companies not 100% debt financed? The answer is because debt is risky. Debt is a contractual obligation that must be met regardless of the company's current financial status. If not met, creditors can ultimately force payment, which can lead to company bankruptcy and liquidation, much to the detriment of shareholders who are *residual claimants* and can potentially lose their entire investment.

Higher financial leverage also results in a higher cost of debt for the company (this is explained later in the module). Several credit-rating companies such as Standard & Poor's and Moody's Investors Service rate publicly traded debt. Those ratings partly determine the debt's interest rate—with lower quality ratings yielding higher interest rates and vice versa. So, all else equal, higher financial leverage lowers a company's debt rating and increases the interest rate it must pay.

Debtholders (creditors) also typically require a company to execute a loan agreement that places varying restrictions on its operating activities. These restrictions, called *covenants*, help safeguard debtholders in the face of increased risk (recall, debtholders do not have a voice on the board of directors). These debt covenants also impose a cost on the company via restrictions on its activities, and these restrictions become more stringent with increased reliance on nonowner financing.

Financial Leverage and Income Variability

Financial leverage can also affect income variability. To illustrate, we must first define variable and fixed costs. **Variable costs** are those that change in proportion to changes in sales volume. **Fixed costs** are those that do not change with changes in sales volume (over a reasonable range).

Debt with a fixed rate of interest introduces fixed costs into the cost structure. The effect of fixed interest costs on income variability is evidenced in Exhibit 3.7.

EXHIBIT 3.7 ■ Cases showing Financial Leverage and Income Variability

	Case 1	Case 2	Case 3
Sales	$10,000	$8,000	$12,000
Variable costs (40%)	4,000	3,200	4,800
Fixed costs	2,000	2,000	2,000
Net income	$ 4,000	$2,800	$ 5,200
Percentage change in sales	—	(20)%	20%
Percentage change in income	—	(30)%	30%

A given percentage change in revenues generates a greater percentage change in income. Exhibit 3.7 shows that a 20% change in revenues (cases 2 and 3) generates a 30% income change. Leverage is a *magnifier*—positive when revenues increase, and negative when revenues decrease.

The effect of financial leverage (fixed costs) on ROE is shown in Exhibit 3.8. For a given increase or decrease in revenues, the change in ROE is greater for a higher leverage (fixed cost) company.

EXHIBIT 3.8 ■ Effect of Leverage on ROE Variability

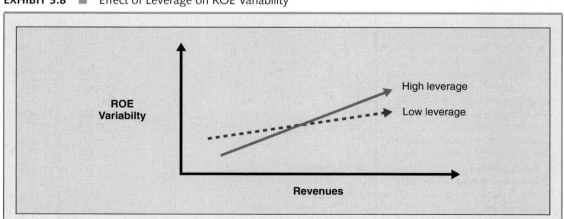

Thus, although a higher level of ROE is desirable, there is a difference between high ROE generated by operating activities (RNOA) and high ROE generated from high levels of financial leverage (FLEV). As illustrated above, use of financial leverage can benefit shareholders. Financial leverage, however, is a double-edged sword. Its downside is an increased level of risk in the form of higher probability for financial distress and bankruptcy if debt payments cannot be made and with greater variability in net income and ROE.

■ MID-MODULE REVIEW 1 ■

Caterpillar, Inc., is a manufacturer of construction equipment. It consists of two segments: one manufactures equipment and the other provides financing (loans and leases) to customers. The finance company is like other financial institutions with high financial leverage and a small spread on loan rates over the cost of debt it incurs to finance those loans. Following is the comparative balance sheets and income statements for Caterpillar, Inc.

CATERPILLAR, INC. Balance Sheets		
December 31 ($ millions)	**2003**	**2002**
Assets		
Current assets		
Cash and short-term investments	$ 342	$ 309
Receivables—trade and other	3,666	2,838
Receivables—finance	7,605	6,748
Deferred and refundable income taxes	707	781
Prepaid expenses	1,424	1,224
Inventories	3,047	2,763
Total current assets	16,791	14,663
Property, plant and equipment—net	7,290	7,046
Long-term receivables—trade and other	82	66
Long-term receivables—finance	7,822	6,714
Investments in unconsolidated affiliated companies	800	747
Deferred income taxes	616	711
Intangible assets	239	281
Goodwill	1,398	1,402
Other assets	1,427	1,117
Total assets	**$36,465**	**$32,747**
Liabilities		
Current liabilities		
Short-term borrowings		
Machinery and engines	$ 72	$ 64
Financial products	2,685	2,111
Accounts payable	3,100	2,269
Accrued expenses	1,638	1,620
Accrued wages, salaries, and employee benefits	1,802	1,779
Dividends payable	127	120
Deferred and current income taxes payable	216	70
Long-term debt due within one year		
Machinery and engines	32	258
Financial products	2,949	3,654
Total current liabilities	12,621	11,945
Long-term debt due after one year		
Machinery and engines	3,367	3,403
Financial products	10,711	8,193
Liability for postemployment benefits	3,172	3,333
Deferred income taxes and other liabilities	516	401
Total liabilities	30,387	27,275
Stockholders' equity		
Common stock of $1.00 par value; Authorized shares: 900,000,000		
Issued shares (2003 and 2002—407,447,312) at paid-in amount	1,059	1,034
Treasury stock (2003—63,685,272 shares; 2002—63,192,245 shares) at cost	(2,914)	(2,669)
Profit employed in the business	8,450	7,849
Accumulated other comprehensive income	(517)	(742)
Total stockholders' equity	6,078	5,472
Total liabilities and stockholders' equity	**$36,465**	**$32,747**

CATERPILLAR, INC. Income Statements		
For Year Ended December 31 ($ millions)	**2003**	**2002**
Sales and revenues		
Sales of machinery and engines	$21,048	$18,648
Revenues of financial products	1,715	1,504
Total sales and revenues	22,763	20,152
Operating costs		
Costs of goods sold	16,945	15,146
Selling, general and administrative expenses	2,470	2,094
Research and development expenses	669	656
Interest expense of financial products	470	521
Other operating expenses	521	411
Total operating costs	21,075	18,828
Operating profit	1,688	1,324
Interest expense excluding financial products	246	279
Other income (expense)	35	69
Consolidated profit before taxes	1,477	1,114
Provision for income taxes	398	312
Profit of consolidated companies	1,079	802
Equity in profit (loss) of unconsolidated affiliated companies	20	(4)
Profit	$ 1,099	$ 798

Required

Using Caterpillar's (CAT) financial information, compute the following for 2003 (refer to Exhibits 3.2 through 3.5 for guidance).

1. Balance sheet amounts
   a. Net operating working capital (NOWC)
   b. Net operating long-term assets (NOLTA)
   c. Net operating assets (NOA) (Note: a + b = c)
   d. Net financial obligations (NFO)
   e. Shareholders' equity
   f. Confirm that $c = d + e$
2. Income statement amounts
   a. Net operating profit after tax (NOPAT)
   b. Net income
   c. Net financial expense
   d. Confirm that $c = a - b$
3. Financial ratios and measures
   a. Return on equity (ROE)
   b. Return on net operating assets (RNOA)
   c. Financial leverage (FLEV)
   d. Net financial rate (NFR)
   e. Spread
   f. Confirm: ROE = RNOA + (FLEV × Spread)
4. What insights do you draw about Caterpillar's financial performance from its *Level 1* analysis of ROE?

Solution

1. a. Net operating working capital (NOWC) . . . . $ 9,908

   NOWC = Current Operating Assets − Current Operating Liabilities
      = ($16,791 − $0) − ($12,621 − [$2,685 + $72] − $2,981)

   b. Net operating long-term assets (NOLTA) 15,986

   NOLTA = Long-Term Operating Assets − Long-Term Operating Liabilities
      = ([$36,465 − $16,791] − $0) − ($516 + $3,172)

   c. Net operating assets (NOA) 25,894

   NOA = Operating Assets − Operating Liabilities
      = ($36,465 − $0) − ($30,387 − $2,757 − $2,981 − $14,078)

      d. Net financial obligations (NFO) $19,816
          NFO = Nonoperating Liabilities − Nonoperating Assets
              = ($2,757 + $2,981 + $14,078) − ($0)
      e. Stockholders' equity (given) 6,078
      f.   c = d + e
          25,894 = 19,816 + 6,078 (confirmed)

2. a. Net operating profit after tax (NOPAT) 1,253
          NOPAT = [Net Operating Profit × (1 − Effective Tax Rate)] + Other Income, net of tax
          NOPAT = [$1,688 × (1 − [$398/$1,477])] + 20
          Note: CAT's income statement references "equity in profit (loss) of unconsolidated affiliated
          companies." We cover the concept of equity income of unconsolidated affiliates in Module 6.
          For now, just know that this amount is presented after tax (so no tax adjustment is necessary).
          Absent knowledge that these affiliates are conducting nonoperating activities, it is customary to
          include them as operating activities.
      b. Net income (given) 1,099
      c. Net financial expense (NFE) = ($246 − $35) × (1 − [$398/$1,477]) 154
      d.   c = a − b
          $154 = $1,253 − $1,099 (confirmed)

3. a. Return on equity (ROE) 19.0%
          ROE = Net Income/Average Stockholders' Equity
              = $1,099/[($6,078 + $5,472)/2]
      b. Return on net operating assets (RNOA) 5.1%
          RNOA = NOPAT/Average NOA
              = $1,253/([$25,894 + $23,155]/ 2)
      c. Financial leverage (FLEV) 324.7%
          FLEV = Average NFO/Average Stockholders' Equity
              = ([$19,816 + $17,683]/2)/([$6,078 + $5,472]/2)
      d. Net financial rate (NFR) 0.8%
          NFR = NFE/Average NFO
              = $154/([$19,816 + $17,683]/2)
      e. Spread 4.3%
          Spread = RNOA − NFR
              = 5.1% − 0.8%
      f.   19.0% = 5.1% + (3.247 × 4.3%)

4. Much of CAT's ROE of 19% is driven by financial leverage, as RNOA is only 5.1%. Remember, CAT's
    financial statements include its manufacturing and financial subsidiaries. The financial subsidiary, like many
    captive finance subsidiaries, is quite large and highly financially leveraged. As a result, the consolidated
    (combined) balance sheet reflects this leverage. Leverage in a financial subsidiary is usually not as problematic
    as if it were solely in the manufacturing company; this is because the financial subsidiary's cash flows are
    unlikely cyclical. As long as its cash flows are relatively stable, it can handle a higher debt load. The business
    model for this financial subsidiary, then, is low margins and high financial leverage to yield the target ROE.
    This is the business model for a typical financial institution.

■ LEVEL 2 ANALYSIS—MARGIN AND TURNOVER

This section focuses on Level 2 analysis, which disaggregates RNOA into net operating profit margin
(NOPM) and net operating asset turnover (NOAT). The purpose here is to identify the key drivers of
RNOA. Nearly all goals of financial analysis are future oriented. Examples are predicting future operating income, pricing companies' securities, forming opinions about companies' debt-paying abilities, evaluating alternate strategies, and making managerial decisions. Understanding the drivers of financial
performance (RNOA) is key to effectively predicting future performance. To highlight the development of
our analytical framework, Exhibit 3.9 presents the Level 1 disaggregation of ROE into operating (RNOA)
and nonoperating components (FLEV × Spread) and the Level 2 disaggregation of RNOA into its components: net operating profit margin (NOPM) and net operating asset turnover (NOAT). The latter is the
focus of this section.

EXHIBIT 3.9 ■ Levels 1 and 2 of ROE Disaggregation

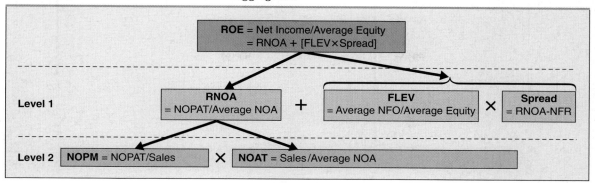

Disaggregation of RNOA

Level 2 analysis focuses on the disaggregation of RNOA into its two basic components, profit margin and asset turnover, as follows:

RNOA = NOPAT/Average Net Operating Assets = NOPAT/Sales × Sales/Average Net Operating Assets

  Margin   Turnover

The ratio of NOPAT (net operating profit after tax) to sales is the *net operating profit margin* (NOPM). It reflects the percentage of each sales dollar that the company is realizing in after-tax operating profit. The ratio of sales to net operating assets is the *net operating asset turnover* (NOAT). Turnover reflects the productivity of assets. Namely, how much revenue does the firm realize from a dollar of operating asset investment.

Management and its stakeholders prefer that both margin and turnover be higher rather than lower as both increase RNOA and, thus, ROE. The next section describes the trade-off between margin and turnover, and how that translates into company performance.

Trade-Off between Margin and Turnover

An infinite number of combinations of net operating profit margin and net operating asset turnover will yield a given RNOA. As depicted in Exhibit 3.10, industries tend to reach RNOA equilibria, which are determined by fundamental business characteristics (data points represent industry medians from over 55,000 observations for the 15 years prior to 2005). That is, some industries, like communication and pharmaceuticals, are capital intensive with relatively low turnover. Accordingly, for such industries to achieve a required RNOA, they must obtain a higher profit margin. Service companies, such as retailers and restaurants, in contrast, carry fewer assets and can operate on lower operating profit margins to achieve a similar RNOA because their asset turnover is far greater.

One implication of Exhibit 3.10 is that we must be careful in evaluating performances of companies in different industries. A higher profit margin in the communication industry than that in the apparel industry is not necessarily the result of better management. Instead, the communication industry requires a higher profit margin to offset its lower asset turnover (resulting from the capital intensity of its industry) to achieve an equivalent return on net operating assets.

The margin and turnover trade-off is obvious when comparing the communication and apparel industries. However, the analysis of conglomerates that are mixtures of several industries is more challenging. Their margins and turnover rates are a weighted average of the margins and turnover rates for the various industries that constitute the company. For example, like Caterpillar, **General Motors Corporation (GM)** is a blend of a manufacturing company and a financial subsidiary (**GMAC**). Each of these industries has its own margin and turnover equilibrium, and the margin and turnover for GM on a consolidated basis is a weighted average of the two.

EXHIBIT 3.10 ■ Margin and Turnover Combinations for a given RNOA

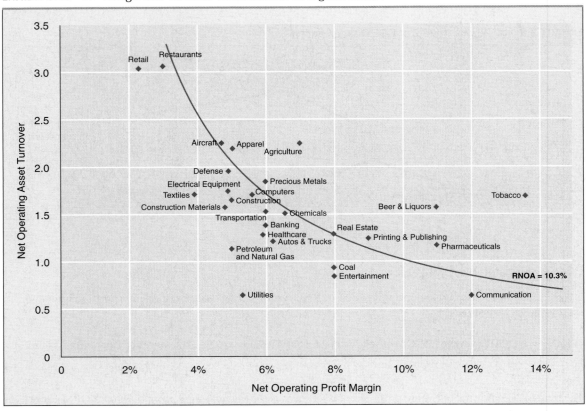

Net Operating Profit Margin (NOPM)

The analysis of profit margin relates to the income statement. Profit margin can be used to compare one income statement number with another, where sales is the usual denominator. It is commonly used to compare the performance of one company over time and/or its performance vis-à-vis its competitors.

The net operating profit (or NOPAT) margin is a useful summary measure of operating performance as it encompasses both the gross profit on sales and operating expenses.[8] It is computed as follows:

Net Operating Profit Margin (NOPM) = NOPAT/Sales

The NOPM is one of the two drivers of RNOA. It is a summary measure of company profitability.

BUSINESS INSIGHT **The 3M Margin**

The following chart shows that 3M's net operating profit margin has increased from 11.6% of sales in 1999 to 13.5% in 2003. The 2001 decline was due to 3M's $568 million pretax restructuring costs, consisting mainly of expected severance costs as it downsized its employee base.

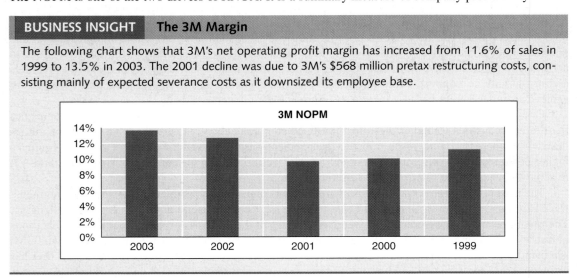

---

[8]Another common measure of performance is **net profit margin** (net income/sales), sometimes called **return on sales**. This measure uses net income, which encompasses both operating and financial components. Our focus on net operating profit margin is to distinguish between operating and nonoperating (financial) components of net profit margin.

Net Operating Asset Turnover (NOAT)

Asset turnover reflects the productivity of company assets. That is, it reflects the amount of capital required to generate a dollar of sales volume. The general form of an asset turnover ratio is:

Asset Turnover = Sales/Average Assets

A turnover ratio uses measures from both the income statement and balance sheet. As depicted in Exhibit 3.10, capital-intensive companies have lower turnover rates than service companies as the amount of assets required to generate a dollar of sales is less for services.

Our interest in asset turnover arises from the following observation: higher turnover reflects greater sales inflow for a given level of assets. Although turnover does not directly impact profitability, it does so indirectly as asset holding costs (such as interest, insurance, warehousing, and logistics) are reduced.

One of the most important measures of turnover is the **net operating asset turnover (NOAT)**, which is defined as:

Net Operating Asset Turnover (NOAT) = Sales/Average Net Operating Assets

For 3M, its 2003 net operating asset turnover is 1.81. Its turnover ratio of 1.81 implies that 3M generates $1.81 in sales from each dollar invested in net operating assets. Another way of interpreting the 1.81 turnover is that for each additional sales dollar, 3M must invest $0.55 in net operating assets (computed as $1/1.81). Thus, each additional sales dollar must generate sufficient operating profit to offset the added investment cost.

3M's net operating assets have increased over the past three years, mainly from acquisitions of other companies. Specifically, its average net operating working capital has not increased to the extent that sales have increased, and its net property, plant, and equipment (PPE) assets have not increased during this period, as capital expenditures have equaled depreciation. Instead, goodwill and other intangible assets account for most of the growth in its net operating assets.

It is crucial that companies monitor their asset utilization. They must also take action if asset growth is excessive. For example, they can sell excess capacity of underutilized assets or outsource production of some products. Later in this module we explore means to monitor, analyze, and interpret the effective use of net operating assets.

BUSINESS INSIGHT   Turnover at 3M

The following chart shows 3M's net operating asset turnover, which is reasonably steady during the past five years. Its largest value is 1.83 times in 2000 and its lowest is 1.75 in 2001 (the restructuring year). 3M's net operating asset turnover is below the 1.97 median for all publicly traded firms.

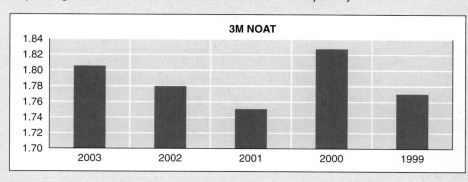

▓ MID-MODULE REVIEW 2 ▓

Refer to the Mid-Module Review 1 for the financial statements of Caterpillar, Inc.

Required

Using Caterpillar's financial information, compute the following for 2003 (refer to Exhibit 3.9 for guidance).

1. Net operating profit margin and net operating asset turnover
   a. Net operating profit margin (NOPM)

  b.   Net operating asset turnover (NOAT)
  c.   Confirm: RNOA = $a \times b$
2.   What insights do you draw about Caterpillar's financial performance from its *Level 2* analysis of ROE?

Solution

1. a.   Net operating profit margin (NOPAT/Sales) 5.5%
    b.   Net operating asset turnover (NOAT) . . . .   0.93 times
          NOAT = $22,763 /([$25,894 + $23,155]/ 2)
    c.   RNOA: 5.1% = 5.5% $\times$ 0.93 (confirms *Mid-Module Review 1*, part 3b) 5.1%
2. CAT's RNOA is relatively low as it is within the bottom quartile of median RNOAs for publicly traded companies (RNOA of under 6%)—see table in the earlier part of this module. Also, CAT is in a capital intensive industry. The median turnover of net operating assets for all companies is 1.94, and CAT is well below that level (0.93). Although its NOPM approximates the median for all companies, its low NOAT hinders its ability to achieve acceptable returns on net operating assets.

MANAGERIAL DECISION   **You Are the Entrepreneur**

You are analyzing the performance of your startup company. Your analysis of RNOA reveals the following (industry benchmarks in parenthesis): RNOA is 16% (10%), NOPM is 18% (17%), and NOAT is 0.89 (0.59). What interpretations do you draw that are useful for managing your company? [Answer, p. 3-30]

■ LEVEL 3 ANALYSIS—DISAGGREGATION OF MARGIN AND TURNOVER

This section focuses on Level 3 analysis, which highlights the disaggregation of profit margin and asset turnover to better understand the drivers of RNOA. Again, understanding the drivers of financial performance (RNOA) is key to predicting future company performance. To help frame our presentation, Exhibit 3.11 shows the full analytical framework for disaggregation of ROE into Level 1 components, the return from operating activities (RNOA) and the return from nonoperating activities (FLEV $\times$ Spread), the Level 2 disaggregation of RNOA into profit margin (NOPM) and asset turnover (NOAT), and the Level 3 analysis of the drivers of operating profit margin and asset turnover.

EXHIBIT 3.11   ■   Framework for ROE Disaggregation

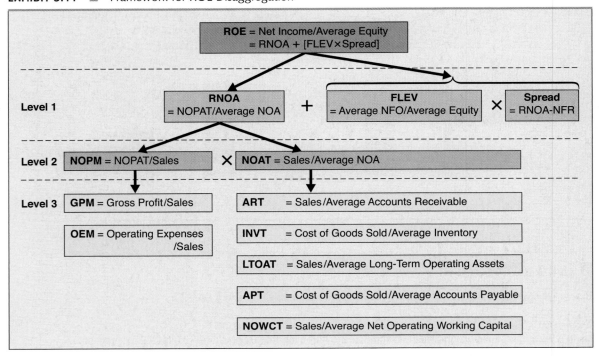

Gross Profit Margin (GPM)

Gross profit is net sales less cost of goods sold. It represents the markup of selling price over costs that the company has incurred in manufacturing or purchasing the goods sold. Analysis of gross profit *dollars* is not usually meaningful as it results from both the unit markup and the number of units sold, either or both can change over time or differ across companies. Instead, we focus on gross profit margin, which is defined as follows:

Gross Profit Margin (GPM) = Gross Profit /Sales

Conducting gross profit analysis in ratio form serves two objectives. First, it mitigates any problem arising when comparing different sized companies. Second, it allows us to focus on average markup per unit sold, which abstracts from the volume of units sold in our analysis.

Analysis of gross profit margin provides insight into a company's average markup on its product cost through selling prices. A higher gross profit margin is preferred to a lower one. A higher gross profit margin also means that a company has more flexibility in product pricing. Such companies are historically more profitable.

Two main factors determine gross profit margin:

1. Competition. When competition intensifies, more substitutes become available, which limits a company's ability to raise prices and pass on cost increases to customers.
2. Product mix. When lower-priced, higher-volume products increase in proportion to higher-priced, lower-volume products, gross profit margin declines.

Absent product mix changes, a decline in gross profit margin is generally viewed negatively as it suggests that a company's products have lost some competitive advantage. Reasons can include failures in product quality, style, or technology.

3M's gross profit margin has improved in recent years. However, in 2001, its GPM declined by 1.9 percentage points, which is substantial. In its 10-K for that year, 3M reports that special items, principally related to its restructuring program, accounted for 1.7 of the 1.9 points of that decline.

3M credits the reductions in its cost of goods sold to its manufacturing efficiencies and purchasing initiatives. Following is an excerpt from its 2003 10-K that provides part of 3M's explanation:

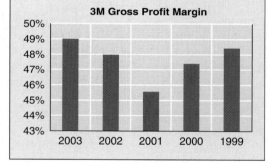

Cost of sales in 2003 benefited from . . . projects aimed at improving manufacturing throughput, yield and productivity. 3M's global sourcing initiative has helped mitigate the impact of raw material price increases. Raw material costs were essentially flat versus 2002. In 2002, gross margins were positively impacted by improved plant efficiencies and lower raw material costs, again helped by 3M's global sourcing initiative. Special items, as a percent of sales, negatively impacted cost of sales by 0.7 percentage points in 2002 and 1.7 percentage points in 2001.

Operating Expense Margin (OEM)

Operating expense ratios (percents) reflect the proportion of sales consumed by each of the major operating expense categories. These ratios are generally computed as follows:

Operating Expense Margin (OEM) = Operating Expenses /Sales

The focus is on any changes over time in the proportion of company sales invested in operating expenses. We can examine any number of separate components of operating expenses divided by sales. These outlays must produce a satisfactory return and create long-term shareholder value. The financial impacts from some expenditures, such as those in advertising and research and development, are self-evident. Also, companies can achieve short-term gains by reducing expenditures in these areas (advertising and R&D outlays are expensed under GAAP). However, persistent underfunding of advertising and R&D can adversely impact a company's competitive position and future performance.

This is an important point. Namely, it is not necessarily better to have a lower operating expense margin. Expenses represent investments, although they are not recognized on the balance sheet as assets. As with any investment, we must expect an acceptable return. This means the objective is not necessarily to reduce operating expenses. Instead, it is to *optimize* them—make sure that they are producing an acceptable return, the aim being to increase RNOA.

3M has two large operating expenses: R&D costs and selling, general, and administrative (SG&A) expenses. 3M's percent of sales invested in R&D has remained constant for the past five years. Its business depends on R&D to maintain its competitive advantage. Cutbacks in R&D for short-run profits are probably at the cost of long-run profits.

3M's SG&A expense as a percentage of sales has decreased from 23.6% to 22.2% in the past five years. This 1.4 percentage point decrease is substantial for a mature company of this size and reflects 3M's commitment to cost control.

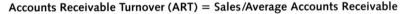

Accounts Receivable Turnover (ART)

Disaggregation of total asset turnover gives further insights into the drivers of RNOA. The accounts receivable turnover (ART) is one of those disaggregates. It provides insights into the sales impact of accounts receivable. That is, receivables are an asset, just like inventories and equipment, and the accounts receivable turnover reflects the investment in receivables required to generate a dollar of sales. This turnover ratio is defined as follows:

Accounts Receivable Turnover (ART) = Sales/Average Accounts Receivable

The higher this turnover ratio, the lower the required investment. Generally, companies want a higher receivables turnover, as this reflects greater sales for a given level of accounts receivable.

3M's accounts receivable turnover ratio increased from 5.79 times in 1999 to 6.96 times in 2003. This is a marked increase that should enhance its profitability and cash flow.

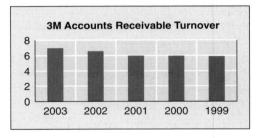

Although companies desire to minimize their investment in accounts receivable, the extension of credit is one of the marketing tools available to a company. Each tool has its cost. While the cost of advertising is easy to see, the cost of credit extension is less evident.

Receivables are an asset that must be financed like any other asset. In addition, receivables entail collection risk and require additional overhead in the form of credit and collection departments. On the other hand, reducing collection overhead costs with an overly restrictive credit policy hurts sales. Receivables must, therefore, be effectively managed.

An intuitive formulation of a measure related to accounts receivable turnover is the **average collection period**, which follows:

Average Collection Period = Accounts Receivable/Average Daily Sales

This metric reflects how long accounts receivable are outstanding, on average.

For 3M, the average collection period has been reduced from 64.4 days in 1999 to 54.3 days in 2003. More timely collection of receivables reduces the probability of noncollection. Also, the reduction in receivables increases cash flow. For these reasons, 3M's more timely collection of receivables over the past five years is a positive development.

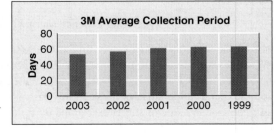

To assess whether an average collection period of 54.3 days is good or bad, we can compare it to the company's credit policies. For example, if invoice terms are net 60 days, experience tells us to expect

$
Cash Effect

$
Cash Effect

the average collection period to be about 30 days. Credit terms vary by industry, but are usually 90 days or less. Accordingly, average collection periods longer than 60 days are unusual and, thus, warrant investigation.[9]

Inventory Turnover (INVT)

The inventory turnover ratio provides insight into the inventory investment required to support the current sales volume. It is computed as follows:

Inventory Turnover (INVT) = Cost of Goods Sold/Average Inventory

This ratio uses cost of goods sold (COGS) as a measure of sales volume because the denominator, inventory, is reported at cost, not retail. Accordingly, both the numerator and denominator are measured at cost.

The inventory turnover for 3M increased from 3.82 times per year in 1999 to 4.96 times per year in 2003. This is a substantial improvement in inventory turns. In its 2003 10-K, 3M attributes much of this success to "projects aimed at improving manufacturing throughput, yield, and productivity." In addition, 3M cites its "global sourcing initiative," which has helped to control raw materials costs, a main component of its inventory.

When inventory turnover declines, concerns arise about uncompetitive products. (Inventory turnover is also determined by changes in product mix.) Further, such declines add costs. Namely, inventory requires warehouse space and logistics, personnel to monitor and manage them, financing costs, and insurance coverage. Also, the longer inventory sits, the greater is the likelihood of its being damaged or stolen, going out of style, or becoming technologically obsolete. Companies want enough inventory to meet customer demand without stock-outs, and no more.

Analysis of inventory is aided by the following complementary measure that reflects the number of days of sales in inventory:

Average Inventory Days Outstanding = Inventory/Average Daily Cost of Goods Sold

This result gives us some indication of the length of time that inventories sit prior to sale.

For 3M, and commensurate with its increased inventory turnover shown above, we see a reduction in its average inventory days outstanding from 91.2 days in 1999 to 71.4 days in 2003. Although 71.4 days can seem like a long time for inventories to remain unsold, remember that this includes the time from the purchase of the raw materials, through the manufacturing process, to the time the finished goods are sold.

We want the company inventory cycle to be as short as possible. One way in which companies can reduce inventory cycle is to minimize their raw materials through good inventory management methods such as just-in-time deliveries—which means that inventory sits with suppliers. Similarly, companies can achieve reductions in work-in-progress inventory by efficient production processes that eliminate bottlenecks. Finally, companies can minimize finished goods inventory by producing to orders, not estimated demand, if possible. These management tools increase inventory turnover and reduce the inventory days outstanding.

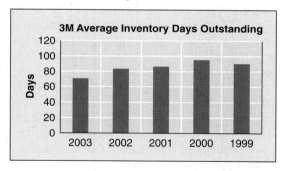

Long-Term Operating Asset Turnover (LTOAT)

Long-term operating asset turnover reflects capital intensity relative to sales and is defined as:

Long-Term Operating Asset Turnover (LTOAT) = Sales/Average Long-Term Operating Assets

Capital intensive industries, like manufacturing companies, require large investments in long-term operating assets. Accordingly, such companies have lower long-term operating asset turnovers than do less capital-intensive companies, like service businesses.

---

[9]Companies with captive finance subsidiaries, and those that offer leasing of their manufactured products, will report longer average collection periods that arise from the length of the financing, not necessarily as a result of uncollectible accounts.

Higher is better for long-term operating asset turnover. Companies desire to minimize the investment in long-term operating assets required to generate a dollar of sales.

Long-term operating asset turnover for 3M in 2003 is 2.8 times, compared with 3.1 times in 1999. During the intervening five years, 3M grew in asset size, but not in terms of long-term operating asset purchases, which have remained fairly constant (capital expenditures approximating depreciation). Instead, 3M's increase in long-term operating assets are in the form of goodwill and other intangible assets acquired from acquisitions of other companies. The LTOAT ratio does not distinguish between long-term operating assets purchased individually or as part of a larger corporate acquisition.

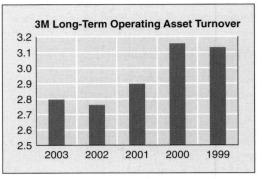

Accounts Payable Turnover (APT)

Net operating working capital, defined as current operating assets less current operating liabilities, is financed in large part by accounts payable (also called *trade credit* or *trade payables*). Accounts payable represent amounts that one company owes another arising from the purchase of goods. Such payables usually represent interest-free financing and are, therefore, less expensive than using available funds or borrowed money to finance purchases or production. Accordingly, companies use trade credit whenever possible. This is called *leaning on the trade*.

The **accounts payable turnover** reflects on management's success in using trade credit to finance purchases of goods. It is computed as:

Accounts Payable Turnover (APT) = Cost of Goods Sold / Average Accounts Payable

Payables are reported at cost, not retail prices. Thus, for consistency with the denominator, cost of goods sold (not sales) is used in the numerator. Management desires to use trade credit to the greatest extent possible for financing. This means that management desires a lower accounts payable turnover.

For 3M, its accounts payable turnover rate has declined from 10.4 times per year in 2001 to 9.1 times per year in 2003. This decline in accounts payable turnover indicates that these obligations are remaining unpaid for a longer period of time. Again, this is generally interpreted as positive, which reflects management's effective use of low-cost financing.

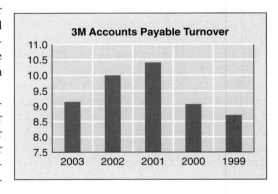

A metric analogous to accounts payable turnover is that of **average payable days outstanding**, which is defined as follows:

Average Payable Days Outstanding = Accounts Payable / Average Daily Cost of Goods Sold

Management hopes to extend the payable days outstanding number to as long as possible provided they do not harm their supply channel relationships.

For 3M, its accounts payable remain unpaid for 40 days in 2003, up from 35 days two years ago. 3M is, therefore, leaning on the trade to a greater extent than it has in the recent past. The increase in payable days outstanding increases cash flow because it reflects greater use of a noninterest-bearing source of funding. So, all else equal, cash flow and profits increase.

Payment policies must be managed with care as increasing payables correspond with increasing

$

Cash Effect

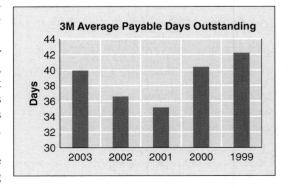

receivables on suppliers' balance sheets, thus increasing suppliers' costs. As a result, if suppliers' bargaining power is greater than the buyers, then suppliers attempt to recoup those costs with higher selling prices. In the extreme, suppliers can refuse to sell to such buyers. Even when buyers possess bargaining leverage, they do not want to exact too high of a cost from suppliers. This is because buyers need a healthy supplier network for a consistent supply source at an acceptable quality level.

Net Operating Working Capital Turnover (NOWCT)

Net operating working capital is the investment in short-term net operating assets. It is one of the two general categories of net operating assets (the other being net long-term operating assets). Management's effectiveness in using operating working capital turnover is reflected in the following metric:

Net Operating Working Capital Turnover (NOWCT) = Net Sales/Average Net Operating Working Capital

A lower operating working capital turnover reflects a greater investment in working capital for each dollar of sales. Working capital turns more quickly when receivables and inventories turn more quickly, and it also turns more quickly when companies lean on the trade (when payables turn more slowly).

3M has been successful in increasing its net operating working capital turnover from 4.7 times a year in 1999 to 5.5 times a year in 2003. This is mainly due to increasing turnover for receivables and inventories, and a decreasing turnover for payables.

RNOA (and ROE) disaggregation gives us insight into the drivers of company success. Knowing the drivers of operating performance is crucial in forecasting future performance, which is the ultimate object of most analyses. Still, we must remember that to fully understand the drivers of operating performance, we must analyze the company's business, not just its financial reports. That analysis entails an understanding of the company's markets, its products, its execution, and a number of other strategic factors.

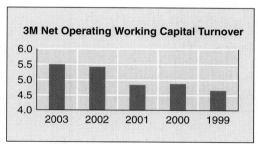

■ MID-MODULE REVIEW 3 ■

Refer to the Mid-Module Review 1 for the financial statements of Caterpillar, Inc.

Required
Using Caterpillar's financial information, compute the following for 2003.

1. Profit margins
   a. Gross profit margin on machinery and engines (GPM)
   b. Selling, general, and administrative costs as a percentage of total sales and revenues (SGAM for short)
2. Asset turnovers
   a. Accounts receivable turnover (ART) for machinery and engines
   b. Average collection period (Accounts Receivable/Average Daily Sales)
   c. Inventory turnover (INVT) on machinery and engines
   d. Average machinery and engine inventory days outstanding (Inventories/Average Daily COGS for Machinery and Engines)
   e. Long-term operating asset turnover (LTOAT); use total sales and revenues in the numerator
   f. Accounts payable turnover (APT); use machinery and engines COGS
   g. Average payable days outstanding (Accounts Payable/Average Daily COGS)

Solution
1. a. Gross profit margin (GPM) . . . . 19.5%   ($21,048 − $16,945)/$21,048
   b. SG&A Expenses / Total Sales and Revenues . . . . 10.9% $2,470/$22,763
2. a. ART (Sales/Average Accounts Receivable) . . . . 6.47 times $21,048/[($3,666 + $2,838)/2]
   b. Average collection period . . . . 63.57 days $3,666/($21,048/365)
   c. INVT (COGS/Average Inventory) . . . . 5.83 times $16,945/[($3,047 + $2,763)/2]

d.	Average inventory days outstanding	65.63 days	$3,047/($16,945/365)
e.	LTOAT (Sales/Average Long-Term Operating Assets)	1.50 times	$22,763/[($15,986 + $14,350)/2]
f.	APT (COGS/Average Accounts Payable)	6.31 times	$16,945/[($3,100 + 2,269)/2]
g.	Average payable days outstanding	66.77 days	$3,100/($16,945/365)

■ LIQUIDITY, SOLVENCY, AND CREDIT ANALYSIS

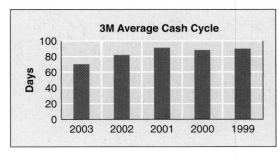

ROE disaggregation focuses mainly on profitability analysis. Yet, liquidity and solvency are also important in analyzing a company. This later analysis is often put under the umbrella of *credit analysis* because of the importance of liquidity and solvency for creditors. However, credit analysis is also important for lenders, underwriters, managers of start-ups and growth companies, and even investors (given that creditors enjoy senior standing in liquidation).

$
Cash Effect

Liquidity refers to cash: how much cash the company has, how much cash the company is generating, and how much can be raised on short notice. Moreover, liquidity is a matter of survival since most obligations are settled with cash. **Solvency** refers to the ability to meet obligations; mainly obligations to creditors, including lessors. Solvency is equally crucial since an insolvent company is a failed company. The following sections introduce measures of liquidity and solvency, and discuss tools and measures of credit analysis.

Liquidity Analysis

This section describes several useful measures in our analysis of liquidity.

Average Cash (Operating) Cycle

$
Cash Effect

The cash (operating) cycle is the period of time from when cash is invested in inventories, until the inventories are sold and receivables are collected. It is the cycle from "cash to cash." Companies generally want to minimize the cash cycle provided that they achieve acceptable inventory levels and customer credit terms, and that relationships with suppliers are not damaged as a result of excessive "leaning on the trade." The average cash cycle is measured as follows:

$$\text{Average Cash Cycle} = \text{Average Collection Period} + \begin{array}{c}\text{Modified Average}\\\text{Inventory Days}\\\text{Outstanding}\end{array} - \begin{array}{c}\text{Modified Average}\\\text{Payable Days}\\\text{Outstanding}\end{array}$$

The modified measures refer to their computation *using sales in the denominator* instead of cost of goods sold. This allows for the summation of days outstanding.

For 3M, the average collection period is 53 days, the modified average inventory days outstanding is 37 days, and the modified average payable days outstanding is 20 days. 3M's average cash cycle (modified to compute all ratios based on sales) follows:

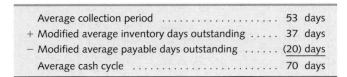

Average collection period	53	days
+ Modified average inventory days outstanding	37	days
− Modified average payable days outstanding	(20)	days
Average cash cycle	70	days

This means 3M takes about 70 days to convert its cash to inventories, then to receivables, and finally back into cash. Over the past five years, 3M has been able to reduce its cash cycle from 91 days in 1999 to 70 days in 2003. This is a marked improvement. The quicker a company is able to cycle from cash to cash, the greater is its cash flow. Its aim, therefore, is to *optimize,* not necessarily minimize, investment in receivables, inventories, and payables. Not extending credit and not having goods available for sale would minimize receivables and inventories, but this would be counterproductive. So, the aim is not to minimize but to optimize receivables, inventories and payables so as to maximize shareholder value. This is known as *working capital management.*

Current Ratio

Current assets are those assets that a company expects to convert into cash within the next year (or operating cycle if longer than one year). Current liabilities are those liabilities that a company expects to mature within the next year (or operating cycle if longer than one year). Companies typically desire more current assets than current liabilities as that implies more expected cash inflows than cash outflows in the short run.

One measure of liquidity is the relative magnitude of current assets and current liabilities. The difference between them is *net working capital.* However, since the dollar amount of net working capital is difficult to compare across companies of different sizes, the current ratio is often used. It is computed as follows:

Current Ratio = Current Assets/Current Liabilities

A current ratio greater than 1.0 implies positive net working capital. In general, companies prefer more liquid assets to less and a higher current ratio to a smaller one. (A too high current ratio is possible, and is indicative of inefficient asset use.) A current ratio less than 1.0 is not always bad for at least two reasons:

$
Cash Effect

1. A cash-and-carry company (like a grocery store where payment is typically made in cash) can have consistently large operating cash inflows and potentially few current assets (and a low current ratio), but still be liquid due to those large cash inflows.
2. A company can efficiently manage its working capital by minimizing receivables and inventories and maximizing payables, and still be liquid. **Dell Computer** and **Wal-Mart**, for example, use their buying power to exact extended credit terms from suppliers. Further, because both companies are mainly cash-and-carry businesses, their current ratios are less than 1.0 and both are liquid.

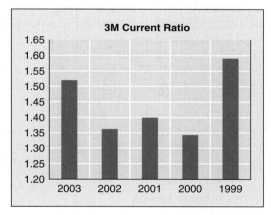

The aim of current ratio analysis is to discern if a company is having, or is likely to have, difficulty meeting short-term obligations. In the case of 3M, its current ratio stands at a healthy 1.52 in 2003. Over the past five years, it has fluctuated within a range of 1.34 to 1.59.

Quick Ratio

The quick ratio is a variant of the current ratio. It focuses on current assets that are considered *quick assets,* which are those assets likely to be converted to cash within a short period of time. Quick assets generally include cash, marketable securities, and accounts receivable; it excludes inventories and prepaid assets. The quick ratio follows:

$
Cash Effect

Quick Ratio = (Cash + Marketable Securities + Accounts Receivables)/Current Liabilities

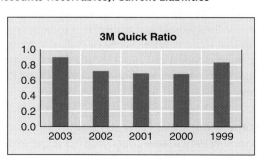

The quick ratio reflects a company's ability to meet its current liabilities without liquidating inventories that could require markdowns. It is a more stringent test of liquidity compared to the current ratio.

3M's quick ratio is 0.90 as of 2003. Over the past five years, 3M's quick ratio has ranged from 0.67 to its current level of 0.90.

Solvency Analysis

Solvency analysis is aided by financial leverage ratios. Financial leverage refers to the extent of borrowed funds in a company's capital structure. We examine financial leverage ratios for insight into company solvency, that is, the risk of bankruptcy. We consider several ratios in addition to FLEV, which we discussed in connection with ROE disaggregation.

Debt-to-Equity

One common measure of financial leverage is the ratio of **debt-to-equity**, which is defined as:

Debt-to-Equity = Total Liabilities/Stockholders' Equity

A higher debt-to-equity ratio reflects a greater proportion of debt in a company's capital structure. 3M's debt-to-equity ratio has fluctuated from 1.21 to 1.56 in the past five years. It currently sits at the lower end of this range at 1.23.

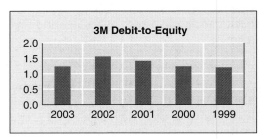

Long-Term Debt-to-Equity

Another common measure of leverage is **long-term debt-to-equity**. It focuses on long-term financing and is defined as follows:

Long-Term Debt-to-Equity = Long-Term Debt/Stockholders' Equity

This ratio implicitly assumes that current liabilities are covered by current assets and, thus, only long-term debt must be funded from operating cash flows. Accordingly, it is important to examine long-term debt relative to the stockholders' investment.

3M's long-term debt-to-equity ratio has fluctuated between 0.15 and 0.36 during the past five years, and the company has a conservative level of 0.22 as of 2003. The marked difference between 3M's debt-to-equity ratio of 1.23 and its long-term debt-to-equity ratio of 0.22 relates to the concentration of its liabilities in short-term noninterest-bearing debt. This is a consequence of 3M's aggressive working capital management program.

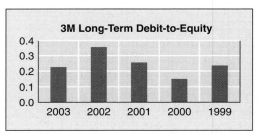

Times Interest Earned

$

Cash Effect

Another useful perspective on solvency analysis is to compare operating flows to liabilities. One approach considers how much income is available to service debt given the debt level and its repayment terms. A common measure is **times interest earned**, defined as follows:

Times Interest Earned = Earnings before Interest and Taxes/Interest Expense

The numerator is similar to net operating profits after-tax (NOPAT), but it is *pre-tax* instead of after-tax. Times interest earned reflects the income available to pay interest expense in relation to interest requirements.

Management wants this ratio to be reasonably high so that there is little risk of default. 3M's times interest earned is robust and currently stands at 65 times. This reflects a comfortable margin of coverage and is at the second highest level in the past five years.

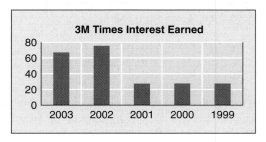

Operating Cash Flow to Labilities

Another variation in comparing operating flows to liabilities is to examine the operating cash flow to liabilities ratio, defined as:

Operating Cash Flow to Liabilities = Net Cash Flow from Operations/Total Liabilities

This ratio links operating cash flows with the debt level. Companies prefer this ratio to be higher rather than lower.

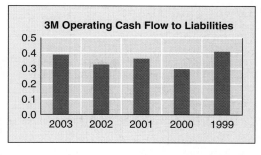

3M's operating cash flow to total liabilities ratio is 0.39 as of 2003. Further, it has fluctuated from a low of 0.29 to a high of 0.41 over the past five years.

Overall, there are several variations in leverage ratios. The basic idea is to construct measures that best reflect a company's credit risk exposure. There is no best financial leverage ratio. As with all ratios, there are several variations in formulas and approaches. Still to be sure we are measuring the risk we wish to measure, we must compute ratios ourselves from raw data and not rely on financial reporting services whose definitions are uncertain, inappropriate, and sometimes wrong.

Bankruptcy Prediction

Lenders, bankers, and debt raters are concerned with default risk, which is the risk a company is unable to honor its debt obligations. One way to assess this risk is to review a company's financial characteristics in relation to prior experience with bankrupt companies. Statistical models often aid in this process and are used to draw inferences on the degree of financial distress.

A well-known model of financial distress is **Altman's Z-score**. Altman's Z-score uses multiple ratios to get a predictor of financial distress. This predictor classifies or predicts the likelihood of bankruptcy or nonbankruptcy. Five financial ratios makeup the Z-score:

$X1$ = Working Capital/Total Assets
$X2$ = Retained Earnings/Total Assets
$X3$ = Earnings before Interest and Taxes/Total Assets
$X4$ = Shareholders' Equity/Total Liabilities
$X5$ = Sales/Total Assets.

In brief, $X1$ reflects liquidity, $X2$ reflects cumulative retained profitability, $X3$ reflects profitability, $X4$ reflects leverage, and $X5$ reflects total asset turnover.

The Altman Z-score is computed as:

$$\text{Z-score} = (0.717 \times X1) + (0.847 \times X2) + (3.107 \times X3) + (0.420 \times X4) + (0.998 \times X5)$$

The Z-score is then interpreted as follows:

$$\text{Z-score} < 1.20 \rightarrow \text{high probability of bankruptcy}$$
$$\text{Z-score} > 2.90 \rightarrow \text{low probability of bankruptcy}$$
$$1.20 \leq \text{Z-score} \leq 2.90 \rightarrow \text{gray or ambiguous area.}[10]$$

Another source of data on default risk is information services. For example, Standard & Poor's, which sells debt ratings, uses several accounting ratios to assess default risk (*S&P Compustat* also provides the Z-score for companies). A discussion of debt ratings and accounting ratios is in Module 7.

■ LIMITATIONS OF RATIO ANALYSIS

The quality of financial statement analysis depends on the quality of financial information. Analysis cannot be blindly conducted because of various accounting conventions and the flexibility afforded companies in preparing financial statements. Instead, any analysis must be aware of GAAP limitations, the current company environment, competitive pressures, and structural and strategic company changes. This section discusses some of the factors that can limit the usefulness of financial accounting information for ratio analysis.

---

[10]The model here is from Altman, *Corporate Financial Distress* (New York: John Wiley, 1983), pp. 120–124. This model is more generalizable than his earlier 1968 model that can only be applied to publicly traded companies.

GAAP Limitations

Several limitations in GAAP can distort financial ratios. They include the following:

1. **Measurability.** Financial statements reflect what can be reliably measured. This results in nonrecognition of some assets, generally items that confer a competitive advantage, and are internally developed. Examples are brand value, a superior management team, employee skills, and a superior supply chain.
2. **Noncapitalized costs.** Related to measurability is the expensing of assets that cannot be identified with enough precision to warrant capitalization. Examples are brand equity costs from promotional activities, and research and development costs on future products.
3. **Historical costs.** Assets and liabilities are typically recorded at original acquisition or issuance costs. Subsequent increases in value are not recorded until realized, and declines in value are only recognized if deemed permanent.

There are other limitations that we subsequently discuss throughout later modules.

Company Changes

Many companies acquire and divest subsidiaries with regularity. Such changes impair the comparability of company ratios across time. Companies also change strategies, such as product pricing, R&D, and financing. We must understand the effects of such changes on ratio analysis and accordingly adjust our inferences.

Companies also behave differently at different points in their life cycles. Specifically, growth companies possess a different profile than do mature companies. Also, seasonal effects can markedly impact analysis of financial statements at different times of the year.

Impact of Conglomerates

Most companies are blends of several businesses. Many consist of a parent company and multiple subsidiaries, often pursuing different lines of business. Several manufacturers, for example, have a finance subsidiary, like the GMAC subsidiary for General Motors. Financial statements of such companies are a combination (consolidation) of the financial statements of the parent and its subsidiaries. Consequently, such consolidated statements impair comparability with other competitors.

Analysis of these conglomerates is difficult and often requires breaking them apart into their component businesses and separately analyzing each line of business. Fortunately, some financial information for major lines of business are provided in the 10-K report, but these disclosures are limited.

A Means to an End

Too many individuals compute and examine ratios in their analysis as if such ratios are reality. Ratios are not reality, but they reflect reality. Reality is the innumerable transactions and events that occur each day between a company and various parties. Reality also is a company's marketing and management philosophies, its human resource activities, its financing activities, its strategic initiatives, and its product management. In our analysis we must learn to look through the numbers and ratios to better understand the operational factors that drive financial results. Our overriding purpose in analysis is to understand the past and present to better predict the future.

■ MODULE-END REVIEW ■

Refer to Mid-Module Review 1 for the financial statements of Caterpillar, Inc.

Required
Using Caterpillar's financial information, compute the following for 2003.

1. Liquidity measures
   a. Average cash operating cycle for machinery and engines
   b. Current ratio
   c. Quick ratio
2. Solvency measures
   a. Debt-to-equity
   b. Long-term debt-to-equity
   c. Times interest earned
   d. Operating cash flow to liabilities (note: CAT's net cash flows from operating activities in 2003 is $2,066 million)
3. What insights do you draw about Caterpillar's liquidity and solvency from the analytical measures in parts 1 and 2?

Solution

1. a. Cash cycle

Average collection period	63.57 days	$3,666/($21,048/365)
Modified average inventory days outstanding	52.84 days	$3,047/($21,048/365)
Modified average payable days outstanding	(53.76) days	$3,100/($21,048/365)
Average cash cycle	62.65 days	63.57 + 52.84 − 53.76

   b. Current ratio .... 1.33 $16,791/$12,621
   c. Quick ratio .... 0.92 ($342 + $3,666 + $7,605)/$12,621
2. a. Debt-to-equity .... 5.00 $30,387/$6,078
   b. Long-term debt-to-equity .... 2.92 ($30,387 − $12,621)/$6,078
   c. Times interest earned .... 3.06 times* ($1,477 + $246 + $470)/($246 + $470)
   d. Operating cash flow to liabilities .... 0.07 $2,066/$30,387

   *Many analysts would properly add the $30.77 million profit from affiliated companies to the numerator, computed as $20/ (1–0.35) assuming a 35% tax rate. This gives a times interest earned of 3.11.

3. The average cash cycle is 62.7 days. This is a reasonably quick conversion from cash-to-cash. John Deere (a competitor), for example, reports a cash-to-cash cycle of 70 days for the same period. Both of these computations are on trade receivables and inventories only and do not include the receivables and inventories arising from long-term financing of equipment sales through their respective financial subsidiaries. CAT's current ratio of 1.33 is also reasonably strong as is its quick ratio of 0.92. Neither ratio indicates liquidity problems.

   CAT's debt-to-equity and long-term debt-to-equity ratios are fairly high and reflect the long-term financing related to its leasing operations. Remember, CAT finances a substantial portion of its equipment sales via its captive finance subsidiary. The balance sheet of that subsidiary, which is consolidated with the manufacturing company parent, is similar to a bank balance sheet (meaning that it is highly leveraged and reliant on a relatively small spread of lease returns over the cost of the financing to support the leasing activities). Given CAT's adequate times interest earned ratio, our concern with CAT's financial leverage is moderated.

APPENDIX 3A

Vertical and Horizontal Analysis

Companies come in all sizes, which presents difficulties in comparing the numbers in financial statements across such companies. There are several methods that attempt to overcome this hurdle.

Vertical analysis is one way to overcome size differences. Its approach is to express the financial statements in ratio form. Specifically, it is common to express income statement items as a percentage of net sales and all balance sheet items as a percentage of total assets. Such a ratio-formed financial statement is prepared by dividing each individual financial statement amount under analysis by its base amount as follows:

Common-Size Percent (%) = (Analysis Period Amount/Base Period Amount) × 100

The resulting *common-size financial statements* facilitate comparative analysis *across companies* of different sizes, and help highlight any changes in strategies or operations *across time*. The common-size balance sheet and income statement for **3M Company** are presented in Exhibits 3A.1 and 3A.2.

EXHIBIT 3A.1 ■ 3M Common-Size Balance Sheet

3M COMPANY Common-Size Balance Sheets						
December 31	2003	2002	2001	2003	2002	2001
Cash	$ 1,836	$ 618	$ 616	10.43%	4.03%	4.22%
Receivables	2,714	2,527	2,482	15.42	16.49	16.99
Inventories	1,816	1,931	2,091	10.32	12.60	14.32
Other current assets	1,354	983	1,107	7.69	6.41	7.58
Total current assets	7,720	6,059	6,296	43.86	39.53	43.11
Property, plant and equipment, net	5,609	5,621	5,615	31.87	36.67	38.44
Investments	218	238	275	1.24	1.55	1.88
Intangibles	2,693	2,167	1,250	15.30	14.14	8.56
Deposits and other assets	1,360	1,244	1,170	7.73	8.12	8.01
Total assets	17,600	15,329	14,606	100.00%	100.00%	100.00%
Notes payable	1,202	1,237	1,373	6.83%	8.07%	9.40%
Accounts payable	1,087	945	753	6.18	6.16	5.16
Accrued liabilities	436	411	539	2.48	2.68	3.69
Income taxes	880	518	596	5.00	3.38	4.08
Other current liabilities	1,477	1,346	1,2488	8.39	8.78	8.54
Total current liabilities	5,082	4,457	4,509	28.88	29.08	30.87
Long-term debt	1,735	2,140	1,520	9.86	13.96	10.41
Other long-term liabilities	2,898	2,739	2,491	16.47	17.87	17.05
Total liabilities	9,715	9,336	8,520	55.20	60.90	58.33
Common stock, net	9	5	5	0.05	0.03	0.03
Capital in excess of par	287	291	291	1.63	1.90	1.99
Retained earnings	14,010	12,748	11,914	79.60	83.16	81.57
Treasury stock	4,641	4,767	4,633	26.37	31.10	31.72
Other equities	(1,780)	(2,284)	(1,491)	(10.11)	(14.90)	(10.21)
Shareholder equity	7,885	5,993	6,086	44.80	39.10	41.67
Total liabilities and equity	17,600	15,329	14,606	100.00%	100.00%	100.00%

EXHIBIT 3A.2 ■ 3M Common-Size Income Statement

3M COMPANY Common-Size Income Statements						
Year Ended Dec. 31	2003	2002	2001	2003	2002	2001
Net sales	$18,232	$16,332	$16,054	100.00%	100.00%	100.00%
Cost of good sold	9,285	8,496	8,749	50.93	52.02	54.50
Gross profit	8,947	7,836	7,305	49.07	47.98	45.50
R & D expenditures	1,102	1,070	1,084	6.04	6.55	6.75
Selling, general & admin exp	4,132	3,720	3,948	22.66	22.78	24.59
Operating Income	3,713	3,046	2,273	20.37	18.65	14.16
Interest expense	56	41	87	0.31	.0.25	0.54
Income before taxes	3,657	3,005	2,186	20.06	18.40	13.62
Income taxes	1,202	966	702	6.59	5.91	4.37
Minority interest income	52	65	54	0.29	0.40	0.34
Net income	2,403	1,974	1,430	13.18%	12.09%	8.91%

3M's total assets in dollars have increased by 26% since 1999. However, it is the *composition* of the balance sheet, the proportion invested in each asset category, that we are interested in. Liquidity has generally improved as cash now represents 10.43% of total assets, up from 4.22% in 2001. Yet, not all of that cash is sitting in 3M's checking account. GAAP categorizes cash and cash equivalents in the same account, the latter being temporary investments. Why would 3M build such liquidity? Perhaps, it desires the capacity to quickly react to strategic moves by competitors and to be able to quickly take advantage of investment opportunities, like the acquisition of a company.

The increased accounts receivable and inventory turnover are evidenced in their reduced proportion of total assets. Receivables now constitute 15.4% of total asserts, down from nearly 20% in 2000 (not shown). Also, inventories make up 10.3% of total assets compared with 14.3% in 2001.

It is interesting that plant assets (net) have decreased as a percentage of total assets, from 38.4% in 2001 to 31.9% in 2003. Yet, this category of assets has not decreased (in dollars), as purchases of plant assets have equaled depreciation expense. All of the growth in long-term operating assets has resulted from acquisitions, in the form of intangible assets, which were nonexistent five years ago, now constitute 15.3% of total assets.

Total liabilities have not changed appreciably as a percentage of total capitalization—55.2% in 2003 versus 58.3% in 2001. Current liabilities are at a slightly higher level. Stockholders' equity stands at 44.8% of total capitalization in 2003 versus 41.7% in 2001.

Exhibit 3A.2 shows the common-size income statement. 3M has done a remarkable job of controlling its cost of goods sold. Gross profit is 49.07% of sales in 2003, up from 45.5% in 2001 when McNerney assumed the top job. Also, overhead cost control has reduced SG&A expenses to 22.66% of sales in 2003, versus 24.59% in 2001. R&D expenses are slightly reduced as a proportion of sales and this is somewhat less than positive given the importance of this cost center to 3M's competitive position and future performance. Finally, 3M is carrying $13.18 cents out of each sales dollar to the bottom line in 2003. This compares favorably with 8.91% in 2001.

Overall, 3M is financially healthy, with high liquidity and relatively low financial leverage, and it is profitable. The operating discipline brought to the company by McNerney is evident in 3M's control over working capital and operating costs.

Horizontal analysis is the scrutiny of financial data *across time*. Comparing data across two or more consecutive periods assists in analyzing company performance and in predicting future performance. Horizontal analysis includes examination of absolute dollar changes and percent changes. The *dollar change* for a financial statement account is computed as follows:

Dollar Change = Analysis Period Amount − Base Period Amount

The *percent change* (%) for an account is computed as follows:

Percent Change = [(Analysis Period Amount − Base Period Amount)/Base Period Amount] × 100

The percent change is not interpretable when the base period amount is negative or zero, or when the analysis period amount is negative.

Trend analysis is a type of horizontal analysis. In this case a base period is chosen, and then all subsequent period amounts are defined relative to the base. Specifically, the *trend period* (%) is defined as follows:

Trend Percent = (Analysis Period Amount/Base Period Amount) × 100

Trend percents are often graphed to give a visual representation of the data.

APPENDIX 3B

ROE Disaggregation into Operating and Nonoperating Components

Following is the detailed disaggregation of ROE into its components: RNOA and FLEV × Spread:

$$ROE = \frac{NI}{SE}$$

$$= \frac{NOPAT - NFE}{SE}$$

$$= \frac{NOPAT}{SE} - \frac{NFE}{SE}$$

$$= \left(\frac{NOA}{SE} \times RNOA \right) - \left(\frac{NFO}{SE} \times NFR \right)$$

$$= \left(\frac{(SE + NFO)}{SE} \times RNOA \right) - \left(\frac{NFO}{SE} \times NFR \right)$$

$$= \left[RNOA \times \left(1 + \frac{NFO}{SE} \right) \right] - \left(\frac{NFO}{SE} \times NFR \right)$$

$$= RNOA + \left(\frac{NFO}{SE} \times RNOA \right) - \left(\frac{NFO}{SE} \times NFR \right)$$

$$= RNOA + \left(\frac{NFO}{SE} \right) (RNOA - NFR)$$

$$= RNOA + (FLEV \times SPREAD)$$

where NI is net income, SE is average stockholders' equity, and all other terms are as defined in Exhibit 3.2.

GUIDANCE ANSWERS

MANAGERIAL DECISION   **You Are the Entrepreneur**

Your company is performing substantially better than its competitors. Namely, your RNOA of 16% is markedly superior to competitors' RNOA of 10%. However, RNOA disaggregation shows that this is mainly attributed to your NOAT of 0.89 versus competitors' NOAT of 0.59. Your NOPM of 18% is essentially identical to competitors' NOPM of 17%. Accordingly, you want to maintain your NOAT as further improvements are probably difficult to achieve. Importantly, you are likely to achieve the greatest benefit with efforts at improving your NOPM of 18%, which is approximately equal to the industry norm of 17%.

Superscript ^{A} denotes assignments based on Appendix 3A.

■ DISCUSSION QUESTIONS

Q3-1. Explain in general terms the concept of return on investment. Why is this concept important in the analysis of financial performance?

Q3-2. (a) Explain how an increase in financial leverage can increase a company's ROE. (b) Given the potentially positive relation between financial leverage and ROE, why don't we see companies with 100% financial leverage (entirely nonowner financed)?

Q3-3. Identify two factors that can yield a decline in the gross profit margin. Should a reduction in the gross profit margin always be interpreted negatively? Explain.

Q3-4. When might a reduction in operating expenses as a percentage of sales denote a short-term gain at the cost of long-term performance?

Q3-5. Describe the concept of asset turnover. What does the concept mean and why it is so important to understanding and interpreting financial performance?

Q3-6. How might a company increase its accounts receivable turnover?

Q3-7. How can a company increase its inventory turnover?

Q3-8. By what means might a company increase its long-term operating asset turnover?

Q3-9. Why might a reduction in the accounts payable turnover rate not be considered favorable?

Q3-10. What is the cash cycle? What objective does management have regarding the cash cycle?

Q3-11. What insights do we take away from the graphical relation between profit margin and asset turnover?

Q3-12. Explain the concept of liquidity and why it is crucial to company survival.

Q3-13. Identify at least two factors that limit the usefulness of ratio analysis.

Q3-14.^{A} What are common-size financial statements? What role do they play in financial statement analysis?

■ MINI EXERCISES

Target Corporation (TGT)

M3-15. **Identify and Compute Net Operating Assets and its Components**   Following is the actual balance sheet for Target Corporation. Identify and compute its net operating assets and its components: net operating working capital and net operating long-term assets.

(millions)	January 31, 2004
Assets	
Cash and cash equivalents	$ 716
Accounts receivable, net	5,776
Inventory	5,343
Other	1,093
Total current assets	12,928
Property and equipment	
Land	3,629
Buildings and improvements	13,091
Fixtures and equipment	5,432
Construction-in-progress	995
Accumulated depreciation	(6,178)
Property and equipment, net	16,969
Other	1,495
Total assets	**$31,392**
Liabilities and shareholders' investment	
Accounts payable	$ 5,448
Accrued liabilities	1,618
Income taxes payable	382
Current portion of long-term debt and notes payable	866
Total current liabilities	8,314
Liabilities and shareholders' investment (continued)	
Long-term debt	$10,217
Deferred income taxes and other	1,796
Shareholders' investment	
Common stock	76
Additional paid-in-capital	1,341
Retained earnings	9,645
Accumulated other comprehensive income	3
Total shareholders' investment	11,065
Total liabilities and shareholders' investment	**$31,392**

M3-16.   Identify and Compute NOPAT and NFE   Following is the actual income statement for Target Corporation. Identify and compute its net operating profit after tax (NOPAT) and its net financial expense (NFE).

Target Corporation (TGT)

(millions)	Year-Ended January 31, 2004
Sales	$46,781
Net credit card revenues	1,382
Total revenues	48,163
Cost of sales	31,790
Selling, general and administrative expense	10,696
Credit card expense	838
Depreciation and amortization	1,320
Interest expense	559
Earnings before income taxes	2,960
Provision for income taxes	1,119
Net earnings	**$ 1,841**

M3-17. Compute RNOA, NOPAT Margin, and NOA Turnover   Selected balance sheet and income statement informa tion for Target Corporation, a department store retailer, follows ($ millions):

Company	Ticker	2004 Sales	2004 NOPAT	2004 Net Operating Working Capital	2003 Net Operating Working Capital	2004 Net Operating Assets	2003 Net Operating Assets
Target Corp	TGT	$48,163	$2,189	$5,480	$5,387	$22,148	$20,604

a. Compute its 2004 return on net operating assets (RNOA).

b. Disaggregate its RNOA from *a* into net operating profit margin (NOPM) and net operating asset turnover (NOAT). Show that RNOA = NOPM × NOAT.

c. Compute its net operating working capital turnover (NOWCT) and its long-term operating asset turnover (LTOAT).

M3-18. Identify and Compute Net Operating Assets and its Components   Following is the actual fiscal year-end 2003 balance sheet for The Walt Disney Company. Identify and compute net operating assets (NOA) and its components: net operating working capital (NOWC) and net operating long-term assets (NOLTA).

(in millions)	September 30, 2003
Assets	
Current assets	
Cash and cash equivalents	$ 1,583
Receivables	4,238
Inventories	703
Television costs	568
Deferred income taxes	674
Other current assets	548
Total current assets	8,314
Film and television costs	6,205
Investments	1,849
Parks, resorts and other property, at cost	
Attractions, buildings and equipment	19,499
Accumulated depreciation	(8,794)
	10,705
Projects in progress	1,076
Land	897
	12,678
Intangible assets, net	2,786
Goodwill	16,966
Other assets	1,190
Total assets	$49,988
Liabilities and Shareholders' Equity	
Current liabilities	
Accounts payable and other accrued liabilities	$ 5,044
Current portion of borrowings	2,457
Unearned royalties and other advances	1,168
Total current liabilities	8,669
Borrowings	10,643
Deferred income taxes	2,712
Other long-term liabilities	3,745
	(continued)

(in millions)	September 30, 2003
Minority interests	428
Shareholders' equity	
Common stock—Disney, $.01 par value	
Authorized—3.6 billion shares, Issued—2.1 billion shares	12,154
Retained earnings	13,817
Accumulated other comprehensive loss	(653)
Treasury stock, at cost, 86.7 million and 81.4 million Disney shares	(1,527)
	23,791
Total liabilities and equity	$49,988

M3-19. Identify and Compute NOPAT and NFE Following is the actual fiscal year-end 2003 income statement for The Walt Disney Company. Identify and compute its net operating profit after tax (NOPAT) and its net financial expense (NFE).

The Walt Disney Company (DIS)

(in millions)	Year Ended September 30, 2003
Revenues	$ 27,061
Costs and expenses	(24,330)
Amortization of intangible assets	(18)
Gain on sale of businesses	16
Net interest expense	(793)
Equity in the income of investees	334
Restructuring and impairment charges	(16)
Income before income taxes, minority interests and the cumulative effect of accounting change	2,254
Income taxes	(789)
Minority interests share of income	(127)
Income before the cumulative effect of accounting changes	1,338
Cumulative effect of accounting change	
Multiple element revenue accounting	(71)
Net income (loss)	$ 1,267

M3-20. Compute RNOA, NOPAT Margin, and NOA Turnover Selected balance sheet and income statement information for The Walt Disney Company, an operator of theme parks and media companies, follows ($ millions):

The Walt Disney Company (DIS)

Company	Ticker	2003 Sales	2003 NOPAT	2003 Net Operating Working Capital	2002 Net Operating Working Capital	2003 Net Operating Assets	2002 Net Operating Assets
Walt Disney	DIS	$27,061	$1,899	$2,102	$1,693	$37,319	$38,009

a. Compute its 2003 return on net operating assets (RNOA).
b. Disaggregate its RNOA from a into net operating profit margin (NOPM) and net operating asset turnover (NOAT). Show that RNOA = NOPM × NOAT.
c. Compute its net operating working capital turnover (NOWCT) and its long-term operating asset turnover (LTOAT).

M3-21. Compute and Interpret Asset Turnover Ratios Selected balance sheet and income statement information from Toys "R" Us, Inc., for 2003 follows ($ millions):

Toys "R" Us, Inc. (TOY)

Company	Sales	Cost of Goods Sold	Average Accounts Receivable	Average Inventory	Average Long-Term Operating Assets
Toys "R" US	$11,566	$7,849	$174	$2,157	$4,821

a. Compute the following asset turnover ratios:
  (1) Accounts receivable turnover
  (2) Inventory turnover
  (3) Long-term operating asset turnover
b. What are some characteristics of the Toys "R" Us business that would likely lead to the levels of turnover identified in (a)?

M3-22. Compute and Interpret Liquidity and Solvency Ratios   Selected balance sheet and income statement information from Toys "R" Us, Inc., for 2002 through 2004 follows ($ millions):

Toys "R" Us, Inc. (TOY)

	2004	2003	2002
Current assets	$4,684	$3,586	$2,631
Current liabilities	2,772	2,378	1,974
Earnings before interest and taxes	265	471	200
Interest expense	127	110	109
Total liabilities	5,987	5,354	4,635
Stockholders' equity	4,231	4,043	3,441

a. Compute the current ratio for each year and discuss any trend in liquidity. What additional information about the accounting numbers comprising this ratio might be useful in helping you assess liquidity? Explain.
b. Compute times interest earned and the debt-to-equity ratio for each year and discuss any trends for each. Do you have any concerns about Toys "R" Us's extent of financial leverage and its ability to meet interest obligations? Explain.
c. What is your overall assessment of Toys "R" Us's liquidity and solvency from the analyses in (a) and (b)? Explain.

■ EXERCISES

E3-23. Compute and Interpret RNOA, Profit Margin, and Asset Turnover of Competitors   Selected balance sheet and income statement information for the department store retailers Target Corporation and Wal-Mart Stores follows ($ millions):

Target Corporation (TGT)

Wal-Mart Stores (WMT)

Company	Ticker	2004 Sales	2004 NOPAT	2004 Net Operating Working Capital	2003 Net Operating Working Capital	2004 Net Operating Assets	2003 Net Operating Assets
Target Corp	TGT	$ 48,163	$2,189	$5,480	$5,387	$22,148	$20,604
Wal-Mart Stores	WMT	258,681	9,601	3,370	3,994	71,573	66,211

a. Compute the 2004 return on net operating assets (RNOA) for each company.
b. Disaggregate RNOA from a into net operating profit margin (NOPM) and net operating asset turnover (NOAT) for each company.
c. Compute the 2004 net operating working capital turnover (NOWCT) and long-term operating asset turnover (LTOAT) for each company.
d. Discuss any differences in these ratios for each company. Your interpretation should reflect the distinct business strategies of each company.

Abercrombie & Fitch (ANF)

The GAP, Inc. (GPS)

E3-24. Compute, Disaggregate, and Interpret RNOA of Competitors   Selected balance sheet and income statement information for the clothing retailers Abercrombie & Fitch and The GAP, Inc., follows ($ millions):

Company	Ticker	2004 Sales	2004 NOPAT	2004 Net Operating Working Capital	2003 Net Operating Working Capital	2004 Net Operating Assets	2003 Net Operating Assets
Abercrombie & Fitch ..... ANF		$ 1,708	$ 203	$ 463	$ 374	$ 861	$ 740
Gap, Inc .... GPS		15,854	1,150	2,056	3,152	5,710	7,314

a. Compute the 2004 return on net operating assets (RNOA) for each company.
b. Disaggregate RNOA from (a) into net operating profit margin (NOPM) and net operating asset turnover (NOAT) for each company.
c. Compute the 2004 net operating working capital turnover (NOWCT) and long-term operating asset turnover (LTOAT) for each company.
d. Discuss any differences in these ratios for each company. Your interpretation should reflect the distinct business strategies of each company.

E3-25. **Compute, Disaggregate, and Interpret RNOA of Competitors** Selected balance sheet and income statement information for the grocery retailers **Albertsons, Inc.**, and **Kroger Company** follows ($ millions):

Albertsons, Inc. (ABS)

Kroger Company (KR)

Company	Ticker	2004 Sales	2004 NOPAT	2004 Net Operating Working Capital	2003 Net Operating Working Capital	2004 Net Operating Assets	2003 Net Operating Assets
Albertsons, Inc ..... ABS		$35,436	$809	$1,254	$939	$10,705	$10,573
Kroger Co .... KR		53,791	562	281	310	12,375	12,424

a. Compute the 2004 return on net operating assets (RNOA) for each company.
b. Disaggregate RNOA from a into net operating profit margin (NOPM) and net operating asset turnover (NOAT) for each company.
c. Compute the 2004 net operating working capital turnover (NOWCT) and long-term operating asset turnover (LTOAT) for each company.
d. Discuss any differences in these ratios for each company. Your interpretation should reflect the distinct business strategies of each company.

E3-26. **Compute, Disaggregate, and Interpret RNOA of Competitors** Selected balance sheet and income statement information for the soft drink manufacturers **Coca-Cola** and **PepsiCo** follows ($ millions):

Coca-Cola (KO)

PepsiCo (PEP)

Company	Ticker	2003 Sales	2003 NOPAT	2003 Net Operating Working Capital	2002 Net Operating Working Capital	2003 Net Operating Assets	2002 Net Operating Assets
Coca-Cola Co ..... KO		$21,044	$4,342	$3,296	$2,581	$19,393	$17,071
PepsiCo Inc .... PEP		26,971	3,649	(75)	716	12,986	12,065

a. Compute the 2003 return on net operating assets (RNOA) for each company.
b. Disaggregate RNOA from a into net operating profit margin (NOPM) and net operating asset turnover (NOAT) for each company.
c. Compute the 2003 net operating working capital turnover (NOWCT) and long-term operating asset turnover (LTOAT) for each company.
d. Discuss any differences in these ratios for each company. Your interpretation should reflect the distinct business strategies of each company.

E3-27. **Compute, Disaggregate, and Interpret RNOA of Competitors** Selected balance sheet and income statement information for the drug retailers **CVS Corporation** and **Walgreen Company** follows ($ millions):

CVS Corporation (CVS)

Walgreen Company (WAG)

Company	Ticker	2003 Sales	2003 NOPAT	2003 Net Operating Working Capital	2002 Net Operating Working Capital	2003 Net Operating Assets	2002 Net Operating Assets
CVS Corp .... CVS		$26,588	$ 877	$3,331	$2,913	$7,098	$6,310
Walgreen Co ..... WAG		32,505	1,150	2,938	2,211	7,196	6,230

a. Compute the 2003 return on net operating assets (RNOA) for each company.
b. Disaggregate RNOA from *a* into net operating profit margin (NOPM) and net operating asset turnover (NOAT) for each company.
c. Compute the 2003 net operating working capital turnover (NOWCT) and long-term operating asset turnover (LTOAT) for each company.
d. Discuss any differences in these ratios for each company. Your interpretation should reflect the distinct business strategies of each company.

Nike, Inc.
(NKE)

Reebok
International
(RBK)

E3-28.   Compute, Disaggregate, and Interpret RNOA of Competitors   Selected fiscal year balance sheet and income statement information for the athletic shoe and apparel manufacturers Nike, Inc., and Reebok International follows ($ millions):

Company	Ticker	2004 Sales	2004 NOPAT	2004 Net Operating Working Capital	2003 Net Operating Working Capital	2004 Net Operating Assets	2003 Net Operating Assets
Nike Inc	NKE	$12,253	$962	$3,255	$3,048	$5,216	$4,824
Reebok Ltd	RBK	3,485	174	1,169	1,053	1,432	1,300

a. Compute the 2004 return on net operating assets (RNOA) for each company.
b. Disaggregate RNOA from *a* into net operating profit margin (NOPM) and net operating asset turnover (NOAT) for each company.
c. Compute the 2004 net operating working capital turnover (NOWCT) and long-term operating asset turnover (LTOAT) for each company.
d. Discuss any differences in these ratios for each company. Your interpretation should reflect the distinct business strategies of each company.

Abercrombie
& Fitch (ANF)

Wal-Mart
Stores (WMT)

E3-29.   Compute and Interpret Asset Turnover Ratios of Competitors   Selected balance sheet and income statement information from Abercrombie & Fitch and Wal-Mart Stores for fiscal 2004 follows ($ millions):

Company	Sales	Cost of Goods Sold	Average Accounts Receivable	Average Inventory	Average Long-Term Operating Assets
Abercrombie & Fitch	$ 1,708	$ 990	$ 8	$ 184	$ 420
Wal-Mart Stores	258,681	198,747	1,411	25,506	67,288

a. Compute the following asset turnover ratios for each company:
   (1) Accounts receivable turnover
   (2) Inventory turnover
   (3) Long-term operating asset turnover
b. What are some characteristics of their respective business activities that would likely lead to the levels of turnover identified in (*a*)?

Harley-
Davidson, Inc.
(HDI)

Target
Corporation
(TGT)

E3-30.   Compute and Interpret Asset Turnover Ratios of Competitors   Selected balance sheet and income statement information from the motorcycle manufacturing company, Harley-Davidson, Inc., and from the retailing company, Target Corporation, follows ($ millions):

Company	Sales	Cost of Goods Sold	Average Accounts Receivable	Average Inventory	Average Long-Term Operating Assets
Harley-Davidson	$ 4,624	$ 2,959	$ 110	$ 213	$ 1,994
Target Corp.	48,163	31,790	5,670	5,052	17,566

a. Compute the following asset turnover ratios for each company:
   (1) Accounts receivable turnover
   (2) Inventory turnover
   (3) Long-term operating asset turnover
b. What are some characteristics of their respective business activities that would likely lead to the levels of turnover identified in (*a*)?

E3-31. **Compute and Interpret Liquidity and Solvency Ratios** Selected balance sheet and income statement information from **The Walt Disney Company** for 2001 through 2003 follows ($ millions):

The Walt Disney Company (DIS)

	Current Assets	Current Liabilities	Pretax Income	Interest Expense	Total Assets	Stockholders' Equity
2001	$7,029	$6,219	$1,283	$606	$43,699	$22,672
2002	7,849	7,819	2,190	759	50,045	23,445
2003	8,314	8,669	2,254	699	49,988	23,791

a. Compute the current ratio for each year and discuss any trend in liquidity. Do you believe the company is sufficiently liquid? Explain. What additional information about the accounting numbers comprising this ratio might be useful in helping you assess liquidity? Explain.

b. Compute times interest earned and the debt-to-equity ratio for each year and discuss any trends for each. Do you have any concerns about the company's extent of financial leverage and its ability to meet interest obligations? Explain.

c. What is your overall assessment of the company's liquidity and solvency from the analyses in (a) and (b)? Explain.

E3-32. **Compute and Interpret Liquidity and Solvency Ratios** Selected balance sheet and income statement information from **Verizon Communications, Inc.,** for 2001 through 2003 follows ($ millions):

Verizon Communications, Inc. (VZ)

	Current Assets	Current Liabilities	Pretax Income	Interest Expense	Total Assets	Stockholders' Equity
2001	$23,187	$38,020	$3,496	$3,737	$170,795	$32,539
2002	20,921	27,047	7,472	3,422	167,468	32,616
2003	18,293	26,570	6,344	2,941	165,968	33,466

a. Compute the current ratio for each year and discuss any trend in liquidity. Do you believe the company is sufficiently liquid? Explain. What additional information about the accounting numbers comprising this ratio might be useful in helping you assess liquidity? Explain.

b. Compute times interest earned and the debt-to-equity ratio for each year and discuss any trends for each. Do you have any concerns about the company's extent of financial leverage and its ability to meet interest obligations? Explain.

c. What is your overall assessment of the company's liquidity and solvency from the analyses in (a) and (b)? Explain.

E3-33. **Compute and Interpret Liquidity and Solvency Ratios** Selected balance sheet and income statement information from **Viacom, Inc.,** for 2001 through 2003 follows ($ millions):

Viacom, Inc. (VIA)

	Current Assets	Current Liabilities	Pretax Income	Interest Expense	Total Assets	Stockholders' Equity
2001	$7,206	$7,562	$ 656	$963	$90,810	$62,717
2002	7,167	7,341	3,695	848	89,754	62,488
2003	7,736	7,585	2,861	776	89,849	63,205

a. Compute the current ratio for each year and discuss any trend in liquidity. Do you believe the company is sufficiently liquid? Explain. What additional information about the accounting numbers comprising this ratio might be useful in helping you assess liquidity? Explain.

b. Compute times interest earned and the debt-to-equity ratio for each year and discuss any trends for each. Do you have any concerns about the company's extent of financial leverage and its ability to meet interest obligations? Explain.

c. What is your overall assessment of the company's liquidity and solvency from the analyses in (a) and (b)? Explain.

E3-34. **Compute and Interpret Liquidity and Solvency Ratios** Selected balance sheet and income statement information from **Wal-Mart Stores, Inc.,** for fiscal 2002 through 2004 follows ($ millions):

Wal-Mart Stores, Inc. (WMT)

	Current Assets	Current Liabilities	Pretax Income	Interest Expense	Total Assets	Stockholders' Equity
2002	$28,246	$27,282	$10,751	$1,456	$ 83,451	$35,102
2003	30,483	32,617	12,719	1,187	94,685	39,337
2004	34,421	37,418	14,193	1,140	104,912	43,623

a. Compute the current ratio for each year and discuss any trend in liquidity. Do you believe the company is sufficiently liquid? Explain. What additional information about the accounting numbers comprising this ratio might be useful in helping you assess liquidity? Explain.

b. Compute times interest earned and the debt-to-equity ratio for each year and discuss any trends for each. Do you have any concerns about the company's extent of financial leverage and its ability to meet interest obligations? Explain.

c. What is your overall assessment of the company's liquidity and solvency from the analyses in (a) and (b)? Explain.

■ PROBLEMS

P3-35. Analysis and Interpretation of Company Profitability   Balance sheets and income statements for Procter & Gamble follow. Refer to these financial statements to answer the requirements below.

Procter & Gamble (PG)

PROCTER & GAMBLE COMPANY Comparative Balance Sheets				
For June 30 ($ millions)	2003	2002	2001	2000
Cash and cash equivalents	$ 5,912	$ 3,427	$ 2,306	$ 1,415
Investment securities	300	196	212	185
Accounts receivable	3,038	3,090	2,931	2,910
Inventories	3,640	3,456	3,384	3,490
Other current (operating) assets	2,330	1,997	2,056	2,146
Total current assets	15,220	12,166	10,889	10,146
Property, plant and equipment, gross	23,542	23,070	22,821	23,221
Accumulated depreciation	10,438	9,721	9,726	9,529
Property, plant and equipment, net	13,104	13,349	13,095	13,692
Goodwill and intangible assets	13,507	13,430	8,300	8,786
Other noncurrent (operating) assets	1,875	1,831	2,103	1,742
Total assets	$43,706	$40,776	$34,387	$34,366
Accounts payable	$ 2,795	$ 2,205	$ 2,075	$ 2,209
Debt due within one year	2,172	3,731	2,233	3,241
Accrued and other liabilities	7,391	6,768	5,538	4,691
Total current liabilities	12,358	12,704	9,846	10,141
Deferred income taxes	1,396	1,077	894	625
Long-term debt	11,475	11,201	9,792	9,012
Other noncurrent liabilities	2,291	2,088	1,845	2,301
Total liabilities	27,520	27,070	22,377	22,079
Preferred stock	1,580	1,634	1,701	1,737
Common stock	1,297	1,301	1,296	1,306
Additional paid-in capital	2,931	2,490	2,057	1,794
Retained earnings	13,692	11,980	10,451	10,710
Other equities	(3,314)	(3,699)	(3,495)	(3,260)
Shareholders' equity	16,186	13,706	12,010	12,287
Total liabilities and equity	$43,706	$40,776	$34,387	$34,366

| PROCTER & GAMBLE COMPANY | | | | |
| Comparative Income Statements | | | | |
Year Ended June 30 ($ millions)	2003	2002	2001	2000
Net sales	$43,377	$40,238	$39,244	$39,951
Cost of goods sold	22,141	20,989	22,102	21,514
Gross profit	21,236	19,249	17,142	18,437
Selling, general & administrative expense	13,383	12,571	12,406	12,483
Operating income	7,853	6,678	4,736	5,954
Other nonoperating income, net	238	308	674	304
Interest expense	561	603	794	722
Income before income taxes	7,530	6,383	4,616	5,536
Income taxes	2,344	2,031	1,694	1,994
Net earnings	$ 5,186	$ 4,352	$ 2,922	$ 3,542

Required

a. Compute the following profitability ratios for each year shown:
   (1) Gross profit margin (GPM).
   (2) Operating expense margin (OEM)—also called SG&A margin.
   (3) Net operating profit margin (NOPM).

b. Your results in part *a* should have revealed an increase in net operating profit margin (NOPM).
   (1) Is this increase due to an increase in the gross profit margin or a decrease in operating expenses, or both? Provide evidence and explain your answer.
   (2) Consider how much control that companies have or do not have over gross profit margin. What factors must exist to allow companies to increase selling prices of their products? In what ways can they improve gross profit margin by lowering product manufacturing costs? Explain.

c. What are the usual components of operating expense for a company like Procter and Gamble? For which of these components are companies likely able to achieve expense reductions? To what extent are these expense reductions a short-term gain at the cost of long-term performance? Explain.

P3-36. Analysis and Interpretation of Asset Turnover Ratios   Refer to the financial information for Procter & Gamble in Problem 3-35 to answer the following.

Procter & Gamble (PG)

Required

a. Compute the following turnover ratios and analysis measures for 2001 through 2003:
   (1) Accounts receivable turnover and the average collection period.
   (2) Inventory turnover and the average inventory days outstanding.
   (3) Long-term operating asset turnover.

b. Results from part *a* should reveal a slight improvement in receivables turnover from 2001 to 2003. How can a company like P&G realize an improvement in this ratio? Explain.

c. Results from part *a* should reveal no discernable improvement in inventory turnover from 2001 to 2003. How can a manufacturer like P&G realize an improvement in its inventory turnover? Explain.

d. Results from part *a* should reveal a slight decline in long-term operating asset turnover from 2001 to 2003. Why is it so difficult for companies to impact this ratio? Can you think of ways in which a company can achieve an improvement in this ratio? Explain.

P3-37. Disaggregation and Interpretation of Company ROE   Refer to the financial information for Procter & Gamble in Problem 3-35 to answer the following.

Procter & Gamble (PG)

Required

a. Compute the following for 2001 through 2003:
   (1) Net operating profit margin (NOPM).
   (2) Return on net operating assets (RNOA).
   (3) Financial leverage (FLEV).
   (4) Net financial rate (NFR)
   (5) Spread
   (6) Return on equity (ROE).
   (7) Confirm that ROE from the formula, ROE = RNOA + (FLEV $\times$ Spread), equals that computed in part (6).

b. Drawing on results from part *a*, does P&G depend more on operations (RNOA) or financial leverage to drive its ROE? Explain.

P3-38.   **Analysis and Interpretation of Liquidity and Solvency**   Refer to the financial information for Procter & Gamble in Problem 3-35 to answer the following.

Required

a.   Compute its current ratio and quick ratio for 2001 through 2003. Do the trends, if any, in these ratios indicate that P&G is becoming more or less liquid? Use computations to support your analysis and inferences.

b.   Compute P&G's debt-to-equity ratio and times interest earned for 2001 through 2003. Do these ratios indicate that P&G is becoming more or less solvent? Explain.

c.   Compute the Altman Z-Score of P&G for 2003. Does this score indicate any concerns about P&G's financial condition? Explain.

P3-39.   **Analysis and Interpretation of Company Profitability**   Actual balance sheets and income statements for Merck & Co. (MRK) follow ($ millions). Refer to these financial statements to answer the requirements below.

MERCK & CO. Comparative Balance Sheets			
December 31 ($ millions)	2003	2002	2001
Assets			
Current Assets			
Cash and cash equivalents	$ 1,201.0	$ 2,243.0	$ 2,144.0
Short-term investments	2,972.0	2,728.2	1,142.6
Accounts receivable	4,023.6	5,423.4	5,215.4
Inventories	2,554.7	2,964.3	3,579.3
Prepaid expenses and taxes	775.9	1,027.5	880.3
Total current assets	11,527.2	14,386.4	12,961.6
Investments	7,941.2	7,255.1	6,983.5
Property, Plant, and Equipment (at cost)			
Land	356.7	336.9	315.2
Buildings	8,016.9	7,336.5	6,653.9
Machinery, equipment and office furnishings	11,018.2	10,883.6	9,807.0
Construction in progress	1,901.9	2,426.6	2,180.4
	21,293.7	20,983.6	18,956.5
Less allowance for depreciation	7,124.7	6,788.0	5,853.1
	14,169.0	14,195.6	13,103.4
Goodwill	1,085.4	4,127.0	4,127.0
Other Intangibles, Net	864.0	3,114.0	3,364.0
Other Assets	5,000.7	4,483.1	3,481.7
	$40,587.5	$47,561.2	$44,021.2
Liabilities and Stockholders' Equity			
Current Liabilities			
Loans payable and current portion of long-term debt	$ 1,700.0	$ 3,669.8	$ 4,066.7
Trade accounts payable	735.2	2,413.3	1,895.2
Accrued and other current liabilities	3,772.8	3,365.6	3,213.2
Income taxes payable	2,538.9	2,118.1	1,573.3
Dividends payable	822.7	808.4	795.8
Total current liabilities	9,569.6	12,375.2	11,544.2
Long-Term Debt	5,096.0	4,879.0	4,798.6
Deferred Income Taxes and Noncurrent Liabilities	6,430.3	7,178.2	6,790.8
Minority Interests	3,915.2	4,928.3	4,837.5
Stockholders' Equity			
Common stock, one cent par value			
Authorized—5,400,000,000 shares			
Issued—2,976,230,393 shares—2003			
—2,976,198,757 shares—2002	29.8	29.8	29.8

(continued)

MERCK & CO. Comparative Balance Sheets (continued)			
December 31 ($ millions)	2003	2002	2001
Stockholders' Equity (continued)			
Other paid-in capital	$ 6,956.6	$ 6,943.7	$ 6,907.2
Retained earnings	34,142.0	35,434.9	31,489.6
Accumulated other comprehensive income (loss)	65.5	(98.8)	10.6
	41,193.9	42,309.6	38,437.2
Less treasury stock, at cost			
754,466,884 shares—2003			
731,215,507 shares—2002	25,617.5	24,109.1	22,387.1
Total stockholders' equity	15,576.4	18,200.5	16,050.1
	$40,587.5	$47,561.2	$44,021.2

MERCK & CO. Comparative Income Statements			
Year Ended December 31 ($ millions)	2003	2002	2001
Sales	$22,485.9	$21,445.8	$21,199.0
Costs, Expenses and Other			
Materials and production	4,315.3	3,907.1	3,624.8
Marketing and administrative	6,394.9	5,652.2	5,700.6
Research and development	3,178.1	2,677.2	2,456.4
Acquired research	101.8	—	—
Equity income from affiliates	(474.2)	(644.7)	(685.9)
Other (income) expense, net	(81.6)	202.3	155.0
	13,434.3	11,794.1	11,250.9
Income from Continuing Operations Before Taxes	9,051.6	9,651.7	9,948.1
Taxes on Income	2,462.0	2,856.9	2,894.9
Income from Continuing Operations	6,589.6	6,794.8	7,053.2
Income from Discontinued Operations, Net of Taxes	241.3	354.7	228.6
Net Income	$ 6,830.9	$ 7,149.5	$ 7,281.8

Required

a. Compute the following profitability ratios for each year shown:
   (1) Gross profit margin (GPM). (*Hint*: Materials and production are MRK's cost of goods sold.)
   (2) Operating expense margin (OEM). (*Hint*: Include acquired research for 2003 in R&D expense.)
   (3) Taxes on income as a percentage of income before taxes.
   (4) Net operating profit margin (NOPM).

b. Your results in part a should have revealed a decrease in net operating profit margin (NOPM) from 2002 to 2003.
   (1) Which component(s) of operating profit (from part a) contribute to this decrease? Provide evidence and explain your answer.
   (2) Consider how much control that companies have or do not have over gross profit margin. What market factors adversely affect GPM? Explain.

c. MRK's R&D costs as a percent of sales have increased over the past 3 years. How do you interpret changes in the level of R&D costs? Explain.

P3-40. **Analysis and Interpretation of Asset Turnover Ratios**   Refer to the financial information for Merck & Co. in Problem 3-39 to answer the following requirements.

Merck & Co. (MRK)

Required

a. Compute the following turnover ratios and analysis measures for 2002 and 2003:
   (1) Accounts receivable turnover and the average collection period.
   (2) Inventory turnover and the average inventory days outstanding.
   (3) Long-term operating asset turnover.

b. Results from part *a* should reveal an improvement in receivables turnover from 2002 to 2003. Considering the customer base for product sales, how can a company like MRK realize an improvement in this ratio? Explain.

c. Results from part *a* should reveal an improvement in inventory turnover from 2002 to 2003. How can a manufacturer like MRK realize an improvement in its inventory turnover? Explain.

d. Results from part *a* should reveal an improvement in long-term operating asset turnover from 2002 to 2003. Why is it so difficult for companies to impact this ratio? Can you think of ways in which a company can achieve an improvement in this ratio? Explain.

Merck & Co. (MRK) **P3-41.** **Disaggregation and Interpretation of Company ROE**   Refer to the financial information for Merck & Co. in Problem 3-39 to answer the following.

Required

a. Compute the following for 2002 and 2003:

(1) Net operating profit margin (NOPM).

(2) Net operating asset turnover ((NOAT).

(3) Return on net operating assets (RNOA).

(4) Confirm that RNOA from the formula, RNOA = NOPM × NOAT, and using results from (1) and (2), equals that computed in part (3).

(5) Financial leverage (FLEV). (*Hint*: FLEV is negative when financial assets exceed financial liabilities.)

(6) Net financial rate (NFR).

(7) Spread.

(8) Return on equity (ROE).

(9) Confirm that ROE from the formula, ROE = RNOA + (FLEV × Spread), and using results from (3), (5) and (7), equals that computed in part (8).

b. Results from part *a* indicate that MRK's RNOA is greater than its ROE for 2003. This means that FLEV has a negative impact. How do you interpret this result? Explain.

Merck & Co. (MRK) **P3-42.** **Analysis and Interpretation of Liquidity and Solvency**   Refer to the financial information for Merck & Co. in Problem 3-39 to answer the following requirements.

Required

a. Compute its current ratio and quick ratio for 2001 through 2003. Do the trends, if any, in these ratios indicate that MRK is becoming more or less liquid? Use computations to support your analysis and inferences.

b. Compute MRK's debt-to-equity ratio and times interest earned for 2001 through 2003. Do these ratios indicate that MRK is becoming more or less solvent? Explain.

Colgate-Palmolive Company (CL) **P3-43.** **Analysis and Interpretation of Company Profitability**   Refer to the actual comparative balance sheets and income statements for Colgate-Palmolive Company that follow to answer the requirements below.

Required

a. Compute the following analysis measures for 2003:

(1) Net operating profit margin (NOPM).

(2) Return on net operating assets (RNOA).

(3) Financial leverage (FLEV).

(4) Net financial rate (NFR).

(5) Spread.

(6) Return on equity (ROE).

(7) Confirm that ROE from the formula, ROE = RNOA + (FLEV × Spread), and using results from (2), (3) and (5), equals that computed in part (6).

b. Drawing on results from part *a,* does Colgate depend more on operations (RNOA) or financial leverage to drive its ROE? Explain.

c. Compute the following profitability ratios for 2003:

(1) Gross profit margin (GPM).

(2) Operating expense margin (OEM)—also called SG&A margin.

(3) Net operating profit margin (NOPM)—*see part a.*

d. Consider how much control that companies have or do not have over gross profit margin. What factors must exist to allow them to increase selling prices of their products? In what ways can they improve gross profit margin by lowering product manufacturing costs? Explain.

e. What components of selling, general and administrative expense are companies likely able to use to achieve expense reductions? To what extent are these expense reductions a short-term gain at the cost of long-term performance? Explain.

f. Compute the following turnover ratios and analysis measures for 2003:
    (1) Accounts receivable turnover.
    (2) Average collection period.
    (3) Inventory turnover.
    (4) Average inventory days outstanding.
g. How can a company like Colgate realize an improvement in its accounts receivable turnover?
    Explain.
h. How can a manufacturer like Colgate realize an improvement in its inventory turnover? Explain.
i. Compute the Altman Z-Score of Colgate for 2003. Does this score indicate any concerns about its
    financial condition? Explain.

COLGATE-PALMOLIVE COMPANY Comparative Income Statements			
Year Ended December 31 ($ millions)	2003	2002	2001
Net sales	$9,903.4	$9,294.3	$9,084.3
Cost of sales	4,456.1	4,224.2	4,234.9
Gross profit	5,447.3	5,070.1	4,849.4
Selling, general & administrative expenses	3,296.3	3,034.0	2,920.1
Other (income) expense, net	(15.0)	23.0	94.5
Operating profit	2,166.0	2,013.1	1,834.8
Interest expense, net	124.1	142.8	166.1
Income before income taxes	2,041.9	1,870.3	1,668.7
Provision for income taxes	620.6	582.0	522.1
Net income	$1,421.3	$1,288.3	$1,146.6

COLGATE-PALMOLIVE COMPANY Comparative Balance Sheets		
December 31 ($ millions)	2003	2002
Assets		
Current Assets		
Cash and cash equivalents	$ 265.3	$ 167.9
Receivables (less allowances of $43.6 and $45.9, respectively)	1,222.4	1,145.4
Inventories	718.3	671.7
Other current assets	290.5	243.1
Total current assets	2,496.5	2,228.1
Property, plant and equipment, net	2,542.2	2,491.3
Goodwill	1,299.4	1,182.8
Other intangible assets, net	597.6	608.5
Other assets	543.1	576.5
Total assets	$ 7,478.8	$ 7,087.2
Liabilities and Shareholders' Equity		
Current Liabilities		
Notes and loans payable	$ 103.6	$94.6
Current portion of long-term debt	314.4	298.5
Accounts payable	753.6	728.3
Accrued income taxes	183.8	121.7
Other accruals	1,090.0	905.6
Total current liabilities	2,445.4	2,148.7
Long-term debt	2,684.9	3,210.8
Deferred income taxes	456.0	488.8
Other liabilities	1,005.4	888.6
Total liabilities	6,591.7	6,736.9
		(continued)

COLGATE-PALMOLIVE COMPANY Comparative Balance Sheets (continued)		
December 31 ($ millions)	2003	2002
Shareholders' Equity		
Preferred stock	292.9	323.0
Common stock, $1 par value (1,000,000,000 shares authorized, 732,853,180 shares issued)	$ 732.9	$ 732.9
Additional paid-in capital	1,126.2	1,133.9
Retained earnings	7,433.0	6,518.5
Accumulated other comprehensive income	(1,866.8)	(1,865.6)
	7,718.2	6,842.7
Unearned compensation	(331.2)	(340.1)
Treasury stock, at cost	(6,499.9)	(6,152.3)
Total shareholders' equity	887.1	350.3
Total liabilities and shareholders' equity	$ 7,478.8	$ 7,087.2

P3-44. **Analysis and Interpretation of Profit Margin, Asset Turnover, and RNOA for Several Companies**
Net operating profit margin (NOPM) and net operating asset turnover (NOAT) for several selected companies for 2003 follow:

Albertsons, Inc. (ABS)

Alcoa, Inc. (AA)

Caterpillar, Inc. (CAT)

Home Depot, Inc. (HD)

McDonalds Corporation (MCD)

SBC Communications, Inc. (SBC)

Southwest Airlines (LUV)

Target Corporation (TGT)

Company	NOPM	NOAT
Albertsons, Inc	2.20%	3.59
Alcoa, Inc	5.93%	1.51
Caterpillar, Inc	6.96%	1.99
Home Depot, Inc	6.64%	2.72
McDonalds Corporation	12.61%	0.89
SBC Communications, Inc	10.62%	0.79
Southwest Airlines	5.08%	0.74
Target Corporation	4.54%	2.23

Required

a. Graph NOPM and NOAT for each of these companies. Do you see a pattern revealed that is similar to that shown in this module? Explain. (Note that the graph in the module is based on medians for selected industries. The graph for this problem uses fewer companies than in the module and, thus, will not be as smooth.)

b. Consider the trade-off between profit margin and asset turnover. How can we evaluate companies on the profit margin and asset turnover trade-off? Explain.

4 Reporting and Analyzing Operating Income

TRANSITORY ITEMS SURFACE AT CISCO

After a decade of 80% annual growth, Cisco Systems, Inc., ran smack into the tech decline in 2001. When its Chief Executive John Chambers failed to implement new strategic initiatives, his reputation as one of the world's top CEOs plummeted like the networking giant's stock. This was especially so after the company took a massive $2.2 billion inventory write-down, which seemed to undermine Cisco's claims of cutting-edge e-efficiency (*BusinessWeek* 2003).

Cisco is the worldwide leader in networking for the Internet. Its engineers have been prominent in the development of Internet Protocol (IP)-based networking technologies in the core areas of routing and switching, along with advancing technologies in areas such as IP telephony, wireless LAN, storage networking, and home networking. Its products are seemingly everywhere:

- Cisco routers and switches are a crucial component of all networks, including the Internet.
- Cisco wireless network and IP telephony products allow people to communicate freely and reduce the cost of long distance communications.
- Cisco wireless technology allows employees to connect to corporate networks over a virtual private network (VPN), and it has medical applications such as telerobotics that aid in surgery. Its commercial application of wireless communication includes wireless displays on shopping carts, targeted advertisements, and quick checkout.
- Virtual classrooms, powered by Cisco's switching technology and web collaboration software, are part of the distance learning evolution.

John Chambers recently commented to *BusinessWeek,* "success in the 1990s was often based on how fast could you get to market and how fast could you blow a product through your distribution [channels]." In the wake of the 2001 market decline, Chambers remarked, "Our market changed dramatically in terms of what customers expected. As the market changed, we needed to have engineering and manufacturing and professional services and [sales] and customer support working together in a way that wasn't required before."

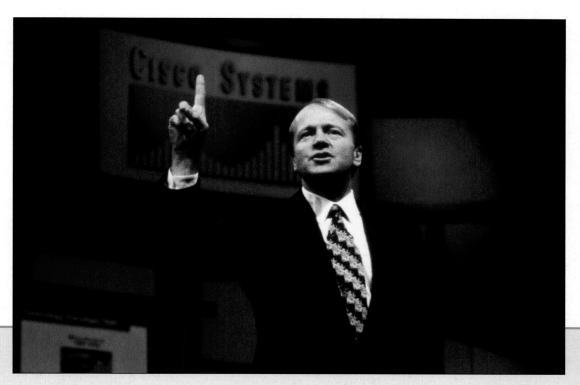

Cisco, in short, had to restructure its business from the ground up. Such a restructuring would be expensive. In a footnote to its annual report, Cisco described its restructuring program as follows:

Due to macroeconomic and capital spending issues affecting the networking industry, the Company announced a restructuring program to prioritize its initiatives around high-growth areas of its business, focus on profit contribution, reduce expenses, and improve efficiency. This restructuring program includes a worldwide workforce reduction, consolidation of excess facilities, and restructuring of certain business functions.

Cisco's restructuring program translated into the following cost implications (10-K report):

- *Workforce reduction*. Elimination of about 6,000 jobs, yielding severance payments and fringe benefits.
- *Facilities consolidation*. Closure of corporate and sales offices and operational centers, yielding lease termination (buyout) costs, losses on disposal of properties and equipment, and vendor payments to terminate supply agreements.
- *Impairment of goodwill and other purchased intangible assets*. These costs reflect the amounts by which asset book values exceed their market values.
- *Inventory write-down*. These costs reflect the amounts by which inventory book values exceed their market values as well as the costs of honoring existing purchase commitments.

Many of the costs comprising Cisco's restructuring program involve considerable estimation. For example, Cisco had to identify the employees to terminate, all 6,000 of them. It had to then separate those that would be retiring and not be replaced, from those that might be induced to accept early retirement packages, from those that would be terminated outright. Further, it had to estimate the severance costs for each. Cisco also had to estimate asset market values and the cost of lease buyouts. Write-down of goodwill and other intangible assets required that it estimate the cash flows to be realized from each investment. Finally, the inventory write-down required that it estimate market values for a substantial amount of unusable inventory.

(Continued on next page)

(Continued from previous page)

As this module will explain, companies must report the expected restructuring costs when they are estimated, *not* when they are subsequently paid. Accordingly, Cisco reported a special charge of $1,170 million as described in the following table from its 2001 restructuring footnote:

	Total Charge	Noncash Charges	Cash Payments	Restructuring Liabilities at July 28, 2001
Workforce reduction	$ 397	$ (71)	$(265)	$ 61
Consolidation of excess facilities and other charges	484	(141)	(18)	325
Impairment of goodwill and purchased intangible assets	289	(289)	—	—
Total	$1,170	$(501)	$(283)	$386

Beyond this $1,170 million charge, Cisco took another charge of $2,250 million. Cisco's total special charges of $3.4 billion contributed to its 2001 net loss of $1 billion.

Cisco's stock had reached a per share high of just over $80 prior to the announcement of its restructuring program. Within three months of that announcement, its stock had declined to $50 per share. By the first anniversary of the announcement, Cisco's stock had plummeted to under $20, one-fourth of its peak value. As the following chart indicates, despite generating nearly $5.5 billion of net income in the two years since its restructuring plan went into effect, the market has yet to embrace Cisco's stock.

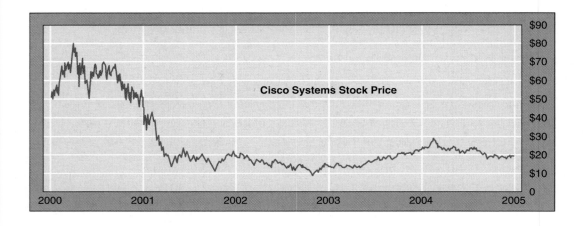

Cisco's restructuring costs fall into a general class of income statement items called *transitory items.* Transitory items result from events that are unlikely to recur. This module describes transitory items, together with other items related to company operating activities. Many of these items reflect important events with enormous dollar amounts.

What does this mean for Cisco? Well, as Chambers noted to *BusinessWeek,* "Jack Welch [former General Electric CEO] said it best. He said, 'John, you'll never have a great company until you go through the really tough times. What builds a company is not just how you handle the successes, but it's the way you handle the real challenges.'" The materials in this module give you insights into how you might better assess the likelihood of such success.

Sources: *Cisco Systems, Inc.,* 2004, 2003 and 2001 10-K Reports; *The Wall Street Journal,* February 7, 2005; *BusinessWeek,* November/December 2003.

■ INTRODUCTION

Operating activities refer to the primary transactions and events of a company. These include the purchase of goods from suppliers, the conversion of goods into finished products, the promotion and distribution of goods, the sale of goods to customers, and post-sale customer support. Operating activities are reported in the income statement under items such as sales, cost of goods sold, and selling, general, and administrative expenses. They represent a company's primary activities, and they must be executed successfully for a company to consistently succeed.

Nonoperating activities relate to the financial (borrowing) and securities investment activities of a company. They are not a company's primary activities. These activities are typically reported in the income statement under items such as interest revenues and expenses, dividend revenues, and gains and losses on sales of securities. Distinguishing income components by operating versus nonoperating is an important part of effective financial statement analysis because operating activities drive future company performance.

Income statement components are also usefully separated into core versus transitory activities. *Core* (or *persistent*) *components* of income are those that are most likely to persist and are, therefore, the most relevant for projecting future financial performance. *Transitory components* of income are those that are not recurring. Presumably, projections of future financial performance are improved if we can identify and exclude transitory components from those projections.

Proper identification of operating and nonoperating components is important for valuation of companies' equity (stock) and debt (note and bond) securities. It is of interest, for example, to know whether company profitability results from operating activities, or whether poor performing operating activities are being masked by income from nonoperating activities. Further, since income from nonoperating activities usually depends on a favorable investment climate, it can be short-lived.

Proper identification of core and transitory components is equally important and are similarly motivated by valuation objectives. Core components, because they are relatively long-lasting, carry a greater weight in the valuation of securities. Importantly, changes in the level of core income per share commonly impact stock price by a factor of 10 or more, while transitory income components normally affect stock price dollar-for-dollar. Since valuation of stock is based on expectations of future company performance, core operating components carry more weight than transitory nonoperating components.

Exhibit 4.1 distinguishes several common income components between operating and nonoperating and between core and transitory.

EXHIBIT 4.1 ■ Distinguishing Operating, Nonoperating, Core, and Transitory Income Components

	Core	Transitory
Operating	Sales; cost of goods sold; selling, general and administrative expenses; research and advertising expenses; income taxes	Gains and losses on sales of operating assets; operating asset write-downs; nonrecurring restructuring accruals
Nonoperating	Interest revenues and expenses; dividend revenues; hedging gains and losses	Debt retirement gains and losses; gains and losses on discontinued operations

Specifically, sales, cost of goods sold, and most selling, general, and administrative expenses are categorized as both operating and core. On the other hand, operating activities such as sales and write-downs of operating assets, and company restructurings are unlikely to recur and, therefore, are transitory. Similarly, investment related income from dividends and interest is nonoperating but recurring, hence its designation as a core activity. Gains and losses on debt retirements and sales of investments are also nonoperating, but are transitory.

This Module is divided into two main sections. The first section focuses on some unique operating components of income. Our presentation includes discussion of revenue recognition and several income components that warrant further explanation: employee stock options, foreign currency translation adjustments, research and development expenses, and income taxes. The second section focuses on concepts of core versus transitory components, including items reported in the income statement after income from continuing operations (*below the line*) such as gains and losses on asset sales, restructuring activities, and asset write-offs.

BUSINESS INSIGHT	Ratio Equilibrium

Each industry tends to evolve and reach an equilibrium level for its operating activities, which depend on its core operations. For example, some industries require a high level of selling, general and administrative (SG&A) expenses, perhaps due to high advertising demands, high level of employee skills required, or necessary research and development (R&D) to remain competitive. To compensate for the required level of expenditures, the pricing activity in an industry must be such to yield a level of gross profit that is sufficient to allow the industry to remain viable. Review the following table of selected operating margins for companies in various industries. (Gross profit divided by sales is GPM; selling, general and administrative expenses divided by sales is SGAM; research and development divided by sales is R&DM; and net income divided by sales is NPM.)

	GPM	SGAM	R&DM	NPM
Cisco Systems 76.5%		41.9%	16.6%	19.0%
Intel Corporation 68.7		31.9	15.1	11.6
Pfizer, Inc. 90.5		49.5	16.0	28.4
Procter & Gamble 53.7		30.0	3.8	12.0
Wal-Mart Stores 23.1		16.7	0.0	3.3

Cisco, Intel, Pfizer, and Proctor & Gamble report high gross profit margins (GPM). This does not necessarily suggest they are better managed than Wal-Mart. Instead, their industries are structured to require higher levels of gross profit to cover other expenses (such as SG&A, R&D, and advertising) necessary for the industry to survive. Wal-Mart, on the other hand, is in a "penny business." Since it sells undifferentiated consumer products, its competitive advantage must lie in cost control. Wal-Mart reports the lowest SGAM of any of the companies listed.

■ OPERATING COMPONENTS

This section focuses on various operating components of income. Revenue recognition is crucial to measuring operating performance. We review revenue recognition criteria and, then, discuss a number of revenue recognition scenarios that warrant special scrutiny. We also explain percentage-of-completion revenue recognition, which is used by many companies whose revenues span multiple accounting periods. The latter part of this section discusses four components of operating income that present reporting and analysis challenges: employee stock options, foreign currency translation adjustments, research and development expenses, and income taxes.

Revenue and its Recognition

Revenue recognition refers to the reporting of company revenue. The decision to recognize revenue depends on relatively simple criteria. Despite their simplicity, most SEC enforcement actions against companies for inaccurate, and sometimes fraudulent, financial reporting are for improper (premature) revenue recognition. Determining whether the criteria for revenue recognition are met is often subjective and subject to abuse. This is especially so for companies facing market pressures to meet income targets.

GAAP dictates two **revenue recognition criteria** that must be met for revenue to be recognized (and reported) on the income statement. Revenue must be (1) **realized or realizable**, and (2) **earned**.[1] *Realized or realizable* means that the company's net assets increase. That is, it receives an asset or satisfies a liability as a result of a transaction or event. *Earned* means that the seller has executed its duties under

---

[1]SEC guidance for revenue recognition is in *Staff Accounting Bulletin (SAB) 101*, which states that revenue is realized, or realizable, and earned when *each* of the following criteria are met: (1) there is persuasive evidence that a sales agreement exists; (2) delivery has occurred or services have been rendered; (3) seller's price to the buyer is fixed or determinable; and (4) collectibility is reasonably assured.

the terms of the sales agreement and that title has passed to the buyer with no right of return or other contingencies.

An unrestricted *right of return*, other than due to product defects, would inhibit revenue recognition. Products delivered on *consignment* would also inhibit revenue recognition until sold by the consignee. Involvement by the seller in product resale such as marketing support (like markdown allowances), retaining possession of the product until resold, or any continuing involvement in product resale would inhibit revenue recognition. Product sales that are contingent upon product performance, product approvals, or similar contingencies would also inhibit revenue recognition.

BUSINESS INSIGHT | **Cisco's Revenue Recognition**

Following is an excerpt from **Cisco Systems'** policies on revenue recognition as reported in footnotes to its recent annual report.

> We recognize product revenue when persuasive evidence of an arrangement exists, delivery has occurred, the fee is fixed or determinable, and collectibility is reasonably assured. In instances where final acceptance of the product, system, or solution is specified by the customer, revenue is deferred until all acceptance criteria have been met . . . Service revenue is generally deferred and, in most cases, recognized ratably over the period during which the services are to be performed . . . Contracts and customer purchase orders are generally used to determine the existence of an arrangement. Shipping documents and customer acceptance, when applicable, are used to verify delivery . . . When a sale involves multiple elements, such as sales of products that include services, the entire fee from the arrangement is allocated to each respective element based on its relative fair value and recognized when revenue recognition criteria for each element are met.

Cisco's criteria for revenue recognition mirror SEC guidance. The key components are that revenue is *earned* and that proceeds are *realized or realizable.* For Cisco, earned means that delivery to and acceptance by the customer occurs, or that Cisco is available to perform service commitments, even if not called upon.

Risks of Revenue Recognition

We identify 10 cases that involve questionable or improper revenue recognition. The SEC is so concerned about aggressive (premature) revenue recognition that it recently issued a special *Staff Accounting Bulletin (SAB) 101* on the matter. Each of the following cases reflect inherent risks for certain industries and companies that are subject to similar transactions and events. We must be cognizant of these risks in both analyzing and interpreting financial performance.

- *Case 1: Pending execution of sales agreements.* Companies seeking to boost current period revenues have resorted to sales recognition upon delivery of product to customers when the requisite sales approval has yet to be received by period-end, although it is expected shortly thereafter. The SEC's position is that if the company's practice is to obtain sales authorization, revenue is *not* recognized until such approval is obtained, even though product delivery is made and approval by the customer is anticipated.

- *Case 2: Gross versus net revenues.* Some companies use their distribution network to act as agents for others, selling other companies' goods at a slight markup for a sales "commission." There are increasing reports of companies that inflate revenues by reporting such transactions on a gross basis (reporting both sales and cost of goods sold) instead of reporting only the commission (sales less cost of goods sold) earned. The incentives for such reporting are high for some dot.com companies and start-ups that believe the market prices of their stocks are based on revenue growth and not profitability. Reporting revenues at gross rather than net would have enormous impact on valuations of those companies. The SEC prescribes that such sales be reported on a net basis.

- *Case 3: Sales on consignment.* Some companies deliver goods to others with the understanding that these goods are ultimately to be sold to third parties. At the time of delivery, however, title to such goods does not pass to the second company, and this second company has no obligation to make payment to the seller until the product is sold. This type of transaction is called a *consignment sale.* The SEC's position is that a sale has not occurred, and revenue is *not* to be recognized by the original company until the product is sold to a third party. Further, the middleman (consignee) cannot report the gross sale, and can only report its commission revenue (see Case 2).

- *Case 4: Barter transactions.* Some barter transactions are concocted to create the illusion of revenue. Examples include the advertising swaps engaged in by some dot.com companies, and the excess capacity swaps of fiber optic communications businesses. An example of the latter is a company selling excess capacity to a competitor and, simultaneously, purchasing excess capacity from that competitor. Although these situations often lead to immediate revenue recognition, they typically are equal exchanges not providing income to either party. Further, these examples do not represent a culmination of the normal earning process (for example, fiber optic networks are created to sell communications services to end users, not to swap capacity with others).

- *Case 5: Failure to take delivery.* Some customers, maybe for lack of storage space or because they prefer to not yet record inventories, do not take delivery by period-end. In this case, revenue is *not* recognized, as it has not yet been earned. The earning process is only complete once the product is delivered and accepted. An example is layaway sales. Even though the product is ordered and even partially paid for, revenue is not recognized, even in part, until the product is delivered and final payment is made or agreed to be made.

- *Case 6: Nonrefundable fees.* Sellers sometimes receive fees that are nonrefundable to the customer. An example is a health club fee or a cellular phone activation fee. Some sellers wish to record these cash receipts as revenue to boost current sales and income. Although cash is received and nonrefundable, revenue is not recognized until the product is delivered or service performed. Until that time, the cash received is reported as an asset on the balance sheet and a liability (deferred revenue) is reported as an obligation to deliver product or perform service. Once the obligation is settled, the liability is removed and revenue is reported.

- *Case 7: Channel stuffing.* Some sellers use their market power over customers to induce (or even require) them to purchase more goods than necessary to satisfy customer demand, thus increasing period-end sales and incomes of sellers. This practice is called *channel stuffing.* If no side agreements exist for product returns, the practice is acceptable per GAAP, but is discouraged. However, when return rights exist, such revenue is not recognized.

- *Case 8: Mischaracterizing extraordinary and unusual items.* Not all revenue recognition irregularities involve questions of when or if revenue is recognized. In some instances, financial statement presentation is the concern. Although presentation concerns usually do not impact net income, they can seriously distort interpretations. The most common concern involves reporting nonoperating gains as operating revenues such as including gains on asset sales with SG&A expenses. A variation on this involves reporting nonoperating gains as offsets to one or more categories of operating expenses, similarly distorting key financial ratios and interpretations— again, without necessarily impacting net income.

- *Case 9: Mischaracterizing transactions as arm's-length.* Transfers of inventories or other assets to related entities typically are not recognized as revenue until later arm's-length sales occur. Sometimes such sales are disguised as being sold to unrelated entities to yield improper revenue recognition when (1) the buyer is a related party to the seller or (2) financing is provided or guaranteed by the seller, or (3) the buyer is a special-purpose entity that fails to meet independence requirements. Revenue is not recognized unless the sale process is complete, that is, goods have been transferred and an obligation exists for payment from a solvent, independent party.

- *Case 10: Selling undervalued assets.* This revenue recognition tactic involves selling specific assets that carry holding gains. An example is the sale of low-cost inventory layers (see Module 5), which boosts gross margin and income for that period, albeit at the cost of having to later replenish inventories with higher-cost goods. Another example is the sale of securities for which unrealized gains exist while holding others with unrealized losses. Such activities are acceptable under GAAP, although required disclosures can be a deterrent.

In sum, revenue can only be recognized when it is earned and when it is realized or realizable. This demands that the seller has performed its obligations (no contingencies exist) and the buyer is an independent party with the financial capacity to cover amounts owed.

$
Cash Effect

Percentage-of-Completion Revenue Recognition

Challenges arise in determining revenue recognition for companies with long-term sales contracts (spanning more than one period) such as construction companies and defense contractors. For these companies, revenue is often recognized using the **percentage-of-completion method**, which recognizes revenue by determining the costs incurred under the contract relative to its total expected costs.

To illustrate, assume that a $10 million contract is signed to construct a building. The construction company estimates $7,500,000 in construction costs, yielding an expected gross profit of $2,500,000. Assume that during the current year the company incurs $4,500,000 in construction costs on that building. The company would report $6 million in revenue, computed as follows:

Total Contract Revenues	Percentage Completed	Revenue Recognized
$10,000,000	$\dfrac{\$4,500,000}{\$7,500,000} = 60\%$	$6,000,000 ($10,000,000 × 60%)

This means that the company would report $1.5 million ($6 million − $4.5 million) in gross profit on this construction project for the current year.

Revenue recognition policies for these types of contracts are disclosed in a manner typical to the following from the 2004 10-K report footnotes of **Raytheon Company**:

> Sales under long-term government contracts are recorded under the percentage of completion method. Incurred costs and estimated gross margins are recorded as sales as work is performed based on the percentage that incurred costs bear to estimated total costs utilizing the Company's estimates of costs and contract value . . . Since many contracts extend over a long period of time, revisions in cost and contract value estimates during the progress of work have the effect of adjusting earnings applicable to performance in prior periods in the current period.

The percentage-of-completion method of revenue recognition requires an estimate of total costs. This estimate is made at the beginning of the contract and is typically the one used to initially bid the contract. However, estimates are inherently inaccurate. If the estimate changes during the construction period, the percentage-of-completion is computed as the total costs incurred to date divided by the *current* estimate of total anticipated costs (costs incurred to date plus total estimated costs to complete).

If total construction costs are underestimated to date, the percentage-of-completion is overestimated (the denominator is too low) and too much revenue and gross profit are recognized to date. The estimation process inherent in this method has the potential for inaccurate or, even, improper revenue recognition. This is also because estimates of remaining costs to complete projects are difficult to verify for auditors. This uncertainty adds additional risk to financial statement analysis.

BUSINESS INSIGHT   **Disney's Revenue Recognition**

The Walt Disney Company uses a method similar to percentage-of-completion to determine the amount of production cost to match against film and television revenues. Following is an excerpt from its 10-K:

> Film and television production and participation costs are expensed based on the ratio of the current period's gross revenues to estimated remaining total gross revenues from all sources on an individual production basis. Television network series costs and multi-year sports rights are charged to expense based on the ratio of the current period's gross revenues to estimated remaining total gross revenues from such programs or straight-line, as appropriate.

Production costs are recorded on the balance sheet as inventory when paid. As film and television revenues are recognized, the company recognizes a portion of production costs to match against revenues in computing income. The costs recognized are equal to the proportion of total revenues recognized in the period to the total expected revenues to be recognized over the life of the film or television show. Thus, estimates of both costs and income depend on the quality of its revenue estimates, an imprecise estimate.

The next section discusses four revenue or expense components, which are part of operating activities, that present us with some unique challenges for financial reporting and analysis.

Employee Stock Option Expense

Employee stock options are a form of compensation that grant a select group of employees the right to purchase a fixed number of company shares at a fixed price for a predetermined time period. The motivation for options is to align employee and shareholder interests. Options aim to provide incentive to employees to work to increase company stock price since they are able to use their options to purchase stock at a fixed price and resell it at the prevailing (expectedly higher) market price, thus realizing a gain. Employees will, thereby, have the same incentives as shareholders (incentives would align)—that is, both desire stock price increases. Unfortunately, stock options cause serious distortions in financial statements.

The initial accounting treatment of employee stock options was enacted prior to development of modern option pricing theory (in *APB 25,* called the *intrinsic value method*). At that time, the prevailing view was that options had value only to the extent that the contractual stock purchase price (exercise price) was *less* than the market stock price on the date that the options were granted to the employee. If a company set the exercise price *equal* to the market price on the date of grant, the view was that no value had been given to the employee. This means that no compensation expense would *ever* be reported from such options. (When the options are ultimately exercised, the company treats the exercise as a normal stock sale at the option's selling price.) The important point is that a company can easily shelter its income statement from this form of compensation expense merely by setting the exercise price equal to the market price of the stock on the date of grant.

Analysts have expressed serious concerns about accounting for stock options and the amount of unrecorded compensation expense tied to options. Consequently, the FASB enacted *SFAS 123* (in 1995) that *encouraged* recognition of compensation expense, but *did not require* such recognition. Companies choosing not to recognize stock option expense are merely required to footnote the pro forma income effects as if they had expensed options at their fair market value.

Cisco Systems presents an example of the currently mandated footnote disclosure related to employee stock options in its 2003 annual report, as shown in Exhibit 4.2.

EXHIBIT 4.2 ■ Stock Option Expense Footnote Disclosure for Cisco

Year Ended ($ millions)	July 26, 2003
Net income (loss)—as reported	$ 3,578
Compensation expense, net of tax	(1,259)
Net income (loss)—pro forma	$ 2,319

Cisco reports net income of $3,578 million, which is absent any stock option compensation expense. It then uses the currently acceptable method of footnoting its $1,259 million in option expense, see Exhibit 4.2. Had Cisco expensed options, its net income would decline by $1,259 million to $2,319 million, a 35% decrease! We should adjust the income statement to include such expenses for analysis purposes when the failure to recognize them does not accurately portray company income.

The International Accounting Standards Board (IASB) requires companies applying its standards to expense the fair value of stock options over the vesting period (effective in 2005). The FASB has issued an exposure draft proposing similar accounting for stock options (*SFAS 123R*, effective in 2006). Financial statements issued prior to the passage of any new standard are not restated. As a result, until all comparable years are accounted for under any new standard, stock options are accounted for as required under *SFAS 123*.

Foreign Currency Translation Effects

Many companies conduct operations outside of their domestic countries and in other currencies. Some companies purchase assets in foreign currencies, borrow money in foreign currencies, and transact business with their customers in foreign currencies. Some companies even have subsidiaries whose entire balance sheet and income statement are stated in foreign currencies.

Financial statements prepared according to U.S. GAAP must be reported in $US. This means that financial statements of any foreign subsidiaries must be translated into $US before they are consolidated with those of the U.S. parent company. This translation process can markedly alter both the balance sheet and income statement.

Balance Sheet Effects

Consider a foreign subsidiary that conducts its business in Euros and prepares its financial statements in Euros. Assume that the Euro strengthens vis-à-vis the $US during the current period—that is, each Euro can now purchase more $US as the $US has weakened. When the balance sheet is translated into $US, the assets and liabilities are reported at higher $US than before the Euro strengthened. This result is shown in accounting equation format in Exhibit 4.3.[2]

EXHIBIT 4.3 ▓ Balance Sheet Effects of Euro Strengthening versus the Dollar

Currency	Assets	=	Liabilities	+	Equity
$US weakens	Increase	=	Increase	+	Increase
$US strengthens	Decrease	=	Decrease	+	Decrease

The amount necessary to balance the accounting equation is reported in the equity section and is called a **foreign currency translation** adjustment. It is included in *other comprehensive income* and does not impact reported net income. Since assets are greater than liabilities for solvent companies, the cumulative translation adjustment is usually positive for local currencies that strengthen vis-à-vis the $US, with the opposite effect when the dollar strengthens. (In the unusual case when liabilities exceed assets, equity exhibits the opposite effects.) The cumulative translation adjustment remains in equity unless the subsidiary is sold, at which time it is recognized in income.

Exhibit 4.4 shows an excerpt from the statement of stockholders' equity of Ford Motor Company. Ford's cumulative foreign currency translation is $(1,291) million at the beginning of 2003, which increases to $1,593 million by year-end. The $2,884 million positive swing primarily reflects a weakening of the $US vis-à-vis the foreign currencies in which Ford conducted its business in 2003. That is, as the $US weakened, assets and liabilities of foreign subsidiaries were translated into more $US, resulting in an increase in equity to maintain the accounting equation. These unrealized gains (and losses) remain in other

EXHIBIT 4.4 ▓ Foreign Currency Translation for Ford Motor Company ($ millions)

Year Ended December 31, 2003	Capital Stock	Capital in Excess of Par Value of Stock	Retained Earnings	Other Comprehensive Income/(Loss)			Other	Total
				Foreign Currency Translation	Minimum Pension Liability	Derivative Instruments and Other		
Balance at beginning of year	$19	$5,420	$8,659	$(1,291)	$(5,776)	$ 536	$(1,977)	$ 5,590
Comprehensive income (loss)								
Net income			495					495
Foreign currency translation . . .				3,075				3,075
Net gain on derivative instruments (net of tax of $430) . .				(191)		989		798
Minimum pension liability (net of tax of $1,208)					2,243			2,243
Net holding gain (net of tax of $1)						1		1
Comprehensive income							6,612	
Common Stock issued for employee benefit plans and other		(46)						(46)
Treasury stock							228	228
Cash dividends			(733)					(733)
Balance at end of year	$19	$5,374	$8,421	$1,593	$(3,533)	$1,526	$(1,749)	$11,651

---

[2]We assume that the company is translating the statements of its foreign subsidiary using the **current rate method**, which is required for subsidiaries operating independently from the parent and is most commonly used. Under the current rate method, most items in the balance sheet are translated using exchange rates in effect at the period-end consolidation date and the income statement is translated using the average exchange rate for the period. An alternative procedure is the *temporal method,* which is covered in advanced courses.

comprehensive income as long as the subsidiary is owned, fluctuating between positive and negative amounts as the value of the $US fluctuates. However, when the subsidiary is sold, any existing foreign currency translation adjustment relating to that subsidiary is immediately recognized in current income with the gain or loss from sale of the subsidiary.

Income Statement Effects

A change in the strength of the $US vis-à-vis foreign currencies does affect reported income in the following manner: changes in foreign currency yield changes in revenues, expenses, and income for the foreign subsidiary (where revenues and expenses are translated at the average exchange rate for the period). Thus, even when translation of the balance sheet does not affect reported income, translation of the income statement does. Specifically, assuming a company is profitable, when the foreign currency strengthens ($US weakens), the subsidiary's revenues, expenses, and income increases. On the other hand, when the $US strengthens, the subsidiary's revenues, expenses, and income decrease.

To illustrate the income statement effects of foreign exchange fluctuations, consider the following footnote to the McDonald's Corporation 2003 10-K:

> In 2003, foreign currency translation had a positive impact on consolidated revenues, operating income and earnings per share due to the strengthening of several major currencies, primarily the Euro.

As the Euro and other currencies strengthen vis-à-vis the $US, McDonald's reported revenues are translated into more $US, resulting in a reported revenues increase. Specifically, McDonald's revenues increased from $15,406 million in 2002 to $17,140 million in 2003. However, 5% of this 11% increase is due to the foreign currency translation effect as evident in the following McDonald's footnote ($ millions):

Total Revenues	2003	2002	Increase (Decrease)	Increase (Decrease) Excluding Currency Translation
U.S.	$ 6,039	$ 5,423	11%	11%
Europe	5,875	5,136	14	—
APMEA	2,447	2,368	3	(3)
Latin America	859	814	6	14
Canada	778	633	23	9
Other	1,142	1,032	11	11
Total revenues	$17,140	$15,406	11%	6%

Although McDonald's reports that 2003 total revenues increase by 11%, the weakening $US accounts for 5% of this increase. That is, excluding currency effects, McDonald's revenues increased only 6%. McDonald's also reports (not shown here) that 9% of its 34% increase in 2003 operating profit was due to the weakening $US.

We must remember that for companies deriving a major portion of their revenues and profits in international currencies, we must be cognizant of the effects of currency fluctuations on reported revenues, expenses, and profits.

Research and Development (R&D) Expense

R&D activities are a major expenditure for most companies, especially for those in technology and pharmaceutical industries where R&D expenses can exceed 10% of revenues. These expenses include employment costs for R&D personnel, R&D related contract services, and R&D plant asset costs.

Accounting for R&D activities follows a uniform method: *expense as incurred*. Although this method is consistent with the accounting for non-R&D costs such as wages and advertising, the expensing of R&D plant assets is in stark contrast to the capitalization-and-depreciation of non-R&D plant assets. The expensing of R&D plant assets is mandated *unless those assets have alternative future uses* (in other R&D projects or otherwise). For example, a general research facility housing multi-use lab equipment is capitalized and depreciated like any other depreciable asset. However, project-directed research buildings and equipment with no alternate uses must be expensed.

Following is a footnote excerpt from Cisco's 2003 annual report related to its research and development expenditures:

> R&D expenses in fiscal 2003 decreased by $313 million or 9.1% from $3.4 billion in fiscal 2002 to $3.1 billion primarily due to a decrease in expenditures on prototypes of approximately $120 million due, in part, to our ongoing cost control measures. In addition, the decrease in R&D expenses was also due to lower depreciation on lab equipment and other reduced discretionary spending. We have continued to invest in R&D efforts in a wide variety of areas . . . All of our R&D costs have been expensed as incurred.

Cisco's general research facilities (those with alternate uses) are capitalized and depreciated. All other R&D costs of Cisco are expensed as incurred.

When a company improperly and immediately expenses its depreciable R&D assets, it yields lower current period income, lower total assets, and lower equity. These effects are mitigated to the extent that a company regularly purchases R&D assets and the amount of purchases is relatively constant from year-to-year. Specifically, after the average useful life is reached, say in 5 to 10 years, the expensing of current year purchases will approximate the depreciation that would have been reported had the assets been capitalized (thus, the income effect is minimal). However, the recorded assets are permanently less, which affects asset turnover ratios and, consequently, analysis of RNOA and ROE —yielding an upward bias due to unrecorded assets (and equity) in the denominator. More generally, the effects of expensing R&D for financial statements is summarized as follows:

$
Cash Effect

Balance Sheet	Income Statement	Statement of Cash Flows
• R&D assets with no alternate use are unrecorded • Unrecorded assets increase return ratios (RNOA and ROE) and asset turnover ratios • R&D expensing reduces income and equity, which can affect ROE	• R&D expensing (versus capitalization-and-depreciation) lowers income; more so when R&D costs are increasing	• No effect from the R&D capitalization versus expense accounting

R&D expenses are core operating activities as they are generally recurring. Since expensing of R&D assets generally depresses profits and equity, the market-to-book ratios (market price per share divided by equity book value per share) for high-R&D industries tend to be higher than those for less-R&D intensive industries. This difference is driven as much by accounting conservatism as it is by fundamental differences in industry characteristics and market expectations about future performance. This emphasizes the need for accounting analysis in any comparison of financial ratios across industries, and particularly for those with substantial R&D activities.

BUSINESS INSIGHT   Cisco R&D

Cisco spends about $3.1 billion annually for R&D compared with its revenues of $18.8 billion, or about 16.5%. This reflects a high percent of revenues devoted to R&D in comparison with nontechnology companies, but typifies companies that compete in the high-tech arena. Following is the R&D-expense-to-sales ratio for Cisco and some of its competitors.

	2003	2002	2001
Cisco Systems	16.5%	18.5%	20.1%
Nortel Networks	20.2	18.7	17.0
Juniper Networks	25.3	44.5	24.8
3Com	12.1	19.2	21.1

Income Tax Expense

Companies maintain two sets of books, one for reporting to their shareholders and another for reporting to tax authorities (this is legal as the tax code is different from GAAP). These two different books can report dramatically different levels of pretax income (in financial reports to shareholders) and taxable income (in tax reports).

One example of a difference relates to plant assets. Companies usually compute depreciation expense using the straight-line method for financial reporting purposes—this means they transfer the same amount of the asset's cost from the balance sheet to the income statement each year. However, for tax reporting, they (legally) transfer more of the asset's cost from the balance sheet to the income statement in the earlier years of the asset's life (referred to as *accelerated depreciation*). This reduces taxable income and the tax liability and, thereby, increases cash flows for the earlier years of an asset's useful life.

Only a fixed amount of asset cost can ultimately be transferred from the balance sheet to the income statement. This means that the amount of depreciation expense for tax reporting will decline in later years of an asset's life and, consequently, taxable income and income taxes paid will be higher than for earlier years.[3] Financial reporting (GAAP) requires that companies recognize this future tax liability. To illustrate, assume that a company's tax expense in its financial report is $100 but taxes paid are $80, reflecting higher depreciation expense for tax reporting. The company's financial statement effects follow:

$
Cash Effect

Tax Expense   100
Cash   80
Deferred
Taxes   20

	Balance Sheet					Income Statement	
Transaction	Cash Asset	+ Noncash Assets	= Liabil- ities	+ Contrib. Capital	+ Retained Earnings	Revenues	− Expenses
Report $100 tax expense, but $80 cash in taxes paid	−80 Cash		+20 Deferred Taxes		−100 Retained Earnings		− 100 Tax Expense

The $80 asset reduction reflects the cash payment of taxes and the $100 equity reduction reflects the income tax expense reported on the income statement for financial reporting. The liability is reported as **deferred taxes** (also called *deferred income taxes*). When reported as a liability it represents taxes to be paid in the future when taxable income is higher than financial reporting income.

Deferred tax liabilities arise when tax reporting income is less than financial reporting income. This implies that the taxes will be paid when the items causing the difference reverse. A common example is the use of accelerated depreciation for tax purposes and straight-line for financial reporting as in our example.

Deferred tax assets arise for the opposite reason: when tax reporting income is higher than financial reporting income. An example might be recording restructuring costs in the year a reorganization plan is approved as described later in this module. For tax purposes, restructuring costs are not deductible until paid in the future. As a result, financial reporting income is less than tax reporting income when the plan is approved, giving rise to a deferred tax asset. This asset represents future benefits to be realized by the company once such deferred costs become deductible for tax purposes and the tax payments are, consequently, reduced.

To see how income tax expense is disclosed, Cisco Systems's tax footnote to its income statement is shown in Exhibit 4.5. Cisco's $1,435 million tax expense reported in its income statement consists of the following two components (organized by federal, state and foreign):

1. *Current tax expense.* Amount currently payable (in cash) to tax authorities.
2. *Deferred tax expense.* Effect on tax expense from changes in deferred tax liabilities and deferred tax assets. In the above example, deferred tax liabilities increase by $20 (reflecting a future liability), which yields a higher income tax expense than taxes paid.

$
Cash Effect

---

[3]To see this, assume we have a $200 plant asset, with a four-year life, and zero salvage. A typical depreciation schedule and pro forma income (assuming $300 income before depreciation and 40% tax rate) follows:

	Year 1	Year 2	Year 3	Year 4	Total
Financial reporting depreciation	$ 50	$ 50	$ 50	$ 50	$ 200
Financial reporting income	250	250	250	250	1,000
Financial reporting tax expense	**100**	100	100	100	400
Tax reporting depreciation	100	50	30	20	200
Tax reporting (taxable) income	200	250	270	280	1,000
Taxes paid	**80**	100	108	112	400

EXHIBIT 4.5 ■ Income Tax Expense Footnote for Cisco

Year Ended ($ millions)	July 26, 2002
Federal	
Current	$1,041
Deferred	6
	1,047
State	
Current	138
Deferred	2
	140
Foreign	
Current	270
Deferred	(22)
	248
Total	$1,435

Companies must disclose the components of deferred tax liabilities and assets. Cisco's deferred tax footnote to its balance sheet (shown in Exhibit 4.6) reports deferred tax assets of $3,826 million. Many of these deferred tax assets relate to expenses that are included in financial reporting income, but are not yet deductible for tax reporting until paid (such as allowance for doubtful accounts, severance accruals in restructuring expenses, inventory allowances, investment provisions, and in-process R&D expenses). These deferred tax assets represent future reductions of the company's tax liability and are, therefore, classified as assets.[4] Deferred tax liabilities arise when expenses are greater for tax purposes than for financial reporting purposes, such as when companies use accelerated depreciation for tax purposes and straight-line for financial reporting.

EXHIBIT 4.6 ■ Deferred Taxes Footnote for Cisco

($ millions)	July 26, 2003
Assets	
Allowance for doubtful accounts and returns	$ 228
Sales-type and direct-financing leases	297
Loan reserves	123
Inventory allowances and capitalization	247
Investment provisions	654
In-process R&D, goodwill, and purchased intangible assets	608
Deferred revenue	899
Credits and net operating loss carryforwards	261
Other	509
Total deferred tax assets	3,826
Liabilities	
Purchased intangible assets	(233)
Unrealized gains on investments	(142)
Total deferred tax liabilities	(375)
Total	$3,451

---

[4]Companies are also required to establish a **deferred tax valuation allowance** for deferred tax assets when the future realization of their benefits is uncertain. The effect on financial statements is to reduce reported assets, increase tax expense, and reduce equity. These effects are reversed if the allowance is reversed in the future when realization of these tax benefits becomes more likely. Cisco established such an allowance in 2000, which was then reversed in 2001 when it determined that the realization of the tax benefits was more certain. The effect of a change (increase or decrease) in the deferred tax valuation allowance on net income is dollar-for-dollar and is, therefore, important for analysis of changes in profitability as this source of the change, although operating, is transitory.

Accounting standards require a company to first compute its tax liability (per its tax return), then to compute any changes in deferred tax liabilities and assets, and finally to compute tax expense reported in the income statement (as a residual figure). Tax expense is, thus, not computed as pretax income multiplied by the company's tax rate as you might first have expected. Instead, tax expense is computed as follows:

Tax Expense = Taxes Paid ± Changes in Deferred Tax Assets and Liabilities

Analysis of deferred taxes can yield useful insights. Generally, income is not taxable until received. Thus, revenue accruals (such as accounts receivable) increase deferred tax liabilities as GAAP income exceeds taxable income (similar to the effect of using straight-line depreciation for financial reporting purposes and accelerated depreciation for tax returns). An increase in deferred tax liabilities indicates that a company is reporting higher GAAP income relative to taxable income.

The difference between reported corporate profits and taxable income increased substantially in the late 1990s, just prior to the stock market decline and the huge asset write-offs that ensued. *CFO Magazine* (November 2002) implies that such differences are important for analysis and must be monitored:

> Fueling the sense that something [was] amiss [was] the growing gap between the two sets of numbers. In 1992, there was no significant difference between pretax book income and taxable net income . . . By 1996, according to IRS data, a $92.5 billion gap had appeared. By 1998 [prior to the market decline], the gap was $159 billion—a fourth of the total taxable income reported . . . If people had seen numbers showing very significant differences between book numbers for trading and tax numbers, they would have wondered if those [income] numbers were completely real.

Although an increase in deferred tax liabilities can legitimately result, for example, from an increase in depreciable assets and the use of accelerated depreciation for tax purposes, we must be aware of the possibility that such is the result of improper revenue recognition as that company may not be reporting those revenues to tax authorities.

■ MID-MODULE REVIEW ■

Following are three footnotes taken from the 2005 annual report of Nissim, Inc.

Note 5. Stock-based compensation
We account for stock-based employee compensation based on the difference, if any, on the date of grant, between the fair value of our stock and the exercise price. Had we elected to recognize the fair value of option grants as an operating expense, our reported net income would have been reduced, as follows:

(in millions)	2005
Net income, as reported	$131
Add: Amortization of stock-based compensation expense using intrinsic value method	14
Less: Total stock-based compensation expense using fair value method, net of tax	(173)
Pro forma net income (loss)	$ (28)

Note 9. Income Taxes
Components of the provision for income taxes for the year ended March 31 follow:

(in millions)	2005
Current provision	
Domestic	$21
Foreign	10
Deferred provision (credit)	
Domestic	(3)
Foreign	1
	$29

Note 14. Foreign Currency Translation

Components of the balance in the foreign currency translation account for the year ended March 31 follow:

(in millions)	2005
Balance, beginning of year	$ 7
Foreign currency translation	(10)
Net loss on derivative instruments—net of tax	2
Balance, end of year	$ (1)

Required

1. Describe the impact of Nissim's accounting for its employee stock options expense on the analysis and interpretation of its performance.
2. (*a*) What is the amount of income tax expense reported on its income statement? (*b*) How much of its income tax expense is payable in cash? (*c*) Assume that its deferred tax liability decreased. Identify an example that could account for such a change.
3. (*a*) What is the foreign currency translation adjustment at the start of fiscal 2005? (*b*) What is the net increase or decrease in the foreign currency translation adjustment for 2005? (*c*) Explain the change in (*b*) within the context of the $US relative to foreign currencies.

Solution

1. Nissim accounts for its employee stock options using a method (intrinsic value) that does not recognize the cost of the options as an expense in the income statement, but instead, footnotes those effects. Nissim's income would have been reduced by $159 million (from $131 million to $(28) million). This is a marked shift downward. Would the reporting of stock option expense in the income statement alter one's analysis and interpretation? Many believe that footnotes are not thoroughly scrutinized and their impacts not fully reflected in most analyses. In that case, such reporting of these expenses in income statements could lower perceptions and stock prices of companies like Nissim.
2. (*a*) $29 million; (*b*) $31 million, computed as $21 million in domestic taxes plus $10 million in foreign taxes; (*c*) Deferred tax liabilities decline when taxable income is more than GAAP income. This can arise when older plant assets are being used because depreciation methods for tax purposes usually yield lower expense in the later years of an asset life vis-à-vis depreciation methods for financial reporting.
3. (*a*) $7 million. (*b*) There is a decrease of $8 million in the cumulative translation adjustment during 2005. (*c*) One cause could be the strengthening of the $US vis-à-vis the foreign currencies in which Nissim operates.

■ TRANSITORY INCOME COMPONENTS

The prior section focused on several operating components of income. This section focuses on another aspect of income components—that of transitory versus core. Estimation of company value involves forecasts of income and cash flows. Such forecasts are better when we can identify any transitory effects in income and cash flows and then eliminate them from projections. Simply put, our goal is to identify the *core* earnings and cash flows of a company. Core earnings and cash flows are more *persistent* and, therefore, are more useful in estimating company value.

Accounting standards attempt to distinguish some transitory income components apart from "income from continuing operations." The transitory components GAAP identifies are discontinued operations, extraordinary items, and changes in accounting principles (the latter will likely disappear under a proposed new standard). This section describes those components and considers their analysis implications. This section also considers additional transitory components, including gains and losses on asset sales, restructuring costs, and goodwill charge-offs.

Discontinued Operations

Discontinued operations refer to any separately identifiable business unit that the company sells or intends to sell. The income or loss of the discontinued operations (net of tax), and the after-tax gain or loss on sale of the unit, are reported in the income statement below income from continuing operations. The segregation of discontinued operations means that its revenues and expenses are *not* reported with revenues and expenses from continuing operations.

To illustrate, assume that Cisco's reported results appeared as follows:

	Continuing Operations	Discontinued Operations	Total
Revenues	$10,000	$3,000	$13,000
Expenses	7,000	2,000	9,000
Pretax income	3,000	1,000	4,000
Tax expense (40%)	1,200	400	1,600
Net income	$ 1,800	$ 600	$ 2,400

The reported income statement would then appear as follows—notice the separate disclosure for discontinued operations shown in bold.

Revenues	$10,000
Expenses	7,000
Pretax income	3,000
Tax expense (40%)	1,200
Income from continuing operations	1,800
Income from discontinued operations, net	600
Net earnings	$ 2,400

Revenues and expenses reflect those of the continuing operations only, and the (persistent) income from continuing operations is reported net of its related tax expense. Results from the (transitory) discontinued operations are collapsed into one line item and reported separately net of its own tax (this includes any gain or loss from sale of the discontinued unit's net assets). The net income figure is unchanged by this presentation.

Importantly, results of the discontinued operations are segregated from those of continuing operations. This presentation facilitates the prediction of results from the (persistent) continuing operations. The segregation of discontinued operations is made in the current year *and* for the two prior years' comparative results reported in the income statement.

Best Buy's 2004 fiscal-year income statement presentation of discontinued operations is in Exhibit 4.7—see boldface numbers. Its income statement reflects the 2004 net loss from its discontinued operations in Musicland up to the point of its sale plus the loss from sale of Musicland's net assets.

EXHIBIT 4.7 ■ Income Statement with Discontinued Operations for Best Buy

($ millions)	2004
Revenue	$24,547
Cost of goods sold	18,350
Gross profit	6,197
Selling, general and administrative expenses	4,893
Operating income	1,304
Net interest (expense) income	(8)
Earnings from continuing operations before income tax expense	1,296
Income tax expense	496
Earnings from continuing operations	800
Loss from discontinued operations, net of $17 tax	**(29)**
Loss on disposal of discontinued operations, net of $0 tax	**(66)**
Net earnings	$ 705

Best Buy also separately identifies the assets and liabilities of its discontinued operations on its 2004 fiscal year-end balance sheet in Exhibit 4.8—see the boldface numbers. Notice that since Best Buy's discontinued operations in Musicland were sold during fiscal year 2004, its net assets in Musicland are no longer a component of its fiscal year-end 2004 balance sheet.

EXHIBIT 4.8 ■ Balance Sheet with Discontinued Operations for Best Buy

($ millions)	February 28, 2004	March 1, 2003
Assets		
Current assets		
Cash and cash equivalents	$2,600	$1,914
Receivables	343	312
Merchandise inventories	2,607	2,077
Other current assets	174	198
Current assets of discontinued operations	—	**397**
Total current assets	5,724	4,898
Property and equipment		
Land and buildings	484	208
Leasehold improvements	861	719
Fixtures and equipment	2,151	2,108
Property under master and capital lease	78	54
	3,574	3,089
Less accumulated depreciation and amortization	1,330	1,027
Net property and equipment	2,244	2,062
Goodwill, net	477	429
Intangible assets	37	33
Other assets	170	115
Noncurrent assets of discontinued operations	—	**157**
Total assets	$8,652	$7,694
Liabilities and Shareholders' Equity		
Current liabilities		
Accounts payable	$2,535	$2,195
Unredeemed gift card liabilities	300	222
Accrued compensation and related expenses	269	174
Accrued liabilities	649	538
Accrued income taxes	380	374
Current portion of long-term debt	368	1
Current liabilities of discontinued operations	—	**320**
Total current liabilities	4,501	3,824
Long-term liabilities	247	287
Long-term debt	482	828
Noncurrent liabilities of discontinued operations	—	**25**
Shareholders' equity		
Common stock, $.10 par value: Authorized—1 billion shares; Issued and outstanding—324,648,000 and 321,966,000 shares, respectively	32	32
Additional paid-in capital	836	778
Retained earnings	2,468	1,893
Accumulated other comprehensive income	86	27
Total shareholders' equity	3,422	2,730
Total liabilities and shareholders' equity	$8,652	$7,694

Extraordinary Items

Extraordinary items refer to transitory events that are both unusual *and* infrequent. Their effects are segregated and reported separately in income statements following income from continuing operations. Management makes the determination of whether an event is unusual and infrequent (with auditor approval) for reporting purposes. Further, management often has incentives to classify unfavorable items as extraordinary, which means they are reported separately from continuing operation (*below-the-line*). These incentives derive from investors who tend to focus more on items included in income from continuing operations and less on those items not included in continuing operations.

GAAP provides the following guidance in determining whether or not an item is extraordinary:

- *Unusual nature.* The underlying event or transaction must possess a high degree of abnormality and be clearly unrelated to, or only incidentally related to, the ordinary activities of the entity, taking into account the entity's operating environment.
- *Infrequency of occurrence.* The underlying event or transaction must be of a type that would not reasonably be expected to recur in the foreseeable future, taking into account the entity's operating environment.

The following items are generally *excluded* from extraordinary items:

- Write-down or write-off of assets
- Foreign currency gains and losses
- Gains and losses from disposal of specific assets or business segment
- Effects of a strike
- Accrual adjustments related to long-term contracts
- Costs of defense against a takeover
- Costs incurred as a result of the September 11, 2001, events

Extraordinary items are reported separately (net of tax) and below income from continuing operations on the income statement.[5]

Changes in Accounting Principle

A **change in accounting principle** results from adoption of a generally accepted accounting principle different from the one previously used for reporting purposes. An example of such a change would be the adoption of a different method of depreciating plant and equipment assets from the method previously used (there are several depreciation methods acceptable under GAAP).

Any change in principle must be justified as preferable from a financial reporting perspective. The usual claim is that its adoption would yield higher quality financial statements. It is unacceptable to change an accounting principle simply because it would have a desirable affect on reported income or tax liabilities.

Accounting for a change in accounting principle involves four steps:

1. Financial statements issued prior to the current period are *not* restated to reflect the change.
2. The cumulative effect of changing to a new accounting principle is included in net income for the period of change. This means that the company is required to compute net income that would have been reported using the new principle for *all* prior periods affected and to compare that cumulative income with the cumulative income previously reported. The difference between these two income figures is reported (net of tax) in the current period of change.
3. The income effect of (and reason for) adopting the new principle is disclosed in the notes to the statements so that readers are informed of the change *and* the income effect of the change.
4. Income computed on a pro forma basis is shown on the face of the income statement for all prior periods reported as if the newly adopted principle had been applied in those periods.

Sometimes the change to a new accounting principle is mandated by the FASB. In these instances the cumulative effect (step 2) outlined above is not used. Instead, the income statements of prior periods are restated and reported as if the new accounting principle were in effect all along. (The FASB has proposed a new standard that would not recognize the cumulative effect of changes in accounting principles. Under

---

[5]Until recently, the majority of extraordinary items were gains and losses on debt retirement. To explain, understand that debt is accounted for at historical cost, just like the accounting for equipment. The *market price* of debt, however, is determined by fluctuations in yield and interest rates. As a result, if a company retires (pays off) its debt before maturity, the purchase price often differs from the debt amount reported on the balance sheet, resulting in gains and losses on retirement. These gains and losses were formerly treated as extraordinary. Following passage of *SFAS 145,* these gains and losses are no longer automatically treated as extraordinary, but instead must meet the usual tests of unusual and infrequent to be designated as extraordinary.

the proposed standard, a change in principle is applied retrospectively to all prior periods for which the effects of the change can be estimated. This standard is proposed to take effect in 2005 or 2006.)

The following footnote from **DuPont**'s 10-K explains its mandated change in accounting principle—the write-down of goodwill in connection with its adoption of *SFAS 142*:

> On January 1, 2002, the company adopted *SFAS No. 142,* "Goodwill and Other Intangible Assets," which requires that goodwill and indefinite-lived intangible assets no longer be amortized. In addition, an initial impairment test of goodwill and indefinite-lived intangible assets as of January 1, 2002, needed to be performed. Thereafter, impairment tests must be performed annually or more frequently if there are triggering events. If the initial test resulted in impairment, an adjustment was to be recorded in net income as a cumulative effect of a change in accounting principle (net of tax). Impairment losses after the initial adoption impairment are to be recorded as part of income from continuing operations.
>
> During the second quarter of 2002, the company completed its initial review of goodwill and recorded a cumulative effect of a change in accounting principle charge of $2,944, effective January 1, 2002, to reduce the carrying value of its goodwill.

A **change in an accounting estimate** is unlike a change in accounting principle. For example, a change from one depreciation method to another is a change in accounting principle. However, if a company continues to use the same depreciation method, but changes the period of time (useful life) over which it depreciates its assets, this is a change in accounting estimate. A change in accounting estimate is applied *prospectively* (current and future periods) from the date of change. No cumulative effect adjustment or restatement of prior periods' income statements are made.

Gains and Losses on Asset Sales

Assets are recorded at cost when purchased. Subsequently, most assets are reported at adjusted historical cost (acquisition cost less any depreciation, amortization, or depletion), even if they appreciate in value. An asset is written down from this book (carrying) value only if a permanent decline in value occurs. However, when an asset is sold, the company recognizes a gain or loss equal to the difference between the selling price and its book value. This gain or loss is computed as follows:

> **Gain or Loss on Asset Sale = Asset Sale Proceeds − Asset Book Value**

To illustrate, assume that Cisco sells a machine for $10,000 when its book value is $8,000, where the latter is computed from its acquisition cost of $12,000 less accumulated depreciation of $4,000. Cisco would report a gain of $2,000 ($10,000 − $8,000). This gain is reported in income from continuing operations (usually included among SG&A expense as an offset to other expense accounts), and it serves to increase reported income.

To generalize, all gains and losses from asset sales are reported in income. Further, gains and losses are reported from sales of both short-term and long-term assets. Companies can even sell assets such as accounts receivable to raise cash, which yield reported gains and losses. Companies sometimes sell investments or entire subsidiaries, which also yield reported gains and losses. Each of these gains and losses is computed in the same manner: Asset Sale Proceeds − Asset Book Value. (Gains and losses are also reported from sales of inventories, but as part of the cost of goods sold computation—that is, sales of goods and services *less* cost of goods (inventories) sold *equals* gross profit.)

$\$$
Cash Effect

Companies usually report gains and losses from asset sales as part of income from continuing operations. However, such gains and losses are transitory in that such sales are not expected to recur. Consequently, our analysis should exclude them from computation of core (persistent) income.

The general challenge for our analysis is to identify such transitory gains and losses. Accounting standards require that companies need only disclose *material* gains and losses.[6] Material items are normally separately disclosed, either as a line item in the income statement or in the notes. However, even when

---

[6]**Materiality** is an accounting term that means it would make a difference to those who rely on financial statements for business decisions. Investors, for example, might find an item material if it is large enough to change their opinion about the desirability of a company as an investment prospect. This *materiality* judgment is in the eye of the beholder, and this subjectivity makes materiality an elusive concept.

material, some companies include gains on asset sales in SG&A expenses as an offset, thereby reducing SG&A expenses and making the company look more efficient than it is.[7]

Restructuring Costs

Restructuring costs are a substantial expense item in many companies' income statements. They tend to be large in magnitude (deemed material) and, as a result, GAAP requires enhanced disclosure, either as a separate line item in the income statement or as a footnote. These costs are typically transitory and require that we reclassify these costs to a transitory category for analysis purposes when companies include them in income from continuing operations. The reporting of restructuring costs in the income statement typically consists of two parts:

1. Employee severance costs
2. Asset write-downs

The first part, **employee severance costs**, represent accrued (estimated) costs for termination of employees as part of a restructuring program. By accruing, we mean:

- Estimating total costs of terminating or relocating selected employees. Costs might include severance pay (typically a number of weeks of pay based on how long the employee has worked for the company), outplacement costs, and relocation or retraining costs for those employees remaining.
- Reporting *total* estimated costs as an expense (and a liability) in the period when those costs are estimated and the restructuring program announced. Subsequent payments reduce this liability and, as a result, do not usually yield any major future expenses.

The second part of restructuring costs is **asset write-downs**, also called *write-offs* or *charge-offs*. Restructuring activities usually involve closure or relocation of manufacturing or administrative facilities. This can require write-down of long-term assets (such as plant assets), write-down of inventories that are no longer salable at current carrying costs, and write-down of goodwill (explained in the next section). Recall that asset cost is first recorded on the balance sheet and is subsequently transferred from the balance sheet to the income statement as expense when the asset is used. The write-down of an asset accelerates this process for a portion, or all, of the asset cost. No cash flow effects occur because of a write-down other than some potential tax benefits.

$ **Cash Effect**

The financial statement effects of restructuring charges can be enormous. We must remember that management determines the amount of restructuring costs and when to recognize them. As such, it is not uncommon for a company to time recognition of restructuring costs in a period when its income is already depressed. This behavior is referred to as a **big bath**.

RESEARCH INSIGHT   Restructuring Costs and Managerial Incentives

Research has investigated the circumstances and effects of restructuring costs. Some research finds that stock prices increase upon announcement of a restructuring as if the market appreciates the company's candor. Research also finds that many companies that reduce income through restructuring costs later reverse those costs, resulting in a substantial income boost for the period of reversal. These reversals often occur when their absence would have yielded an earnings decline. Whether or not the market responds favorably to trimming the fat or simply disregards such transitory items as uninformative, managers have incentives to exclude such income-decreasing items from operating income. These incentives are contractually-based, extending from debt covenants and restrictions to managerial bonuses.

The FASB has tightened rules relating to restructuring costs in an effort to mitigate abuses. For example, a company is required to have a formal restructuring plan that is approved by its board of directors before any restructuring charges are reported. Also, a company must identify the relevant employees and

---

[7]To illustrate, IBM sold its Global Network to AT&T, the gain for which was included in (and as an offset to) its 1999 SG&A expenses. By including this gain as part of SG&A expense, its quarterly expenses were reduced by 13.7% from the previous year's quarter and made IBM appear more efficient that it was. Analysis reveals that without this gain, IBM's quarterly SG&A expenses actually *increased* by 0.7% over the prior year's quarter.

notify them of its plan. In each subsequent year, the company must disclose in its footnotes the original amount of the liability (accrual), how much of that liability is settled in the current period (such as employee payments), how much of the original liability has been reversed because of cost overestimation, any new accruals for unforeseen costs, and the current balance of the liability.

BUSINESS INSIGHT Cisco's Restructuring

Cisco's restructuring activity in 2001 included a $397 million charge for workforce reduction (mainly severance and benefit payments) and a $484 million charge for consolidation of facilities, including the write-down of plant assets and lease termination payments to landlords. The status of these charges and the ensuing two years' results are shown in the following footnote to Cisco's 2003 annual report:

($ millions)	Workforce Reduction	Consolidation of Excess Facilities and Other Charges
Initial charge in the third quarter of fiscal 2001	$ 397	$ 484
Noncash charges	(71)	(141)
Cash payments	(265)	(18)
Balance at July 28, 2001	61	325
Adjustments	(35)	128
Cash payments	(26)	(131)
Balance at July 27, 2002	—	322
Adjustments	—	45
Cash payments	—	(72)
Balance at July 26, 2003	$ —	$ 295

For its $397 million initial workforce reduction charge, $265 million cash was paid to employees and $71 million was noncash charges, leaving a $61 million first-year balance. In the second year, $26 million cash was paid to employees and the remaining $35 million was eliminated as an adjustment. Cisco reports that this $35 million was transferred from the workforce reduction account to the consolidation of facilities account.

For the $484 million initial accrual on facilities consolidation, $18 million was paid in cash and $141 million was noncash charges, leaving a $325 million first-year balance. In the second year, the accrual was increased by $128 million, including the $35 million reclassification discussed above and a further $93 million "due to changes in real estate market conditions." This additional $93 million impacted its 2002 income. The second-year's accrual balance was $322 million after a reduction of $131 million for cash payments. In fiscal 2003, continued deterioration of the real estate market yielded a further accrual of $45 million, which also affected 2003 income. Cisco ended 2003 with a balance of $295 million after cash payments of $72 million.

In sum, of the total restructuring charges relating to workforce reduction and consolidation of facilities, $881 million ($397 million + $484 million) affected 2001 income, $93 million ($128 million − $35 million) affected 2002 income, and $45 million affected 2003 income.

MANAGERIAL DECISION You Are the Financial Analyst

You are analyzing the 10-K of a company that has reported a large restructuring cost, involving both employee severance and asset write-downs, in its income statement. How do you interpret and treat this cost in your analysis of its current and future period profitability? [Answer, p. 4-28]

Goodwill Write-Down

Goodwill is the excess of the purchase price paid for a company over the fair market value of its net assets (assets less liabilities assumed in the acquisition). The goodwill asset is recorded at its acquisition (historical) cost and its carrying amount on the balance sheet is not reduced unless it is deemed to be *impaired*, at which time it is written down to this new value or written off entirely.

Goodwill write-down, also called goodwill write-off or charge-off, refers to the immediate transfer of some or all of a company's goodwill (asset) book value from the balance sheet to the income statement as expense. The asset book value is immediately reduced and a corresponding expense is reported that often yields a net loss. Like the write-down of tangible assets, the write-down of goodwill is a *discretionary expense* whose amount and timing are largely determined by management (with auditor acceptance).

It is commonplace to see goodwill write-downs for unsuccessful acquisitions, particularly those from the acquisition boom of the late 1990s. Goodwill write-downs usually represent material amounts. For example, AOL Time-Warner wrote off $54 billion of goodwill in the second quarter of 2002, which arose from the $106 billion merger of AOL and Time-Warner. This write-off exceeded the *total revenues* of 483 of the Fortune 500 companies (*Fortune*, 2002). Goodwill write-downs are usually transitory, but are typically reported by companies in income from continuing operations. For analysis purposes we normally classify them as operating and transitory, unless they are recurring.

The following footnote from Cisco Systems's 2001 annual report discloses its $289 million goodwill (and purchased intangibles) write-down:

> Due to the decline in current business conditions, the Company restructured certain of its businesses and realigned resources to focus on profit contribution, high-growth markets, and core opportunities. As a result, the Company recorded a charge of $289 million related to the impairment of goodwill and purchased intangible assets, measured as the amount by which the carrying amount exceeded the present value of the estimated future cash flows for goodwill and purchased intangible assets, as follows (in millions):

Acquired Company	Amount Impaired
Monterey Networks, Inc.	$108
HyNEX, Ltd.	79
Clarity Wireless, Inc. (Broadband Customer Premises Equipment)	53
Other	49
Total	$289

Goodwill is *impaired* when the market value of the acquired business is less than its book value on the balance sheet. If that occurs, goodwill is written down to an imputed value (described in Module 6). It is important to remember that management determines whether goodwill has become impaired and, if so, by what amount. The timing and magnitude of the impairment charge is, therefore, subject to management influence.

BUSINESS INSIGHT   Pro Forma Income and Managerial Motives

Income from continuing operations per GAAP, once a key measure of company performance, is often supplemented or even supplanted by pro forma income in company financial statements and press releases. **Pro forma income** begins with the GAAP income from continuing operations (that excludes discontinued operations, extraordinary items, and changes in accounting principle), and then excludes other transitory items (most notably, restructuring charges), and some additional items such as expenses arising from acquisitions (goodwill amortization and other acquisition costs), compensation expense in the form of stock options, and research and development expenditures.

The purported motive of pro forma income is to eliminate transitory items so as to enhance year-to-year comparability. Although this might be justified on the basis that the resulting income has greater predictive ability, important information is lost in the process. Accounting is beneficial in reporting how effective management has been in its stewardship of invested capital. Asset write-downs, liability accruals, and other charges that are eliminated in the process often reflect outcomes of poor management decisions. Our analysis must not blindly eliminate information contained in nonrecurring and noncore items by focusing solely on pro forma income.

Critics of pro forma income argue that the items excluded by managers from GAAP income are inconsistent across companies and time. They contend that a major motive for pro forma income is to mislead stakeholders. Legendary investor Warren Buffet puts pro forma in context (Berkshire Hathaway, Annual Report): "When companies or investment professionals use terms such as 'EBITDA' and 'pro forma,' they want you to unthinkingly accept concepts that are dangerously flawed."

■ SUMMARY OF CORE, TRANSITORY, OPERATING, AND NONOPERATING DISTINCTIONS

We conclude this module with a summary of our analysis of the income statement utilizing the core versus transitory and operating versus nonoperating dimensions. Exhibit 4.9 presents common income statement items categorized along these dimensions.

EXHIBIT 4.9 ■ Income Items Categorized by Core versus Transitory and Operating versus Nonoperating

	Core	Transitory
Operating	• Revenues • Cost of goods sold • Selling, general and administrative expense • Footnoted employee stock option expense • Severance cost portion of pension expense • Gains and losses from hedging of foreign currencies and commodities	• Restructuring costs (unless recurring) • Asset write-downs • Goodwill impairment expense • Gains and losses from asset sales • Merger and acquisition expense, including purchased research and development expense* • Litigation settlements and insurance proceeds • Extraordinary items tied to operations
Nonoperating	• Interest revenue and expense • Dividend revenue • Interest, expected return, and amortization portions of pension expense • Unrealized gains and losses from income on investments categorized as trading securities • Gains and losses from hedging related to interest costs	• Gains and losses on sales of investments, excluding "trading securities" • Income and losses on discontinued operations and gains and losses on disposal of discontinued operations • Extraordinary items not tied to operations (gains and losses on early debt retirement)

*Purchased (in-process) R&D relates to R&D projects acquired in conjunction with the acquisition of a company. Under GAAP, the cost of these projects must be expensed immediately like other R&D costs. We discuss this topic further in Module 6.

Core operating components include sales, cost of goods sold, and the usual selling, general, and administrative expenses. It also includes footnoted employee stock option expenses (at least until they are, if ever, reported in the income statement) as they are compensation expenses. The severance cost portion of pension expense is also included in core operating activities (both interest cost and expected return offset portions of pension expense included as a core nonoperating item). The severance portion of pension expense derives from the increase in pension obligation due to employees working another year, which is viewed as compensation expense (covered in Module 9). Gains and losses deriving from foreign currency translation and commodity hedges are included as they relate to management of risks as part of operations (gains and losses on interest rate hedges and swaps are included in core nonoperating income).

Core nonoperating components include interest revenue and expense, and dividend revenue. Also included are the interest cost and expected return portions of pension expense as well as gains and losses from hedging related to interest costs. The interest and expected return portions of pension expense relate to the financing of the pension obligation and the returns on pension investments, which are considered nonoperating. Unrealized gains and losses from trading securities (reported in income) and gains and losses from hedging related to mitigation of interest rate risk are both viewed as nonoperating.

Transitory operating components include restructuring costs (assuming nonrecurring), goodwill (and other impaired asset) write-downs, and gains and losses from asset sales. Determining transitory (nonrecurring) components from those that are not requires judgment. For example, merger and acquisition expense, including in-process R&D expense, are considered transitory unless acquisitions are regular, and are considered operating unless the acquisition is for nonstrategic reasons. Extraordinary items are transitory, but are operating or nonoperating depending on their source.

Transitory nonoperating components include gains and losses on sales of investments, and any income, gains, and losses from discontinued operations and their disposal (discontinued operations are not part of continuing operations). Extraordinary gains and losses from early retirement of debt is a transitory nonoperating item.[8]

---

[8]Gains and losses on early debt retirement are not an extraordinary item under current GAAP unless they meet the tests of both unusual and infrequent. Instead, they are reported in income from continuing operations. Regardless, these gains and losses are regarded as both transitory (unless recurring) and nonoperating.

We conclude this section with Cisco's 2003 income statement which follows:

Year Ended ($ millions)	July 26, 2003
Net sales	
Product	$15,565
Service	3,313
Total net sales	18,878
Cost of sales	
Product	4,594
Service	1,051
Total cost of sales	5,645
Gross margin	13,233
Operating expenses	
Research and development	3,135
Sales and marketing	4,116
General and administrative	702
Amortization of purchased intangible assets	394
In-process research and development	4
Total operating expenses	8,351
Operating income (loss)	4,882
Interest income	660
Other income (loss), net	(529)
Interest and other income (loss), net	131
Income (loss) before provision for income taxes	5,013
Provision for income taxes	1,435
Net income (loss)	$ 3,578

Cisco's income statement components are generally viewed as operating with the exception of its $660 million interest income and $(529) million in other income (loss). The footnotes to Cisco's 10-K reveal that other income (loss) relates primarily to its investments that are deemed impaired. Cisco's sole transitory item is its $4 million in-process R&D expense as this is normally nonrecurring for Cisco. Amortization expense is the regular recurring cost allocation of intangible assets (similar to depreciation for tangible assets) and is not transitory.[9]

RESEARCH INSIGHT   Pro Forma Income

Transitory items in income such as discontinued operations, restructuring charges, extraordinary items, and the effects of changes in accounting principle make it difficult for investors to determine what portion of income is sustainable into the future. The past decade has seen more companies reporting pro forma income, which purportedly exclude the effects of nonrecurring or noncash items that companies feels are unimportant for valuation purposes. Research, however, provides no evidence that more exclusions via pro forma income leads to more predictable future cash flows. More important, investors appear to be misled by the exclusions at the time of the pro forma income release. Research also finds that companies issuing pro forma income are more likely to be young companies concentrated in technology and business services. Too often, these companies are characterized by below-average sales and income when they choose to report pro forma income. Evidence also shows that the pro forma income can exceed GAAP income by as much as 20 percent.

---

[9]**Standard & Poor's** (S&P) is a major player in the analyst community, providing investment information to equity investors and bond ratings to fixed-income investors. S&P has its own definition of "core income," which is similar to the one here: including items such as employee stock options expense and gains and losses from hedging of foreign currencies and commodities, and excluding items such as goodwill write-downs, gains and losses from asset sales, merger and acquisition costs, and litigation expenses and insurance proceeds.

MODULE-END REVIEW ■

Following is the 2005 income statement reported by Aboody, Inc.

(in millions, except per share amounts)	2005
Revenues	$973
Cost of sales	425
Selling, general and administrative expenses	82
Purchased in-process research and development charges	15
Loss on sale of subsidiary	33
Merger-related costs	11
Restructuring costs	91
Equity in earnings of unconsolidated affiliates	9
Other costs (revenues)—net	(27)
Income from continuing operations before taxes and other items	334
Provision for income taxes	120
Minority interests' share of income	4
Income from continuing operations	210
Discontinued operations	
Income from operations of discontinued business—net of tax	22
Gain on sale of discontinued business—net of tax	8
Discontinued operations—net of tax	30
Net income	$240

Required

a. Identify the components in its income statement that are likely transitory.
b. Compute a net income figure absent the transitory components identified in (a).

Solution

a. The following five income components of Aboody are usually identified as transitory by analysts:
  • *Purchased in-process research and development charges.* GAAP requires that research and development projects purchased in an acquisition of a company be written off immediately if they have not reached technological feasibility when acquired. This is a one-time write-off and is properly characterized as transitory.
  • *Loss on sale of subsidiary.* This item rests in the category of gains and losses on asset sales. This is considered a one-time loss and is characterized as transitory.
  • *Merger-related costs.* These are one-time (transitory) costs incurred in connection with the acquisition of another company.
  • *Restructuring costs.* These are one-time (transitory) costs as part of a restructuring plan.
  • *Discontinued operations.* This item reflects income earned in connection with a business unit that was sold. The gain on sale is transitory as it is a one-time occurrence. The income from operations was not a past transitory item as it regularly occurred, but it is properly identified as transitory this period because it will not persist into the future.
b. Net income absent the transitory items identified in part (a) is computed as follows ($ millions):
  $240 + [($15 + $33 + $11 + $91) \times (1 - \{120/334\})] - $30 = \underline{$306}$

The *adjusted* income number of $306 million is markedly higher ($66 million) from the reported net income of $240 million. This case emphasizes the importance of adjusting income for any transitory items when analyzing current performance and forecasting future performance. (The ratio $120/$334 is the effective tax rate. Items reported "net of tax" do not require adjustment for tax.)

APPENDIX 4A

Earnings Per Share

The income statement reports earnings per share (EPS) numbers. At least one, and potentially two, EPS figures are reported: basic and diluted. The difference between the two measures follows:

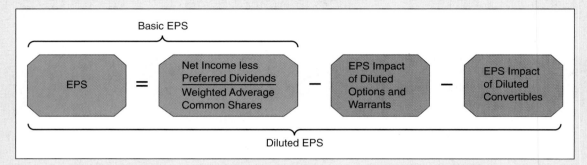

Basic EPS is computed as: (Net income − Dividends on preferred stock)/Weighted average of common shares outstanding for the year. The subtraction of preferred stock dividends yields the income per common share available for dividend payments to common shareholders.

Computation of **diluted EPS** reflects the added shares to be issued if all stock options and convertible securities had been exercised at the beginning of the year. To illustrate, assume a company has outstanding employee stock options for 10,000 shares. To compute diluted EPS, we assume that the options are exercised at the beginning of the year and, thus, increase the denominator by 10,000 shares. Notice that diluted EPS never exceeds basic EPS.[10]

The earnings per share section of Cisco's income statement is in Exhibit 4A.1. Notice that diluted EPS never exceeds basic EPS. Given the near identical results for basic and diluted EPS, we know that Cisco has few dilutive securities.[11]

EXHIBIT 4A.1 ■ Earnings per Share Section of Cisco's Income Statement

($ millions, except per share data)	July 26, 2003	July 27, 2002
Net sales	$18,878	$18,915
Net income (loss)	3,578	1,893
Net income (loss) per share—basic	0.50	0.26
Net income (loss) per share—diluted	0.50	0.25
Shares used in per-share calculation—basic	7,124	7,301
Shares used in per-share calculation—diluted	7,223	7,447

EPS figures are often used as a method of comparing operating results for companies of different sizes under the assumption that the number of shares outstanding is proportional to the income level (that is, a company twice the size of another will report double the income and will have double the common shares outstanding, leaving EPS approximately equal for the two companies). This assumption is erroneous. Management controls the number of common shares outstanding. Different companies also have different philosophies regarding share issuance and repurchase. For

---

[10]Companies can have a variety of convertible securities, like convertible bonds, that are potentially converted into common stock. To compute diluted EPS for convertible bonds, the company would increase the denominator by the number of shares that would be issued to the holders and eliminate the after-tax interest that would have been foregone had the bonds been converted. Similar adjustments can be made for convertible preferred stock by reflecting the additional common shares outstanding and eliminating the dividends that would have been paid on the preferred stock. The increase in the number of shares for the diluted EPS computation would be reduced by the shares that could have been repurchased with the proceeds of the option exercise, thus reducing the net increase in common shares outstanding.

[11]The effects of dilutive securities are only included if they are, in fact, dilutive. If they are *antidilutive,* inclusion would actually increase EPS. As a result, they are excluded from the computation. An example of an antidilutive security is employee stock options whose exercise price is greater than the current market price. These *underwater* options are antidilutive and are therefore excluded from the EPS computation. Cisco excludes 838 million of underwater stock options from its 2003 EPS computation.

example, consider that most companies report annual EPS of less than $5, while Berkshire Hathaway reported EPS of $5,308 for 2003! This is because Berkshire Hathaway has so few common shares outstanding, not necessarily because it has stellar profits.

GUIDANCE ANSWERS

MANAGERIAL DECISION   You Are the Financial Analyst

There are two usual components to a restructuring charge: asset write-downs (such as inventories, property, plant, and goodwill) and severance costs. Write-downs occur when the cash flow generating ability of an asset declines, thus reducing its current market value below its book value reported on the balance sheet. Arguably, this decline in cash flow generating ability did not occur solely in the current year and, most likely, has developed over several periods. Delays in loss recognition, such as write-downs of assets, are not uncommon. Thus, prior period income is arguably not as high as reported, and the current period loss is not as great as is reported. Turning to severance costs, their recognition can be viewed as an investment decision by the company that is expected to increase future cash flows (through decreased wages). If this cost accrual is capitalized on the balance sheet, current period income is increased and future period income would bear the amortization of this "asset" to match against future cash flow benefits from severance. This implies that current period income is not as low as reported; however, this adjustment is not GAAP as such severance costs cannot be capitalized. Yet, we can make such an adjustment in our analysis.

Superscript ^A^ denotes assignments based on Appendix 4A.

■ DISCUSSION QUESTIONS

Q4-1. What are the criteria that guide firms in recognition of revenue? What does each of the criteria mean? How are the criteria met for a company like Abercrombie & Fitch, a clothing retailer? How are the criteria met for a construction company that builds offices under long-term contracts with developers?

Abercrombie & Fitch (ANF)

Q4-2. Why are discontinued operations reported separately from continuing operations in the income statement?

Q4-3. What are the criteria for categorizing an event as an extraordinary item? Provide an example of an event that would properly be categorized as an extraordinary item and one that would not.

Q4-4. How does the proper accounting treatment for a change in accounting *principle* differ from that for a change in accounting *estimate*?

Q4-5. What is the concept of *materiality* and why is it so important to an understanding of financial statements?

Q4-6. Identify the two typical categories of restructuring costs and their effects on the balance sheet and the income statement. Explain the concept of a *big bath* and why restructuring costs are often identified with this event.

Q4-7. What is the proper accounting treatment for research and development costs? Why are R&D costs normally not capitalized under GAAP?

Q4-8. Under what circumstances will deferred taxes likely result in a cash outflow?

Q4-9. What is the concept of *pro forma income* and why has this income measure been criticized?

■ MINI EXERCISES

M4-10. Computing Percentage-of-Completion Revenues   Bartov Corporation agreed to build a warehouse for $2,500,000. Expected (and actual) costs for the warehouse follows: 2003, $400,000; 2004, $1,000,000; and 2005, $500,000. The company completed the warehouse in 2005. Compute revenues, expenses, and income for each year 2003 through 2005 using the percentage-of-completion method.

M4-11. Assessing Revenue Recognition of Companies   Identify and explain when each of the following companies should recognize revenue.

a. The GAP: The GAP is a retailer of clothing items for all ages.

b. Merck & Company: Merck engages in the development, manufacturing, and marketing of pharmaceutical products. It sells its drugs to retailers like CVS and Walgreen.

The GAP (GPS)

Merck & Company (MRK)

John Deere
(DE)

Bank of
America (BAC)

Johnson
Controls (JCI)

BannerAD
Corporation
(BANR)

The GAP (GPS)

Abbott
Laboratories
(ABT)

Bristol-Myers
Squibb (BMY)

Merck &
Company
(MRK)

c. **John Deere**: Deere manufactures heavy equipment. It sells equipment to a network of independent distributors, who in turn sell the equipment to customers. Deere provides financing and insurance services both to distributors and customers.

d. **Bank of America**: Bank of America is a banking institution. It lends money to individuals and corporations and invests excess funds in marketable securities.

e. **Johnson Controls**: Johnson Controls manufactures products for the US Government under long-term contracts.

M4-12. Assessing Risk Exposure to Revenue Recognition   BannerAD Corporation manages a Website in which it sells products on consignment from sellers. It pays these sellers a portion of the sales price, absent its commission. Identify at least two potential revenue recognition problems relating to such sales.

M4-13. Estimating Revenue Recognition with Right of Return   The GAP offers an unconditional return policy. It normally expects 2% of sales at retail selling prices to be returned at some point prior to the expiration of the return period. Assuming that it records total sales of $5 million for the current period, how much revenue can it record for this period?

M4-14. Assessing Research and Development Expenses   Abbott Laboratories reports the following income statement (in partial form):

Year Ended December 31 ($ 000s)	2003
Net sales	$19,680,561
Cost of products sold	9,473,416
Research and development	1,733,472
Acquired in-process research and development	100,240
Selling, general and administrative	5,050,901
Total operating cost and expenses	16,358,029
Operating earnings	$ 3,322,532

a. Compute the percent of net sales that Abbott Laboratories spends on research and development (R&D). How would you assess the appropriateness of its R&D expense level?

b. Describe how accounting for R&D expenditures affects Abbott Laboratories' balance sheet and income statement.

M4-15. Interpreting Foreign Currency Translation Disclosure   Bristol-Myers Squibb (BMY) reports accumulated other comprehensive income (loss) as part of its statement of stockholders' equity as reported in the following footnote from its 10-K report:

Dollars in Millions	Foreign Currency Translation	Available for Sale Securities	Deferred Loss on Effective Hedges	Minimum Pension Liability Adjustment	Accumulated Other Comprehensive Income/(Loss)
Balance at December 31, 2002 (Restated)	$(724)	$ 1	$ (87)	$ (94)	$(904)
Other comprehensive income (loss)	233	23	(171)	(36)	49
Balance at December 31, 2003	$(491)	$24	$(258)	$(130)	$(855)

a. What effect(s) does the $233 million foreign currency translation amount have on BMY's stockholders' equity?

b. Describe the exchange rate environment ($US vis-à-vis other world currencies) that gives rise to the effect identified in part a.

M4-16. Analyzing Stock Option Expense for Income   Merck & Company reports the following footnote disclosure to its 10-K report:

The effect on net income and earnings per common share if the Company had applied the fair value method for recognizing employee stock-based compensation is as follows:

Years Ended December 31 ($ millions)	2003	2002	2001
Net income, as reported	$6,830.9	$7,149.5	$7,281.8
Compensation expense, net of tax			
Reported	4.9	1.2	(0.1)
Fair value method	(559.4)	(487.9)	(400.9)
Pro forma net income	$6,276.4	$6,662.8	$6,980.8

a. How much expense is currently reported in Merck's income statement relating to its stock options?

b. How much expense would have been reported had Merck valued its employee stock options using the fair value method? What woud have been the effect on net income if this alternative method had been applied?

c. Is the expense in (b) a cash expense? How would your answer change, if at all, if you knew that Merck repurchases shares of its stock in the open market to offset the dilutive effect of shares issued when these stock options are exercised?

M4-17.[A] **Defining and Computing Earnings per Share**   3M Company reports the following basic and diluted earnings per share in its 2002 10-K report (shares in million). (a) Describe the accounting definitions for basic and diluted earnings per share. (b) Identify the 3M numbers that make up both EPS computations.

Weighted average common shares outstanding—basic	390.0
Earnings per share—basic	$5.06
Weighted average common shares outstanding—diluted	395.5
Earnings per share—diluted	$4.99

■ EXERCISES

E4-18.   **Assessing Revenue Recognition Timing**   Discuss and justify when each of the following businesses should recognize revenues:

a. A clothing retailer like The Limited.

b. A contractor like Boeing Corporation that performs work under long-term government contracts.

c. A grocery store like Albertsons.

d. A producer of television shows like MTV that syndicates its content to television stations.

e. A residential real estate developer who constructs only speculative houses and later sells these houses to buyers.

f. A banking institution like Bank of America that lends money for home mortgages.

g. A manufacturer like Harley-Davidson.

h. A publisher of magazines such as Time-Warner.

E4-19.   **Assessing Revenue Recognition Timing and Income Measurement**   Discuss and justify when each of the following businesses should recognize revenue and identify any income measurement issues that are likely to arise.

a. RealMoney.Com, a division of TheStreet.Com provides investment advice to customers for an up-front fee. It provides these customers with password-protected access to its Website where customers can download certain investment reports. Real Money has an obligation to provide updates on its Website.

b. Oracle develops general ledger and other business application software that it sells to its customers. The customer pays an up-front fee to gain the right to use the software and a monthly fee for support services.

c. Intuit develops tax preparation software that it sells to its customers for a flat fee. No further payment is required and the software cannot be returned, only exchanged if defective.

d. A developer of computer games sells its software with a 10-day right of return period during which the software can be returned for a full refund. After the 10-day period has expired, the software cannot be returned.

E4-20.   **Constructing and Assessing Income Statements Using Percentage-of-Completion**   Assume that General Electric Company agreed in May 2004 to construct a nuclear generator for NSTAR, a utility serving the Boston area. The contract price of $500 million is to be paid as follows: $200 million at the time of signing; $100 million on December 31, 2004; and $200 million at completion in May 2005. General Electric incurred the following costs in constructing the generator: $100 million in 2004, and $300 million in 2005.

a. Compute the amount of General Electric's revenue, expense, and income for both 2004 and 2005 under the percentage-of-completion revenue recognition method.

b. Discuss whether or not you believe the percentage-of-completion method provides a good measure of General Electric's performance under the contract.

E4-21.   Constructing and Assessing Income Statements Using Percentage-of-Completion   On March 15, 2003, Frankel Construction contracted to build a shopping center at a contract price of $120 million. The schedule of expected (equals actual) cash collections and contract costs follows:

Year	Cash Collections	Cost Incurred
2003	$ 30 million	$15 million
2004	50 million	40 million
2005	40 million	30 million
Total	$120 million	$85 million

a. Calculate the amount of revenue, expense, and net income for each of the three years 2003 through 2005 using the percentage-of-completion revenue recognition method.

b. Discuss whether or not the percentage-of-completion method provides a good measure of this construction company's performance under the contract.

E4-22.   Interpreting the Income Tax Expense Footnote Disclosure   The income tax footnote to the financial statements of FedEx follows.

FedEx (FDX)

The components of the provision for income taxes for the years ended May 31 were as follows:

In millions	2002	2001
Current provision		
Domestic		
Federal	$333	$310
State and local	39	43
Foreign	41	36
	413	389
Deferred provision (credit)		
Domestic		
Federal	21	(43)
State and local	3	(3)
Foreign	(2)	—
	22	(46)
	$435	$343

a. What is the amount of income tax expense reported in FedEx's 2002 income statement?

b. How much of its 2002 income tax expense is payable in cash? Explain.

c. One possible reason for the $22 million deferred tax expense in 2002 is that deferred tax liabilities increased during that year. Provide an example that gives rise to an increase in the deferred tax liability.

Dow Chemical (DOW)

E4-23.   Identifying Operating and Transitory Income Components   Following is the Dow Chemical income statement.

a. Identify the components in its statement that you would consider operating.

b. Identify those components that you would consider transitory.

(In millions) For Year Ended December 31	2002
Net sales	$27,609
Cost of sales	23,780
Research and development expenses	1,066
Selling, general, and administrative expenses	1,598
Amortization of intangibles	65
Merger-related expenses and restructuring	280
Asbestos-related charge	828
Equity in earnings of nonconsolidated affiliates	40
Sundry income—net	54
Interest income	66
Interest expense and amortization of debt discount	774
Income (loss) before income taxes and minority interests	(622)
Provision (credit) for income taxes	(280)
Minority interests' share of income	63
Income (loss) before cumulative effect of changes in accounting principles	(405)
Cumulative effect of changes in accounting principles	67
Net income (loss) available for common stockholders	$ (338)

E4-24. Identifying Operating and Transitory Income Components Following is the Pfizer, Inc., income statement. **Pfizer, Inc. (PFE)**

a. Identify the components in its statement that you would consider operating.

b. Identify those components that you would consider transitory.

Year Ended December 31 (millions)	2002
Revenues	$32,373
Costs and expenses	
Cost of sales	4,045
Selling, informational and administrative expenses	10,846
Research and development expenses	5,176
Merger-related costs	630
Other (income) deductions—net	(120)
Income from continuing operations before provision for taxes on income, minority interests and cumulative effect of a change in accounting principle	11,796
Provision for taxes on income	2,609
Minority interests	6
Income from continuing operations before cumulative effect of a change in accounting principle	9,181
Discontinued operations	
Income from operations of discontinued businesses—net of tax	278
Gain on sale of discontinued business—net of tax	77
Discontinued operations—net of tax	355
Income before cumulative effect of a change in accounting principle	9,536
Cumulative effect of a change in accounting principle—net of tax	(410)
Net income	$ 9,126

E4-25. Assessing Effects of Employee Stock Options for Income and EPS Viacom, Inc., reports the following footnote disclosure in its 10-K report ($ millions, except per share): **Viacom, Inc. (VIA)**

Year Ended December 31	2003	2002
Net earnings (loss)	$1,416.9	$ 725.7
Option expense, net of tax	(252.9)	(200.3)
Net earnings (loss) after option expense	$1,164.0	$ 525.4
Basic earnings (loss) per share		
Net earnings (loss) as reported	$ .81	$ .41
Net earnings (loss) after option expense	$ .67	$ .30
Diluted earnings (loss) per share		
Net earnings (loss) as reported	$ .80	$ .41
Net earnings (loss) after option expense	$ .66	$ .30

a. Viacom is currently accounting for its employee stock options using *APB 25*. Summarize the accounting for stock options under this current standard.

b.[A] By what amount (and percent) would Viacom's 2003 net earnings be affected had it valued employee stock options when granted and recognized using the fair value as expense? By what amount (and percent) would diluted earnings per share be affected by this alternate accounting treatment?

c. Is stock options expense a cash expense? How would your answer differ, if at all, if you knew that Viacom repurchases shares of its stock in the open market to offset the dilutive effects of the issuance of additional shares to employees under its stock option program?

d.[A] Following declines in the stock market, the market price of the shares under option can fall below the exercise price. How would this affect diluted earnings per share?

Agilent Technologies, Inc. (A)

Hewlett-Packard (HPQ)

E4-26. Analyzing and Assessing Research and Development Expenses Agilent Technologies, Inc., the high-tech spin-off from Hewlett-Packard, reports the following operating loss for 2003 in its 10-K ($ millions):

Net revenue	
Products	$5,240
Services and other	816
Total net revenue	6,056
Costs and expenses	
Cost of products	3,195
Cost of services and other	567
Total costs	3,762
Research and development	1,051
Selling, general and administrative	1,968
Total costs and expenses	6,781
Loss from operations	$ (725)

a. What percentage of its total net revenue is Agilent spending on research and development?

b. How are its balance sheet and income statement affected by the accounting for R&D costs?

c. Agilent reports a loss from operations for 2003. Identify and explain the implications if Agilent had reduced its 2003 R&D spending by $800 million and reported an operating profit. Consider its reduction of R&D costs relative to the no reduction scenario.

Honeywell International, Inc. (HON)

E4-27. Analyzing and Interpreting Foreign Currency Translation Adjustments Honeywell International, Inc., reports $10,729 million of stockholders' equity in its 2003 10-K, which is reported as follows:

(In millions, except per share amounts)	Common Stock Issued		Additional Paid-in Capital	Common Stock Held in Treasury		Accumulated Other Nonowner Changes	Retained Earnings	Total Shareowners' Equity
	Shares	Amount		Shares	Amount			
Balance at December 31, 2002	957.6	$958	$3,409	(103.1)	$(3,783)	$(1,109)	$ 9,450	$ 8,925
Net income							1,324	1,324
Foreign exchange translation adjustments						551		551
Minimum pension liability adjustment						369		369
Nonowner changes in shareowners' equity								2,244
Common stock issued for employee savings and option plans (including related tax benefits of $19)			75	9.3	182			257
Repurchases of common stock				(1.9)	(62)			(62)
Cash dividends on common stock ($.75 per share)							(645)	(645)
Other owner changes			2	.4	8			10
Balance at December 31, 2003	957.6	$958	$3,486	(95.3)	$(3,655)	$ (189)	$10,129	$10,729

a. How did foreign currency translation adjustments affect stockholders' equity for Honeywell in 2003? Explain.
b. Describe the accounting for foreign currency translation. What scenario of exchange rates for the $US vis-à-vis foreign currency is consistent with the translation adjustments reported for Honeywell?
c. How did the foreign currency translation adjustments reported in its stockholders' equity affect Honeywell's 2003 reported income? What other related effects might be reflected in its 2003 income statement?
d. Under what circumstances will the cumulative foreign currency translation adjustments in stockholders' equity impact reported income in the income statement?

■ PROBLEMS

P4-28. Analyzing and Interpreting Revenue Recognition Policies and Risks   Amazon.com, Inc., provides the following explanation of its revenue recognition policies from its 10-K report.   **Amazon.com (AMZN)**

> The Company generally recognizes revenue from product sales or services rendered when the following four revenue recognition criteria are met: persuasive evidence of an arrangement exists, delivery has occurred or services have been rendered, the selling price is fixed or determinable, and collectibility is reasonably assured.
>
> The Company evaluates the criteria outlined in EITF Issue No. 99-19, "Reporting Revenue Gross as a Principal versus Net as an Agent," in determining whether it is appropriate to record the gross amount of product sales and related costs or the net amount earned as commissions. Generally, when the Company is the primary obligor in a transaction, is subject to inventory risk, has latitude in establishing prices and selecting suppliers, or has several but not all of these indicators, revenue is recorded gross as a principal. If the Company is not the primary obligor and amounts earned are determined using a fixed percentage, a fixed-payment schedule, or a combination of the two, the Company generally records the net amounts as commissions earned.

Product sales (including sales of products through the Company's Syndicates Stores program), net of promotional gift certificates and return allowances, are recorded when the products are shipped and title passes to customers. Return allowances are estimated using historical experience.

Commissions received on sales of products from Amazon Marketplace, Auctions and zShops are recorded as a net amount since the Company is acting as an agent in such transactions. Amounts earned are recognized as net sales when the item is sold by the third-party seller and our collectibility is reasonably assured. The Company records an allowance for refunds on such commissions using historical experience.

The Company earns revenues from services, primarily by entering into business-to-business strategic alliances, including providing the Company's technology services such as search, browse and personalization; permitting third parties to offer products or services through the Company's Websites; and powering third-party Websites, providing fulfillment services, or both. These strategic alliances also include miscellaneous marketing and promotional agreements. As compensation for the services the Company provides under these agreements, it receives one or a combination of cash and equity securities. If the Company receives non-refundable, up-front payments, such amounts are deferred until service commences, and are then recognized on a straight-line basis over the estimated corresponding service period. Generally, the fair value of consideration received, whether in cash, equity securities, or a combination thereof, is measured when agreement is reached, and any subsequent appreciation or decline in the fair value of the securities received does not affect the amount of revenue recognized over the term of the agreement. To the extent that equity securities received or modified after March 16, 2000 are subject to forfeiture or vesting provisions and no significant performance commitment exists upon signing of the agreements, the fair value of the securities and corresponding revenue is determined as of the date of the respective forfeiture or as vesting provisions lapse. The Company generally recognizes revenue from these services on a straight-line basis over the period during which the Company performs services under these agreements, commencing at the launch date of the service.

Outbound shipping charges to customers are included in net sales.

Required

a. Identify and discuss the main revenue recognition policies for its two primary sources of business revenues.

b. Identify and describe at least three potential areas for revenue recognition shams in a business such as Amazon.

AOL Time-Warner (AOL)   **P4-29.   Analyzing, Interpreting, and Forecasting with Discontinued Operations**   AOL Time-Warner reports the following footnote relating to its discontinued operations in its 2002 10-K report.

In the third quarter of 2002, the Company's results of operations have been adjusted to reflect the results of certain cable television systems held in the TWE-Advance/Newhouse Partnership ("TWE-A/N") as discontinued operations for all periods presented herein. For 2002, for the six months ended June 30, 2002 (e.g., the most recent reported period prior to the deconsolidation), the net impact of the deconsolidation of these systems was a reduction of the Cable segment's previously reported revenues, EBITDA and operating income of $715 million, $333 million and $206 million, respectively. For the year ended December 31, 2001, the net impact of the deconsolidation of these systems was a reduction of the Cable segment's previously reported revenues, EBITDA and operating income of $1,247 billion, $571 million and $313 million, respectively. The discontinued operations did not impact the Company's results in 2000 because the Company's ownership interest in these cable television systems was acquired in the Merger. As of December 31, 2001, the discontinued operations had current assets and total assets of approximately $64 million and $2.7 billion, respectively, and current liabilities and total liabilities of approximately $210 million and $963 million, respectively, including debt assumed in the restructuring of TWE-A/N.

Required

a. Describe the accounting treatment according to GAAP for discontinued operations

b. How did AOL Time-Warner's treatment of its discontinued operations impact its 2001 (1) income statement and (2) balance sheet?

c. How do you believe the operating results of the discontinued segment should be interpreted when evaluating the 2002 financial performance for AOL Time-Warner?

P4-30.   Analyzing and Interpreting Income Components and Disclosures   The income statement for Xerox   Xerox
Corporation follows.   Corporation
    (XRX)

Year Ended December 31 (in millions)	2002	2001	2000
Revenues			
Sales	$ 6,752	$ 7,443	$ 8,839
Service, outsourcing and rentals	8,097	8,436	8,750
Finance income	1,000	1,129	1,162
Total revenues	15,849	17,008	18,751
Costs and Expenses			
Costs of sales	4,197	5,170	6,080
Cost of service, outsourcing and rentals	4,530	4,880	5,153
Equipment financing interest	401	457	498
Research and development expenses	917	997	1,064
Selling, administrative and general expenses	4,437	4,728	5,518
Restructuring and asset impairment charges	670	715	475
Gain on sale of half of interest in Fuji Xerox	—	(773)	—
Gain on affiliate's sale of stock	—	(4)	(21)
Gain on sale of China operations	—	—	(200)
Other expenses, net	445	444	551
Total costs and expenses	15,597	16,614	19,118
Income (Loss) before Income Taxes (Benefits), Equity Income, Minorities' Interests and Cumulative Effect of Change in Accounting Principle	252	394	(367)
Income taxes (benefits)	60	497	(70)
Income (Loss) before Equity Income, Minorities' Interests and Cumulative Effect of Change in Accounting Principle	192	(103)	(297)
Equity in net income of unconsolidated affiliates	54	53	66
Minorities' interests in earnings of subsidiaries	(92)	(42)	(42)
Income (Loss) before Cumulative Effect of Change in Accounting Principle	154	(92)	(273)
Cumulative effect of change in accounting principle	(63)	(2)	—
Net Income (Loss)	$ 91	$ (94)	$ (273)

Required

a.   Xerox reports three main sources of income: sales, services, and finance income. Describe the usual and proper revenue recognition policy for each of these sources.

b.   Xerox reports research and development (R&D) expenses of $917 million in 2002, which is 13.5% of its sales. (1) How are R&D expenses accounted for under GAAP? (2) Why do you believe regulators resist the capitalization of expenses such as R&D?

c.   Xerox reports restructuring costs of $670 million in 2002. It also reports restructuring costs in each of 2001 and 2000. (1) Describe the two typical categories of restructuring costs and the accounting for each. (2) How do you recommend treating these costs for analysis purposes? (3) Should regular recurring restructuring costs be treated differently than isolated occurrences of such costs for analysis purposes?

d.   Xerox reports various gains on the sales of its subsidiaries as *negative expenses* in 2000 and 2001. (1) Describe in general terms how Xerox computes these gains. (2) How should such gains be treated for analysis purposes? (3) Do you believe Xerox is trying to influence the reader of its income statement by inclusion of these gains in its expense section?

e.   Xerox reports $445 million in expenses labeled as 'Other expenses, net.' How can a company use the concept of materiality to minimize the disclosure relating to such items and, therefore, to potentially obscure its actual financial performance?

P4-31.   Analyzing and Interpreting Employee Stock Option Disclosures and Adjustments   eBay, Inc., reports   eBay, Inc.
the following footnote for its employee stock options from its 10-K report.   (EBAY)

Generally accepted accounting principles provide companies with the option of either recognizing the fair value of option grants as an operating expense or disclosing the impact of fair value accounting in a note to the financial statements. Consistent with predominant industry practice, we account for stock-based employee compensation arrangements using the intrinsic value method, which calculates compensation expense based on the difference, if any, on the date of the grant, between the fair value of our stock and the exercise price and have elected to disclose the impact of fair value accounting for option grants. Had we elected to recognize the fair value of option grants as an operating expense, our reported net income would have been substantially reduced, as follows (in thousands):

Year Ended December 31	2001	2002
Net income, as reported	$ 90,448	$ 249,891
Add: Amortization of stock-based compensation expense determined under the intrinsic value method	3,091	5,953
Deduct: Total stock-based compensation expense determined under fair value based method for all awards, net of tax	(211,526)	(192,902)
Pro forma net income (loss)	$(117,987)	$ 62,942

Required

a. Describe the accounting for employee stock options under GAAP.

b. How does eBay's accounting for its stock options impact its reported 2002 income? Explain.

Dell Computer Corporation (DELL)

P4-32. Analyzing and Interpreting Restructuring Costs and Effects   Dell Computer Corporation reported $587 million of charges in connection with a prior year restructuring of its operations as described in the following footnote from its 2003 10-K report.

($ millions)	Total Charge	Cumulative Payments	Noncash Charges	Liability at January 31, 2003
Employee separations	$184	$(184)	$ —	$—
Facility consolidations	224	(130)	(79)	15
Other asset impairments and exit costs	179	(27)	(152)	—
Total	$587	$(341)	$(231)	$15

Required

a. Identify the three components of Dell's restructuring charge and the related expense amounts for each. For each component, what portion of its charge was paid in cash?

b. What was the effect on the balance sheet and the income statement of Dell's noncash charges?

Altria Group, Inc. (MO)

Miller Brewing (MLR)

P4-33. Analyzing and Interpreting Gains and Losses on Asset (Subsidiary) Sales   Altria Group, Inc., formerly Phillip Morris Companies, Inc., sold its Miller Brewing subsidiary. Following is a footnote to its 10-K report, which describes that transaction.

On May 30, 2002, ALG announced an agreement with SAB to merge Miller into SAB. The transaction closed on July 9, 2002, and SAB changed its name to SABMiller plc ("SABMiller"). At closing, ALG received 430 million shares of SABMiller valued at approximately $3.4 billion, based upon a share price of 5.12 British pounds per share, in exchange for Miller, which had $2.0 billion of existing debt. The shares in SABMiller owned by ALG resulted in a 36% economic interest in SABMiller and a 24.9% voting interest. The transaction resulted in a pre-tax gain of approximately $2.6 billion or approximately $1.7 billion after-tax. The gain was recorded in the third quarter of 2002. Beginning with the third quarter of 2002, ALG's ownership interest in SABMiller is being accounted for under the equity method. Accordingly, ALG's investment in SABMiller of approximately $1.9 billion is included in other assets on the consolidated balance sheet at December 31, 2002. In addition, ALG records its share of SABMiller's net earnings, based on its economic ownership percentage, in minority interest in earnings and other, net, on the consolidated statement of earnings.

Required

a.   Identify (1) the total value received by Altria in exchange for Miller, (2) the book value of Altria's investment in the Miller Brewing subsidiary, and (3) the pretax and after-tax gains recognized by Altria from the Miller transaction.

b.   How much of the purchase price was received in cash by Altria? Explain.

c.   How should the gain from this transaction be interpreted in an analysis of Altria, especially with respect to projections of Altria's future cash flows?

5 Reporting and Analyzing Operating Assets

A HAIR-RAISING TURNAROUND

"Three years ago, we made a commitment. We said that we're going to transform this Company from a chronic underperformer to a producer of consistent, sustainable earnings growth—the kind of growth that would take us to the top tier of industry performers over time . . . I'm pleased to report that we are delivering on those commitments. Three years of solid progress allows us to say something . . . that this Company hasn't been able to say in several years . . . Gillette had record earnings per share." (The Gillette Company 2003 Annual Report, Chair's letter)

Gillette reported record sales and earnings in 2003, three years after James Kilts assumed the top job. Sales rose 9%, to $9.25 billion, up from $8.45 billion in 2002. Net income rose 14%, to $1.39 billion, up from $1.22 billion in 2002.

Gillette's turnaround and its recent results "trounced Wall Street's estimates . . . 'If anybody had doubted the company's ability to produce solid numbers, that has got to be put to bed,' said William H. Steele, an analyst at Banc of America Securities. Mr. Steele credits Mr. Kilts for much of the improvement. Shares rose $2.41, or 6.2%, to $41.20 a share . . . [and] marks the first time in more than four years that Gillette shares have surpassed $40." (*The Wall Street Journal,* April 2004)

Gillette is a global manufacturer of a variety of consumer products. It has five major segments:

- **Blades and Razors.** Gillette is the world leader in blades and razors with such brands as M3Power, Mach3Turbo, Mach3, SensorExcel, Sensor, Atra, and Trac II.

- **Duracell.** Gillette is the world leader in alkaline batteries with such products as Duracell CopperTop, Duracell Ultra alkaline batteries, and Duracell primary lithium, zinc air, and rechargeable batteries.

- **Oral Care.** Gillette is the world leader in manual and power toothbrushes, all sold under the Oral-B brand.

- **Braun.** Gillette sells electric shavers under the Braun brand and hair epilators under the Silk-Epil brand. It also sells Braun household and personal diagnostic appliances.

- **Personal Care.** Gillette sells shaving preparations, skin care products, and antiperspirants/deodorants under brands such as Gillette Series, Satin Care, Right Guard, Soft & Dri, and Dry Idea.

As the following chart shows, Gillette's stock price has consistently trotted upward, after reaching a low point shortly after Kilts, formerly CEO of Nabisco, joined the company in early 2001:

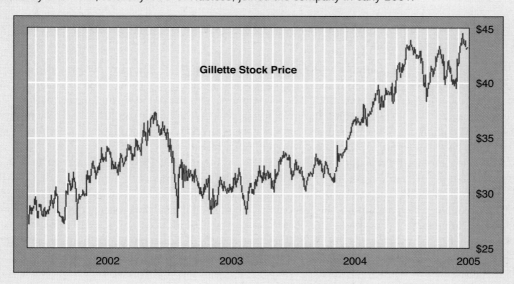

The company hailed its earnings and stock price turnaround as evidence that its multiyear restructuring aimed at both slimming a bloated manufacturing process and renegotiating supplier agreements was bearing fruit. A heavy investment in advertising and marketing also paid off with higher sales, and two new Gillette disposable razors were well received.

Management of its net operating assets, including working capital and long-term plant assets, was crucial to creation of shareholder value. Gillette focused intently on its management of net operating assets and has realized substantial accomplishments, including the following:

- It reorganized its supply chain and gained a better handle on receivables. Its receivables are turning over at a rate of 6.6 times a year, up from 3.5 times a year five years ago.

(Continued on next page)

(Continued from previous page)

- It pursues a cost-reduction program. The program aims to build more efficient production lines, offer some workers early retirement, and consolidate operations. These efforts have trimmed costs from its bloated inventories and its inefficient manufacturing process. Inventories are turning over at a rate of three times a year, up from two times a year just four years ago.
- It is shifting factory and warehouse operations from London to Eastern Europe to trim costs, it is moving manufacturing of its Sensor razor from its high-tech Berlin plant to Eastern European, and it is realigning some razor production from the Czech Republic to St. Petersburg.

This module focuses on the reporting and analysis of receivables, inventories, and plant assets. As with Gillette, these assets comprise the bulk of operating assets for most companies and must be managed effectively to achieve high performance.

There are choices for managers in accounting for their operating assets, and the amounts reported are impacted by numerous estimates. Management decisions in accounting for operating assets can markedly affect both the balance sheet and the income statement. We discuss these and other issues, including the accounting, reporting and analysis of investing activities. We explain the processes and the effects of accounting choices for the reporting of these assets on financial statements. This knowledge is used to conduct better analysis and interpretation of companies' investing activities.

As one analyst points out, "It would have been easy for [CEO] Kilts to say, 'Let's cut back on marketing, let's cut back on . . . spending and make our number.' He didn't," said Joseph Altobello, an analyst at CIBC World Markets. "He's managing for the longer term." (*The Wall Street Journal*, 2003) Gillette management has made some razor sharp decisions that are now bearing fruit. [A final note: In 2005, Procter & Gamble made a bid (subject to regulatory approvals) to acquire 100% of Gillette. P&G's offer would yield an 18% premium to Gillette stockholders.]

Sources: *The Wall Street Journal* 2004 and 2003; *Gillette* 2004 and 2003 Annual Report; *Gillette* 2004 10-K Report and 2005 press release.

■ INTRODUCTION

Management of net operating assets is crucial to achieving high company performance and creating shareholder value. To manage and assess net operating assets, we need to understand how they are measured and reported. This module describes the reporting and measuring of operating working capital, mainly receivables and inventories, and of long-term operating assets such as property, plant, and equipment. We do not discuss nonoperating investments and financing activities (current and long-term debt and equity) as they are covered in other modules.

Receivables are usually a major part of operating working capital. They must be carefully managed as they represent a substantial asset for most companies and are an important marketing tool. GAAP requires companies to report receivables at the amount they expect to collect. This requires estimation of uncollectible accounts, which determines the receivables reported on the balance sheet and expenses reported on the income statement. Accordingly, it is important that companies accurately assess uncollectible accounts and timely report them. It is also necessary that readers of financial reports understand management's accounting choices and their effects on reported balance sheets and income statements.

Inventory is another major component of operating working capital. Inventories usually constitute one of the three largest asset amounts (with receivables and long-term operating assets). Also, cost of goods sold, which flows from inventory, is often the largest expense category for retailing and manufacturing companies. GAAP allows several acceptable methods for inventory accounting, and these choices can markedly impact the balance sheets and income statements, especially for companies experiencing relatively high inflation, coupled with slowly turning inventories.

Long-term plant assets are often the largest component of operating assets. Indeed, long-term operating assets often are the largest asset for manufacturing companies, and their related depreciation expense is typically second only to cost of goods sold in the income statement. GAAP allows different accounting methods for computing depreciation, which we discuss in this module. We also explain the reporting of gains and losses on asset sales and accounting for asset write-downs, as it is important to understand their effects for current and future profitability.

■ ACCOUNTS RECEIVABLE

Our focus on operating assets begins with accounts receivable. To help frame our discussion, we refer to the following graphic as we proceed through the module:

Income Statement
Sales
Cost of goods sold
Selling, general & administrative
Income taxes
Net income

Balance Sheet	
Cash	Current liabilities
Accounts receivable	Long-term liabilities
Inventory	
Property, plant, and equipment, net	Shareholders' equity
Investments	

We highlight the financial statement item (accounts receivable) that is the focus of this section. We also highlight the income statement items that are impacted by uncollectible accounts receivable and by credit sales. This section explains the accounting, reporting, and analysis of these and related items.

When companies sell to other companies, they usually do not expect cash upon delivery as is common with retail customers. Instead, they offer credit terms, and the resulting sales are called *credit sales* or *sales on account*.[1] An account receivable on the seller's balance sheet is always matched by a corresponding account payable on the buyer's balance sheet. Accounts receivable are reported on the balance sheet of the seller at *net realizable value*, which is the net amount the seller expects to collect.

Sellers expect that some buyers will be unable to pay their accounts when they come due and that sellers will be unable to collect on them. Buyers, for example, can suffer business downturns that are beyond their control, which limit their cash available to meet liabilities. They must, then, make choices concerning which of their liabilities to pay. Liabilities to the IRS, to banks, and to bondholders are usually paid, as those creditors have enforcement powers and can quickly seize assets and disrupt operations, leading to bankruptcy and eventual liquidation. Buyers also try to cover their payroll, as they cannot exist without employees. Then, if there is cash remaining, buyers will pay suppliers to ensure continued flow of goods.

The buyers' accounts payable are *unsecured liabilities*, meaning that buyers have not pledged collateral to guarantee payment of amounts owed. As a result, when a company declares bankruptcy, suppliers' claims (accounts payable) are lumped in with other unsecured creditors (after the IRS and the secured creditors), and are typically not paid in full. Consequently, there is risk in the collectibility of accounts receivable. This *collectibility risk* is crucial to analysis of accounts receivable.

Gillette reports $920 million of trade accounts receivable (the term *trade* refers to customers) in the following current asset section from its 2003 balance sheet ($ millions):

Cash and cash equivalents	$ 681
Trade receivables, less allowances of $53	920
Other receivables	351
Inventories	1,094
Deferred income taxes	322
Other current assets	282
Total current assets	3,650

---

[1] An example of common credit terms are 2/10, net 30. These terms indicate that the seller offers the buyer an early-pay incentive, which in this case is a 2% discount off the cost if the buyer pays within 10 days of billing. If the buyer does not take advantage of the discount, it must pay 100% of the invoice cost within 30 days of billing. From the seller's standpoint, offering the discount is often warranted because it receives cash more quickly, and it hopes to invest the monies to yield a return greater than the discount it is offering. The buyer often wishes to avail itself of attractive discounts even if it has to borrow money to do so. If the discount is not taken, however, the buyer should withhold payment as long as it can (at least for the full net period) so as to maximize its available cash while the seller will exert whatever pressure it can to collect the amount due as quickly as possible. There is normal tension between sellers and buyers in this regard.

Its receivables are reported net of allowances for uncollectible accounts of $53 million. This means the total amount owed to Gillette is $973 million ($920 million + $53 million), but Gillette *estimates* that $53 million are uncollectible and reports on its balance sheet only the amount expected to be collected.

We might ask why buyers would sell to companies from whom they will not collect amounts owed. The answer is they would not *if* they knew beforehand who those companies were. For example, Gillette probably cannot identify those companies that constitute the $53 million in uncollectible accounts as of its statement date. Yet, it knows from past experience that a certain portion of its receivables will prove uncollectible. GAAP requires it to estimate the dollar amount of uncollectible accounts each time it issues its financial statements (even if it cannot identify specific accounts that are uncollectible), and to report its accounts receivable at the resulting *net realizable value* (total receivables less an allowance for uncollectible accounts).

Allowance for Uncollectible Accounts

The amount of expected uncollectible accounts is usually computed based on an *aging analysis*. When aging the accounts, an analysis of receivables is performed as of the balance sheet date. Specifically, each customer's account balance is categorized by the number of days or months that the related invoices are outstanding. Based on prior experience, or on other available statistics, uncollectible (bad debt) percentages are applied to each of these categorized amounts, with larger percentages applied to older accounts. The result of this analysis is a dollar amount for the allowance for uncollectible accounts (also called allowance for doubtful accounts) at the balance sheet date.

To illustrate, Exhibit 5.1 shows an aging analysis for a seller that began operations this period and is owed $100,000 of accounts receivable at period-end. Those accounts listed as current consist of those outstanding that are still within their original credit period. As an example, an invoice with terms 2/10, net 30, which has been outstanding for 30 days or less as of the financial statement date is current. Accounts listed as 1–60 days past due are those 1 to 60 days past their due date. This would include an account that is 45 days outstanding for a net 30-day invoice. This same logic applies to all aged categories.

EXHIBIT 5.1 ■ Aging of Accounts Receivable

Age of Accounts Receivable	Receivable Balance	Estimated Percent Uncollectible	Estimated Uncollectible Accounts
Current	$ 50,000	2%	$1,000
1–60 days past due	30,000	3	900
61–90 days past due	15,000	4	600
Over 90 days past due	5,000	8	400
Total	$100,000		$2,900

Exhibit 5.1 also reflects the seller's experience with uncollectible accounts, which manifests itself in the uncollectible percentages for each aged category. For example, on average, 3% of buyers' accounts that are 1–60 days past due prove uncollectible for this seller. Hence, it estimates a potential loss of $900 for those $30,000 in receivables for that aged category.[2]

The seller represented in Exhibit 5.1 reports its accounts receivable on the balance sheet as follows:

> Accounts receivable, net of $2,900 in allowances $97,100

---

[2]Another means to estimate uncollectible accounts is to use the *percentage of sales*. To illustrate, if a company reports sales of $100,000 and estimates the provision at 3% of sales, it would report a bad debts expense of $3,000 instead of $2,900. This results in an allowance balance of $3,000 instead of $2,900 using the aging analysis. The percentage of sales method computes bad debts expense (the addition to the allowance balance), whereas the aging method computes the allowance balance (with bad debts expense being the amount needed to yield that balance). Thus, these methods nearly always report different values for the allowance, net accounts receivable, and bad debts expense.

The *reconciliation* of its allowance account from the beginning of the period to its end follows (assuming a zero beginning allowance amount):

Beginning allowance for uncollectible accounts ...... $	0
Add: Provision for uncollectible accounts	2,900
Less: Write-offs of accounts receivable	0
Ending allowance for uncollectible accounts .... $	2,900

The allowance for uncollectible accounts is increased by new provisions (additions) of expected uncollectible accounts and it is decreased by accounts that are written off. Individual accounts are written off when the seller identifies them as uncollectible. (A write-off reduces both accounts receivable and the allowance for uncollectible accounts as described below.) The ending balance of the allowance account for a period becomes the beginning balance of the allowance account for next period.

To illustrate a write-off, assume that subsequent to the period-end shown above, the seller receives notice that one of its customers, owing $500 at the time, has declared bankruptcy. The seller's attorneys believe that legal costs in attempting to collect this receivable would likely exceed the amount owed. So, the seller decides not to pursue collection and to write off this account. The write-off has the following effects:

1. Accounts receivable are reduced from $100,000 to $99,500.
2. Allowance for uncollectible accounts is reduced from $2,900 to $2,400.

After the write-off, the seller's accounts receivable are reported on its balance sheet as follows:

Accounts receivable, net of $2,400 in allowances	$97,100

Exhibit 5.2 shows the effects of this write-off on the individual accounts.

EXHIBIT 5.2 ■ Effects of an Accounts Receivable Write-Off

Account	Before Write-Off	Effects of Write-Off	After Write-Off
Accounts receivable	$100,000	$(500)	$99,500
Less: Allowance for uncollectible accounts	2,900	500	2,400
Accounts receivable, net of allowance	$ 97,100		$97,100

The balance of net accounts receivable that is reported on the balance sheet after the write-off is the same net balance that the company reported before the write-off. This is always the case. The write-off of an account is a nonevent from an accounting point of view. That is, total assets do not change, liabilities stay the same, and equity is unaffected as there is no net income effect. Only individual asset accounts are affected, not the total.

Let's next consider what happens when additional information arrives that alters management's expectations of uncollectible accounts. To illustrate, assume that sometime after the write-off above, the seller realizes that it has underestimated uncollectible accounts and that $3,000 (not $2,400) of the remaining $99,500 accounts receivable are uncollectible. It must then increase the allowance for uncollectible accounts by $600. The additional $600 provision has the following financial statement effects:

1. Allowance for uncollectible accounts is increased by $600 to the revised estimated balance of $3,000; and accounts receivable (net of the allowance for uncollectible accounts) declines by $600 from $97,100 to $96,500 (or $99,500 − $3,000).
2. A $600 expense is added to the income statement, which reduces net income. This expense is called *bad debts expense* and is usually included among selling, general, and administrative expenses (not reported separately). This added expense is reported in the current period. In the prior period, the seller reported $2,900 of bad debts expense when the allowance account was originally estimated.

To summarize, the *main balance sheet and income statement effects occur when the provision is made to the allowance for uncollectible accounts.* Accounts receivable (net) is reduced, and that reduction is reflected in the income statement as bad debts expense (usually part of selling, general, and administrative expenses). The net income reduction yields a corresponding equity reduction (via reduced retained earnings). Importantly, the main financial statement effects are at the point of *estimation*, not upon the event of *write-off*. In this way, sales are matched with bad debts expense, and accounts receivable are matched with its expected uncollectible accounts. Exhibit 5.3 illustrates each of the transactions discussed in this section using the financial statement effects template:

EXHIBIT 5.3 ■ Financial Statement Effects of Key Accounts Receivable Transactions

	Balance Sheet						Income Statement	
Transaction	Cash Asset	+ Noncash Assets	= Liabil- ities	+ Contrib. Capital	+ Retained Earnings		Revenues	− Expenses
a. Sales of $100,000 on credit		+100,000 Accounts Receivable			+100,000		+100,000 Sales	
b. Estimate $2,900 in bad debts		−2,900 Allowance for Uncollectibles			−2,900			− 2,900 Bad Debts Expense
c. Write-off $500 in accounts receivable		−500 Accounts Receivable +500 Allowance for Uncollectibles						
d. Increase allowance account by $600		−600 Allowance for Uncollectibles			−600			− 600 Bad Debts Expense

Margin notes:

Accounts Rec. 100,000
Sales 100,000

Bad Debts Exp. 2,900
Allow. for Uncol. 2,900

Allow. for Uncol. 500
Accounts Rec. 500

Bad Debts Exp. 600
Allow. for Uncol. 600

Footnote Disclosures

To illustrate the typical footnote disclosure related to accounts receivable, let's consider **Gillette** and its disclosure relating to its allowance for uncollectible accounts:

> With respect to trade receivables, concentration of credit risk is limited, due to the diverse geographic areas covered by Gillette operations. The Company's largest customer, Wal-Mart Stores, Inc. and its affiliates, accounted for 13% of consolidated net sales in 2003, and 12% of consolidated net sales in both 2002 and 2001. These sales occurred primarily in North America and were across all product segments. At December 31, 2003 and 2002, 44% and 40% of the Company's accounts receivable were from customers in North America, respectively. Wal-Mart Stores, Inc. represented 23% and 17% of the North American accounts receivable at December 31, 2003 and 2002, respectively. Using the best information available, the Company has provided an allowance for doubtful accounts based on estimated bad-debt loss.

Given the large concentration of its receivables with **Wal-Mart**, Gillette does not have much risk related to their collection. (Witness Wal-Mart's power over suppliers—it represents 23% of Gillette's receivables but only 13% of its sales.)

Gillette provides a footnote reconciliation of its allowance for uncollectible (doubtful) accounts for the past three years as shown in Exhibit 5.4.

EXHIBIT 5.4 ■ Reconciliation of Gillette's Allowance for Uncollectible Accounts

Allowance for Doubtful Accounts Years ended December 31 (millions)	2003	2002	2001
Balance at beginning of year	$73	$69	$81
Additions	19	37	30
Deductions	(39)	(33)	(42)
Balance at end of year	$53	$73	$69

The reconciliation of Gillette's allowance account provides insight into the level of its provision (additional allowances) per year relative to its actual write-offs. For example, the 2003 provision of $19 million was much less than the 2003 write-offs of $39 million. Its allowance account declined as a result; that is, Gillette utilized amounts accrued in one or more prior years to absorb losses in the current year. For this entire three-year period, Gillette has increased the allowance account by a cumulative total of $86 million ($19 million + $37 million + $30 million) and has written off accounts equal to an aggregate amount of $114 million ($39 million + $33 million + $42 million). As a result, the allowance account has been reduced by a cumulative amount of $28 million during the past three years.

On a percentage basis, the 2003 allowance account represents 5.4% of gross accounts receivable [$53 million/($920 million + $53 million)]. The 2002 allowance account represents 5.7% of gross accounts receivable [$73 million/($1,202 million + $73 million)]. Gillette, therefore, has reduced the 2003 allowance account as a percentage of gross accounts receivable compared to 2002.

The reduction in Gillette's allowance account results from greater write-offs and a lower allowance. Since 2003 additions to the allowance account are reduced relative to 2002, Gillette is, loosely speaking, living off the allowance account established in prior years. A question we must ask at the end of 2003 is whether the allowance account is adequate to absorb expected losses. If not, then Gillette's receivables are overstated on its balance sheet and its income is overstated (because too little bad debt expense is recognized).

Analysis Implications

This section considers analysis of accounts receivable and its provision for uncollectible accounts.

Adequacy of Allowance Account

A company makes two representations when reporting accounts receivable (net) in the current asset section of its balance sheet:

1. It expects to collect the asset amount reported on the balance sheet (remember, accounts receivable are reported net of allowance for uncollectible accounts).
2. It expects to collect the asset amount within the next year (implied from its classification as a current asset).

From an analysis viewpoint, we scrutinize the adequacy of a company's provision for its uncollectible accounts. If the provision is inadequate, the cash ultimately collected will be less than what the company is reporting as net receivables.

How can an outsider assess the adequacy of the allowance account? One answer is to examine the percentage of the allowance account to gross accounts receivable. For Gillette, the 2003 percentage is 5.4% (see above), a slight decline from the prior year. What does such a decline signify? Perhaps the overall economic environment has improved, rendering write-offs less likely. Perhaps the company has improved its credit underwriting or receivables collection efforts. Such new initiatives are likely to be discussed in the MD&A section of its financial report. Or perhaps the company's customer mix has changed and it is now selling to more creditworthy customers (or, it eliminated a risky class).

The important point is that we must be comfortable with the percentage of uncollectible accounts reported by the company. We must remember that management has control over the adequacy and reporting of the allowance account—albeit with audit assurances.

Income Shifting

We noted that the main financial statement effects of uncollectible accounts are normally at the point of estimation, not on the event of write-off. It is also important to recall that the amount and timing of the uncollectible provision is largely controlled by management. Although external auditors assess the reasonableness of the allowance for uncollectible accounts, they do not possess the inside knowledge and experience of management and are, therefore, at an information disadvantage, particularly if any dispute arises.

Experience tells us that many companies have previously used the allowance for uncollectible accounts to shift income from one year into another. For example, by underestimating the provision, bad debt expense is reduced in the current period, thus increasing current period income. In one or more future periods, when write-offs occur for which the company should have provisioned earlier, it must then increase the provision to make up for the underestimated provision for that earlier period. This reduces income in one or more future periods. Income has, thus, been shifted (borrowed) from a future period into the current period.

Why would a company want to engage in shifting income from a later period into the current period? Perhaps it is a lean year and the company is in danger of missing income targets. For example, internal targets influence manager bonuses and external targets set by the market influence stock prices. Perhaps the company is in danger of defaulting on loan agreements tied to income levels. The reality is that income pressures are great and these pressures can cause companies to bend the rules.

We should also consider whether a company engages in shifting income from the current period to one or more future periods. For example, when a company overestimates the current period uncollectible provision it reduces current period income. Then, in future lean periods, the company can reduce its allowance account as a percentage of gross accounts receivable, thereby increasing income for one or more future periods.

Why would a company want to shift income from the current period to one or more future periods? Perhaps current times are good and the company wants to "bank" some of that income for future periods—sometimes called a *cookie jar reserve*. It can then draw on that reserve, if necessary, to boost income in one or more future lean years. Perhaps another reason for a company to shift income from the current period is that it does not wish to unduly inflate current market expectations and pressures for future period income. Or, perhaps the company is experiencing a very bad year and it feels that overestimating the provision will not drive income materially lower than it is. Thus, it decides to take a big bath (a large loss) and create a reserve that can be used in future periods. Sears provides an interesting case as described in the Business Insight below.

Use of the allowance for uncollectible accounts to shift income is a source of concern. This is especially so for banks because the allowance for loan losses is usually a large component of their balance sheets and loan loss expense is a major component of reported income. Our analysis must scrutinize the allowance for uncollectible accounts to identify any changes from past practices or industry norms and, then, to justify those changes before accepting them as valid.

BUSINESS INSIGHT   **Sears' Cookie Jar**

The Heard on the Street column in *The Wall Street Journal* (1996) reported the following: "Analyst David Poneman argues that Sears' earnings growth this year of 24%, or $134 million, has been aided by a 1993 balance-sheet maneuver that softens the impact of soaring levels of bad credit-card debt among its 50 million cardholders. Wall Street got a wake-up call in the second quarter, when Sears increased its provision for bad credit-card debt by $254 million, up 73% from the year earlier. Then in the third quarter, it made another $286 million provision, a 53% increase. Yet the retailer posted a 22% gain in third-quarter net. How so? 'Sears is using its superabundant balance sheet to smooth out its earnings,' says Mr. Poneman. He says Sears has a 'quality-of-earnings' issue."

Poneman is referring to a $2 billion reserve for credit losses that Sears set up in 1993. As it turned out, the reserve was higher than needed. Three years later, Sears still had a nearly $1 billion reserve on its balance sheet. That's nearly twice the size of reserves at most credit-card companies as a percentage of receivables. The credit-card reserve was part of a big bath that also included restructuring charges that Sears took in 1993. Such charges and reserves can be a big help for a new CEO (which Sears had) who wishes to show a pattern of improving results in future years. Poneman says the big addition to reserves "moved income out of 1992 and 1993 and into 1995 and 1996." Why is that bad? The overly large reserve allowed Sears to prop up its earnings at a time when losses in its credit-card unit were soaring. Sears' credit-card delinquencies had risen by $420 million in 1996. Poneman asserts that "Considering that increased delinquencies exceed year-to-date increased earnings, it could be argued that the increase in Sears' year-to-date earnings has depended entirely on its over-reserved condition."

Accounts Receivable Turnover and Average Collection Period

Total asset turnover is sales divided by average total assets. An important component of this measure is the accounts receivables turnover (ART), which is defined as:[3]

Accounts Receivable Turnover = Sales/Average Accounts Receivable

---

[3]Technically, net credit sales should be used in the numerator as receivables arise from credit sales and the inclusion of cash sales inflates the ratio. Typically, however, outsiders do not know the level of cash sales and total sales must be used.

Accounts receivable turnover reveals how many times receivables have turned (been collected) during the period. More turns indicate that receivables are being collected more quickly.

A companion measure to accounts receivable turnover is the average collection period (ACP) for accounts receivable, also called days sales outstanding (DSO), which is defined as:

> **Average Collection Period = Accounts Receivable /Average Daily Sales**

where average daily sales equals sales divided by 365 days. The average collection period indicates how long, on average, the receivables are outstanding before being collected.

To illustrate, assume that sales are $1,000, ending accounts receivable are $230, and average accounts receivable are $200. The accounts receivable turnover is 5, computed as $1,000/200, and the average collection period (days sales outstanding) is 84 days, computed as $230/($1,000/365).

The accounts receivable turnover and the average collection period yield valuable insights on at least two dimensions:

1. *Receivables quality* Changes in receivable turnover (and collection period) give insights into accounts receivable quality. If turnover slows (collection period lengthens), the reason could be deterioration in collectibility of receivables. However, before reaching this conclusion, consider at least three alternative explanations:

    a. A seller can extend its credit terms. If the seller is attempting to enter new markets or take market share from competitors, it may extend credit terms to attract buyers.

    b. A seller can take on longer-paying customers. For example, facing increased competition, many computer and automobile companies began leasing their products, thus reducing the cash outlay for customers and stimulating sales. The change in mix away from cash sales and toward leasing had the effect of reducing receivables turnover and increasing the collection period.

    c. The seller can increase the allowance provision. Receivables turnover is often computed using net receivables (after the allowance for uncollectible accounts). Overestimating the provision reduces net receivables and increases its turnover.

2. *Asset utilization* Asset turnover is an important measure of financial performance, both by managers for internal performance goals, as well as by the market in evaluating companies. High-performing companies must be both efficient (controlling margins and operating expenses) and productive (getting the most out of their asset base). An increase in receivables ties up cash as the receivables must be financed, and slower-turning receivables carry increased risk of loss. One of the first "low hanging fruits" that companies pursue in efforts to improve asset utilization is efficiency in receivables collection.

$
Cash Effect

The following chart shows the accounts receivable turnover for Gillette and three of its peer competitors as identified by Gillette in its 10-K.

Accounts Receivable Turnover for Gillette and Competitors

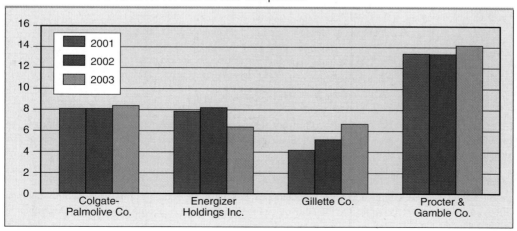

The improvement in Gillette's receivable turnover over the 2001–2003 period from 4.2 times to 6.6 times is evident, and it is now in excess of the turnover for **Energizer**. Nevertheless, Gillette's turnover is still less than **Colgate-Palmolive** and markedly lower than **Procter & Gamble**. The two latter companies also have large sales to **Wal-Mart**.

A possible cause for these differences in turnover is the relative sizes of these companies. Gillette is a $9.3 billion (sales) company, Colgate-Palmolive is a $9.9 billion company, and Proctor & Gamble is a $43.4 billion company. P&G's greater size likely confers some negotiating advantage even against a behemoth like Wal-Mart (with 2003 sales of $256 billion).

To appreciate differences in accounts receivable turnover rates across industries, let's compare Gillette with companies in other industries as follows:

Accounts Receivable Turnover for Companies in Different Industries

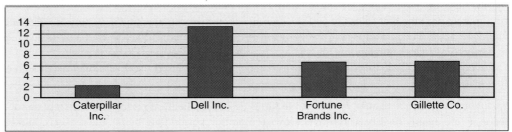

Gillette and **Fortune Brands** yield similar accounts receivable turnover. These companies are comparable in that both manufacture and sell consumer products. Fortune Brands' products include Titleist golf balls and equipment, Moen faucets, and Jim Beam whiskey. **Caterpillar**, on the other hand, is a heavy equipment producer that finances much of its equipment sales with intermediate-term loans and leases. Thus, its accounts receivable turnover is much lower. At the other end is **Dell Computer**. Much of Dell's sales occur on a cash basis via the Internet and, hence, its accounts receivable turnover is very high.

MANAGERIAL DECISION   You Are the Receivables Manager

You are analyzing your receivables turnover report for the period and you are concerned that the average collection period is lengthening. What specific actions can you take to reduce the average collection period? [Answer, p. 5-33]

▓ MID-MODULE REVIEW 1 ▓

At December 31, 2005, Engel Company had a balance of $770,000 in its Accounts Receivable account and an unused balance of $7,000 in its Allowance for Uncollectible Accounts. The company then analyzed and aged its accounts receivable as follows:

Current	$468,000
1–60 days past due	244,000
61–180 days past due	38,000
Over 180 days past due	20,000
Total accounts receivable	$770,000

In the past, the company experienced losses as follows: 1% of current balances, 5% of balances 0–60 days past due, 15% of balances 61–180 days past due, and 40% of balances over 180 days past due. The company bases its provision for credit losses on the aging analysis.

Required
1. What amount of uncollectible accounts (bad debts) expense will Engel report in its 2005 income statement?
2. Show how Accounts Receivable and the Allowance for Uncollectible Accounts appear in its December 31, 2005, balance sheet.
3. Assume that Engel's allowance for uncollectible accounts has maintained an historical average of 2% of gross accounts receivable. How do you interpret the level of the current allowance percentage?

Solution

1. As of December 31, 2005:

Current . . . . $468,000 × 1% = $	4,680
1–60 days past due . . . . 244,000 × 5% =	12,200
61–180 days past due . . . . 38,000 × 15% =	5,700
Over 180 days past due . . . . 20,000 × 40% =	8,000
Amount required	$ 30,580
Unused allowance balance	7,000
Provision	$ 23,580 2005 bad debts expense

2. Current assets section of balance sheet:

Accounts receivable, net of $30,580 in allowances . . .	$739,420

3. Engel Company has markedly increased the percentage of the allowance for uncollectible accounts to gross accounts receivable—from the historical 2% to the current 4% ($30,580/$770,000). There are at least two possible interpretations:
    a. The quality of Engel Company's receivables has declined. Possible causes include the following: (1) Sales can stagnate and the company can feel compelled to sell to lower quality accounts to maintain sales volume; (2) It may have introduced new products for which average credit losses are higher; and (3) Its administration of accounts receivable can become lax.
    b. The company has intentionally increased its allowance account above the level needed for expected future losses so as to reduce current period income and "bank" that income for future periods (income shifting).

■ INVENTORY

The second of the two major components of operating working capital is inventory. To help frame this discussion, we again refer to the following graphic. We highlight inventory, which is a major asset for most manufacturers and merchandisers. We also highlight cost of goods sold on the income statement, which reflects the flow of inventory costs to match against related sales. This section explains the accounting, reporting, and analysis of inventory and related items.

Income Statement	Balance Sheet	
Sales	Cash	Current liabilities
Cost of goods sold	Accounts receivable	Long-term liabilities
Selling, general & administrative	**Inventory**	
Income taxes	Property, plant, and equipment, net	Shareholders' equity
Net income	Investments	

Inventory is reported on the balance sheet at its purchase price or the cost to manufacture those goods if internally produced. Such prices and costs typically vary over time with changes in market conditions. Consequently, the cost per unit of the goods available for sale likely varies from period to period—even if the quantity of goods available remains the same.

Once inventory is purchased or produced, it is carried on the balance sheet as an asset until it is sold, at which time its cost is transferred from the balance sheet to the income statement as an expense (cost of goods sold). The process by which costs are removed from the balance sheet is important. For example, if higher cost units are transferred from the balance sheet when a sale is recorded, then gross profit (sales less cost of goods sold) is lower. Conversely, if lower cost units are transferred to cost of goods sold, gross profit is higher. The remainder of this section discusses inventory cost capitalization and recognition including the mechanics, reporting, and analysis of inventory costing.

Capitalization of Inventory Cost

Capitalization means that a cost is recorded on the balance sheet and is not immediately expensed on the income statement. Once costs are capitalized, they remain on the balance sheet as assets until they are used up, at which time they are transferred from the balance sheet to the income statement as expense. If costs are capitalized rather than expensed, then assets, current income, and current equity are higher.

For purchased inventories (such as those with merchandisers), the amount of cost capitalized is the purchase price. For manufacturers, cost capitalization is more difficult, as **manufacturing costs** consist of three components: cost of direct materials used in the product, cost of direct labor to manufacture the product, and manufacturing overhead. Direct materials cost is relatively easy to compute. Design specifications list the components of each product, and their purchase costs are readily determined. The direct labor cost per unit of inventory is based on how long each unit takes to construct and the rates for each labor class working on that product. Overhead costs are also capitalized into inventory, and include the costs of plant asset depreciation, utilities, supervisory personnel, and other costs that contribute to manufacturing activities—that is, all costs of manufacturing other than direct materials and direct labor. (How these costs are assigned to individual units and across multiple products is a *managerial accounting* topic and beyond the scope of this book.)

When inventories are used up in production or are sold, their costs are transferred from the balance sheet to the income statement as cost of goods sold (COGS). COGS is then matched against sales revenue to yield **gross profit**:

$$\text{Gross Profit} = \text{Sales Revenue} - \text{Cost of Goods Sold}$$

The manner in which inventory costs are transferred from the balance sheet to the income statement affects both the level of inventories reported on the balance sheet and the amount of gross profit (and net income) reported on the income statement.

Inventory Costing Methods

Computation of cost of goods sold is important and is shown in Exhibit 5.5.

EXHIBIT 5.5 ■ Cost of Goods Sold Computation

	Beginning inventory (prior period balance sheet)
+	Inventory purchases and/or production
	Cost of goods available for sale
−	Ending inventory (current period balance sheet)
	Cost of goods sold (current income statement)

The cost of inventory available at the beginning of a period is a carryover from the ending inventory balance of the prior period. Current period purchases of inventory (or costs of newly manufactured inventories) are added to the costs of beginning inventory on the balance sheet, yielding the total cost of goods (inventory) available for sale. Then, the total cost of goods available either end up in cost of goods sold for the period (reported on the income statement) or is carried forward as inventory to start the next period (reported on the balance sheet). This cost flow is graphically shown in Exhibit 5.6.

EXHIBIT 5.6 ■ Inventory Cost Flows to Financial Statements

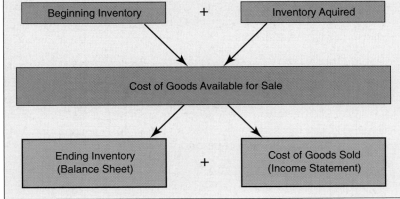

Understanding the flow of inventory costs is important. If all inventory purchased or manufactured during the period is sold, then COGS is equal to the cost of the goods purchased or manufactured. However, when inventory remains at the end of a period, companies must identify the cost of those inventories that have been sold and the cost of those inventories that remain. The issue involves determining the order in which inventories have been sold and GAAP allows for several options.

To illustrate the possible cost flow assumptions that companies can adopt, assume that Exhibit 5.7 reflects the inventory records of a company.

EXHIBIT 5.7 ■ Summary Inventory Records for a Company

Inventory on January 1, 2005	500 units @ $100 each	$50,000
Inventory purchased in 2005	200 units @ $150 each	30,000
Total cost of goods available for sale in 2005	700 units	$80,000

This company began the period with inventories consisting of 500 units that it either purchased or manufactured at a total cost of $50,000 ($100 each). During the period the company purchased and/or manufactured an additional 200 units costing $30,000. The total cost of goods that are available for sale for this period equals $80,000.

This company sold 450 units during 2005 at a selling price of $250 per unit for total sales of $112,500. Accordingly, the company must remove the cost of the goods sold from its reported inventories on the balance sheet and match this cost against the revenues generated from the goods sold (reported as cost of goods sold). An important question is which costs should management remove from the balance sheet and report as cost of goods sold in the income statement. Three inventory costing methods are commonly used, and all are acceptable under GAAP.

First-In, First-Out (FIFO)

The FIFO inventory costing method transfers costs from inventory in the order that they were initially recorded. That is, FIFO assumes that the first costs recorded in inventory (first-in) are the first costs transferred from inventory (first-out). Applying FIFO to the data in Exhibit 5.7 means that the costs relating to the 450 units sold are all taken from its *beginning* inventory, which consists of 500 units. The company's cost of goods sold and gross profit, using FIFO, is computed as follows:

Sales	$112,500
COGS (450 @ $100 each)	45,000
Gross profit	$ 67,500

The cost remaining in inventory and reported on its 2005 year-end balance sheet is $35,000 ($80,000 − $45,000).

Last-In, First-Out (LIFO)

The LIFO inventory costing method transfers the most recent costs that were recorded in inventory. That is, we assume that the most recent costs recorded in inventory (last-in) are the first costs transferred from inventory (first-out). The company's cost of goods sold and gross profit, using LIFO, is computed as follows:

Sales	$112,500
COGS: (200 @ $150 each = $30,000)	
(250 @ $100 each = $25,000)	55,000
Gross profit	$ 57,500

The cost remaining in inventory and reported on its 2005 balance sheet is $25,000 (80,000 − $55,000).

Average Cost (AC)

The average cost method computes the cost of goods sold as an average of the cost to purchase or manufacture all of the inventories that were available for sale during the period as follows:

Sales	$112,500
COGS (450 @ $114.286 [$80,000/700 units] each)	51,429
Gross profit	$ 61,071

The average cost of $114.286 per unit is determined from the total cost of goods available for sale divided by the number of units available for sale ($80,000/700 units). The cost remaining in inventory and reported on its 2005 balance sheet is $28,571 ($80,000 − $51,429).

Footnote Disclosures

Notes to financial statements describe, at least in general terms, the inventory accounting method used by a company. To illustrate, Gillette reports $1,094 million in inventory on its 2003 balance sheet as a current asset. Gillette includes a general footnote on inventory along with more specific disclosures in other footnotes. Following is an excerpt from Gillette's general footnote related to inventories:

> Inventories are stated at the lower of cost or market. Cost is determined on a first-in, first-out (FIFO) basis.

This footnote includes at least two items of interest for our analysis of inventory:

1. Gillette uses the FIFO method of inventory costing.
2. Inventories are reported at the lower of cost or market—lower of cost or market (LCM) means that inventory is written down if its replacement cost declines below its FIFO cost reported on the balance sheet (see impairment cost discussion that follows).

Gillette includes another footnote that provides further details on its manufacturing inventories as follows:

Inventories At December 31 (millions)	2003	2002
Raw materials and supplies	$ 114	$115
Work in process	196	191
Finished goods	784	622
Total inventories	$1,094	$928

This disclosure separately reports its inventory costs by the following stages in its production cycle:

- *Raw materials and supplies* These are costs of direct materials and inputs into the production process, including for example base chemicals in raw state, plastic and steel for manufacturing, and incidental direct materials such as screws and lubricants.
- *Work in process* These are costs of partly finished products (also called work-in-progress) in the manufacturing process.
- *Finished goods* These are the costs of products that are completed and awaiting sale.

Gillette's raw materials and work-in-process inventories have roughly remained at 2002 levels despite a 9.5% increase in sales. This likely reflects its cost reduction and production efficiency programs initiated in 2002–2003. On the downside, its finished goods inventory has increased.

Why do companies disclose such details on inventory, and why is so much attention paid to inventory in financial statement analysis? First, the magnitude of a company's investment in inventory is typically huge—impacting both balance sheets and income statements. Second, risks of inventory losses are often high, as they are tied to technical obsolescence and consumer tastes. Third, it can give us insight into future performance—both good and bad. Fourth, high inventory levels result in substantial costs for the company, such as the following:

- Financing costs to purchase inventories (when not purchased on credit)
- Storage costs of inventories (such as warehousing and related facilities)
- Handling costs of inventories (including wages)
- Insurance costs of inventories

Consequently, companies seek to minimize the amount of inventories available provided this does not exceed the cost of insufficient inventory (stock-out and resulting lost sales and delays in production as machines and employees sit idle awaiting inventories to process).

Lower of Cost or Market

Gillette's inventory disclosures make reference to the cost of its inventories not exceeding market value. This is important as companies are required to write down the carrying amount of inventories on the balance sheet *if* the reported cost (using FIFO, for example) exceeds market value (determined by current replacement cost). This process is called reporting inventories at the **lower of cost or market**. Should the replacement cost (market value) be less than reported cost, the inventories must be written down from cost to market, resulting in the following financial statement effects:

- Inventory book value is written down to current market value (replacement cost); reducing total assets.
- Inventory write-down is reflected as an expense (part of cost of goods sold) on the income statement; reducing current period gross profit, income, and equity.

The most common occurrence of inventory write-downs is in connection with restructuring activities. These write-downs are included in cost of goods sold. They are *not* reported in selling, general, and administrative expenses, which is common for other asset write-downs.

The write-down of inventories can potentially shift income from one period to another. If, for example, inventories were written down below current replacement cost (too conservative), future gross profit would be increased as lower future costs would be reflected in cost of goods sold. GAAP anticipates this possibility by requiring that inventories not be written down below a floor that is equal to net realizable value less a normal markup. Although this does allow some discretion (and the ability to manage income), the net realizable value and markup values must be substantiated by auditors.

Financial Statement Effects of Inventory Costing

This section describes the financial statement effects of different inventory costing methods.

Income Statement Effects

The three inventory costing methods described yield differing levels of gross profit for our illustrative example as shown in Exhibit 5.8.

EXHIBIT 5.8 ■ Income Effects from Inventory Costing Methods

	Sales	Cost of Goods Sold	Gross Profit
FIFO	$112,500	$45,000	$67,500
LIFO	112,500	55,000	57,500
Average cost	112,500	51,429	61,071

It is important to keep in mind the underlying cost behavior of this case: the illustrative company's unit costs are subject to inflation and, as a result, inventory costs have risen during this period (from $100 per unit to $150 per unit). The higher gross profit reported under FIFO is because it matches older, lower cost inventory (vis-à-vis LIFO) against current selling prices. To generalize: in an inflationary environment, FIFO yields higher gross profit than does LIFO or average cost.

The gross profit impact from FIFO is determined by two effects, First, goods previously purchased at a lower cost can now be sold at a higher selling price (due to inflation). Second, the longer those goods sit in inventory as inflation occurs, the greater the holding gain from inflation. In recent years, such gains have been minimal due to minimal inflation and increased management focus on reducing inventory quantities through improved manufacturing processes and better inventory controls. The FIFO gross profit effect can still arise, however, with companies subject to high inflation and slow inventory turnover.

Balance Sheet Effects

The ending inventory using LIFO for our illustration is less than that reported using FIFO. In periods of rising costs, using LIFO generally yields ending inventories that are markedly lower than FIFO. As a result, balance sheets using LIFO do not accurately represent the cost that a company would incur to replace its current investment in inventories.

Caterpillar (CAT), for example, reports 2003 inventories under LIFO costing $3,047 million. As disclosed in the footnotes to its 10-K, if CAT valued these inventories using FIFO, the reported amount would be $1,863 million greater, a 61% increase. This suggests that over $1,863 million currently invested in inventories is omitted from CAT's balance sheet.

Cash Flow Effects

$
Cash Effect

The increased gross profit using FIFO results in higher pretax income and, consequently, higher taxes payable (assuming FIFO is also used for tax reporting). Conversely, the use of LIFO in an inflationary environment results in a reduced tax liability.[4]

Caterpillar, Inc. reports the following disclosure to its 2003 10-K regarding its inventories:

> Inventories are stated at the lower of cost or market. Cost is principally determined using the last-in, first-out (LIFO) method. The value of inventories on the LIFO basis represented about 80% of total inventories at December 31, 2003, 2002 and 2001.
>
> If the FIFO (first-in, first-out) method had been in use, inventories would have been $1,863 million, $1,977 million and $1,923 million higher than reported at December 31, 2003, 2002 and 2001, respectively.

Most of CAT's inventories are reported using LIFO.[5] The use of LIFO has reduced the carrying amount of its 2003 inventories by $1,863 million. Had it used FIFO, its inventories would have been reported at $4,910 million rather than the $3,047 million that is reported on its balance sheet as of 2003. This difference, referred to as the **LIFO reserve**, is the amount LIFO inventories must be adjusted to equal FIFO inventories.

Use of LIFO has reduced the dollar amount of CAT's inventories by $1,863 million, resulting in a cumulative increase in cost of goods sold and a cumulative decrease in gross profit and pretax profit of that same amount.[6] The decrease in pretax profits reduces CAT's tax bill by $652 million ($1,863 million × 35% assumed corporate tax rate), which increases CAT's cumulative operating cash flow by that same amount. The increased cash flow from tax savings is often cited as a compelling reason for management to adopt LIFO.

We can use the LIFO reserve to adjust for analysis purposes the balance sheet and income statement to achieve comparability between companies that utilize different inventory costing methods. For example, if we wanted to compare CAT with another company using FIFO, we can add the LIFO reserve to its LIFO inventory. As explained above, this $4,910 million increase in 2003 inventories would have increased its pretax profits by $1,863 million and taxes by $652 million. Thus, the balance sheet adjustments involve increasing inventories by $1,863 million, tax liabilities by $652 million, and equity by the remaining after-tax amount of $1,211 million (computed as $1,863 − $652).

To adjust the income statement from LIFO to FIFO, we use the *change* in LIFO reserve (for CAT, it changes from $1,977 million in 2002 to $1,863 million in 2003). CAT's 2003 pretax income *increases* by $113 million from the *decrease* in LIFO reserve. This means that had it been using FIFO, its COGS would have been $113 million higher, and gross profit and pretax income would have been $113 million lower. This shows that use of LIFO does not always yield lower pretax profit as costs do not always rise. (Companies can also sustain reductions in the LIFO reserve if inventories are liquidated as described below.)

RESEARCH INSIGHT   LIFO and Stock Prices

The value-relevance of inventory disclosures depends at least partly on whether investors rely more on the income statement or the balance sheet to assess future cash flows. Under LIFO, cost of goods sold reflects current costs, whereas FIFO ending inventory reflects current costs. This implies that LIFO enhances the usefulness of the income statement to the detriment of the balance sheet. This trade-off partly motivates the required LIFO reserve disclosure (the adjustment necessary to restate LIFO ending inventory and cost of good sold to FIFO).

Research suggests that LIFO-based income statements better reflect stock prices than do FIFO income statements that are restated using the LIFO reserve. Research also shows a negative relation between stock prices and LIFO reserve—meaning that higher magnitudes of LIFO reserve are associated with lower stock prices. This is consistent with the LIFO reserve being viewed as an inflation indicator (for either current or future inventory costs) detrimental to company value.

---

[4]When a company adopts LIFO in its tax filings, the IRS requires it to use LIFO for reporting to its shareholders (in its 10-K). This requirement is known as the *LIFO conformity rule.*

[5]Neither the IRS nor GAAP requires use of a single inventory costing method. That is, companies are allowed to, and frequently do, use different inventory costing methods for different pools of their inventories (such as spare parts versus finished goods).

[6]Recall: Cost of Goods Sold = Beginning Inventories + Purchases − Ending Inventories. Thus, as ending inventories decrease, cost of goods sold increases.

Tools of Inventory Analysis

This section describes several useful tools for analysis of inventory and related accounts.

Gross profit analysis

The **gross profit margin (GPM)** is gross profit divided by sales. This is an important ratio that is monitored by management and outsiders. The gross profit margin of Gillette for each of the past three years is shown in Exhibit 5.9.

EXHIBIT 5.9 ▓ Gross Profit Margin for Gillette

	2003	2002	2001
Revenues	$9,252	$8,453	$8,084
Cost of goods sold	3,708	3,511	3,407
Gross profit	$5,544	$4,942	$4,677
Gross profit margin	59.9%	58.5%	57.9%

The gross profit margin is commonly used instead of the dollar amount of gross profit as it allows for comparisons across companies and over time. A decline in GPM is usually cause for concern since it indicates that the company has less ability to pass on to customers increased costs in its products. Since companies try to charge the highest price the market will bear, we can safely assume that a decline in GPM is the result of market forces beyond the company's control. Some possible reasons for a GPM decline follow:

- Product line is stale. Perhaps it is out of fashion and the company must resort to markdowns to reduce overstocked inventories. Or, perhaps the product lines have lost their technological edge, yielding reduced demand.
- New competitors enter the market. Perhaps substitute products are now available from competitors, yielding increased pressure to reduce selling prices.
- General decline in economic activity. Perhaps an economic downturn reduces product demand. The recession of the early 2000s led to reduced gross profits for many companies.
- Inventory is overstocked. Perhaps the company overproduced goods and finds itself in an overstock position. This can require reduced selling prices to move inventory.

Gillette increased its 2003 gross profit margin 2 percentage points above that for 2001, a substantial increase for a two-year period. Following is Gillette's discussion of its gross profit improvement from its 2003 10-K:

> Gross profit was $5.54 billion in 2003, $4.94 billion in 2002, and $4.68 billion in 2001. As a percent of net sales, gross profit was 59.9% in 2003, 58.5% in 2002, and 57.9% in 2001. The improvement in gross profit was due to favorable product mix, cost-savings initiatives, and manufacturing efficiencies, which more than offset higher European-based costs due to exchange and $50 million in incremental provisions to realign European blade and razor manufacturing and distribution.

Competitive pressures mean that companies rarely have the opportunity to affect gross profit with price increases. Most improvements in gross profit that we witness are likely the result of better management of supply chains, production processes, or distribution networks. Companies that win typically do so because of better performance on basic business processes. This is one of Gillette's primary objectives.

Inventory Turnover

Inventory turnover (INVT) is a useful measure of inventory management and is computed as follows:

Inventory Turnover = Cost of Goods Sold/Average Inventory

Cost of goods sold is in the numerator because inventory is reported at cost. Inventory turnover indicates how many times inventory turns (is sold) during a period. More turns indicate that inventory is being sold more quickly.

Average inventory days outstanding (AIDO), also called *days inventory outstanding,* is a companion measure to inventory turnover and is computed as follows:

Average Inventory Days Outstanding = Inventory/Average Daily Cost of Goods Sold

where average daily cost of goods sold equals cost of goods sold divided by 365 days.

Average inventory days outstanding indicates how long, on average, inventories are *on the shelves* before being sold. For example, if cost of goods sold is $1,200 and average (and ending) inventories are $300, inventories are turning four times and are on the shelves 91.25 days ($300/[$1,200/365]) on average. This performance might be an acceptable turnover for the retail fashion industry where it needs to sell out its inventories each retail selling season, but it would not be acceptable for the grocery industry.

Analysis of inventory turnover is important for at least two reasons:

1. *Inventory quality.* Inventory turnover can be compared with those of prior periods and competitors. Higher turnover is viewed favorably, implying that products are salable, preferably without undue discounting of selling prices. Conversely, lower turnover implies that inventory is on the shelves for a longer period of time, perhaps from excessive purchases or production, missed fashion trends or technological advances, increased competition, and so forth. Our conclusions about higher or lower turnover must consider alternative explanations such as the following:
   a. Company product mix can change to higher margin, slower turning inventories or vice-versa. This can occur from business acquisitions and the resulting consolidated inventories.
   b. A company can change its promotion policies. Increased, effective advertising is likely to increase inventory turnover. Advertising expense is in SG&A, not COGS. This means the cost is in operating expenses, but the benefit is in gross profit and turnover. If the promotion campaign is successful, the positive effects in margin and turnover should offset the promotion cost in SG&A.
   c. A company can realize improvements in manufacturing efficiency and lower investments in direct materials and work-in-process inventories. Such improvements reduce inventory and, consequently, increase inventory turnover. Although positive, it does not yield any information about the desirability of a company's product line.
2. *Asset utilization.* Companies strive to optimize their inventory investment. Carrying too much inventory is expensive, and too little inventory risks stock-outs and lost sales (current and future). There are operational changes that companies can make to reduce inventory:
   a. Improved manufacturing processes can eliminate bottlenecks and the consequent build-up of work-in-process inventories.
   b. Just-in-time (JIT) deliveries from suppliers that provide raw materials to the production line when needed can reduce the level of raw materials required.
   c. Demand-pull production, in which raw materials are released into the production process when final goods are demanded by customers instead of producing for estimated demand, can reduce inventory levels. Dell Computer produces for actual, rather than estimated, demand; as its computers are manufactured after the customer order is received.

$
Cash Effect

Reducing inventories reduces inventory carrying costs, thus improving profitability and increasing cash flow (asset reduction is reflected as a cash inflow adjustment in the statement of cash flows).

There is normal tension between the sales side of a company that argues for depth and breadth of inventory and the finance side that monitors inventory carrying costs and seeks to maximize cash flow. Companies, therefore, seek to *optimize* inventory investment, not *minimize* it.

Following is a chart comparing Gillette's inventory turnover with the peer companies it identifies in its 2003 10-K. Although Gillette's inventory turnover has improved over the past two years, it is about the same as Energizer, which is the lower performer. Further, inventory turnover for both Procter and Gamble and Colgate-Palmolive are markedly better than that for Gillette.

Inventory Turnover for Gillette and Competitors

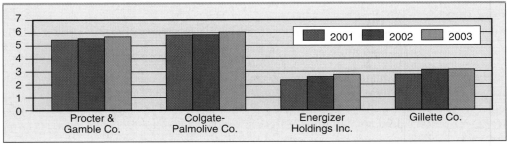

It is also instructive to compare the consumer products manufacturing industry represented by Gillette against some other companies and industries as follows:

Inventory Turnover for Companies from Different Industries

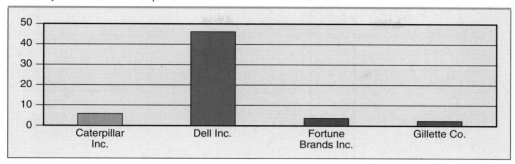

Dell's production management expertise is well known. It effectively utilizes its buying power over suppliers and its just-in-time delivery processes to minimize the investment in and cost of raw materials. Its production process is so efficient that work-in-process inventories are virtually zero. (Dell reports less work-in-process inventories than Gillette and has nearly four times the sales!) Dell also produces to order instead of for finished goods inventory. As a result, it reports finished goods inventories that are less than one-tenth of those for Gillette. Consequently, Dell's inventory turnover is nearly off the chart. However, Gillette reasonably compares with the others. For example, Gillette's inventory turnover is slightly less than that for Fortune Brands (3.0 times versus 3.6 times per year) but is less than the 5.4 times per year of Caterpillar.

MANAGERIAL DECISION   You Are the Plant Manager

You are analyzing your inventory turnover report for the month and are concerned that the average inventory days outstanding is lengthening. What actions can you take to reduce average inventory days outstanding? [Answer, p. 5-33]

LIFO Liquidations

When companies acquire inventory at different costs, they are required to maintain each cost level as a separate inventory *pool* or *layer* (for example, the $100 and $150 cost units in our Exhibit 5.7 illustration). When companies reduce inventory levels, current selling prices are matched with older inventory costs. If the company uses FIFO inventory costing, its older costs are not that much different from its current replacement costs (FIFO inventories are the most recent purchases). As a result, profits do not markedly change. Yet, when companies use LIFO inventory costing, older costs are often markedly different than current replacement costs. Given the usual inflationary environment, sales of older pools often yield a boost to gross profit as older, lower costs are matched against current selling prices.

The increase in gross profit, resulting from a reduction of inventory quantities in the presence of rising costs is called **LIFO liquidation**. The effect of LIFO liquidation is evident in the following footnote from General Motors Corporation's 2003 10-K:

> Inventories are stated generally at cost, which is not in excess of market. The cost of approximately 92% of U.S. inventories is determined by the last-in, first-out (LIFO) method. Generally, the cost of all other inventories is determined by either the first-in, first-out (FIFO) or average cost methods.
>
> During 2003, U.S. LIFO eligible inventory quantities were reduced. This reduction resulted in a liquidation of LIFO inventory quantities carried at lower costs prevailing in prior years as compared with the cost of 2003 purchases, the effect of which decreased cost of goods sold by approximately $200 million, pre-tax.

GM reports that reductions in inventory quantities led to the sale (at current selling prices) of products that carried costs from prior years that were less than current costs. As a result of these inventory reductions, pretax income increased by $200 million from lower COGS. In this case, the inventory LIFO liquidation yielded a profit increase. We must be aware, however, of potentially different income effects from LIFO liquidations when inventory costs fluctuate.

▩ MID-MODULE REVIEW 2 ▩

At the beginning of the current period, Hutton Company holds 1,000 units of its only product with a per unit cost of $18. A summary of purchases during the current period follows:

	Units	Unit Cost	Cost
Beginning Inventory	1,000	$18.00	$18,000
Purchases: #1	1,800	18.25	32,850
#2	800	18.50	14,800
#3	1,200	19.00	22,800
Goods available for sale	4,800		$88,450

During the current period, Hutton sells 2,800 units.

Required

1. Assume that Hutton uses the first-in, first-out (FIFO) method. Compute the cost of goods sold for the current period and the ending inventory balance.
2. Assume that Hutton uses the last-in, first-out (LIFO) method. Compute the cost of goods sold for the current period and the ending inventory balance.
3. Assume that Hutton uses the average cost (AC) method. Compute the cost of goods sold for the current period and the ending inventory balance.
4. As manager, which one of these three inventory costing methods would you choose:
    a. To reflect what is probably the physical flow of goods? Explain.
    b. To minimize income taxes for the period? Explain.
5. Assume that Hutton utilizes the LIFO method and instead of purchasing lot #3, the company allows its inventory level to decline and delays purchasing lot #3 until the next period. Compute cost of goods sold under this scenario and discuss the effect of LIFO liquidation on profit.

Solution

Preliminary computation: Units in ending inventory = 4,800 available − 2,800 sold = 2,000

1. First-in, first-out (FIFO)

Cost of goods sold computation:	Units		Cost		Total
	1,000	@	$18.00	=	$18,000
	1,800	@	$18.25	=	32,850
	2,800				$50,850
Cost of goods available for sale			$88,450		
Less: Cost of goods sold			50,850		
Ending inventory ($22,800 + $14,800)			**$37,600**		

2. Last-in, first-out (LIFO)

Cost of goods sold computation:	Units		Cost		Total
	1,200	@	$19.00	=	$22,800
	800	@	$18.50	=	14,800
	800	@	$18.25	=	14,600
	2,800				$52,200
Cost of goods available for sale			$88,450		
Less: Cost of goods sold			52,200		
Ending inventory ($18,000 + [1,000 × $18.25])			**$36,250**		

3.　Average cost (AC)

$$\text{Average unit cost } = \$88,450/4,800 \quad = \$18.427$$
$$\text{Cost of goods sold} = 2,800 \times \$18.427 = \mathbf{\$51,596}$$
$$\text{Ending inventory } \quad = 2,000 \times \$18.427 = \mathbf{\$36,854}$$

4.　a.　FIFO in most circumstances reflects physical flow. For example, FIFO would apply to the physical flow of perishables and to situations where the earlier items acquired are moved out first because of risk of deterioration or obsolescence.

　　b.　LIFO results in the lowest ending inventory amount during periods of rising costs, which in turn yields the lowest net income and the lowest income taxes.

5.　Last-in, first-out with LIFO liquidation

Cost of goods sold computation:	Units		Cost		Total
	800	@	$18.50	=	$14,800
	1,800	@	$18.25	=	32,850
	200	@	$18.00	=	3,600
	2,800				$51,250
Cost of goods available for sale			$65,650		
Less: Cost of goods sold			51,250		
Ending inventory (800 × $18)			$14,400		

The company's LIFO gross profit has increased by $950 ($52,200 − $51,250). This increase is from LIFO liquidation, which is the reduction of inventory quantities that results in matching older (lower) cost layers against current selling prices. The company has, in effect, dipped into lower cost layers to boost current period profit—all from a simple delay of inventory purchases.

■ PROPERTY, PLANT, AND EQUIPMENT (PPE)

For many companies, the largest of operating assets is that of its long-term property, plant, and equipment assets. To frame this discussion, we again refer to the following graphic where we highlight long-term operating assets on the balance sheet, and selling, general and administrative expenses on the income statement.[7] The latter includes the allocation of those asset costs, such as depreciation and asset write-downs, to match against sales benefited by those assets. This section explains the accounting, reporting, and analysis of those long-term operating assets and related items.

Income Statement
Sales
Cost of goods sold
Selling, general & administrative
Income taxes
Net income

Balance Sheet	
Cash	Current liabilities
Accounts receivable	Long-term liabilities
Inventory	
Property, plant, and equipment, net	Shareholders' equity
Investments	

Capitalization of Asset Costs

An expenditure is reported as an asset on the balance sheet only if it possesses each of the following two characteristics:

1.　The asset is owned or controlled by the company.
2.　The asset provides future expected benefits.

---

[7] Depreciation on any manufacturing facilities is included in cost of goods sold.

Owning the asset means the company has title to the asset as provided in a purchase contract.[8] Future expected benefits usually refer to future cash inflows.

Companies can only capitalize those asset costs that are *directly linked* to future cash inflows, and the costs capitalized as an asset can be no greater than the expected future cash inflows from that asset. This means that if a company reports a $200 asset, we can reasonably expect that it will derive *at least* $200 in expected cash inflows from the use and ultimate disposition of the asset.

BUSINESS INSIGHT   **WorldCom and Improper Cost Capitalization**

Federal authorities arrested **WorldCom**'s chief financial officer, Scott Sullivan, and its controller (chief accounting officer), David Myers, in August 2002 for allegedly conspiring to alter the telecommunications giant's financial statements to meet analyst expectations. They were accused of *cooking the books* so the company would not show a loss for 2001 and subsequent quarters (U.S. v. Sullivan et al., No. 02-1511, complaint unsealed, S.D.N.Y., 8/1/2002). According to the criminal complaint, WorldCom failed to generate enough revenue to offset its costs. These costs were fees charged by third-party telecommunications companies for access to their networks that allowed WorldCom to enlarge its service area. Many of these access-leases required WorldCom to pay a fixed sum to the outside network regardless of whether WorldCom actually made use of all or part of the capacity agreed upon.

WorldCom obtained these leases in anticipation of an increase in Internet-related business that did not materialize. Instead of reporting the loss, its executives shifted operating costs to its capitalized assets. By capitalizing these costs (moving them from the income statement to the balance sheet), WorldCom was able to disguise these costs as an asset to be allocated as future costs. When questioned by internal auditors, Sullivan allegedly said the costs were "pre-paid capacity" associated with underutilized lines.

Contrary to WorldCom's usual practices and prevailing accounting principles, no support existed for its capitalization, alleges FBI agents. Further, other officials within WorldCom expressed concerns about the propriety of its capitalization to no avail. Myers did admit that the amounts were capitalized based on historical margins (ratio of line costs to revenues), and he acknowledged no support for that. Myers also said he was uncomfortable with capitalization, but that once it started it was difficult to stop.

Although the WorldCom case also involved alleged fraud, an astute analyst would have suspected something was amiss from analysis of WorldCom's long-term asset turnover (Sales/Average long-term assets) as shown below. The obvious decline in turnover reveals that its assets constituted an ever-increasing percent of total sales during 1995 to 2002, by quarter. This finding does not, in itself, imply fraud. It does, however, raise serious questions that should have been answered by WorldCom executives in meetings with analysts.

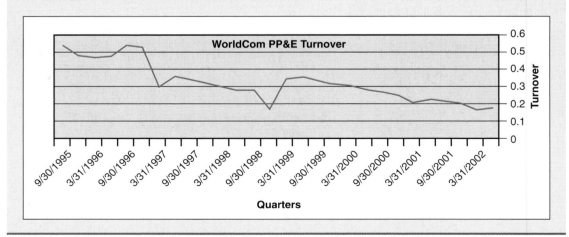

---

[8]Assets acquired under leases are also capitalized *if* certain conditions are met—see Module 9.

The *directly linked* condition for capitalization of asset cost is important. When a company acquires a machine, it expects the machine's output to yield cash inflows (from the sale of product and eventual disposition). It can, therefore, capitalize those asset costs. On the other hand, when it expends funds for research and development (R&D) activities, it cannot directly link expected cash inflows with those expenditures since R&D activities are often unsuccessful. Further, it cannot estimate with relative certainty the future cash flows from successful R&D activities. Accordingly, GAAP requires that R&D expenditures be expensed when paid.

To further understand this directly linked condition, let's consider two additional expenditures. First, a company expects its advertising costs to yield future cash inflows from increased sales. Yet, a company cannot link specific future cash inflows with a particular ad campaign. Advertising expenditures are, therefore, expensed. Second, a company pays wages to employees with the expectation they generate cash inflows. Although employees are expected to provide future benefits, a company cannot link those expected benefits directly with the output of specific workers and, therefore, it cannot capitalize wage costs.

Each of these examples relate to items or activities that we generally think of as *assets*. That is, we reasonably expect R&D efforts and advertising campaigns to produce results. If not, companies would not pursue them. We also generally view employee activities as generating future benefits. Indeed, we often refer to the *human resources* (asset) of a company.

However, the link between these items or activities and their outputs is not as direct as GAAP requires for capitalizing such costs. As a result, these asset types are not reported on balance sheets. It is important to note that these activities (R&D, advertising, and wages) are more prevalent in knowledge-based industries. Yet, even traditional retailers and manufacturers are concerned with management of their intangible knowledge-based assets. The nonrecognition of these assets is one reason it is difficult to analyze and value knowledge-based companies. Such companies are less suited to traditional ROE disaggregation analysis. Capitalization and non-capitalization of costs can markedly impact financial statements and, therefore, our analysis inferences and a company's investment prospects.

Depreciation

Once a depreciable cost is recognized on the balance sheet as an asset, it must then be systematically transferred from the balance sheet to the income statement as depreciation expense to match asset cost with the revenues it generates. The depreciation process requires the following estimates:

1. **Useful life.** Period of time over which the asset is expected to generate cash inflows
2. **Salvage value.** Expected disposal amount for the asset at the end of its useful life
3. **Depreciation rate.** An estimate of how the asset will be used up over its useful life

Each of these factors must be estimated when the asset is acquired. Depreciation commences immediately upon asset acquisition and use. Estimates that determine depreciation are revised, if necessary, during the life of the asset.

The **depreciation base**, also called *nonrecoverable cost,* of an asset is what is depreciated. The depreciation base is the acquisition cost less estimated salvage value. This means that at the end of its useful life, only salvage value remains on the balance sheet. If this estimate of salvage value proves correct, the company will dispose of the asset for that salvage value and no gain or loss on disposal is reported. If the company receives more (less) than salvage value, then a gain (or loss) is reported equal to the sales proceeds less the book value of the asset disposed.

Depreciation rate refers to the manner in which the asset is used up. One of the following three assumptions is typically made about the depreciation rate:

1. Asset is used up by the same amount each period.
2. Asset is used up more in the early years of its useful life.
3. Asset is used up in proportion to its actual usage.

A company can depreciate different assets using different depreciation rates (and different useful lives). Whatever depreciation rate is chosen, however, it must generally be used throughout the useful life of that asset. Changes to depreciation rates can be made, but they must be justified as providing more useful financial reports.

The using up of an asset generally relates to physical or technological obsolescence. *Physical obsolescence* relates to an asset's diminished capacity to produce output. *Technological obsolescence* relates to an asset's diminished efficiency in producing output in a competitive manner. The decline of the U.S. steel-producing industry in the face of more efficient imports is an example of the latter.

All depreciation methods have the following general formula:

$$\text{Depreciation Expense} = \text{Depreciation Base} \times \text{Depreciation Rate}$$

Remembering this general form helps us understand the depreciation process. Also, each depreciation method reports the same amount of depreciation expense *over the life of the asset.* The only difference is in the amount of depreciation expense reported *for a given period.*

To illustrate depreciation mechanics, consider an asset (machine) with the following details: $100,000 cost, $10,000 salvage value, and a five-year useful life.

Straight-Line Method

Under the straight-line (SL) method, depreciation expense is recognized evenly over the estimated useful life of the asset as follows:

Depreciation Base	Depreciation Rate
Cost − Salvage value	1/Estimated useful life
= $100,000 − $10,000	= 1/5 years = 20%
= $90,000	

Depreciation expense per year for this asset is $18,000, computed as $90,000 × 20%.[9] For the asset's first full year of usage, $18,000 of depreciation expense is reported in the income statement. At the end of that first year the asset is reported on the balance sheet as follows:

Machine, at cost	$100,000
Less accumulated depreciation	18,000
Machine, net	$ 82,000

Accumulated depreciation is the sum of all depreciation expense that has been recorded to date. The asset **book value (BV)**, or *net book value* or *carrying value,* is cost less accumulated depreciation. Although the word value is used here, it does not refer to market value. Depreciation is a cost allocation concept (transfer of costs from the balance sheet to the income statement), not a valuation concept.

In the second year of usage, another $18,000 of depreciation expense is recorded in the income statement and the net book value of the asset on the balance sheet follows:

Machine, at cost	$100,000
Less accumulated depreciation	36,000
Machine, net	$ 64,000

Accumulated depreciation now includes the sum of the first and second years' depreciation ($36,000), and the net book value of the asset is now reduced to $64,000. After the fifth year, a total of $90,000 of accumulated depreciation will be recorded, yielding a net book value for the machine of $10,000, its estimated salvage value.

Double-Declining-Balance Method

GAAP also allows *accelerated* methods of depreciation, the most common being the double-declining-balance method. This method records more depreciation in the early years of an asset's useful life (hence

---

[9]If an asset is purchased in midyear, it is typically depreciated only for the portion of the year it is used. For example, had the asset in this illustration been purchased on May 1, the company would report $10,500 of depreciation in the first year, computed as 7/12 × $18,000.

the term *accelerated*) and less depreciation in later years. At the end of the asset's useful life, the balance sheet will still report a net book value equal to the asset's salvage value. The difference between straight-line and accelerated depreciation methods, then, is not in the total amount of depreciation, but in the rate at which costs are periodically transferred from the balance sheet to income statement.

For the double-declining-balance (DDB) method, the depreciation base and the depreciation rate are computed as follows:

Depreciation Base	Depreciation Rate
Net Book Value = Cost − Accumulated Depreciation	2 × SL rate = 2 × 20% = 40%

The depreciation expense for the first year of usage for this asset is $40,000, computed as $100,000 × 40%. At the end of the first full year, $40,000 of depreciation expense is reported on the income statement (compared with $18,000 under the SL method), and the asset is reported on the balance sheet as follows:

Machine, at cost	$100,000
Less accumulated depreciation	40,000
Machine, net	$ 60,000

In the second year, $24,000 ($60,000 × 40%) of depreciation expense is reported in the income statement and the net book value of the asset on the balance sheet follows:

Machine, at cost	$100,000
Less accumulated depreciation	64,000
Machine, net	$ 36,000

The double-declining-balance method continues to record depreciation expense in this manner until the salvage amount is reached, at which point the depreciation process is discontinued. This leaves a net book value equal to the salvage value as with the straight-line method.[10] The DDB depreciation schedule for the life of this asset is in Exhibit 5.10.

EXHIBIT 5.10 ▓ Double-Declining-Balance Depreciation Schedule

Year	Book Value at Beginning of Year	Depreciation Expense	Book Value at End of Year
1	$100,000	$40,000	$60,000
2	60,000	24,000	36,000
3	36,000	14,400	21,600
4	21,600	8,640	12,960
5	12,960	2,960*	10,000

*The formula value of $5,184 ($12,960 × 40%) is not reported because it would depreciate the asset below salvage value. Only the $2,960 needed to reach salvage value is reported as depreciated.

Exhibit 5.11 shows the depreciation expense and net book value for both the SL and DDB methods. During the first two years, the DDB method transfers more cost from the balance sheet to the income statement in the form of depreciation expense in comparison with the SL method. Beginning in the third year, this pattern reverses and the SL method produces higher depreciation expense. Over the asset's life, the same $90,000 of asset cost is transferred, leaving a salvage value of $10,000 on the balance sheet under both methods.

---

[10]A variant of DDB allows for a switchover from DDB to SL at the point when SL depreciation exceeds that for DDB.

EXHIBIT 5.11 ▪ Comparison of Straight-Line and Double-Declining-Balance Depreciation

	Straight-Line		Double-Declining-Balance	
Year	Depreciation Expense	Book Value at End of Year	Depreciation Expense	Book Value at End of Year
1	$18,000	$82,000	$40,000	$60,000
2	18,000	64,000	24,000	36,000
3	18,000	46,000	14,400	21,600
4	18,000	28,000	8,640	12,960
5	18,000	10,000	2,960	10,000
	$90,000		$90,000	

All depreciation methods yield the same salvage value

Total depreciation over asset life is identical for all methods

$
Cash Effect

Companies typically use the SL method for financial reporting purposes and an accelerated depreciation method for tax returns.[11] The reason is that in early years the SL depreciation yields higher income on shareholder reports, whereas accelerated depreciation yields lower taxable income. Even though this relation reverses in later years, companies prefer to have the tax savings early rather than later so that the cash savings can be invested to produce earnings. Further, even with the reversal, if depreciable assets are growing at a fast enough rate, the additional first year's depreciation on acquired assets more than offsets the lower depreciation expense on older assets, yielding a "permanent" reduction in taxable income and taxes paid.[12]

Asset Sales, Estimates, and Impairments

This section discusses gains and losses from asset sales, changes in accounting estimates, and computation and disclosure of asset impairments.

Gains and Losses on Asset Sales

The gain or loss on the sale (disposition) of a long-term asset is computed as follows,

Gain or Loss on Asset Sale = Proceeds from Sale − Book Value of Asset Sold

The book (carrying) value of an asset is its acquisition cost less accumulated depreciation. When an asset is sold, its acquisition cost and related accumulated depreciation are removed from the balance sheet and any gain or loss is reported in income from continuing operations.

Gains and losses on asset sales can be large, and analysts must be aware of these *transitory operating* income components. Further, if not deemed material, companies often include such gains and losses in general line items of the income statement—often as an offset to selling, general and administrative expenses.

To illustrate, **DuPont** provides the following footnote disclosure to its 10-K relating to the sale of DuPont Pharmaceuticals' net assets to **Bristol-Myers Squibb Company** ($ millions):

GAIN ON SALE OF DUPONT PHARMACEUTICALS. On October 1, 2001, the company sold substantially all of the net assets of DuPont Pharmaceuticals to Bristol-Myers Squibb Company and recorded

---

[11]The IRS mandates the use of MACRS (Modified Accelerated Cost Recovery System) for tax purposes. This method fixes the useful life for various classes of assets, assumes no salvage value, and generally uses the double-declining-balance method.

[12]We sometimes see two other depreciation methods: (1) **Units-of-production**—a method that depreciates assets according to use. Specifically, the depreciation base is cost less salvage value, and the depreciation rate is the units produced and sold during the year compared with the total expected units to be produced and sold. For example, if a truck is driven 10,000 miles out of a total expected 100,000 miles, 10% of its nonrecoverable cost is reflected as depreciation expense. This method is common for extractive industries like timber and coal. (2) **Sum-of-the-years'-digits**—an accelerated method. Specifically, the depreciation base is cost less salvage value and the depreciation rate is (years in reverse)/(sum of all years). For example, for a 5-year asset, the depreciation rate in year 1 is 5/15, year 2 is 4/15 and so on, where the sum of all years is $1 + 2 + 3 + 4 + 5 = 15$.

net proceeds of $7,798. The net assets sold to Bristol-Myers Squibb as of the date of sale and included within the accompanying Consolidated Balance Sheet at December 31, 2000, consisted of the following:

	October 1, 2001	December 31, 2000
Current assets	$ 584	$ 484
Property, plant and equipment, net	356	374
Other assets, net	1,041	1,139
Current liabilities	(282)	(392)
Noncurrent liabilities	(288)	(244)
Net assets sold	$1,411	$1,361

As a result of this transaction, the company recorded a pretax gain of $6,136, which included charges that are a direct result of the decision to divest DuPont Pharmaceuticals. The after-tax gain on this transaction was $3,866.

DuPont sold a subsidiary company, carried on its balance sheet at a net book value of $1,411 million, for $7,798 million. The gain of 6,387 million, less transaction costs of $251 million and taxes of $2,270 million, resulted in an after-tax gain of $3,866 million. DuPont reported net income of $4,339 million in that year, 89% of which is attributable to the gain on the sale of this subsidiary.

Accounting Estimate Change

Estimates required in the depreciation process are made when the asset is acquired. These include the useful life, salvage value, and depreciation rate (straight-line vs. accelerated). Companies can, and do, change these estimates when necessary during the useful lives of assets. When either the useful life or salvage value estimates change, companies use the new estimates from the date of the change going forward.

To illustrate, Delta and several other airlines changed their depreciation lives on aircraft in the late 1990s and early 2000s. Following is a disclosure relating to this action in Delta Air Lines' 10-K:

Depreciation and Amortization Effective July 1, 1998, the Company increased the depreciable life of certain new generation aircraft types from 20 to 25 years. Owned flight equipment is depreciated on a straight-line basis to a residual value equal to 5% of cost.

Analysts are usually critical of changes in estimates, especially when they result in an increase in current income. For example, the *Center for Financial Research and Analysis (CFRA)* assessed the Delta announcement as follows:

Delta Air Lines, Inc. ("DAL") extended the life of certain new generation aircraft types on July 1, 1998 to 25 years from 20 years. Furthermore, the Company's residual values for aircraft changed from a policy of 5% of the cost of the aircraft to *between* 5% to 10% of the cost. This change reduced depreciation expense by $92 million for the fiscal year ended June 1999, resulting in a boost to reported earnings of $0.37 [per share]. Absent the change CFRA estimates DAL's fiscal 1999 earnings would have been $6.83 rather than the reported $7.20. Furthermore, we find this change particularly unusual since DAL recorded a charge of $107 million to write-down to estimated fair value aircraft parts and obsolete flight equipment and parts during the September 1999 quarter.

Delta's change in the depreciable life (and salvage value) of its aircraft is a change in estimate. A change in estimate is reflected *prospectively* from the date of change—for current and future periods. (A change in accounting principle is different from a change in estimate. The reporting for a change in accounting principle is described in Module 4.)

Asset Impairments

Property, plant, and equipment (PPE) assets are reported at their net book values (original cost less accumulated depreciation). This is the case even if market values of these assets increase subsequent to acquisition. As a result, there can be unrecognized gains *buried* in the balance sheet.

However, if market values of PPE assets subsequently decrease—and the asset value is deemed as permanently impaired—then companies must recognize losses on those assets. **Impairment** of PPE assets is determined by comparing the sum of *expected* future (undiscounted) cash flows from the asset with its net book value. If these expected cash flows are greater than net book value, no impairment is deemed to exist. However, if the sum of expected cash flows is less than net book value, the asset is deemed impaired and it is written down to its current market value (generally, the present value of those expected cash flows). Exhibit 5.12 depicts this impairment analysis.

EXHIBIT 5.12 ▦ Impairment Analysis of Long-Term Assets

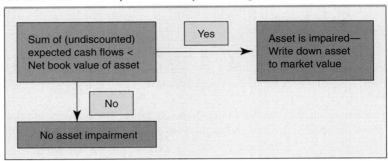

When a company takes an impairment charge, assets are reduced by the amount of the write-down and the loss is recognized in the income statement, which reduces current period income. These impacts are depicted in Exhibit 5.13.

EXHIBIT 5.13 ▦ Financial Statement Effects of Asset Impairment

Balance Sheet									Income Statement		
Cash Asset	+	Noncash Assets	=	Liabilities	+	Contrib. Capital	+	Retained Earnings	Revenues	−	Expenses
		Decrease						Decrease			Increase

Once a depreciable asset is written off, future depreciation is reduced by the amount written off. This is because that portion of the asset's cost that is written off is permanently removed from the balance sheet and cannot be subsequently depreciated. It is important to note that management determines if and when to recognize asset impairments. Write-downs of long-term assets are often recognized in connection with a restructuring program.

Analysis of asset write-downs present at least two potential challenges:

1. *Insufficient write-down.* Assets sometimes are impaired to a larger degree than is recognized. This can arise if management is overly optimistic about future prospects or is reluctant to recognize the full loss in income. Underestimation of an impairment yields a succession of smaller (depreciation) charges rather than one large charge.
2. *Aggressive write-down.* This *big bath* scenario can arise if income is currently and severely depressed. Management's view is that the market will not penalize them for an extra write-off, and that doing so purges the balance sheet of costs that would otherwise hit future years' income.

Neither of these cases is condoned under GAAP. Yet, since management is estimating future cash flows for the impairment test, it has some degree of control over the timing and amount of the write-off and can use that discretion to manage reported income.

Footnote Disclosures

Gillette reports the following PPE asset amounts in its balance sheet:

At December 31 ($ millions)	2003	2002
Property, Plant and Equipment, net	3,642	3,565

In addition to its balance sheet disclosure, Gillette provides the following two footnotes that more fully describe its PPE assets:

1. *Summary of Significant Accounting Policies.* This footnote contains the following general description of Gillette's accounting for PPE assets:

   Property, plant and equipment are stated at cost. Depreciation is computed primarily on a straight-line basis over the estimated useful lives of assets: buildings and building equipment, five to 40 years; machinery and equipment, three to 20 years.

   There are a two items of interest in this disclosure: (a) Gillette, like most publicly traded companies, depreciates its PPE assets using the straight-line method. For tax purposes, however, it uses an accelerated method. (b) Gillette provides general disclosures on the useful lives of its assets: 3–40 years. We will discuss a method to estimate the useful lives a bit more accurately in the next section.

2. *Supplemental balance sheet information.* This footnote provides a breakdown of PPE assets by category:

Property, Plant, and Equipment At December 31 ($ millions)	2003	2002
Land	$ 79	$ 81
Buildings	929	844
Machinery and equipment	6,077	5,504
	7,085	6,429
Less accumulated depreciation	3,443	2,864
Total	$3,642	$3,565

Analysis Implications

This section considers measures useful for analysis of long-term asset utilization and age.

PPE Turnover

A crucial issue in analysis of PPE assets is their productivity (utilization). For example, what level of plant assets is necessary to generate a dollar of revenues? How capital intensive is the company and its competitors? PPE turnover is often used for insights into asset utilization and to address these and similar questions. It is defined as follows:

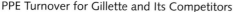

PPE Turnover (PPET) = Sales/Average PPE Assets

Gillette's 2003 PPE asset turnover is 2.6 times. Although its turnover has improved over the past three years, it remains less than those of companies that Gillette identifies as its peers, as shown in the following chart:

PPE Turnover for Gillette and Its Competitors

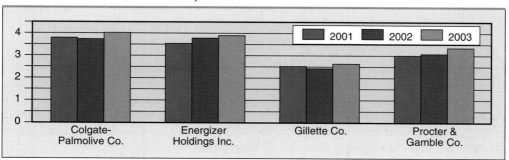

We prefer that PPE turnover be higher rather than lower. A higher PPE turnover implies a lower capital investment for a given level of sales. The result is an increase in profitability (as asset carrying costs are less) and an increase in cash flow (as reduced assets increase operating cash flow).

PPE turnover is lower for capital-intensive manufacturing companies like Gillette than it is for companies in service or knowledge-based industries. To this point, consider the following chart of plant asset turnover for companies from different industries:

PPE Turnover for Companies from Different Industries

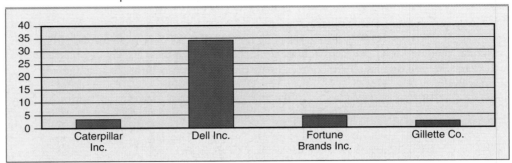

Dell's PPE turnover is as impressive as its inventory turnover, which far surpasses that of these other companies. Gillette's PPE turnover of 2.6 times compares more favorably with the remaining companies (Caterpillar is 3.2 times and Fortune Brands is 4.6 times). Nevertheless, Gillette still must work to increase its PPE asset utilization.

MANAGERIAL DECISION   You Are the Division Manager

You are the division manager for a main operating division of your company. You are concerned that a declining PPE turnover is adversely affecting your division's RNOA. What specific actions can you take to increase PPE turnover? [Answer, p. 5-33]

Useful Life and Percent Used Up

Gillette reports that the useful lives of its depreciable assets range from 5 to 40 years for buildings and 3 to 20 years for machinery and equipment. The longer the useful life, the less depreciation expense reported in the annual income statement and the higher is current income. It might be of interest, therefore, to know whether a company is more conservative (closer to 3 years) or more aggressive (closer to 40 years) than its competitors.

If we assume straight-line (SL) depreciation and zero salvage value, we can estimate the average useful life for depreciable assets as follows:

Estimated Useful Life = Depreciable Asset Cost / Depreciation Expense

For Gillette, the estimated useful life for its plant assets is 12.1 years, computed as ($7,085 million − $79 million)/$578 million. In this computation, $79 million in land cost is subtracted in the numerator since it is not a depreciable asset, and $578 million in depreciation expense is taken from the statement of cash flows (or from the footnotes or income statement, if reported as a separate line item).

We can also estimate the percent of a company's depreciable assets that are used up—reflecting the percent of depreciable assets that are no longer productive—as follows:

Percent Used Up = Accumulated Depreciation / Depreciable Asset Cost

Gillette's assets are 49.1% used up, computed as $3,443 million/($7,085 million − $79 million). If all assets were replaced evenly each year, the average asset would be 50% used up. Gillette's depreciable assets are slightly younger than this benchmark. Knowing the estimated percentage by which assets are used up is of interest in forecasting future cash flows. If, for example, depreciable assets are 80% used up, we might need to project a higher level of capital expenditures to replace assets in the near future. We also expect that older assets are less efficient and carry higher maintenance costs.

■ MODULE-END REVIEW ■

On January 2, Lev Company purchases equipment for use in fabrication of a part for one of its key products. The equipment costs $95,000, and its estimated useful life is five years, after which it is expected to be sold for $10,000.

Required

1. Compute depreciation expense for each year of the equipment's useful life for each of the following depreciation methods:
   a. Straight-line
   b. Double-declining-balance
2. Show how the equipment is reported on Lev's balance sheet at the end of the third year assuming straight-line depreciation.
3. Assume that this is the only depreciable asset the company owns and that it uses straight-line depreciation. Using the depreciation expense computed in *1a* and the balance sheet presentation from 2, estimate the useful life and the percent used up for this asset at the end of the third year.

Solution

1*a.* Straight-line
Depreciation expense = ($95,000 − $10,000)/5 years = $17,000 per year

1*b.* Double-declining-balance (twice straight-line rate = 2 × (100%/5) = 40%

Year	Book Value × Rate	Depreciation Expense
1	$95,000 × 0.40 =	$38,000
2	($95,000 − $38,000) × 0.40 =	22,800
3	($95,000 − $60,800) × 0.40 =	13,680
4	($95,000 − $74,480) × 0.40 =	8,208
5	($95,000 − $82,688) × 0.40 =	2,312*

*The formula value of $4,925 is not reported because it would depreciate the asset below salvage value. Only the $2,312 needed to reach salvage value is depreciated.

2.

Equipment, cost	$95,000
Less accumulated depreciation	51,000
Equipment, net	$44,000

Equipment is reported on Lev's balance sheet at its net book value of $44,000.

3. The estimated useful life is computed as: Depreciable Asset Cost/Depreciation Expense = $95,000/ $17,000 = 5.6 years. As you can see, since salvage values are not usually disclosed by companies (not required disclosure), our estimate is a bit high for the useful life of this asset. This estimate is useful information since companies typically only provide a range of useful lives for depreciable assets in the footnotes.

   The percent used up is computed as: Accumulated Depreciation/Depreciable Asset Cost = $51,000/$95,000 = 53.7%. The equipment is more than one-half used up at the end of the third year. Again, the lack of knowledge of salvage value has resulted in an underestimate of the percent used up. Still, this estimate is useful in that we know that the company's asset is over one-half used up and is likely to require replacement in about 2 years (estimated as less than one-half of its estimated useful life of 5.6 years). This replacement will become a cash outflow or financing need when it arises and should be considered in our projections of future cash flows.

GUIDANCE ANSWERS

MANAGERIAL DECISION   You Are the Receivables Manager

First, you must realize that the extension of credit is an important tool in the marketing of your products, often as important as advertising and promotion. Given that receivables are necessary, there are some methods we can use to speed their collection. (1) We can better screen the customers to whom we extend credit. (2) We can negotiate advance or progress payments from customers. (3) We can use bank letters of credit or other automatic drafting procedures so that billings must not be sent. (4) We can make sure products are sent as ordered to reduce disputes. (5) We can improve administration of past due accounts to provide for more timely notices of delinquencies and better collection procedures.

MANAGERIAL DECISION   You Are the Plant Manager

Companies need inventories to avoid lost sales opportunities; however, there are several ways to minimize inventory needs. (1) We can reduce product costs by improving product design to eliminate costly features not valued by customers. (2) We can use more cost-efficient suppliers; possibly including production in lower wage-rate parts of the world. (3) We can reduce raw material inventories with just-in-time delivery from suppliers. (4) We can eliminate bottlenecks in the production process that increase work-in-process inventories. (5) We can manufacture for orders rather than for estimates of demand to reduce finished goods inventories. (6) We can improve warehousing and distribution to reduce duplicate inventories. (7) We can monitor product sales and adjust product mix as demand changes to reduce finished goods inventories.

MANAGERIAL DECISION   You Are the Division Manager

PPE is a difficult asset to reduce. Since companies need long-term operating assets, managers usually try to maximize throughput to reduce unit costs. Also, many companies form alliances to share administrative, production, logistics, customer service, IT and other functions. These alliances take many forms (such as joint ventures) and are designed to spread ownership of assets among many users. The goal is to identify underutilized assets and to increase capacity utilization. Another solution might be to reconfigure the value chain from raw material to end user. Examples includes the sharing of IT or manufacturing facilities, outsourcing of production or administration such as customer service centers, and the use of variable interest entities for asset securitization (see Module 9).

■ DISCUSSION QUESTIONS

Q5-1. Explain how management can shift income from one period into another by its estimation of uncollectible accounts.

Q5-2. Why do relatively stable inventory costs reduce the importance of management's choice of an inventory costing method?

Q5-3. What is one explanation for increased gross profit during periods of rising inventory costs when FIFO is used?

Q5-4. If inventory costs are rising, which inventory costing method—first-in, first-out; last-in, first-out; or average cost—yields the (a) lowest ending inventory? (b) lowest net income? (c) largest ending inventory? (d) largest net income? (e) greatest cash flow assuming that method is used for tax purposes?

Q5-5. Even though it may not reflect their physical flow of goods, why might companies adopt last-in, first-out inventory costing in periods when costs are consistently rising?

Q5-6. In a recent annual report, **Kaiser Aluminum Corporation** made the following statement in reference to its inventories: "The Company recorded pretax charges of approximately $19.4 million because of a reduction in the carrying values of its inventories caused principally by prevailing lower prices for alumina, primary aluminum, and fabricated products." What basic accounting principle caused Kaiser Aluminum to record this $19.4 million pretax charge? Briefly describe the rationale for this principle.

Q5-7. Why is the recognition of depreciation expense necessary to properly match revenues and expenses?

Q5-8. How does a company treat a revision of depreciation due to a change in an asset's estimated useful life or salvage value? Which period(s)—past, present, or future—is affected by such revisions? Explain.

Q5-9. When is a PPE asset considered to be impaired? How is an impairment loss computed?

Q5-10. What is the benefit of accelerated depreciation for income tax purposes when the total depreciation taken over the asset's life is identical to that from straight-line depreciation?

Q5-11. What factors determine the gain or loss on the sale of a PPE asset?

■ MINI EXERCISES

M5-12. **Estimating Uncollectible Accounts and Reporting Accounts Receivables**   Mohan Company estimates its uncollectible accounts by aging its accounts receivable and applying percentages to various aged categories of accounts. Mohan computes a total of $2,100 in estimated losses as of December 31, 2005. Its Accounts Receivable has a balance of $98,000, and its Allowance for Uncollectible Accounts has an unused balance of $500 before adjustment at December 31, 2005.

a.   What is the amount of bad debt expense that Mohan will report in 2005?

b.   Determine the net amount of accounts receivable reported in current assets at December 31, 2005.

M5-13. **Explaining the Allowance Method for Accounts Receivable**   At a recent board of directors meeting of Ascot, Inc., one of the directors expressed concern over the allowance for uncollectible accounts appearing in the company's balance sheet. "I don't understand this account," he said. "Why don't we just show accounts receivable at the amount owed to us and get rid of that allowance?" Respond to that director's question, include in your response (a) an explanation of why the company has an allowance account, (b) what the balance sheet presentation of accounts receivable is intended to show, and (c) how the matching principle relates to the analysis and presentation of accounts receivable.

M5-14. **Analyzing the Allowance for Uncollectible Accounts**   Following is the current asset section from **Kraft Foods, Inc.**, balance sheet:

Kraft Foods, Inc. (KFT)

At December 31 ($ millions)	2003	2002
Cash and cash equivalents	$ 514	$ 215
Receivables (less allowances of $114 and $119)	3,369	3,116
Inventories		
Raw materials	1,375	1,372
Finished product	1,968	2,010
	3,343	3,382
Deferred income taxes	681	511
Other current assets	217	232
Total current assets	$8,124	$7,456

a.   Compute the gross amount of accounts receivable for both 2003 and 2002. Compute the percentage of the allowance for uncollectible accounts relative to the gross amount of accounts receivable for each of these years.

b.   How do you interpret the change in the percentage of the allowance for uncollectible accounts relative to total accounts receivable computed in (*a*)?

M5-15. **Evaluating Accounts Receivable Turnover for Competitors**   **Procter & Gamble** (PG) and **Colgate-Palmolive** (CL) report the following sales and accounts receivable balances ($ millions):

Procter & Gamble (PG)

Colgate-Palmolive (CL)

	Procter & Gamble		Colgate-Palmolive	
	Sales	Accounts Receivable	Sales	Accounts Receivable
2003	$43,373	$3,038	$9,903	$1,222
2002	40,169	3,090	9,294	1,145

a.   Compute the 2003 accounts receivable turnover for both companies.

b.   Identify and discuss a potential explanation for the difference between these competitors' accounts receivable turnover.

M5-16. Computing Cost of Goods Sold and Ending Inventory under FIFO, LIFO, and Average Cost   Assume that Gode Company reports the following initial balance and subsequent purchase of inventory:

Beginning inventory, 2005	1,000 units @ $100 each	$100,000
Inventory purchased in 2005	2,000 units @ $150 each	300,000
Cost of goods available for sale in 2005	3,000 units	$400,000

Assume that 1,700 units are sold during 2005. Compute the cost of goods sold for 2005 and the balance reported as ending inventory on its 2005 balance sheet under the following inventory costing methods:
a.   FIFO
b.   LIFO
c.   Average Cost

M5-17. Computing Cost of Goods Sold and Ending Inventory   Bartov Corporation reports the following beginning inventory and purchases for 2005:

Beginning inventory, 2005	400 units @ $10 each	$ 4,000
Inventory purchased in 2005	700 units @ $12 each	8,400
Cost of goods available for sale in 2005	1,100 units	$12,400

Bartov sells 600 of these units in 2005. Compute its cost of goods sold for 2005 and the ending inventory reported on its 2005 balance sheet under each of the following inventory costing methods:
a.   FIFO
b.   LIFO
c.   Average Cost

Sears (S)

Kmart (KMRT)

M5-18. Computing and Evaluating Inventory Turnover   Sears (S) and Kmart (KMRT) reported the following information in their respective 10-K reports, prior to their merger:

($ millions)	Sears			K-Mart		
	Sales	COGS	Inventories	Sales	COGS	Inventories
2003	$41,124	$26,202	$5,335	$23,253	$17,638	$3,238
2002	41,366	25,646	5,115	30,762	24,228	4,825

a.   Compute the 2003 inventory turnover for each of these two retailers.
b.   Discuss any changes that are evident in inventory turnover across years and companies from (a).
c.   Describe ways that a retailer can improve its inventory turnover.

M5-19. Computing Depreciation under Straight-Line and Double-Declining-Balance   A delivery van costing $18,000 is expected to have a $1,500 salvage value at the end of its useful life of 5 years. Assume that the truck was purchased on January 1, 2005. Compute the depreciation expense for 2006 (its second year) under each of the following depreciation methods:
a.   Straight-line.
b.   Double-declining-balance.

M5-20. Computing Depreciation under Straight-Line and Double-Declining-Balance for Partial Years   A machine costing $145,800 is purchased on May 1, 2005. The machine is expected to be obsolete after three years (36 months) and, thereafter, no longer useful to the company. The estimated salvage value is $5,400. Compute depreciation expense for both 2005 and 2006 under each of the following depreciation methods:
a.   Straight-line.
b.   Double-declining-balance.

Texas Instruments (TXN)

Intel Corporation (INTC)

M5-21. Computing and Comparing PPE Turnover for Two Companies   Texas Instruments (TXN) and Intel Corporation (INTC) report the following information:

| ($ millions) | Texas Instruments | | Intel Corp | |
	Sales	PPE, net	Sales	PPE, net
2003	$9,834	$4,132	$30,141	$16,661
2002	8,383	4,794	26,764	17,847

a. Compute the 2003 PPE turnover for both companies. Comment on any difference you observe.

b. Discuss ways in which high-tech manufacturing companies like these can increase their PPE turnover.

■ EXERCISES

E5-22. **Estimating Uncollectible Accounts and Reporting Accounts Receivable** LaFond Company analyzes its accounts receivable at December 31, 2005, and arrives at the aged categories below along with the percentages that are estimated as uncollectible.

Age Group	Accounts Receivable	Estimated Loss %
1–30 days past due	$ 90,000	1%
31–60 days past due	20,000	2
61–120 days past due	11,000	5
121–180 days past due	6,000	10
Over 180 days past due	4,000	25
Total accounts receivable	$131,000	

The unused balance of the allowance for uncollectible accounts is $520 on December 31, 2005, before any adjustments.

a. What amount of bad debts expense will LaFond report for 2005?

b. What is the balance of accounts receivable that it reports on its December 31, 2005, balance sheet?

E5-23. **Analyzing and Reporting Receivable Transactions and Uncollectible Accounts (using percentage of sales method)** At the beginning of 2005, Penman Company had the following account balances in its financial records:

Accounts Receivable	$122,000
Allowance for Uncollectible Accounts	7,900

During 2005, its credit sales were $1,173,000 and collections on credit sales were $1,150,000. The following additional transactions occurred during the year:

Feb. 17 Wrote off Nissim's account, $3,600.

May 28 Wrote off Weiss's account, $2,400.

Dec. 15 Wrote off Ohlson's account, $900.

Dec. 31 Recorded the provision for uncollectible accounts at 0.8% of credit sales for the year. (*Hint*: The allowance account is increased by 0.8% of credit sales regardless of any prior write-offs.)

Compute and show how accounts receivable and the allowance for uncollectible accounts are reported in its December 31, 2005, balance sheet.

E5-24. **Interpreting the Accounts Receivable Footnote** Hewlett-Packard Company (**HP**) reports the following trade accounts receivable in its 10-K report:

Hewlett-
Packard (HPQ)

October 31 (In millions)	2003	2002
Accounts receivable, net of allowance for doubtful accounts of $347 and $410 as of October 31, 2003 and 2002, respectively	$8,921	$8,456

HP's footnotes to its 10-K provide the following additional information relating to its allowance for doubtful accounts:

For Year Ended October 31 (In millions)	2003	2002	2001
Allowance for doubtful accounts			
Balance, beginning of period	$410	$275	$171
Amount acquired through acquisition.	—	141	—
Additions to allowance.	29	90	206
Deductions, net of recoveries	(92)	(96)	(102)
Balance, end of period	$347	$410	$275

a. What is the gross amount of accounts receivables for HP in each of its fiscal years 2002 and 2003?
b. What is the percentage of the allowance for doubtful accounts to gross accounts receivable for each of its fiscal years 2002 and 2003?
c. What amount of bad debt expense has HP reported in each of its fiscal years 2001 through 2003? How does its reported expense compare with the amounts of its accounts receivable actually written off? (Identify the amounts and explain.)
d. Explain the changes in the allowance for doubtful accounts from 2001 through 2003. Does it appear that HP increased or decreased its allowance for doubtful accounts in any particular year beyond what seemed reasonable?

E5-25. **Estimating Bad Debts Expense and Reporting of Receivables** At December 31, 2005, Sunil Company had a balance of $375,000 in its accounts receivable and an unused balance of $4,200 in its allowance for uncollectible accounts. The company then aged its accounts as follows:

Current	$304,000
0–60 days past due	44,000
61–180 days past due	18,000
Over 180 days past due	9,000
Total accounts receivable	$375,000

The company has experienced losses as follows: 1% of current balances, 5% of balances 0–60 days past due, 15% of balances 61–180 days past due, and 40% of balances over 180 days past due. The company continues to base its provision for credit losses on this aging analysis and percentages.
a. What amount of bad debt expense does Sunil report on its 2005 income statement?
b. Show how accounts receivable and the allowance for uncollectible accounts are reported in its December 31, 2005, balance sheet.

E5-26. **Estimating Uncollectible Accounts and Reporting Receivables over Multiple Periods** Barth Company, which has been in business for three years, makes all of its sales on credit and does not offer cash discounts. Its credit sales, customer collections, and write-offs of uncollectible accounts for its first three years follow:

Year	Sales	Collections	Accounts Written Off
2003	$751,000	$733,000	$5,300
2004	876,000	864,000	5,800
2005	972,000	938,000	6,500

a. Barth uses the allowance method of recognizing credit losses that provides for such losses at the rate of 1% of sales. (*Hint*: This means the allowance account is increased by 1% of credit sales regardless of any write-offs and unused balances.) What amounts for accounts receivable and the allowance for uncollectible accounts are reported on its balance sheet at the end of 2005? What total amount of bad debts expense appears on its income statement for each of the three years?
b. Comment on the appropriateness of the 1% rate used to provide for bad debts based on your results in part (a).

E5-27. Applying and Analyzing Inventory Costing Methods At the beginning of the current period, Chen carried 1,000 units of its product with a unit cost of $20. A summary of purchases during the current period follows:

	Units	Unit Cost	Cost
Beginning Inventory	1,000	$20	$20,000
Purchases: #1	1,800	22	39,600
#2	800	26	20,800
#3	1,200	29	34,800

During the current period, Chen sold 2,800 units.

a. Assume that Chen uses the first-in, first-out method. Compute its cost of goods sold for the current period and the ending inventory balance.

b. Assume that Chen uses the last-in, first-out method. Compute its cost of goods sold for the current period and the ending inventory balance.

c. Assume that Chen uses the average cost method. Compute its cost of goods sold for the current period and the ending inventory balance.

d. Which of these three inventory costing methods would you choose to:
   1. Reflect what is probably the physical flow of goods? Explain.
   2. Minimize income taxes for the period? Explain.
   3. Report the largest amount of income for the period? Explain.

E5-28. Analysis of Inventory Footnote Disclosure General Electric Company reports the following footnote in its 10-K report:

General Electric Company (GE)

INVENTORIES December 31 (In millions)	2003	2002
Raw materials and work in process	$4,530	$4,894
Finished goods	4,376	4,379
Unbilled shipments	281	372
	9,187	9,645
Less revaluation to LIFO	(632)	(606)
	$8,555	$9,039

The company reports its inventories using the LIFO inventory costing method.

a. At what dollar amount are inventories reported on its 2003 balance sheet?

b. At what dollar amount would inventories have been reported on GE's 2003 balance sheet had it used FIFO inventory costing?

c. What *cumulative* effect has the use of LIFO inventory costing had, as of year-end 2003, on its pretax income compared with the pretax income it would have reported had it used FIFO inventory costing? Explain.

d. Assuming a 35% income tax rate, by what *cumulative* dollar amount has GE's tax liability been affected by use of LIFO inventory costing as of year-end 2003? Has the use of LIFO inventory costing increased or decreased its cumulative tax liability?

e. What effect has the use of LIFO inventory costing had on GE's pretax income and tax liability for 2003 (assume a 35% income tax rate)?

E5-29. Computing Cost of Sales and Ending Inventory Stocken Company has the following financial records for the current period:

	Units	Unit Cost
Beginning inventory	100	$46
Purchases: #1	650	42
#2	550	38
#3	200	36

Ending inventory at the end of this period is 350 units. Compute the ending inventory and the cost of goods sold for the current period using (a) first-in, first out, (b) average cost, and (c) last-in, first-out.

Kraft Foods, Inc. (KFT)

E5-30.   Analysis of Inventory and Footnote Disclosure   The current asset section of the Kraft Foods, Inc., balance sheet follows ($ millions):

At December 31	2003	2002
Cash and cash equivalents	$ 514	$ 215
Receivables (less allowances of $114 and $119)	3,369	3,116
Inventories		
Raw materials	1,375	1,372
Finished product	1,968	2,010
	3,343	3,382
Deferred income taxes	681	511
Other current assets	217	232
Total current assets	$8,124	$7,456

Kraft also reports the following footnote to its 2003 10-K report:

Note 6. Inventories

The cost of approximately 39% and 43% of inventories in 2003 and 2002, respectively, was determined using the LIFO method. The stated LIFO amounts of inventories were approximately $155 million and $215 million higher than the current cost of inventories at December 31, 2003 and 2002, respectively.

Notice that not all of Kraft's inventories are reported using the same inventory costing method (companies can use different inventory costing methods for different inventory pools).

a.   At what dollar amount are Kraft's inventories reported on its 2003 balance sheet?

b.   At what dollar amount would inventories have been reported on Kraft's 2003 balance sheet had it used FIFO inventory costing?

c.   What *cumulative* effect has the use of LIFO inventory costing had, as of year-end 2003, on its pretax income compared with the pretax income it would have reported had it used FIFO inventory costing? Explain.

d.   Assuming a 35% income tax rate, by what *cumulative* dollar amount has Kraft's tax liability been affected by use of LIFO inventory costing as of year-end 2003? Has the use of LIFO inventory costing increased or decreased its cumulative tax liability?

e.   What effect has the use of LIFO inventory costing had on Kraft's pretax income and tax liability for 2003 (assume a 35% income tax rate)?

E5-31.   Computing Straight-Line and Double-Declining-Balance Depreciation   On January 2, Haskins Company purchases a laser cutting machine for use in fabrication of a part for one of its key products. The machine cost $80,000, and its estimated useful life is five years, after which the expected salvage value is $5,000. Compute depreciation expense for each year of the machine's useful life under each of the following depreciation methods:

a.   Straight-line

b.   Double-declining-balance

E5-32.   Computing Depreciation, Asset Book Value, and Gain or Loss on Asset Sale   Sloan Company uses its own executive charter plane that originally cost $800,000. It has recorded straight-line depreciation on the plane for six full years, with an $80,000 expected salvage value at the end of its estimated 10-year useful life. Sloan disposes of the plane at the end of the sixth year.

a.   At the disposal date, what is the (1) cumulative depreciation expense and (2) net book value of the plane?

b.   How much gain or loss is reported at disposal if the sales price is for:

   1.   Cash equal to book value (of plane)

   2. $195,000 cash

   3. $600,000 cash

E5-33.   Computing Straight-Line and Double-Declining-Balance Depreciation   On January 2, 2005, Dechow Company purchases a machine to help manufacture a part for one of its key products. The machine cost $218,700 and is estimated to have a useful life of six years, with an expected salvage value of $23,400.

Compute each year's depreciation expense for 2005 and 2006 for each of the following depreciation methods.
a. Straight-line.
b. Double-declining-balance.

E5-34. **Computing Depreciation, Asset Book Value, and Gain or Loss on Asset Sale** Palepu Company owns and operates a delivery van that originally cost $27,200. Straight-line depreciation on the van has been recorded for three years, with a $2,000 expected salvage value at the end of its estimated six-year useful life. Depreciation was last recorded at the end of the third year, at which time Palepu disposes of this van.
a. Compute the net book value of the van on the sale date.
b. Compute the gain or loss on sale of the van if its sales price is for:
1. Cash equal to book value (of van).
2. $15,000 cash.
3. $12,000 cash.

E5-35. **Estimating Useful Life and Percent Used Up** The property and equipment footnote from the Deere & Company balance sheet follows ($ millions):

Deere & Company (DE)

PROPERTY AND DEPRECIATION

A summary of property and equipment at October 31 in millions of dollars follows:

	Useful Lives (Years)	2003
Land		$ 68
Buildings and building equipment	10–33	1,366
Machinery and equipment	12	2,705
Dies, patterns, tools, etc.	8	932
All other	3–8	671
Construction in progress		92
Total at cost		5,834
Less accumulated depreciation		3,758
Property and equipment—net		$2,076

During 2003, the company reported $631.4 million of depreciation expense.
a. Compute the estimated useful life of Deere's depreciable assets (*Hint:* exclude land and construction in progress). How does this estimate compare with the useful lives footnote disclosure from Deere?
b. Estimate the percent used up of Deere's depreciable assets. How do you interpret this figure?

E5-36. **Computing and Evaluating Receivables, Inventory and PPE Turnovers** 3M Company reports the following financial statement amounts in its 10-K report:

3M Company (MMM)

($ millions)	Sales	Cost of Sales	Receivables	Inventories	PPE
2003	$18,232	$8,321	$3,162	$1,816	$5,609
2002	16,332	7,482	2,840	1,931	5,621
2001	16,079	7,462	2,786	2,091	5,615

Required
a. Compute the receivables, inventory, and PPE turnover ratios for both 2003 and 2002.
b. What changes are evident in the turnover rates of 3M for these years? Discuss ways in which a company such as 3M can improve its turnover within each of these three areas.

E5-37. **Computing and Assessing Plant Asset Impairment** Zeibart Company purchases equipment for $225,000 on July 1, 2000, with an estimated useful life of 10 years and expected salvage value of $25,000. Straight-line depreciation is used. On July 1, 2004, economic factors cause the market value of the equipment to decline to $90,000. On this date, Zeibart examines the equipment for impairment and estimates $125,000 in future cash inflows related to use of this equipment.
a. Is the equipment impaired at July 1, 2004? Explain.
b. If the equipment is impaired at July 1, 2004, compute the impairment loss.

■ PROBLEMS

P5-38. Evaluating Turnover Rates for Different Companies   Following are asset turnover rates for accounts receivable; inventory; and property, plant, and equipment (PPE) for **Best Buy** (retailer of consumer products), **Carnival** (vacation cruise line), **Caterpillar** (manufacturer of heavy equipment), **Harley-Davidson** (manufacturer of motorcycles), **Microsoft** (software company), **Oracle** (software company), and **Sharper Image** (retailer of specialty consumer products):

Best Buy (BBY)

Carnival (CCL)

Caterpillar (CAT)

Harley-Davidson (HDI)

Microsoft (MSFT)

Oracle (ORCL)

Sharper Image (SHRP)

	Receivables Turnover	Inventory Turnover	PPE Turnover
Best Buy Co., Inc.	74.94	7.16	10.58
Carnival Corporation	43.88	25.23	0.47
Caterpillar Inc.	2.18	5.37	3.18
Harley-Davidson, Inc.	4.96	12.97	4.47
Microsoft Corporation	6.24	7.00	14.33
Oracle Corporation	4.17	n.a.	9.25
Sharper Image Corporation	50.57	4.21	10.79

Required

a. Interpret and explain differences in receivables turnover for the retailers (Best Buy and Sharper Image) vis-à-vis that for the manufacturers (Caterpillar and Harley-Davidson).

b. Interpret and explain the difference in inventory turnover for Harley-Davidson versus Sharper Image. Why do you believe Oracle's inventory turnover is reported as n.a.?

c. Interpret and explain the difference in PPE turnover for Carnival versus Microsoft.

d. What are some general observations you might draw regarding the relative levels of these turnover rates across the different industries?

P5-39. Interpreting Accounts Receivable and Footnote Disclosure   Following is the current asset section from the **W.W. Grainger, Inc.**, balance sheet:

W.W. Grainger, Inc. (GWW)

($ 000s)	2003	2002	2001
Cash and cash equivalents	$ 402,824	$ 208,528	$ 168,846
Accounts receivable (less allowances for doubtful accounts of $24,736, $26,868 and $30,552, respectively)	431,896	423,240	454,180
Inventories	661,247	721,178	634,654
Prepaid expenses and other assets	37,947	36,665	37,477
Deferred income taxes	99,499	95,336	97,454
Total current assets	$1,633,413	$1,484,947	$1,392,611

Grainger reports the following footnote relating to its receivables:

ALLOWANCE FOR DOUBTFUL ACCOUNTS
The following table shows the activity in the allowance for doubtful accounts:

	For Years Ended December 31		
($ 000s)	2003	2002	2001
Balance at beginning of period	$26,868	$30,552	$23,436
Provision for uncollectible accounts	9,263	13,328	21,483
Write-off of uncollectible accounts, less recoveries	(11,713)	(17,054)	(14,290)
Miscellaneous adjustments	318	42	(77)
Balance at end of period	$ 24,736	$ 26,868	$ 30,552

Required

a. What amount do customers owe Grainger at each of the year-ends 2001 through 2003?

b. What percentage of those accounts receivable in a does Grainger feel are uncollectible? (*Hint*: Percentage of uncollectible accounts = Allowance for uncollectible accounts/Gross accounts receivable.)

c. What amount of bad debts expense did Grainger report in its income statement for each of the years 2001 through 2003?

d. Explain the change in the balance of the allowance for uncollectible accounts from 2002 to 2003. Specifically, did the allowance increase or decrease as a percentage of gross accounts receivable, and why?

e. If Grainger had kept its 2003 allowance for uncollectible accounts at the same percentage of gross accounts receivable as it was in 2002, by what amount would its profit have changed (ignore taxes)? Explain.

P5-40. Analyzing and Interpreting Receivables and its Related Ratios   Following is the current asset section from **AOL Time Warner**'s balance sheet ($ millions):

AOL Time-Warner (AOL)

December 31	2002	2001
Current assets		
Cash and equivalents	$ 1,730	$ 719
Receivables, less allowances of $2,379 and $1,889 million	5,667	6,054
Inventories	1,896	1,791
Prepaid expenses and other current assets	1,862	1,687
Total current assets	$11,155	$10,251

During 2002, AOL reported a $98,700 million net loss, all of which was attributed to the write off of goodwill that it recognized in the merger of AOL and Time Warner. Sales were $40,961 million in 2002 and $37,166 million in 2001.

Required

a. What is AOL's gross amount of receivables at the end of (1) 2002 and (2) 2001?

b. For both 2002 and 2001, compute the ratio of (1) the allowance for uncollectible accounts to gross receivables and (2) gross receivables to sales. Identify and interpret the changes in these ratios over these two years.

c. Compute both the receivables turnover and the average collection period for 2002. Does the collection period (days sales in receivables) appear reasonable given AOL's lines of business? Explain.

d. Given the large loss reported in 2002, it is reasonable to consider whether AOL took a big bath by writing off other assets or padding reserves such as the allowance for uncollectible accounts. Do your results from (b) suggest that this might be the case? Explain. What might be another explanation for the relative increase in the allowance for uncollectible accounts?

P5-41. Analysis of Inventory and its Footnote Disclosure   The current asset section of the **Caterpillar, Inc.**, balance sheet follows ($ millions):

Caterpillar, Inc. (CAT)

December 31	2003	2002
Current assets		
Cash and short-term investments	$ 342	$ 309
Receivables—trade and other	3,666	2,838
Receivables—finance	7,605	6,748
Deferred and refundable income taxes	707	781
Prepaid expenses	1,424	1,224
Inventories	3,047	2,763
Total current assets	$16,791	$14,663

CAT also provides the following footnote to its 2003 10-K report:

Inventories are stated at the lower of cost or market. Cost is principally determined using the last-in, first-out (LIFO) method. The value of inventories on the LIFO basis represented about 80% of total inventories at December 31, 2003, 2002 and 2001.

If the FIFO (first-in, first-out) method had been in use, inventories would have been $1,863 million, $1,977 million and $1,923 million higher than reported at December 31, 2003, 2002 and 2001, respectively.

Notice that not all of CAT's inventories are reported using the same inventory costing method (companies can use different inventory costing methods for different inventory pools).

a.   At what dollar amount is CAT's inventories reported on its 2003 balance sheet?
b.   At what dollar amount would inventories have been reported on CAT's 2003 balance sheet had it used FIFO inventory costing?
c.   What *cumulative* effect has the use of LIFO inventory costing had, as of year-end 2003, on its pretax income compared with the pretax income it would have reported had it used FIFO inventory costing? Explain.
d.   Assuming a 35% income tax rate, by what *cumulative* dollar amount has CAT's tax liability been affected by use of LIFO inventory costing as of year-end 2003? Has the use of LIFO inventory costing increased or decreased its cumulative tax liability?
e.   What effect has the use of LIFO inventory costing had on CAT's pretax income and tax liability for 2003 (assume a 35% income tax rate)?

P5-42.   **Analyzing and Interpreting Inventories and its Related Ratios and Disclosures**   The current asset section from The Stride Rite Corporation's annual report follows ($ thousands):

Stride Rite
Corporation
(SRR)

	November 28, 2003	November 29, 2002
Current Assets		
Cash and cash equivalents	$103,272	$ 73,105
Accounts and notes receivable, less allowances of $9,406 in 2003 and $12,250 in 2002	51,058	48,075
Inventories	81,925	98,213
Deferred income taxes	14,393	20,588
Prepaid expenses and other current assets	19,452	14,131
Total current assets	$270,100	$254,112

Stride Rite reports the following related to its gross profit ($ thousands):

	Years Ended	
	2003	2002
Net sales	$550,124	$532,400
Cost of sales	340,614	337,951
Gross profit	$209,510	$194,449

Stride Rite further reports the following footnote related to its inventories:

INVENTORIES   The cost of inventories, which consist primarily of finished product, at November 28, 2003 and November 29, 2002 was determined on a last-in, first-out (LIFO) basis. During 2003, the LIFO reserve decreased by $1,610,000 to $10,875,000 at November 28, 2003. If all inventories had been valued on a first-in, first-out (FIFO) basis, net income would have been lower by $1,019,000 ($.03 per share) in 2003. The LIFO reserve decreased in 2002 and increased in 2001, by $758,000 and $314,000, respectively. If all inventories had been valued on a FIFO basis, net income would have been lower by $516,000 ($.01 per share) in 2002 and would have been higher by $223,000 (less than $.01 per share) in 2001.

During 2003 and 2002, reductions in certain inventory quantities resulted in the sale of products carried at costs prevailing in prior years which were different from current costs. As a result of these inventory reductions, net income was increased by $141,000 (less than $.01 per share) and decreased by $120,000 (less than $.01 per share) in 2003 and 2002, respectively.

Required
a.   Compute the ratio of inventories to total current assets for both 2003 and 2002. Is the change you observe for the ratio a positive development for a company such as Stride Rite? Explain.
b.   Compute inventory turnover for both 2003 and 2002 (2001 ending inventories were $112,481). Interpret and explain the change in inventory turnover as positive or negative for the company.
c.   What inventory costing method does Stride Rite use? What effect has the use of this method (relative to FIFO or LIFO) had on its reported income over the three years, 2001–2003? Explain.

d. Stride Rite reports that it decreased certain inventory quantities. Why do you believe Stride Rite reduced its inventory quantities? Is this development positive or negative for a company such as Stride Rite? Explain.

e. What effect did reductions in inventory quantities have on Stride Rite's reported income for 2003 and for 2002? Explain.

P5-43. Estimating Useful Life and Percent Used Up   The property and equipment section of the Abbott Laboratories 2003 balance sheet follows ($000s):

Abbott Laboratories (ABT)

Property and Equipment, at Cost	
Land	$ 356,757
Buildings	2,662,023
Equipment	9,479,044
Construction in progress	792,923
	13,290,747
Less: accumulated depreciation and amortization	7,008,941
Net Property and Equipment	$ 6,281,806

The company also provides the following disclosure relating to the useful lives of its depreciable assets:

Property and Equipment—Depreciation and amortization are provided on a straight-line basis over the estimated useful lives of the assets. The following table shows estimated useful lives of property and equipment:

Classification	Estimated Useful Lives
Buildings	10 to 50 years (average 27 years)
Equipment	3 to 20 years (average 11 years)

During 2003, the company reported $910,785 ($000s) for depreciation expense.

a. Compute the estimated useful life of Abbott Laboratories' depreciable assets. How does this compare with its useful lives footnote disclosure shown above?

b. Compute the estimated percent used up of Abbott Laboratories' depreciable assets. How do you interpret this figure?

P5-44. Interpreting and Applying Disclosures on Property and Equipment   Following are selected income statement; balance sheet; and land, buildings, and equipment (PPE) disclosures from Rohm and Haas Company (a specialty chemical company).

Rohm and Haas Company (ROH)

For Years Ended December 31 ($ millions)	2002	2001	2000
Net sales	$5,727	$5,666	$6,349
Cost of goods sold	3,910	4,008	4,342
Gross profit	1,817	1,658	2,007
Selling and administrative expense	879	861	933
Research and development expense	260	230	224
Interest expense	132	182	241
Amortization of goodwill and other intangibles	69	156	159
Purchased in-process research and development	—	—	13
Provision for restructuring and asset impairments	177	320	13
Share of affiliate earnings, net	15	12	18
Other income, net	5	15	46
Earnings (loss) from continuing operations before income taxes, extraordinary item and cumulative effect of accounting change	320	(64)	488

December 31 ($ millions)	2002	2001
Assets		
Cash and cash equivalents	$ 295	$ 92
Receivables, net	1,184	1,220
Inventories	765	712
Prepaid expenses and other current assets	299	397
Total current assets	2,543	2,421
Land, buildings and equipment, net of accumulated depreciation	2,954	2,905
Investments in and advances to affiliates	170	152
Goodwill, net of accumulated amortization	1,617	2,159
Other intangible assets, net of accumulated amortization	1,861	2,257
Other assets	561	484
Total Assets	$9,706	$10,378

Note 15: Land, Building and Equipment, net

(in millions)	2002	2001
Land	$ 142	$ 114
Buildings and improvements	1,541	1,421
Machinery and equipment	4,926	4,482
Capitalized interest	292	272
Construction in progress	345	318
Less: accumulated depreciation	4,292	3,702
Total	$2,954	$2,905

The principal lives (in years) used in determining depreciation rates of various assets are: buildings and improvements (10–50); machinery and equipment (5–20); automobiles, trucks and tank cars (3–10); furniture and fixtures, laboratory equipment and other assets (5–10); capitalized interest (11).

Note 5: Provision for Restructuring and Asset Impairments

2002   In 2002, we recognized $177 million for restructuring and asset impairments. This charge is comprised of $191 million for the impairment of certain long-lived assets and costs associated with workforce reductions initiated in 2002. Of the total 2002 charges, $158 million was non-cash in nature and comprised of asset impairments recorded to reduce the carrying value of certain identified assets to their fair values, which were calculated using cash flow analyses . . . The largest, single asset write-down was $121 million, recorded to write-down certain long-lived intangible and fixed assets of the Printed Wiring Board business in the Electronic Materials segment in accordance with SFAS No. 144, "Accounting for the Impairment or Disposal of Long-Lived Assets." The remaining $37 million of non-cash charges, recorded during 2002, related largely to the closure of two European plants and other building and equipment impairments.

2001   In 2001, we launched a repositioning initiative to enable several of our businesses to respond to structural changes in the global marketplace. In connection with these repositioning initiatives, we recognized a $330 million restructuring and asset impairment charge in the second quarter of 2001 . . . The largest component of the 2001 repositioning charge related to the full and partial closure of certain manufacturing and research facilities across all business groups and included exit costs related to the liquid polysulfide sealants business in Adhesives and Sealants and part of the dyes business in Performance Chemicals. Approximately 75% of the asset write-downs were in the North American region.

Required

a. Compute the PPE (land, buildings and equipment) asset turnover for 2002 and 2001 (net PPE assets for 2000 is $2,916 million). Interpret and explain any change in turnover. Does the level of its PPE turnover suggest that Rohm and Haas is capital intensive? Explain. Do you believe that Rohm and Haas' balance sheet reflects all of the assets it uses to conduct operations? Explain.

b. Rohm and Haas reported depreciation expense of $388 million in 2002. Assuming that Rohm and Haas uses straight-line depreciation, estimate the useful life, on average, for its depreciable PPE assets?

c. By what percentage are Rohm and Haas' assets "used up" at year-end 2002? What implication does the assets used up computation have for forecasting cash flows?

d. Rohm and Haas reported large expenses in 2002 and 2001 related to asset impairment charges with its restructuring program. Describe the accounting process by which the impairment charge is determined. How do these charges affect its cash flows for 2002 and 2001? How should you treat these charges for analysis purposes?

6 Reporting and Analyzing Intercorporate Investments

HEWLETT-PACKARD

HP GAMBLES ON COMPAQ

The Wall Street Journal ran an article in August 2002 on Hewlett-Packard Company under the heading, "H-P Posts Big Loss Due to Compaq Purchase." *The WSJ* reported that "HP posted a $2.03 billion fiscal third-quarter net loss . . . reflecting nearly $3 billion of restructuring costs and merger-related charges." This article further fueled the ongoing debate over the wisdom of HP's recent merger with Compaq Computer Corporation.

One year later, *Forbes* concluded, "Carleton [Carly] S. Fiorina should take a little time out to celebrate. The chief executive of Hewlett-Packard has pulled off the biggest merger in high-tech history. . . . One year into the [$24.2 billion] purchase of Compaq Computer, she has cut $3.5 billion in annual costs, a billion dollars more and a year earlier than promised. And despite erasing 17,000 jobs since the merger, HP has gained market share in key categories, scored 3,000 new patents and debuted 367 new products. It just won a ten-year, $3 billion outsourcing deal with Procter & Gamble. No wonder HP is promoting itself with a $400 million brand blitz while the rest of tech reels." (*Forbes*, August 2003)

HP was a $45 billion (in sales) company prior to its merger with Compaq. Carly Fiorina felt strongly that the merger was necessary to save HP from falling behind on technological development. She cited the example of photo company Eastman Kodak, which Fiorina said was slow to recognize the growth of digital photography (*Associated Press Newswires*, 2003).

Fiorina framed the Compaq merger decision for her directors as follows: "Do you think the information-technology industry needs to consolidate and, if so, is it better to be a consolidator or a consolidatee? How important is it to our strategic goals to be No. 1 or No. 2 in our chief product categories? Finally: Can we achieve our strategic goals without something drastic?" (*WSJ*, 2003) The response was less than enthusiastic. "Outside director Pattie Dunn started out doubtful. 'There's scant history of these things working,' she said. 'What will make our odds better?' When the McKinsey consultants cited $2.5 billion a year of cost savings, her face lit up." (*WSJ*, 2003)

HP's sales now exceed $70 billion and its operations are organized into five business segments:

- **Imaging and Printing Group**—provides home and business imaging, printing and publishing devices and systems, digital imaging products, printer supplies, and consulting services.
- **Personal Systems Group**—provides commercial personal computers (PCs), consumer PCs, workstations, handheld computing devices, digital entertainment systems, calculators, and other accessories, software and services for commercial and consumer markets.

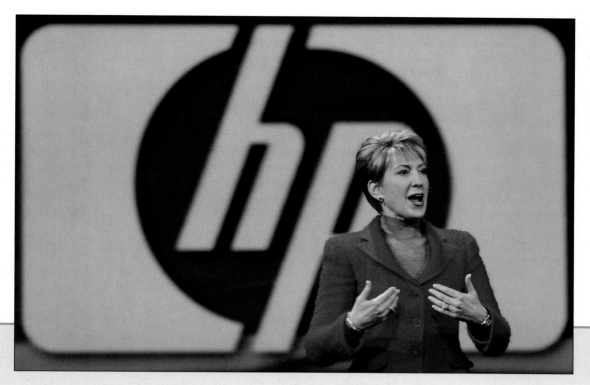

- **Enterprise Systems Group**—provides servers, storage, and software solutions.
- **HP Services**—provides a portfolio of IT services including customer support, consulting and integration, and managed services.
- **HP Financial Services**—supports and enhances HP's global product and service solutions, providing a range of financial management services.

In 2003, its first full year following the Compaq merger, HP reported net income of $2.5 billion. *Forbes* lauded its performance: "HP has slashed billions in costs by overhauling its data processing operations and its supply chain. . . . In merging its systems with Compaq's, HP erected a single communications network linking more than a quarter of a million PCs and handhelds; it handles 26 million e-mails a day. HP also cut the number of software applications it uses from 7,000 to 5,000, and of components it buys from 250,000 to 25,000. A huge part of the company's success so far has come from the $3 billion in annual cost cuts. Half the savings comes from cutting jobs. However, a large portion comes from the price concessions that HP can extract from its suppliers now that it orders huge volumes of PC components and other supplies. That, in turn, allows it to pressure rivals, even the ultra-lean Dell, on price." (*Forbes*, 2003)

Mergers, acquisitions, and alliances have become a crucial part of corporate strategy as companies strive for increased market power throughout their value chains and seek to provide a greater array of solutions for their customer base. *Forbes* quotes Fiorina: " 'Some companies will get rolled up; others will slowly slip away.' She adds that her rivals at Dell will find that 'the growth they achieved in the past doesn't prepare them for the growth they have to have in the future.' Sun Microsystems chief Scott McNealy 'will be one of those guys who tries to hang on,' but 'the business model doesn't work.' Companies that can't create new markets or steal business from competitors, she says, will be valued more like an old-line maker of washing machines." (*Forbes*, 2003)

HP purchased Compaq for $24.2 billion. From an accounting standpoint, acquiring a company is like acquiring any other asset. That is, it is recorded on the balance sheet at its fair market value on the date of acquisition. Each tangible asset (such as receivables, inventories, and plant assets) and any liabilities assumed by the purchaser must be appraised, as must any acquired identifiable intangible assets (such as trademarks, customer lists, licenses, franchise agreements, leases, contracts, software, and patented and unpatented technology). Any purchase price in excess of the fair market value of the tangible and identifiable intangible net assets is assigned to *goodwill*.

(Continued on next page)

(Continued from previous page)

The purchaser's financial reports reflect the operating activities of the acquired company from the date of acquisition. For HP, that meant Compaq's results are reflected in HP's income statement from the May 2001 acquisition date, which involved five months in the initial year of acquisition given HP's year-end is October. From the purchaser's view, this accounting is the same whether it acquires 25% or 100%, the difference lies in whether the acquired company is treated as an equity method investment or is consolidated. We cover both methods in this module.

There is subjectivity in the allocation of the purchase price in acquisitions, and some assets are depreciated and amortized over longer periods than others. Such allocation decisions can materially impact near-term and long-term profitability. Further, the cost of goodwill never impacts the income statement unless it becomes impaired and is written down. Finally, many financial statements reflect results of acquisitions made under a previous accounting standard (pooling-of-interest) that reported acquired assets at the acquired company's book value rather than fair market value at the time of sale, as is current practice. This module covers all of these issues for the reporting and analysis of consolidation accounting.

There are three methods of accounting for intercorporate investments depending on the perceived level of influence or control that the acquiring company has over the company that is acquired. The choice of method is typically determined by the percent of the company that is acquired. Each of these accounting methods affects the balance sheet and the income statement differently. We will consider the reporting and analysis of intercorporate investments, and their effects on the various financial statements. We will also consider what is being reported on the balance sheet *and* what is not. We highlight these issues as we progress through the discussion. [A final note: HP's directors forced Fiorina out in 2005. Says *Fortune* (February 7, 2005) "Buying Compaq hasn't paid off . . . nearly three years after the merger, there is still no easy solution to HP's problems."]

Sources: Hewlett-Packard 10-K report, 2004 and 2003; *The Wall Street Journal*, August 2002 and 2003; *Forbes,* August 2003; Associated Press Newswires, 2003.

■ INTRODUCTION

Many companies purchase the common stock of other companies. These purchases, called *intercorporate investments,* are often aimed at strategic activities such as the following:

- **Short-term investment of excess cash.** Companies often generate excess cash for investment either during slow times of the year (after receivables are collected and before seasonal production begins) or for liquidity needs (such as to counter strategic moves by competitors or to quickly respond to acquisition opportunities).
- **Alliances for strategic purposes.** Companies often acquire an equity interest in others for strategic purposes, such as gaining access to their research and development activities, to supply or distribution markets, or to their production and marketing expertise.
- **Market penetration or expansion.** Acquisitions of controlling interests in other companies can achieve vertical or horizontal integration in existing markets or can be avenues to penetrate new and growth markets.

Accounting for intercorporate investments follows one of three different methods, each of which affects the balance sheet and the income statement differently, often substantially. To help assimilate the materials in this module, Exhibit 6.1 provides a graphical depiction of accounting for investments.

The accounting for intercorporate investments depends on the degree of influence or control that the investor company (purchaser) can exert over the investee company (the company whose securities are being purchased). GAAP identifies three levels of influence/control:

1. **Passive.** In this case the purchasing company is merely an investor and cannot exert influence over the investee company. The purchaser's goal for this investment is to realize dividends and capital gains. Generally, passive investor status is presumed if the investor company owns less than 20% of the outstanding voting stock of the investee.
2. **Significant influence.** A company can sometimes exert significant influence over, but not control, the activities of the investee company. This level of influence can result from the percentage of

EXHIBIT 6.1 ■ Intercorporate Investment Diagram

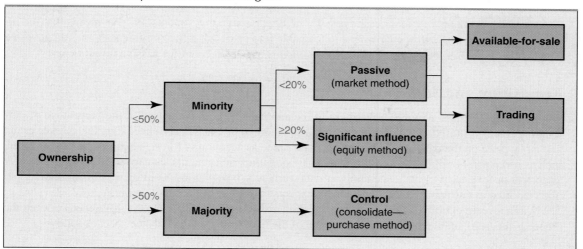

voting stock owned. It also can result from legal agreements, such as a license to use technology, a formula, or a trade secret like production know-how. It also can occur when the investor company is the sole supplier or customer of the investee. Generally, significant influence is presumed if the investor company owns 20% to 50% of the voting stock of the investee.

3. **Control.** When a company has control over another, it has the ability to elect a majority of the board of directors and, as a result, the ability to affect its strategic direction and hiring of executive management. Control is generally presumed if the investor company owns more than 50% of the outstanding voting stock of the investee company. Control can sometimes occur at less than 50% stock ownership by virtue of legal agreements, technology licensing, or other contractual means.

Once the level of influence/control is determined, the appropriate accounting method is applied as outlined in Exhibit 6.2.

EXHIBIT 6.2 ■ Investment Type, Accounting Treatment, and Financial Statement Effects

	Accounting	Balance Sheet Effects	Income Statement Effects	Cash Flow Effects
Passive	Market method	Investment account is reported at current market value	Dividends and capital gains affect income Interim changes in market value may or may not affect income depending on classification	Dividend and sale proceeds are cash inflows Purchases are cash outflows
Significant influence	Equity method	Investment account equals percent owned of investee company's equity*	Dividends reduce investment account Investor reports income equal to percent owned of investee income Capital gains are income	Dividend and sale proceeds are cash inflows Purchases are cash outflows
Control	Consolidation	Balance sheets of investor and investee are combined	Income statements of investor and investee are combined (and sale of investee yields capital gain or loss)	Cash flows of investor and investee are combined (and sale/purchase of investee yields cash inflow/outflow)

*Investments are often acquired at purchase prices in excess of book value (on average, market prices are 1.5 times book value for public companies). In this case the investment account exceeds the proportionate ownership of the investee's equity. We discuss this later in the module.

There are two basic reporting issues with investments: (1) how investment income should be recognized and (2) at what amount (cost or fair market value) the investment should be reported on the balance sheet. We next discuss both of these issues as we consider each of the three investment types.

■ PASSIVE INVESTMENTS

Short-term investments of excess cash typically involve passive investments. Passive means that the investor does not possess sufficient ownership to enable it to exert "significant influence" over the investee company or to control it outright. The *market method* is used to account for passive investments.

Acquisition and Sale

When an investment is acquired, regardless of the amount of shares purchased or the percentage of outstanding shares acquired, the investment is initially recorded on the balance sheet at its fair market value, that is, its price on the date of purchase. This is the same as accounting for the acquisition of other assets such as inventories or plant assets. Subsequent to acquisition, investments are carried on the balance sheet as current or long-term assets, depending on management's expectations about their ultimate holding period (reported as current assets if management expects to dispose of them within one year).

When investments are sold, any recognized gain or loss on sale is equal to the difference between the proceeds received and the book (carrying) value of the investment on the balance sheet as follows:

Gain or Loss on Sale = Proceeds from Sale − Book Value of Investment Sold

To illustrate the acquisition and sale of a passive investment, assume that Pownall Company purchases an investment in King Company consisting of 1,000 shares for $20 cash per share (this includes transaction costs such as brokerage). Near year-end, Pownall sells 400 of the 1,000 shares for $30 cash per share. The financial statement effects of these transactions for Pownall follow:

	Balance Sheet						Income Statement	
Transaction	Cash Asset	+ Noncash Assets	= Liabil- ities	+ Contrib. Capital	+ Retained Earnings		Revenues	− Expenses
1. Purchase 1,000 shares of King common stock for $20 cash per share	−20,000	+20,000 Investments						
2. Sell 400 shares of King common stock for $30 cash per share	+12,000	−8,000 Investments			+4,000		+4,000 Gain on Sale	

Margin notes:

Investments 20,000
　Cash 20,000

Cash 12,000
　Investments 8,000
　Gain on Sale 4,000

The gain or loss on sale is reported as a component of *other income,* which is commonly commingled with interest and dividend revenue.

Accounting for the purchase and sale of investments is the same as with any other asset. Further, there is no difference in accounting for purchases and sales across the different types of passive investments discussed in this section. However, there are differences in accounting for the different passive investments *between* their purchase and their sale. We next address this issue.

Mark-to-Market versus Cost

If an investment in securities has an active market with published prices, that investment is reported on the balance sheet at its market value as of the balance sheet date. If such a market does not exist, that investment is reported at its historical cost (or adjusted cost in the case of equity method investments that we describe in the next section). **Market value** is the published price (as listed on a stock exchange) multiplied by the number of shares owned. This is one of very few assets that are reported at market value instead of historical cost.[1]

---

[1]Other assets reported at market value include (1) derivative securities (such as forward contracts, options, and futures) that are purchased to provide a hedge against price fluctuations or to eliminate other business risks (such as interest or exchange rate fluctuations), and (2) inventories and long-term assets that must be written down to market when permanent declines in value occur.

There is a trade-off between the *objectivity* of historical cost and the *relevance* of market value. All things equal, we prefer to know current market values of assets as these are more relevant in determining the market value of the company. However, for most assets, market values cannot be reliably determined. Their use would introduce excess subjectivity into the financial reporting process.

In the case of marketable securities, market prices result from numerous transactions between willing buyers and sellers. Market prices in this case provide an unbiased (objective) estimate of value to report on balance sheets. This market method of accounting for marketable securities yields fluctuations in the asset side of the balance sheet with corresponding fluctuations in equity (liabilities are unaffected). This is reflected in the following accounting equation:

$$\text{Assets} \uparrow\downarrow = \text{Liabilities} + \text{Equity} \uparrow\downarrow$$

An important issue is whether such changes in equity should be reported as income (with a consequent change in retained earnings), or whether they should bypass the income statement and directly impact equity via *other comprehensive income (OCI)*. The answer differs depending on the classification of securities, which we explain in the next section.

Investments Marked to Market

The following two classifications of marketable securities require the investment to be reported on the balance sheet at current market value (*marked-to-market*):

1. **Available-for-sale (AFS).** These are investments in securities that management intends to hold for capital gains and dividend revenue; although it may sell them if the price is right.
2. **Trading (T).** These are investments in securities that management intends to actively buy and sell for trading profits as market prices fluctuate.

Investments in both equity and debt securities qualify for these classifications. (Equity securities refer to those with ownership interest, whereas debt securities have no ownership interest.) Management's assignment of securities between these two classifications depends on the degree of turnover (transaction volume) it expects in the investment portfolio, which reflects its intent to actively trade the securities or not. Available-for-sale portfolios exhibit less turnover than that for trading portfolios.[2] Once that classification is established, reporting for a portfolio follows that in Exhibit 6.3.

EXHIBIT 6.3 ■ Accounting Treatment for Available-for-Sale and for Trading Investments

Investment Classification	Reporting of Market Value Changes	Reporting Dividends Received and Gains and Losses on Sale
Available-for-Sale (AFS)	Market value changes bypass the income statement and are reported directly in *other comprehensive income* (OCI) of equity	Reported as *other income* in income statement
Trading (T)	Market value changes are reported in the income statement as unrealized gains or losses; impacts equity via retained earnings	Same as above

Both available-for-sale and trading investments are reported at current market values (marked-to-market) on the statement date. Whether the change in market value affects current income depends on the investment classification: available-for-sale has no income affect; trading has an income affect. The impact on equity is similar for both classifications, with the only difference being whether the change is reflected in retained earnings or in the other comprehensive income (OCI) of equity. Dividends and any gains or losses on security sales are reported in the other income section of the income statement for both classifications.

$

Cash Effect

---

[2]GAAP permits companies to have multiple portfolios, each with a different classification, and management can change portfolio classification provided it adheres to strict disclosure and reporting requirements if its expectations of turnover change.

Market Adjustments

To illustrate the accounting for changes in market value subsequent to purchase (and before sale), assume that Pownall's investment in King Co. (600 remaining shares purchased for $20 per share) increases in value to $25 per share at year-end. The investment must be marked to market to reflect the $3,000 unrealized gain ($5 per share increase for 600 shares). The financial statements are affected as follows:

	Balance Sheet					Income Statement	
Transaction	Cash Asset +	Noncash Assets =	Liabil-ities +	Contrib. Capital +	Retained Earnings	Revenues −	Expenses
If available-for-sale portfolio:							
$5 increase in market value of King Co. investment	+3,000 Investments				+3,000 OCI		
If trading portfolio:							
$5 increase in market value of King Co. investment	+3,000 Investments				+3,000 Retained Earnings	+3,000 Unrealized Gain	

Investments   3,000
 Unrealized gain
  (OCI)   3,000

Investments   3,000
 Unrealized gain
  (Income)   3,000

Under both classifications, the investment account is increased by $3,000 to reflect the increase in market value of the shares owned. When accounted for as available-for-sale, the unrealized gain is reflected as an increase in Other Comprehensive Income (OCI), typically viewed as a component of retained earnings. However, when accounted for as trading, the unrealized gain is recorded as income, thus increasing both reported income and retained earnings for that period. (Our illustration uses a portfolio with only one security for simplicity. Portfolios usually consist of multiple securities, and the unrealized gain or loss is computed based on the total cost and total market value of the entire portfolio.)

These market adjustments are only applied to publicly traded securities as companies sometimes purchase securities for which current market values are unavailable. Examples are investments in start-up companies, privately held corporations, and in local bond offerings. Investments in nonpublicly traded companies are accounted for at cost as we discuss later in this section.

Financial Statement Disclosures

Companies are required to disclose cost and market value information on their investment portfolios in footnotes to financial statements. **American Express Company (AXP)** reports its accounting policies for its investments in the following footnote to its 10-K report:

> **Investments**   Generally, investment securities are carried at fair value on the balance sheet with unrealized gains (losses) recorded in equity, net of income tax provisions (benefits). Gains and losses are recognized in results of operations upon disposition of the securities. In addition, losses are also recognized when management determines that a decline in value is other-than-temporary, which requires judgment regarding the amount and timing of recovery.

This footnote reveals that American Express generally accounts for its investments as available-for-sale. We know this because it reports that unrealized gains and losses are "recorded in equity." It also reports that these investments are reported on its balance sheet at market value. Following is the investments line item from the asset section of American Express' balance sheet ($ millions):

December 31	2003
Investments	$57,067

Its investment portfolio is carried as an asset with a current market value of $57,067 million. Unrealized gains and losses on its available-for-sale investments bypass its income statement (do not affect current income), and are reported as a component of equity called other comprehensive income (OCI). Gains and losses on the *sale* of investments, however, are reported in current income. Also, as American Express reports in its footnote, if investments suffer a decline in value prior to sale that is deemed "other-than-temporary," they are written down to current market value and that loss is reported in current income.

Footnotes to the American Express 10-K provide further information about the composition of its investment portfolio ($ millions):

The following is a summary of investments at December 31:

	2003
Available-for-Sale, at fair value	$52,278
Investment loans (fair value: $4,116)	3,794
Trading	995
Total	$57,067

This note reveals that of the $57,067 million in investments, $52,278 million are classified as available-for-sale, with the remainder classified as either investment (commercial) loans or trading securities. Investment loans are reported at cost since no liquid market exists for these investments.[3] The trading portfolio is reported at current market value with unrealized gains and losses reported in current income.

American Express provides additional (required) disclosures on both the cost and unrealized gains and losses for its available-for-sale investments as follows:

(Millions)	Cost	Gross Unrealized Gains	Gross Unrealized Losses	Fair Value
Corporate debt securities	$20,144	$ 883	$(110)	$20,917
Mortgage and other asset-backed securities	16,674	279	(84)	16,869
State and municipal obligations	7,138	479	(5)	7,612
Structured investments	2,828	24	(60)	2,792
Foreign government bonds and obligations	1,378	60	(3)	1,435
U.S. Government and agencies obligations	1,150	17	—	1,167
Other	1,474	21	(9)	1,486
Total	$50,786	$1,763	$(271)	$52,278

For each investment, American Express reports its cost, fair market value, and gross unrealized gains and losses; the latter reflect differences between cost and market. American Express reports that the cost of its investment portfolio is $50,786 million, and that there are unrealized gains (losses) of $1,763 ($271) million as of December 31, 2003. The total market value of $52,278 million at December 31, 2003 is the amount reported on its balance sheet.

---

[3]The reported "fair value" is computed based on projected cash flows and prevailing interest rates, and is not based on reference to a published market price.

American Express' net unrealized gain of $1,492 million ($1,763 million − $271 million) is reported net of $561 million in estimated tax; yielding a reported balance of $931 million in the other comprehensive income section of its stockholders' equity as follows ($ millions):

December 31	2003
Shareholders' Equity	
Common shares, $.20 par value, authorized 3.6 billion shares; issued and outstanding 1,284 million shares in 2003	$ 257
Additional paid-in capital	6,081
Retained earnings	8,793
Other comprehensive income (loss), net of tax	
Net unrealized securities gains	931
Net unrealized derivatives losses	(446)
Foreign currency translation adjustments	(278)
Minimum pension liability	(15)
Accumulated other comprehensive income	192
Total shareholders' equity	$15,323

There is sometimes confusion because of the difference between the amount reported in the investment footnote and the amount reported in other comprehensive income. This difference arises because the net unrealized gain of $1,492 million ($1,763 million − $271 million) reported in the investment footnote is pretax and the $931 million reported in the other comprehensive income section of stockholders' equity is after-tax (reflecting a nearly 38% tax rate).

Investments Marked to Cost

$
Cash Effect

Investments for which no current market values exist must be accounted for using the cost method. Under the **cost method**, the investment is continually reported at its historical cost, and any cash dividends and interest received are recognized in current income.

Debt securities that management intends to hold to maturity are reported using the cost method. These debt securities are classified as **held-to-maturity** (HTM). Exhibit 6.4 identifies the reporting of these securities.

EXHIBIT 6.4 ■ Accounting Treatment for Held-to-Maturity Investments

Investment Classification	Reporting of Market Value Changes	Reporting Dividends Received and Gains and Losses on Sale
Held-to-Maturity (HTM)	Market value changes are *not* reported in either the balance sheet or income statement	Reported as *other income* in income statement

Changes in market value are not reflected on either the balance sheet or the income statement. The presumption is that these investments are held to maturity, at which time they are received at their face value. Fluctuations in market value, as a result, are less relevant for this investment classification. Finally, any interest received, and gains and losses on the sale of these investments, are recorded in current income.

■ MID-MODULE REVIEW 1 ■

Part 1: Available-for-sale securities
Using the financial statement effects template, enter the effects (amount and account) relating to the following four transactions involving investments in marketable securities classified as available-for-sale.

1. Purchased 1,000 shares of Pincus common stock for $15 cash per share.
2. Received cash dividend of $2 per share on Pincus common stock.
3. Year-end market price of Pincus common stock is $17 per share.
4. Sold all 1,000 shares of Pincus common stock for $17,000 cash.

Solution for Part 1:

Transaction	Balance Sheet									Income Statement		
	Cash Asset	+	Noncash Assets	=	Liabil-ities	+	Contrib. Capital	+	Retained Earnings	Revenues	−	Expenses
1. Purchased 1,000 shares of Pincus common stock for $15 cash per share	−15,000		+15,000 Investments									
2. Received cash dividend of $2 per share on Pincus common stock	+2,000								+2,000 Retained Earnings	+2,000 Dividend Income		
3. Year-end market price of Pincus common stock is $17 per share			+2,000 Investments						+2,000 OCI			
4. Sold all 1,000 shares of Pincus common stock for $17,000 cash	+17,000		−17,000 Investments						−2,000 OCI +2,000 Retained Earnings	+2,000 Gain on Sale		

Part 2: Trading securities

Using the financial statement effects template and the same transaction information 1 through 4 from part 1, enter the effects (amount and account) relating to these transactions assuming that the investments are classified as trading securities.

Solution for Part 2:

Transaction	Balance Sheet									Income Statement		
	Cash Asset	+	Noncash Assets	=	Liabil-ities	+	Contrib. Capital	+	Retained Earnings	Revenues	−	Expenses
1. Purchased 1,000 shares of Pincus common stock for $15 cash per share	−15,000		+15,000 Investments									
2. Received cash dividend of $2 per share on Pincus common stock	+2,000								+2,000 Retained Earnings	+2,000 Dividend Income		
3. Year-end market price of Pincus common stock is $17 per share			+2,000 Investments						+2,000 Retained Earnings	+2,000 Unrealized Gain		
4. Sold all 1,000 shares of Pincus common stock for $17,000 cash	+17,000		−17,000 Investments									

■ INVESTMENTS WITH SIGNIFICANT INFLUENCE

Many companies make investments in other companies that yield them significant influence over those other companies. These intercorporate investments are usually made for strategic reasons such as the following:

- **Prelude to acquisition.** Significant ownership can allow the investor company to gain a seat on the board of directors from which it can learn much about the investee company, its products, and its industry.
- **Strategic alliance.** One example of a strategic alliance is an investment in a company that provides inputs for the investor's production process. This relationship is closer than the usual supplier-buyer relationship, often because the investor company provides trade secrets or technical know-how of its production process.
- **Pursuit of research and development.** Many research activities in the pharmaceutical, software, and oil and gas industries are conducted jointly. The common motivation is to reduce risk or the amount of capital invested by the investor. The investor company's equity investment often carries an option to purchase additional shares or the entire company, which it can exercise if the research activities are fruitful.

A crucial feature in each of these investments is that the investor company has ownership sufficient to exert *significant influence* over the investee company. GAAP requires that such investments be accounted for using the *equity method.*

Significant influence is the ability of the investor to affect the financing or operating policies of the investee. Ownership levels of 20% to 50% of the outstanding common stock of the investee presume significant influence. Significant influence can also exist when ownership is less than 20%. Evidence of such influence can be that the investor company is able to gain a seat on the board of directors of the investee by virtue of its equity investment, or the investor controls technical know-how or patents that are used by the investee, or the investor is able to exert significant influence by virtue of legal contracts between it and the investee. (There is growing pressure for determining significant influence by the facts and circumstances of the investment instead of a strict ownership percentage rule.)

Accounting for Investments with Significant Influence

Investments with significant influence must be accounted for using the **equity method**. The equity method of accounting for investments reports the investment on the balance sheet at an amount equal to the percentage of the investee's equity owned by the investor; hence the name equity method. (This assumes acquisition at book value. Acquisition at an amount greater than book value is covered later in this section.) Contrary to passive investments that are reported at market value, equity method investments increase (decrease) with increases (decreases) in the equity of the investee.

Equity method accounting is summarized as follows:

Cash Effect

- Investments are initially recorded at their purchase cost.
- Dividends received are treated as a recovery of the investment and, thus, reduce the investment balance (dividends are *not* reported as income as with passive investments).
- The investor reports income equal to its percentage share of the reported income of the investee; the investment account is increased by that income or decreased by its share of any loss.
- The investment is *not* reported at market value as passive market investments are.

To illustrate the accounting for investments using the equity method, consider the following scenario: Assume that HP acquires a 30% interest in Mitel Networks, a company seeking to develop a new technology in a strategic alliance with HP. At acquisition, Mitel reports $1,000 of stockholders' equity, and HP purchases its 30% stake for $300. At the first year-end, Mitel reports profits of $100 and pays $20 in cash dividends to its shareholders ($6 to HP). Following are the financial statement effects for HP (the investor company) for this investment using the equity method:

	Balance Sheet					Income Statement		
Transaction	Cash + Asset	Noncash = Assets	Liabil- + ities	Contrib. + Capital	Retained Earnings	Revenues	−	Expenses
1. Purchase 30% invest- ment in Mitel for $300 cash	−300	+300 Investment in Mitel						
2. Mitel reports $100 income		+30 Investment in Mitel			+30 Retained Earnings	+30 Investment Income		
3. Mitel pays $20 cash dividends, $6 to HP	+6	−6 Investment in Mitel						
Ending balance of HP's investment account		324						

Investments	300	
Cash		300

Investments	30	
Investment income		30

Cash	6	
Investments		6

$ Cash Effect

The investment is initially reported on HP's balance sheet at its purchase price of $300, representing a 30% interest in Mitel's equity of $1,000. During the year, Mitel's equity increases to $1,080 ($1,000 plus $100 income and less $20 dividends). Likewise, HP's investment increases by $30 to reflect its 30% share of Mitel's $100 income and decreases by $6 from Mitel's $20 of dividends. After these transactions, HP's investment in Mitel is reported on HP's balance sheet at 30% of $1,080, or $324.

Companies sometimes pay more than book value when acquiring equity interest in other companies. For example, if HP paid $400 for its 30% stake in Mitel, HP would initially report its investment at its $400 purchase price. The $400 investment consists of two parts: the $300 equity investment described above and the $100 additional investment. HP is willing to pay the higher purchase price because it be-lieves that Mitel's reported equity is below its current market value (such as when its assets are reported at costs that are below market values or when intangible assets like internally generated goodwill are not recorded on its balance sheet). The $300 portion of the investment is accounted for as described above. The $100 additional investment is accounted for like the purchase of any other asset. That is, if the $100 relates to undervalued depreciable assets, it is depreciated over the estimated useful lives. Or, if it relates to identifiable intangible assets that have a determinable useful life (like patents), it is amortized over the useful lives of the intangible assets. If it relates to goodwill, it is not amortized and remains on the balance sheet at $100 unless and until it is deemed to have become impaired. (See Appendix 6A for an expanded illustration.)

Two final points about equity method accounting: First, just as the equity of a company is different from its market value, so is the balance of the equity investment account different from its market value. Indeed, there can be a substantial difference between the book value of an investment and its market value (as is the case with every asset other than passive market investments that are recorded at market value).[4] Second, if the investee company reports income, the investor company does as well. Recognition of equity income by the investor, however, does not mean that it has received that income in cash. Cash is only re-ceived if the investee's directors declare a dividend payment.[5] To highlight this, investors subtract the dif-ference between reported equity income and dividends received in the operating section of the statement of cash flows. The net amount is the *cash* income received.

$ Cash Effect

---

[4]However, if the market value of an investment has permanently declined, the investment is deemed impaired and it is written down to that lower market value.

[5]Investee dividend-paying ability can be (a) restricted by regulatory agencies or foreign governments, (b) prohibited under debt agreements for highly leveraged borrowers, and/or (c) influenced by directors that the investor does not control.

> **RESEARCH INSIGHT**   **Equity Income and Stock Prices**
>
> The equity method of accounting for investments does not recognize any dividends received from the investee nor any market value changes for the investee in the investor's income until the investment is sold. However, research has found a positive relation between investors' and investees' stock prices at the time of investees' earnings and dividend announcements. This suggests that the market includes information regarding investees' earnings and dividends when assessing the stock prices of investor companies. This implies the market looks beyond the book value of the investment account in determining stock prices of investor companies.

Equity Method Accounting and ROE Effects

The balance sheet amount for equity method investments is equal to the percentage owned of the equity of the investee company when the investment is acquired at book value. To illustrate, consider the case of SBC Communications Inc, which owns 60% of Cingular Wireless, a nationwide wireless provider formed as a joint venture with BellSouth. SBC accounts for its investment in Cingular using the equity method as described in the following footnote to its 10-K report:

> We account for our 60% economic interest in Cingular under the equity method of accounting in our consolidated financial statements since we share control equally (i.e., 50/50) with our 40% economic partner in the joint venture. We have equal voting rights and representation on the board of directors that controls Cingular.

(SBC's investment is accounted for using the equity method despite its "60% economic interest." Economic interest means that it receives 60% of the income, cash flow, and net asset ownership. Guidelines for use of the equity method versus consolidation are based on whether SBC has the ability to exert "significant influence" or "control" over Cingular. Since voting rights are shared equally, SBC does not have "control" and, as a result, consolidation is inappropriate.)

SBC reports an investment balance at December 31, 2003, of $5,090 million, which is equal to its 60% share of Cingular's equity as reported in the following footnote to the SBC 10-K report:

Cingular Wireless ($ millions)	2003
Income Statements	
Operating revenues	$15,483
Operating income	2,289
Net income	1,022
Balance Sheets	
Current assets	$ 3,300
Noncurrent assets	22,226
Current liabilities	3,187
Noncurrent liabilities	13,855

Specifically, Cingular's equity is equal to $8,484 million ($3,300 + $22,226 − $3,187 − $13,855) and, thus, SBC's 60% economic interest represents an investment balance of $5,090 million (60% × $8,484).

However, note that the balance sheet of Cingular reports total assets of $25,526 million and total liabilities of $17,042 million. The $5,090 million investment balance on SBC's balance sheet fails to reflect the full asset investment and financial obligations of Cingular—as it reflects only its share of net assets.

SBC also reports equity income of $613 million as reported in the following footnote:

($ millions)	2003	2002
Beginning of year	$10,468	$ 9,441
Contributions	—	299
Equity in net income	613	759
Other adjustments	(78)	(31)
End of year	$11,003	$10,468

The $613 million represents 60% of Cingular's net income of $1,022 million as reported in the Cingular footnote previously presented. Cingular did not pay any cash dividends to SBC in 2003 and, thus, SBC's reported income did not reflect any operating cash inflows for 2003 from the investment in Cingular.

$
Cash Effect

Under equity method accounting, only the net equity owned is reported on the balance sheet (not the assets and liabilities to which the investment relates), and only the net equity in earnings is reported in the income statement (not the investee's sales and expenses). Both the balance sheet and income statements are, therefore, markedly affected. Further, because the assets and liabilities are left off the balance sheet, and because the sales and expenses are omitted from the income statement, the *components* of ROE are also markedly affected as follows:

- **Net operating profit margin (NOPM = NOPAT/Sales).** Most analysts include equity income in NOPAT since it relates to operating investments. The reported NOPM is, thus, *overstated* due to nonrecognition of investee sales and the recognition of investee income.
- **Net operating asset turnover (NOAT = Sales/Average NOA).** The equity investment balance is typically included in operating assets. This means that NOAT is *understated* due to nonrecognition of investee sales and *overstated* by nonrecognition of investee assets in excess of the investment balance. The net effect is, therefore, *indeterminate* (NOAT is overstated provided NOA exceeds sales, and understated otherwise.)
- **Financial leverage (FLEV = Net financial obligations/Average equity).** Financial leverage is *understated* due to nonrecognition of investee liabilities and the recognition of investee equity (the proportionate share of investee earnings is included in SBC's income).

Although ROE components are affected, ROE is unaffected by use of equity method accounting. Still, the evaluation of the *quality* of ROE is affected. Analysis reveals that ROE is impacted from a lower net operating profit margin (actual NOPM is overstated) and higher financial leverage (actual FLEV is understated) than was apparent based on the reported balance sheet and income statement. As we discuss in a later module, analysts frequently adjust reported financial statements for these types of items before conducting analysis. One such adjustment might be to consolidate the equity method investee with the investor company.

MANAGERIAL DECISION | **You Are the Chief Financial Officer**

You are receiving capital expenditure requests for long-term operating asset purchases from various managers. You are concerned that capacity utilization is too low. What potential courses of action can you consider? Explain. [Answer, p. 6-29]

MID-MODULE REVIEW 2

Using the financial statement effects template, enter the effects (amount and account) relating to the following four transactions involving investments in marketable securities accounted for using the equity method.

1. Purchased 5,000 shares of Cheng common stock at $10 cash per share. These shares reflect 30% ownership of Cheng.
2. Received a $2 per share cash dividend on Cheng common stock.
3. Made an adjustment to reflect $100,000 income reported by Cheng.
4. Sold all 5,000 shares of Cheng common stock for $90,000.

Solution:

		Balance Sheet									Income Statement		
Transaction or Event		Cash Asset	+	Noncash Assets	=	Liabil-ities	+	Contrib. Capital	+	Retained Earnings	Revenues	−	Expenses
Investments 50,000 Cash 50,000	1. Purchased 5,000 shares of Cheng common stock at $10 cash per share. These shares reflect 30% owner-ship of Cheng	−50,000		+50,000 Investments									
Cash 10,000 Investments 10,000	2. Received a $2 per share cash dividend on Cheng common stock	+10,000		−10,000 Investments									
Investments 30,000 Equity Income 30,000	3. Made an adjustment to reflect $100,000 income reported by Cheng			+30,000 Investments						+30,000 Retained Earnings	+30,000 Equity Income		
Cash 90,000 Gain on Sale 20,000 Investments 70,000	4. Sold all 5,000 shares of Cheng common stock for $90,000	+90,000		−70,000 Investments						+20,000 Retained Earnings	+20,000 Gain on Sale		

■ INVESTMENTS WITH CONTROL

This section discusses accounting for investments where the investor company "controls" the investee company. For example, in its footnote describing its accounting policies, **Hewlett-Packard** reports the following:

> **Principles of Consolidation** The Consolidated Financial Statements include the accounts of HP and its wholly-owned and controlled majority-owned subsidiaries. All significant intercompany accounts and trans-actions have been eliminated.

This means that HP financial statements are an aggregation (an adding up) of those of the parent company and all its subsidiary companies, less any intercompany activities.

Accounting for Investments with Control

Accounting for business combinations (acquisitions) involves one additional step to equity method accounting. Under the equity method, the investment balance represents the proportion of the investee's equity owned by the investor, and that the investor company income statement includes its proportionate share of the investee's income. Consolidation accounting (1) replaces the investment balance with the investee's assets and liabilities to which it relates, and (2) replaces the equity income reported by the investor with the investee's sales and expenses to which it relates. Specifically, the consolidated balance sheet includes the gross assets and liabilities of the investee company, and the income statement includes the gross sales and expenses.

To illustrate, consider the following scenario. Penman Company acquires all of the common stock of Nissim Company by exchanging newly issued shares for all of Nissim's common stock. The purchase price is equal to the $3,000 book value of Nissim's stockholders' equity (contributed capital of $2,000 and retained earnings of $1,000). The investment in Nissim Co. on Penman's balance sheet is accounted for using the equity method (GAAP only requires consolidation for financial statements issued to the public, not for the internal financial records of the separate companies). Penman records an initial balance in the investment account of $3,000, which equals the purchase price. The balance sheets for Penman and Nissim immediately after the acquisition, together with the required consolidating adjustments (or eliminations), and the consolidated balance sheet that the two companies report are shown in Exhibit 6.5.

EXHIBIT 6.5 ■ Mechanics of Consolidation Accounting (Purchased at Book Value)

	Penman Company	Nissim Company	Consolidating Adjustments	Consolidated
Current assets	$ 5,000	$1,000		$ 6,000
Investment in Nissim	3,000	0	(3,000)	0
PPE, net	10,000	4,000		14,000
Total assets	$18,000	$5,000		$20,000
Liabilities	$ 5,000	$2,000		$ 7,000
Contributed capital	10,000	2,000	(2,000)	10,000
Retained earnings	3,000	1,000	(1,000)	3,000
Total liabilities and equity	$18,000	$5,000		$20,000

Since Penman "controls" the activities of Nissim, GAAP requires consolidation of the two balance sheets. This process involves summing the individual lines for each balance sheet less the elimination of any intercompany transactions (investments and loans, or sales and purchases, within the consolidated group). The consolidated balances for current assets, PPE, and liabilities are, for example, the sum of those accounts on each balance sheet. The equity investment, however, represents an intercompany transaction that must be eliminated prior to consolidation. This is accomplished by removing the equity investment of $3,000, and removing Nissim's equity to which that investment relates.[6]

---

[6]In the event that Penman acquires less than 100% of the stock of Nissim, Penman's equity must increase to maintain the accounting equation. This equity account is titled **minority interest**. For example, assume that Penman acquires 80% of Nissim for $2,400 (80% of $3,000). The consolidating adjustments follow:

Balance Sheet									Income Statement		
Cash Asset	+	Noncash Assets	=	Liabil- ities	+	Contrib. Capital	+	Retained Earnings	Revenues	−	Expenses
		−2,400 Investment in Nissim				−2,000 Nissim's Common Stock		−1,000 Nissim's Retained Earnings			
						+600 Minority Interest					

The claim of noncontrolling shareholders is recognized in stockholders' equity just like those of majority shareholders.

The consolidated balance sheet is shown in the far right column of Exhibit 6.5. It shows total assets of $20,000, total liabilities of $7,000 and stockholders' equity of $13,000. Consolidated equity equals that of the parent company—this is always the case.[7]

The illustration above assumes that the purchase price of the acquisition equals book value. What changes, if any, occur when the purchase price and book value are different? To explore this case, consider an acquisition where purchase price exceeds book value. This might arise, for example, if an investor company believes it is acquiring something of value that is not reported on the investee's balance sheet—such as tangible assets whose market values have risen above book value, or unrecorded intangible assets like patents or corporate synergies. If an acquisition is made at a price in excess of book value, all net assets acquired (both tangible and intangible) must be recognized on the consolidated balance sheet.

To illustrate an acquisition where purchase price exceeds book value, assume that Penman Company acquires Nissim Company for $4,000 instead of the $3,000 purchase price we used in the previous illustration. Also assume that in determining its purchase price, Penman feels that the additional $1,000 ($4,000 vs. $3,000) is justified because (1) Nissim's PPE is worth $300 more than its book value, and (2) Penman realizes $700 in additional value from corporate synergies.

The $4,000 investment account reflects two components: the book value acquired of $3,000 (as before) and an additional $1,000 of newly acquired assets. The post-acquisition balance sheets of the two companies, together with the consolidating adjustments and the consolidated balance sheet, are shown in Exhibit 6.6.

EXHIBIT 6.6 ■ Mechanics of Consolidation Accounting (Purchased above Book Value)

	Penman Company	Nissim Company	Consolidating Adjustments	Consolidated
Current assets	$ 5,000	$1,000		$ 6,000
Investment in Nissim	4,000	0	(4,000)	0
PPE, net	10,000	4,000	300	14,300
Goodwill			700	700
Total assets	$19,000	$5,000		$21,000
Liabilities	5,000	$2,000		$ 7,000
Contributed capital	11,000	2,000	(2,000)	11,000
Retained earnings	3,000	1,000	(1,000)	3,000
Total liabilities and equity	$19,000	$5,000		$21,000

The consolidated balances for current assets, PPE, and liabilities are the sum of those accounts on each company's balance sheet. The investment account, however, includes newly acquired assets that must be reported on the consolidated balance sheet. The consolidation process in this case has two steps. First, the $3,000 equity of Nissim Company is eliminated against the investment account as before. Then, the remaining $1,000 of the investment account is eliminated through the adjustments for newly acquired assets ($300 of PPE and $700 of goodwill not reported on Nissim's balance sheet) on the consolidated balance sheet. Thus, the consolidated balance sheet reflects the book value of Penman and the *fair market value* (book value plus the excess of Nissim's market value over book value) for Nissim Company at the acquisition date.

To illustrate consolidation mechanics with an actual case, consider the consolidated balance sheet (parent company, subsidiary and consolidated balance sheet) that General Electric reports in a supplemental schedule to its 10-K report as shown in Exhibit 6.7.

---

[7]Also, consolidated net income always equals the parent company's net income as the subsidiary's net income is already reflected in the parent's income statement as equity income from its investment.

EXHIBIT 6.7 ■ General Electric's Consolidated Balance Sheet

At December 31, 2003 (In millions)	General Electric Company and Consolidated Affiliates	GE	GECS
ASSETS			
Cash and equivalents	$ 12,664	$ 1,670	$ 11,273
Investment securities	120,724	380	120,344
Current receivables	10,732	10,973	—
Inventories	8,752	8,555	197
Financing receivables (investments in time sales, loans and financing leases)—net	226,029	—	226,029
Insurance receivables—net	27,053	—	27,053
Other GECS receivables	9,545	—	11,901
Property, plant and equipment (including equipment leased to others)—net	53,382	14,566	38,816
Investment in GECS	—	45,308	—
Intangible assets—net	55,025	30,204	24,821
Consolidated, liquidating securitization entities	26,463	—	26,463
All other assets	97,114	30,448	67,629
TOTAL ASSETS	**$647,483**	**$142,104**	**$554,526**
LIABILITIES AND EQUITY			
Short-term borrowings	$134,917	$ 2,555	$132,988
Accounts payable, principally trade accounts	19,824	8,753	13,440
Progress collections and price adjustments accrued	4,433	4,433	—
Dividends payable	2,013	2,013	—
All other current costs and expenses accrued	15,343	15,343	—
Long-term borrowings	170,004	8,388	162,540
Insurance liabilities, reserves and annuity benefits	136,264	—	136,264
Consolidated, liquidating securitization entities	25,721	—	25,721
All other liabilities	41,357	18,449	22,828
Deferred income taxes	12,647	1,911	10,736
Total liabilities	562,523	61,845	504,517
Minority interest in equity of consolidated affiliates	5,780	1,079	4,701
Common stock (10,063,120,000 shares outstanding)	669	669	1
Accumulated gains/(losses)—net			
Investment securities	1,620	1,620	1,823
Currency translation adjustments	2,987	2,987	2,639
Derivatives qualifying as hedges	(1,792)	(1,792)	(1,727)
Other capital	17,497	17,497	12,268
Retained earnings	82,796	82,796	30,304
Less common stock held in treasury	(24,597)	(24,597)	—
Total shareowners' equity	79,180	79,180	45,308
TOTAL LIABILITIES AND EQUITY	**$647,483)**	**$142,104**	**$554,526**

General Electric Company (GE) owns 100% of its financial products' subsidiary, General Electric Capital Services (GECS), whose stockholder's equity is $45,308 million as of 2003. The Investment in GECS account is also reported at $45,308 million on GE's (parent company) balance sheet. This investment account is subsequently removed (eliminated) in the consolidation process, together with the equity of GECS to which it relates. Following this elimination, and the *elimination of all other intercompany sales and advances,* the adjusted balance sheets of the two companies are summed to yield the consolidated balance sheet.

Reporting of Acquired Intangible Assets

Acquisitions are often made at a purchase price in excess of the book value of the investee company's equity. The purchase price is first allocated to the fair market values of tangible assets and liabilities (such as PPE in our example). Then, the remainder is allocated to acquired *intangible* assets.

Hewlett-Packard reported the following allocation of its $24,170 million purchase price for **Compaq Computer** in the footnotes to its 10-K report ($ millions).

Tangible assets	Cash and cash equivalents	$ 3,615
	Accounts receivable	4,305
	Financing receivables	1,241
	Inventory	1,661
	Current deferred tax assets	1,475
	Other current assets	1,146
	Property, plant and equipment	2,998
	Long-term financing receivables and other assets	1,914
Acquired intangible assets	Amortizable intangible assets	
	Customer contracts and lists, distribution agreements	1,942
	Developed and core technology, patents	1,501
	Product trademarks	74
	Intangible asset with an indefinite life	1,422
	Goodwill	14,450
Liabilities assumed	Accounts payable	(2,804)
	Short- and long-term debt	(2,704)
	Accrued restructuring	(960)
	Other current liabilities	(5,933)
	Other long-term liabilities	(1,908)
IPR&D →	In-process research and development	735
	Total purchase price	$24,170

Tangible assets acquired and liabilities assumed in the purchase are valued by the purchasing company as of the acquisition date and are recorded on the consolidated balance sheet at fair market value. (In the Exhibit 6.6 example, we sum the $4,000 PPE book value of Nissim with the $300 excess of market over book value to yield the $4,300 PPE fair market value that is included among the assets on the consolidated balance sheet.) Any remaining purchase price above book value is allocated to acquired identifiable *intangible* assets, also valued at the acquisition date. A sampling of the types of intangible assets that are often recognized for such acquisitions follows:

- Marketing-related assets like trademarks and Internet domain names
- Customer-related assets like customer lists and customer contracts
- Artistic-related assets like plays, books, and video
- Contract-based assets like licensing, franchise and royalty agreements, and lease contracts
- Technology-based assets like patents, software, databases, and trade secrets

In its acquisition of Compaq, HP allocated $4.9 billion ($1,942 million + $1,501 million + $74 million + $1,422 million) of its purchase price to identifiable intangible assets (absent goodwill), as described in the following footnote to its 10-K:

> **Amortizable intangible assets**   Of the total purchase price, approximately $3.5 billion [$1,942 million + $1,501 million + $74 million] was allocated to amortizable intangible assets including customer contracts and developed and core technology. . . . HP is amortizing the fair value of these assets on a straight-line basis over a weighted average estimated useful life of approximately 9 years. Developed technology, which consists of products that have reached technological feasibility, includes products in most of Compaq's product lines. . . . Core technology and patents represent a combination of Compaq processes, patents and trade secrets. . . . HP is amortizing the developed and core technology and patents on a straight-line basis over a weighted average estimated useful life of approximately 6 years.

Intangible asset with an indefinite life   The estimated fair value of the intangible asset with an indefinite life was $1.4 billion, consisting of the estimated fair value allocated to the Compaq trade name. This intangible asset will not be amortized because it has an indefinite remaining useful life based on many factors and considerations, including the length of time that the Compaq name has been in use, the Compaq brand awareness and market position and the plans for continued use of the Compaq brand.

HP discloses that it allocated a portion of the purchase price to the following identifiable intangible assets:

- Customer contracts
- Customer lists and distribution agreements
- Developed technology
- Core technology and patents
- Compaq trade name

HP deems the first four of these identifiable intangible assets as *amortizable assets,* which are those having a finite useful life. HP, subsequently, amortizes them over their useful lives (similar to depreciation). The last asset (Compaq trade name) is deemed to have an indefinite useful life. It is not amortized, but is tested annually for impairment like goodwill.

Once the purchase price has been allocated to identifiable tangible and intangible assets (net of liabilities assumed), any remainder of the purchase price is allocated to goodwill. HP allocated $14.45 billion (60%) of the Compaq purchase price to goodwill. The SEC is scrutinizing companies that assign an excessive proportion of the purchase price to goodwill; companies have been identified as doing this in a desire to avoid the future earnings drag from amortization expense.

Reporting of Goodwill

Goodwill is no longer amortized, as it was prior to 2001. Instead, GAAP requires companies to test it annually for impairment just like any other asset. The impairment test is a two-step process:

1. The market value of the investee company is compared with the book value of the investor's equity investment account.[8]
2. If the market value is less than the investment balance, the investment is deemed impaired. The company must then estimate the goodwill value as if the subsidiary were acquired for its current market value, and the imputed balance for goodwill becomes the amount at which it is recorded. If this imputed amount is less than its book value, goodwill must be written down, resulting in an impairment loss that is reported in the consolidated income statement.

To illustrate the impairment computation, assume that an investment, currently reported at $1 million on the investor's balance sheet, has a current fair market value of $900,000. The consolidated balance sheet reports net assets (absent goodwill) at $700,000 and goodwill at $300,000. Analysis reveals that the current fair market value of the net assets of the investee company (absent goodwill) is $700,000. This indicates goodwill is impaired by $100,000, which is computed as follows:

Fair market value of investee company	$ 900,000
Fair market value of net assets (absent goodwill)	(700,000)
Implied goodwill	200,000
Current goodwill balance	(300,000)
Impairment loss	$(100,000)

This analysis of investee company implies that goodwill must be written down by $100,000. The impairment loss is reported as a separate line item in the consolidated income statement. The related footnote disclosure describes the reasons for the write-down and the computations involved.

---

[8]The fair market value of the investee company can be determined using market comparables or another valuation method (such as the discounted cash flow model, residual operating income model, or P/E multiples—see Module 11).

Intel provides an example of a goodwill impairment disclosure in its 10-K report:

During the fourth quarter of 2003, the company completed its annual impairment review for goodwill and found indicators of impairment for the Wireless Communications and Computing Group (WCCG). . . . The impairment review requires a two-step process. The first step of the review compares the fair value of the reporting units with substantial goodwill against their aggregate carrying values, including goodwill. The company estimated the fair value of the WCCG . . . reporting unit using the income method of valuation, which includes the use of estimated discounted cash flows. Based on the comparison, the carrying value of the WCCG reporting unit exceeded the fair value. Accordingly, the company performed the second step of the test, comparing the implied fair value of the WCCG reporting unit's goodwill with the carrying amount of that goodwill. Based on this assessment, the company recorded a non-cash impairment charge of $611 million, which is included as a component of operating income in the "all other" category.

Nonamortization of goodwill is GAAP policy post-2001. No retroactive adjustment to goodwill is made for years prior to 2001. This means that it is difficult to compare operating results for 2002 and later years to those for earlier years when goodwill amortization was a major item. To alleviate this problem, required footnote disclosures provide pro forma income numbers assuming that nonamortization of goodwill is applied to periods prior to adoption of the new goodwill accounting policy.

BUSINESS INSIGHT   Pitfalls of Acquired Growth

It may be the greatest destruction of shareholder value in history, and it happened in the bull market between 1995 and 2001. That is, the subsequent year's returns of most shareholders of purchasing companies that were hit with merger and acquisition fever fell below those of their peers. The winners were shareholders of target companies who sold their stock within the first week of takeover. What went wrong? The short answer is that companies overpaid as a result of overestimating the cost-cuttings and synergies such takeovers would bring. Then, they failed to quickly integrate operations. The results? Fully 61% of corporate buyers of intercorporate investments decreased their shareholders' wealth.

Reporting of Purchased In-Process R&D

Companies allocate the purchase price to assets acquired in a purchase, including any intangible assets. An intangible asset a company often acquires is *in-process research & development (IPR&D)*. IPR&D is an asset that is purchased just like PPE and other assets. Under GAAP, however, R&D is generally expensed. Thus, the cost of acquired IPR&D assets must be written off immediately upon purchase. This write-off is called *in-process R&D expense,* and is generally reported as a separate item in the income statement if it is material.

An investor company must value the IPR&D assets of an investee company before it can allocate any of the purchase price to them and then write them off. That valuation can use any one of several accepted valuation methods. **Hewlett-Packard**, for example, in its $24.1 billion acquisition of **Compaq Computer**, allocated $735 million to IPR&D (see table on page 6-19), which it immediately expensed in its income statement. HP described its IPR&D valuation process as follows:

In-Process Research & Development

Of the total purchase price, $735 million was allocated to IPR&D and was expensed in the third quarter of fiscal 2002. Projects that qualify as IPR&D represent those that have not yet reached technological feasibility and for which no future alternative uses exist. Technological feasibility is defined as being equivalent to a beta-phase working prototype in which there is no remaining risk relating to the development.

The value assigned to IPR&D was determined by considering the importance of each project to the overall development plan, estimating costs to develop the purchased IPR&D into commercially viable products, estimating the resulting net cash flows from the projects when completed and discounting the net cash flows to their present value. The revenue estimates used to value the purchased IPR&D were based on estimates of the relevant market sizes and growth factors, expected trends in technology and the nature and expected timing of new product introductions by Compaq and its competitors.

The rates utilized to discount the net cash flows to their present values were based on Compaq's weighted average cost of capital. The weighted average cost of capital was adjusted to reflect the difficulties and uncertainties in completing each project and thereby achieving technological feasibility, the percentage-of-completion of each project, anticipated market acceptance and penetration, market growth rates and risks related to the impact of potential changes in future target markets. Based on these factors, discount rates that range from 25%–42% were deemed appropriate for valuing the IPR&D.

IPR&D refers to acquired projects that have not yet reached technological feasibility at the acquisition date, and for which no alternative uses exist. They might have been useful to the acquired company, but are not to the investor, perhaps because they do not fit into the investor's strategic plans.

Excessive allocation of a purchase price to IPR&D artificially reduces current period income and inflates income in successive periods (by the elimination of future depreciation or amortization expense). The SEC monitors purchase allocations closely and challenges those with which it disagrees. As a result of these reviews, a number of companies have subsequently been forced to restate the amounts of their initial IPR&D write-offs. (The FASB recently issued an exposure draft that proposes that IPR&D no longer be expensed at acquisition; instead, the proposal is to record IPR&D as an intangible asset that is subsequently tested for impairment.)

Reporting Subsidiary Stock Issuances

Subsidiaries can issue stock, just like their parent companies do. If issued to outside investors, the result is an infusion of cash into the subsidiary and a reduction in the percentage of the company owned by the parent company. For example, **Citigroup Inc.** reports the following stock issuance in its 10-K report by one of its subsidiaries:

$

Cash Effect

> **Travelers Property Casualty Corp.** (an indirect wholly owned subsidiary of Citigroup on December 31, 2001) sold 231 million shares of its class A common stock representing approximately 23.1% of its outstanding equity securities in an initial public offering (the IPO) on March 27, 2002. In 2002, Citigroup recognized an after-tax gain of $1.158 billion as a result of the IPO.

Gains on subsidiary stock issuances result from an increase in the investment balance on the parent's balance sheet.

To illustrate, assume that an investor company owns 100% of its investee company and the latter has a book value of stockholders' equity of $500. The investment on the parent's balance sheet, using the equity method, is at $500 (assuming the investment was acquired at book value). Next, assume that the investee company issues previously unissued shares to outsiders for $100 and, thereby, reduces the investor company's ownership to 90%. The investor company now owns 90% of a subsidiary with a book value of $600 for an investment equivalent of $540 (90% × $600). The value of its investment account has, thus, risen by $40 ($540 vs. $500).

The SEC allows the parent company to report this increase in the book value of the investment as either a gain in the computation of net income (with a consequent increase in retained earnings), as Citigroup did, or as an increase in additional paid-in capital. **Barnes & Noble**'s IPO of its **GameStop** subsidiary provides an example of the latter alternative method as follows:

> GameStop completed an initial public offering of shares of its Class A common stock at a price of $18.00 per share, raising net proceeds of approximately $348,000. The Company recorded an increase in additional paid-in capital of $155,490 ($90,184 after taxes), representing the Company's incremental share in the equity of GameStop.

Although equity of the parent company is the same under both accounting methods, recognition of the gain boosts reported income. We need to be aware of this transitory, nonoperating component of income— most analysts exclude it from the net operating profit (NOPAT) computation for analysis purposes.

Limitations of Consolidation Reporting

Consolidation of financial statements is meant to present a financial picture of the entire set of companies under control of the parent. Since investors typically purchase stock in the parent company and not in the subsidiaries, the view is more relevant than would be one of the parent company's own balance sheet with subsidiaries reported as equity investments. Still, we must be aware of certain limitations that the consolidation process entails:

$
Cash Effect

1. Consolidated income does not imply that cash is received by the parent company and is available for subsidiaries. The parent can only receive cash via dividend payments. It is quite possible, therefore, for an individual subsidiary to experience cash flow problems even though the consolidated group has strong cash flows. Likewise, debts of a subsidiary are not obligations of the consolidated group. Thus, even if the consolidated balance sheet is strong, creditors of a failing subsidiary are often unable to sue the parent or other subsidiaries to recoup losses.

2. Consolidated balance sheets and income statements are a mix of the subsidiaries, often from different industries. Comparisons across companies, even if in similar industries, are often complicated by the different mix of subsidiary companies.

3. Segment disclosures on individual subsidiaries are affected by intercorporate transfer pricing policies that can artificially inflate the profitability of one segment at the expense of another. Companies also have considerable discretion in the allocation of corporate overhead to subsidiaries, which can markedly affect segment profitability.

BUSINESS INSIGHT   **HP's Post-Acquisition Accounting under Fire**

Post-acquisition accounting can get complicated. Consider the following critique in *The Wall Street Journal*'s Heard on the Street column (March 5, 2003) regarding HP's earnings release:

IT DOESN'T TAKE an H-P 12C calculator to figure out that the fiscal-first-quarter earnings improvement touted by Hewlett-Packard Co. for its personal-computing business may not be as impressive as it appears . . . they are just doing some simple math. They are adding back in estimates of certain expenses—such as research-and-development and corporate-governance costs—that H-P moved out of the profit calculation for the business in the quarter ended Jan. 31, in contrast to earlier quarters. H-P executives had held aloft the PC unit's profitability—$33 million, the first in-the-black result in about two years—to highlight how its contentious, [$24.2 billion] acquisition of Compaq Computer Corp. last year had paid off.

The upshot: H-P's PC unit, as well as a few other divisions, looked quite a bit healthier. To get a sense of the effect of the changes, consider that, before the recategorizations, H-P's PC business posted a full-year 2002 operating loss of $532 million. But after taking the reclassifications into account, the PC group's fiscal 2002 loss narrowed to $372 million, according to H-P. In other words, the loss shrinks by an average of $40 million a quarter, a pretty hefty sum when compared with the segment's most-recent quarterly profit of $33 million. . . . Mr. Wayman, H-P's chief financial officer, says of the reclassifications: "This is just what happens when two large companies come together."

Reporting Consolidations under Pooling-of-Interests

Prior to 2001, companies had a choice in their accounting for business combinations. They could use the *purchase method* as described in this module (now required for all acquisitions), or they could use the *pooling-of-interests (pooling) method*. A large number of acquisitions were accounting for under pooling-of-interest, and its impact on financial statements will linger for many years.

The main difference between the pooling-of-interest and the purchase method of accounting for acquisitions is this: under the purchase method the investment account is initially recorded at the *fair market value* of the acquired company at acquisition. Under the pooling-of-interest method, the investment account is initially recorded at the *book value* of equity for the acquired company, regardless of the amount of purchase price. As a result, no goodwill is created. Further, since goodwill amortization was required under previous GAAP, subsequent income was larger under pooling in part because no goodwill amortization was recorded. This feature spawned widespread use of the pooling-of-interest, especially for high-tech companies.

Acquisitions previously accounted for under pooling-of-interest remain unaffected under current GAAP. We must be aware of at least two points for analysis purposes:

1. Assets were usually understated when using pooling-of-interest because investee companies were recorded at book rather than market value. This implies that consolidated asset turnover ratios are overstated.

2. Incomes of companies using pooling-of-interest were nearly always overstated due to elimination of goodwill amortization. This continues to create difficulties for comparative analysis when looking at companies that previously applied pooling-of-interest accounting.

■ MODULE-END REVIEW ■

On January 1 of the current year, Bradshaw Company purchased all of the common shares of Jeter Company for $600,000 cash—this is $200,000 in excess of Jeter's book value of its equity. The balance sheets of the two firms immediately after the acquisition follow:

	Bradshaw (Parent)	Jeter (Subsidiary)	Consolidating Adjustments	Consolidated
Current assets	$1,000,000	$100,000		
Investment in Jeter	600,000	—		
PPE, net	3,000,000	400,000		
Goodwill	—	—		
Total assets	$4,600,000	$500,000		
Liabilities	$1,000,000	$100,000		
Contributed capital	2,000,000	200,000		
Retained earnings	1,600,000	200,000		
Total liabilities and equity	$4,600,000	$500,000		

During purchase negotiations, Jeter's PPE was appraised at $500,000, and all of Jeter's remaining assets and liabilities were appraised at values approximating their book values. Also, Bradshaw concluded that payment of an additional $100,000 was warranted because of anticipated corporate synergies. Prepare the consolidating adjustments and the consolidated balance sheet at acquisition.

Solution

	Bradshaw (Parent)	Jeter (Subsidiary)	Consolidating Adjustments	Consolidated
Current assets	$1,000,000	$100,000		$1,100,000
Investment in Jeter	600,000	—	$(600,000)	
PPE, net	3,000,000	400,000	100,000	3,500,000
Goodwill	—	—	100,000	100,000
Total assets	$4,600,000	$500,000		$4,700,000
Liabilities	$1,000,000	$100,000		$1,100,000
Contributed capital	2,000,000	200,000	(200,000)	2,000,000
Retained earnings	1,600,000	200,000	(200,000)	1,600,000
Total liabilities and equity	$4,600,000	$500,000		$4,700,000

Notes: The $600,000 investment account is eliminated together with the $400,000 book value of Jeter's equity to which it mainly relates. The remaining $200,000 consists of the additional $100,000 in PPE assets and the $100,000 in goodwill from expected corporate synergies. Following these adjustments, the balance sheet items are summed to yield the consolidated balance sheet.

A P P E N D I X   6A

Equity Method Mechanics

The appendix provides a comprehensive example of accounting for an equity method investment. Assume that Petroni Company acquires a 30% interest in the outstanding voting shares of Wahlen Company on January 1, 2005. To obtain these shares, Petroni pays $126,000 cash and issues 6,000 of its $10 par value common stock. On that date, Petroni's stock has a fair market value of $18 per share, and Wahlen's book value of equity is $560,000. Petroni agrees to pay $234,000 ($126,000 plus 6,000 shares at $18 per share) for a company with a book value of equity equivalent to $168,000 ($560,000 × 30%) because it feels that (1) Wahlen's balance sheet is undervalued by $140,000 (Petroni estimates PPE is undervalued by $50,000 and that Wahlen has unrecorded patents valued at $90,000) and (2) the investment is expected to yield intangible benefits valued at $24,000.[9]

The effect of the investment on Petroni's books is to reduce cash by $234,000 and to report the investment in Wahlen for $234,000. The investment is reported at its fair market value at acquisition, just like all other asset acquisitions, and it is reported as a noncurrent asset since the expected holding period of equity method investments is in excess of one year. Subsequent to this purchase there are three main aspects of equity method accounting:

$
Cash Effect

1. Dividends received from the investee are treated as a return *of* the investment rather than a return *on* the investment (investor company records an increase in cash received and a decrease in the investment account).
2. When the investee company reports net income for a period, the investor company reports its percentage ownership of that income. This is usually reported in the other income section of its income statement. Thus, both equity and the investment account increase from equity method income. If the investee company reports a net *loss* for the period, income of the investor company is reduced as well as its investment account by its proportionate share.
3. The investment balance is not marked-to-market as with passive investments. Instead, it is recorded at its historical cost and is increased (decreased) by the investor company's proportionate share of investee income (loss) and decreased by any cash dividends received. Unrecognized gains (losses) can, therefore, occur if the market value of the investment differs from this adjusted cost.

To illustrate these mechanics, let's return to our illustration and assume that subsequent to acquisition, Wahlen reports net income of $50,000 and pays $10,000 cash dividends. Petroni's balance sheet and income statement are impacted as follows:

Transaction	Change in Investment Account on Petroni's Balance Sheet	Equity Income on Petroni's Income Statement
Acquisition balance	$234,000	
Wahlen reports income of $50,000 (30% for Petroni)	15,000	$15,000
Wahlen pays a $10,000 cash dividend ($3,000 to Petroni)	(3,000)	
Updated balance	$246,000	

$
Cash Effect

Petroni's ending investment balance is $246,000 and its cash balance increased by the $3,000 dividend received (note, the market value of the investment can differ from its book value). Corresponding to the $15,000 increase in assets from Wahlen's income is a $15,000 increase in retained earnings (following the reporting of income to retained earnings). Petroni reports this $15,000 as investment income. Dividends received are treated as a return of the capital invested in Wahlen and, thus, the investment account is reduced.

---

[9]The $140,000 by which the balance sheet is undervalued translates into an investment equivalent of $42,000 ($140,000 × 30%). This, plus the intangible benefits valued at $24,000, comprises the $66,000 difference between the purchase price ($234,000) and the book value equivalent ($168,000).

There is symmetry between Petroni's investment account and Wahlen's stockholders' equity as follows:

Investment Account on Petroni's Balance Sheet		Wahlen's Stockholders' Equity	
Acquisition balance	$234,000	Acquisition balance	$560,000
Income	15,000	Income	50,000
Dividends	(3,000)	Dividends	(10,000)
Ending balance	$246,000	Ending balance	$600,000

Petroni's ending investment balance of $246,000 is 30% of Wahlen's $600,000 stockholders' equity plus the original $66,000 excess. This explains why the equity investment balance we see reported on a balance sheet does not always equal the percentage owned of the investee company.[10]

APPENDIX 6B

Consolidation Accounting Mechanics

This appendix is a continuation of the example we introduced in Appendix 6A, extended to the consolidation of a parent company and one wholly owned subsidiary. Assume that Petroni Company acquires 100 percent (rather than 30% as in Appendix 6A) of the outstanding voting shares of Wahlen Company on January 1, 2005. To obtain these shares, Petroni pays $420,000 cash and issues 20,000 shares of its $10 par value common stock. On this date, Petroni's stock has a fair market value of $18 per share, and Wahlen's book value of equity is $560,000. Petroni is willing to pay $780,000 ($420,000 plus 20,000 shares at $18 per share) for this company with a book value of equity of $560,000 because it believes Wahlen's balance sheet is understated by $140,000 (its PPE is undervalued by $50,000 and it has unrecorded patents valued at $90,000). The remaining $80,000 of the purchase price excess over book value is ascribed to corporate synergies and other unidentifiable intangible assets (goodwill). Thus, the purchase price consists of the following three components:

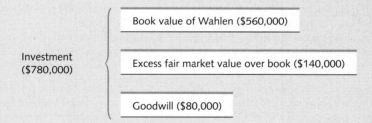

The investment in Wahlen on Petroni's books is accounted for using the equity method of accounting.[11] This means that at acquisition, Petroni's assets (investments) increase by $780,000 and its equity (contributed capital) increases by the same amount. The balance sheets of Petroni and Wahlen at acquisition follow, including the adjustments that occur in the consolidation process and the ultimate consolidated balance sheet.

---

[10]To the extent that the excess is attributed to depreciable (amortizable) assets of the subsidiary, the excess is depreciated (amortized) and that amount is reflected in the parent's income statement as expense. Eventually, the excess is entirely depreciated (amortized) and the investment balance equals the percentage owned (30%) of the subsidiary's stockholders' equity with no excess. Any portion of the excess attributed to goodwill is not amortized, resulting in a permanent difference unless and until the goodwill is deemed to be impaired and written down.

[11]The equity method is used for all investments other than passive investments. Once "control" is achieved, the investor company is required to consolidate its financial statements with those of other entities in the control set. The investment account remains unchanged on the parent's books, it is merely replaced with the assets and liabilities of the subsidiaries to which it relates for the consolidation process.

Accounts	Petroni Company	Wahlen Company	Consolidation Adjustments*		Consolidated Balance Sheet
Cash	$ 168,000	$ 80,000			$ 248,000
Receivables, net	320,000	180,000			500,000
Inventory	440,000	260,000			700,000
Investment in Wahlen	780,000	0	[S]	(560,000)	0
			[A]	(220,000)	
Land	200,000	120,000			320,000
PPE, net	1,040,000	320,000	[A]	50,000	1,410,000
Patent	0	0	[A]	90,000	90,000
Goodwill	0	0	[A]	80,000	80,000
Totals	$2,948,000	$960,000			$3,318,000
Accounts payable	$320,000	$60,000			$380,000
Long-term liabilities	760,000	340,000			1,100,000
Contributed capital	1,148,000	80,000	[S]	(80,000)	1,148,000
Retained earnings	720,000	480,000	[S]	(480,000)	720,000
Totals	$2,948,000	$960,000			$3,318,000

*[S] refers to elimination of stockholders' equity and [A] refers to recognition of assets acquired.

The initial balance of the investment account at acquisition ($780,000) reflects the $700,000 market value of Wahlen's net tangible assets ($560,000 book value + $140,000 undervaluation of assets) plus the goodwill ($80,000) acquired. Goodwill is the excess of the purchase price over the fair market of the net assets acquired. It does not appear on Petroni's balance sheet as an explicit asset at this point. It is, however, included in the investment balance and will emerge as a separate asset during consolidation.

The process of completing the initial consolidated balance sheet involves eliminating the investment account and replacing it with the assets and liabilities of Wahlen Company to which it relates. Recall the investment account consists of three items: the book value of Wahlen ($560,000), the excess of market price over book value ($140,000), and goodwill ($80,000). The consolidation process eliminates each item as follows:

[S]   Elimination of Wahlen's book value of equity: Investment account is reduced by the $560,000 book value of Wahlen, and each of the components of Wahlen's equity ($80,000 common stock and $480,000 retained earnings) are eliminated.

[A]   Elimination of the excess of purchase price over book value: Investment account is reduced by $220,000. The remaining adjustments increase assets (A) by the additional purchase price paid. PPE is written up by $50,000, and a $90,000 patent asset and an $80,000 goodwill asset are reported.

Consolidation is similar in successive periods. To the extent that the excess purchase price has been assigned to depreciable assets, or identifiable intangible assets that are amortized over their useful lives, the new assets recognized initially are depreciated. For example, if the PPE has an estimated life of 20 years with no salvage value, we can depreciate 1/20 of the $50,000 each year. Likewise, the $90,000 patent is amortized over its remaining life. Depreciation and amortization are reflected in Petroni's income statement (depreciation of the book value portion is on Wahlen's income statement). Finally, since goodwill is not amortized under GAAP, it remains at its carrying amount of $80,000 on the consolidated balance sheet unless and until it is impaired and written down.

As the excess of the purchase price over book value acquired is depreciated/amortized, the investment account gradually declines. Assuming goodwill is not impaired, the investment reaches a balance equal to the percentage of the investee's equity owned (100% in this case) plus the balance of goodwill. Generally, the investment account equals the percentage of the equity owned plus any remaining undepreciated/unamortized excess over purchase price.

APPENDIX 6C

Accounting for Derivatives

Derivatives refer to financial instruments that are utilized by companies to reduce various kinds of risks. Some examples follow:

- A company expects to purchase raw materials for its production process and wants to reduce the risk that the purchase price increases prior to the purchase.
- A company has an accounts receivable on its books that is payable in a foreign currency and wants to reduce the risk that exchange rates move unfavorably prior to collection.
- A company borrows funds on a floating rate of interest (such as linked to the prime rate) and wants to convert the loan to a fixed rate of interest.

Companies are commonly exposed to these and many similar types of risk. Although companies are generally willing to assume the normal market risks that are inherent in their business, many of these financial-type risks can add variability to income and are uncontrollable. Fortunately, commodities, currencies, and interest rates are all traded on various markets and, further, securities have been developed to manage all of these risks. These securities fall under the label of derivatives. They include forward contracts, futures contracts, option contracts, and swap agreements.

Companies use derivatives to manage many of these financial risks. The reduction of risk comes at a price: the fee that another party (called the counterparty) is charging to assume that risk. Most counterparties are financial institutions, and managing financial risk is their business and is a source of their profits. Although derivatives can be used effectively to manage financial risk, they can also be used for speculation with potentially disastrous results. It is for this reason that regulators passed standards regarding their disclosure in financial statements.

Reporting of Derivatives

Derivatives work by offsetting the gain or loss for the asset or liability to which they relate. Derivatives thus shelter the company from such fluctuations. For example, if a hedged receivable denominated in a foreign currency declines in value (due to a strengthening of the $US), the derivative security will increase in value by an offsetting amount, at least in theory. As a result, net equity remains unaffected and no gain or loss arises, nor is reported in income.[12]

Although accounting for derivatives is complex, it essentially boils down to this: the derivative contract, and the asset or liability to which it relates, are both reported on the balance sheet at market value. The asset and liability are offsetting *if* the hedge is effective and, thus, net equity is unaffected. Likewise, the related gains and losses are largely offsetting, leaving income unaffected. Income is impacted only to the extent that the hedging activities are ineffective or result from speculative activities. It is this latter activity, in particular, that regulators were concerned about in formulating accounting standards for derivatives.

Disclosure of Derivatives

Companies are required to disclose both qualitative and quantitative information about derivatives in notes to their financial statements and elsewhere (usually in Management's Discussion and Analysis section). The aim of these disclosures is to inform outsiders about potential risks underlying derivative securities.

Following is **Midwest Air**'s disclosures from its 10-K report relating to its use of derivatives:

Derivative Instruments and Hedging Activities
The Company periodically utilizes option contracts to mitigate the exposure to the fluctuation in aircraft fuel prices in accordance with the Company's financial risk management policy. This policy was adopted by the Company to document the Company's philosophy toward financial risk and outline acceptable use of derivatives to mitigate that financial risk. The options establish ceiling prices for anticipated jet fuel purchases and serve as hedges of those purchases. The Company does not hold or issue derivative instruments for trading purposes. At December 31, 2002, the Company had options in place to hedge approximately 20% and 15% of its projected fuel purchases in the first quarter and second quarter of 2003, respectively. These contracts expired at various dates through June 30, 2003. At December 31, 2002, the options were valued at $1.0 million and are included in other prepaid expense in the consolidated balance sheet. The value of any options is determined using estimates of fair market value provided by major financial institutions. At December 31, 2003, the Company had no options for current or future periods.

The Company accounts for its fuel hedge derivative instruments as cash flow hedges, as defined in SFAS No. 133, "Accounting for Derivative Instruments and Hedging Activities" and the corresponding amendments under SFAS No. 138, "Accounting for Certain Derivative Instruments and Certain Hedging Activities." Therefore, all changes in the fair value of the derivative instruments that are considered effective are recorded in other comprehensive income until the

---

[12]Unrealized gains and losses on derivatives classified as *cash flow hedges* (such as those relating to planned purchases of commodities) are accumulated in other comprehensive income (OCI) and are not recognized in current income until the transaction is complete (such as when both the purchase and sale of inventory occurs). Unrealized gains and losses on derivatives classified as *fair value hedges* (such as those relating interest rate hedges and swaps, and the hedging of asset values such as relating to securities) as well as the changes in value of the hedged asset (liability) are recorded in current income.

underlying hedged fuel is consumed, when they are reclassified to the income statement as an offset of fuel expense. The Company reclassified $1.1 million and $1.5 million to the income statement in 2003 and 2002, respectively, as an offset to fuel expense when the hedges expired.

Midwest Air's derivative use is mainly to hedge against fuel cost. Those hedges act to place a ceiling on fuel cost and are used for about 15% to 20% of Midwest Air's fuel purchases.

From a reporting standpoint, unrealized gains and losses on these option contracts are accumulated in the Other Comprehensive Income (OCI) portion of its stockholders' equity until the fuel is purchased. Once that fuel is purchased, those unrealized gains and losses are removed from OCI and the gain (loss) on the option is used to offset the loss (gain) on fuel. In 2003, $1.1 million of hedging gains were used to offset fuel expense for Midwest Air.

Although the market value of derivatives and their related assets or liabilities can be large, the net effect on stockholders' equity is usually minor. This is because companies are mainly using them as hedges and not as speculative securities. SFAS 133, 'Accounting for derivative instruments and hedging activities,' was enacted in response to a concern that speculative activities were not adequately disclosed. However, subsequent to its passage the financial effects have been minimal. Either these companies were not speculating to the extent expected, or they have since reduced their level of speculation in response to increased scrutiny from better disclosures.

GUIDANCE ANSWERS

MANAGERIAL DECISION   You Are the Chief Financial Officer

Capacity utilization is important. If long-term operating assets are not sufficiently utilized, cost per unit produced is too high. Cost per unit does not relate solely to manufacturing products, but also applies to the cost of providing services and many other operating activities. However, if we purchase assets with little productive slack, our costs of production at peak levels can be excessive. Further, the company may be unable to service peak demand and risk losing customers. In response, many companies have explored alliances. These take many forms. Some require a simple contract to use another company's manufacturing, service, or administrative capability for a fee (note: these executory contracts are not recorded under GAAP). Another type of alliance is that of a joint venture to share ownership of manufacturing or IT facilities. In this case, if demand can be coordinated with that of a partner, perhaps operating assets can be more effectively used. Finally, a variable interest entity (VIE) can be formed to acquire the asset for use by the company and its partner—explained in Module 9.

Superscript ^A(^B,C) denotes assignments based on Appendix 6A (6B, 6C).

■ DISCUSSION QUESTIONS

Q6-1. What measure (fair market value or amortized cost) is used for the balance sheet to report (a) trading securities, (b) available-for-sale securities, and (c) held-to-maturity securities?

Q6-2. What is an unrealized holding gain (loss)? Explain.

Q6-3. Where are unrealized holding gains and losses related to trading securities reported in the financial statements? Where are unrealized holding gains and losses related to available-for-sale securities reported in the financial statements?

Q6-4. What does *significant influence* imply regarding intercorporate investments? Describe the accounting procedures used for such investments.

Q6-5. On January 1 of the current year, Yetman Company purchases 40% of the common stock of Livnat Company for $250,000 cash. During the year, Livnat reports $80,000 of net income and pays $60,000 in cash dividends. At year-end, what amount should appear in Yetman's balance sheet for its investment in Livnat?

Q6-6. What accounting method is used when a stock investment represents more than 50% of the investee company's voting stock? Explain.

Q6-7. What is the underlying objective of consolidated financial statements?

Q6-8. Finn Company purchases all of the common stock of Murray Company for $750,000 when Murray Company has $300,000 of common stock and $450,000 of retained earnings. If a consolidated balance sheet is prepared immediately after the acquisition, what amounts are eliminated in preparing it? Explain.

Q6-9.^B Bradshaw Company owns 100% of Dee Company. At year-end, Dee owes Bradshaw $75,000. If a consolidated balance sheet is prepared at year-end, how is the $75,000 handled? Explain.

Q6-10. What are some limitations of consolidated financial statements?

■ MINI EXERCISES

M6-11. **Interpreting Disclosures of Available-for-Sale Securities**   Use the following year-end footnote disclosure from **Pfizer**'s 10-K report to answer parts (a) and (b):

Pfizer (PFE)

(Millions of Dollars)	2003
Cost of available-for-sale equity securities	$234)
Gross unrealized gains	263
Gross unrealized losses	(6)
Fair value of available-for-sale equity securities	$491

a. At what amount is its available-for-sale equity securities reported on Pfizer's 2003 balance sheet?
Explain.

b. How is its net unrealized gain of $257 million ($263 million − $6 million) reported by Pfizer in its
financial statements?

M6-12. **Accounting for Available-for-Sale and Trading Securities**   Assume that Wasley Company purchases
6,000 common shares of Pincus Company for $12 cash per share. During the year, Wasley receives a cash
dividend of $1.10 per common share from Pincus, and the year-end market price of Pincus common stock
is $13 per share. How much income does Wasley report relating to this investment for the year if it accounts
for the investment as:

a. Available-for-sale investment

b. Trading investment

M6-13. **Interpreting Disclosures of Investment Securities**   **Abbott Laboratories** reports the following disclosure relating to its December 31 after-tax comprehensive income. How is Abbott accounting for its
investment in securities? How do you know?

**Abbott
Laboratories
(ABT)**

Comprehensive Income, net of tax ($ 000s)	2003
Foreign currency translation adjustments	$1,162,004
Minimum pension liability adjustments, net of taxes of $57,219	(99,155)
Unrealized (losses) gains on marketable equity securities	106,673
Net (losses) gains on derivative instruments designated as cash flow hedges	3,550
Reclassification adjustments for realized (gains)	(20,538)
Other comprehensive income	1,152,534
Net earnings	2,753,233
Comprehensive income	$3,905,767

M6-14. **Analyzing and Interpreting Equity Method Investments**   Stober Company purchases an investment in
Lang Company at a purchase price of $1 million cash, representing 30% of the book value of Lang. During
the year, Lang reports net income of $100,000 and pays cash dividends of $40,000. At the end of the year,
the market value of Stober's investment is $1.2 million.

a. At what amount is the investment reported on Stober's balance sheet at year-end?

b. What amount of income from investments does Stober report? Explain.

c. Stober's $200,000 unrealized gain in investment market value (choose one and explain):

   (1) Is not reflected on either its income statement or balance sheet.

   (2) Is reported in its current income.

   (3) Is reported on its balance sheet only.

   (4) Is reported in its other comprehensive income.

M6-15. **Computing Income for Equity Method Investments**   Kross Company purchases an equity investment in
Penno Company at a purchase price of $5 million, representing 40% of the book value of Penno. During the
current year, Penno reports net income of $600,000 and pays cash dividends of $200,000. At the end of the
year, the market value of Kross's investment is $5.3 million. What amount of income does Kross report re-
lating to this investment in Penno for the year? Explain.

M6-16. **Interpreting Disclosures on Investments in Affiliates**   Merck's 10-K report included the following foot-note disclosure:

> **Joint Ventures and Other Equity Method Affiliates**   Investments in affiliates accounted for using the equity method . . . totaled $2.2 billion at December 31, 2003 and 2002, respectively. These amounts are reported in Other assets. Dividends and distributions received from these affiliates were $553.4 million in 2003, $488.6 million in 2002 and $572.2 million in 2001.

a.   At what amount are the equity method investments reported on Merck's balance sheet? Does this amount represent Merck's adjusted cost or market value?

b.   How does Merck account for the dividends received on these investments?

M6-17. **Computing Consolidating Adjustments and Minority Interest**   Philipich Company purchases 80% of Hirst Company's common stock for $600,000 cash when Hirst Company has $300,000 of common stock and $450,000 of retained earnings. If a consolidated balance sheet is prepared immediately after the acquisition, what amounts are eliminated when preparing that statement? What amount of minority interest appears in the consolidated balance sheet?

M6-18. **Computing Consolidated Net Income**   Benartzi Company purchased a 90% interest in Liang Company on January 1 of the current year. Benartzi Company had $600,000 net income for the current year *before* recognizing its share of Liang Company's net income. If Liang Company had net income of $150,000 for the year, what is the consolidated net income for the year?

M6-19. **Earnings under Pooling-of-Interest Method**   DeFond Company acquired 100% of Verduzco Company on September 1 of the current year. Why might the consolidated earnings of the two companies for the current year be higher if the transaction had been treated as a pooling-of-interest (which is no longer accepted under GAAP) rather than as a purchase?

■ EXERCISES

E6-20. **Assessing Financial Statement Effects of Trading and Available-for-Sale Securities**

a.   Complete the following financial statement effects template (with amounts and accounts) for the four transactions involving investments in marketable securities classified as trading.

(1)   Purchased 6,000 common shares of Liu, Inc., for $12 cash per share.

(2)   Received a cash dividend of $1.10 per common share from Liu.

(3)   Year-end market price of Liu common stock is $11.25 per share.

(4)   Sold all 6,000 common shares of Liu for $66,900.

	Balance Sheet						Income Statement		
Transaction	Cash Asset	+ Noncash Assets	= Liabil- ities	+ Contrib. Capital	+ Retained Earnings		Revenues	−	Expenses

b.   Using the same transaction information as above, complete the financial statement effects template (with amounts and accounts) assuming the investments in marketable securities are classified as available-for-sale.

E6-21. **Assessing Financial Statement Effects of Trading and Available-for-Sale Securities**   Use the template in E6-20 to indicate the financial statement effects (with amounts and accounts) for the following transactions involving investments in marketable securities assuming that:

a.   Investments are classified as trading.

(1)   Ohlson Co. purchases 5,000 common shares of Freeman Co. at $16 cash per share.

(2)   Ohlson Co. receives a cash dividend of $1.25 per common share from Freeman.

(3)   Year-end market price of Freeman common stock is $17.50 per share.

(4)   Ohlson Co. sells all 5,000 common shares of Freeman for $86,400 cash.

b.   Investments are classified as available-for-sale (for same four transactions from *a*).

E6-22.   Interpreting Footnotes on Security Investments   Berkshire Hathaway reports the following footnotes with its 10-K report ($ millions):

Berkshire
Hathaway
(BRKA)

Years Ended December 31	2003	2002	2001
Accumulated Other Comprehensive Income			
Unrealized appreciation of investments	$12,049	$ 3,140	$ (5,583)
Applicable income taxes	(4,158)	(1,147)	1,956
Reclassification adjustment for appreciation included in net earnings	(4,129)	(918)	(1,488)
Applicable income taxes	1,379	341	536
Foreign currency translation of adjustments and other	267	272	(114)
Applicable income taxes	(127)	(65)	24
Minimum pension liability adjustment	1	(279)	(35)
Applicable income taxes	(3)	29	12
Other	6	7	40
Other comprehensive income (loss)	5,285	1,380	(4,652)
Accumulated other comprehensive income at beginning of year	14,271	12,891	17,543
Accumulated other comprehensive income at end of year	$19,556	$14,271	$12,891

Investments in equity securities

Data with respect to investments in equity securities are shown below. Amounts are in millions.

American
Express
Company
(AXP)

December 31, 2003	Cost	Unrealized Gains	Fair Value
Common stock of			
American Express Company	$1,470	$ 5,842	$ 7,312
The Coca-Cola Company	1,299	8,851	10,150
The Gillette Company	600	2,926	3,526
Wells Fargo & Company	463	2,861	3,324
Other equity securities	4,683	6,292	10,975
	$8,515	$26,772	$35,287

The Coca-Cola
Company (KO)

The Gillette
Company (G)

Wells Fargo &
Company
(WFC)

a.   At what amount is its equity securities investment portfolio reported on its balance sheet? Does that amount include any unrealized gains or losses? Explain.

b.   How is Berkshire Hathaway accounting for its equity securities investment portfolio—as an available-for-sale or trading portfolio? How do you know?

c.   What does the number $12,049 represent in the Accumulated Other Comprehensive Income footnote? Is this number pretax or after-tax? Explain.

E6-23.   Interpreting Footnote Disclosures for Investments   CNA Financial Corporation provides the following footnote to its 10-K report:

CNA Financial
Corporation
(CNA)

Valuation of investments: CNA classifies its fixed maturity securities (bonds and redeemable preferred stocks) and its equity securities as available-for-sale, and as such, they are carried at fair value. The amortized cost of fixed maturity securities is adjusted for amortization of premiums and accretion of discounts to maturity, which are included in net investment income. Changes in fair value are reported as a component of other comprehensive income. Investments are written down to fair value and losses are recognized in income when a decline in value is determined to be other-than-temporary.

Summary of Fixed Maturity and Equity Securities

December 31, 2003 (In millions)	Cost or Amortized Cost	Gross Unrealized Gains	Gross Unrealized Losses		Estimated Fair Value
			Less than 12 Months	Greater than 12 Months	
Fixed maturity securities					
U.S. Treasury securities and obligations of government agencies	$ 1,823	$ 91	$ 10	$ 4	$ 1,900
Asset-backed securities	8,634	146	22	1	8,757
States, municipalities and political subdivisions—tax-exempt	7,787	207	22	2	7,970
Corporate securities	6,061	475	40	14	6,482
Other debt securities	2,961	311	4	4	3,264
Redeemable preferred stock	97	7	—	—	104
Options embedded in convertible debt securities	201	—	—	—	201
Total fixed maturity securities	27,564	1,237	98	25	28,678
Equity securities					
Common stock	163	222	2	—	383
Nonredeemable preferred stock	130	16	2	—	144
Total equity securities	293	238	4	—	527
Total	$27,857	$1,475	$102	$25	$29,205

    a.   At what amount is its investment portfolio reflected on its balance sheet? In your answer identify its market value, cost, and any unrealized gains and losses.

    b.   How are its unrealized gains and/or losses reflected in CNA's balance sheet and income statement?

    c.   How are any impairment losses and the gains and losses realized from the sale of securities reflected in CNA's balance sheet and income statement?

E6-24.   **Assessing Financial Statement Effects of Equity Method Securities**   Use the template in E6-20 to indicate the financial statement effects (with amounts and accounts) for the following transactions involving investments in marketable securities accounted for using the equity method:

    a.   Purchased 12,000 common shares of Barth Co. at $9 cash per share; the shares represent 30% ownership in Barth.

    b.   Received a cash dividend of $1.25 per common share from Barth.

    c.   Recorded income from Barth stock investment when Barth's net income is $80,000.

    d.   Sold all 12,000 common shares of Barth for $120,500.

E6-25.   **Assessing Financial Statement Effects of Equity Method Securities**   Use the template in E6-20 to indicate the financial statement effects (with amounts and accounts) for the following transactions involving investments in marketable securities accounted for using the equity method:

    a.   Healy Co. purchases 15,000 common shares of Palepu Co. at $8 cash per share; the shares represent 25% ownership of Palepu.

    b.   Healy receives a cash dividend of $0.80 per common share from Palepu.

    c.   Palepu reports annual net income of $120,000.

    d.   Healy sells all 15,000 common shares of Palepu for $140,000 cash.

E6-26.   **Assessing Financial Statement Effects of Passive and Equity Method Investments**   On January 1, 2005, Ball Corporation purchased, as a stock investment, 10,000 shares of Leftwich Company common stock for $15 cash per share. On December 31, 2005, Leftwich announced net income of $80,000 for the year and paid a cash dividend of $1.10 per share. At December 31, 2005, the market value of Leftwich's stock was $19 per share.

    a.   Assume that the stock acquired by Ball represents 15% of Leftwich's voting stock and that Ball classifies it as available-for-sale. Use the template in E6-20 to indicate the financial statement effects (with amounts and accounts) for the following transactions:

(1) Ball purchased 10,000 common shares of Leftwich at $15 cash per share; the shares represent a 15% ownership in Leftwich.

(2) Leftwich reported annual net income of $80,000.

(3) Received a cash dividend of $1.10 per common share from Leftwich.

(4) Year-end market price of Leftwich common stock is $19 per share.

b. Assume that the stock acquired by Ball represents 30% of Leftwich's voting stock and that Ball accounts for this investment using the equity method since it is able to exert significant influence. Use the template in E6-20 to indicate the financial statement effects (with amounts and accounts) for the following transactions:

(1) Ball purchased 10,000 common shares of Leftwich at $15 cash per share; the shares represent a 30% ownership in Leftwich.

(2) Leftwich reported annual net income of $80,000.

(3) Received a cash dividend of $1.10 per common share from Leftwich.

(4) Year-end market price of Leftwich common stock is $19 per share.

E6-27. Interpreting Equity Method Investment Footnotes DuPont reports the following footnote to its 10-K report relating to its equity method investments ($ millions): DuPont (DD)

Financial Position at December 31	2003	2002
Current assets	$3,367	$3,463
Noncurrent assets	5,441	5,814
Total assets	$8,808	$9,277
Short-term borrowings[1]	$1,339	$1,178
Other current liabilities	1,814	1,756
Long-term borrowings[1]	915	1,199
Other long-term liabilities	628	730
Total liabilities	$4,696	$4,863
DuPont's investment in affiliates (includes advances)	$1,304[2]	$2,047

[1]DuPont's pro rata interest in total borrowings was $1,004 in 2003 and $1,098 in 2002, of which $639 in 2003 and $681 in 2002 were guaranteed by the company.

[2]Reflects a $293 reduction in carrying values due to impairment charges recorded in 2003. In addition, $329 is excluded from the 2003 balance and reported as Assets held for sale on the Consolidated Balance Sheet.

a. DuPont reports its investment in equity method affiliates on its balance sheet at $1,304 million. Does this reflect the adjusted cost or market value of its interest in these companies?

b. Approximately what percentage does DuPont own, on average, of these affiliates? Explain.

c. DuPont reports that its equity interest in reported losses of these affiliates is approximately $55 million (46.8% of $118 million in net losses reported by these affiliates) in 2003, and that it received $58 million in dividends from these affiliates in 2003. Use this information, and the above footnote, to explain much of the change in the investment balance from $2,047 million in 2002 to $1,304 million in 2003.

d. How does use of the equity method impact DuPont's ROE and its components (asset turnover and profit margin)?

E6-28. Analyzing and Interpreting Disclosures on Equity Method Investments Caterpillar, Inc. (CAT), owns 50% of Shin Caterpillar Mitsubishi, Ltd. It reports the investment on its balance sheet at $432 million, and provides the following footnote in its 10-K report: Caterpillar, Inc. (CAT)

Shin Caterpillar Mitsubishi, Ltd.

The company's investment in affiliated companies accounted for by the equity method consists primarily of a 50% interest in Shin Caterpillar Mitsubishi Ltd. (SCM) located in Japan. Combined financial information of the unconsolidated affiliated companies accounted for by the equity method (generally on a three-month lag, e.g., SCM results reflect the periods ending September 30) was as follows:

Years Ended December 31 (Millions of Dollars)	2003	2002	2001
Results of operations			
Sales	$2,946	$2,734	$2,493
Cost of sales	2,283	2,168	1,971
Gross profit	663	566	522
Profit (loss)	$ 48	$ (1)	$ 9
Caterpillar's profit (loss)	$ 20	$ (4)	$ 3

December 31 (Millions of Dollars)	2003	2002	2001
Financial position			
Assets			
Current assets	$1,494	$1,389	$1,451
Property, plant and equipment—net	961	1,209	986
Other assets	202	493	290
	2,657	3,091	2,727
Liabilities			
Current liabilities	$1,247	$1,117	$1,257
Long-term debt due after one year	343	808	414
Other liabilities	257	249	281
	1,847	2,174	1,952
Ownership	$810	$ 917	$ 775

December 31 (Millions of Dollars)	2003	2002	2001
Caterpillar's investment in unconsolidated affiliated companies			
Investment in equity method companies	$ 432	$ 437	$ 437
Plus: Investment in cost method companies	368	310	350
Investment in unconsolidated affiliated companies	$ 800	$ 747	$ 787

a. Did CAT acquire this investment at book value (with no goodwill)? Show computations supporting your response.
b. What assets and liabilities of SCM are omitted from CAT's balance sheet as a result of the equity method of accounting for this investment?
c. Do the liabilities of the investee company affect CAT? Explain.
d. How is use of the equity method impacting CAT's ROE and its components (asset turnover and profit margin)?

E6-29. Reporting and Interpreting Stock Investment Performance Kasznik Company began operations in 2005 and, by year-end (December 31), had made six stock investments. Year-end information on these stock investments follows.

Company	Cost or Equity Basis (as appropriate)	Year-End Market Value	Market Classification
Barth, Inc.	$ 68,000	$ 65,300	Trading
Foster, Inc.	162,500	160,000	Trading
McNichols, Inc.	197,000	192,000	Available-for-sale
Patell, Inc.	157,000	154,700	Available-for-sale
Ertimur, Inc.	100,000	102,400	Equity method
Soliman, Inc.	136,000	133,200	Equity method

a. At what total amount is the trading stock investments reported at in the December 31, 2005, balance sheet?

b. At what total amount is the available-for-sale stock investments reported at in the December 31, 2005, balance sheet?

c. At what total amount is the equity method stock investments reported at in the December 31, 2005, balance sheet?

d. What total amount of unrealized holding gains or unrealized holding losses related to stock investments appear in the 2005 income statement?

e. What total amount of unrealized holding gains or unrealized holding losses related to stock investments appear in the stockholders' equity section of the December 31, 2005, balance sheet?

f. What total amount of market value adjustment to stock investments appears in the December 31, 2005, balance sheet? Which category of stock investments does the market value adjustment relate to? Does the market value adjustment increase or decrease the financial statement presentation of these stock investments?

E6-30. **Interpreting Equity Method Investment Footnotes**   Abbott Laboratories reports the following footnote to its 10-K report:

Abbott
Laboratories
(ABT)

Equity Method Investments *(dollars in millions)*   Abbott's 50 percent-owned joint venture, TAP Pharmaceutical Products Inc. (TAP), is accounted for under the equity method of accounting. The investment in TAP was $340, $370, and $392 at December 31, 2003, 2002, and 2001, respectively. Dividends received from TAP were $606, $695, and $433 in 2003, 2002, and 2001, respectively. Abbott's income from the TAP joint venture is recognized net of consolidating adjustments. Abbott performs certain administrative, selling and manufacturing services for TAP at negotiated rates that approximate fair market value for the services performed. Summarized financial information for TAP is as follows:

Year Ended December 31	2003	2002	2001
Net sales	$3,979.6	$4,037.4	$3,787.2
Cost of sales	1,066.8	884.1	938.6
Income before taxes	1,815.5	2,081.4	1,204.1
Net income	1,161.9	1,333.5	669.9

December 31	2003	2002	2001
Current assets	$1,451.6	$1,176.8	$1,191.2
Total assets	1,718.1	1,580.3	1,568.3
Current liabilities	965.8	791.6	713.1
Total liabilities	1,037.2	839.8	804.7

Undistributed earnings of investments accounted for under the equity method amounted to $315 as of December 31, 2003.

a. At what amount is Abbott's equity investment in TAP reported on Abbott's balance sheet? Confirm that this amount is equal to its proportionate share of TAP's equity.

b. How did the receipt of $606 in dividends from TAP affect Abbott's balance sheet and income statement?

c. How much income did Abbott report in 2003 relating to this investment in TAP?

d. Interpret the Abbott statement that "undistributed earnings of investments accounted for under the equity method amounted to $315 as of December 31, 2003."

e. How does use of the equity method impact Abbott's ROE and its components (asset turnover and profit margin)?

E6-31. **Constructing the Consolidated Balance Sheet at Acquisition**   On January 1 of the current year, Healy Company purchased all of the common shares of Miller Company for $500,000 cash. Balance sheets of the two firms at acquisition follow:

	Healy Company	Miller Company	Consolidating Adjustments	Consolidated
Current assets	$1,700,000	$120,000		
Investment in Miller	500,000	—		
Plant assets, net	3,000,000	410,000		
Goodwill	—	—		
Total assets	$5,200,000	$530,000		
Liabilities	$ 700,000	$ 90,000		
Contributed capital	3,500,000	400,000		
Retained earnings	1,000,000	40,000		
Total liabilities and equity	$5,200,000	$530,000		

During purchase negotiations, Miller's plant assets were appraised at $425,000; and, all of its remaining assets and liabilities were appraised at values approximating their book values. Healy also concluded that an additional $45,000 (in goodwill) demanded by Miller's shareholders was warranted because Miller's earning power was better than the industry average. Prepare the consolidating adjustments and the consolidated balance sheet at acquisition.

E6-32.   Constructing the Consolidated Balance Sheet at Acquisition   Rayburn Company purchased all of Kanodia Company's common stock for cash on January 1, at which time the separate balance sheets of the two corporations appeared as follows:

	Rayburn Company	Kanodia Company	Consolidating Adjustments	Consolidated
Investment in Kanodia	$ 600,000	—		
Other assets	2,300,000	$700,000		
Goodwill	—	—		
Total assets	$2,900,000	$700,000		
Liabilities	$ 900,000	$160,000		
Contributed capital	1,400,000	300,000		
Retained earnings	600,000	240,000		
Total liabilities and equity	$2,900,000	$700,000		

During purchase negotiations, Rayburn determined that the appraised value of Kanodia's Other Assets was $720,000; and, all of its remaining assets and liabilities were appraised at values approximating their book values. The remaining $40,000 of the purchase price was ascribed to goodwill. Prepare the consolidating adjustments and the consolidated balance sheet at acquisition.

E6-33.   Financial Statement Effects from a Subsidiary Stock Issuance   Ryan Company owns 80% of Lev Company. Information reported by Ryan Company and Lev Company as of January 1, 2005, follows:

Ryan Company
Shares owned of Lev   40,000
Book value of investment in Lev $320,000

Lev Company
Shares outstanding   50,000
Book value of equity $400,000
Book value per share $8

Assume Lev Company issues 30,000 additional shares of previously authorized but unissued common stock solely to outside investors (none to Ryan Company) for $12 cash per share. Indicate the financial statement effects of this stock issuance on Ryan Company using the following template (show computations) for both of the reporting options available under GAAP. Identify and explain both options.

Ryan Company's Financial Statements

Transaction	Balance Sheet					Income Statement	
	Cash Asset	+ Noncash Assets	= Liabil- ities	+ Contrib. Capital	+ Retained Earnings	Revenues	- Expenses
Lev Co. issues 30,000 shares (Option A)							
Lev Co. issues 30,000 shares (Option B)							

E6-34. **Goodwill Impairment**   On January 1, 2005, Engel Company purchases 100% of Ball Company for $16.8 million. At the time of acquisition, Ball's stockholders' equity is reported at $16.2 million. Engel ascribes the excess of $600,000 to goodwill. Assume that the market value of Ball declines to $12.5 million and that the fair market value of Ball's tangible net assets is estimated at $12.3 million as of December 31, 2005.

 a.   Provide computations to determine if the goodwill has become impaired and, if so, the amount of the impairment.

 b.   What impact does the impairment of goodwill have on Engel's financial statements?

E6-35. **Purchase Price Allocation including In-Process R&D**   Amgen Inc., reports the following footnote to its 10-K report:

Amgen Inc.
(AMGN)

> **Immunex acquisition.** On July 15, 2002, the Company acquired all of the outstanding common stock of Immunex in a transaction accounted for as a business combination. Immunex was a leading biotechnology company dedicated to developing immune system science to protect human health. The acquisition enhanced Amgen's strategic position within the biotechnology industry by strengthening and diversifying its (1) product base and product pipeline in key therapeutic areas, and (2) discovery research capabilities in proteins and antibodies. The purchase price was allocated to the tangible and identifiable intangible assets acquired and liabilities assumed based on their estimated fair values at the acquisition date. The following table summarizes the estimated fair values of the assets acquired and liabilities assumed as of the acquisition date (in millions):

Current assets, principally cash and marketable securities	$ 1,619.1
Deferred tax assets	200.2
Property, plant, and equipment	571.6
In-process research and development	2,991.8
Identifiable intangible assets, principally developed product technology and core technology	4,803.2
Goodwill	9,774.2
Other assets	26.2
Current liabilities	(579.0)
Deferred tax liabilities	(1,635.5)
Net assets	$17,771.8

> The allocation of the purchase price was based, in part, on a third-party valuation of the fair values of in-process research and development, identifiable intangible assets, and certain property, plant, and equipment. The estimated fair value of the in-process R&D projects was determined based on the use of a discounted cash flow model. For each project, the estimated after-tax cash flows were probability weighted to take into account the stage of completion and the risks surrounding the successful development and commercialization. These cash flows were then discounted to a present value using discount rates ranging from 12% to 14%.

 a.   Of the total assets acquired, what portion is allocated to tangible assets and what portion to intangible assets?

b. Are the assets (both tangible and intangible) of the acquired company reported on the consolidated balance sheet at the book value as reported on the acquired company's balance sheet immediately prior to the acquisition, or at the fair market value on the date of the acquisition? Explain.

c. How are the tangible and intangible assets accounted for subsequent to the acquisition?

d. Comment on the valuation of the in-process R&D and the accounting for this portion of the purchase price.

e. If the amount allocated to in-process R&D was decreased, what effect would this have on the allocation of the purchase price to the remaining acquired assets? What effect would this have on current and future earnings?

E6-36.[B] **Constructing the Consolidated Balance Sheet at Acquisition**   Easton Company acquires 100 percent of the outstanding voting shares of Harris Company on January 1, 2005. To obtain these shares, Easton pays $210,000 in cash and issues 5,000 of its $10 par value common stock. On this date, Easton's stock has a fair market value of $36 per share, and Harris's book value of stockholders' equity is $280,000. Easton is willing to pay $390,000 for a company with a book value for equity of $280,000 because it believes that (1) Harris's buildings are undervalued by $40,000, and (2) Harris has an unrecorded patent that Easton values at $30,000. Easton considers the remaining balance sheet items to be fairly valued (no book-to-market difference). The remaining $40,000 of the purchase price excess over book value is ascribed to corporate synergies and other general unidentifiable intangible assets (goodwill). The January 1, 2005, balance sheets at the acquisition date follow:

	Easton Company	Harris Company	Consolidating Adjustments	Consolidated
Cash	$ 84,000	$ 40,000		
Receivables	160,000	90,000		
Inventory	220,000	130,000		
Investment in Harris	390,000	—		
Land	100,000	60,000		
Buildings, net	400,000	110,000		
Equipment, net	120,000	50,000		
Total assets	$1,474,000	$480,000		
Accounts payable	$ 160,000	$ 30,000		
Long-term liabilities	380,000	170,000		
Common stock	500,000	40,000		
Additional paid-in capital	74,000	—		
Retained earnings	360,000	240,000		
Total liabilities & equity	$1,474,000	$480,000		

a. Show the breakdown of the investment into the book value acquired, the excess of fair value over book value, and the portion of the investment representing goodwill.

b. Prepare the consolidating adjustments and the consolidated balance sheet. Identify the adjustments by whether they relate to the elimination of stockholders' equity [S] or the excess of purchase price over book value [A].

c. How will the excess of the purchase price over book value acquired be treated in years subsequent to the acquisition?

Hewlett-
Packard (HP)

E6-37[C] **Reporting and Analyzing Derivatives**   Hewlett Packard reports the following schedule of comprehensive income (net income plus other comprehensive income) in its 2003 20-K report:

(In millions)	Accumulated Other Comprehensive Income (Loss)	Total
Net earnings		$2,539
Net unrealized gain on available-for-sale securities	$ 33	33
Net unrealized loss on derivative instruments	(48)	(48)
Reduction of minimum pension liability	211	211
Cumulative translation adjustment	2	2
Comprehensive income		$2,737

a. Identify and describe the usual applications for derivatives.
b. How are derivatives and their related assets (and/or liabilities) reported on the balance sheet?
c. By what amount has the unrealized gain or loss on the HP derivatives affected its current income? What are the analysis implications?

■ PROBLEMS

P6-38. Analyzing and Interpreting Available-for-Sale Securities Disclosures Following is a portion of the investments footnote from MetLife's 10-K report. Investment earnings are a crucial component of the financial performance of insurance companies such as MetLife, and investments comprise a large part of its assets. Met Life accounts for its bond investments as available-for-sale securities.

MetLife (MET)

December 31, 2002 ($ millions)	Cost or Amortized Cost	Gross Unrealized Gain	Gross Unrealized Loss	Estimated Fair Value
Fixed maturities				
Bonds:				
U.S. corporate securities	$ 47,021	$3,193	$ 957	$ 49,257
Mortgage-backed securities	33,256	1,649	22	34,883
Foreign corporate securities	18,001	1,435	207	19,229
U.S. treasuries/agencies	14,373	1,565	4	15,934
Asset-backed securities	9,483	228	208	9,503
Foreign government securities	7,012	636	52	7,596
States and political subdivisions	2,580	182	20	2,742
Other fixed income assets	609	191	103	697
Total bonds	$132,335	$9,079	$1,573	$139,841

December 31, 2001 ($ millions)	Cost or Amortized Cost	Gross Unrealized Gain	Gross Unrealized Loss	Estimated Fair Value
Fixed maturities				
Bonds:				
U.S. corporate securities	$ 43,141	$1,470	$ 748	$ 43,863
Mortgage-backed securities	25,506	866	192	26,180
Foreign corporate securities	16,836	688	539	16,985
U.S. treasuries/agencies	8,297	1,031	43	9,285
Asset-backed securities	8,115	154	206	8,063
Foreign government securities	5,488	544	37	5,995
States and political subdivisions	2,248	68	21	2,295
Other fixed income assets	1,874	238	142	1,970
Total bonds	$111,505	$5,059	$1,928	$114,636

MetLife also discloses the following for its net investment income and its realized gains (losses) on its fixed-income (bonds) portfolio:

Net Investment Income

The components of net investment income were as follows (dollars in millions):

	Years Ended December 31,		
	2002	2001	2000
Fixed maturities	$8,384	$8,574	$8,538

Sales of fixed maturities and equity securities classified as available-for-sale were as follows

| ($ millions) | Years Ended December 31, | | |
	2002	2001	2000
Proceeds	$37,427	$28,105	$46,205
Gross investment gains	$ 1,661	$ 646	$ 599
Gross investment losses	$ (979)	$ (948)	$ (1,520)

Required

a. At what amount does MetLife's report its bond investments on its balance sheets for 2002 and 2001?

b. What are its net unrealized gains (losses) for 2002 and 2001? By what amount did these unrealized gains (losses) affect its reported income in 2002 and 2001?

c. What is the difference between *realized* and *unrealized* gains and losses? Are realized gains and losses treated differently in the income statement than unrealized gains and losses?

d. Many analysts compute a *mark-to-market investment return* as follows: Net investment income + Realized gains and losses + Change in unrealized gains and losses. Compute this mark-to-market investment return for 2002 and 2001 (note: unrealized gains were $1,677 million in 2000). Do you think that this metric provides insights into the performance of MetLife's investment portfolio beyond that which is included in GAAP income statements? Explain.

General Mills (GIS)

P6-39. **Analyzing and Interpreting Disclosures on Equity Method Investments**   General Mills invests in a number of joint ventures to manufacture and distribute its food products as discussed in the following footnote to its fiscal year 2002 10-K report:

INVESTMENTS IN JOINT VENTURES

We have a 50 percent equity interest in Cereal Partners Worldwide (CPW), a joint venture with Nestlé that manufactures and markets ready-to-eat cereals outside the United States and Canada. We have a 40.5 percent equity interest in Snack Ventures Europe (SVE), our joint venture with PepsiCo that manufactures and markets snack foods in continental Europe. We have a 50 percent equity interest in 8th Continent, LLC, a domestic joint venture formed in 2001 with DuPont to develop and market soy foods and beverages. As a result of the Pillsbury acquisition, we have 50 percent interests in . . . joint ventures for the manufacture, distribution and marketing of *Häagen-Dazs* frozen ice cream products and novelties . . . We also have a 50 percent interest in Seretram, a joint venture with Co-op de Pau for the production of *Green Giant* canned corn in France.

The joint ventures are reflected in our financial statements on an equity accounting basis. We record our share of the earnings or losses of these joint ventures. (The table that follows reflects the joint ventures on a 100 percent basis.) We also receive royalty income from certain of these joint ventures, incur various expenses (primarily research and development) and record the tax impact of certain of the joint venture operations that are structured as partnerships.

Our cumulative investment in these joint ventures (including our share of earnings and losses) was $326 million, $218 million and $198 million at the end of 2002, 2001 and 2000, respectively. We made aggregate investments in the joint ventures of $38 million, $25 million and $29 million (net of a $6 million loan repayment) in 2002, 2001 and 2000, respectively. We received aggregate dividends from the joint ventures of $17 million, $3 million and $5 million in 2002, 2001 and 2000, respectively. Summary combined financial information for the joint ventures on a 100 percent basis follows.

Combined Financial Information—Joint Ventures—100% Basis

In Millions, Fiscal Year Ending in May	2002	2001
Net sales	$1,468	$1,429
Gross profit	664	619
Earnings (losses)	61	(4)

In Millions	May 26, 2002	May 27, 2001
Current assets	$587	$476
Noncurrent assets	712	614
Current liabilities	630	585
Noncurrent liabilities	9	2

Required

a. How does General Mills account for its investments in joint ventures? How are these investments reflected on its balance sheet, and how generally is income recognized on these investments?

b. General Mills reports the total of all of these investments on its May 26, 2002, balance sheet at $326 million. Approximately what percent of these joint ventures does it own, on average? Given this percent, approximately how much income would you expect that General Mills reports relating to these investments?

c. Does the $326 million investment reported on General Mills' balance sheet sufficiently reflect the assets and liabilities required to conduct these operations? Explain.

d. Do you believe that the liabilities of these joint venture entities represent actual obligations of General Mills? Explain.

e. What potential problem(s) does equity method accounting present for analysis purposes?

P6-40. Analyzing and Interpreting Disclosures on Consolidations   Caterpillar Inc. consists of two business units: the manufacturing company (parent corporation) and a wholly owned finance subsidiary. These two units are consolidated in Caterpillar's 10-K report. Following is a supplemental disclosure that Caterpillar includes in its 10-K report that shows the separate balance sheets of the parent and its subsidiary, as well as consolidating adjustments and the consolidated balance sheet presented to shareholders. This supplemental disclosure is not mandated under GAAP, but is voluntarily reported by Caterpillar as useful information for investors and creditors. Using this disclosure, answer the following questions: **Caterpillar Inc. (CAT)**

Required

a. Does each individual company (unit) maintain its own financial statements? Explain. Why does GAAP require consolidation instead of providing the financial statements of individual companies (units)?

b. What is the balance of Investments in Financial Products Subsidiaries as of December 31, 2003, on the parent's balance sheet? What is the equity balance of the financial products subsidiary to which this relates as of December 31, 2003? Do you see a relation? Will this relation always exist?

c. Refer to your answer for (a). How does the equity method of accounting for the investment in the subsidiary company obscure the actual financial condition of the parent company that is revealed in the consolidated financial statements?

d. Refer to the Consolidating Adjustments column reported—it is used to prepare the consolidated balance sheet. Generally, what do these adjustments accomplish?

e. Compare the consolidated balance of stockholders' equity with the stockholders' equity of the parent company (Machinery and Engines). Will the relation that is evident always hold? Explain.

f. Recall that the parent company uses the equity method of accounting for its investment in the subsidiary, and that this account is eliminated in the consolidation process. What is the relation between consolidated net income and the net income of the parent company? Explain.

g. What do you believe is the implication for the consolidated balance sheet if the market value of the Financial Products subsidiary is greater than the book value of its stockholders' equity?

| | | Supplemental Consolidating Data | | |
December 31, 2003 (Millions of Dollars)	Consolidated	Machinery and Engines	Financial Products	Consolidating Adjustments
Assets				
Current assets				
Cash and short-term investments	$ 342	$ 220	$ 122	$ —
Receivables—trade and other	3,666	2,993	1,642	(969)
Receivables—finance	7,605	—	7,605	—
Deferred and refundable income taxes	707	645	62	—
Prepaid expenses	1,424	1,403	27	(6)
Inventories	3,047	3,047	—	—
Total current assets	16,791	8,308	9,458	(975)
Property, plant and equipment—net	7,290	4,682	2,608	—
Long-term receivables—trade and other	82	81	1	—
Long-term receivables—finance	7,822	—	7,822	—
Investments in unconsolidated affiliated companies	800	426	374	—
Investments in Financial Products subsidiaries	—	2,547	—	(2,547)

(Continued on next page)

(Continued from previous page)

| December 31, 2003 (Millions of Dollars) | Supplemental Consolidating Data | | | |
	Consolidated	Machinery and Engines	Financial Products	Consolidating Adjustments
Assets *(Continued)*				
Deferred income taxes	$ 616	$ 819	$ 19	$ (222)
Intangible assets	239	230	9	—
Goodwill	1,398	1,398	—	—
Other assets	1,427	719	708	—
Total assets	**$36,465**	**$19,210**	**$20,999**	**$(3,744)**
Liabilities				
Current liabilities				
Short-term borrowings	$ 2,757	$ 72	$ 3,160	$ (475)
Accounts payable	3,100	3,078	243	(221)
Accrued expenses	1,638	857	802	(21)
Accrued wages, salaries and employee benefits	1,802	1,788	14	—
Dividends payable	127	127	—	—
Deferred and current income taxes payable	216	166	50	—
Deferred liability	—	—	259	(259)
Long-term debt due within one year	2,981	32	2,949	—
Total current liabilities	12,621	6,120	7,477	(976)
Long-term debt due after one year	14,078	3,367	10,711	—
Liability for postemployment benefits	3,172	3,172	—	—
Deferred income taxes and other liabilities	516	473	264	(221)
Total liabilities	30,387	13,132	18,452	(1,197)
Shareholders' equity				
Common stock	1,059	1,059	890	(890)
Treasury stock	(2,914)	(2,914)	—	—
Profit employed in the business	8,450	8,450	1,495	(1,495)
Accumulated other comprehensive income	(517)	(517)	162	(162)
Total stockholders' equity	6,078	6,078	2,547	(2,547)
Total liabilities and stockholders' equity	**$36,465**	**$19,210**	**$20,999**	**$(3,744)**

7 Reporting and Analyzing Nonowner Financing

VERIZON COMMUNICATIONS

WHERE CHANGE IS THE NORM

Verizon Communications Inc., began doing business in 2000, when Bell Atlantic Corporation merged with GTE Corporation. Verizon is one of the world's leading providers of communications services. It is the largest provider of wireline and wireless communications in the U.S., and is the largest of the Baby Bells as of 2004 with $68 billion in revenues and $166 billion in assets. Verizon is the third largest long distance carrier for U.S. consumers, and it is the largest directory publisher in the world (Verizon 2004 10-K).

When Ivan Seidenberg became sole CEO of Verizon in mid-2002 (and its chairman in late 2003), the Internet frenzy had cooled and Verizon's stock price had plunged, falling from an all-time high of $70 in late 1999 to $27 in mid-2002. Since then, the stock has rebounded somewhat, but continued to trade below $45 per share in early 2005.

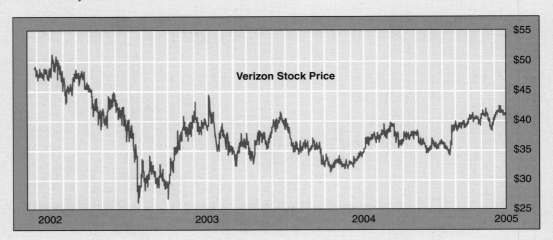

Version survived the internet and telecom downturn, but it faces a formidable new challenger: cable. Cable companies spent an estimated $75 billion in recent years upgrading their infrastructure to offer customers discounted bundled packages of local voice, high-speed Internet connections, and video. They could grab a

quarter of the local voice market over the next decade as they deploy new voice over Internet protocol (VOIP) technology, estimates John Hodulik, a UBS telecom analyst." (*BusinessWeek* 2004)

Phone companies have historically drawn their power and profits from both networks of switches and the lines that lead to nearly every home. "Having watched this industry for 35 years," says Bruce Gordon, president of Verizon's retail division, "I don't believe it's a network that will take us into the next decade." (*BusinessWeek* 2003) Further, Verizon's revenue mix has changed in the past two years as illustrated in the following graphic drawn from its 2003 10-K report:

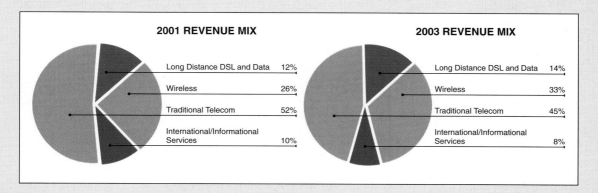

2001 REVENUE MIX		2003 REVENUE MIX	
Long Distance DSL and Data	12%	Long Distance DSL and Data	14%
Wireless	26%	Wireless	33%
Traditional Telecom	52%	Traditional Telecom	45%
International/Informational Services	10%	International/Informational Services	8%

The change in revenue mix is as much due to the declining land-line segment as it is to the rise in newer technologies, as traditional phone service revenues declined another 7 percentage points in 2003 (Verizon 2003 10-K). Despite the enormous investment in physical plant to support this segment of its business, Verizon must now shift its strategic focus to wireless and high-speed connectivity.

Faced with growing competition from cable-TV companies and others, Verizon plans to spend $20 billion to $40 billion over the next decade to build fiber-optic connections to every home and business it serves. *BusinessWeek* says "this means speeds of 5 to 10 megabits per second, up to 20 times faster than today's

(Continued on next page)

(Continued from previous page)

typical broadband connections . . . that's fast enough to provide voice, video, and digital-TV signals on a single connection to the customer." Verizon is also deploying wireless technology faster than rivals and setting up Wi-Fi hotspots, committing itself to a massive network upgrade.

The demand for new capital spending is coming at an inopportune time for Verizon. Saddled with a debt load of over $45 billion as of 2003, half of which matures over the next five years, Verizon must also provide for the payment of over $4 billion in stock dividends annually plus nearly $17 billion in accumulated employee pensions and health-care costs. Verizon is concerned. Faced with a question from a stockholder why Verizon isn't repurchasing its stock given its decline in value, Seidenberg said "our number-one priority for using free cash flow over the last two years has been reducing debt." (Verizon 2003 10-K)

" 'Verizon, like the rest of the industry, is in a tough spot,' says Moody's analyst Dennis Saputo, who has the company's A1 credit rating on review for a possible downgrade. 'They have an increasing business risk with substitution and competition, and they are trying to offset that risk by lowering debt and improving the balance sheet. They're dammed if the do and dammed if they don't . . . Right now, as competition is increasing, this isn't a good time to be cutting capital investments." (TheStreet.Com 2003)

This module focuses on liabilities—that is, short-term and long-term obligations. Liabilities (also called debt) are one of two financing sources for a company. The other is shareholder financing. Bonds and notes are a major part of most companies' liabilities. In this module, we show how to price liabilities and how the issuance and subsequent payment of the principal and interest on them affect financial statements. We also discuss the required disclosures that enable us to effectively analyze a company's ability to make its liability payments as they mature.

The actor, James Earl Jones, intones in the Verizon ad, "make progress every day." Verizon is seeking to do just that as it allocates its available cash flow between strategic investment and debt payments.

Sources: *BusinessWeek* 2003; *TheStreet.Com* 2003; *Verizon* 2004 and 2003 Annual Reports; *Verizon* 2004 and 2003 10-Ks.

■ INTRODUCTION

The accounting equation (Assets = Liabilities + Equity) is a useful tool in helping us think about how the balance sheet and income statement are constructed, the linkages between the financial statements, and the effects of transactions on financial statements. The accounting equation is also useful in helping us think about the statements from another perspective, namely, how the business is financed. Consider the following representation of the accounting equation:

$$\underbrace{\text{Assets}}_{\text{Uses}} = \underbrace{\text{Liabilities} + \text{Equity}}_{\text{Sources}}$$

Assets represent investments (uses of funds) that management has made. It includes current operating assets such as cash, accounts receivable, and inventories. It also includes long-term operating assets such as manufacturing and administrative facilities. Most companies also invest a portion of funds in nonoperating assets that provide the liquidity a company needs to conduct transactions and to react to market opportunities and changes.

Just as asset disclosures provide us with information on where a company invests its funds, the disclosures on liabilities and equity inform us as to how those assets are financed. These are the sources of funds. To be successful, a company must not only invest funds wisely, but must also be astute in the manner in which it raises funds.

Companies hope to finance their assets at the lowest possible cost. Current liabilities (such as accounts payable and accrued liabilities) are generally non-interest-bearing. As a result, firms try to maximize the financing of their assets with these sources of funds.

Current liabilities, as the name implies, are short-term in nature, generally requiring payment within the coming year. As a result, they are not a suitable source of funding for long-term assets that generate cash flows over several years. Instead, companies often finance long-term assets with long-term liabilities that require payments over several years. Generally, companies try to link the cash outflows of the financing source with the cash inflows of the asset class to which they relate. As such, long-term financing is usually in the form of bonds, notes, and stock issuances.

$
Cash Effect

We know that when a company acquires assets, and finances them with liabilities, its financial leverage increases. Also, the magnitude of required liability payments increases proportionally with the level of liability financing, and those larger payments imply a higher probability of default should a downturn in business occur. Increasing levels of liabilities, then, make the company riskier to investors who, consequently, demand a higher return on the financing provided to that company. This assessment is part of liquidity and solvency analysis.

This module describes and assesses *on-balance-sheet financing,* namely current and noncurrent liabilities, where the financing effects are reported on financial statements. If companies can find a way to purchase assets and have neither the asset, nor its related financing, appear on the balance sheet, they can report higher levels of income (and asset turnover) and appear less risky. It is this basic idea that has spawned off-balance-sheet financing, which is the focus of Module 9.

■ CURRENT LIABILITIES

Liabilities are separated into current and long-term. The focus of this section is on current liabilities. Most current liabilities such as those related to utilities, wages, insurance, rent, and taxes, generate a corresponding impact on selling, general and administrative expenses. **Verizon**'s current liabilities as taken from its balance sheet follows:

At December 31 ($ millions)	2003	2002
Current liabilities		
Debt maturing within one year	$ 5,967	$ 9,267
Accounts payable and accrued liabilities	14,699	12,642
Liabilities of discontinued operations	—	1,007
Other	5,904	5,013
Total current liabilities	$26,570	$27,929

Verizon reports four categories of current liabilities: (1) long-term liability (debt) obligations that are scheduled for payment in the upcoming year, (2) accounts payable and accrued liabilities, (3) current liabilities from discontinued operations (these operations were sold in 2003, hence they are no longer part of Verizon's operations), and (4) other current liabilities, which consist mainly of customer deposits, dividends payable, and miscellaneous.

Analysis and interpretation of return on net operating assets (RNOA) requires that we separate current liabilities into operating and nonoperating components. These two components primarily consist of the following:

1. Current operating liabilities
   - **Accounts payable** Obligations to others for amounts owed on purchases of goods and services. These are usually non-interest-bearing.
   - **Accrued liabilities** Obligations for which there is no related external transaction in the current period. These include, for example, accruals for employee wages earned but yet unpaid, accruals for taxes (usually quarterly) on payroll and current period profits, and accruals for other liabilities such as rent, utilities, and insurance. Accruals are made to properly reflect the liabilities owed as of the statement date and the expenses incurred in the period.
2. Current nonoperating liabilities
   - **Short-term interest-bearing debt** Short-term bank borrowings and notes expected to mature in whole or in part during the upcoming year; including any accrued interest payable.

- **Current maturities of long-term debt** Long-term borrowings that are scheduled to mature in whole or in part during the upcoming year.

The remainder of this section describes current operating liabilities followed by a discussion of current nonoperating liabilities.

Accounts Payable

Accounts payable, which are part of current operating liabilities, arise from the purchase of goods and services from others. Accounts payable are normally non-interest-bearing and, thus, are an inexpensive financing source. Verizon reports $14,699 million in accounts payable and accrued liabilities. Its accounts payable represent $4,130 million, or 28%, of this total amount.

Accounting for a typical purchase of goods on account, which results in accounts payable, and the ultimate sale of those goods follows:

		Balance Sheet					Income Statement	
Transaction	Cash Asset	+ Noncash Assets	= Liabil- ities	+ Contrib. Capital	+ Retained Earnings		Revenues	− Expenses
1. Purchase $100 of inventory on credit		+100 Inventory	+100 Accounts Payable					
2a. Sale of $100 inventory on credit for $140		+140 Accounts Receivable			+140 Retained Earnings		+140 Sales	
2b. Record $100 cost of sales with transaction 2a		−100 Inventory			−100 Retained Earnings			−100 Cost of Goods Sold
3. Cash received from accounts receivable	+140	−140 Accounts Receivable						
4. Cash paid to settle accounts payable	−100		−100 Accounts Payable					

Side journal entries:

Inventory 100
  Accounts Payable 100

Accounts Receivable 140
  Sales 140

Cost of Goods Sold 100
  Inventory 100

Cash 140
  Accounts Receivable 140

Accounts Payable 100
  Cash 100

$ Cash Effect

The financial statement effects template reveals several impacts related to the usual purchase of goods on account and their ultimate sale:

- Purchase of inventory is reflected on the balance sheet as an increase in inventory and an increase in accounts payable.
- Sale of inventory involves two components—revenue and cost. The revenue part reflects the increase in sales revenue and the increase in accounts receivable (revenue is recognized when earned, even though cash is not yet received).
- The cost part of the sales transaction reflects the decrease in inventory and the increase in cost of goods sold (COGS). COGS is reported in the income statement and matched against revenues reported (this expense is recognized because the inventory asset is sold, even though inventory-related payables may not yet be paid).
- Cash payment of accounts payable is solely a balance sheet transaction and does not impact income statement accounts (expense relating to purchase of inventories is recognized when the asset is sold or used up, not when the liability is paid).
- Collection of the receivable reduces accounts receivable and increases cash. It is solely a balance sheet transaction and does not impact income statement accounts.

Accounts payable reflect a source of interest-free financing. Increased payables reduce the amount of net operating working capital as these payables are deducted from current operating assets in the computation of net operating working capital. Also, increased payables mean increased cash flow (as increased liabilities increase net cash from operating activities) and increased profitability (reduction in the level of interest-bearing debt that is required to finance operating assets). RNOA increases when companies make use of this low cost financing source. Our analysis, however, must be aware of excessive 'leaning on the trade' as short-term income gains can yield long-term costs such as damaged supply channels.[1,2]

$ Cash Effect

MID-MODULE REVIEW 1

3M's accounts payable turnover (cost of goods sold/average accounts payable—see Module 3 for a discussion) decreased from 10.4 in 2001 to 9.1 in 2003.

a. Does this change indicate that accounts payable have increased or decreased relative to cost of goods sold? Explain.

b. What effect does this change have on 3M's net cash flows from operating activities?

c. What management concerns, if any, might this change in accounts payable turnover pose?

Solution

a. We know that accounts payable turnover is computed as cost of goods sold divided by accounts payable. Thus, a decline in accounts payable turnover indicates that accounts payable have increased relative to cost of goods sold (all else equal).

b. An increase in accounts payable results in an increase in net cash flows from operating activities. This is a case of the company *leaning on the trade.*

c. Increased accounts payable (and accrued liabilities) reduce net operating working capital, with consequent improvement in profitability and cash flow. As a result, the increase in payables is desirable, provided that the company does not damage relations with its suppliers. Analysts must be aware of the potentially damaging consequences of leaning on the trade to a much greater extent than is customary.

Accrued Liabilities

Accrued liabilities are identified at the end of an accounting period to reflect liabilities and expenses that have been incurred during the period but are not yet recognized in financial statements.[3] **Verizon** reports details of its $10,569 million accrued liabilities and its $4,130 million accounts payable in the following footnote to its 10-K report:

December 31 ($ millions)	2003	2002
Accounts payable	$ 4,130	$ 4,851
Accrued expenses	2,995	2,796
Accrued vacation pay	824	960
Accrued salaries and wages	3,376	2,171
Interest payable	633	669
Accrued taxes	2,741	1,195
Total	$14,699	$12,642

---

[1]We must be aware, however, that excessive delays in payment of payables can result in suppliers charging a higher price for their goods or, ultimately, refusing to sell to certain buyers. This is a hidden "financing" cost that, although it is not interest, is a real cost.

[2]Accounts payable often carry credit terms such as 2/10, net 30. These terms give the buyer, for example, 2% off the invoice price of goods purchased if paid within 10 days. Otherwise the entire invoice is payable within 30 days. By its failure to take a discount, the buyer is effectively paying 2% interest charge to use its funds for an additional 20 days. Since there are approximately 18 such 20-day periods in a year (365/20), this equates to an annual rate of interest of about 36%. Thus, borrowing funds at less than 36% to pay this liability within the discount period would be cost effective and good management.

[3]Accruals can also be made for recognition of revenue and a corresponding receivable. An example of this might be revenue recognition on a long-term contract that has reached a particular milestone, or for interest earned on an investment in bonds that is still outstanding at period-end.

$

Cash Effect

Verizon accrues liabilities for the following expenses: miscellaneous accrued expenses, accrued vacation pay, accrued salaries and wages, interest payable, and accrued taxes. These accruals are typical of most companies. The accruals are recognized with a liability on the balance sheet and a corresponding expense on the income statement. This means that liabilities increase, current income decreases, and equity decreases. When an accrued liability is ultimately paid, both cash and the liability is decreased (but no expense is recorded as it was recognized previously).

Accounting for Accruals

Accounting for a typical accrued liability, that of accrued wages, follows:

Transaction or Event	Balance Sheet					Income Statement	
	Cash Asset	+ Noncash Assets	= Liabil- ities	+ Contrib. Capital	+ Retained Earnings	Revenues	− Expenses
1. Accrued $75 for employee wages earned			+75 Wages Payable		−75 Retained Earnings		− 75 Wages Expense
2. Next period's cash payment of wages	−75		−75 Wages Payable				

Wages Expense 75
  Wages Payable 75

Wages Payable 75
  Cash 75

The following financial statement effects result from this accrual of employee wages:

- Employees have worked during a period and have not yet been paid. The effect of this accrual is to increase wages payable on the balance sheet and to recognize wages expense on the income statement. Failure to recognize this liability and associated expense would understate liabilities on the balance sheet and overstate income.

$

Cash Effect

- Employees are paid in the following period, resulting in a cash decrease and a reduction in wages payable. This payment does not result in expense because the expense was recognized in the prior period when incurred.

The accrued wages illustration relates to events that are fairly certain. We know, for example, when wages are incurred but not paid. Other examples of such accruals are rental costs, insurance premiums, and taxes owed.

Some accrued liabilities are less certain than others. Consider a company facing a lawsuit. Should it record the possible liability and related expense? The answer depends on the likelihood of occurrence and the ability to estimate the obligation. Specifically, if the obligation is *probable* and the amount *estimable,* then a company will recognize this obligation, called a *contingent liability.* If an obligation is only *reasonably possible,* regardless of the company's ability to estimate the amount, the contingent liability is not reported on the balance sheet and is merely disclosed in the footnotes. All other contingent liabilities that are less than reasonably possible are not disclosed.

All accrued liabilities result in a liability on the balance sheet and an expense on the income statement. Management has some latitude in determining the amount and timing for accruals. This latitude can lead to misreporting of income and liabilities (unintentional or otherwise). Here's how: If accruals are underestimated, then liabilities are underestimated, income is overestimated, and retained earnings are overestimated. In subsequent periods when an understated accrued liability is reversed, reported income is lower than it should be; this is because prior period income was higher than it should have been. (The reverse holds for overestimated accruals.) The over and under reporting of accruals, therefore, results in the shifting of income from one period into another. We must be keenly aware of this potential for income shifting as we analyze the financial condition of a company.

Experience tells us that accrued liabilities that are linked with restructuring programs (including severance accruals and accruals for asset write-downs), with legal and environmental liabilities, and with business acquisitions are too often problematic. Namely, these accruals too often represent early (aggressive) recognition of expenses, some as part of a *big bath,* in a desire to relieve future periods of these expenses. Accordingly, we must monitor any change or unusual activity with accrued liabilities.

Estimating Accruals

Several accrued liabilities require estimates of their amounts. Warranty liabilities are an important case of accrued liabilities. Warranties are commitments that manufacturers make to their customers to repair or replace defective products within a specified period of time. The expected cost of this commitment usually is reasonably estimated at the time of sale based on past experience. As a result, GAAP requires manufacturers to record the expected cost of warranties as a liability, and to record the related expected warranty expense in the income statement to match against the sales revenue reported for that period.

To illustrate, the effects of an accrual of a $1,000 warranty liability are as follows:

Transaction or Event	Balance Sheet							Income Statement				
	Cash Asset	+	Noncash Assets	=	Liabil- ities	+	Contrib. Capital	+	Retained Earnings	Revenues	−	Expenses	
1. Accrue $1,000 of expected warranty costs on goods sold this period					+1,000 Warranty Payable				−1,000 Retained Earnings		−	1,000 Warranty Expense	Warranty Expense 1,000 / Warranty Payable 1,000
2. Next period's costs (sent $950 in replacement products) to cover failures under warranty			−950 Inventory		−950 Warranty Payable								Warranty Payable 950 / Inventory 950

Reporting of warranty liabilities has the same effect on financial statements as does the accrual of wages expense in the previous section. That is, a liability is recorded on the balance sheet and an expense is reported in the income statement, reducing income by the warranty accrual. When the defective product is later replaced (or repaired), the liability is reduced together with the cost of the inventory (or other assets) spent to satisfy the claim. (Only a portion of the products estimated to fail does so in the current period; we expect other product failures in future periods. Management monitors this estimate and adjusts it if failure is higher or lower than expected.) As in the accrual of wages, the expense is reported when it is incurred and the liability is estimated, not when it is paid.

Ford Motor Company reports $5,443 million of warranty liability on its 2003 balance sheet. Its footnotes reveal the following additional information:

Product Performance, Warranty—Estimated warranty costs and additional service actions are accrued for at the time the vehicle is sold to a dealer. Included in the warranty cost accruals are costs for basic warranty coverages on vehicles sold. Estimates for warranty costs are made based primarily on historical warranty claim experience. The following is a tabular reconciliation of the product warranty accrual (in millions):

Product Warranty Liability	2003	2002
Beginning balance	$ 5,401	$ 4,739
Payments made during the year	(3,524)	(3,508)
Changes in accrual related to warranties issued during the year	3,562	3,489
Changes in accrual related to pre-existing warranties	(266)	595
Foreign currency translation and other	270	86
Ending balance	$ 5,443	$ 5,401

Of the $5,401 million balance at the beginning of 2003, $3,524 million in cost was incurred to replace or repair defective products during the year, reducing the liability by this amount. This cost can be in the form of cash paid to customers or to employees as wages, and in the form of parts used for repairs. Ford accrued an additional $3,562 million in new warranty liabilities in 2003 and recorded additional miscellaneous adjustments amounting to a net increase in the liability of $4 million ($270 million − $266 million). It is important to understand that only the increase in the liability resulting from additional accruals impacts the income statement (like the provision for uncollectible accounts receivable), reducing income through additional warranty expense. Payments per the warranty obligation reduce the preexisting liability.

GAAP requires that the warranty liability reflects the estimated amount of cost that the company expects to incur as a result of warranty claims. This is often a difficult estimate to make and is prone to error. There is also the possibility that a company might underestimate its warranty liability to report higher current income, or overestimate it so as to depress current income and create an additional liability on the balance sheet (*cookie jar reserve*) that can be used to absorb future warranty costs without the need to record additional expense. The latter would shift income from the current period to one or more future periods. Warranty liabilities must, therefore, be examined closely and compared with sales levels. Any deviations from the historical relation of the warranty liability to sales, or that reported by competitors, should be investigated.

■ MID-MODULE REVIEW 2 ■

Hayn Company's employees worked during the current month and earned $10,000 in wages, which are not paid until the first of next month. Must Hayn recognize any wages liability and expense for the current month? Explain with reference to the financial statement effects template.

Solution

Yes. Liabilities and expenses must be recognized when incurred, regardless of when payment is made, and matched with the revenues they helped generate. Failure to recognize the wages owed and wages expense to employees for the period would understate liabilities and overstate income. Hayn must reflect the wages earned and the related expense in its financial statements as follows:

		Balance Sheet				Income Statement	
Transaction	Cash Asset	+ Noncash Assets	= Liabil- ities	+ Contrib. Capital	+ Retained Earnings	Revenues	− Expenses
Accrue $10,000 in wages expense			+10,000 Wages Payable		−10,000 Retained Earnings		− 10,000 Wages Expense

Wage Expense 10,000
Wages
    Payable   10,000

Current Nonoperating (Financial) Liabilities

Current nonoperating (financial) liabilities include short-term bank loans, the accrual of interest on those loans, and the current maturities of long-term debt. Companies generally try to structure their financing so that debt service requirements (payments) of those financing obligations coincide with the cash inflows from the assets financed. This means that current assets are usually financed with current liabilities, and that long-term assets are financed with long-term liabilities (and equity) sources.

To illustrate, a seasonal company's investment in current assets tends to fluctuate during the year as depicted in the graphic below:

$ **Cash Effect**

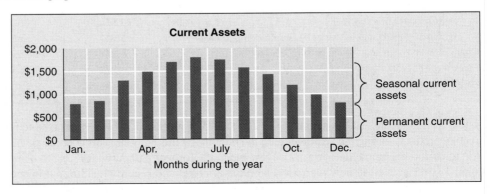

This particular company does most of its selling in the summer months. More inventory is purchased and manufactured in the early spring than at any other time of the year. Sales of inventory are also greater during the summer months, giving rise to accounts receivable that are higher than normal during the fall. The peak working capital level is reached at the height of the selling season and is lowest as the business slows in the off-season. There is a permanent level of working capital required for this business (about $750), and a seasonal component (maximum of about $1,000). Different businesses exhibit different patterns in their working capital requirements, but many have permanent and seasonal components.

The existence of permanent and seasonal current operating assets often require financing sources for liabilities that consist of permanent and seasonal components. Again, let's assume the company exhibits current asset levels according to the graphic above. Since a portion of these assets is in inventories that are financed, in part, with accounts payable and accruals, we expect there is a relatively permanent level of current operating liabilities that also exhibit a seasonal component that fluctuates with the level of operations. These payables are generally non-interest-bearing and, thus, provide low-cost financing that should be used to the greatest extent possible. Additional financing needs are covered by short-term interest-bearing debt.

This section focuses on current nonoperating liabilities, which include short-term debt (and its interest) and any current maturities of long-term liabilities. Corresponding to these liabilities are their related interest expenses.

Short-Term Interest-Bearing Debt

Seasonal swings in working capital are often financed with a bank line of credit (short-term debt). In this case the bank provides a commitment to lend up to a given level with the understanding that the amounts borrowed are repaid in full sometime during the year. An interest-bearing note evidences any such borrowing.

$\$$

Cash Effect

When these short-term funds are borrowed, the cash received is reported on the balance sheet together with an increase in liabilities (notes payable). The note is reported as a current liability since the expectation is that it will be paid within a year. This borrowing has no effect on income or equity. The borrower incurs (and the lender earns) interest on the note as time passes. GAAP requires the borrower to accrue the interest liability and the related interest expense each time financial statements are issued.

To illustrate, assume that Verizon borrows $1,000 cash on January 1. The note bears interest at a 12% annual (3% quarterly) rate, and the interest is payable on the first of each subsequent quarter (April 1, July 1, October 1, January 1). Assuming that Verizon issues calendar-quarter financial statements, this borrowing results in the following financial statement effects for January 1 through April 1:

	Balance Sheet					Income Statement			
Transaction	Cash Asset	+ Noncash Assets	= Liabil- ities	+ Contrib. Capital	+ Retained Earnings	Revenues	– Expenses		
Jan 1, Borrowed $1,000 cash by issuing note payable	+1,000 Cash		+1,000 Note Payable					Cash 1,000 Note Payable 1,000	
Mar 31, Interest accrues on 12% note payable			+30 Interest Payable		−30 Retained Earnings		− 30 Interest Expense	Interest Expense 30 Interest Payable 30	
Apr 1, Cash paid to cover interest due	−30 Cash		−30 Interest Payable					Interest Payable 30 Cash 30	

The January 1 borrowing is reflected by an increase in cash and notes payable. On March 31, this company issues its quarterly financial statements. Although interest is not paid until April 1, the company has incurred three months' interest obligation as of March 31. Failure to recognize this liability and the expense incurred would not fairly present the financial condition of the company. Accordingly, the quarterly accrued interest is computed as follows:

$$\textbf{Interest Expense} = \textbf{Principal} \times \textbf{Annual Rate} \times \textbf{Portion of Year Outstanding}$$
$$\$30 \quad = \quad \$1,000 \quad \times \quad 12\% \quad \times \quad 3/12$$

$ Cash Effect

The subsequent interest payment on April 1 is reflected in the financial statements as a reduction of cash and a reduction of the interest payable liability accrued on March 31. There is no expense reported on April 1, as it was recorded the previous day (March 31) when financial statements were prepared. (For fixed-maturity borrowings specified in days, such as a 90-day note, we use a 365-day year for interest accrual computations, see Mid-Module Review 3 below.)

Current Maturities of Long-Term Debt

Payments that must be made during the upcoming 12 months on long-term debt (such as for a mortgage) or the maturity of a bond or note are reported as current liabilities called *current maturities of long-term debt*. All companies are required to provide a schedule of the maturities of its long-term debt in the footnotes to financial statements. To illustrate, the current liability section from the balance sheet of Verizon follows. Verizon reports $5,967 million in long-term debt due within one year.

December 31 ($ millions)	2003
Current liabilities	
Debt maturing within one year	$ 5,967
Accounts payable and accrued liabilities	14,699
Liabilities of discontinued operations	—
Other	5,904
Total current liabilities	$26,570

■ MID-MODULE REVIEW 3 ■

Gigler Company borrowed $10,000 on a 90-day, 6% note payable dated January 15. The bank accrues interest daily based on a 365-day year. Use the financial statement effects template to show the implications (amounts and accounts) of the January 31 month-end interest accrual.

Solution

Interest Expense   26
Interest Payable   26

	Balance Sheet							Income Statement		
Transaction	Cash Asset	+	Noncash Assets	=	Liabil- ities	+	Contrib. Capital	+	Retained Earnings	Revenues − Expenses
Accrued $26 of interest as of January 31*					+26 Interest Payable				−26 Retained Earnings	− 26 Interest Expense

*Accrued interest for a 16-day period at January 31 = $10,000 × 0.06 × 16/365 = $26.

■ LONG-TERM LIABILITIES

Companies usually desire some long-term liabilities in their capital structure to fund their long-term assets. Long-term liabilities of smaller amounts can be readily obtained from banks, private placements with insurance companies, and other credit sources. However, when a large amount of financing is required, the issuance of bonds (and notes) in capital markets is a cost-efficient way to raise capital. The following discussion uses bonds for illustration, but much of it is readily applied to notes.

$ Cash Effect

Bonds and notes are structured like any other borrowing. The borrower receives cash and agrees to pay it back with interest. Generally, the entire **face amount** (principal) of the bond or note is repaid at maturity and interest payments are made (usually semiannually) in the interim.

Companies wishing to raise funds in the bond market normally work with an underwriter (like Merrill Lynch) to set the terms of the bond issue. The underwriter, then, sells individual bonds (usually in $1,000 denominations) from this general bond issue to its retail clients and professional portfolio managers (like **The Vanguard Group**), and it receives a fee for underwriting the bond issue. These bonds often become investments for retirement plans and insurance companies.

Once sold, the bonds can be traded in the secondary market between investors just like stocks. Market prices of bonds fluctuate daily despite the fact that the company's obligation for payment of principal and interest normally remains fixed throughout the life of the bond. This is because bonds compete with other possible investments, and become more or less desirable depending on the general level of interest rates offered by competing securities and the financial condition of the borrowing company.

This section analyzes and interprets the reporting for bonds. We also examine the mechanics of bond pricing and describe the accounting for and reporting of bonds.

Pricing of Debt

We must understand two different interest rates that are crucial for pricing debt:

- **Coupon (contract** or **stated) rate**   The coupon rate of interest is stated in the bond contract. It is used to compute the dollar amount of (semiannual) interest payments that are paid to bondholders during the life of the bond issue.
- **Market (yield) rate**   This is the interest rate that investors expect to earn on the investment for this debt security. This rate is used to price the bond issue.

The coupon (contract) rate is used to compute interest payments and the market (yield) rate is used to price the bond. The coupon rate and the market rate are nearly always different. This is because the coupon rate is fixed prior to issuance of the bond and normally remains so throughout its life. Market rates of interest, on the other hand, fluctuate continually with the supply and demand for bonds in the market place, general macroeconomic conditions, and the financial condition of borrowers.

The bond price, both its initial sales price and the price it trades at in the secondary market subsequent to issuance, equals the present value of the expected cash flows to the bondholder. Specifically, bondholders normally expect to receive two different cash flows:

$

Cash Effect

1. **Periodic interest payments** (usually semiannual) during the bond life. These payments are often in the form of equal cash flows at periodic intervals, called an **annuity**.
2. **Single payment** of the face (principal) amount of the bond at maturity.

The bond price equals the present value of the periodic interest payments plus the present value of the principal payment at maturity. We next illustrate the purchase of bonds at three different prices: at par, at a discount, and at a premium.

Bonds Issued at Par

To illustrate bond pricing, assume that investors wish to value a bond with a face amount of $10 million, a 6% annual coupon rate payable semiannually (3% semiannual rate), and a maturity of 10 years.[4] Investors purchasing this issue receive the following cash flows:

	Number of Payments	Dollars per Payment	Total Cash Flows
Semiannual interest payments	10 years × 2 = 20	$10,000,000 × 3% = $ 300,000	$ 6,000,000
Principal payment at maturity	1	$10,000,000	10,000,000
			$16,000,000

Specifically, the bond agreement dictates that the borrower makes 20 semiannual payments of $300,000 each, computed as $10,000,000 × (6%/2), plus the $10,000,000 face amount at maturity, for a total of $16 million in cash flows. (When pricing bonds, identify the *number* of interest payments and use that

---

[4]Semiannual interest payments are typical for bonds. This means that the issuer pays bondholders two interest payments per year. In this case, the semiannual interest rate is the annual rate divided by two.

number when computing the present value of both the interest payments and the principal (face) payment at maturity.)

The bond price is the present value of the interest annuity plus the present value of the principal payment. Assuming that investors desire a 6% annual market rate (yield), the bond sells for $10,000,000 million, which is computed as follows:

> Present value factors are from Appendix A near end of the book

	Payment	Present Value Factor[a]	Present Value
Interest	$ 300,000	14.87747[b]	$ 4,463,200[d]
Principal	$10,000,000	0.55368[c]	5,536,800
			$10,000,000

[a]Mechanics of using tables to compute present values are explained in Appendix 7A. Present value factors are taken from Appendix A near the end of the book.

[b]Present value of ordinary annuity for 20 periods discounted at 3% per period.

[c]Present value of single payment in 20 periods hence discounted at 3% per period.

[d]Rounded.

Since the bond contract pays investors a 6% annual rate when investors demand a 6% market rate given the bond's (company's) credit rating and term, then investors purchase those bonds at the **par (face) value** of $10 million.

Discount Bonds

As a second illustration, assume that the company's risk characteristics are such that investors demand an 8% annual yield (4% semiannual) for the 6% coupon bond, while all other details remain the same. The bond now sells for $8,640,999, computed as follows:

	Payment	Present Value Factor	Present Value
Interest	$ 300,000	13.59033[a]	$ 4,077,099
Principal	$10,000,000	0.45639[b]	4,563,900
			$ 8,640,999

[a]Present value of ordinary annuity for 20 periods discounted at 4% per period.

[b]Present value of single payment in 20 periods hence discounted at 4% per period.

Since the bond carries a coupon rate *lower* than that which investors demand, the bond is less desirable and sells at a **discount**. More generally, bonds sell at a discount whenever the coupon rate is less than the market rate.[5]

Premium Bonds

As a third illustration, assume that investors demand a 4% annual yield (2% semiannual) for the 6% coupon bonds, while all other details remain the same. The bond now sells for $11,635,129, computed as follows:

	Payment	Present Value Factor	Present Value
Interest	$ 300,000	16.35143[a]	$ 4,905,429
Principal	$10,000,000	0.67297[b]	6,729,700
			$11,635,129

[a]Present value of ordinary annuity for 20 periods discounted at 2% per period.

[b]Present value of single payment in 20 periods hence discounted at 2% per period.

Since the bond carries a coupon rate *higher* than that which investors demand, the bond is more desirable and sells at a **premium**. More generally, bonds sell at a premium whenever the coupon rate is greater than the market rate. Exhibit 7.1 summarizes this relation for bond pricing.

----

[5]Bond prices are often stated in percent form. For example, a bond sold at par is said to be sold at 100 (that is, 100% of par). The bond sold at $8,640,999 is said to be sold at 86.41 (86.41% of par, computed as $8,640,999/$10,000,000).

EXHIBIT 7.1 ■ Coupon Rate, Market Rate, and Bond Pricing

Coupon rate > market rate	→	Bond sells at a **premium** (above face amount)
Coupon rate = market rate	→	Bond sells at **par** (at face amount)
Coupon rate < market rate	→	Bond sells at a **discount** (below face amount)

Exhibit 7.2 shows an announcement (called a *tombstone*) of the recent **General Electric** $5 billion debt issuance. It is 5% debt, paying 2.5% semiannual interest, maturing in 2013, with an issue price of 99.626 (valued at a discount). GE's underwriters took 0.425 in fees (more than $21 million) for underwriting and selling this debt issue.[6]

EXHIBIT 7.2 ■ Announcement (Tombstone) of Debt Offering to Public

General Electric Company

$5,000,000,000
5% Notes due 2013

Issue price: 99.626%

We will pay interest on the notes semiannually on February 1 and August 1 of each year, beginning August 1, 2003. The notes will mature on February 1, 2013. We may not redeem the notes prior to maturity.

The notes will be unsecured obligations and rank equally with our other unsecured debt securities that are not subordinated obligations. The notes will be issued in registered form in denominations of $1,000.

Neither the Securities and Exchange Commission nor any state securities commission has approved or disapproved of the notes or determined if this prospectus supplement or the accompanying prospectus is truthful or complete. Any representation to the contrary is a criminal offense.

	Per Note	Total
Public Offering Price(1)	99.626%	$4,981,300,000
Underwriting Discounts	.425%	$ 21,250,000
Proceeds to General Electric Company (before expenses)	99.201%	$4,960,050,000

(1) Plus accrued interest from January 28, 2003, if settlement occurs after that date.

The underwriters expect to deliver the notes in book-entry form only through the facilities of The Depository Trust Company, Clearstream, Luxembourg or the Euroclear System, as the case may be, on or about January 28, 2003.

Joint Bookrunners

Lehman Brothers	**Morgan Stanley**	**Salomon Smith Barney**

Senior Co-Managers

Banc of America Securities LLC	Credit Suisse First Boston	Deutsche Bank Securities
Goldman. Sachs & Co.	JPMorgan	Merrill Lynch & Co.
	UBS Warburg	

Co-Managers

Banc One Capital Markets, Inc.	Barclays Capital	Blaylock & Partners, L.P.
BNP PARIBAN	Dresdner Kleinwort Wasserstein	Guzman & Company
HSBC	Loop Capital Markets	Ormes Capital Markets, Inc.
Utendahl Capital Partners, L.P.	The Williams Capital Group, L.P.	

---

[6]The tombstone makes clear that if we purchase any of these notes (in denominations of $1,000) after the semiannual interest date, we must pay accrued interest in addition to the purchase price. This interest is returned to us in the regular interest payment. (This procedure makes the bookkeeping easier for the issuer/underwriter.)

Effective Cost of Debt

$

Cash Effect

When a bond sells for par, the cost to the issuing company is the cash interest paid. In our first illustration above, the *effective cost* of the bond is the 6% interest paid by the issuer.

When a bond sells at a discount, the issuer's effective cost consists of two parts: (1) the cash interest paid and (2) the discount incurred. The discount, which is the difference between par and the lower issue price, is a cost that must eventually be reflected in the issuer's income statement as an expense. This means that the effective cost of a discount bond is greater than if the bond had sold at par. A discount is a cost and, like any other cost, must eventually be transferred from the balance sheet to the income statement as an expense.

When a bond sells at a premium, the issuer's effective cost consists of (1) the cash interest paid and (2) a cost reduction due to the premium received. The premium is a benefit that must eventually find its way from the balance sheet to the income statement as a *reduction* of interest expense. As a result of the premium, the effective cost of a premium bond is less than if the bond had sold at par.

Bonds are priced to yield the return (market rate) demanded by investors, which results in this fact: the effective rate of a bond *always* equals the yield (market) rate demanded by investors, regardless of the coupon (stated) rate of the bond. Bond prices are set by the market so as to always yield the rate demanded by investors based on the terms and qualities of the bond. This means that companies cannot influence the effective cost of debt by raising or lowering the coupon rate. We discuss the factors affecting the yield demanded by investors later in the module.

$

Cash Effect

The effective cost of debt is ultimately reflected in the amount reported in the issuer's income statement as interest expense. This can be, and usually is, different from the cash interest paid. The next section discusses how management reports bonds on the balance sheet and interest expense on the income statement.

■ REPORTING OF DEBT FINANCING

This section identifies and describes the financial statements effects of bond transactions.

Financial Statement Effects of Debt Issuance

Bonds Issued at Par

$

Cash Effect

When a bond sells at par, the issuing company receives the cash proceeds and accepts an obligation to make payments per the bond contract. Specifically, cash is increased and a liability (bonds payable) is increased by the same amount. Using the facts from our illustration above, the issuance of bonds at par has the following financial statement effects (there is no revenue or expense at bond issuance):

Cash   10,000,000
  Bonds
    Payable 10,000,000

	Balance Sheet							Income Statement		
Transaction	Cash Asset	+	Noncash Assets	=	Liabil- ities	+	Contrib. Capital	+	Retained Earnings	Revenues − Expenses
Issue bonds at par for cash	+10,000,000				+10,000,000 Bond Payable, net					

Discount Bonds

When a bond is sold at a discount, the cash proceeds and net bond liability are recorded at the amount of the proceeds received (not the face amount of the bond). Again, using the facts above from our bond discount illustration, the financial statement effects follow:

Cash   8,640,999
Bond
  Discount 1,359,001
  Bonds
    Payable 10,000,000

	Balance Sheet							Income Statement		
Transaction	Cash Asset	+	Noncash Assets	=	Liabil- ities	+	Contrib. Capital	+	Retained Earnings	Revenues − Expenses
Issue bonds at a discount for cash	+8,640,999				+8,640,999 Bond Payable, net					

For the discount bond case, cash is increased by the proceeds from the sale of the bonds, and the liability increases by the same amount. However, this net liability consists of two components as follows:

Bonds payable, face	$10,000,000
Less bond discount	(1,359,001)
Bonds payable, net	$ 8,640,999

Bonds are reported on the balance sheet net of any discount (or premium). When the bond matures, however, the company is obligated to repay $10 million. Accordingly, at maturity, the bond liability needs to read $10 million, the amount that is owed. This means that between the bond issuance and its maturity, the discount must decline to zero. This reduction of the discount over the life of the bond is called **amortization**. The next section shows how discount amortization results in additional interest expense in the income statement. This amortization causes the effective interest expense to be greater than the periodic cash interest payments.

BUSINESS INSIGHT   **Verizon's Zero Coupon Debt**

Zero coupon bonds and notes, called *zeros,* do not carry a coupon rate. The pricing of these bonds and notes is done in the same manner as those with coupon rates—the exception is the absence of an interest annuity. This means that the price is the present value of the principal payment at maturity; hence the bond is sold at a *deep discount.* Following is an example from Verizon's 10-K report:

> *Zero-Coupon Convertible Notes*
> In May 2001, Verizon . . . issued approximately $5.4 billion in principal amount at maturity of zero-coupon convertible notes due 2021, resulting in gross proceeds of approximately $3 billion. The notes are convertible into shares of our common stock at an initial price of $69.50 per share if the closing price of Verizon common stock on the NYSE exceeds specified levels or in other specified circumstances. The conversion price increases by at least 3% a year. The initial conversion price represents a 25% premium over the May 8, 2001 closing price of $55.60 per share. There are no scheduled cash interest payments associated with the notes. The zero-coupon convertible notes are callable by Verizon . . . on or after May 15, 2006. In addition, the notes are redeemable at the option of the holders on May 15th in each of the years 2004, 2006, 2011 and 2016. As of December 31, 2003, the zero-coupon notes were classified as long-term debt maturing within one year since they are redeemable on May 15, 2004.

Verizon's zero-coupon convertible notes have a maturity value of $5.4 billion and mature in 2021. No interest is paid in the interim. The notes were sold for $3 billion. The difference between the $3 billion sales proceeds and the $5.4 billion maturity value represents Verizon's interest costs, which is the return to the investor. The effective cost of the debt is the interest rate that equates the issue price and maturity value, or approximately 3%. These notes are also convertible—an increasingly popular form of debt discussed in Module 8.

Premium Bonds

When a bond is sold at a premium, the cash proceeds and net bond liability are recorded at the amount of the proceeds received (not the face amount of the bond). Again, using the facts above from our premium bond illustration, the financial statement effects follow:

	Balance Sheet					Income Statement		
Transaction	Cash Asset	+ Noncash Assets	= Liabil- ities	+ Contrib. Capital	+ Retained Earnings	Revenues	−	Expenses
Issue bonds at a premium for cash	+11,635,129		+11,635,129 Bond Payable, net					

Cash   11,635,129
  Bond
    Premium 1,635,129
  Bonds
    Payable 10,000,000

The bond liability amount reported on the balance sheet, again, consists of two parts:

Bonds payable, face	$10,000,000
Add bond premium	1,635,129
Bonds payable, net	$11,635,129

The $10 million must be repaid at maturity, and the premium is amortized to zero over the life of the bond. The premium represents a *benefit,* which yields a *reduction* in interest expense on the income statement.

Effects of Discount and Premium Amortization

$
Cash Effect

For bonds issued at par, interest expense reported on the income statement equals the cash interest payment. However, for bonds issued at a discount or premium, interest expense reported on the income statement consists of one of the following two components:

Cash interest paid		Cash interest paid
+ Amortization of discount	or	− Amortization of premium
Interest expense		Interest expense

$
Cash Effect

Specifically, periodic amortization of a discount is added to the cash interest paid to get interest expense for a discount bond. Amortization of the discount reflects the additional cost the issuer incurs from issuance of the bonds at a discount and its recognition, via amortization, as an increase to interest expense. For a premium bond, the premium is a benefit the issuer receives at issuance. Amortization of the premium reduces interest expense over the debt term. In both cases, interest expense on the income statement represents the *effective cost* of debt (the *nominal cost* of debt is the cash interest paid).

Companies amortize discounts and premiums using the effective interest method. To illustrate, recall the assumptions of the discount bond above—face amount of $10 million, a 6% annual coupon rate payable semiannually (3% semiannual rate), a maturity of 10 years, and a market (yield) rate of 8% annual (4% semiannual). These facts resulted in a bond issue price of $8,640,999. Exhibit 7.3 shows the first two and final two periods of a bond discount amortization table for this bond.

EXHIBIT 7.3 ■ Bond Discount Amortization Table

Period	[A] ([E] × market%) Interest Expense	[B] (Face × coupon%) Cash Interest Paid	[C] ([A] − [B]) Discount Amortization	[D] (Prior bal − [C]) Discount Balance	[E] (Face − [D]) Bond Payable, Net
0				$1,359,001	$ 8,640,999
1	$345,640	$300,000	$45,640	1,313,361	8,686,639
2	347,466	300,000	47,488	1,265,895	8,734,105
⋮	⋮	⋮	⋮	⋮	⋮
19	392,458	300,000	92,458	96,087	9,902,188
20	396,088	300,000	96,088	0	10,000,000

The interest period is denoted in the left-most column. Period 0 is the point at which the bond is issued, and period 1 and following are successive six-month periods (recall, interest is paid semiannually). Column [A] is interest expense, which is reported in the income statement. This is computed as the carrying amount of the bond at the beginning of the period (column [E]) multiplied by the 8% yield rate (4% semiannual) used to compute the bond issue price. Column [B] is cash interest paid, which is a constant $300,000 per the bond contract (face amount × coupon rate). Column [C] is discount amortization, which is the difference between interest expense and cash interest paid. Column [D] is the discount balance, which is the previous balance of the discount less the discount amortization in column [C]. Column [E] is the net bond payable, which is the $10 million face amount less the unamortized discount from column [D].

Amounts for interest periods 0, 1, 2, 19, and 20 are shown in the table. The amortization process continues until period 20, at which time the discount balance is 0 and the net bond payable is $10 million

$
Cash Effect

(the maturity value). An amortization table reveals the financial statement effects of the bond for its duration.[7] Specifically, we see the income statement effects in column [A], the cash effects in column [B], and the balance sheet effects in columns [C], [D] and [E].

To illustrate amortization of a premium bond, we use the assumptions of the premium bond above—$10 million face value, a 6% annual coupon rate payable semiannually (3% semiannual rate), a maturity of 10 years, and a 4% annual market (yield) rate (2% semiannual). These parameters resulted in a bond issue price of $11,635,129. Exhibit 7.4 shows the first and last two periods of a bond premium amortization table for this bond.

EXHIBIT 7.4 ■ Bond Premium Amortization Table

Period	[A] ([E] × market%) Interest Expense	[B] (Face × coupon%) Cash Interest Paid	[C] ([B] − [A]) Premium Amortization	[D] (Prior bal − [C]) Premium Balance	[E] (Face + [D]) Bond Payable, Net
0				$1,635,129	$11,635,129
1	$232,703	$300,000	$67,297	1,567,832	11,567,832
2	231,357	300,000	68,643	1,499,188	11,499,188
⋮	⋮	⋮	⋮	⋮	⋮
19	203,883	300,000	96,117	98,018	10,099,068
20	201,981	300,000	98,018	0	10,000,000

Interest expense is computed using the same process that we used for discount bonds. The difference is that the yield rate is 4% (2% semiannual) in the premium case. Also, cash interest paid follows from the bond contract (face amount × coupon rate), and the other columns' computations reflect the premium amortization. After period 20, the premium is fully amortized (equals zero) and the net bond payable balance is $10 million, the amount owed at maturity. Again, an amortization table reveals the financial statement effects of the bond—the income statement effects in column [A], the cash effects in column [B], and the balance sheet effects in columns [C], [D] and [E].

$
Cash Effect

Financial Statement Effects of Bond Repurchase

Companies report bonds payable at *historical (adjusted) cost.* Specifically, net bonds payable amounts follow from the amortization table, as do the related cash flows and income statement numbers. All financial statement relations are set at bond issuance and do not subsequently change.

$
Cash Effect

Once issued, however, bonds are free to trade in secondary markets between bondholders. The yield rate used in these transactions to compute bond prices changes based on the level of interest rates in the economy and the perceived creditworthiness of the bond issuer.

Companies can and sometimes do repurchase (also called *redeem*) their bonds prior to maturity. The bond indenture (contract agreement) may include provisions giving the company the right to repurchase its bond. Or, the company can repurchase bonds in the open market. When a bond repurchase occurs, a gain or loss usually results, and is computed as follows:

Gain or Loss on Bond Repurchase = Bonds Payable, Net − Repurchase Payment

The net bonds payable, also referred to as the *book (carrying) value of the bond,* is the net amount reported on the balance sheet. If the issuer pays more to retire the bonds than the amount carried on its balance sheet, a loss is reported on its income statement, usually called *loss on bond retirement.* The issuer reports a *gain on bond retirement* if the repurchase price is less than the net bonds payable.

GAAP dictates that any gains or losses on bond repurchases are reported as part of ordinary income unless they meet the criteria for treatment as an extraordinary item (unusual and infrequent, see Module 2). Relatively few debt retirements meet these criteria and, hence, most gains and losses on bond repurchases are reported as part of income from continuing operations.

---

[7]A fully completed amortization table is shown in Appendix 7B for illustrative purposes.

$

Cash Effect

How should we treat these gains and losses for analysis purposes? That is, do they carry economic effects? The answer is no—the gain or loss on repurchase is exactly offset by the present value of the future cash flow implications of the repurchase (Appendix 7B demonstrates this).

Another analysis issue involves assessing the market values of bonds and other long-term liabilities. This information is relevant for some investors and creditors in revealing unrealized gains and losses (similar to that reported for marketable securities). GAAP requires companies to provide information about current market values of their long-term liabilities in footnotes (see Verizon's fair value of debt disclosure in the next section). However, these market values are *not* reported on the balance sheet and changes in these market values are not reflected in net income. We must make our own adjustments to the balance sheet and income statement if we want them to reflect changes in market values of liabilities.

Financial Statement Footnotes

Companies are required to disclose details about their long-term liabilities, including the amounts borrowed under each debt issuance, the interest rates, maturity dates, and other key provisions. Following is **Verizon**'s disclosure for its long-term debt ($ millions):

Long-Term Debt

Outstanding long-term obligations are as follows:

At December 31	Interest Rates %	Maturities	2003
Notes payable	1.24–10.05	2004–2032	$17,364
Telephone subsidiaries—debentures and first/refunding mortgage bonds	2.00– 7.00	2004–2042	13,417
	7.15– 7.65	2006–2032	3,625
	7.85– 9.67	2010–2031	2,184
Other subsidiaries—debentures and other	6.36– 8.75	2004–2028	3,926
Zero-coupon convertible notes, net of unamortized discount of $2,198	3.00% yield	2021	3,244
Employee stock ownership plan loans:			
GTE guaranteed obligations	9.73	2005	119
NYNEX debentures	9.55	2010	175
Capital lease obligations (average rate 7.9%) other lease-related debt (average rate 6.0%)			521
Property sale holdbacks held in escrow, vendor financing and other	4.00– 6.00	2004–2005	99
Unamortized discount, net of premium			(81)
Total long-term debt, including current maturities			44,593
Less: debt maturing within one year			(5,180)
Total long-term debt			$39,413

Verizon reports a book value for long-term debt of $44,593 million at year-end 2003. Of this amount, $5,180 million matures in the next year, hence its classification as a current liability (current maturities of long-term debt) and the remainder matures after 2004. Verizon also reports $81 million in unamortized discount (net of premium) on this debt.

In addition to amounts, rates, and due dates on its long-term debt, Verizon reports aggregate maturities for the five years subsequent to its balance sheet date as follows:

Maturities of Long-Term Debt

Maturities of long-term debt outstanding at December 31, 2003 are $5.2 billion in 2004, $5.5 billion in 2005, $3.9 billion in 2006, $2.5 billion in 2007, $2.5 billion in 2008 and $25.1 billion thereafter.

This reveals that Verizon is required to make principal payments of $19.6 billion in the next five years, with $10.7 billion of that coming due in the next two years. Such maturities are important as a company must meet its required payments, negotiate a rescheduling of the indebtedness, or refinance the debt to avoid default. The latter (default) usually has severe consequences as debtholders have legal remedies available to them, that can result in bankruptcy of the company.

Verizon's disclosure on the market value of its total debt follows:

At December 31, 2003 ($ millions)	Carrying Amount	Fair Value
Short- and long-term debt	$45,140	$48,685

As of 2003, indebtedness with a book value of $45,140 million had a market value of $48,685 million, resulting in an unrecognized liability (and loss if redeemed) of $3,545 million (due mainly to a decline in interest rates subsequent to bond issuance). The justification for not recognizing unrealized gains and losses on the balance sheet and income statement is that such amounts can reverse with future fluctuations in interest rates. Further, since only the face amount of debt is repaid at maturity, unrealized gains and losses that arise during intervening years are not necessarily relevant. This is the same logic for nonrecognition of gains and losses on held-to-maturity investments in debt securities.

■ DEBT RATINGS AND THE COST OF DEBT

Earlier in the module we explained that the effective cost of debt to the issuing company is the market (yield) rate of interest used to price the bond, regardless of the bond coupon rate. The market rate of interest is usually defined as the yield on U.S. Government borrowings such as treasury bills, notes, and bonds, called the *risk-free rate,* plus a *spread* (also called risk premium).

Yield Rate = Risk-Free Rate + Spread

Treasury yields (risk-free rates) vary with the maturity of the security, generally increasing as the term increases as shown in the following graph as of 2005:

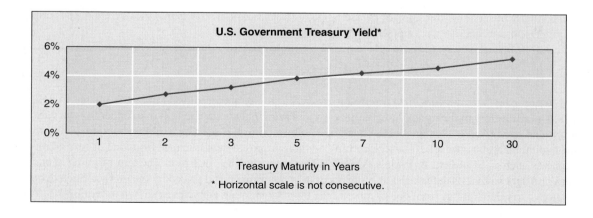

The rate of interest that a company must pay on its debt is a function of the maturity of that debt and the creditworthiness of the issuing company. The rate it pays in excess of the treasury (risk-free) rate for a given debt maturity and risk level of issuer is illustrated in the following graph as of 2005:

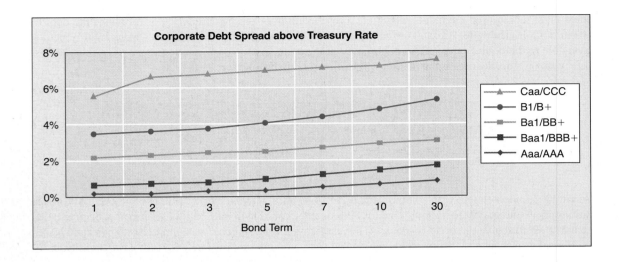

For all maturities, the required market rate increases (shifts upward) as debt quality moves from Aaa/AAA debt, which is the highest quality debt reflected in the line nearest to zero, to the Caa/CCC debt, which is the lowest quality debt reflected in the line nearest to 8%. That is, higher credit-rated issuers warrant a lower rate than lower credit-rated issuers. This difference is substantial. For example, for the 10-year bond, the treasury bond yield is 4.71%, while the Aaa/AAA corporate bond yield is 5.31% (a 0.60% or 60 basis-point spread). However, the low quality, high risk Caa/CCC bond yield is 11.86% (4.71% + 7.15%), which is a 7.15% or 715 basis point spread.

RESEARCH INSIGHT   **Accounting Conservatism and Cost of Debt**

Research indicates that companies applying more conservative accounting incur a lower cost of debt. Research also suggests that while accounting conservatism can lead to lower quality accounting income (because such income does not fully reflect economic reality), creditors are more confident in the numbers and view them as more credible. Evidence also implies that companies can lower the required return demanded by creditors (the spread) by issuing high quality financial reports that include enhanced footnote disclosures and detailed supplemental reports.

A company's debt rating, also referred to as credit quality and creditworthiness, is related to default risk. **Default** refers to the nonpayment of interest and principal and/or the failure to adhere to the various terms and conditions (covenants) of the bond indenture. Companies seeking to obtain bond financing from the capital markets, normally first seek a rating on their proposed debt issuance from one of several rating agencies such as **Standard & Poor's, Moody's Investors Service,** or **Fitch**. The aim of rating agencies is to rate debt so that its default risk is more accurately determined and priced by the market. Such debt issuances carry debt ratings from one or more of the three large rating agencies as shown in Exhibit 7.5. This exhibit includes the general description attached to the debt for each rating class—for example, AAA is assigned to debt of prime maximum safety (maximum creditworthiness).

EXHIBIT 7.5 ▩ Corporate Debt Ratings and Descriptions

Moody's	S&P	Fitch	Description
Aaa	AAA	AAA	Prime Maximum Safety
Aa1	AA+	AA+	High Grade, High Quality
Aa2	AA	AA	
Aa3	AA−	AA−	
A1	A+	A+	Upper-Medium Grade
A2	A	A	
A3	A−	A−	
Baa1	BBB+	BBB+	Lower-Medium Grade
Baa2	BBB	BBB	
Baa3	BBB−	BBB−	
Ba1	BB+	BB+	Non-Investment Grade
Ba2	BB	BB	Speculative
Ba3	BB−	BB−	
B1	B+	B+	Highly Speculative
B2	B	B	
B3	B−	B−	
Caa1	CCC+	CCC	Substantial Risk
Caa2	CCC		In Poor Standing
Caa3	CCC−		
Ca			Extremely Speculative
C			May be in Default
		DDD	Default
		DD	
	D	D	

MANAGERIAL DECISION **You Are the Vice President of Finance**

Your company is currently rated B1/B+ by credit rating agencies. You are considering possible financial and other restructurings of the company to increase your credit rating. What types of restructurings might you consider? What benefits will your company receive from those restructurings? What costs will your company incur to implement such restructurings? [Answer, p. 7-29]

Verizon bonds are rated A1/A+ as of 2004. It is this rating that, in conjunction with the maturity of its bonds, establishes the market interest rate and consequent selling price. There are a number of considerations that affect the rating of a bond. **Standard & Poor's** list the following factors among its credit rating criteria:

Business Risk
  Industry characteristics
  Competitive position (e.g., marketing, technology, efficiency, regulation)
  Management
Financial Risk
  Financial characteristics
  Financial policy
  Profitability
  Capital structure
  Cash flow protection
  Financial flexibility

Debt ratings are set from the point of view of the debt investor. Debt investors are mainly interested in assessing the probability that the interest and principal payments are made on time by the borrower. If a company defaults on its debt, debtholders possess several legal remedies, including the potential to require asset liquidation to settle obligations. However, in this eventuality, debtholders rarely realize the entire amounts owed to them.

Standard and Poor's uses several financial ratios to assess default risk. A listing of these ratios, together with median averages for various risk classes as of 2005, is in Exhibit 7.6. In examining the ratios, recall that debt is regarded as increasingly more risky as we move from the first column, AAA, to the last, CCC.[8]

EXHIBIT 7.6 ■ Ratio Values for Different Risk Classes of Corporate Debt*

Three-Year Medians	AAA	AA	A	BBB	BB	B	CCC
EBIT interest coverage (×)	21.4	10.1	6.1	3.7	2.1	0.8	0.1
EBITDA interest coverage (×)	26.5	12.9	9.1	5.8	3.4	1.8	1.3
FFO/total debt (%)	128.8	55.4	43.2	30.8	18.8	7.8	1.6
Free oper. cash flow/total debt (%)	84.2	25.2	15.0	8.5	2.6	(3.2)	(12.9)
Return on capital (%)	34.9	21.7	19.4	13.6	11.6	6.6	1.0
Operating income/sales (%)	27.0	22.1	18.6	15.4	15.9	11.9	11.9
Long-term debt/capital (%)	13.3	28.2	33.9	42.5	57.2	69.7	68.8
Total debt/capital (incl. STD) (%)	22.9	37.7	42.5	48.2	62.6	74.8	87.7

*Corporate Ratings Criteria—Adjusted Key Financial Ratios, Standard & Poor's Ratings, Released 2002, Standard & Poor's, a division of The McGraw-Hill Companies (reproduced with permission).

A review of these ratios indicates that the following factors are considered relevant by S&P in evaluating the ability of a company to meet its debt service requirements:

1. Liquidity (ratios 1 through 4)
2. Profitability (ratios 5 and 6)
3. Solvency (ratios 7 and 8)

Further, these ratios are variants of many of the ratios we describe in Module 3.

[8]Definitions for the key ratios in this Exhibit follow:

$$\text{EBIT interest coverage} = \frac{\text{Earnings from continuing operations before interest and taxes}}{\text{Gross interest incurred before subtracting (1) capitalized interest and (2) interest income}}$$

$$\text{EBITDA interest coverage} = \frac{\text{Earnings from continuing operations before interest and taxes, depreciation, and amortization}}{\text{Gross interest incurred before subtracting (1) capitalized interest and (2) interest income}}$$

$$\text{Funds from operations/total debt} = \frac{\text{Net income from continuing operations plus depreciation, amortization, deferred income taxes, and other noncash items}}{\text{Long-term debt plus current maturities, commercial paper, and other short-term borrowings}}$$

$$\text{Free operating cash flow/total debt} = \frac{\text{Funds from operations minus capital expenditures, minus (plus) the increase (decrease) in working capital (excluding changes in cash, marketable securities, and short-term debt)}}{\text{Long-term debt plus current maturities, commercial paper, and other short-term borrowings}}$$

$$\text{Return on capital} = \frac{\text{Earnings from continuing operations before interest and taxes}}{\text{Average of beginning of year and end of year capital, including short-term debt, current maturities, long-term debt, noncurrent deferred taxes, and equity}}$$

$$\text{Operating income/sales} = \frac{\text{Sales minus cost of goods manufactured (before depreciation and amortization), selling, general and administrative, and research and development costs}}{\text{Sales}}$$

$$\text{Long-term debt/capital} = \frac{\text{Long-term debt}}{\text{Long-term debt + shareholders' equity (including preferred stock) plus minority interest}}$$

$$\text{Total debt/capital} = \frac{\text{Long-term debt plus current maturities, commercial paper, and other short-term borrowings}}{\text{Long-term debt plus current maturities, commercial paper, and other short-term borrowings + shareholders' equity (including preferred stock) plus minority interest}}$$

There are other relevant factors in setting debt ratings such as the following:

- **Collateral**   Companies can provide security for debt in the form of mortgages on assets. To the extent debt is secured, the debtholder is in a preferred position vis-à-vis other creditors.
- **Covenants**   Debt agreements (indentures) can contain restrictions on the issuing company to protect debtholders. Examples are restrictions on excessive dividend payment, on other company acquisitions, on further borrowing, and on maintaining minimum levels for key liquidity and solvency ratios. These covenants provide debtholders some means of control over the issuer's operations since, unlike equity investors, they do not have voting rights.
- **Options**   Debt obligations involve contracts between the borrowing company and debtholders. Options are sometimes written into debt contracts. Examples are options to convert debt into stock (so that debtholders have a stake in value creation) and options allowing the issuing company to repurchase its debt before maturity (usually at a premium).

RESEARCH INSIGHT   **Valuation of Debt Options**

Debt instruments can include features such as conversion options, under which the debt can be converted to common stock. Such conversion features are not accounted for separately under GAAP. Instead, convertible debt is accounted for just like debt with no conversion features (unless the conversion option can be separately traded). However, option-pricing models can be used to estimate the value of such debt features even when no market for those features exist. Empirical results suggest that those debt features represent a substantial part of debt value. These findings contribute to the current debate regarding the separation of compound financial instruments into debt and equity portions for financial statement presentation and analysis.

■ MODULE-END REVIEW ■

On January 1, 2005, Hogan Company issues $300,000 of 15-year, 10% bonds payable for $351,876, yielding an effective interest rate of 8%. Interest is payable semiannually on June 30 and December 31. (1) Show computations to confirm the issue price of $351,876, and (2) complete Hogan's financial statement effects template for (a) bond issuance, (b) semiannual interest payment and premium amortization on June 30, 2005, and (c) semiannual interest payment and premium amortization on December 31, 2005.

Solution

1.

Issue price for $300,000, 15-year, 10% semiannual bonds discounted at 8%:	
Present value of principal payment ($300,000 × 0.30832)	$ 92,496
Present value of semiannual interest payments ($15,000 × 17.29203)	259,380
Issue price of bonds	$351,876

2.

	Balance Sheet					Income Statement		
Transaction	**Cash Asset** +	**Noncash Assets** =	**Liabil- ities** +	**Contrib. Capital** +	**Retained Earnings**	**Revenues** −	**Expenses**	
a. Issuance	+351,876		+351,876 Bond Payable, net					
b. Interest and amortization[1]	− 15,000		− 925 Bond Payable, net		−14,075		− 14,075 Bond Interest Expense	
c. Interest and amortization[2]	− 15,000		− 962 Bond Payable, net		−14,038		− 14,038 Bond Interest Expense	

Cash	351,876
Bond Premium	51,876
Bond Payable	300,000
Bond Int. Exp.	14,075
Bond Premium	925
Cash	15,000
Bond Int. Exp.	14,038
Bond Premium	962
Cash	15,000

[1]$300,000 × 0.10 × 6/12 = $15,000 cash payment; 0.04 × $351,876 = $14,075 interest expense; the difference is the bond premium amortization, a reduction of the net bond carrying amount.

[2]0.04 × ($351,876 − $925) = $14,038 interest expense. The difference between this amount and the $15,000 cash payment is the premium amortization, a reduction of the net bond carrying amount.

APPENDIX 7A

Compound Interest

This appendix explains the concepts of present and future value.

Present Value Concepts

Would we rather receive a dollar now or a dollar one year from now? Most people would answer, 'a dollar now.' Intuition tells us that a dollar received now is more valuable than the same amount received sometime in the future. Sound reasons exist for choosing the earlier dollar, the most obvious of which concerns risk. Since the future is uncertain, an event can prevent us from receiving the dollar at the later date. To avoid this risk, we choose the earlier date. Another reason for choosing the earlier date is that the dollar received now could be invested. That is, one year from now, we have the dollar and the interest earned on that dollar.

Present Value of a Single Amount

Risk and interest factors yield the following generalizations: (1) the right to receive an amount of money now—its **present value**—is worth more than the right to receive the same amount later—its future value; (2) the longer we must wait to receive an amount, the less attractive the receipt is (the difference between the present value of an amount and its future value is a function of interest, that is, Principal × Interest Rate × Time); and (3) the more risk associated with any situation, the higher the interest rate.

To illustrate, let's compute the present value equivalent to receiving $100 one year from now if money can be invested at 10%. We recognize intuitively that, with a 10% interest rate, we should accept less than $100. We base this estimate on the realization that the $100 received in the future must equal the present value (100%) plus interest (10%) on the present value. Thus, the $100 future receipt must be 1.10 times the present value. Dividing $100/1.10, we obtain a present value of $90.91 (rounded). This means that we would do as well to accept $90.91 now as to wait one year and receive $100. To confirm the equality of the $90.91 receipt now to a $100 receipt one year later, we calculate the future value of $90.91 at 10% for one year as follows:

$$\$90.91 \times 1.10 \times 1 \text{ year} = \$100 \text{ (rounded)}$$

To generalize, we compute the present value of a future receipt by *discounting* the future receipt back to the present at an appropriate interest rate. We present this schematically below:

Present Value	←	Discounted for	←	Future Value
$90.91		1 year at 10%		$100

If either the time period or the interest rate were increased, the resulting present value would decrease. If more than one time period is involved, our future receipts include interest on interest. This is called *compounding*.

Present Value Tables

Table 1 in Appendix A near the end of the book can be used to compute the present value amounts in this section. A present value table provides multipliers for many combinations of time periods and interest rates that, when applied to the dollar amount of a future cash flow, determines its present value.

Present value tables are used as follows. First, determine the number of interest compounding periods involved (three years compounded annually are 3 periods, and three years compounded semiannually are 6 periods). The extreme left-hand column indicates the number of periods.

Next, determine the interest rate per compounding period. Interest rates are usually quoted on a *per year* (annual) basis. The rate per compounding period is the annual rate divided by the number of compounding periods per year. For example, an interest rate of 10% per year would be 10% per period if compounded annually, and 5% per period if compounded semiannually.

Finally, locate the present value factor, which is that value to the right of the appropriate number of compounding periods and beneath the appropriate interest rate per compounding period. Multiply this factor by the number of dollars involved.

All values in Table 1 are less than 1.0 because the present value is always smaller than the $1 future amount. As the interest rate increases (moving from left to right in the table) or the number of periods increases (moving from top to bottom), the present value multipliers decline. This illustrates two important facts: (1) present values decline as interest rates increase, and (2) present values decline as the time to receipt lengthens. Consider the following two cases:

Case 1. Compute the present value of $100 to be received one year from today, discounted at 10% interest compounded annually:

Number of periods (one year, annually) = 1
Rate per period (10%/1) = 10%
Multiplier = 0.90909
Present value = $100.00 × 0.90909 = $90.91 (rounded)

Case 2. Compute the present value of $116.99 to be received two years from today, discounted at 8% compounded *semiannually*:

Number of periods (two years, semiannually) = 4
Rate per period (8%/2) = 4%
Multiplier = 0.85480
Present value = $116.99 × 0.85480 = $100.00 (rounded)

Present Value of an Annuity

We can compute the present value of any single future amount (or series of future amounts) using present value tables like Table 1. One frequent pattern of amounts, however, is subject to a more convenient treatment. This pattern, known as an **annuity**, can be described as *equal amounts equally spaced over a period.*

To illustrate, assume $100 is to be received at the end of each of the next three years as an annuity. When annuity amounts occur at the *end of each period*, the annuity is called an *ordinary annuity.* As shown below, the present value of this ordinary annuity can be computed from Table 1 by computing the present value of each of the three individual receipts and summing them (assume a 5% annual rate).

Case 3.

Future Receipts (ordinary annuity)			PV Multiplier (Table 1)		Present Value
Year 1	Year 2	Year 3			
$100			× 0.95238	=	$ 95.24
	$100		× 0.90703	=	90.70
		$100	× 0.86384	=	86.38
			2.72325		$272.32

Table 2 in Appendix A provides a single multiplier for computing the present value of a series of future amounts in the ordinary annuity form. Referring to Table 2 in the three periods hence row and the 5% column, we see that the multiplier is 2.72325. When applied to the $100 annuity amount, the multiplier gives a present value of $272.33. As shown above, the same present value (with 1 cent rounding error) is derived using several multipliers from Table 1. For annuities of 5, 10, or 20 years, considerable computations are avoided by using annuity tables.

Bond Valuation

We already explained that (1) a bond agreement specifies a pattern of future cash flows—usually a series of interest payments and a single payment of the face amount at maturity, and (2) bonds are sold at premiums or discounts to adjust their coupon rates to the prevailing market rate at issuance. The selling price (or valuation) of a bond that yields a specific rate is determined as follows:

1. Use Table 1 to compute the present value of the future principal payment at the desired (effective) rate.
2. Use Table 2 to compute the present value of the future series of interest payments at the desired (effective) rate.
3. Add the present values from steps 1 and 2.

We illustrate in Exhibit 7A.1 the pricing of a $100,000 issuance of 8%, 4-year bonds paying interest semiannually and sold on the date of issue to yield (1) 8%, (2) 10% or (3) 6%. Note that the price of 8% bonds sold to yield 8% is the face (or par) value of the bonds. A bond issue price of $93,537 (discount bond) yields 10%. A bond issue price of $107,019 (premium bond) yields 6%.

EXHIBIT 7A.1 ▦ Calculation of Bond Price Using Present Value Tables

(1) $100,000 of 8%, 4-year bonds with interest payable semiannually priced to yield 8%.

Future Cash Flows	Multiplier (Table 1)	Multiplier (Table 2)	Present Values at 4% Semiannually
Principal payment, $100,000 (a single amount received 8 semiannual periods hence)	0.73069		$ 73,069
Interest payments, $4,000 at end of each of 8 semiannual periods		6.73274	26,931
Present value (issue price) of bonds			$100,000

(2) $100,000 of 8%, 4-year bonds with interest payable semiannually priced to yield 10%.

Future Cash Flows	Multiplier (Table 1)	Multiplier (Table 2)	Present Values at 5% Semiannually
Principal payment, $100,000 (a single amount received 8 semiannual periods hence)	0.67684		$67,684
Interest payments, $4,000 at end of each of 8 semiannual periods		6.46321	25,853
Present value (issue price) of bonds			$93,537

(3) $100,000 of 8%, 4-year bonds with interest payable semiannually priced to yield 6%.

Future Cash Flows	Multiplier (Table 1)	Multiplier (Table 2)	Present Values at 3% Semiannually
Principal repayment, $100,000 (a single amount received 8 semiannual periods hence)	0.78941		$ 78,941
Interest payments, $4,000 at end of each of 8 semiannual periods		7.01969	28,078
Present value (issue price) of bonds			$107,019

Future Value Concepts

Future Value of a Single Amount

The **future value** of a single sum is the amount that a specific investment is worth at a future date if invested at a given rate of compound interest. To illustrate, suppose that we decide to invest $6,000 in a savings account that pays 6% annual interest and we intend to leave the principal and interest in the account for five years. We assume that interest is credited to the account at the end of each year. The balance in the account at the end of five years is determined using Table 3 in Appendix A, which gives the future value of a dollar after a given number of time periods, as follows:

Principal	×	Factor	=	Future Value
$6,000	×	1.33823	=	$8,029

The factor 1.33823 is in the row for five periods and the column for 6%.

Next, suppose that the interest is credited to the account semiannually rather than annually. In this situation, there are 10 compounding periods, and we use a 3% semiannual rate (one-half the annual rate since there are two compounding periods per year). The future value calculation follows:

Principal	×	Factor	=	Future Value
$6,000	×	1.34392	=	$8,064

Future Value of an Annuity

If, instead of investing a single amount at the beginning of a series of periods, we invest a specified amount *each period*, then we are investing in an annuity. To illustrate, assume that we decide to invest $2,000 at the end of each year for five years at an 8% annual rate of return. To determine the accumulated amount of principal and interest, we refer to Table 4 in Appendix A, which furnishes the future value of a dollar invested at the end of each period. The factor 5.867 is in the row for five periods and the column for 8%, and the calculation is as follows:

Periodic Payment	×	Factor	=	Future Value
$2,000	×	5.86660	=	$11,733

If we decide to invest $1,000 at the end of each six months for five years at an 8% annual rate of return, we would use the factor for 10 periods at 4%, as follows:

Periodic Payment	×	Factor	=	Future Value
$1,000	×	12.00611	=	$12,006

APPENDIX 7B

Economics of Gains and Losses on Bond Repurchases

Is a reported gain or loss on bond repurchases before maturity of economic substance? The short answer is no. To illustrate, assume that on January 1, a company issues $50 million face value bonds with an 8% annual coupon rate. The interest is to be paid semiannually (4% each semiannual period) for a term of five years (10 semiannual periods), at which time the principal is due and payable. The bond issue price, if investors demand a 10% annual return (5% semiannually) on their investment, is computed as follows:

Present value of semiannual interest ($2,000,000 × 7.72173)	=	$15,443,460
Present value of principal ($50,000,000 × 0.61391)	=	30,695,500
Present value of bond	=	$46,138,960

This bond's amortization table follows:

Period	[A] ([E] × market%) Interest Expense	[B] (Face × coupon%) Cash Interest Paid	[C] ([A] − [B]) Discount Amortization	[D] (Prior bal − [C]) Discount Balance	[E] (Face − [D]) Bond Payable, Net
0				$3,861,040	$46,138,960
1	$2,306,948	$2,000,000	$306,948	3,554,092	46,445,908
2	2,322,295	2,000,000	322,295	3,231,797	46,768,203
3	2,338,410	2,000,000	338,410	2,893,386	47,106,614
4	2,355,331	2,000,000	355,331	2,538,056	47,461,944
5	2,373,097	2,000,000	373,097	2,164,959	47,835,041
6	2,391,752	2,000,000	391,752	1,773,206	48,226,794
7	2,411,340	2,000,000	411,340	1,361,867	48,638,133
8	2,431,907	2,000,000	431,907	929,960	49,070,040
9	2,453,502	2,000,000	453,502	476,458	49,523,542
10	2,476,458	2,000,000	476,458	0	50,000,000

Next, assume we are at period 6 (three years after issuance) and the market rate of interest for this bond has risen from 10% at the time of issuance to 12% currently. The firm then decides to retire (redeem) the outstanding bond issue and finances it through issuance of a new bond issue. That is, it issues bonds with a face amount equal to the market value of the existing issue and uses the proceeds to retire the existing issue. The new issue will have a term of two years (four semiannual periods), the remaining life of the existing bond issue.

At the end of the third year, there are four semiannual payments of interest remaining in the amount of $2,000,000 each plus the repayment of the face amount of the bond at the end of the fourth period. The present value of this cash flow stream, discounted at the current 12% annual rate (6% semiannual rate) is:

Present value of semiannual interest ($2,000,000 × 3.46511)	=	$ 6,930,220
Present value of principal ($50,000,000 × 0.79209)	=	39,604,500
Present value of bond	=	$46,534,720

This means the company pays $46,534,720 to redeem a bond that is on its books at a carrying amount of $48,226,794. The difference of $1,692,074 is reported as a gain on repurchase (also called *redemption*). GAAP requires this gain be reported in income from continuing operations unless it meets the tests for treatment as an extraordinary item (both unusual and infrequent).

Although the company reports a gain in its income statement, has it actually realized an economic gain? Consider that this company issues new bonds when the previous ones are redeemed that carry a coupon rate of 12% (6% semiannually) for $46,534,720. Since we assume that those bonds are sold with a coupon rate equal to the market rate, they will sell at par (no discount or premium). The interest expense per six-month period, therefore, equals the interest paid in the amount of $2,792,083 ($46,534,720 × 6%). Total expense for the four-period life of the bond is $11,168,333 ($2,792,083 × 4). That amount, plus the $46,534,720 face amount of bonds due at maturity, results in total bond payments of $57,703,053. Had this company not redeemed the bonds, it would have paid four additional interest payments of $2,000,000 each plus the face amount of $50,000,000 at maturity, for total bond payments of $58,000,000. On the surface, it appears that the firm is able to save $296,947 by redeeming the bonds and, therefore, reports a gain.[9]

However, this gain is misleading. Specifically, this gain has two components. First, interest payments increase by $792,083 per year ($2,792,083 − $2,000,000). Second, the face amount of the bond that must be repaid in four years decreases by $3,465,280 ($50,000,000 − $46,534,720). To evaluate whether a real gain has been realized, we must consider the present value of these cash outflows and savings. The present value of the increased interest outflow, a four-period annuity of $792,083 discounted at 6% per period, is **$2,744,655** ($792,083 × 3.46511). The present value of the reduced maturity amount, $3,465,280 in four periods hence, is **$2,744,814** ($3,465,280 × 0.79209)—note: the two amounts differ by $159, and would be equal if we used more significant digits.

This analysis shows there is no real economic gain. The present value of the increased interest payments exactly offsets the present value of the decreased amount due at maturity. Why, then, does GAAP yield a gain? The answer lies in use of historical costing. Bonds are reported at amortized cost, that is, the face amount less any applicable discount or plus any premium. These amounts are a function of the bond issue price and its yield rate at issuance, which are both fixed for the bond duration. Market prices for bonds, however, vary continually with changes in market interest rates. Companies do not adjust bond liabilities for these changes in market value. As a result, when bonds are redeemed, their carrying amount differs from market value and GAAP reports a gain or loss equal to this difference.

GUIDANCE ANSWERS

> **MANAGERIAL DECISION**   **You Are the Vice President of Finance**
>
> The types of restructurings you might consider are those yielding a strengthening of the financial ratios typically used to assess liquidity and solvency by the rating agencies. Such restructurings typically include inventory reduction to generate cash, the reallocation of cash outflows from investing activities (PPE) to debt reduction, and issuing stock for cash used to reduce debt (an equity for debt recapitalization). These actions increase liquidity or reduce financial leverage and, thus, should yield an improved debt rating. An improved debt rating gives your company access to more debtholders as your current debt rating is below investment grade and is not a suitable investment for many professionally managed portfolios. It also yields a lower interest rate on your debt. Offsetting these benefits are costs such as the following: (1) potential loss of sales from inventory stockouts; (2) potential future cash flow reductions and loss of market power from reduced investing in PPE; and (3) costs of equity issuances (which is more than debt since investors demand a higher return to compensate for added risk and the lack of tax deductibility of dividends vis-à-vis interest payments), which can yield a net increase in the total cost of capital. All cost and benefits must be assessed before you pursue any restructurings.

Superscript ᴬ(ᴮ) denotes assignments based on Appendix 7A (7B).

■ DISCUSSION QUESTIONS

Q7-1. What does the term *current liabilities* mean? What assets are usually used to settle current liabilities?

Q7-2. What is an accrual? How do accruals impact the balance sheet and the income statement?

Q7-3. What is the difference between a bond coupon rate and its market interest rate (yield)?

---

[9]Also, total interest expense on the new bond issue is $3,168,333 ($11,168,333 − $8,000,000) more than it would have recorded under the old issue. So, although it is recording a present gain, it also incurs future higher interest costs which are not recognized under GAAP.

Q7-4. How does issuing a bond at a premium or discount affect the bond's *effective* interest rate vis-à-vis the coupon (stated) rate?

Q7-5. Why do companies report a gain or loss on the repurchase of their bonds (assuming the repurchase price is different from bond book value)? Is this gain or loss a real economic gain or loss?

Q7-6. How do debt ratings affect the cost of borrowing for a company?

Q7-7.[B] How would you interpret a company's reported gain or loss on the repurchase of its bonds?

■ MINI EXERCISES

M7-8. Analyzing and Computing Financial Statement Effects of Bond Interest   DeFond Company gave a creditor a 90-day, 8% note payable for $7,200 on December 16. Complete the following template to illustrate the effects of the year-end December 31 accounting adjustment DeFond must make.

	Balance Sheet										Income Statement		
Transaction	Cash Asset	+	Noncash Assets	=	Liabil- ities	+	Contrib. Capital	+	Retained Earnings		Revenues	−	Expenses

M7-9. Analyzing and Determining the Amount of a Liability   For each of the following situations, indicate the liability amount, if any, that is reported on the balance sheet of Basu, Inc., at December 31, 2005.

    a.   Basu owes $110,000 at year-end 2005 for its inventory purchases.

    b.   Basu agreed to purchase a $28,000 drill press in January 2006.

    c.   During November and December of 2005, Basu sold products to a firm and warranted them against product failure for 90 days. Estimated 2006 costs of honoring this warranty are $2,200.

    d.   Basu provides a profit-sharing bonus for its executives equal to 5% of its reported pretax annual income. The estimated pretax income for 2005 is $600,000. Bonuses are not paid until January of the following year.

M7-10. Interpreting Relations between Bond Price, Coupon, Yield, and Rating   The following notice appeared in *The Wall Street Journal* regarding a bond issuance by Boston Scientific (BSX):

> **Boston Scientific Corp.**—$500 million of notes was priced with the following terms in two parts via joint lead managers Merrill Lynch & Co., UBS Securities and Wachovia:
>
>   Amount: $250 million; Maturity: Jan. 12, 2011; Coupon: 4.25%; Price: 99.476;
>   Yield: 4.349%; Ratings: Baa1 (Moody's), A− (S&P).
>   Amount: $250 million; Maturity: Jan. 12, 2017; Coupon: 5.125%; Price: 99.926;
>   Yield: 5.134%; Ratings: Baa1 (Moody's), A− (S&P).

    a.   Discuss the relation between the coupon rate, issuance price, and yield for the 2011 issue.

    b.   Compare the yields on the two bond issues. Why are the yields different when the bond ratings are the same?

M7-11. Determining Gain or Loss on Bond Redemption   On April 30, 2005, one year before maturity, Easton Company retired $200,000 of its 9% bonds payable at the current market price of 101 (101% of the bond face amount, or $200,000 × 1.01= $202,000). The bond book value on April 30, 2005, is $197,600 reflecting an unamortized discount of $2,400. Bond interest is presently fully paid and recorded up to the date of retirement. What is the gain or loss on retirement of these bonds? Is this gain or loss a real economic gain or loss? Explain.

M7-12. Interpreting Bond Footnote   Bristol-Myers Squibb (BMY) reports the following maturities schedule for its long-term debt in its 2003 10-K report:

		Payments Due by Period			
Dollars in Millions	Total	2004	2005–2006	2007–2008	Later Years
Long-Term Debt	$8,522	$13	$2,616	$545	$5,348

    a.   What does the $2,616 million indicate for the 2005–2006 time period?

    b.   What implications does this payment schedule have for your evaluation of BMY's liquidity and solvency?

M7-13. **Classifying Debt Accounts into the Balance Sheet or Income Statement**   Indicate the proper financial statement classification (balance sheet or income statement) for each of the following accounts:

a.   Gain on Bond Retirement   e.   Bond Interest Expense
b.   Discount on Bonds Payable   f.   Bond Interest Payable (due next period)
c.   Mortgage Notes Payable   g.   Premium on Bonds Payable
d.   Bonds Payable   h.   Loss on Bond Retirement

Comcast Corporation (CMC)

M7-14. **Interpreting Bond Footnote Disclosures**   Comcast Corporation reports the following footnote to the long-term debt section of its 2003 10-K report:

> **Debt Covenants**
>
> Certain of our subsidiaries' loan agreements require that we maintain financial ratios based on debt, interest and operating income before depreciation and amortization, as defined in the agreements. In addition, certain of our subsidiary loan agreements contain restrictions on dividend payments and advances of funds to us. We were in compliance with all financial covenants for all periods presented. As of December 31, 2003, $50 million of our cash, cash equivalents and short-term investments is restricted under contractual or other arrangements. Restricted net assets of our subsidiaries were approximately $368 million as of December 31, 2003.

a.   The financial ratios to which Comcast refers are similar to those discussed in the section on debt ratings and the cost of debt. What effects might these ratios have on the degree of freedom that management has in running Comcast?

b.   Violation of debt covenants is a serious event that typically triggers an 'immediately due and payable' provision in the debt contract. What pressures might you envision for management if the company's ratios are near their covenant limits?

c.   Comcast reports that certain of its assets are restricted by its bond covenants. What implications do these restrictions have on your analysis of the company and its liquidity and solvency position?

M7-15. **Analyzing Financial Statement Effects of Bond Redemption**   Holthausen Corporation issued $400,000 of 11%, 20-year bonds at 108 on January 1, 2000. Interest is payable semiannually on June 30 and December 31. Through January 1, 2005, Holthausen amortized $5,000 of the bond premium. On January 1, 2005, Holthausen retires the bonds at 103. Using the financial statement effects template from M7-8, indicate the financial statement effects of the bond retirement for January 1, 2005.

M7-16. **Analyzing Financial Statement Effects of Bond Redemption**   Dechow, Inc., issued $250,000 of 8%, 15-year bonds at 96 on July 1, 2000. Interest is payable semiannually on December 31 and June 30. Through June 30, 2006, Dechow amortized $3,000 of the bond discount. On July 1, 2006, Dechow retired the bonds at 101. Using the financial statement effects template from M7-8, indicate the financial statement effects of the bond retirement for June 30, 2006.

M7-17. **Analyzing and Computing Accrued Interest on Notes**   Compute any interest accrued for each of the following notes payable owed by Penman, Inc., as of December 31, 2005 (use a 365-day year):

Lender	Issuance Date	Principal	Coupon Rate (%)	Term
Nissim	11/21/05	$18,000	10%	120 days
Klein	12/13/05	14,000	9	90 days
Bildersee	12/19/05	16,000	12	60 days

General Mills (GIS)

M7-18. **Debt Ratings and Capital Structure**   General Mills reports the following information in the Management Discussion & Analysis section of its 2003 10-K report:

> Free cash flow allowed us to reduce debt to $9.0 billion at the end of 2003. As we complete the integration of Pillsbury, we expect our free cash flow to increase, and have set a target to pay down a cumulative $2 billion of our total adjusted debt over the next three years, including at least $450 million in fiscal 2004. The goal of our debt reduction plan is to return to a mid-A rating for our corporate debt. Currently, Standard and Poor's Corporation has ratings of "BBB+" on our publicly held long-term debt.

a.   Why will debt reduction result in a higher debt rating for General Mills' bonds?
b.   What effect will a higher debt rating have on General Mills' financing costs? Explain.

M7-19. **Computing Bond Issue Price**   Bushman, Inc., issues $500,000 of 9% bonds that pay interest semiannually and mature in 10 years. Compute the bond issue price assuming that the bonds' market rate is:

    a.   8% per year compounded semiannually.

    b.   10% per year compounded semiannually.

M7-20. **Computing Issue Price for Zero Coupon Bonds**   Bushman, Inc., issues $500,000 of zero coupon bonds that mature in 10 years. Compute the bond issue price assuming that the bonds' market rate is:

    a.   8% per year compounded semiannually.

    b.   10% per year compounded semiannually.

M7-21. **Financial Statement Effects of Accounts Payable Transactions**   Petroni Company had the following transactions relating to its accounts payable:

    a.   Purchases $300 of inventory on credit.

    b.   Sells $300 of inventory for $420 on credit (cost side recorded in part *c*).

    c.   Records $300 cost of sales with transaction *b*.

    d. $300 cash paid to settle accounts payable from *a*.

    e. $420 cash received from accounts receivable in *b*.

Use the financial statement effects template shown in M7-8 to identify the effects (both amounts and accounts) of these transactions.

M7-22. **Computing Bond Issue Price and Preparing an Amortization Table in Excel**   On January 1, 2005, Bushman, Inc., issues $500,000 of 9% bonds that pay interest semiannually and mature in 10 years (December 31, 2014).

    a.   Using the Excel PRICE worksheet function, compute the issue price assuming that the bonds' market rate is 8% per year compounded semiannually. (Use 100 for the redemption value to get a price as a percentage of the face amount, and use 1 for the basis.)

    b.   Prepare an amortization table in Excel to demonstrate the amortization of the book (carrying) value to the $500,000 maturity value at the end of the 20th semiannual period.

■ EXERCISES

E7-23. **Analyzing and Computing Accrued Warranty Liability and Expense**   Waymire Company sells a motor that carries a 60-day unconditional warranty against product failure. Waymire estimates that between the sale and lapse of the product warranty, 2% of the 69,000 units sold this period will require repair at an average cost of $50 per unit. Warranty costs for 1,000 known failures are already reflected in its financial statements, resulting in a current warranty liability of $10,000 on the balance sheet.

    a.   How much *additional* warranty expense must Waymire report in its income statement and what amount of *additional* warranty liability must it report on its balance sheet for this year?

    b.   What analysis issues do we need to consider with respect to the amount of reported warranty liability?

E7-24. **Analyzing Contingencies and Assessing Liabilities**   The following independent situations represent various types of liabilities. Analyze each situation and indicate which of the following is the proper accounting treatment for the company in boldface type: (a) record in accounts, (b) disclose in a financial statement footnote, or (c) neither record nor disclose.

    1.   A stockholder has filed a lawsuit against **Clinch Corporation**. Clinch's attorneys have reviewed the facts of the case. Their review revealed that similar lawsuits have never resulted in a cash award and it is highly unlikely that this lawsuit will either.

    2.   **Foster Company** signed a 60-day, 10% note when it purchased items from another company.

    3.   The Department of Environment Protection notifies **Shevlin Company** that a state where it has a plant is filing a lawsuit for groundwater pollution against Shevlin and another company that has a plant adjacent to Shevlin's plant. Test results have not identified the exact source of the pollution. Shevlin's manufacturing process often produces by-products that can pollute ground water.

    4.   **Sloan Company** manufactured and sold products to a retailer that sold the products to consumers. The Sloan Company warranty offers replacement of the product if it is found to be defective within 90 days of the sale to the consumer. Historically, 1.2% of the products are returned for replacement.

E7-25. **Analyzing and Computing Accrued Wages Liability and Expense**   Demski Company pays its employees on the 1st and 15th of each month. It is March 31 and Demski is preparing financial statements for this quarter. Its employees have earned $25,000 since the 15th of this month and have not yet been paid. How will Demski's balance sheet and income statement change to reflect the accrual of wages that must be made at March 31? What balance sheet and income statement accounts would be incorrectly reported if Demski failed to make this accrual (for each account indicate whether it would be overstated or understated)?

E7-26.   Analyzing and Reporting Financial Statement Effects of Bond Transactions   On January 1, 2005, Hutton Corp. issued $300,000 of 15-year, 10% bonds payable for $351,876, yielding an effective interest rate of 8%. Interest is payable semiannually on June 30 and December 31. (a) Show computations to confirm the issue price of $351,876. (b) Indicate the financial statement effects using the following template for (1) bond issuance, (2) semiannual interest payment and premium amortization on June 30, 2005, and (3) semiannual interest payment and premium amortization on December 31, 2005.

Transaction	Balance Sheet									Income Statement		
	Cash Asset	+	Noncash Assets	=	Liabil- ities	+	Contrib. Capital	+	Retained Earnings	Revenues	−	Expenses
1.												
2.												
3.												

E7-27.   Analyzing and Reporting Financial Statement Effects of Bond Transactions   On January 1, 2005, Piotroski, Inc., borrowed $700,000 on a 12%, 15-year mortgage note payable. The note is to be repaid in equal semiannual installments of $50,854 (payable on June 30 and December 31). Indicate the financial statement effects using the following template for (a) issuance of the mortgage note payable, (b) payment of the first installment on June 30, 2005, and (c) payment of the second installment on December 31, 2005.

Transaction	Balance Sheet									Income Statement		
	Cash Asset	+	Noncash Assets	=	Liabil- ities	+	Contrib. Capital	+	Retained Earnings	Revenues	−	Expenses
a.												
b.												
c.												

E7-28.   Computing the Bond Issue Price   D'Souza, Inc., issues $900,000 of 10% bonds that pay interest semiannually and mature in five years. Assume that the market interest (yield) rate is 12% per year compounded semiannually. Compute the bond issue price.

AT&T (T)   **E7-29.   Effects of Bond Credit Ratings Changes**   AT&T reports the following footnote to its 2003 10-K:

Credit Ratings and Related Debt Implications
During 2003, AT&T's long-term credit ratings were lowered by both Standard & Poor's (S&P) and Fitch. As of December 31, 2003, our credit ratings were as follows:

Credit Rating Agency	Short-Term Rating	Long-Term Rating	Outlook
Standard & Poor's	A-2	BBB	Stable
Fitch	F-2	BBB	Negative
Moody's	P-2	Baa2	Negative

Our access to capital markets as well as the cost of our borrowings are affected by our debt ratings. The rating action by S&P in July 2003, triggered a 25 basis point interest rate step-up on approximately $10 billion in notional amount of debt ($1.3 billion of which matured in November 2003). This step-up was effective for interest payment periods that began after November 2003, resulting in an expected increase in interest expense of approximately $15 million in 2004. Further debt rating downgrades could require AT&T to pay higher rates on certain existing debt and post cash collateral for certain interest-rate and equity swaps if we are in a net payable position.

If AT&T's debt ratings are further downgraded, AT&T's access to the capital markets may be restricted and/or such replacement financing may be more costly or have additional covenants than we had in connection with our debt at December 31, 2003. In addition, the market environment for financing in general, and within the telecommunications sector in particular, has been adversely affected by economic conditions and bankruptcies of other telecommunications providers. If the financial markets become more cautious regarding the industry/ratings category we operate in, our ability to obtain financing would be further reduced and the cost of any new financings may be higher.

a. What are some typical financial ratios that credit rating companies use to evaluate the relative riskiness of borrowers?

b. Why might a reduction its credit ratings result in higher interest costs and restrict AT&T's access to credit markets?

c. What type of actions can AT&T take to improve its credit ratings?

E7-30. Analyzing and Reporting Financial Statement Effects of Bond Transactions Lundholm, Inc., which reports financial statements each December 31, is authorized to issue $500,000 of 9%, 15-year bonds dated May 1, 2005, with interest payments on October 31 and April 30. Assuming the bonds are sold at par on May 1, 2005, complete the following template to reflect the financial statement effects for the following events: (a) bond issuance, (b) payment of the first semiannual period's interest, and (c) retirement of $300,000 of the bonds at 101 on November 1, 2006.

	Balance Sheet									Income Statement		
Transaction	Cash Asset	+	Noncash Assets	=	Liabil- ities	+	Contrib. Capital	+	Retained Earnings	Revenues	−	Expenses
a.												
b.												
c.												

E7-31. Analyzing and Reporting Financial Statement Effects of Bond Transactions On January 1, 2005, McKeown, Inc., issued $250,000 of 8%, 9-year bonds for $220,775, yielding a market (yield) rate of 10%. Semiannual interest is payable on June 30 and December 31 of each year. (a) Show computations to confirm the bond issue price. (b) Indicate the financial statement effects using the following template for (1) bond issuance, (2) semiannual interest payment and discount amortization on June 30, 2005, and (3) semiannual interest payment and discount amortization on December 31, 2005.

	Balance Sheet									Income Statement		
Transaction	Cash Asset	+	Noncash Assets	=	Liabil- ities	+	Contrib. Capital	+	Retained Earnings	Revenues	−	Expenses
1.												
2.												
3.												

E7-32. Analyzing and Reporting Financial Statement Effects of Bond Transactions On January 1, 2005, Shields, Inc., issued $800,000 of 9%, 20-year bonds for $878,948, yielding a market (yield) rate of 8%. Semiannual interest is payable on June 30 and December 31 of each year. (a) Show computations to confirm the bond issue price. (b) Indicate the financial statement effects using the following template for (1) bond issuance, (2) semiannual interest payment and premium amortization on June 30, 2005, and (3) semiannual interest payment and premium amortization on December 31, 2005.

	Balance Sheet									Income Statement		
Transaction	Cash Asset	+	Noncash Assets	=	Liabil- ities	+	Contrib. Capital	+	Retained Earnings	Revenues	−	Expenses
1.												
2.												
3.												

E7-33. Bond Pricing, Interest Rates, and Financial Statements Following is a price quote for $1.6 billion of 5.625% coupon bonds issued by Abbott Laboratories that mature in July 2006 (from www.bondpage.com):

Abbott Laboratories (ABT)

Ratings Industry	Issue Call Information	Coupon Maturity Pmt Months	Price YTM
A1/AA Industrial	Abbott Labs Non Callable, Make Whole Calls	5.625 07-01-2006 Jan,Jul	104.069 2.982

This quote indicates that Abbott's bonds have a market price of 104.069 (104.069% of face value), resulting in a yield of 2.982%.

a. Assuming that these bonds were originally issued at or close to par value, what does the above market price reveal about the direction that interest rates have changed since Abbott issued its bonds? (Assume that Abbott's debt rating has remained the same.)

b. Does the change in interest rates since the issuance of these bonds affect the amount of interest expense that Abbott is reporting in its income statement? Explain.

c. If Abbott Labs was to repurchase its bonds at the above market price of 104.069, how would the repurchase affect its current income?

d. Assuming that the bonds remain outstanding until their maturity, at what market price will the bonds sell on their due date of July 1, 2006?

E7-34.ᴬ **Computing Present Values of Single Amounts and Annuities**   Refer to Tables 1 and 2 in Appendix A near the end of the book to compute the present value for each of the following amounts:

a. $90,000 received 10 years hence if the annual interest rate is
1. 8% compounded annually.
2. 8% compounded semiannually.

b. $1,000 received at the end of each year for the next eight years if money is worth 10% per year compounded annually.

c. $600 received at the end of each six months for the next 15 years if the interest rate is 8% per year compounded semiannually.

d. $500,000 inheritance 10 years hence if money is worth 10% per year compounded annually.

E7-35. **Analyzing and Reporting Financial Statement Effects of Bond Transactions**   On January 1, 2005, Trueman Corp. issued $600,000 of 20-year, 11% bonds for $554,860, yielding a market (yield) rate of 12%. Interest is payable semiannually on June 30 and December 31. (a) Confirm the bond issue price. (b) Indicate the financial statement effects using the following template for (1) bond issuance, (2) semiannual interest payment and discount amortization on June 30, 2005, and (3) semiannual interest payment and discount amortization on December 31, 2005.

Transaction	Balance Sheet							Income Statement		
	Cash Asset	+	Noncash Assets	=	Liabil- ities	+	Contrib. Capital	+	Retained Earnings	Revenues − Expenses
1.										
2.										
3.										

E7-36. **Analyzing and Reporting Financial Statement Effects of Bond Transactions**   On January 1, 2005, Verrecchia Company issued $400,000 of 5-year, 13% bonds for $446,208, yielding a market (yield) rate of 10%. Interest is payable semiannually on June 30 and December 31. (a) Show computations to confirm the bond issue price. (b) Indicate the financial statement effects using the following template for (1) bond issuance, (2) semiannual interest payment and premium amortization on June 30, 2005, and (3) semiannual interest payment and premium amortization on December 31, 2005.

Transaction	Balance Sheet							Income Statement		
	Cash Asset	+	Noncash Assets	=	Liabil- ities	+	Contrib. Capital	+	Retained Earnings	Revenues − Expenses
1.										
2.										
3.										

■ PROBLEMS

P7-37. Interpreting Term Structures of Coupon and Yield Rates Lockheed Martin reports $6,072 million of long-term debt outstanding as of December 2003 in the following schedule to its 10-K report:

Lockheed Martin (LMT)

Type (Maturity Dates) (In millions, except interest rate data)	Range of Interest Rates	2003	2002
Floating rate convertible debentures (2033)	0.93%	$1,000	$ —
Other debentures (2013–2036)	7.0–9.1%	3,388	4,198
Notes (2004–2022)	6.5–9.0%	1,778	3,099
Other obligations (2004–2017)	1.0–10.5%	42	260
		6,208	7,557
Less current maturities		(136)	(1,365)
		$6,072	$6,192

Bond pricing information relating to its Other Debentures follows (from www.bondpage.com):

Ratings Industry	Issue Call Information	Coupon Maturity Pmt Months	Price YTM LY
Baa2/BBB Industrial	Lockheed Martin Corp Non Callable	8.200 12-01-2009 Jun,Dec	119.002 3.976 Mat
Baa2/BBB Industrial	Lockheed Martin Corp Non Callable	7.650 05-01-2016 May,Nov	122.278 5.058 Mat
Baa2/BBB Industrial	Lockheed Martin Corp Non Callable, Make Whole Calls	8.500 12-01-2029 Jun,Dec	137.654 5.666 Mat

Required

a. Although the coupon rates on these debentures range from 7.65% to 8.5%, the market (yield) rate ranges from 3.976% to 5.666%. Discuss how and why these two rates differ.

b. Rank the yields in order of maturity. Do you see a pattern? Discuss the relation between the yield rate and the term to maturity.

P7-38. Interpreting Debt Footnotes on Interest Rates and Expense CVS Corporation discloses the following footnote in its 10-K relating to its debt:

CVS Corporation (CVS)

BORROWING AND CREDIT AGREEMENTS
Following is a summary of the Company's borrowings as of the respective balance sheet dates:

In millions	Jan. 3, 2004	Dec. 28, 2002
Commercial paper	$ —	$ 4.8
5.5% senior notes due 2004	300.0	300.0
5.625% senior notes due 2006	300.0	300.0
3.875% senior notes due 2007	300.0	300.0
8.52% ESOP notes due 2008	163.2	194.4
Mortgage notes payable	12.2	13.0
Capital lease obligations	0.9	0.9
	1,076.3	1,113.1
Less:		
Short-term debt	—	(4.8)
Current portion of long-term debt	(323.2)	(32.0)
	$ 753.1	$1,076.3

CVS also discloses the following:

Interest expense, net—Interest expense was $53.9 million, $54.5 million and $65.2 million and interest income was $5.8 million, $4.1 million and $4.2 million in 2003, 2002 and 2001, respectively. Interest paid totaled $64.9 million in 2003, $60.7 million in 2002 and $75.2 million in 2001.

Required

a. What is the average interest rate that CVS paid on its long-term debt (all of the reported interest rates relate to long-term debt)?

b. Does your computation in (a) seem reasonable given the disclosure relating to specific bond issues? Explain.

c. Why can the amount of interest paid be different from the amount of interest expense recorded in the income statement?

P7-39.   Analyzing and Interpreting Liability Accruals in Financial Statements and Notes   Refer to the financial statements and disclosures for International Paper (IP)—selected pages are shown below—to answer the following requirements.

International
Paper (IP)

In millions, for Year Ended December 31	2000
Net Sales	$28,180
Costs and Expenses	
Cost of products sold	20,082
Selling and administrative expenses	2,283
Depreciation and amortization	1,916
Distribution expenses	1,104
Taxes other than payroll and income taxes	287
Merger integration costs	54
Restructuring and other charges	949
Total Costs and Expenses	26,675
Reversals of reserves no longer required	34
Earnings before Interest, Income Taxes, Minority Interest and Extraordinary Items	1,539
Interest expense, net	816
Earnings before Income Taxes, Minority Interest and Extraordinary Items	723
Income tax provision	117
Minority interest expense, net of taxes	238
Earnings before Extraordinary Items	368
Impairment losses on businesses to be sold, net of taxes	(541)
Net gain on sales of investments and businesses, net of taxes and minority interest	315
Net Earnings	$ 142

In millions at December 31	2000
Assets	
Current Assets	
Cash and temporary investments	$ 1,198
Accounts and notes receivable, less allowances of $128	3,433
Inventories	3,182
Assets of businesses held for sale	1,890
Other current assets	752
Total Current Assets	10,455
Plants, Properties and Equipment, net	16,011
Forestlands	5,966
Investments	269

(Continued on next page)

(Continued from previous page)

In millions at December 31	2000
Assets (continued)	
Goodwill	$ 6,310
Deferred Charges and Other Assets	3,098
Total Assets	$42,109
Liabilities and Common Shareholders' Equity	
Current Liabilities	
Notes payable and current maturities of long-term debt	$ 2,115
Accounts payable	2,113
Accrued payroll and benefits	511
Liabilities of businesses held for sale	541
Other accrued liabilities	2,133
Total Current Liabilities	7,413
Long-Term Debt	12,648
Deferred Income Taxes	4,699
Other Liabilities	2,155
Minority Interest	1,355
International Paper-Obligated Mandatorily Redeemable Preferred Securities	
of Subsidiaries Holding International Paper Debentures	1,805
Common Shareholders' Equity	
Common stock, $1 par value, 484.2 shares	484
Paid-in capital	6,501
Retained earnings	6,308
Accumulated other comprehensive income (loss)	(1,142)
	12,151
Less: Common stock held in treasury, at cost, 2.7 shares	117
Total Common Shareholders' Equity	12,034
Total Liabilities and Common Shareholders' Equity	$42,109

6. Special Items Including Restructuring and Business Improvement Actions

2000: Special items reduced 2000 net earnings by $601 million, 1999 net earnings by $352 million and 1998 net earnings by $98 million. The following table and discussion presents the impact of special items for 2000:

In millions, Year-Ended December 31, 2000	Earnings (Loss) Before Income Taxes and Minority Interest	Earnings (Loss) After Income Taxes and Minority Interest
Before special and extraordinary items	$1,692	$ 969
Merger-related expenses	(54)	(33)
Restructuring and other charges	(824)	(509)
Provision for legal reserves	(125)	(80)
Reversals of reserves no longer required	34	21
After special items	$ 723	$ 368

During 2000, special charges before taxes and minority interest of $969 million ($601 million after taxes and minority interest) were recorded. These special items included a $54 million pre-tax charge ($33 million after taxes) for merger-related expenses, an $824 million charge before taxes and minority interest ($509 million after taxes and minority interest) for asset shutdowns of excess internal capacity and cost reduction actions, a $125 million pre-tax charge ($80 million after taxes) for additional Masonite legal reserves and a $34 million pre-tax credit ($21 million after taxes) for the reversals of reserves no longer required.

The merger-related expenses of $54 million consisted primarily of travel, systems integration, employee retention, and other one-time cash costs related to the Champion acquisition and Union Camp merger.

The $824 million charge for the asset shutdowns of excess internal capacity and cost reduction actions consisted of a $71 million charge in the second quarter of 2000 and a $753 million charge in the fourth quarter of 2000. The second quarter charge of $71 million consisted of $40 million of asset write-downs and $31 million of severance and other charges. The fourth quarter charge of $753 million consisted of $536 million of asset write-downs and $217 million of severance and other charges.

7. Businesses Held for Sale

During 2000, International Paper announced plans to sell by the end of 2001, approximately $5 billion of assets that are not strategic to its core businesses.

In the third quarter of 2000, the assets of Masonite and Zanders were written down to their fair market values based on estimated sales proceeds. This resulted in an extraordinary pre-tax charge of $460 million ($310 million after taxes). In the fourth quarter of 2000, Fine Papers, the Chemical Cellulose pulp business and International Paper's Flexible Packaging businesses in Argentina (included in Other) were written down to their fair market values based on estimated sales proceeds, resulting in an extraordinary pre-tax charge of $373 million ($231 million after taxes). These charges are presented as extraordinary items, net of taxes, in the consolidated statement of earnings in accordance with the pooling-of-interests rules.

The assets of the businesses held for sale, totaling $1.9 billion, are included in "assets of businesses held for sale" in current assets in the accompanying consolidated balance sheet. The liabilities of these businesses, totaling $541 million, are included in "liabilities of businesses held for sale" in current liabilities in the accompanying consolidated balance sheet.

Required

a. What amount of net income did IP report for 2000? List the descriptions and amounts of all transitory items in IP's income statement.

b. In Note 6, IP reports a $969 million charge for 2000. What are the four major components of this charge?

c. IP reports a total charge of $824 million relating to "asset shutdowns of excess internal capacity and cost reduction actions" in its Note 6. What amount of this charge related to asset write-downs and what amount related to severance and other charges?

d. What did the $125 million (pretax) special charge item relate to (per Note 6)?

e. IP reports $541 million (net of tax) in "Impairment losses on businesses to be sold, net of tax" on its income statement. To what does this item relate?

f. IP reports $34 million in "Reversals of reserves no longer required" on its income statement. Briefly interpret what this item means.

g. Do you believe that IP's accruals provide investors with relevant information? Explain. How might a company use accruals to misrepresent its financial condition? What might you examine to analyze the appropriateness of accruals?

P7-40. **Analyzing Bond Rates, Yields, Prices, and Credit Ratings**   Reproduced below is the long-term debt footnote from the 10-K report of Southwest Airlines:

Southwest Airlines (LUV)

Long-Term Debt

(In thousands)	2002
8¾% Notes due 2003	$ 100,000
Aircraft Secured Notes due 2004	175,000
8% Notes due 2005	100,000
Pass Through Certificates	585,661
7⅞% Notes due 2007	100,000

(Continued on next page)

(Continued from previous page)

(In thousands)	2002
French Credit Agreements	$ 50,024
6½% Notes due 2012	385,000
7⅜% Debentures due 2027	100,000
Capital leases	100,563
	1,696,248
Less current maturities	130,454
Less debt discount and issue costs	13,013
	$1,552,781

On March 1, 2002, the Company issued $385 million senior unsecured Notes (Notes) due March 1, 2012. The Notes bear interest at 6.5 percent, payable semi-annually beginning on September 1, 2002. Southwest used the net proceeds from the issuance of the Notes, approximately $380.2 million, for general corporate purposes, including the repayment of the Company's credit facility in March 2002.

As of December 31, 2002, aggregate annual principal maturities (not including interest on capital leases) for the five-year period ending December 31, 2007, were $130 million in 2003, $207 million in 2004, $142 million in 2005, $542 million in 2006, $114 million in 2007, and $561 million thereafter.

Reproduced below is the rating of Southwest Airlines's $385 million, 6.5% note issuance, due in 2012. The rating is from **Fitch Ratings, Ltd.**:

				Ratings			
Maturity Date	Currency	Total Amount	Coupon Rate	Long Term	Short Term	CUSIP	ISIN
01-MAR-2012	USD	$385,000,000	6.5%	A	—	844741AV0	US844741AV08

Following is a price quote on those same Southwest Airline's $385 million notes:

Ratings	Ticker	Description	Coupon	Maturity	YTC/YTM	Price
Baa1/A	LUV	Southwest Airls Co	6.500	03-01-2012	4.721	111.631

This quote indicates that the Southwest Airlines notes with a 6.5% coupon rate trades at 111.631 (111.631% of par) resulting in a yield to the investor of 4.721%.

Required

a. What is the amount of long-term debt reported on Southwest's 2002 balance sheet? What are the scheduled maturities for this indebtedness? Why is information relating to a company's scheduled maturities of debt useful in an analysis of its financial condition?

b. Southwest reported $106 million in interest expense in its 2002 income statement. In the note to its statement of cash flows, Southwest indicates that the cash portion of this expense is $80 million. What could account for the difference between interest expense and interest paid? Explain.

c. Southwest's long-term debt is rated "A" by Fitch and similarly by other credit rating agencies. What factors would be important to consider in attempting to quantify the relative riskiness of Southwest compared with other borrowers? Explain.

d. Southwest's $385 million 6.5% notes traded at 111.631, or 111.631% of par. What is the current dollar value of these notes per this trading price? How is the difference between this value and the $385 million face amount of the issue reflected in Southwest's financial statements? What effect would the repurchase of this entire note issue have on Southwest's financial statements? What does the 111.631 price tell you about the general trend in interest rates since Southwest sold this bond issue? Explain.

8 Reporting and Analyzing Owner Financing

SURVIVING DRUG WARS

Pfizer is a research-based, global pharmaceutical company that discovers, develops, manufactures, and markets leading prescription medicines for humans and animals. The following six drugs account for $23.5 billion (52%) of its $45.2 billion in sales (Pfizer 2004 and 2003 10-K reports):

$ Millions	2003	2002	Percent Change
Lipitor	$9,231	$7,972	16%
Norvasc	4,336	3,846	13
Zoloft	3,118	2,742	14
Neurontin	2,702	2,269	19
Zithromax	2,010	1,516	33
Celebrex	2,132	0	—

While Pfizer's products enjoy success, they highlight the challenge of managing a large, modern pharmaceutical company. For example, Lipitor, the bestselling drug in the world, loses its patent protection in six years. Pfizer's current answer to this challenge is to combine Lipitor with a powerful new drug in the hope of even greater market share and a new patent. The new compound, Torcetrapib, is aimed at reducing heart attacks at a greater level than the one-third or so seen with Lipitor alone.

The question is whether the new duo (Torcetrapib) will arrive in time to stop the usual 80% plunge in sales that occurs when a drug goes off-patent. Pfizer is spending a staggering $800 million putting the combo pill through final-stage trials in an all-out effort to show it prevents both plaque buildup and heart disease deaths. Another $90 million has already been committed to build a factory in Ireland to produce the combo.

If the pill falls short, Pfizer's income could plummet in the next decade. However, if it works, the drugmaker could easily dominate the industry for many years to come. Best of all, the new combo would get Pfizer patent protection, which Lipitor loses, until 2020 (Forbes 2004).

Loss of patent protection on key drug products is not the only problem facing Pfizer's Hank McKinnell, its CEO since 2001. A bitter fight continues over U.S. trade policy and the lives of millions of Americans involving whether the U.S. should permit imports of prescription drugs from Canada. Presently, it is generally illegal

for U.S. residents to buy pharmaceuticals north of the border or from anywhere abroad without a federal waiver. Yet, for many Americans, the lure of such purchases is intense because many of the same products are available in the U.S. are also in Canada at prices 30% to 50% lower.

The reason for the price difference is that Canada, like most major governments except the U.S., heavily regulates medicine prices. Companies such as Pfizer, Wyeth, and Eli Lilly say that imports from Canada undercut their U.S. income and hurt research and development. They want Canada either to raise its prices for patented drugs or to embargo drug exports.

While the U.S. pharmaceutical industry is certainly profitable, America's scientists have produced the overwhelming share of medical breakthroughs. This is why the research operations of non-American companies such as Switzerland's Novartis are migrating to the U.S. Further, as Merck & Co. Chairman and CEO Raymond V. Gilmartin cautions, U.S. competitiveness hinges on industries such as pharmaceuticals that are at the forefront of innovation.

Still, despite its high-tech image, the pharmaceutical industry is less adept at manufacturing than we might expect. Factory processes are often so antiquated that companies typically can't even pinpoint the causes of snafus. "Manufacturing has been the poor stepchild of the pharmaceutical industry," asserts Jeffrey T. Macher of Georgetown University. (*BusinessWeek* 2004)

Drugmakers are now tackling manufacturing concerns with new approaches, such as process analytical technology (PAT). The idea is that instead of putting a drug lot on hold to test it after each step, the company will peer into the process itself and measure what's going on—as it's happening. It is possible, for instance, to shine a laser through a window in a blender. The constituents absorb or reflect the light differently, creating a spectrograph that can tell operators if the ingredients are mixing properly.

A host of other technologies, such as Raman spectroscopy and chemical imaging are also being investigated in the desire to help determine the distribution of active ingredients in a pill or the size of the granules. Companies such as Pfizer and Abbott Laboratories are spending tens of millions per year to install such new technology and processes in plants. (*BusinessWeek* 2004)

Pfizer's stock price by late 2004, as the following chart illustrates, is in the $30 per share range, which is approximately what its shares sold for in early 2000. During this same time period, Pfizer's income has roughly doubled.

(Continued on next page)

(Continued from previous page)

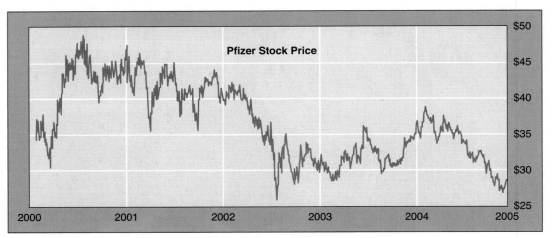

Pfizer now commands a below-average market multiple of 16.5 based on projected 2004 earnings per share of $2.11. That's a rare position for Pfizer, which typically has traded at a large premium to the S&P 500. Pfizer's admirers believe its growth potential is underappreciated and that the stock could rise to the mid $40s over the next year. But the market remains cautious because of the challenges facing the pharmaceutical industry. (*Barron's* 2004)

One of the keys to Pfizer's present strategy has been to increase its size to spread its high overhead over a broader sales base. As part of this growth strategy, in 2000, Pfizer merged with Warner-Lambert Company, and in 2003, it acquired Pharmacia for $56 billion, making it the largest pharmaceutical company in the world. Under the terms of the merger agreement, each outstanding share of Pharmacia common stock was exchanged for 1.4 shares of Pfizer common stock. Also, each share of Pharmacia Series C convertible perpetual preferred stock was exchanged for a newly created class of Pfizer Series A convertible perpetual preferred stock with substantially similar rights.

Companies like Pfizer issue stock for several reasons, including acquisitions and share purchases by employees under stock purchase and stock option plans. They also frequently engage in share repurchase programs and seek to unlock hidden value through sales, spin-offs, and split-offs of subsidiaries.

This module describes the accounting for equity transactions, including sales and repurchases of stock, dividends and stock splits, equity carve-outs, comprehensive income, and convertible securities. During 2003, Pfizer's stockholders' equity was impacted by earnings and other comprehensive income, issuance of stock in the Pharmacia acquisition, repurchases of common stock in the open market, the payment of dividends, issuance of stock for employee stock option exercise, and the conversion to common of preferred shares. We discuss each of these transactions in this module.

Sources: *The Wall Street Journal* (2004), *Barrons* (2004), *Forbes* (2004), *BusinessWeek* (2004), *Pfizer* 2004 and 2003 10-K Report

■ INTRODUCTION

Acompany finances its assets (through other than operating cash flows) from one of two sources: either it borrows funds from debtholders or it obtains funds from shareholders. On average, companies obtain about half of their external financing from borrowed sources and the other half from shareholder investment. This module describes the issues relating to stockholders' equity, including the accounting for stock transactions (sales and repurchases of stock, and dividends). We also discuss the issue of equity carve outs, a process by which companies seek to unlock substantial shareholder value via spin-offs and split-offs of business units into separate companies. Finally, we discuss the accounting for convertible securities, an increasingly prevalent financing vehicle.

When a company issues stock to the investing public, it records the receipt of cash (or other assets) and an increase in stockholders' equity, representing investment in the company by shareholders. The increase in cash and equity is equal to the market price of the stock on the issue date multiplied by the number of shares sold.

$
Cash Effect

Like bonds, stockholders' equity is accounted for at *historical cost.* Consequently, fluctuations in the market price of the issuer's stock subsequent to the initial public offering do not directly affect the financial statements of the issuing company. This is because these transactions are between outside parties not involving the issuer. When and if stock is repurchased and subsequently resold, the issuer's stockholders' equity decreases (increases) by the purchase (sales) price of the shares.

There is an important difference between accounting for stockholders' equity and accounting for transactions involving assets and liabilities: *there is never any gain or loss reported on the purchase and sale of stock or the payment of dividends.* Instead, these "gains and losses" are reflected as increases and decreases in the contributed capital component of the issuing company's stockholders' equity.

This module focuses on the two broad categories of shareholder investment: contributed capital and earned capital. Exhibit 8.1 provides an illustration of this breakdown using **Pfizer**'s stockholders' equity as of 2003. Its equity consists of the following four groupings: two classes of stock (preferred and common, including additional paid-in capital and the employee benefit trust), treasury (repurchased) stock, retained earnings, and accumulated other comprehensive income.

EXHIBIT 8.1 ■ Stockholders' Equity from Pfizer's Balance Sheet

	Shareholders' Equity (millions, except preferred shares issued)	Dec. 31, 2003
Contributed capital	Preferred stock, without par value, at stated value; 27 shares authorized; 5,445 issued in 2003	$ 219
	Common stock, $.05 par value; 12,000 shares authorized; issued: 2003—8,702	435
	Additional paid-in capital	66,396
	Employee benefit trust	(1,898)
	Treasury stock, shares at cost; issued: 2003—1,073	(29,352)
Earned capital	Retained earnings	29,382
	Accumulated other comprehensive income	195
	Total shareholders' equity	$ 65,377

Pfizer, like other companies, has two broad categories of stockholders' equity:

1. **Contributed capital**   This section reports the proceeds received by the issuing company from original stock issuances. It often includes common stock, preferred stock, and additional paid-in capital. Netted against these capital accounts is treasury stock, the amounts paid to repurchase shares of the issuer's stock from its investors less the proceeds from the resale of such shares. Collectively, these accounts are generically referred to as contributed capital (or *paid-in capital*).

2. **Earned capital**   This section consists of (a) retained earnings, which represent the cumulative income and losses of the company less any dividends to shareholders, and (b) accumulated other comprehensive income (AOCI), which includes changes to equity that have not impacted income and are, therefore, not reflected in retained earnings. For Pfizer, AOCI includes foreign currency translation adjustments, changes in market values of derivatives, unrecognized gains and losses on available-for-sale securities, and minimum pension liability adjustments.

We discuss each of these two categories in turn. For each section, we provide a graphic that displays the part of stockholders' equity in the balance sheet impacted by the discussion of that section.

■ CONTRIBUTED CAPITAL

We begin our discussion with contributed capital. Contributed capital represents the cumulative cash inflow that the company has received from the sale of various classes of stock, less the net cash that it has paid out to repurchase its stock from the market. The contributed capital of Pfizer is highlighted in the following graphic:

Shareholders' Equity (millions, except preferred shares issued)	Dec. 31, 2003
Preferred stock, without par value, at stated value; 27 shares authorized; 5,445 issued in 2003	$ 219
Common stock, $.05 par value; 12,000 shares authorized; issued: 2003—8,702	435
Additional paid-in capital	66,396
Employee benefit trust	(1,898)
Treasury stock, shares at cost; issued: 2003—1,073	(29,352)
Retained earnings	29,382
Accumulated other comprehensive income	195
Total shareholders' equity	$ 65,377

Pfizer's contributed capital consists of paid-in and additional paid-in capital for both its preferred and common stock, less costs of treasury stock (repurchased shares) and the reduction of stockholders' equity arising from its employee benefit trust.[1]

Classes of Stock

There are two general classes of stock: preferred and common. The difference between the two lies in the respective legal rights conferred upon each class.

Preferred Stock

Preferred stock generally has some preference, or priority, with respect to common stock. Two usual preferences follow:

1. **Dividend preference**   Preferred shareholders receive dividends on their shares before common shareholders do. If dividends are not paid in a given year, those dividends are normally forgone. However, some preferred stock contracts include a *cumulative provision* stipulating that any forgone dividends must first be paid to preferred shareholders, together with the current year's dividends, before any dividends are paid to common shareholders.
2. **Liquidation preference**   If a company fails, its assets are sold (liquidated) and the proceeds are paid to the debtholders and shareholders, in that order. Shareholders, therefore, have a greater risk of loss than do debtholders. Among shareholders, the preferred shareholders receive payment in full before common shareholders. This liquidation preference makes preferred shares less risky than common shares. Any liquidation payment to preferred shares is normally at its par value, although it is sometimes specified in excess of par; called a *liquidating value.*

The preferred stock of Pfizer is described as follows in its financial statement notes:

> In connection with our acquisition of Pharmacia in 2003, we issued a newly created class of Series A convertible perpetual preferred stock (7,500 shares designated) in exchange for and with rights substantially similar to Pharmacia's Series C convertible perpetual preferred stock. The Series A convertible perpetual preferred stock is held by an Employee Stock Ownership Plan ("Preferred ESOP") Trust and provides dividends at the rate of 6.25% which are accumulated and paid quarterly. The per-share stated value is $40,300 and the preferred stock ranks senior to our common stock as to dividends and liquidation rights. Each share is convertible, at the holder's option, into 2,547.87 shares of our common stock with equal voting rights. The Company may redeem the preferred stock, at any time or upon termination of the Preferred ESOP, at its option, in cash, in shares of common stock or a combination of both at a price of $40,300 per share.

Following are several important features of the Pfizer preferred stock:

* Shareholders control the number of shares issued—called *authorized shares*. The number of authorized shares can only be increased by an affirmative shareholder vote. There are 27 million

---

[1]Its employee benefit trust (also called *employee stock ownership plan,* or *ESOP*) purchases company stock for the benefit of its employees with borrowed funds. Common stock increases from those purchases of shares; but until the debt is paid, the company reports an offset (reduction) in stockholders' equity equal to the unpaid debt. This explains the negative amount reported in its employee benefit trust account. As of 2003, Pfizer reports an unpaid balance of $1,898 million.

preferred shares authorized, of which 5,445 shares are issued as of 2003. The articles of incorporation set the number of shares authorized for issuance. Once that limit is reached, shareholders must approve any increase in authorized shares.

- Preferred stock is convertible into common stock at the option of the holder and at a predetermined exchange rate. A preferred share is convertible, at the holder's option, into 2,547.87 common shares.
- Preferred stock pays a dividend of 6.25% of its par (stated) value of $40,300. This means that each preferred share is entitled to annual dividends of $2,518.75 ($40,300 × 6.25%), payable quarterly.
- Preferred stock is *cumulative*. This feature provides preferred shareholders with protection that unpaid dividends (called *dividends in arrears*) must be paid before any dividends are paid to common shareholders.
- Preferred stock has a preference with respect to dividends and liquidation; meaning that preferred shareholders are paid before common shareholders.
- Pfizer can redeem (repurchase) preferred stock at any time in cash, common stock, or both.

Pfizer's cumulative preferred shares carry a dividend yield of 6.25%. This dividend yield compares favorably with the $0.60 per share (1.7% yield on a $35 share price) paid to its common shareholders in 2003. Generally, preferred stock can be an attractive investment for shareholders seeking higher dividend yields, especially when tax laws wholly or partially exempt such dividends from taxation. Such exemption is not available for interest payments received by debtholders.

There are two additional features sometimes seen in preferred stock agreements:

1. **Conversion feature** The yield on preferred stock, especially when coupled with a cumulative feature, is similar to the interest rate on a bond or note. Further, preferred shareholders receive the par value at liquidation like debtholders receive face value. The fixed yield and liquidation value for the preferred stock limit the upside potential return of preferred shareholders. This constraint can be overcome by inclusion of a *conversion feature* that allows preferred stockholders to convert their shares into common shares at their option at a predetermined conversion ratio (some preferred contracts give the company an option to force conversion).
2. **Participation feature** Preferred shares sometimes carry a *participation feature* that allows preferred shareholders to share ratably with common stockholders in dividends. The dividend preference over common shares can be a benefit when dividend payments are meager, but a fixed dividend yield limits upside potential if the company performs exceptionally well. This limitation can be overcome with a participation feature.

Common Stock

Pfizer has also issued common stock, which it describes as follows (shares in millions):

> Common stock, $.05 par value; 12,000 shares authorized; issued: 2003—8,702

The Pfizer common stock has the following important characteristics:

- Pfizer common stock has a par value of $0.05 per share. The **par value** is an arbitrary amount set by company organizers at the time of formation. Generally, par value has no substance from a financial reporting or statement analysis perspective (there are some legal implications, which are usually minor). Its main impact is in specifying the allocation of proceeds from stock issuances between the two contributed capital accounts on the balance sheet: common stock and additional paid-in capital.
- Pfizer has authorized the issuance of 12,000 million shares. As of 2003, 8,702 million shares are issued. When shares are first issued the number of shares outstanding equals those issued. Any shares subsequently repurchased as treasury stock are deducted from issued shares to derive *outstanding shares*.[2]

Accounting for Stock Transactions

We cover the accounting for stock transactions in this section, including the accounting for stock issuances and for stock repurchases.

---

[2]Generally, issued shares equal outstanding shares plus treasury shares.

Stock Issuance

Stock issuances, whether common or preferred, yield an increase in both assets and stockholders' equity. Companies use stock issuances to obtain cash and other assets for use in their business. (The chart to the side shows the largest stock issuances for 2004.)

Stock issuances increase assets (cash) by the number of shares sold multiplied by the issuance price of the stock on the issue date. Equity increases by the same amount, which is reflected in contributed capital accounts. Specifically, assuming the issuance of common stock (initial public offering, or IPO for short), the common stock account increases by the number of shares sold multiplied by its par value and the additional paid-in capital account increases for the remainder.

2004's Top 10 Global Stock Issuances	
ISSUER	AMOUNT (billions)
ENEL	$9.5
France Telecom	6.2
Royal Bank of Scotland	4.8
Belgacom	4.4
GE	3.8
Bayerische Hypo-Vereinsbk	3.7
Deutsche Telekom	3.7
Electric Power Dev.	3.4
Total	3.2
Genworth Financial	2.9

To illustrate, assume that Pfizer issues 10,000 shares at a market price of $43 cash per share. This stock issuance has the following financial statement effects:

Cash   430,000
  Common Stock   500
  Additional
    Paid-In
    Capital   429,500

	Balance Sheet						Income Statement		
Transaction	Cash Asset	+	Noncash Assets	=	Liabil- ities	+	Contrib. Capital	+	Retained Earnings	Revenues	−	Expenses
Issue 10,000 common shares with $0.05 par value for $43 cash per share	+430,000						+500 Common Stock +429,500 Additional Paid-In Capital		

Specifically, the following financial statement effects of the stock issuance are evident:

1. Cash increases by $430,000 (10,000 shares × $43 per share)
2. Common stock increases by the $500 par value of shares sold (10,000 shares × $0.05 par value)[3]
3. Additional paid-in capital increases by the $429,500 difference between the issue price and par value ($430,000 − $500)[4]

Once shares are issued, they are freely traded among investors. The proceeds of those sales and their associated gains and losses on sales do not affect the issuing company and are not recorded in its accounting records. Further, fluctuations in the issuing company's stock price subsequent to issuance do not directly affect its financial statements.

Refer again to the following report of common stock on Pfizer's balance sheet (in millions):

Common stock, $.05 par value; 12,000 shares authorized; issued: 2003—8,702	$ 435
Additional paid-in capital	66,396

$
Cash Effect

---

[3]Stock can also be issued as "no par" or as "no par with a stated value." For no par stock, the common stock account is increased by the entire proceeds of the sale and no amount is assigned to additional paid-in capital. For no par stock with a stated value, the stated value is treated just like par value, that is, common stock is increased by the number of shares multiplied by the stated value, and the remainder is assigned to the additional paid-in capital account.

[4]Stock issuance affects only the balance sheet. There is never any revenue or gain from stock issuance reported in the income statement.

Its common stock, in the amount of $435 million, equals the number of shares issued multiplied by the common stock's par value: 8,702 million × $0.05 = $435 million. Total proceeds from stock issuances are $66,831 million, or $7.68 per share ($66,831 million/8,702 million shares). The balance of the proceeds from stock issuances ($66,396 million) is included in the additional paid-in capital account.

RESEARCH INSIGHT	Stock Issuance and Stock Returns

Research shows that, historically, companies issuing equity securities experience unusually low stock returns for several years following those offerings. Evidence suggests that this poor performance is partly due to overly optimistic estimates of long-term growth for these companies by equity analysts that impact the offering price. This over-optimism is most pronounced when the analyst is employed by the brokerage firm that underwrites the issue. There is also evidence that companies manage earnings upward prior to an equity offering. This means the observed decrease in returns following an issuance likely reflects the market's negative reaction, on average, to earnings management. This yields a classic "chicken or the egg" dilemma: do stock returns decline following issuance because analysts/managers are skewing performance measures upward, or do managers skew performance measures upward because they anticipate that investors rationally adjust downward those measures?

Stock Repurchase

Pfizer provides the following description of its stock repurchase program in notes to its 10-K report:

> We continue to purchase our common stock via open market purchases or in privately negotiated transactions as circumstances and prices warrant. Purchased shares under each of the share-purchase programs are available for general corporate purposes.

> In December 2003, we announced a $5 billion share-purchase program, which we expect to be completed by the end of 2004. In July 2002, we announced a $16 billion share-purchase program (increased from the initial $10 billion) authorized by our board of directors, which we completed in November 2003. In total, under the June 2002 program we purchased approximately 508 million shares. In May 2002, we completed the share-purchase program authorized in June 2001. In total, under the June 2001 program we purchased 120 million shares at a total cost of approximately $4.8 billion.

Pfizer initiated several stock buyback programs in the past three years. One reason a company repurchase shares is if it feels that the market undervalues them. The logic is that the repurchase sends a positive signal to the market about the company's financial condition that positively impacts its share price and, thus, allows it to resell those shares for a "gain." Any such gain on resale is *never* reflected in the income statement. Instead, the excess of the resale price over the repurchase price is added to additional paid-in capital. GAAP prohibits companies from reporting gains via stock transactions with their own shareholders.

Another reason shares are repurchased is to offset the dilutive effects of an employee stock option program. When an employee exercises stock options, the number of shares outstanding increases together with cash received. These additional shares reduce earnings per share and are, therefore, viewed as *dilutive*. In response, many companies repurchase an equivalent number of shares in a desire to keep outstanding shares constant.

A stock repurchase represents a downsizing of the company. It has the opposite financial statement effects from a stock issuance. That is, cash is reduced by the price of the shares repurchased (number of shares repurchased multiplied by the purchase price per share) and stockholders' equity is reduced by the same amount. The reduction in equity is achieved by increasing a contra equity account called **treasury stock**. *A contra equity account is a negative equity account,* which reduces stockholders' equity. Thus, when a contra equity account increases, total equity decreases.

Any subsequent reissuance of treasury stock does not yield a gain or loss. Instead, the difference between the proceeds received and the repurchase price of the treasury stock is reflected as an increase or decrease to additional paid-in capital.

To illustrate, assume that 3,000 common shares of Pfizer previously issued for $43 are later repurchased for $40. This repurchase has the following financial statement effects:

Transaction	Balance Sheet										Income Statement		
	Cash Asset	+	Noncash Assets	=	Liabil- ities	+	Contrib. Capital	+	Retained Earnings		Revenues	−	Expenses
Repurchase 3,000 common shares for $40 cash per share	−120,000						−120,000 Treasury Stock Increase						

Margin note:
Treasury
Stock 120,000
  Cash   120,000

Assets (cash) and equity both decrease. Treasury stock (a contra equity account) increases by $120,000, which reduces stockholders' equity by that same amount.

Assume that these 3,000 shares are then subsequently resold for $42 cash per share. This resale of treasury stock has the following financial statement effects:

Transaction	Balance Sheet										Income Statement		
	Cash Asset	+	Noncash Assets	=	Liabil- ities	+	Contrib. Capital	+	Retained Earnings		Revenues	−	Expenses
Reissue 3,000 treasury (common) shares for $42 cash per share	+126,000						+120,000 Treasury Stock Decrease +6,000 Additional Paid-In Capital						

Margin note:
Cash   126,000
  Treasury
    Stock   120,000
  Additional
    Paid-In
    Capital   6,000

Margin icon: $ Cash Effect

Cash assets increase by $126,000 (3,000 shares × $42 per share), the treasury stock account is reduced by the $120,000 cost of the treasury shares issued, and the $6,000 excess (3,000 shares × $2 per share) is reported as an increase in additional paid-in capital.[5] Again, there is no effect on the income statement—companies are prohibited from reporting gains and losses from repurchases and reissuances of their own stock.

The treasury stock section of **Pfizer**'s balance sheet is reproduced below:

At December 31 (millions)	2003
Treasury stock, shares at cost; issued: 2003—1,073	$(29,352)

Pfizer has repurchased a cumulative total of 1,073 million shares of its common stock for $29,352 million, an average repurchase price of $27.35 per share. This compares with total contributed capital of $65,152 million ($219 million + $435 million + $66,396 million − $1,898 million; see page 8-5). Thus, about 45% of its original contributed capital has been repurchased. Although some of Pfizer's treasury purchases were to offset increases in shares outstanding due to the exercise of stock options, it appears that most of these purchases are motivated by a perceived low stock price by Pfizer management.

MANAGERIAL DECISION   You Are the Chief Financial Officer

You believe that your company's stock price is lower than its real value. You are considering various alternatives to increase that price, including the repurchase of company stock in the market. What are some considerations relating to this decision? [Answer, p. 8-22]

---

[5]If the reissue price is below the repurchase price, then additional paid-in capital is reduced until it reaches a zero balance, after which retained earnings is reduced.

▩ MID-MODULE REVIEW 1 ▩

Plesko Corporation reported the following transactions relating to its stock accounts in 2005:

Jan 15   Issued 10,000 shares of $5 par value common stock at $17 cash per share
Mar 31   Purchased 2,000 shares of its own common stock at $15 cash per share.
June 25 Reissued 1,000 shares of its treasury stock at $20 cash per share.

Use the financial statement effects template to identify the effects of these stock transactions.

Solution

Transaction	Balance Sheet						Income Statement		
	Cash Asset	+ Noncash Assets	= Liabil- ities	+ Contrib. Capital	+ Retained Earnings		Revenues	− Expenses	
Jan. 15	+170,000			+170,000ᵃ					
Mar. 31	− 30,000			− 30,000ᵇ					
June 25	+ 20,000			+ 20,000ᶜ					

Cash	170,000
Common Stock	50,000
Additional Paid-In Capital	120,000

Treasury Stock	30,000
Cash	30,000

Cash	20,000
Treasury Stock	15,000
Additional Paid-In Capital	5,000

ᵃCommon stock increases by $50,000 and additional paid-in capital by $120,000.

ᵇTreasury stock increases by $30,000, which reduces contributed capital by that same amount.

ᶜTreasury stock declines by its $15,000 cost (1,000 shares × $15 per share) and additional paid-in capital increases by $5,000. Total contributed capital, thus, increases by $20,000.

■ EARNED CAPITAL

We now turn our attention to the earned capital portion of stockholders' equity. Earned capital represents the cumulative profit that has been retained by the company. Recall that earned capital is increased by income earned and decreased by any losses incurred. Earned capital is also decreased by dividends paid to shareholders. Not all dividends are paid in the form of cash, however. In fact, companies can pay dividends in many forms, including property (like land, for example) or additional shares of stock. We cover both cash and stock dividends in this section. Earned capital also includes the positive or negative effects of accumulated other comprehensive income (AOCI). The earned capital of Pfizer is highlighted in the following graphic:

Shareholders' Equity (millions, except preferred shares issued)	Dec. 31, 2003
Preferred stock, without par value, at stated value; 27 shares authorized; 5,445 issued in 2003 . . .	$ 219
Common stock, $.05 par value; 12,000 shares authorized; issued: 2003—8,702	435
Additional paid-in capital	66,396
Employee benefit trust	(1,898)
Treasury stock, shares at cost; issued: 2003—1,073	(29,352)
Retained earnings	29,382
Accumulated other comprehensive income	195
Total shareholders' equity	$ 65,377

Cash Dividends

$
Cash Effect

Many companies, but not all, pay dividends. Their reasons for dividend payments are varied. Most dividends are paid in cash on a quarterly basis. The following is a description of **Pfizer**'s dividend policy from its 2003 10-K:

Dividends on Common Stock

Our dividend payout ratios [dividends/net income] were approximately 111.1% in 2003 and 35.6% in 2002. The significant change in the ratio in 2003 compared to 2002 is primarily a result of the impact that certain non-cash charges relating to purchase accounting had on our 2003 net income combined with increasing our dividend payments in 2003.

2004's Top 10 Global Underwriters of Equity Issuances		
MANAGER	AMOUNT (billions)	MARKET SHARE
Morgan Stanley	$54.3	10.7%
Goldman Sachs	51.3	10.2
Citigroup	47.7	9.5
Merrill Lynch	43.3	8.6
UBS	36.7	7.3
JP Morgan	30.6	6.1
Deutsche Bank	26.6	5.3
Credit Suisse F.B.	24.4	4.8
Lehman Brothers	21.0	4.2
Nomura	16.2	3.2

In December 2003, our Board of Directors declared a first-quarter 2004 dividend of $.17 per share. The 2004 cash dividend marks the 37th consecutive year of dividend increases.

Outsiders closely monitor dividend payments. It is generally perceived that the level of dividend payments is related to the expected long-term core income. Accordingly, dividend increases are usually accompanied by stock price increases, and companies rarely reduce their dividends unless absolutely necessary. Dividend reductions are, therefore, met with substantial stock price declines.

Pfizer's short-run dividend payment history, as reported in its 10-K, follows:

	Quarter			
	First	Second	Third	Fourth
2003				
Cash dividends paid per common share	$.15	$.15	$.15	$.15
2002				
Cash dividends paid per common share	$.13	$.13	$.13	$.13

This dividend information shows that Pfizer increased its quarterly dividend from $0.13 cents per share in 2002 to $0.15 cents per share in 2003.

Financial Effects of Cash Dividends

$
Cash Effect

Cash dividends reduce both cash and retained earnings by the amount of the cash dividends paid. To illustrate, Pfizer paid $4,771 million in 2003 cash dividends on its common and preferred shares. The financial statement effects of this cash dividend payment are reflected as a reduction in assets (cash) and a reduction in retained earnings as follows:

Retained
Earnings 4,771 M
Cash   4,771 M

	Balance Sheet						Income Statement	
Transaction	Cash Asset	+ Noncash Assets	= Liabil- ities	+ Contrib. Capital	+ Retained Earnings		Revenues	− Expenses
Paid $4,771 million cash dividends on common and preferred shares	−4,771 mil.				−4,771 mil. Retained Earnings			

Dividend payments have no effect on profitability. They are a direct reduction to retained earnings and bypass the income statement.

Preferred stock dividends have priority over those for common shares, including unpaid prior years' preferred dividends (dividends in arrears) when preferred stock is cumulative. To illustrate, assume that Pfizer has 15,000 shares of $50 par value, 8% preferred stock outstanding and 50,000 shares of $5 par value common stock outstanding. During its first three years in business, assume that Pfizer declares $20,000 dividends in the first year, $260,000 of dividends in the second year, and $60,000 of dividends in the third year. If the preferred stock is cumulative, the total amount of dividends paid to each class of stock in each of the three years follows:

	Preferred Stock	Common Stock
Year 1		
Current year dividend ($750,000 × 8%; but only $20,000 paid, leaving $40,000 in arrears)	$20,000	
Balance to common		$ 0
Year 2		
Arrearage from Year 1 ([$750,000 × 8%] − $20,000)	40,000	
Current year dividend ($750,000 × 8%)	60,000	
Balance to common		160,000
Year 3		
Current year dividend ($750,000 × 8%)	60,000	
Balance to common		0

■ MID-MODULE REVIEW 2 ■

Finn Corporation has outstanding 10,000 shares of $100 par value, 5% preferred stock and 50,000 shares of $5 par value common stock. During its first three years in business, Finn declared no dividends in the first year, $300,000 of cash dividends in the second year, and $80,000 of cash dividends in the third year.

a. If preferred stock is cumulative, determine the total amount of dividends paid to each class of stock for each of the three years.

b. If preferred stock is noncumulative, determine the total amount of dividends paid to each class of stock for each of the three years.

Solution

a.

	Preferred Stock	Common Stock
Year 1	$ 0	$ 0
Year 2		
Arrearage from Year 1 ($1,000,000 × 5%)	50,000	
Current year dividend ($1,000,000 × 5%)	50,000	
Balance to common		200,000
Year 3		
Current year dividend ($1,000,000 × 5%)	50,000	
Balance to common		30,000

b.

	Preferred Stock	Common Stock
Year 1	$ 0	$ 0
Year 2		
Current year dividend ($1,000,000 × 5%)	50,000	
Balance to common		250,000
Year 3		
Current year dividend ($1,000,000 × 5%)	50,000	
Balance to common		30,000

Stock Dividends and Splits

Dividends need not be paid in cash. Many companies pay dividends in the form of additional shares of stock. Companies can also distribute additional shares to their stockholders with a stock split. We cover both of these distributions in this section.

Stock Dividends

When dividends are paid in the form of the company's stock, retained earnings are reduced and contributed capital is increased. However, the amount by which retained earnings are reduced depends on the proportion of the outstanding shares distributed to the total outstanding shares on the issue date. Exhibit 8.2 illustrates two possibilities depending on whether stock dividends are classified as either small stock dividends or large stock dividends. The break point is 20–25% of the outstanding shares. (When the number of additional shares issued as a stock dividend is so great that it has, or is reasonably expected to have, the effect of materially reducing the share market value, the transaction is of the nature of a stock split; the 20–25% guideline is used for that purpose.)

EXHIBIT 8.2 ■ Analysis of Stock Dividend Effects

Percentage of Outstanding Shares Distributed	Retained Earnings	Contributed Capital
Less than 20–25% (*small stock dividend*)	Reduce by **market value** of shares distributed	Common stock increased by (dividend shares × par value per share); additional paid-in capital increased for the balance
More than 20–25% (*large stock dividend*)	Reduce by **par value** of shares distributed	Common stock increased by (dividend shares × par value per share)

For *small stock dividends,* retained earnings are reduced by the *market* value of the shares distributed (dividend shares × market price per share) and contributed capital is increased by the same amount. For the contributed capital increase, the common stock is increased by the par value of the shares distributed and the remainder (dividend shares × [market value per share − par value per share] increases additional paid-in capital. For *large stock dividends,* retained earnings are reduced by the *par* value of the shares distributed (dividend shares × par value per share), and common stock is increased by the same amount (no change to additional paid-in capital).

To illustrate the financial statement effects of dividends, assume that a company has 1 million shares of $5 par common stock outstanding. It then declares a small stock dividend of 15% of the outstanding shares (1,000,000 shares × 15% = 150,000 shares) when the market price of the stock is $30 per share. This small stock dividend has the following financial statement effects:

Retained Earnings 4,500,000
Common Stock 750,000
Additional Paid-In Capital 3,750,000

	Balance Sheet					Income Statement	
Transaction	Cash Asset	+ Noncash Assets	= Liabil- ities	+ Contrib. Capital	+ Retained Earnings	Revenues	− Expenses
Distribute 150,000 shares as a *small* stock dividend				+750,000 Common Stock +$3,750,000 Additional Paid-In Capital	−$4,500,000 Retained Earnings		

Retained earnings are reduced by $4,500,000, which equals the market value of the small stock dividend (150,000 shares × $30 market price per share). The increase in contributed capital is treated as follows: common stock is increased by the par value of $750,000 (150,000 shares × $5 par value), and the remainder of $3,750,000 increases additional paid-in capital. Similar to cash dividend payments, the stock dividends, whether large or small, never impact income.

Next, let's instead assume that a company declares a large stock dividend of 70% of the 1 million outstanding common ($5 par) shares when the market price of the stock is $30 per share. This large stock dividend has the following financial statement effects:

Transaction	Balance Sheet						Income Statement	
	Cash Asset	+ Noncash Assets	= Liabil- ities	+ Contrib. Capital	+ Retained Earnings		Revenues	− Expenses
Distribute 700,000 shares as a *large* stock dividend				+$3,500,000 Common Stock	−$3,500,000 Retained Earnings			

Retained
 Earnings 3,500,000
Common
 Stock   3,500,000

Retained earnings are reduced by $3,500,000, which equals the par value of the large stock dividend (700,000 shares × $5 par value per share). Common stock is increased by the par value of $3,500,000. There is no effect on additional paid-in capital since the dividend is reported at par value.

For both large and small stock dividends, companies are required to show comparable shares outstanding for all prior periods for which earnings per share (EPS) is reported in the statements. The reasoning is that a stock dividend has no effect on the ownership percentage of each common stockholder. As such, to show a dilution in reported EPS would erroneously suggest a decline in profitability when it is simply due to an increase in shares outstanding.

Stock Splits

A stock split is a proportionate distribution of shares and, as such, is similar in substance to a stock dividend. A typical stock split is 2-for-1, which means that the company distributes one additional share for each share owned by a shareholder. Following the distribution, and even though each investor owns twice as many shares, their percentage ownership in the company is unchanged.

A stock split is not a monetary transaction and, as such, there are no financial statement effects. However, companies must disclose the new number of shares outstanding for all periods presented in the financial statements. Further, many states require that the par value of shares be proportionately adjusted as well (for example, halved for a 2-for-1 split).

If state law requires that par value not be reduced for a stock dividend, this event should be described as a *stock split affected in the form of a dividend*. The following disclosure from **Pfizer**'s annual report provides such an example:

> We affected a three-for-one stock split of our common stock in the form of a 200% stock dividend in 1999 and a two-for-one split of our common stock in the form of a 100% stock dividend in 1997. All share and per share information in this report reflects both splits.

■ MID-MODULE REVIEW 3 ■

The stockholders' equity of Zhang Corporation at December 31, 2005, follows.

5% preferred stock, $100 par value, 10,000 shares authorized; 4,000 shares issued and outstanding	$ 400,000
Common stock, $5 par value, 200,000 shares authorized; 50,000 shares issued and outstanding	250,000
Paid-in capital in excess of par value—Preferred stock	40,000
Paid-in capital in excess of par value—Common stock	300,000
Retained earnings	656,000
Total stockholders' equity	$1,646,000

Identify the financial statement effects for each of the following transactions that occurred during 2006:

Apr. 1 Declared and issued an 100% stock dividend on all outstanding shares of common stock when the market value of the stock was $11 per share.

Dec. 7 Declared and issued a 3% stock dividend on all outstanding shares of common stock when the market value of the stock was $7 per share.

Dec 31 Declared and paid a cash dividend of $1.20 per share on all outstanding shares

Solution

	Balance Sheet							Income Statement		
Transaction	Cash Asset	+	Noncash Assets	=	Liabil- ities	+	Contrib. Capital	+ Retained Earnings	Revenues	− Expenses
Apr. 1							+ 250,000	− 250,000[1]		
Dec. 7							+ 21,000	− 21,000[2]		
Dec. 31	−123,600							− 123,600[3]		

[1]This large stock dividend reduces retained earnings at the par value of shares distributed (50,000 shares × 100% × $5 par value = $250,000). Contributed capital (common stock) increases by the same amount.

[2]This small stock dividend reduces retained earnings at the market value of shares distributed (3% × 100,000 shares × $7 per share = $21,000). Contributed capital increases by the same amount ($15,000 to common stock and $6,000 to paid-in capital).

[3]At the time of the cash dividend, there are 103,000 shares outstanding. The cash paid is, therefore, 103,000 shares × $1.20 per share = $123,600.

Comprehensive Income

Comprehensive income is a more inclusive notion of company performance than net income. It includes all recognized changes in equity that occur during a period except those resulting from contributions by and distributions to owners.

Specifically, comprehensive income includes (and net income excludes) foreign currency adjustments, unrealized changes in market values of available-for-sale securities, minimum pension liability adjustments, and changes in market values of certain derivative investments. Comprehensive income includes the effects on a company of some economic events that are often outside of management's control. Accordingly, some assert that net income is a measure of management's performance, while comprehensive income is a measure of company performance.

Pfizer reports the following components of its comprehensive income from its 10-K report:

(Millions)	Retained Earnings	Accumulated Other Comprehensive Income (Expense)
Balance December 31, 2002	$30,243	$(1,875)
Comprehensive income		
Net income	3,910	
Other comprehensive income—net of tax		
Currency translation adjustment		2,070
Net unrealized gain on available-for-sale securities		68
Minimum pension liability		(68)
Total other comprehensive income		2,070
Cash dividends declared—		
common stock	(4,764)	
preferred stock	(7)	
Balance December 31, 2003	**$29,382**	**$ 195**

Pfizer's total other comprehensive income includes the three following items that affect stockholders' equity and are not reflected in net income:

1. **Currency translation adjustment** ($2,070 million). This is the unrecognized gain on assets and liabilities denominated in foreign currencies. A gain implies that the $US has weakened relative to foreign currencies; such as when assets denominated in foreign currencies are translated in more $US. (Module 4 explains accounting for foreign currency translation.)
2. **Net unrealized gain on available-for-sale securities** ($68 million). Unrealized gains and losses on available-for-sale securities are not reflected in net income. Instead, they are accumulated in a

separate equity account until the securities are sold. (Module 6 explains accounting for investments).

3. **Minimum pension liability** ($68 million). This is the additional pension liability that must be recorded under GAAP because some of Pfizer's pension plans are underfunded. The $68 million unrealized gain on available-for-sale securities and the $68 million minimum pension liability are unrelated and the same dollar amount is coincidental. (Module 9 explains pension accounting.)

Summary of Stockholders' Equity

A summary of transactions that affect stockholders' equity is included in the statement of shareholders' equity. This statement reports a reconciliation of the beginning and ending balances of important stockholders' equity accounts. **Pfizer**'s statement of stockholders' equity follows:

(Millions, Except Preferred Shares)	Preferred Stock Shares	Preferred Stock Stated Value	Common Stock Shares	Common Stock Par Value	Additional Paid-In Capital	Employee Benefit Trust Shares	Employee Benefit Trust Fair Value	Treasury Stock Shares	Treasury Stock Cost	Retained Earnings	Accum. Other Compre- hensive Inc./(Exp.)	Total
Balance December 31, 2002 .	—	—	6,829	$341	$ 9,368	(58)	$(1,786)	(667)	$(16,341)	$30,243	$(1,875)	$ 19,950
Comprehensive income:												
Net income										3,910		3,910
Other comprehensive income—net of tax:												
Currency translation adjustment											2,070	2,070
Net unrealized gain on available-for-sale securities											68	68
Minimum pension liability											(68)	(68)
Total other comprehensive income											2,070	2,070
Total comprehensive income .												5,980
Pharmacia acquisition	6,019	$242	1,817	91	55,402							55,735
Cash dividends declared—												
common stock										(4,764)		(4,764)
preferred stock										(7)		(7)
Stock option transactions . . .			52	3	1,374	5	175	(1)	(20)			1,532
Purchases of common stock .								(407)	(13,037)			(13,037)
Employee benefit trust transactions—net					112	(1)	(287)	1	10			(165)
Preferred stock—conversions and redemptions	(574)	(23)			23				6			6
Other			4	—	117			1	30	—		147
Balance December 31, 2003 .	5,445	$219	8,702	$435	$66,396	(54)	$(1,898)	(1,073)	$(29,352)	$29,382	$ 195	$ 65,377

Pfizer's statement of shareholders' equity reveals the following key transactions for 2003:

- Net income plus other comprehensive income increased shareholders' equity by $5,980 million.
- Pfizer issued 6,019 preferred shares with a total par (stated) value of $242 million as part of Pharmacia's acquisition in 2003. It also issued 1,817 million common shares, which increased common stock by $91 million (1,817 million shares × $0.05 par value) and additional paid-in (contributed) capital by $55,402 million, representing the remaining value of the shares issued.
- Dividend payments to preferred and common shareholders decreased stockholders' equity by $4,771 million ($4,764 million + $7 million).
- Issuance of shares as a result of the exercise of employee stock options increased equity by $1,532 million.
- Stock repurchases decreased equity by $13,037 million.

- Employee benefit trust transactions reduced stockholders' equity by $165 million.
- Conversion of preferred stock into common stock reduced the preferred stock account and increased the common stock account, for a net increase in stockholders' equity of $6 million.
- Other transactions increased stockholders' equity by $147 million.

One final point: the financial press sometimes refers to a measure called **book value per share**. This is the net book value of the company that is available to common shareholders, defined as: stockholders' equity less preferred stock (and preferred additional paid-in capital) divided by the number of common shares outstanding (issued common shares less treasury shares). Pfizer's book value per share is computed as: ($65,377 million − $219 million)/(8,702 million shares − 1,073 million shares) = $8.54 book value per common share.

▓ MID-MODULE REVIEW 4 ▓

The stockholders' equity of Sloan Corporation at December 31, 2005, follows.

Common stock, $5 par value, 400,000 shares authorized; 160,000 shares issued and outstanding	$800,000
Paid-in capital in excess of par value	920,000
Retained earnings	513,000

During 2006, the following transactions occurred:

June 28   Declared and issued a 10% common stock dividend when the market value is $11 per share.
Dec. 5   Declared and paid a cash dividend of $1.25 per share.
Dec. 31   Updated retained earnings for net income of $412,000.

Compute the year-ending balance of retained earnings for 2005.

Solution

Retained Earnings Reconciliation For Year Ended December 31, 2006		
Retained earnings, December 31, 2005		$513,000
Add: Net income		412,000
		925,000
Less: Cash dividends declared	$220,000	
Stock dividends declared	176,000	396,000
Retained earnings, December 31, 2006		$529,000

■ EQUITY CARVE OUTS AND CONVERTIBLES

Corporate divestitures, or **equity carve outs**, are increasingly common as companies seek to increase shareholder value through partial or total divestiture of operating units. Generally, equity carve outs are motivated by the notion that consolidated financial statements often obscure the performance of individual business units, thus complicating their evaluation by outsiders. Corporate managers are concerned that this difficulty in assessing the performance of individual business units limits their ability to reach full valuation. Maximization of shareholder value is, therefore, not attained. In response, conglomerates have divested subsidiaries so that the market can individually price them.

Sell-Offs

Equity carve outs take many forms. The first and simplest form of divestiture is the outright sale of a business unit, called a **sell-off**. In this case, the company sells its equity interest to an unrelated party. When a company sells the business unit, it accounts for this sale similar to the sale of any other asset. Specifically, any excess (deficit) of cash received over the book value of the business unit sold is recorded as a gain (loss) on the sale.

$
Cash Effect

To illustrate, **Pfizer** reported a 2003 gain on the sale of its Adams confectionery products business unit in its income statement as follows:

> In March 2003, we sold the Adams confectionery products business, formerly part of our Consumer Health-care segment, to Cadbury Schweppes plc for $4.2 billion in cash. We recognized a gain on the sale of this business of $3,091 million ($1,824 million net of tax) in 2003.

The financial statement effects of this transaction follow:

- Pfizer received $4,200 million cash.
- The Adams's subsidiary was carried on Pfizer's balance sheet as an equity method investment with a book value of $1,109 million.
- Pfizer's gain on sale equaled the sale proceeds less the book value: $4,200 million − $1,109 million = $3,091 million gain on sale.
- The gain on sale, though transitory, is reported in its 2003 income from continuing operations.
- Pfizer subtracts the gain from net income in its statement of cash flows to compute net cash flows from operations since it is not deemed an operating cash flow. Instead, the $4,200 million cash proceeds are reported as a cash inflow from investing activities.

Spin-Offs

A **spin-off** is another form of divestiture. In this case, the company distributes the subsidiary shares that it owns as a dividend to its shareholders who, then, own shares in the subsidiary directly rather than through the parent company. In recording this dividend, retained earnings are reduced by the book value of the equity method investment and the subsidiary's investment account is removed from the balance sheet.

The spin-off of **Limited Too** subsidiary by its parent company, **The Limited, Inc.** (now Limited Brands), is an example of this form of equity carve out. The Limited described this spin-off as follows:

> On July 15, 1999, the Company's Board of Directors approved a formal plan to spin-off Limited Too. The record date for the spin-off was August 11, 1999, with Limited shareholders receiving one share of Too, Inc. (the successor company to Limited Too) common stock for every seven shares of Limited common stock held on that date. The spin-off was completed on August 23, 1999. The Company recorded the spin-off as a $25 million dividend, which represented the carrying value of the net assets underlying the common stock distributed. As part of the transaction, the Company received total proceeds of $62 million that included a $50 million dividend from TOO and a $12 million repayment of advances to TOO. During the second quarter of 1999, the Company recognized a $13.1 million charge for transaction costs related to the spin-off.

The important financial statement facts and effects of this transaction follow:

- Limited's shareholders received 1 share of Limited Too stock for every 7 shares of The Limited that they owned.
- Limited recorded the distribution as a dividend. Retained earnings were reduced by the book value (carrying amount) of the equity method investment, and the investment was removed from its assets.
- This distribution had no effect on The Limited's profitability in the year of the distribution. Instead, the distribution reduced the retained earnings component of its shareholders' equity.

Split-Offs

The **split-off** is a third form of equity carve out. In this case, the parent exchanges stock in the subsidiary that it owns in return for shares in the parent owned by its shareholders. After completing this transaction, the subsidiary is an independent publicly traded company.

The parent treats acquisition of its own shares from its shareholders like the purchase of treasury stock. As such, the treasury stock account is increased and the equity method investment account is reduced, reflecting the distribution of that asset. The dollar amount recorded for this treasury stock depends on how the distribution is set up. There are two possibilities:

1. **Pro rata distribution.** Shares are distributed to stockholders on a pro rata basis. Namely, a shareholder owning 10% of the outstanding stock of the parent company receives 10% of the shares of the subsidiary distributed. The treasury stock account is recorded at the book value of the investment in the subsidiary. The accounting is similar to repurchase of treasury stock for cash, except that shares of the subsidiary are paid to shareholders instead of cash.
2. **Non pro rata distribution.** This case is like a tender offer where stockholders can accept or reject the distribution. The treasury stock account is recorded at the *market value* of the shares of the subsidiary distributed. Since the investment account can only be reduced by its book value, a gain or loss on distribution is recorded in the income statement for the difference.[6]

The Limited split-off of Abercrombie & Fitch (A&F) in 1998 provides an excellent example of both variants of the split-off. To illustrate, we begin with the following 2000 income statement of The Limited ($ 000s):

	2000	1999	1998
Net sales	$10,104,606	$ 9,766,220	$ 9,364,750
Costs of goods sold, buying and occupancy	(6,667,389)	(6,443,063)	(6,424,725)
Gross income	3,437,217	3,323,157	2,940,025
General, administrative and store operating expenses	(2,561,201)	(2,415,849)	(2,256,332)
Special and nonrecurring items, net	(9,900)	23,501	1,740,030
Operating income	866,116	930,809	2,423,723
Interest expense	(58,244)	(78,297)	(68,528)
Other income, net	20,378	40,868	59,915
Minority interest	(69,345)	(72,623)	(63,616)
Gain on sale of subsidiary stock	—	11,002	—
Income before income taxes	758,905	831,759	2,351,494
Provision for income taxes	331,000	371,000	305,000
Net income	$ 427,905	$ 460,759	$ 2,046,494

Limited reports "special and nonrecurring items" of $1,740 million in 1998. This amount includes $1,651 million in gain from the A&F split-off. Although Limited describes this gain as special and nonrecurring, Limited *included* it in income from continuing operations. This highlights the potential for large transitory items in income from continuing operations.

Limited describes this split-off in the notes to its 2000 annual report as follows:

On May 19, 1998, the Company completed a tax-free exchange offer to establish A&F as an independent company. A total of 94.2 million shares of the Company's common stock were exchanged at a ratio of 0.86 of a share of A&F common stock for each Limited share tendered. In connection with the exchange, the Company recorded a $1.651 billion tax-free gain. This gain was measured based on the $21.81 per share market value of the A&F common stock at the expiration date of the exchange offer. In addition, on June 1, 1998, a $5.6 million dividend was effected through a pro rata spin-off to shareholders of the Company's remaining 6.2. million A&F shares. Limited shareholders of record as of the close of trading on May 29, 1998 received .013673 of a share of A&F for each Limited share owned at that time.

Key financial statement facts and effects of this transaction follow:

*   Limited exchanged shares that it owned in A&F for some of the Limited shares owned by its shareholders. This splits off the subsidiary as an independent company.
*   Limited recorded treasury stock at the market value of A&F on the exchange date. Since the investment is removed from its balance sheet at its book value, the difference between these two amounts is recorded as a gain of $1,651 million.

---

[6]The SEC also allows companies to record the difference as an adjustment to additional paid-in capital. The usual practice, as might be expected, is for companies to report any gain as part of income.

- Limited's statement of cash flows adds back the gain to remove it from operating cash flows because the A&F split-off does not involve any cash flows.
- Limited was unable to exchange all of the A&F shares it owned via the tender offer. It then distributed the remaining 6.2 million shares on a pro rata basis. No gain is recorded on this part of the transaction.

$

Cash Effect

Analysis of Equity Carve Outs

Sell-offs, spin-offs, and split-offs all involve the divestiture of an operating segment. They are usually stock transactions and, as a result, do not involve cash inflow. Finally, they are all one-time occurrences. Yet, since they can result in substantial gains and can markedly alter the balance sheet, we must think about how they should be interpreted.

Equity carve outs are usually noncash and are always transitory. The company does, of course, lose the cash flows (positive or negative) of the divested business unit. As such, the divestiture should be treated like any other discontinued operation. Any recognized gain or loss from divestiture is treated as a nonoperating (investing) activity. The sale price of the divested unit reflects the valuation of *future expected* cash flows by the purchaser and is best viewed as a nonoperating (investing) activity by the seller. Income (and cash flows) of the divested unit up to the date of sale, however, is part of operations.

▣ MID-MODULE REVIEW 5 ▣

Blacconiere Company announced the split-off of its Salamon subsidiary. Blacconiere reported a gain from the split-off. (1) Describe the accounting for a split-off. (2) Why was Blacconiere able to report a gain on this transaction?

Solution
1. In a split-off, shares of the parent company owned by its shareholders are exchanged for shares of the subsidiary owned by the parent. If the distribution is non pro rata, the parent can report a gain equal to the difference between the fair market value of the subsidiary and its book value on the parent's balance sheet.
2. Blacconiere met the conditions described in part 1, which enabled it to report a gain.

Convertible Securities

Convertible securities are debt and equity securities that provide the holder with an option to convert those securities into other securities. Convertible debentures, for example, are debt securities that give the holder the option to convert the debt into common stock at a predetermined conversion price. Preferred stock can also contain a conversion privilege. Pfizer provides an example of the latter in its description of the Pharmacia acquisition:

> On April 16, 2003, Pfizer acquired Pharmacia for a purchase price of approximately $56 billion, which included the issuance of approximately 1.8 billion shares of Pfizer common stock, 180 million options on Pfizer common stock, six thousand shares of Pfizer Series A convertible perpetual preferred stock (convertible into 15.5 million shares of Pfizer common stock), and vested share awards, as well as transaction costs.

Conversion privileges offer an additional benefit to the holder of a security. That is, debtholders and preferred stockholders carry senior positions as claimants in bankruptcy, and carry a fixed or dividend yield. With a conversion privilege, they can enjoy the residual benefits of common shareholders should the company perform well.

A conversion option is valuable and yields a higher price for the securities than they would otherwise command. However, conversion privileges impose a cost on common shareholders. That is, the higher market price received for convertible securities is offset by the cost imposed on the subordinate (common) securities.

Accounting for the issuance of a convertible security is straightforward: the conversion option is *not* valued on the balance sheet unless it is detachable from the security (and, thus, separately salable). Instead, the convertible preferred stock or convertible debt is recorded just like preferred stock or debt that does not have a conversion feature.

When securities are converted, the book value of the converted security is removed from the balance sheet and a corresponding increase is made to contributed capital. To illustrate, assume that Pfizer has convertible bonds with a face value of $1,000 and an unamortized premium of $100. Its holders convert them into 20 shares of $10 par value common stock. The financial statement effects of this conversion follow:

Bonds Payable 1,100
  Common Stock   200
  Additional
    Paid-In
    Capital   900

Transaction	Balance Sheet					Income Statement	
	Cash Asset	+ Noncash Assets	= Liabil- ities	+ Contrib. Capital	+ Retained Earnings	Revenues	− Expenses
$1,100 book value bonds are converted into 20 common shares of $10 par value			−1,100 Bonds Payable, net	+200 Common Stock +900 Additional Paid-In Capital			

Following are key financial statement effects of this transaction:

* Face value ($1,000) and unamortized premium ($100) of the bonds are removed from the balance sheet
* Common stock increases by the par value of the shares issued (20 shares $\times$ $10 par = $200) and additional paid-in capital increases for the balance ($900)
* There is no effect on income from this conversion.

Accounting for conversion of preferred shares is similar. That is, preferred stock is removed from the balance sheet and common stock is issued at a price equal to the book value of the converted preferred shares.

One final note, the potentially dilutive effect of convertible securities is taken into account in the computation of diluted earnings per share (EPS). Specifically, the diluted EPS computation assumes conversion at the beginning of the year (or when the security is issued if during the year). The earnings available to common shares in the numerator are increased by any forgone after-tax interest expense or preferred dividends, and the additional shares to be issued in the conversion increase the shares outstanding in the denominator.

MODULE-END REVIEW

Kallapur, Inc. has issued convertible debentures: each $1,000 bond is convertible into 200 shares of $1 par common. Assume that the bonds were sold at a discount, and that each bond has a current unamortized discount equal to $150. Using the following template, illustrate the effects on the financial statements of the conversion of one of its bonds.

Transaction	Balance Sheet					Income Statement	
	Cash Asset	+ Noncash Assets	= Liabil- ities	+ Contrib. Capital	+ Retained Earnings	Revenues	− Expenses

Solution

Transaction	Balance Sheet					Income Statement	
	Cash Asset	+ Noncash Assets	= Liabil- ities	+ Contrib. Capital	+ Retained Earnings	Revenues	− Expenses
Convert an $850 book value bond into 200 common shares of $1 par value			−850 Bonds Payable, net	+200 Common Stock +650 Additional Paid-In Capital			

GUIDANCE ANSWERS

| MANAGERIAL DECISION | You Are the Chief Financial Officer |

Several points must be considered. (1) Treasury shares are likely to prop up earnings per share (EPS). While the numerator (earnings) is likely dampened by the use of cash for the stock repurchase, EPS is likely to increase because of the reduced shares in the denominator. (2) Another motivation is that, if the shares are sufficiently undervalued (in management's opinion), the stock repurchase and subsequent re-sale can provide a better return than some alternative investments. (3) Stock repurchases send a strong signal to the market that management feels its stock is undervalued. This is more credible than merely making that argument with analysts. On the other hand, company cash is diverted from other investments. This is bothersome if such investments are mutually exclusive either now or in the future.

■ DISCUSSION QUESTIONS

Q8-1. Define *par value stock*. What is the significance of a stock's par value from an accounting and analysis perspective?

Q8-2. What are the basic differences between preferred stock and common stock? What are the typical features of preferred stock?

Q8-3. What features make preferred stock similar to debt? Similar to common stock?

Q8-4. What is meant by dividend arrearage on preferred stock? If dividends are two years in arrears on $500,000 of 6% preferred stock, and dividends are declared at the end of this year, what amount of total dividends must preferred shareholders receive before any distributions are made to common shareholders?

Q8-5. Distinguish between authorized stock and issued stock. Why might the number of shares issued be more than the number of shares outstanding?

Q8-6. Describe the difference between contributed capital and earned capital. Specifically, how can earned capital be considered as an investment by the company's shareholders?

Q8-7. How does the account "additional paid-in capital" (APIC) arise? What inferences, if any, can you draw from the amount of APIC as reported on the balance sheet relative to the common stock amount in relation to the financial condition of the company?

Q8-8. Define *stock split*. What are the major reasons for a stock split?

Q8-9. Define *treasury stock*. Why might a corporation acquire treasury stock? How is treasury stock reported in the balance sheet?

Q8-10. If a corporation purchases 600 shares of its own common stock at $10 per share and resells them at $14 per share, where would the $2,400 increase in capital be reported in the financial statements? Why is no gain reported?

Q8-11. A corporation has total stockholders' equity of $4,628,000 and one class of $2 par value common stock. The corporation has 500,000 shares authorized; 300,000 shares issued; 260,000 shares outstanding; and 40,000 shares as treasury stock. What is its book value per share?

Q8-12. What is a stock dividend? How does a common stock dividend distributed to common shareholders affect their respective ownership interests?

Q8-13. What is the difference between the accounting for a small stock dividend and the accounting for a large stock dividend?

Q8-14. Employee stock options have a potentially dilutive effect on earnings per share (EPS) that is recognized in the diluted EPS computation. What can companies do to offset these dilutive effects and how might this action affect the balance sheet?

Q8-15. What information is reported in a statement of stockholders' equity?

Q8-16. What items are typically reported under the stockholders' equity category of other comprehensive income (OCI)?

Q8-17. What is the difference between a spin-off and a split-off? Under what circumstances can either result in the recognition of a gain in the income statement?

Q8-18. Describe the accounting for a convertible bond. Can the conversion ever result in the recognition of a gain in the income statement?

■ MINI EXERCISES

M8-19. Analyzing and Identifying Financial Statement Effects of Stock Issuances　On June 1, 2005, Beatty Corp., issues (*a*) 8,000 shares of $50 par value preferred stock at $68 cash per share and it issues (*b*) 12,000 shares of $1 par value common stock at $10 cash per share. Indicate the financial statement effects of these two issuances using the following template:

	Balance Sheet							Income Statement		
Transaction	Cash Asset	+	Noncash Assets	=	Liabil- ities	+	Contrib. Capital	+ Retained Earnings	Revenues	− Expenses

M8-20. **Analyzing and Identifying Financial Statement Effects of Stock Issuances** On September 1, 2005, Magliolo, Inc., (*a*) issues 18,000 shares of $10 par value preferred stock at $48 cash per share and (*b*) issues 120,000 shares of $2 par value common stock at $37 cash per share. Indicate the financial statement effects of these two issuances using the template in M8-19.

M8-21. **Distinguishing between Common Stock and Additional Paid-in Capital** Following is the 2003 stockholders' equity section from the Cisco Systems, Inc., balance sheet (in millions, except par value).

Cisco Systems, Inc. (CSCO)

Shareholders' equity	July 26, 2003
Preferred stock, no par value: 5 shares authorized; none issued and outstanding	$ —
Common stock and additional paid-in capital, $0.001 par value: 20,000 shares authorized: 6,998 shares issued and outstanding	21,116
Retained earnings	6,559
Accumulated other comprehensive income	354
Total shareholders' equity	$28,029

For the $21,116 million reported as "common stock and additional paid-in capital," what portion is common stock and what portion is additional paid-in capital? Explain.

M8-22. **Identifying and Analyzing Financial Statement Effects of Stock Issuance and Repurchase** On January 1, 2005, Bartov Company issues 5,000 shares of $100 par value preferred stock at $250 cash per share. On March 1, the company repurchases 5,000 shares of previously issued $1 par value common stock at $83 cash per share. Indicate the financial statement effects of these two issuances using the template in M8-19.

Procter & Gamble Company (PG)

M8-23. **Assessing the Financial Statement Effects of a Stock Split** Procter & Gamble Company discloses the following footnote to its 2004 10-K report:

> **Stock Split** In March 2004, the Company's Board of Directors approved a two-for-one stock split effective for common and preferred shareholders of record as of May 21, 2004. The financial statements, notes and other references to share and per share data have been restated to reflect the stock split for all periods presented.

This note to its 2004 balance sheet further indicates that amounts have been "restated for two-for-one stock split effective May 21, 2004." What restatements has P&G made to its balance sheet as a result of this action?

M8-24. **Proving Common Stock and Treasury Stock Balances** Following is the stockholders' equity section from the Abercrombie & Fitch balance sheet ($ thousands):

Abercrombie & Fitch (ANF)

Shareholders' Equity	Feb. 1, 2003
Common stock—$.01 par value: 150,000,000 shares authorized, 97,268,877 shares outstanding	$ 1,033
Paid-in capital	142,577
Retained earnings	714,475
	858,085
Less: Treasury stock, at average cost	(108,558)
Total shareholders' equity	$ 749,527

Assuming that A&F has repurchased 6,031,123 shares that comprise its 2003 treasury stock account, show the computation to yield the $1,033,000 balance reported for its common stock.

M8-25. **Identifying and Analyzing Financial Statement Effects of Cash Dividends**   Freid Corp. has outstanding 6,000 shares of $50 par value, 6% preferred stock, and 40,000 shares of $1 par value common stock. The company has $328,000 of retained earnings. At year-end, the company declares and pays the regular $3 per share cash dividend on preferred stock and a $2.20 per share cash dividend on common stock. Indicate the financial statement effects of these two dividend payments using the template in M8-19.

M8-26. **Analyzing and Identifying Financial Statement Effects of Stock Dividends**   Dutta Corp. has outstanding 70,000 shares of $5 par value common stock. At year-end, the company declares and issues a 4% common stock dividend when the market price of the stock is $21 per share. Indicate the financial statement effects of this stock dividend declaration and payment using the template in M8-19.

M8-27. **Analyzing, Identifying and Explaining the Effects of a Stock Split**   On September 1, 2005, Weiss Company has 250,000 shares of $15 par value ($165 market value) common stock that are issued and outstanding. Its balance sheet on that date shows the following account balances relating to the common stock:

Common stock	$3,750,000
Paid-in capital in excess of par value	2,250,000

On September 2, Weiss splits its stock 3-for-2 and reduces the par value to $10 per share.
a. How many shares of common stock are issued and outstanding immediately after the stock split?
b. What is the dollar balance of the common stock account immediately after the stock split?
c. What is the likely reason that Weiss Company split its stock?

M8-28. **Distributing Cash Dividends to Preferred and Common Shareholders**   Dechow Company has outstanding 20,000 shares of $50 par value, 6% cumulative preferred stock and 80,000 shares of $10 par value common stock. The company declares and pays cash dividends amounting to $160,000.
a. If no arrearage on the preferred stock exists, how much in total dividends, and in dividends per share, is paid to each class of stock?
b. If one year's dividend arrearage on the preferred stock exists, how much in total dividends, and in dividends per share, is paid to each class of stock?

M8-29. **Analyzing and Preparing a Retained Earnings Reconciliation**   Use the following data to prepare the 2005 retained earnings reconciliation for Bamber Company:

Total retained earnings, December 31, 2004	$347,000
Stock dividends declared and paid in 2005	28,000
Cash dividends declared and paid in 2005	35,000
Net income for 2005	94,000

M8-30. **Interpretation of a Spin-Off Disclosure**   Bristol-Myers Squibb discloses the following in notes to its 2003 10-K report:

Bristol-Myers Squibb (BMY)

The Company spun off Zimmer Holdings, Inc. (Zimmer), in a tax-free distribution, resulting in a common stock dividend of $156 million.

a. Describe the difference between a spin-off and a split-off.
b. What effects did BMY's spin-off have on its balance sheet and its income statement?

M8-31. **Interpretation of a Proposed Split-Off Disclosure**   Viacom, Inc. reports the following footnote in its 2003 10-K:

Viacom, Inc. (VIA)

SUBSEQUENT EVENT
On February 10, 2004, the Company announced that its Board of Directors authorized the Company to pursue the divestiture of Viacom's approximately 81.5% interest in Blockbuster, based on the conclusion that Blockbuster would be better positioned as a company completely independent of Viacom. The Company anticipates that the divestiture would be achieved through a tax-free split-off, but will also continue to consider other alternatives. The transaction is subject to further approval of the Viacom Board and an assessment of market conditions. The split-off, which would result in a reduction of Viacom's outstanding shares, is expected to be completed by mid-2004. If the Company determines to split-off Blockbuster any difference between the fair market value of Blockbuster and its net book value at the time of the split-off will be recognized as a gain or loss for accounting purposes. The actual amount of the gain or loss will depend upon the fair market

value and the net book value of Blockbuster at the time of the split-off as well as the exchange ratio used in the split-off.

a.   Describe the accounting for a split-off.
b.   How will the proposed split-off result in a reduction of Viacom's outstanding shares?
c.   Under what circumstances will Viacom be able to report a gain for this proposed split-off?

AT&T (T)   M8-32.   Interpretation of Disclosure related to the Split-Off of AT&T Wireless   AT&T reports the following footnote to its 2003 10-K:

> In 2001, we realized a tax-free noncash gain on the disposition of discontinued operations of $13.5 billion, representing the difference between the fair value of the AT&T Wireless tracking stock at the date of the split-off and our book value of AT&T Wireless.

a.   Describe the accounting for a split-off.
b.   Describe the circumstances that allowed AT&T to recognize a gain on this split-off.
c.   How should you interpret the gain from this split-off in your analysis of AT&T for 2003?

Jetblue   M8-33.   Analyzing Financial Statement Effects of Convertible Securities   Jetblue Airways Corporation re-
Airways   ports the following footnote to its 2002 10-K:
Corporation
(JBLU)

> **Convertible Redeemable Preferred Stock and Stockholders' Equity**
> Effective with our initial public offering on April 17, 2002, our authorized shares of capital stock were increased to 500 million shares of common stock and 25 million shares of preferred stock and all outstanding shares of our convertible redeemable preferred stock were converted to common stock on a one-for-one basis. The holders of our common stock are entitled to one vote per share on all matters which require a vote by the Company's stockholders as outlined in the articles of incorporation and the by-laws.

a.   Describe the effects on Jetblue's balance sheet of the conversion of its preferred stock.
b.   Did this conversion impact its 2002 net earnings? Explain.

■ EXERCISES

E8-34.   Identifying and Analyzing Financial Statement Effects of Stock Transactions   Lipe Company reports the following 2005 transactions relating to its stock accounts:

Feb 20	Issued 10,000 shares of $1 par value common stock at $25 cash per share.
Feb 21	Issued 15,000 shares of $100 par value, 8% preferred stock at $275 cash per share.
Jun 30	Purchased 2,000 shares of its own common stock at $15 cash per share.
Sep 25	Sold 1,000 shares of the treasury stock at $21 cash per share.

Indicate the financial statement effect of these transactions using the following template:

	Balance Sheet						Income Statement		
Transaction	Cash Asset	+	Noncash Assets	=	Liabil-ities	+ Contrib. Capital + Retained Earnings	Revenues	−	Expenses

E8-35.   Analyzing and Identifying Financial Statement Effects of Stock Transactions   McNichols Corp. reports the following transactions relating to its stock accounts in 2005:

Jan 15	Issued 25,000 shares of $5 par value common stock at $17 cash per share
Jan 20	Issued 6,000 shares of $50 par value, 8% preferred stock at $78 cash per share.
Mar 31	Purchased 3,000 shares of its own common stock at $20 cash per share.
June 25	Sold 2,000 shares of the treasury stock at $26 cash per share.
July 15	Sold the remaining 1,000 shares of treasury stock at $19 cash per share.

Indicate the financial statement effects of these transactions using the template in E8-34.

Abercrombie   E8-36.   Analyzing and Computing Average Issue Price and Treasury Stock Cost   Following is the stockhold-
& Fitch (ANF)   ers' equity section from the Abercrombie & Fitch balance sheet:

(Thousands)	February 1, 2003
Shareholders' Equity	
Common stock—$.01 par value: 150,000,000 shares authorized, 97,268,877 shares outstanding	$ 1,033
Paid-in capital	142,577
Retained Earnings	714,475
	858,085
Less: Treasury stock, at average cost	(108,558)
Total shareholders' equity	$ 749,527

    a. Assuming that A&F has repurchased 6,031,123 shares that constitute its treasury stock, compute the number of shares that it has issued?

    b. At what average issue price were the A&F shares issued?

    c. At what average cost were the A&F treasury stock shares purchased?

E8-37. **Analyzing and Distributing Cash Dividends to Preferred and Common Stocks** Moser Company began business on March 1, 2003. At that time, it issued 20,000 shares of $60 par value, 7% cumulative preferred stock and 100,000 shares of $5 par value common stock. Through the end of 2005, there has been no change in the number of preferred and common shares outstanding.

    a. Assume that Moser declared and paid cash dividends of $0 in 2003, $183,000 in 2004, and $200,000 in 2005. Compute the total cash dividends and the dividends per share paid to each class of stock in 2003, 2004, and 2005.

    b. Assume that Moser declared and paid cash dividends of $0 in 2003, $84,000 in 2004, and $150,000 in 2005. Compute the total cash dividends and the dividends per share paid to each class of stock in 2003, 2004, and 2005.

E8-38. **Analyzing and Distributing Cash Dividends to Preferred and Common Stocks** Potter Company has outstanding 15,000 shares of $50 par value, 8% preferred stock and 50,000 shares of $5 par value common stock. During its first three years in business, it declared and paid no cash dividends in the first year, $280,000 in the second year, and $60,000 in the third year.

    a. If the preferred stock is cumulative, determine the total amount of cash dividends paid to each class of stock in each of the three years.

    b. If the preferred stock is noncumulative, determine the total amount of cash dividends paid to each class of stock in each of the three years.

E8-39. **Analyzing and Computing Issue Price, Treasury Stock Cost, and Shares Outstanding** Following is the stockholders' equity section from Altria's balance sheet ($ million):

Altria (MO)

December 31,	2003
Stockholders' Equity	
Common stock, par value $0.331/3 per share (2,805,961,317 shares issued)	$ 935
Additional paid-in capital	4,813
Earnings reinvested in the business	47,008
Accumulated other comprehensive losses (including currency translation of $1,578)	(2,125)
Cost of repurchased stock (768,697,895 shares)	(25,554)
Total stockholders' equity	$ 25,077

    a. Show the computation to derive the $935 million for common stock.

    b. At what average price has Altria issued its common stock?

    c. How many shares of Altria common stock are outstanding as of December 31, 2003?

    d. At what average cost has Altria repurchased its treasury stock as of December 31, 2003?

    e. Why would a company such as Altria want to repurchase more than $25 billion of its common stock?

E8-40. **Analyzing and Distributing Cash Dividends to Preferred and Common Stocks** Skinner Company began business on June 30, 2003. At that time, it issued 18,000 shares of $50 par value, 6% cumulative preferred stock and 90,000 shares of $10 par value common stock. Through the end of 2005, there has been no change in the number of preferred and common shares outstanding.

a.   Assume that Skinner declared and paid cash dividends of $63,000 in 2003, $0 in 2004, and $378,000 in 2005. Compute the total cash dividends and the dividends per share paid to each class of stock in 2003, 2004, and 2005.

b.   Assume that Skinner declared and paid cash dividends of $0 in 2003, $108,000 in 2004, and $189,000 in 2005. Compute the total cash dividends and the dividends per share paid to each class of stock in 2003, 2004, and 2005.

E8-41.   Analyzing and Identifying Financial Statement Effects of Dividends   Chaney Company has outstanding 25,000 shares of $10 par value common stock. It also has $405,000 of retained earnings. Near the current year-end, the company declares and pays a cash dividend of $1.90 per share and declares and issues a 4% stock dividend. The market price of the stock at the declaration date is $35 per share. Indicate the financial statement effects of these two separate dividends using the template in E8-34.

E8-42.   Identifying and Analyzing Financial Statement Effects of Dividends   The stockholders' equity of Revsine Company at December 31, 2004, appears below:

Common stock, $10 par value, 200,000 shares authorized;	
80,000 shares issued and outstanding	$800,000
Paid-in capital in excess of par value	480,000
Retained earnings	305,000

During 2005, the following transactions occurred:

May 12   Declared and issued a 7% stock dividend; the common stock market value was $18 per share.

Dec. 31   Declared and paid a cash dividend of 75 cents per share.

a.   Indicate the financial statement effects for each of these transactions using the template in E8-34.

b.   Prepare a retained earnings reconciliation for 2005 assuming that the company reports 2005 net income of $283,000.

E8-43.   Analyzing and Identifying Financial Statement Effects of Dividends   The stockholders' equity of Kinney Company at December 31, 2004, is shown below:

5% preferred stock, $100 par value, 10,000 shares authorized;	
4,000 shares issued and outstanding	$ 400,000
Common stock, $5 par value, 200,000 shares authorized;	
50,000 shares issued and outstanding	250,000
Paid-in capital in excess of par value—preferred stock	40,000
Paid-in capital in excess of par value—common stock	300,000
Retained earnings	656,000
Total stockholders' equity	$1,646,000

The following transactions, among others, occurred during 2005:

Apr. 1   Declared and issued a 100% stock dividend on all outstanding shares of common stock. The market value of the stock was $11 per share.

Dec. 7   Declared and issued a 3% stock dividend on all outstanding shares of common stock. The market value of the stock was $14 per share.

Dec. 20   Declared and paid (1) the annual cash dividend on the preferred stock and (2) a cash dividend of 80 cents per common share.

a.   Indicate the financial statement effects of these separate transactions using the template in E8-34.

b.   Prepare a 2005 retained earnings reconciliation assuming that the company reports 2005 net income of $253,000.

E8-44.   Analyzing, Identifying and Explaining the Effects of a Stock Split   On March 1 of the current year, Xie Company has 400,000 shares of $20 par value common stock that are issued and outstanding. Its balance sheet shows the following account balances relating to common stock:

Common stock	$8,000,000
Paid-in capital in excess of par value	3,400,000

On March 2, Xie Company splits its common stock 2-for-1 and reduces the par value to $10 per share.

a.   How many shares of common stock are issued and outstanding immediately after the stock split?
b.   What is the dollar balance in its common stock account immediately after the stock split?
c.   What is the dollar balance in its paid-in capital in excess of par value account immediately after the stock split?

E8-45.   Analyzing and Computing Issue Price, Treasury Stock Cost, and Shares Outstanding   Following is the stockholders' equity section of the Caterpillar, Inc., balance sheet:

Caterpillar, Inc. (CAT)

December 31 ($ millions)	2003	2002
Stockholders' equity		
Common stock of $1.00 par value:		
Authorized shares: 900,000,000		
Issued shares (2003 and 2002—407,447,312) at paid-in amount	**$ 1,059**	$ 1,034
Treasury stock (2003—63,685,272 shares;		
2002—63,192,245 shares) at cost	**(2,914)**	(2,669)
Profit employed in the business	**8,450**	7,849
Accumulated other comprehensive income	**(517)**	(742)
Total stockholders' equity	**$ 6,078**	$ 5,472

a.   How many shares of Caterpillar common stock are outstanding at year-end 2003?
b.   What does the phrase "at paid-in amount" mean?
c.   At what average cost has Caterpillar repurchased its stock as of year-end 2003?
d.   Why would a company such as Caterpillar want to repurchase its common stock?

E8-46.   Effects of Equity Changes from Convertible Preferred and Employee Stock Options   Following is the 2002 statement of stockholders' equity for JetBlue Airways Corporation ($ 000s):

JetBlue Airways Corporation (JBLU)

($ thousands)	Convertible Redeemable Preferred Stock	Common Stock	Additional Paid-In Capital	Accumulated Deficit/ Retained Earnings	Unearned Compensation	Accumulated Other Comprehensive Income	Total
Balance at December 31, 2001	$ 210,441	$ 65	$ 3,868	$(33,117)	$(2,983)	$ —	$ (32,167)
Net income	—	—	—	54,908	—	—	54,908
Other comprehensive income	—	—	—	—	—	187	187
Total comprehensive income							55,095
Accrued undeclared dividends on preferred stock	5,955	—	—	(5,955)	—	—	(5,955)
Proceeds from initial public offering, net of offering expenses	—	101	168,177	—	—	—	168,278
Conversion of redeemable preferred stock	(216,394)	461	215,933	—	—	—	216,394
Exercise of common stock options	—	8	1,058	—	—	—	1,066
Tax benefit of stock options exercised	—	—	6,568	—	—	—	6,568
Unearned compensation on common stock options, net of forfeitures	—	—	8,144	—	(8,144)	—	—
Amortization of unearned compensation	—	—	—	—	1,713	—	1,713
Stock issued under crewmember stock purchase plan	—	3	3,711	—	—	—	3,714
Other	(2)	—	12	(45)	—	—	(33)
Balance at December 31, 2002	$ —	$638	$407,471	$ 15,791	$(9,414)	$187	$414,673

a. Discuss the linkage between changes in convertible redeemable preferred stock, common stock, and additional paid-in capital accounts for 2002.

b. Assuming that 811,623 shares were issued to employees under the stock option plan in 2002, discuss the effects on stockholders' equity of the exercise of employee stock options in 2002. JetBlue's stock traded in the $20 per share range during that same period.

E8-47. **Analyzing and Computing Issue Price, Treasury Stock Cost, and Shares Outstanding**   Following is the stockholders' equity and minority interest sections of the **Merck & Co., Inc.**, balance sheet:

Merck & Co., Inc. (MRK)

($ millions)	Dec. 31, 2003
Minority interests	$ 3,915.2
Stockholders' equity	
Common stock, one cent par value	
Authorized—5,400,000,000 shares	
Issued—2,976,230,393 shares—2003	29.8
Other paid-in capital	6,956.6
Retained earnings	34,142.0
Accumulated other comprehensive income	65.5
	41,193.9
Less treasury stock, at cost	
754,466,884 shares—2003	25,617.5
Total stockholders' equity	$15,576.4

a. Explain the derivation of the $29.8 million in the common stock account.
b. At what average issue price were the Merck common shares issued at?
c. At what average cost was the Merck treasury stock purchased at?
d. How many common shares are outstanding as of December 31, 2003?

IMS Health (RX)

E8-48. **Interpretation of a Split-Off Disclosure**   **IMS Health** reports the following footnote to its 2003 10-K related to the split-off of its CTS subsidiary:

CTS Split-OFF

On February 6, 2003, the Company completed an exchange offer to distribute its majority interest in CTS. The Company exchanged 0.309 shares of CTS class B common shares for each share of the Company that was tendered. Under terms of the offer, the Company accepted 36,540 IMS common shares tendered in exchange for all 11,291 CTA common shares that the Company owned. As the offer was oversubscribed, the Company accepted tendered IMS shares on a pro-rata basis in proportion to the number of shares tendered. The proration factor was 21.115717%.

As a result of this exchange offer, during 2003, the Company recorded a net gain from discontinued operations of $496,887. This gain was based on the Company's closing market price on February 6, 2003 multiplied by the 36,540 shares of IMS common shares accepted in the offer, net of the Company's carrying value of CTS and after deducting direct and incremental expenses related to the exchange offer.

a. Describe the accounting procedures for a split-off.
b. Describe the circumstances that allowed IMS to recognize a gain on this split-off.
c. How should you interpret this gain in your analysis of the company for 2003?

■ PROBLEMS

P8-49. **Analyzing and Identifying Financial Statement Effects of Stock Transactions**   The stockholders' equity section of Gupta Company at December 31, 2004, follows:

8% preferred stock, $25 par value, 50,000 shares authorized; 6,800 shares issued and outstanding	$170,000
Common stock, $10 par value, 200,000 shares authorized; 50,000 shares issued and outstanding	500,000
Paid-in capital in excess of par value—preferred stock	68,000
Paid-in capital in excess of par value—common stock	200,000
Retained earnings	270,000

During 2005, the following transactions occurred:

Jan. 10   Issued 28,000 shares of common stock for $17 cash per share.
Jan. 23   Purchased 8,000 shares of common stock for the treasury at $19 cash per share.
Mar. 14   Sold one-half of the treasury shares acquired January 23 for $21 cash per share.
July 15   Issued 3,200 shares of preferred stock for $128,000 cash.
Nov. 15   Sold 1,000 of the treasury shares acquired January 23 for $24 cash per share.

Required

a.   Indicate the financial statement effects of each separate transaction using the following template:

	Balance Sheet							Income Statement		
Transaction	Cash Asset	+	Noncash Assets	=	Liabil- ities	+	Contrib. Capital	+ Retained Earnings	Revenues	− Expenses

b.   Prepare the December 31, 2005, stockholders' equity section of the balance sheet assuming the company reports 2005 net income of $59,000.

P8-50. Analyzing and Identifying Financial Statement Effects of Stock Transactions The stockholders' equity of Sougiannis Company at December 31, 2004, follows:

7% Preferred stock, $100 par value, 20,000 shares authorized; 5,000 shares issued and outstanding	$ 500,000
Common stock, $15 par value, 100,000 shares authorized; 40,000 shares issued and outstanding	600,000
Paid-in capital in excess of par value—preferred stock	24,000
Paid-in capital in excess of par value—common stock	360,000
Retained earnings	325,000
Total stockholders' equity	$1,809,000

The following transactions, among others, occurred during the year:

Jan. 12   Announced a 3-for-1 common stock split, reducing the par value of the common stock to $5 per share. The authorized shares were increased to 300,000 shares.
Sept. 1   Acquired 10,000 shares of common stock for the treasury at $10 cash per share.
Oct. 12   Sold 1,500 treasury shares acquired September 1 at $12 cash per share.
Nov. 21   Issued 5,000 shares of common stock at $11 cash per share.
Dec. 28   Sold 1,200 treasury shares acquired September 1 at $9 cash per share.

Required

a.   Indicate the financial statement effects of each separate transaction using the template in P8-49.
b.   Prepare the December 31, 2005, stockholders' equity section of the balance sheet assuming that the company reports 2005 net income of $83,000.

P8-51. Identifying and Analyzing Financial Statement Effects of Stock Transactions The stockholders' equity of Verrecchia Company at December 31, 2004, follows:

Common stock, $5 par value, 350,000 shares authorized; 150,000 shares issued and outstanding	$750,000
Paid-in capital in excess of par value	600,000
Retained earnings	346,000

During 2005, the following transactions occurred:

Jan. 5   Issued 10,000 shares of common stock for $12 cash per share.
Jan. 18   Purchased 4,000 shares of common stock for the treasury at $14 cash per share.
Mar 12   Sold one-fourth of the treasury shares acquired January 18 for $17 cash per share.

July 17   Sold 500 shares of the remaining treasury stock for $13 cash per share.

Oct. 1   Issued 5,000 shares of 8%, $25 par value preferred stock for $35 cash per share. This is the first issuance of preferred shares from the 50,000 authorized shares.

Required

a.   Indicate the financial statement effects of each transaction using the template in P8-49.

b.   Prepare the December 31, 2005, stockholders' equity section of the balance sheet assuming that the company reports net income of $72,500 for the year.

P8-52.   Identifying and Analyzing Financial Statement Effects of Stock Transactions   Following is the stockholders' equity of Dennis Corporation at December 31, 2004:

8% preferred stock, $50 par value, 10,000 shares authorized; 7,000 shares issued and outstanding	$ 350,000
Common stock, $20 par value, 50,000 shares authorized; 25,000 shares issued and outstanding	500,000
Paid-in capital in excess of par value—preferred stock	70,000
Paid-in capital in excess of par value—common stock	385,000
Retained earnings	238,000
Total stockholders' equity	$1,543,000

The following transactions, among others, occurred during the year:

Jan. 15   Issued 1,000 shares of preferred stock for $62 cash per share.

Jan. 20   Issued 4,000 shares of common stock at $36 cash per share.

May 18   Announced a 2-for-1 common stock split, reducing the par value of the common stock to $10 per share. The authorization was increased to 100,000 shares.

June 1   Issued 2,000 shares of common stock for $60,000 cash.

Sept. 1   Purchased 2,500 shares of common stock for the treasury at $18 cash per share.

Oct. 12   Sold 900 treasury shares at $21 cash per share.

Dec. 22   Issued 500 shares of preferred stock for $59 cash per share.

Required

Indicate the financial statement effects of each transaction using the template in P8-49.

P8-53.   Analyzing and Interpreting Equity Accounts and Comprehensive Income   Following is the stockholders' equity section of the balance sheet for Procter & Gamble Company and its statement of stockholders' equity.

Procter &
Gamble
Company (PG)

	June 30	
Amounts in millions	**2003**	**2002**
Shareholders' Equity		
Convertible Class A preferred stock, stated value $1 per share (600 shares authorized)	$ 1,580	$ 1,634
Non-Voting Class B preferred stock, stated value $1 per share (200 shares authorized)	—	—
Common stock, stated value $1 per share (5,000 shares authorized; shares outstanding: 2003—1,297.2, 2002—1,300.8)	1,297	1,301
Additional paid-in capital	2,931	2,490
Reserve for ESOP debt retirement	(1,308)	(1,339)
Accumulated other comprehensive income	(2,006)	(2,360)
Retained earnings	13,692	11,980
Total Shareholders' Equity	**$16,186**	**$13,706**

Dollars in millions/ Shares in thousands	Common Shares Outstanding	Common Stock	Preferred Stock	Additional Paid-In Capital	Reserve for ESOP Debt Retirement	Accumulated Other Comprehensive Income	Retained Income	Total	Total Comprehensive Income
Balance June 30, 2002	1,300,770	$1,301	$1,634	$2,490	$(1,339)	$(2,360)	$11,980	$13,706	
Net earnings							5,186	5,186	$5,186
Other comprehensive income									
Financial statement translation						804		804	804
Net investment hedges,									
net of $251 tax						(418)		(418)	(418)
Other, net of tax benefits						(32)		(32)	(32)
Total comprehensive income									$5,540
Dividends to shareholders									
Common							(2,121)	(2,121)	
Preferred, net of tax benefit							(125)	(125)	
Treasury purchases	(14,138)	(14)		6			(1,228)	(1,236)	
Employee plan issuances	7,156	7		384				391	
Preferred stock conversions	3,409	3	(54)	51				—	
ESOP debt guarantee reduction					31			31	
Balance June 30,2003	1,297,197	$1,297	$1,580	$2,931	$(1,308)	$(2,006)	$13,692	$16,186	

Required

a. How many shares of convertible class A preferred stock are issued at fiscal year-end 2003?

b. What does the term *convertible* mean?

c. Show (confirm) the computation yielding the $1,297 million for common stock at year-end 2003.

d. Assuming that the convertible class A preferred stock was sold at par value, at what average price were the common shares issued at as of year-end 2003?

e. What is the accumulated other comprehensive income account? Explain.

f. What items are included in the $5,540 million 'total comprehensive income' at year-end 2003? How do these items affect stockholders' equity?

g. What amount of cash dividends was paid in 2003 for each of P&G's classes of stock?

P8-54.   Analyzing and Interpreting Equity Accounts and Comprehensive Income   Following is the stockholders' equity section of **Fortune Brands** balance sheet and its statement of stockholders' equity.

Fortune
Brands (FO)

	December 31	
(In millions, except per share amounts)	2003	2002
Minority interest in consolidated subsidiaries	$ 369.5	$ 398.9
Stockholders' equity		
$2.67 Convertible Preferred stock	7.5	7.9
Common stock, par value $3.125 per share, 229.6 shares issued	717.4	717.4
Paid-in capital	126.7	116.0
Accumulated other comprehensive loss	(106.2)	(177.6)
Retained earnings	4,942.2	4,529.9
Treasury stock, at cost	(2,968.1)	(2,880.4)
TOTAL STOCKHOLDERS' EQUITY	$ 2,719.5	$ 2,313.2

(In millions except per share amounts)	$2.67 Convertible Preferred Stock	Common Stock	Paid-In Capital	Accumulated Other Comprehensive Loss	Retained Earnings	Treasury Stock, At Cost	Total
Balance at December 31, 2002	$ 7.9	$717.4	$116.0	$(177.6)	$4,529.9	$(2,880.4)	$2,313.2
Comprehensive income							
Net income	—	—	—	—	579.2	—	579.2
Foreign exchange adjustments	—	—	—	76.0	—	—	76.0
Minimum pension liability adjustments	—	—	—	(4.6)	—	—	(4.6)
Total comprehensive Income	—	—	—	71.4	579.2	—	650.6
Dividends ($1.14 per share)	—	—	—	—	(166.9)	—	(166.9)
Purchases (4.1 shares)	—	—	—	—	—	(204.5)	(204.5)
Tax benefit on exercise of stock options	—	—	27.6	—	—	—	27.6
Conversion of preferred stock and delivery of stock plan shares (3.3 shares) and sale of stock in a subsidiary	(0.4)	—	(16.9)	—	—	116.8	99.5
Balance at December 31, 2003	$ 7.5	$717.4	$126.7	$(106.2)	$4,942.2	$(2,968.1)	$2,719.5

Required

a. Explain the "$2.67" as reported in the convertible preferred stock account title.

b. Show (confirm) the computation that yields the $717.4 million common stock in 2003.

c. Assuming that the convertible preferred stock was sold at par value, at what average price were the common shares issued at as of year-end 2003?

d. What accounts typically comprise the accumulated other comprehensive income (or loss) account? What accounts are included in Fortune Brands' accumulated comprehensive income and loss adjustments for 2003?

e. Assuming that there are 83,305,000 shares in treasury at year-end 2003, show how the $166.9 million in dividends is computed. What effect did the dividend payment of $1.14 per common share have on the stockholders' equity of Fortune Brands?

Lucent Technologies (LU)

E8-55.   Interpretation of Footnote on Convertible Debentures   Lucent Technologies reports the following footnote to its 2003 10-K related to its convertible debentures:

2.75% series A and B debentures
During the third quarter of fiscal 2003, we sold 2.75% Series A Convertible Senior Debentures and 2.75% Series B Convertible Senior Debentures for an aggregate amount of $1.6 billion, net of the underwriters discount and related fees and expenses of $46 million. The debentures were issued at a price of $1,000 per debenture and were issued under our universal shelf. The debentures rank equal in priority with all of the existing and future unsecured and unsubordinated indebtedness and senior in right of payment to all of the existing and future subordinated indebtedness. The terms governing the debentures limit our ability to create liens, secure certain indebtedness and merge with or sell substantially all of our assets to another entity.

The debentures are convertible into shares of common stock only if (1) the average sale price of our common stock is at least equal to 120% of the applicable conversion price, (2) the average trading price of the debentures is less than 97% of the product of the sale price of the common stock and the conversion rate, (3) the debentures have been called for redemption by us or (4) certain specified corporate actions occur.

Required

a. How did Lucent initially account for the issuance of its bonds, assuming that the conversion option is not detachable and separately salable?

b. How will Lucent account for the conversion of its bonds, if and when conversion occurs? Specifically, will Lucent recognize any gain or loss related to conversion? Explain.

    c. How is the convertible bond treated in the computation of basic and diluted earnings per share (EPS)?

    d. How should you treat the existence of its convertible bonds in your analysis of the company?

P8-56.   **Interpretation of Disclosure on Convertible Preferred Securities**   **Lucent Technologies** reports the following footnote to its 2003 10-K related to its convertible preferred stock:

Mandatorily Redeemable Convertible Preferred Stock
We have 250,000,000 shares of authorized preferred stock. During fiscal 2001, we designated and
sold 1,885,000 shares of non-cumulative 8% redeemable convertible preferred stock having an
initial liquidation preference of $1,000 per share, subject to accretion. The net proceeds were
$1.8 billion, including fees of $54 million. . . . Holders of the preferred stock have no voting
rights, except as required by law, and rank junior to our debt obligations. In addition, upon our
dissolution or liquidation, holders are entitled to the liquidation preference plus any accrued and
unpaid dividends prior to any distribution of net assets to common shareowners . . . Each trust
preferred security is convertible at the option of the holder into 206.6116 shares of our common stock.

Required

    a. Describe the meaning of the terms or phrases: *non-cumulative, 8%, convertible,* and *liquidation preference.*

    b. Describe the general impact on Lucent's balance sheet when it issued the preferred shares.
      (*Hint:* Aggregate all equity into the contributed capital account, that is, do not break out par value and additional paid-in capital.)

    c. Assume that its preferred stock is converted in full. Describe the general impact on Lucent's balance sheet at the conversion of the preferred shares if:
      (1) The conversion is paid in cash.
      (2) The preferred stock is converted into common stock
      (*Hint:* Aggregate all equity into the contributed capital account, that is, do not break out par value and additional paid-in capital).

    d. How should you treat the existence of its convertible stock for your analysis of the company?

MODULE

9 Reporting and Analyzing Off-Balance-Sheet Financing

MIDWEST AIRLINES

A HARD LANDING

The following headline has become all too familiar for companies in the airline industry: **Midwest Express Holding and its Unions Agree to Concessions in Bid to Avert Reorganization**. This article in *The Wall Street Journal* reports that: "Midwest Air Group's three unions tentatively agreed to concessions meant to help the airline company avoid Chapter 11 bankruptcy reorganization. The pilots union for the regional carrier . . . accepted the concessions in a new contract for its 223 pilots [and] . . . it reached tentative agreements with two other unions—the pilots union for national carrier Midwest Airlines and the 285-member flight-attendants union. The company seeks to save $600,000 a month through union workers' wage reductions, work-rule changes or productivity increases and also seeks concessions from aircraft lessors and banks." (*TWSJ* 2003)

Midwest Air Group, Inc. (formerly Midwest Express) is a regional carrier operating out of Milwaukee. Until earnings became losses in the wake of the September 11, 2001, terrorist attack, Midwest Air was a profitable carrier. It had found its niche and was successfully defending its turf against larger and more cumbersome national carriers. It was in an elite group, with Southwest Airlines and JetBlue.

Midwest Air was not, however, a no-frills airline. It was one of the first to offer all leather seating and a wider, less crowded, all-business class. Food service was high quality, served on china with metal utensils, and featured baked on-board chocolate chip cookies. The service was excellent. Passengers willingly paid a premium price for luxury air travel.

By 2000, Midwest Air had amassed nearly $134 million in retained earnings on an initial capital investment of $11.4 million (in 1984). Midwest Air reported 1999 net income of nearly $39 million on revenues of nearly $450 million. Then, the revenue stream sharply declined and the company lost $40 million during 2001–2003. Although technically solvent, with stockholders' equity of $124 million as of 2003, Midwest Air is fighting for its financial survival.

The hard landing endured by Midwest Air's shareholders during the past five years is graphically illustrated in the following stock price chart:

Midwest Air Stock Price

The company, in an effort to stave off bankruptcy, negotiated the following lease, debt, and stock transactions:

- **Lease Restructuring.** In August 2003, the company reached final agreement on renegotiating its contracts with 11 aircraft lessors and lenders. The lessors and lenders, in return for amending its contracts, received warrants to purchase shares of common stock at their option.

- **Debt Financing.** In September 2003, the company sold convertible senior secured notes to qualified institutional and accredited investors. The notes are generally convertible at any time at the option of the note holders into shares of common stock.

(Continued on next page)

(Continued from previous page)

- **Equity Financing.** In November 2003, the company sold 1,882,353 shares of common stock to qualified institutional and accredited investors at a price of $4.25 per share in a private placement for an aggregate purchase price of approximately $8 million.

These transactions have served to effectively convert the standing of its creditors to more like that of equity investors.

This module focuses on financing tools, such as those utilized by Midwest Air to fund its investing and operating activities. As we know, both investors and creditors are vitally concerned with the efficient utilization of assets and the manner in which those assets are financed. Chief financial officers (CFOs) are aware of this concern, and they seek alternatives to on-balance-sheet recognition of debt and assets in an effort to *window-dress* (meaning to cosmetically massage) their balance sheets.

One important financing tool, known as *off-balance-sheet financing*, refers to financing of investing activities where both the financing and investing accounts are not reported on the balance sheet. If CFOs can obtain a revenue stream from an asset without reporting either the asset or the liability on the balance sheet, then all of the usual measures of financial performance appear better than they would with on-balance-sheet financing.

CFOs have become increasingly clever in constructing contracts to finance assets in a manner where both the assets and liabilities are off-balance-sheet. For example, many companies employ the use of operating leases. More recently, activities accounted for as equity method investments (see Module 6) have been effectively used (these sometimes involve the use of variable interest entities or VIEs). Even most pension obligations are reported off-balance-sheet.

We cover each of these topics in this module. As we describe these techniques, keep in mind that it is often what is *not* reported on the face of the financial statements, particularly the balance sheet, that is of great informational value. However, information on these activities is available in the notes to financial statements. We will learn how to read, analyze and interpret such notes in this module.

Sources: *Midwest Airlines* 2004 and 2003 Annual Reports; *Midwest Airlines* 2004 10-K; *The Wall Street Journal*, 14 July 2003.

■ INTRODUCTION

Company stakeholders pay close attention to the composition of the balance sheet and its relation to the income statement. This attention extends to their analysis and valuation of both equity and debt securities. Of particular importance in this valuation process is the analysis of return on equity (ROE) and its components: return on net operating assets (RNOA)—including its components of net operating profit margin (NOPM) and net operating asset turnover (NOAT)—and financial leverage (FLEV) and spread. (Module 3 explains these measures.)

Valuation of debt securities (bonds and notes) must concern itself with financial leverage (claims against assets) and the level of debt service requirements compared with expected cash flows. If analysis reveals that ROE and cash flows are inadequate, companies likely face the prospect of declining debt ratings. The resulting higher cost of debt capital places limitations on the number of investment projects that yield a return greater than their financing cost. This restricts the ability of the company to grow and be profitable.

Financial managers are aware of the importance of how financial markets perceive their companies. They also recognize the market attention directed at the quality of their balance sheets and income statements. This reality yields pressure on companies to *window dress* their financial statements to present their financial condition and performance in the best possible light. Consider the following cases:

- **Case 1.** A company is concerned that its liquidity is perceived as insufficient. Prior to the end of the present financial reporting period it takes out a short-term loan from its bank and delays payment of accounts payable. The company's cash and current assets increase, yielding a balance sheet that appears more liquid.

- **Case 2.** A company's level of accounts receivable is perceived as too high, suggesting possible collection problems and reduced liquidity. Prior to the statement date, the company offers customers an additional discount to induce them to pay the accounts more quickly. Although profits on these sales are reduced by the discount, the company reduces its accounts receivable, increases its reported cash balance, and presents a healthier current financial picture. Further, if inventory is too high, the company can reduce its available quantities and increase its liquidity position by delaying purchases or by promoting sales via markdowns on selling prices.

- **Case 3.** A company faces the maturity of a long-term liability, such as the maturity of a bond or note. The amount coming due is reported as a current liability (current maturities of long-term debt), thus reducing net working capital. Prior to the end of its accounting period, the company renegotiates the debt to extend the maturity date of the payment or refinances the indebtedness with longer-term debt. The indebtedness is, thus, reported as a long-term liability and net working capital is increased.

- **Case 4.** The company's financial leverage is deemed excessive, resulting in lower debt ratings and increased borrowing costs. To remedy the problem, the company issues new common equity and utilizes the proceeds to reduce its indebtedness.

Companies generally wish to present a balance sheet with sufficient liquidity, less debt, and fewer assets. The rationale for the first two factors, those of liquidity and debt levels, are due to their link with solvency. Companies that are more liquid and less financially leveraged are viewed as less likely to go bankrupt. As a result, the risk of default on their debt is less, resulting in a higher debt rating and a lower interest rate on its debt.

The third factor, desire for fewer assets, is driven by return considerations. The components of ROE are net operating profit margin (NOPM), net operating asset turnover (NOAT), and financial leverage (FLEV) with its related spread. We generally prefer a company's ROE to be derived from operating results (RNOA) rather than leverage. So, if a company can maintain a given level of profitability with fewer assets, the related increase in ROE is due to higher RNOA (asset turnover), and not to increased financial leverage.

Off-balance-sheet financing means that assets or liabilities, or both, are not reported on the balance sheet. Even though GAAP requires detailed footnote disclosures, managers generally believe that keeping such assets and liabilities off the balance sheet improves market perception of their operating performance and financial condition. This belief presumes that the market is somewhat inefficient, a perception that persists despite empirical evidence suggesting that we can adjust balance sheets to include assets and liabilities that are excluded by managers.

This module explains and illustrates several techniques that managers utilize to achieve off-balance-sheet financing. Some topics we discuss are leases, pensions, and variable interest entities (and SPEs). This is not an exhaustive list of the myriad of techniques that managers have invented to achieve off-balance-sheet financing, but it includes the methods that are commonly used to achieve this objective. One point to keep in mind: since we are discussing off-balance-sheet financing, the relevant information for such financing is mainly in footnotes. GAAP footnote disclosures on such financing are fairly good, and we must have the skills to analyze and interpret them to understand these techniques. This module provides those skills.

■ LEASES

We begin the discussion of off-balance-sheet financing with leasing. The following graphic shows that leasing impacts both the balance sheet (liabilities and assets) and the income statement (leasing expenses are often, but not necessarily, reported in selling, general and administrative).

Income Statement	Balance Sheet	
Sales	Cash	Current liabilities
Cost of goods sold	Accounts receivable	**Long-term liabilities**
Selling, general & administrative	Inventory	
Income taxes	**Long-term operating assets**	Shareholders' equity
Net income	Investments	

Footnote Disclosures—Off-Balance-Sheet Financing		
Leases	Pensions	VIEs

A lease is a contact between the owner of an asset (the **lessor**) and the party desiring to use that asset (the **lessee**). Since this is a private contract between two willing parties, it is governed only by applicable commercial law, and can include whatever provisions are negotiated between the parties. The lessor and lessee can be any legal form of organization, including private individuals, corporations, partnerships, and joint ventures.

Leases generally provide for the following terms:

* Lessor allows the lessee the unrestricted right to use the asset during the lease term.
* Lessee agrees to make periodic payments to the lessor and to maintain the asset.
* Asset title remains with the lessor, who usually takes physical possession of the asset at lease-end. A lessee often negotiates the right to purchase the asset at its market or other predetermined price at lease-end.

From the lessor's standpoint, lease payments are set at an amount that yields an acceptable return on investment, commensurate with the credit standing of the lessee. The lessor, thus, obtains a quality investment, and the lessee gains use of the asset.

The lease serves as a financing vehicle, similar to an intermediate term secured bank loan. However, there are several advantages to leasing over bank financing:

* Leases often require less equity investment than bank financing. That is, banks often only lend a portion of the asset's cost and require the borrower to make up the difference from its available cash. However, leases usually require the first lease payment be made at the inception of the lease. For a 60-month lease, this amounts to 1/60 (1.7%) equity investment by the lessee, compared with 20%–30% equity that is often required by a bank.
* Since leases are contracts between two parties, their terms can be structured in any way to meet their respective needs. For example, a lease can allow variable payments to match seasonal cash inflows of the lessee, or have graduated payments for start-ups.
* If the lease is properly structured, neither the leased asset nor the lease liability is reported on the balance sheet. Accordingly, leasing can be a form of off-balance-sheet financing.

Lessee Reporting of Leases

GAAP identifies two different approaches for the reporting of leases by the lessee:

* **Capital lease method**. This method requires that both the lease asset and the lease liability be reported on the balance sheet. The lease asset is depreciated like any other long-term asset. The lease liability is amortized like debt, where lease payments are separated into interest expense and principal repayment.
* **Operating lease method**. Under this method, neither the lease asset nor the lease liability is on the balance sheet. Lease payments are recorded as rent expense by the lessee when paid.

The lessee's financial statement effects of these methods are summarized in Exhibit 9.1

EXHIBIT 9.1 ■ Financial Statement Effects of Lease Methods for the Lessee

Lease Type	Assets	Liabilities	Expenses	Cash Flows
Capital	Lease asset reported	Lease liability reported	Depreciation and interest expense	Payments per lease contract
Operating	Lease asset not reported	Lease liability not reported	Rent expense	Same as above

GAAP defines criteria to determine the classification of a lease as capital or operating, and only the operating method achieves off-balance-sheet financing.[1] Accordingly, managers seeking off-balance-sheet financing structure their leases so as to fail the "capitalization tests" that require the capital method to be used.

When the operating method for leases is applied, lease assets and liabilities are *not* recorded on the balance sheet. The company merely footnotes their existence and key details of the lease transaction. The income statement reports the lease payment as rent expense (instead of depreciation and interest expense when using the capital method). The cash outflows (payments to lessor) are per the contract, and are identical whether or not the lease is capitalized on the balance sheet.

---

[1]The four criteria for lease capitalization follow (must capitalize when one or more criteria are met): (1) The lease automatically transfers ownership of the lease asset from the lessor to the lessee at termination of the lease. (2) The lease provides that the lessee can purchase the lease asset for a nominal amount (a bargain purchase) at termination of the lease. (3) The lease term is at least 75% of the economic useful life of the lease asset. (4) The present value of the lease payments is at least 90% of the fair market value of the lease asset at inception of the lease.

Reporting of leases using the operating method has four important benefits for the lessee:

1. The lease asset is not reported on the balance sheet. This means that net operating asset turnover is higher because reported operating assets are lower and revenues are unaffected.
2. The lease liability is not reported on the balance sheet. This means that common balance sheet measures of leverage (like liabilities divided by equity) are improved. Consequently, many managers believe the company would then command a better debt rating and lower interest rate on borrowed funds.
3. Without analytical adjustments (see later section on capitalization of operating leases), the portion of ROE derived from operating activities (RNOA) appears higher, and the company's ROE is perceived of higher quality.
4. For the early years of the lease term, rent expense reported for an operating lease is less than the depreciation and interest expense reported for a capital lease.[2] This means that net income is higher in those early years with an operating lease.[3] Further, if the company is growing and adding operating lease assets at a sufficient rate, since the reported rent expense is less than the first year's depreciation and interest on capital leases, the level of profits will continue to remain higher during the growth period.

The benefits of applying the operating method for leases are obvious to managers, thus leading them to avoid lease capitalization. Furthermore, the lease accounting standard is structured around rigid requirements relating to capitalization. Whenever accounting standards (such as that for leasing) are rigidly defined, clever managers that are so inclined can structure lease contracts to meet the letter of the standard to achieve a desired accounting result when the essence of the transaction would suggest a different accounting treatment. This is *form over substance*.

Footnote Disclosures of Leases

Disclosures of expected payments for leases are required under both operating and capital lease methods. Midwest Air provides a typical disclosure from its 2003 annual report:

The Company leases aircraft, terminal space, office space and warehouse space. Future minimum lease payments required under operating leases having initial or remaining noncancellable lease terms in excess of one year as of December 31, 2003 were as follows (in thousands):

Year Ended December 31,	
2004	$ 43,248
2005	40,331
2006	38,989
2007	36,931
2008	35,341
2009 and thereafter	413,071

As of December 31, 2003, Midwest had 19 jet aircraft in service financed by operating leases. These leases have expiration dates ranging from 2004 through 2023 and can generally be renewed, based on the fair market value at the end of the lease term, for one to four years. Most of the leases include purchase options at or near the end of the lease term at fair market value.

As of December 31, 2003, Midwest Connect's 14 turboprop aircraft were financed under operating leases with a lease term of 12 years and an expiration date of 2008. These leases permit renewal for various periods at rates approximating fair market value and purchase options at or near the end of the lease term at fair market value. In the fourth quarter 1999, the Company entered into lease agreements to finance the acquisition of five Fairchild 328JETs. The leases run for a term of 16.5 years, with expiration of all leases

---

[2]This is true even if the company employs straight-line depreciation for the lease asset since interest expense accrues on the outstanding balance of the lease liability, which is higher in the early years of the lease life. Total expense is the same *over the life of the lease,* regardless of whether the lease is capitalized or not. That is: Total rent expense (from operating lease) = Total depreciation expense (from capital lease) + Total interest expense (from capital lease).

[3]However, NOPAT is *lower* for an operating lease (when not capitalized) because rent expense is an operating expense whereas only depreciation expense (not interest expense) is an operating expense for a capital lease.

occurring in 2016. These leases permit renewal for various periods at rates approximating fair market value and purchase options at or near the end of the lease term at fair market value.

Rent expense for all operating leases, excluding landing fees, was $47,889,000, $40,723,000 and $39,021,000 for 2003, 2002 and 2001, respectively.

The purpose of lease disclosures such as this is to provide information concerning current and future payment obligations. These contractual obligations are similar to debt payments and must be factored into our evaluation of the company's financial condition.

The Midwest Air footnote disclosure reports minimum (base) contractual lease payment obligations for each of the next five years and the total lease payment obligations that come due after that five-year period. This is similar to disclosures of future maturities for long-term debt. The company must also provide separate disclosures for operating leases and capital leases. (We know that all of Midwest Air's leases are operating because its footnote does not disclose any payments relating to capital leases.)

MANAGERIAL DECISION   **You Are the Division President**

You are the president of an operating division. Your CFO recommends operating lease treatment for asset acquisitions to reduce reported assets and liabilities on your balance sheet. To achieve this classification, you must negotiate leases with terms that you feel are not advantageous to your company. What is your response? [Answer, p. 9-22]

Capitalization of Operating Leases

Failure to capitalize operating leases when they should be capitalized, excludes a potentially large amount of assets and liabilities from the balance sheet. Most would probably agree, however, that these leased properties represent assets as defined under GAAP. That is, the company controls the assets and they provide future benefits. Also, lease liabilities represent real contractual obligations that should properly be recognized on the balance sheet.

Failure to recognize lease assets and lease liabilities when they should be capitalized yields distortions in ROE disaggregation analysis (see Module 3)—specifically:

• Net operating asset turnover (NOAT) is overstated due to nonreporting of lease assets.
• Financial leverage is understated by the nonreporting of lease liabilities—recall that lease liabilities are nonoperating.
• Net operating profit margin (NOPM) is understated. Although, over the life of the lease, rent expense under operating leases equals depreciation plus interest expense under capital leases, only depreciation expense is included in net operating profit (NOPAT)—interest is a nonoperating expense.[4]

Although aggregate ROE is relatively unaffected (assuming that the leases are at their midpoint on average so that rent expense is approximately equal to depreciation plus interest) failure to capitalize an operating lease results in a balance sheet that, arguably, neither reflects all of the assets that are used in the business, nor the nonoperating obligations for which the company is liable. Such noncapitalization of leases makes ROE appear to be of higher quality since it results from higher RNOA (due to higher NOA turnover) and not from higher financial leverage (FLEV). This is, of course, the main reason why managers want to exclude leases from the balance sheet.

Despite structuring leases to achieve off-balance-sheet financing, required lease disclosures allow us to capitalize operating leases for analysis purposes. This capitalization process involves three steps (this is the process that would have been used if the leases had been classified as capital leases):

1. Determine the discount rate.[5]
2. Compute the present value of operating lease payments.
3. Include the present value from step 2 as both a lease asset and a lease liability.

---

[4]While cash payments are the same whether the lease is classified as operating or capital, *operating cash flow* is higher with capital leases since depreciation is an add-back, and the reduction of the capital lease obligation is classified as a *financing* outflow rather than operating.

[5]There are at least two means to determine the rate: (1) If the company discloses capital leases, we can infer it to be the rate that yields the present value computed by the company given the projected capital leases payments (see Business Insight box later in this section). (2) Use the rate that corresponds to the company's debt rating or the rate from any recent borrowings involving intermediate term secured obligations.

To illustrate the capitalization of operating leases, we use **Midwest Air**'s footnote and its long-term secured borrowing rate of 7% as the discount rate to compute the present value of its operating leases in Exhibit 9.2.[6]

EXHIBIT 9.2 ■ Present Value of Operating Lease Payments ($ 000s)

Year	Operating Lease Payment	Discount Factor (i=0.07)	Present Value
1	$ 43,248	0.93458	$ 40,419
2	40,331	0.87344	35,227
3	38,989	0.81630	31,827
4	36,931	0.76290	28,175
5	35,341	0.71299	25,198
		7.80743* × 0.71299	196,729†
>5	413,071		$357,575
Average life	$413,071/$35,341 = 11.688 years		

*We compute the annuity factor for 11.688 years as 7.80743 from the formula $\dfrac{1 - \dfrac{1}{(1 + .07)^{11.688}}}{0.07}$.

†$35,341 × 7.80743 × 0.71299 = $196,729.

Specifically, each of the first five lease payments is discounted at the factor for that year. The remaining payments of $413,071 are assumed to reflect an annuity equal to the year 5 payment of $35,341 for a time period necessary to accumulate to the total payments due after year 5, computed as $413,071/$35,341 = 11.688 years. That is, after year 5, we *assume* that the company makes annual lease payments of $35,341 for a period of 11.688 years (sufficient to exhaust the $413,071 disclosed in the lease footnote as the total payments after year 5). The present value of this annuity is computed as $35,341 × 7.80743. Since this present value is at year 5, it must then be discounted to the present (year 0) by multiplying it by the year 5 present value factor of 0.71299. Thus, the present value of this 11.688 year annuity of $35,341, beginning in year 5 and discounted back to year 0, is $196,729. We then add this amount to the earlier years' present values to get Midwest Air's present value of its operating leases of $357,575.

Next, this present value is added to Midwest Air's assets and liabilities to capitalize the operating leases for analysis purposes. These adjustments yield the comparisons in Exhibit 9.3 for Midwest Air at year-end 2003.

EXHIBIT 9.3 ■ Analytical Adjustments from Capitalization of Operating Leases ($ 000s)

	Reported	Adjustments	Adjusted
Net operating assets	$291,624	$357,575	$649,199
Net nonoperating liabilities	167,307	357,575	524,882
Equity	124,317		124,317

The capitalization of operating leases has a marked impact on Midwest Air's balance sheet. For the airline and retailing industries, in particular, lease assets (airplanes and real estate) comprise a large portion of net operating assets and these leases are usually classified as operating.

These adjustments can change perception of ROE components. The net operating asset turnover is lower (net operating assets increase and revenues remain constant) than we would infer from reported financial statements. Using the year-end data presented in Exhibit 9.3 and given revenues of $383,948 the NOA turnover (using year-end figures) decreases from 1.32 ($383,948/$291,624) to 0.59 ($383,948/$649,199). Likewise, leverage (liabilities to equity) is higher than we would infer from reported financial

---

[6]The factors for individual payment amounts for years 1 through 5 are discounted using the present value for a single payment formula $1/(1 + r)^t$. The payment amount for each year is multiplied by this factor with r equal to 7% and t equal to the year number. The payments to be made after year 5 represent an annuity of $35,341 per year for 11.688 years. The present value of this annuity is computed by the formula $\dfrac{1 - \dfrac{1}{(1 + r)^t}}{r}$ with r equal to 7% and t equal to 11.688.

statements. Using the same data, liabilities-to-equity ratio is 4.22 times ($524,882/$124,317) versus 1.35 times ($167,307/$124,317) computed from the reported statements. Financial leverage is, therefore, revealed to play a greater role in ROE. The adjusted assets and liabilities arguably present a more realistic picture of the invested capital required to operate Midwest Air and of the amount of leverage represented by the leasing of assets.

BUSINESS INSIGHT   **Imputed Discount Rate for Leases**

When companies report both operating and capital leases, the average rate used to discount capital leases can be imputed from disclosures in the leasing footnote. Consider the following lease payment schedule reported by Wal-Mart Stores, Inc. in its 10-K report ($ millions):

Fiscal Year	Operating Leases	Capital Leases
2005	$ 665	$ 430
2006	651	427
2007	599	419
2008	553	411
2009	519	397
Thereafter	5,678	3,002
Total minimum rentals	$8,665	5,086
Less estimated executory costs		44
Net minimum lease payments		5,042
Less imputed interest at rates ranging from 4.2% to 14.0%		1,849
Present value of minimum lease payments		$3,193

Wal-Mart reports total undiscounted minimum capital lease payments of $5,042 and a discounted value for those lease payments of $3,193. Using Excel, we can estimate by trial and error the discount rate that yields the present value—which is about 8% (see chart below). The 8% discount rate can then be used to capitalize the operating lease payments ($ millions).

Year	Capital Lease Payment	Discount Factor (i=0.08)	Present Value
1	$ 430	0.92593	$ 398
2	427	0.85734	366
3	419	0.79383	333
4	411	0.73503	302
5	397	0.68058	270
		5.51496* × 0.68058	1,490[†]
>5	3,002		$3,159
Avg. life	$3,002/$397 = 7.562 years		

*The annuity factor for 7.562 years is 5.51496, from the formula $\dfrac{1 - \dfrac{1}{(1 + 0.08)^{7.562}}}{0.08}$.

[†]$397 × 5.51496 × 0.68058 = $1,490.

▨ MID-MODULE REVIEW 1 ▨

Following is the leasing footnote disclosure from Gap Inc.'s 10-K report.

> We lease most of our store premises and some of our headquarters facilities and distribution centers. These operating leases expire at various dates through 2033. The aggregate minimum non-cancelable annual lease payments under leases in effect on January 31, 2004, are as follows:

Fiscal Year	(In millions)
2004	$ 924
2005	835
2006	693
2007	564
2008	484
Thereafter	1,929
Total minimum lease commitment	$5,429

1. Does Gap classify these leases as operating or capital leases? Explain.
2. Assuming its leases are operating leases, compute the adjustments that you would consider for analysis of Gap's balance sheet? (Gap's recent intermediate term borrowing rate is 7%.)
3. Assuming the same facts as in part 2, what income statement adjustments might you consider?

Solution

1. Gap's leases are classified as operating leases—see footnote. Also, since there are no disclosures in the leasing footnote related to capital leases, we know that all of the leases are classified as operating.
2. Using a 7% discount rate, the present value of its operating leases follows ($ millions):

Year	Operating Lease Payment	Discount Factor (i=0.07)	Present Value
1	$ 924	0.93458	$ 864
2	835	0.87344	729
3	693	0.81630	566
4	564	0.76290	430
5	484	0.71299	345
		3.37654* × 0.71299	1,165†
>5	1,929		$4,099
Average life	$1,929/$484 = 3.9855 years		

*The annuity factor for 3.9855 years is 3.37654, from the formula $\dfrac{1 - \dfrac{1}{(1 + .07)^{3.9855}}}{0.07}$.

†$484 × 3.37654 × 0.71299 = $1,165.

Gap's operating leases represent $4,099 million of unreported operating assets and unreported nonoperating liabilities. These amounts should be added to the balance sheet for analysis purposes.

3. Potential income statement adjustments would include elimination of the rent expense currently reported in Gap's SG&A expenses and replacing it with the depreciation of the capitalized lease asset and the interest on the capitalized lease liability. Whereas rent expense is considered as an operating expense, only the depreciation expense is similarly classified. The interest is, of course, a nonoperating expense. NOPAT, as a result, is increased following the financial statement adjustment for operating lease capitalization.

■ PENSIONS

Companies frequently offer pension plans as a benefit for their employees. There are two general types of pension plans:

1. **Defined contribution plan.** This plan has the company make periodic contributions to an employee's account (usually with a third party trustee like a bank), and many plans require an employee matching contribution. Following retirement, the employee makes periodic withdrawals from that account. A tax-advantaged 401(k) account is a typical example. Under a 401(k) plan, the

employee makes contributions that are exempt from federal taxes until they are withdrawn after retirement.

2. **Defined benefit plan.** This plan has the company make periodic payments to an employee after retirement. Payments are usually based on years of service and the employee's salary. The company may or may not set aside sufficient funds to make these payments. As a result, defined benefit plans can be overfunded or underfunded. All pension investments are retained by the company until paid to the employee. In the event of bankruptcy, employees have the standing of a general creditor, but usually have additional protection in the form of government pension benefit insurance.

For a defined contribution plan, the company contribution is recorded as an expense in the income statement when the cash is paid or the liability accrued. For a defined benefit plan, it is not so simple. This is because the company holds pension investments, and the pension obligation is not satisfied until paid. How a defined benefit plan impacts financial statements is a major focus of this section.

There are two major accounting issues. First, how can companies best report their balance sheet presentation of pension investments and obligations? Managers are concerned that presenting both the asset (pension investments) and liability (pension obligation) would adversely impact the market's perception of their companies' financial condition (recall our previous discussion on leases). These managers lobbied for, and the FASB agreed to, a method that allows companies to report only the *net* pension liability on the balance sheet. This means that if the pension obligation is greater than the fair market value of pension investments, the underfunded amount is reported on the balance sheet as a long-term liability (pension obligations maturing in the upcoming year are current liabilities). Conversely, if pension investments exceed the pension obligation, the overfunded amount is reported as a long-term asset.

As a preview to pension accounting, Midwest Air is obligated to pay its employees $17.743 million in pension benefits at year-end 2003. Further, it has only $3.383 million set aside in pension plan investments to pay for this liability for a net unfunded pension balance of $14.360 million. Yet, Midwest Air reports a net pension liability of only $2,354 million on its balance sheet! The difference between the balance sheet amount of $2.354 million and the actual net pension obligation of $14.360 million ($17.743 million − $3.383 million) represents *unrecognized* pension liabilities of $12.006 million. This accounting conforms to GAAP. This section will interpret the information provided in company footnotes for us to better understand the full liability.

The second major accounting issue is the potential effect on the income statement from fluctuations in the market values of pension investments (assets) and pension obligations (liabilities). Given the accounting equation (assets = liabilities + equity) net changes in pension investments and pension obligations would impact equity, and these equity changes are normally first reported in the income statement and, then, in retained earnings. This would mean that income statements would be much more volatile, fluctuating with swings in the market value of pension investments and with changes in estimates of pension obligations. To alleviate this issue, GAAP allows companies to report pension income based on *expected* long-run returns on pension investments (rather than actual investment returns) and to defer recognition of unrealized gains and losses on both pension investments and pension obligations.[7] This *income smoothing* effect was a deliberate outcome of the FASB's pension deliberations and consequent reporting requirements.

The following graphic shows that pensions impact both the balance sheet (liabilities and assets) and the income statement (pension expense).

Income Statement	Balance Sheet	
Sales	Cash	Current liabilities
Cost of goods sold	Accounts receivable	**Long-term liabilities**
Selling, general & administrative	Inventory	
Income taxes	**Long-term operating assets**	Shareholders' equity
Net income	Investments	

Footnote Disclosures—Off-Balance-Sheet Financing		
Leases	**Pensions**	VIEs

---

[7]Unrealized gains and losses on pension obligations can arise from changes in estimates used to compute the present value of the pension obligations.

Reporting of Defined Benefit Plans

Exhibit 9.4 presents the balance sheet and income statement effects from the accounting for defined benefit pension plans assuming that the company has a net pension liability.[8]

EXHIBIT 9.4 ■ Financial Statement Effects of Defined Benefit Plans

Balance Sheet				Income Statement		
Cash + Noncash Assets	=	Liabilities	+	Contributed Capital + Retained Earnings	Revenues −	Expenses
	Pension Obligation					− { Service Cost / Interest Cost
	− Pension Investments				Investment Returns	
	Net Pension Liability			Net Pension Cost		

Actuaries hired by the company typically estimate the pension obligation.[9] Changes in any one of the assumptions used to estimate the pension obligation can markedly alter the liability reported on the balance sheet. Once this obligation is estimated, the company reports the present value of that obligation, net of the fair market value of the pension investments, on its balance sheet.

Changes to the net pension liability can arise from either changes in the estimated pension obligation, or changes in the market value of the plan investments, or both. As the net pension liability changes, however, equity must change in response to maintain the accounting equation. Changes in equity are usually reflected as an increase in income if equity is increasing or as a decrease in income if equity is decreasing.

Changes to the pension obligation arise from three sources as illustrated in Exhibit 9.5.[10]

EXHIBIT 9.5 ■ Sources of Financial Statement Effects of Defined Benefit Plans

Source	Balance Sheet Effect*	Income Statement Effect*
Service cost: Increase in pension obligation from additional year of employee work.[†]	Net pension liability **increases**	Income **decreases**
Interest cost: Increase in pension obligation from additional year of accrued interest.	Net pension liability **increases**	Income **decreases**
Investment return: Increase in pension investments from interest, dividends, and capital gains.	Net pension liability **decreases**	Income **increases**

*Exact opposite effects arise for any decreases in service cost, interest cost, and investment return.

[†]Since pension payments are usually based on ending salaries and years of service, service cost will increase each year as employees continue to work.

As net pension liability increases, that increase is reflected as increased pension expense in the income statement, and decreased income. Conversely, as the net pension liability decreases, that decrease is reflected in decreased pension expense in the income statement, and increased income.

Footnote Disclosures of Pensions

Since pension reporting is, for the most part, off-balance-sheet, GAAP requires extensive footnote disclosures. This means that an understanding of pension footnotes is key to proper analysis and interpretation of the financial effects of pensions for companies. This section looks at the effects of these disclosures on our analysis and interpretation of (1) financial condition—balance sheet, and (2) financial performance—income statement.

---

[8]If the market value of pension investments is greater than the pension obligation, the company reports a net pension asset instead of a net pension liability.

[9]Estimates reflect several key assumptions including the portion of current employees that is expected to remain with the company until retirement, employees' final salaries on which pension payments are usually based, and employees' remaining life spans for collecting the pension benefits after retirement.

[10]The pension liability can also increase or decrease as a result of changes in the assumptions used to compute it. We discuss the treatment of the changes arising from differing actuarial assumptions in the next section.

Balance Sheet Effects

A reconciliation of the pension obligation (called the *projected benefit obligation,* or *PBO*) from the beginning to the end of the year takes on the following form:

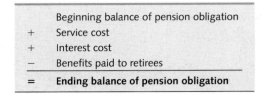

	Beginning balance of pension obligation
+	Service cost
+	Interest cost
−	Benefits paid to retirees
=	**Ending balance of pension obligation**

Although actual disclosures are a bit more complicated, this general format can be seen in the following defined benefit pension disclosure from the **Midwest Air** 10-K report ($000s):

Change in Pension Benefit Obligation	2003
Net benefit obligation at beginning of year	$13,665
Service cost	924
Interest cost	838
Benefits paid	(25)
Plan amendments	226
Actuarial loss	2,115
Net benefit obligation at end of year	$17,743

For Midwest Air's plan, its pension obligation was $13,665,000 at the beginning of 2003. It increased by $924,000 as a result of service costs, and $838,000 as a result of the interest accrual. The obligation decreased by $25,000 due to benefits paid during the year to retirees. It also increased by $226,000 as a result of plan amendments that provided employees with additional benefits, and the obligation increased by $2,115,000 as a result of actuarial losses (changes in assumptions used to compute the pension obligation).[11]

The reconciliation of the pension investment account (sometimes referred to as plan assets) from the beginning to the end of the year has the following general form:

	Beginning balance of pension investment account
+	Actual returns on invested assets
+	Company contributions to pension plan assets
−	Benefits paid to retirees
=	**Ending balance of pension investment account**

Midwest Air's reconciliation of its 2003 pension investments account follows ($000s):

Change in Pension Plan Assets	2003
Fair value of assets at beginning of year	$1,680
Actual return on plan assets	(15)
Employer contributions	1,743
Benefits paid	(25)
Fair value of plan assets at end of year	$3,383

Midwest Air's pension investments began the year with a fair market value of $1,680,000. A realized investment *loss* of $15,000 reduced the investment portfolio. Midwest Air contributed $1,743,000 to the

---

[11]Changes in actuarial assumptions yielding increases (decreases) in the pension obligation are labeled as losses (gains). A typical actuarial change resulting in a 'loss' is the decrease in the discount rate used to compute the present value of the pension obligation. As the discount rate decreases the pension obligation increases, resulting in a 'loss.' Midwest Air decreased its discount rate from 6.75% to 6% in 2003.

plan investment account (this is a cash outflow of the company for 2003). Benefits of $25,000 were paid to retirees, which reduced the pension obligation, and also reduced the plan investments as benefits are paid from this fund.

The difference between its pension obligation ($17,743,000) and the fair market value of its plan investments ($3,383,000) is $14,360,000, the **funded status**. This status reveals that the Midwest Air Pension Plan is underfunded by $14,360,000 as of 2003. Midwest Air reports the funded status of the plan, as detailed in the following disclosure ($000s):

Funded status at end of year	$(14,360) ◄——— Actual
Unrecognized net actuarial loss	8,707
Unrecognized prior service cost	3,299
Accrued benefit liability	$ (2,354) ◄——— Reproted

Even though its plan is underfunded by $14,360,000, a net pension obligation of only $2,354,000 appears on Midwest Air's balance sheet. The *unrecognized* liabilities, called net actuarial loss and prior service cost, are not reported on the balance sheet as a liability.

Pension obligations can change from changes in actuarial assumptions (actuarial loss resulting from a decrease in the discount rate in this case) and from company amendments to the pension plan to confer additional benefits on its employees (this is called a *prior service cost*). Managers were concerned about changes in pension obligations affecting their liabilities and lobbied the FASB to not require immediate recognition of these liabilities. The FASB conceded, and such increases in pension obligations are recorded off-balance-sheet. However, they are gradually recognized on-balance-sheet via an 'amortization' process, which we discuss below.

In sum, Midwest Air is obligated to its employees for $17,743,000 at year-end 2003. Its investments to cover this obligation total $3,383,000, for a net liability of $14,360,000. However, only $2,354,000 of this amount is reported on its balance sheet at year-end 2003. The remainder of $12,006,000 ($8,707,000 + $3,299,000) is unrecognized per GAAP, but disclosed in its notes.

How should we treat this information for analysis purposes? One option is to adjust the balance sheet to include the full liability. Although making the increased liability adjustment is not difficult, the offsetting adjustments (maintaining the accounting equation) can be complex and are beyond the scope of this book. A second option is to focus on the potential cash outflows that will be required to settle this liability. We discuss these cash flow implications later in this section.

RESEARCH INSIGHT   Valuation of Pension Footnote Disclosures

The FASB requires footnote disclosure of the major components of pension cost presumably because it is useful for investors. Pension-related research has examined whether investors assign different valuation multiples to the components of pension cost when assessing company market value. Research finds that pension components differ from one another reflecting differences in information about perceived permanent earnings.

Income Statement Effects

This section examines the income statement effects of pensions. Computation of pension expense, which usually appears as a component of SG&A expense when not reported as a separate line in the income statement, takes on the following general form:

	Service cost
+	Interest cost
−	Expected return on pension plan investments
±	Amortization of deferred losses (gains)
=	**Pension expense**

Midwest Air's defined benefit pension footnote for 2003 indicates that $2,038,000 of pension expense is reported in its income statement ($000s) and consists of the following components:

Components of Net Pension Benefit Cost	2003
Service cost	$924
Interest cost	838
Expected return on assets	(233)
Amortization of	
Prior service cost	310
Actuarial loss (gain)	199
Total net periodic benefit cost	$2,038

Service and interest costs that increase the pension liability are reflected in Midwest Air's income statement as expenses of $924,000 and $838,000, respectively. Investment returns that increase the pension investment balance (reduce the net pension obligation) decrease pension cost by $233,000. A portion of the pension liability relating to prior service cost and actuarial adjustments is *recognized* on-balance-sheet; this amortization increases the net pension liability and yields a corresponding increase in pension cost on the income statement. These elements yield the net pension cost of $2,038,000 in Midwest Air's 2003 income statement.

Computation of pension expense uses the *expected* return on pension investments (assets), not the *actual* return. The reason for this is that the value of pension investments fluctuate—often greatly during bull and bear markets. Consequently, if we used *actual* returns as the offset in computing pension expense, reported income would sharply increase in bull markets but would decline to potentially loss levels in bear markets. This potential for income volatility from use of actual investments returns in the computation of pension expense, and the potential to adversely impact companies' stock prices, worried corporate managers. As a result, they lobbied the FASB, and it agreed to accept expected long-run returns instead of actual returns to smooth reported earnings.

So, what is done with the difference between actual and expected returns? That is, because these unexpected returns are not now reported in income, what, if anything, is done with them? The answer is they are accumulated off-balance-sheet, just like the unrecognized prior service cost and actuarial losses discussed above.

What should be our reaction to this reporting and disclosure? Stock and bond prices tend to fluctuate around a long-term average. This means that if a company uses the long-run average as the expected return, then sometimes the actual return will exceed this level, and sometimes the actual return will be less. Over time, the unrealized gains and losses should hover around zero. The rationale for the off-balance-sheet disclosure of unrealized gains and losses is that, over time, they will not be realized and, thus, income statements are not distorted by using the expected long-run average return.[12]

For Midwest Air, it reports an expected return on its 2003 pension investments of $233,000, thus reducing pension expense by that amount. During 2003, its pension investments actually *lost* $15,000. This illustrates the smoothing mechanism of the expected return computation. Midwest Air's 2003 income was not impacted by the market decline under the *assumption* that the market will rebound in the future.

Pension Assumptions and Their Effects

Pension obligations depend on several assumptions. These include the expected rate of wage inflation used to estimate the pension obligation, the discount rate used to compute the present value of the pension obligation, and the expected return on plan investments. Given their importance, GAAP requires disclosure of these key rates for both the current and preceding year. Midwest Air's disclosure of these rates for its defined benefit plan follows:

Weighted-Average Assumptions	2003	2002
Discount rate	6.00%	6.75%
Expected return on plan assets	9.00%	9.00%
Rate of compensation increase	5.44%	5.44%

---

[12]This is the same logic underlying the accounting for held-to-maturity debt securities. That is, since the expectation is that the debt securities will not be sold until maturity, intervening fluctuation in market value are not important and should not be recognized in income for the intervening periods. The logic is more difficult to apply to equity securities.

Decreases in the discount rate, as evident for Midwest Air, yields two results: (1) the pension obligation is larger since the future payments are discounted at a lower rate, and (2) the interest cost can be either higher or lower, as a lower interest rate is applied to a higher pension liability. Midwest Air's decision to reduce its discount rate reflects the general decline in long-term borrowing rates in the early 2000s.

The expected return on plan assets impacts the expected dollar return offset to service and interest cost. Namely, the higher that return, the larger the offset (and the lower the pension expense). Thus, an increase in that return results in income increases. Understandably, the SEC scrutinizes these return assumptions and challenges managers that assume an unreasonably high return. Midwest Air's use of 9% is on the high end of that range, especially in light of the decline in long-run borrowing rates evidenced in its reduced discount rate. It could even be viewed as aggressive.

The rate of compensation increase directly impacts the pension obligation and, indirectly, reported income. Namely, the higher that rate, the higher the pension obligation, and the lower the income. Midwest Air's expected compensation increase was unchanged for this period.

Finally, we must be mindful of the classification of pension expense. Most consider the service cost component an operating expense, since it reflects the cost of employees working another year. However, the interest cost component is generally viewed as a nonoperating (financing) cost, and the expected return on plan assets is likewise viewed as nonoperating. Consequently, analysis and adjustment entails the parsing of pension expense into operating and nonoperating components.

To illustrate, Midwest Air recognized 2003 net pension expense of $2,038,000. This amount includes $924,000 of service cost, $838,000 of interest costs, $233,000 of expected return on pension assets, amortization of prior service costs of $310,000, and amortization of deferred actuarial losses of $199,000.[13] Analysis would adjust these income effects to exclude the interest cost, the expected return from plan assets, and the amortization of the deferred actuarial losses from its operating income. This would leave the service cost ($924,000) and the amortization of the prior service cost ($310,000) as operating expenses in computation of NOPAT.

BUSINESS INSIGHT | **How Pensions Confound Income Analysis**

Overfunded pension plans and boom markets can balloon income. When the stock market is booming, pension investments realize large gains that flow to income. This is because even though pension assets do not belong to shareholders (as they are the legal entitlement of current and future retirees), the gains and losses from those assets are reported in income. For example, in 2002, GE's reported net pension *income* was $1.6 billion, or 8.2%, of its pretax income, while its actual return on plan assets was a *loss* of $5.3 billion. Many analysts consider investment returns and interest expense on the pension obligation as nonoperating activities, so as to highlight the pension impact on profitability.

Future Cash Flow Effects

Midwest Air's pension plan is underfunded (has a negative funded status) by $14,360,000. However, only $2,354,000 is reported on the company's balance sheet as a liability. The difference is due to the fact that $12,006,000 of the liability is not recognized on-balance-sheet and *will not* be recognized unless the total unrecognized amount exceeds prescribed limits (even then, most of the unrecognized amount will continue to remain off-balance-sheet).

The unrecognized (off-balance-sheet) pension liabilities can be enormous. Consider this: in 2003, GM reported total pension and health benefit obligations of $169.9 billion and total pension investments to pay for this obligation of $103.7 billion for an underfunded balance (liability) of $66.2 billion. Yet GM reported a net pension *asset* on its balance sheet of $0.2 billion. The reason for this is that $66.4 billion (39%) of its pension obligation is not recognized on-balance-sheet.

The off-balance-sheet treatment of pension obligations is acceptable under GAAP. The fact is, however, that GM and many other companies with sizable pension plans have a substantial liability to their

---

[13]The amortization of prior service costs relates to plan amendments that have increased the pension obligation and are recognized on-balance-sheet gradually over time via the amortization process (presumably to match against the increased revenues generated by employees as a result of their added benefits). This cost is generally viewed as operating. The amortization of deferred actuarial losses relates to the cost of an increase in pension obligation as a result of decreases in the discount rate. This cost is generally viewed as nonoperating.

employees. In booming investment markets, like that which we witnessed in the 1990s, pension investments grow faster than pension obligations and provide a suitable source of payment for those liabilities. However, when markets reverse, like in the bear market of the early 2000s, pension investments shrink considerably and do not provide sufficient funds to meet such obligations. It is at times like these that unions put pressure on management to fund the pension deficit with cash. That cash must come, generally, either from borrowed money or operating cash flows.

For example, in 2002–2003, GM contributed $23.2 billion in cash to its pension plan investment account. This represented 50% of its operating cash flow of $46.4 billion during that period. These pension liabilities are real liabilities, even if not recognized on-balance-sheet. Further, they must be funded with cash if investments fail to provide a sufficient return. The potential cash drain is real and contributes to future declines in company stock price.

RESEARCH INSIGHT   Why do Companies provide Pensions?

Research examines why companies choose to offer pension benefits. It finds that company owners establish deferred compensation and pensions to align the long-term interests of owners and emloyees. Research also examines the composition of pension investments. It finds that a large portion of pension fund assets are invested in fixed-income instruments, which are lower risk than other investment securities; this implies that pension assets are less risky than nonpension assets.

■ MID-MODULE REVIEW 2 ■

Following is the pension disclosure footnote from **Altria**'s 10-K report. All required questions relate only to the U.S. plan.

The benefit obligations, plan assets and funded status of Altria Group. Inc.'s pension plans at December 31, 2003 and 2002, were as follows:

(In millions)	2003	2002
Benefit obligation at January 1	$9,002	$ 8,818
Service cost	234	215
Interest cost	579	590
Benefits paid	(604)	(845)
Miller transaction		(650)
Termination, settlement and curtailment	46	126
Actuarial losses	428	756
Other	(2)	(8)
Benefit obligation at December 31	9,683	9,002
Fair value of plan assets at January 1	7,535	9,448
Actual return on plan assets	1,821	(1,304)
Contributions	853	705
Benefits paid	(648)	(858)
Miller transaction		(476)
Actuarial (losses) gains	(6)	20
Fair value of plan assets at December 31	9,555	7,535
Funded status (plan assets less than benefit obligations) at December 31	(128)	(1,467)
Unrecognized actuarial losses	3,615	4,052
Unrecognized prior service cost	130	134
Additional minimum liability	(196)	(1,096)
Net prepaid pension asset (liability) recognized	$3,421	$ 1,623

1. In general, what factors impact a company's pension benefit obligation during a period?
2. In general, what factors impact a company's pension plan investments during a period?
3. What is the funded status (net dollars) of the Altria pension plan at year-end 2003?

4. What amount for funded status is reported on Altria's 2003 balance sheet? Is this an asset or a liability?
5. Identify and explain the difference between the funded status and the pension liability reported for Altria at year-end 2003. What factor is the largest source of this difference for Altria?

Following is Altria's footnote for its pension costs reported in its income statement.

(In millions)	2003	2002
Service cost	$ 234	$ 215
Interest cost	579	590
Expected return on plan assets	(936)	(943)
Amortization		
Net gain on adoption of SFAS No. 87	—	(1)
Unrecognized net loss (gain) from experience differences	46	23
Prior service cost	16	14
Termination settlement and curtailment	68	133
Net periodic pension cost (income)	$ 7	$ 31

6. What effect does the expected return on plan assets play in determination of pension cost?
7. How does Altria's expected return on plan assets compare with its actual return (in $s) for 2003?
8. How much net pension cost is reflected in Altria's 2003 income statement?

Solution

1. A pension benefit obligation is increased primarily by service cost, interest cost, and actuarial losses (increases in the pension liability as a result of changes in actuarial assumptions). It is decreased by the payment of benefits to retirees.
2. Pension investments are increased by positive investment returns for the period and cash contributions made by the company. Investments are decreased by benefits paid to retirees and by investment losses.
3. Altria's funded status is: $9,683 million (obligation) − $9,555 million (assets) = $128 million (net pension liability).
4. Altria reports a net *asset* of $3,421 million.
5. The difference between Altria's funded amount ($128 million liability) and the reported amount ($3,421 million asset) is due mainly to unrecognized actuarial losses of $3,615 million. As a result, $3,615 million of pension liabilities that contribute to the lower funded status are not recognized on-balance-sheet.
6. Expected return on plan assets acts as an offset to service cost and interest cost in computing net pension cost. As the expected return increases, net pension cost is reduced.
7. Altria expected return of $936 million is less than its actual return of $1,821 million in this year. Also, in 2003, it deferred unrealized gains that are neither recognized on-balance-sheet nor on the income statement.
8. Altria reports a net pension cost of $7 million in its 2003 income statement.

RESEARCH INSIGHT   Valuation of Nonpension Postretirement Benefits

The FASB requires employers to accrue the costs of all nonpension postretirement benefits; known as *accumulated postretirement benefit obligation* (APBO). These benefits consist primarily of health care and insurance. This requirement is controversial due to concerns about the reliability of the liability estimate. Research finds that the APBO (alone) is associated with company value. However, when other pension-related variables are included in the research, the APBO liability is no longer useful in explaining company value. Research concludes that the pension-related variables effectively convey the information in APBO for valuation purposes.

VARIABLE INTEREST ENTITIES (VIES)

Variable interest entities (VIEs), formerly called **special purpose entities** (SPEs), have been legitimate financing tools for decades and are an integral part of corporate finance. The VIE concept is as follows:

- A VIE is formed by a sponsoring company with minimal equity investment.
- The VIE purchases assets from, or for, the sponsoring company using borrowed funds in addition to its equity capital.

- Cash flows from the acquired assets are used to repay the debt and earn a return for the equity investors.
- The sponsoring company benefits either from the asset reduction arising from the sale of assets or from placement of newly acquired assets on another entity's balance sheet. These benefits yield an improved asset turnover ratio (assets are less in the denominator) and an improved financial leverage ratio (liabilities are less in the numerator).

The following graphic shows that VIEs impact both the balance sheet (liabilities and assets) and the income statement.

Income Statement
Sales
Cost of goods sold
Selling, general & administrative
Income taxes
Net income

Balance Sheet	
Cash	Current liabilities
Accounts receivable	**Long-term liabilities**
Inventory	
Long-term operating assets	Shareholders' equity
Investments	

Footnote Disclosures—Off-Balance-Sheet Financing		
Leases	Pensions	**VIEs**

Applying VIEs as Financing Tools

This section describes two common means of using VIEs as financing tools.

Asset Securitization

Consumer finance companies and retailers commonly use VIEs to securitize (sell) assets. **Sears** provides a common example as illustrated in the footnotes to its 2003 10-K report:

> **Accounting for Credit Card Securitizations**
>
> Credit card securitizations are utilized as part of the Company's overall funding strategy. Sears sells certain of its credit card receivable balances to various subsidiaries that in turn transfer those balances to master trusts ("trusts"). The trusts then securitize the receivable balances by issuing certificates representing undivided interests in the trusts' receivables to both outside investors and to the Company (as a retained interest). These certificates entitle the holder to a series of scheduled cash flows under preset terms and conditions, the receipt of which is dependent upon cash flows generated by the related trusts' assets. In each securitization transaction, a Sears subsidiary has retained certain subordinated interests which serve as a credit enhancement to the certificates held by the outside investors. As a result, the credit quality of certificates held by outside investors is enhanced. However, the investors and the trusts have no recourse against the Company beyond the trust assets.

Sears' use of its VIE is typical. As customers use the Sears credit card for their purchases, Sears accumulates the credit card receivables on its balance sheet. Periodically, it packages certain amounts of those receivables and sells them to a VIE trust, which funds the purchase by selling certificates entitling the holder to a portion of the cash receipts arising from the collection of the receivables (this funding can also be accomplished by issuing debt to be repaid from the collection of the receivables). Sears also purchases some of these certificates. Its certificates, however, do not receive cash from collections until the other certificates have been fully paid and, therefore, serve as a type of equity capital for the VIE. Sears does not provide any other form of protection to the outside certificate holders (the certificates are sold "without recourse," that is, without collection rights against Sears).

Project and Real Estate Financing

Another common use of VIEs is to finance construction projects. For example, say a sponsoring company desires to construct a manufacturing plant. It establishes a VIE and executes a contract with the VIE to purchase output from the plant. The VIE uses the contract and the newly constructed manufacturing plant assets to collateralize debt that it issues to finance the plant's construction. The sponsoring company obtains the benefits of the plant, but does not recognize either the asset or the liability since executory contracts (commitments) are not reported on the balance sheet under GAAP. Further, GAAP does not even require disclosure of these contracts in the footnotes.

Clothing retailers such as Gap and Abercrombie & Fitch are major users of executory contracts with outside manufacturers. The manufacturing assets, and related liabilities of the VIEs, are consequently kept off the balance sheet.

A slight variation is to add leasing to this transaction. To illustrate, assume a company desires to construct an office building. It establishes a VIE to construct and finance the building and then lease it back to the company under an operating lease. As we explained earlier in this module, if the lease is structured as an operating lease, neither the lease asset nor the lease obligation is reported on the company's balance sheet.

In summary, each of these cases demonstrates the financing capabilities of VIEs. Further, there are two main reasons for the popularity of VIEs:

1. **Lower cost of capital.** VIEs can provide lower cost financing for a company. Since the VIE is not burdened with the myriad of business risks that can affect a company (for example, in Sears' case the VIE only has the risk of uncollectibility), its investors do not need to be compensated for additional risk. Further, it is generally perceived that VIEs are protected from the bankruptcy of the sponsoring company, thus further reducing investment risk.
2. **Nonconsolidation.** VIEs can provide a mechanism for off-balance-sheet financing if unconsolidated with the sponsoring company. As we discuss in the next section, however, recent accounting standards have made it more difficult to avoid consolidation.

Reporting of Consolidated VIEs

Nonconsolidation of VIEs allows assets and liabilities related to the business to be reported off-balance-sheet. As a result, net operating asset turnover (Sales/NOA) is improved, which in turn improves return on net operating assets (RNOA), an important metric of financial performance.[14]

In recent years, regulators have passed legislation to make it difficult, if not impossible, to conduct VIE-related transactions off-balance-sheet. For instance, in 2001 the FASB published *SFAS 140,* which prescribed the conditions for asset securitization as a sale (where the company can remove the asset from the balance sheet and record its purchase as a sale, to affect financing of the asset off-balance-sheet). Essentially, the VIE must be an independent entity with sufficient equity capital to finance its ongoing operations without the support of the sponsoring company. Many previously existing VIEs did not qualify and, as a result, the sponsoring companies were forced to consolidate the VIE balance sheets with their own balance sheets. This consolidation recognizes the assets and related liabilities on-balance-sheet, thus negating any cosmetic effects of the off-balance-sheet financing.

Subsequent to passage of *SFAS 140,* the FASB issued *FIN 46* in 2003.[15] This interpretation identified the characteristics of VIEs that require consolidation. Generally, any entity that lacks independence from the sponsoring company and lacks sufficient capital to conduct its operations apart from the sponsoring company, must be consolidated with whatever entity bears the greatest risk of loss and stands to reap the greatest rewards from its activities.

Companies consolidating these VIEs will realize a marked increase in assets and related liabilities. Sears provides an example as evident in its following securitization footnote:

> On March 31, 2001, the Company adopted the requirements of *Statement of Financial Accounting Standards* (SFAS) *No. 140,* "Accounting for Transfers and Servicing of Financial Assets and Extinguishments of Liabilities," which superceded *SFAS No. 125.* Under *SFAS No. 125,* the Company's securitization transactions were accounted for as sales of receivables. *SFAS No. 140* established new conditions for a securitization to be accounted for as a sale of receivables. Accordingly, the Company recorded on the balance sheet approximately $8.1 billion of previously unconsolidated securitized credit card receivables and related securitization borrowings in the second quarter of 2001. In addition, approximately $3.9 billion of assets were reclassified to credit card receivables from retained interest in transferred credit card receivables. In connection with the consolidation of the securitization structure, the Company recognized a non-cash, pretax charge of $522 million in 2001 to establish an allowance for uncollectible accounts related to the receivables

---

[14]RNOA is improved so long as the increase in asset turnover (NOAT) is not offset by a reduction in operating profit margin (NOPM) due to the increased cost using the VIE structure (such as purchasing goods in a finished state from wholesalers rather than manufacturing those goods, selling receivables at a discount, or leasing property from outside investors). This is a reasonable assumption. Otherwise, transfer of the assets to other entities would be unwise.

[15]FIN refers to FASB Interpretations. These interpretations are issued periodically and represent modifications or extensions of existing accounting standards.

which were previously considered as sold or accounted for as retained interests in transferred credit card receivables. In 2003, the Company either repaid or transferred to Citicorp all of its domestic debt securitized by credit card receivables.

This new standard required Sears to consolidate previously unconsolidated VIEs. Its assets (accounts receivable) increased by $8.1 billion, and liabilities relating to these receivables were recorded on Sears' balance sheet. Also, Sears recorded a $522 million allowance for uncollectible accounts relating to these receivables, reducing pretax income by that amount in the year of consolidation. Probably not surprisingly, in the following year, Sears unloaded its receivable portfolio and related debt to Citicorp.

To summarize, if not consolidated, VIEs are typically accounted for under the equity method of accounting (these investments are neither passive in nature nor controlling). Under this method of accounting, the investor company only reports the investment asset in an amount equal to the percentage of the investee company's equity that it owns (see Module 6 for a discussion of equity method accounting). One option for analysis purposes, is to replace the investment account with the assets and the liabilities of the VIE to which it relates. This amounts to consolidation of the VIE (see Module 6 for a discussion of consolidations).

We must be aware of two issues relating to the use of unconsolidated VIEs. First, more operating assets will be required to manage the business than are reported on the balance sheet. Second, the obligations of the business will be greater than are reported on the balance sheet. These are the same issues we highlight in our discussion of operating leases. Further, the benefits to the company of the nonconsolidation of VIEs are similar to those resulting from the treatment of leases as operating, which we discuss above. As a result, VIEs have grown in popularity, and we must be aware of their implications for our analysis of the financial statements.

■ MODULE-END REVIEW ■

Following is the footnote disclosure relating to Target's accounts receivable, and its VIE Target Receivables Corporation (TRC), from its 2003 10-K report:

> **Accounts Receivable and Receivable-backed Securities**
>
> Through our special purpose subsidiary, Target Receivables Corporation (TRC), we transfer, on an ongoing basis, substantially all of our receivables to the Target Credit Card Master Trust (the Trust) in return for certificates representing undivided interests in the Trust's assets. TRC owns the undivided interest in the Trust's assets, other than the Trust's assets securing the financing transactions entered into by the Trust and the 2 percent of Trust assets held by Retailers National Bank (RNB). RNB is a wholly owned subsidiary of the Corporation that also services receivables. The Trust assets and the related income and expenses are reflected in each operating segment's assets and operating results based on the origin of the credit card giving rise to the receivable.
>
> Beginning on August 22, 2001, our consolidated financial statements reflected the obligation to holders of previously sold receivable-backed securities as debt of TRC and the receivables at fair value in place of the previously recorded retained interests related to the sold securities. This resulted in a pre-tax charge of $67 million ($.05 per share). On August 22, 2001, the Trust's entire portfolio of receivables was reflected on our consolidated financial statements at its fair value, which was based upon the expected performance of the underlying receivables portfolio. At that point in time, fair value was equivalent in amount to face value, net of an appropriate allowance.

1. Why might a company such as Target have accounts receivable?
2. How is Target managing its accounts receivable?
3. What effect do recent accounting standards relating to receivables have on Target's balance sheet?

Solution

1. Target maintains a proprietary credit card. Accordingly, charges made by its customers using this card are reflected as receivables on its balance sheet.
2. Target sells its receivables to a variable interest entity (VIE), the Target Receivables Corporation (TRC), which finances the purchase by borrowing from the capital markets.
3. Recent accounting standards relating to VIEs have led to the consolidation of TRC with Target. The receivables are now reflected on Target's balance sheet because of the consolidation.

GUIDANCE ANSWERS

MANAGERIAL DECISION   **You are the Division President**

You must take care in accepting lease terms that are not advantageous to your company merely to achieve off-balance-sheet financing. Long-term shareholder value is created by managing your operation well, including negotiating leases with acceptable terms. Lease footnote disclosures also provide sufficient information for skilled analysts to undo the operating lease treatment. This means that you can end up with effective capitalization of a lease with lease terms that are not in the best interests of your company and with few benefits from off-balance-sheet financing. There is also the potential for lost credibility with stakeholders.

■ DISCUSSION QUESTIONS

Q9-1. What are the financial reporting differences between an operating lease and a capital lease? Explain.

Q9-2. Are footnote disclosures sufficient to overcome nonrecognition on the balance sheet of assets and related liabilities for operating leases? Explain.

Q9-3. Is the expense of a lease over its entire life the same whether or not it is capitalized? Explain.

Q9-4. What are the economic and accounting differences between a defined contribution plan and a defined benefit plan?

Q9-5. Under what circumstances will a company report a net pension asset? A net pension liability?

Q9-6. What are the components of pension expense that is reported in the income statement?

Q9-7. What effect does the use of expected returns on pension investments and the deferral of unexpected gains and losses on those investments have on income?

Q9-8. What is a variable interest entity (VIE)? Provide an example of the use of a VIE as a financing vehicle.

Q9-9. What effect does FIN 46 have on both accounting for VIEs and the balance sheets of companies that sponsor them?

■ MINI EXERCISES

M9-10.   Analysis and Interpretation of Leasing Footnote Disclosures   YUM! Brands, Inc., discloses the following footnote to its 2003 10-K report relating to its leasing activities:

YUM! Brands, Inc. (YUM)

> We have non-cancelable commitments under both capital and long-term operating leases, primarily for our restaurants. Capital and operating lease commitments expire at various dates through 2087 and, in many cases, provide for rent escalations and renewal options. Most leases require us to pay related executory costs, which include property taxes, maintenance and insurance.

a. Yum reports the existence of both capital and operating leases. In general, what effects does each of these lease types have on Yum's balance sheet and its income statement?

b. What types of adjustments might you consider to Yum's balance sheet for analysis purposes?

M9-11.   Analysis and Capitalization of Operating Lease Payments Disclosed in Footnotes   Southwest Airlines Co. discloses the following in the footnotes to its 10-K report relating to its leasing activities:

Southwest Airlines Co. (LUV)

(In millions)	Capital leases	Operating leases
2004	$ 18	$ 283
2005	24	273
2006	14	219
2007	16	202
2008	13	190
After 2008	39	1,328
Total minimum lease payments	124	$2,495
Less amount representing interest	33	
Present value of minimum lease payments	91	
Less current portion	10	
Long-term portion	$ 81	

Operating leases are not reflected on-balance-sheet. In our analysis of a company, we often desire to capitalize these operating leases, that is, add the present value of these lease payments to both the reported assets and liabilities. (*a*) Compute the present value of Southwest's operating lease payments assuming a 7% discount rate. (*b*) What effect does capitalization of Southwest's operating leases have on its total liabilities (it reported total liabilities of $4,826 million for 2003).

American Express (AXP)

M9-12. Analysis and Interpretation of Pension Disclosures—Expenses and Returns   American Express discloses the following pension footnote in its 10-K report:

(Millions)	2003
Service cost	$ 115
Interest cost	118
Expected return on plan assets	(146)
Amortization of	
Prior service cost	(8)
Transition obligation	(2)
Recognized net actuarial loss (gain)	18
Settlement/curtailment loss (gain)	10
Net periodic pension benefit cost	$ 105

a. How much pension expense does American Express report in its 2003 income statement?
b. What effect does its 'expected return on plan assets' have on its reported pension expense? Explain.
c. Explain use of the word 'expected' as it relates to results of pension plan investments.

YUM! Brands, Inc. (YUM)

M9-13. Analysis and Interpretation of Pension Disclosures—Expenses and Returns   YUM! Brands, Inc., discloses the following pension footnote in its 10-K report:

	Pension Benefits		
(In millions)	2003	2002	2001
Service cost	$ 26	$ 22	$ 20
Interest cost	34	31	28
Amortization of prior service cost	4	1	1
Expected return on plan assets	(30)	(28)	(29)
Recognized actuarial loss	6	1	1
Net periodic benefit cost	$ 40	$ 27	$ 21

a. How much pension expense does Yum report in its 2003 income statement?
b. What effect does its "expected return on plan assets" have on its reported pension expense? Explain.
c. Explain use of the word *expected* as it relates to results of pension plan investments.

Abercrombie and Fitch (ANF)

M9-14. Analysis and Interpretation of Retirement Benefit Footnote   Abercrombie and Fitch disclose the following footnote relating to its retirement plans in its 2002 10-K report:

RETIREMENT BENEFITS The Company participates in a qualified defined contribution retirement plan and a nonqualified supplemental retirement plan. Participation in the qualified plan is available to all associates who have completed 1,000 or more hours of service with the Company during certain 12-month periods and attained the age of 21. Participation in the nonqualified plan is subject to service and compensation requirements. The Company's contributions to these plans are based on a percentage of associates' eligible annual compensation. The cost of these plans was $5.6 million in 2002, $3.9 million in 2001 and $3.0 million in 2000.

a. Does Abercrombie have a defined contribution or defined benefit pension plan? Explain.
b. How does Abercrombie account for its contributions to its retirement plan?
c. How is Abercrombie's obligation to its retirement plan reported on its balance sheet?

Target Corporation (TGT)

M9-15. Analysis and Interpretation of Pension Plan Benefit Footnote   Target Corporation provides the following footnote relating to its retirement plans in its 2003 10-K report:

Defined Contribution Plans   Employees who meet certain eligibility requirements can participate in a defined contribution 401(k) plan by investing up to 80 percent of their compensation. We match 100 percent of each employee's contribution up to 5 percent of respective total compensation. Our contribution to the plan is initially invested in Target Corporation common stock. Benefits expense related to these matching contributions was $117 million, $111 million and $97 million in 2003, 2002 and 2001, respectively.

a. Does Target have a defined contribution or defined benefit pension plan? Explain.
b. How does Target account for its contributions to its retirement plan?
c. How is Target's obligation to its retirement plan reported on its balance sheet?

M9-16. Analysis and Interpretation of Footnote on Variable Interest Entities (VIEs) The Dow Chemical Company provides the following footnote in its 2002 10-K report relating to special purpose entities, now known as variable interest entities (VIEs):

Dow Chemical Company (DOW)

> **Variable Interest Entities** Dow has operating leases with various special purpose entities. Nine of these entities qualify as variable interest entities ("VIEs") under *FIN No. 46*, "Consolidation of Variable Interest Entities." Based on the current terms of the lease agreements and the residual value guarantees Dow provides to the lessors, the Company expects to be the primary beneficiary of the VIEs. As a result, if the facts and circumstances remain the same, Dow would be required to consolidate the assets and liabilities held by these VIEs in the third quarter of 2003.

a. In general, for what business reason(s) were these VIEs established?
b. How are these VIEs accounted for in Dow's financial statements?
c. What effect does the accounting for VIEs per *FIN 46* have on Dow's balance sheet?

M9-17. Analysis and Interpretation of Footnote on Contract Manufacturers Reebok reports the following information relating to its manufacturing activities in the footnotes to its 2003 10-K report:

Reebok (RBK)

> **MANUFACTURING** Most of our products are produced by independent manufacturers that are principally located outside the United States. We source some of our apparel and some of the component parts used in our footwear, however, from independent manufacturers located in the United States. In addition, we operate facilities in Indianapolis, Indiana and Mattapoisett, Massachusetts that provide apparel and accessory finishing for our sports licensing business.

a. What effect does the use of contract manufacturers have on Reebok's balance sheet?
b. How might Reebok's return on net operating assets (RNOA) and its components be affected by use of contract manufacturers? Explain.
c. Reebok executes purchase contracts with its contract manufacturers to purchase their output. How are executory contracts reported under GAAP? Does your answer suggest a possible motivation for the use of contract manufacturing?

■ EXERCISES

E9-18. Analysis and Interpretation of Leasing Footnote Fortune Brands, Inc., reports the following footnote relating to its leased facilities in its 2002 10-K report:

Fortune Brands, Inc. (FOPRA)

Future minimum rental payments under noncancelable operating leases as of December 31, 2001 are as follows:

(In millions)	
2002	$ 49.0
2003	38.0
2004	31.7
2005	25.5
2006	19.7
Remainder	54.3
Total minimum rental payments	218.2
Less minimum rentals to be received under noncancelable subleases	1.2
	$217.0

a. Assuming that this is the only information available about its leasing activities, does Fortune Brands classify its leases as operating or capital? Explain.
b. What effect has its lease classification had on Fortune Brands' balance sheet? Over the life of the lease, what effect does this classification have on net income?

E9-19.   Analysis and Interpretation of Footnote on both Operating and Capital Leases   Verizon Communications, Inc., provides the following footnote relating to its leasing activities in its 10-K report:

The aggregate minimum rental commitments under noncancelable leases for the periods shown at December 31, 2002, are as follows:

Years (dollars in millions)	Capital Leases	Operating Leases
2003	$ 75	$ 825
2004	89	739
2005	31	643
2006	24	698
2007	19	353
Thereafter	93	1,047
Total minimum rental commitments	331	$4,305
Less interest and executory costs	(90)	
Present value of minimum lease payments	241	
Less current installments	(54)	
Long-term obligation at December 31, 2002	$187	

a.   Assuming that this is the only available information relating to its leasing activities, what amount does Verizon report on its balance sheet for its lease obligations? Does this amount represent its total obligation to lessors? How do you know?

b.   What effect has its lease classification as capital or operating had on Verizon's balance sheet? Over the life of its leases, what effect does this lease classification have on its net income?

E9-20.   Analyzing, Interpreting and Capitalizing Operating Leases   Staples, Inc., reports the following footnote relating to its capital and operating leases in its 2003 10-K report ($ thousands):

Other long-term obligations at January 31, 2004 include $90.0 million relating to future rent escalation clauses and lease incentives under certain existing store operating lease arrangements. These rent expenses are recognized on a straight-line basis over the respective terms of the leases. Future minimum lease commitments due for retail and support facilities (including lease commitments for 6 retail stores not yet opened at January 31, 2004) and equipment leases under noncancellable operating leases are as follows (in thousands):

Fiscal Year:	Total
2004	$ 504,964
2005	484,560
2006	451,712
2007	421,610
2008	395,472
Thereafter	2,336,640
	$4,594,958

Rent expense approximated $480.0 million, $445.2 million, and $419.8 million for fiscal years 2003, 2002 and 2001, respectively.

What dollar adjustment(s) might you consider to Staples' balance sheet given this information and assuming that Staples intermediate-term borrowing rate is 7%? Explain. (Staples reported total liabilities of $2,840,146 ($ 000s) for 2003.)

E9-21.   Analysis, Interpretation and Capitalization of Operating Leases   YUM! Brands, Inc., reports the following footnote relating to its capital and operating leases in its 2003 10-K report ($ millions):

Future minimum commitments and amounts to be received as lessor or sublessor under non-cancelable leases are set forth below:

| (In millions) | Commitments | | Lease Receivables | |
	Capital	Operating	Direct Financing	Operating
2004	$ 15	$ 320	$ 8	$ 22
2005	15	290	8	20
2006	14	250	7	19
2007	13	227	7	18
2008	13	204	6	17
Thereafter	122	1,193	63	102
	$192	$2,484	$99	$198

What adjustment(s), assuming a discount rate of 7%, might you consider making to Yum's balance sheet given this information? Explain. Yum reported total liabilities of $4,500 million for 2003. (*Hint*: Net the respective operating commitments and lease receivables columns.)

E9-22. **Analyzing, Interpreting and Capitalizing Operating Leases**   Reebok reports the following footnote relating to its capital and operating leases in its 2003 10-K report: Reebok (RBK)

Minimum annual rentals under operating leases for the five years subsequent to December 31, 2003 and in the aggregate are as follows ($ thousands):

	Total Amount	Less: Amounts Representing Sublease Income	Net Amount
2004	$ 47,102	$1,417	$ 45,685
2005	36,439	1,236	35,203
2006	28,960	1,232	27,728
2007	22,306	1,042	21,264
2008	17,324	433	16,891
2009 and thereafter	12,753	0	12,753
	$164,884	$5,360	$159,524

Total rent expense for all operating leases amounted to $58,919, $58,768 and $55,999 for the years ended December 31, 2003, 2002 and 2001, respectively.

What adjustment(s) might you consider to Reebok's balance sheet given this information and assuming that Reebok's discount rate is 7%? Explain.

E9-23. **Analysis and Interpretation of Pension Footnote—Funded and Reported Amounts**   YUM! Brands, Inc., reports the following pension footnote in its 10-K report: YUM! Brands, Inc. (YUM)

| September 30 (In millions) | Pension Benefits | |
	2003	2002
Change in benefit obligation		
Benefit obligation at beginning of year	$501	$420
Service cost	26	22
Interest cost	34	31
Plan amendments	—	14
Curtailment gain	(1)	(3)
Benefits and expenses paid	(21)	(16)
Actuarial loss	90	33
Benefit obligation at end of year	$ 629	$ 501

(Continued on next page)

(Continued from previous page)

September 30 (In millions)	Pension Benefits	
	2003	2002
Change in plan assets		
Fair value of plan assets at beginning of year	$ 251	$ 291
Actual return on plan assets	52	(24)
Employer contributions	157	1
Benefits paid	(21)	(16)
Administrative expenses	(1)	(1)
Fair value of plan assets at end of year	$ 438	$ 251
Funded status	$(191)	$(250)
Employer contributions	—	25
Unrecognized actuarial loss	230	169
Unrecognized prior service cost	12	16
Net amount recognized at year-end	$ 51	$ (40)

a. Describe what is meant by *service cost* and *interest cost.*
b. What is the source of funds to make payments to retirees?
c. Show the computation of the 2003 funded status for Yum.
d. What net pension amount is reported on its 2003 balance sheet? Why is the reported amount different from the funded status?

Xerox
(XRXPRC)

E9-24. **Analysis and Interpretation of Pension Footnote—Funded and Reported Amounts** Xerox reports the following pension footnote as part of its 2003 10-K report:

(In millions)	Pension Benefits	
	2003	2002
Change in Benefit Obligation		
Benefit obligation, January 1	$ 7,931	$ 7,606
Service cost	197	180
Interest cost	934	(210)
Plan participants' contributions	15	18
Plan amendments	1	(31)
Actuarial loss	312	736
Currency exchange rate changes	486	327
Divestitures	(45)	(1)
Curtailments	1	2
Special termination benefits	—	39
Benefits paid/settlements	$(861)	(735)
Benefit obligation, December 31	$ 8,971	$ 7,931
Change in Plan Assets		
Fair value of plan assets, January 1	$ 5,963	$7,040
Actual return on plan assets	1,150	(768)
Employer contribution	672	138
Plan participants' contributions	15	18
Currency exchange rate changes	401	271
Divestitures	(39)	(1)
Benefits paid/settlements	(861)	(735)
Fair value of plan assets, December 31	$ 7,301	$ 5,963

(Continued on next page)

(Continued from previous page)

(In millions)	Pension Benefits	
	2003	2002
Funded status (including under-funded and non-funded plans)	$(1,670)	$(1,968)
Unamortized transition assets	(2)	—
Unrecognized prior service cost	(24)	(27)
Unrecognized net actuarial loss	1,870	1,843
Net amount recognized	$ 174	$ (152)

(In millions)	Pension Benefits	
	2003	2002
Components of Net Periodic Benefit Cost		
Defined benefit plans		
Service cost	$ 197	$ 180
Interest cost	934	(210)
Expected return on plan assets	(940)	134
Recognized net actuarial loss	53	7
Amortization of prior service cost	—	3
Recognized net transition asset	—	(1)
Recognized curtailment/settlement loss (gain)	120	55
Net periodic benefit cost	364	168
Special termination benefits	—	27
Defined contribution plans	62	10
Total	$ 426	$ 205

a. Describe what is meant by *service cost* and *interest cost* (the service and interest costs appear both in the reconciliation of the PBO and in the computation of pension expense).

b. What is the actual return on pension investments in 2003? Was Xerox's profitability impacted exactly by this amount?

c. Provide an example under which an "actuarial loss," such as the $312 million charge that Xerox reports, might arise.

d. What is the source of funds to make payments to retirees?

e. How much cash did Xerox contribute to its pension plans in 2003?

f. How much cash did the company pay to retirees in 2003?

g. Show the computation of its 2003 funded status.

h. What net pension amount is reported on its 2003 balance sheet? Why is the reported amount different from the funded status?

E9-25. Analysis and Interpretation of Pension Footnote—Funded and Reported Amounts   Verizon reports   Verizon (VZ)
the following pension footnote as part of its 2003 10-K report:

At December 31 ($ millions)	Pension	
	2003	2002
Change in Benefit Obligation		
Beginning of year	$37,908	$36,391
Service cost	788	718
Interest cost	2,439	2,488

(Continued on next page)

(Continued from previous page)

At December 31 ($ millions)	Pension	
	2003	2002
Plan amendments	$ 854	$ 114
Actuarial loss, net	1,214	2,560
Benefits paid	(3,925)	(3,356)
Termination benefits	2,588	286
Acquisitions and divestitures, net	23	885
Settlements and curtailments	(900)	(2,256)
Other	54	78
End of year	41,043	37,908
Change in Plan Assets		
Beginning of year	38,676	48,558
Actual return on plan assets	8,671	(4,678)
Company contributions	285	157
Benefits paid	(3,925)	(3,356)
Settlements	(900)	(2,536)
Acquisitions and divestitures, net	34	531
End of year	42,841	38,676
Funded Status		
End of year	1,798	768
Unrecognized		
Actuarial loss, net	5,079	8,295
Prior service (benefit) cost	1,512	752
Transition asset	(3)	(44)
Net amount recognized	$ 8,386	$ 9,771

a. Describe what is meant by *service cost* and *interest cost*.
b. What is the source of funds to make payments to retirees?
c. Show the computation of Verizon's 2003 funded status.
d. What net pension amount is reported on its 2003 balance sheet? Why is the reported amount different from the funded status?

General Motors (GM)

E9-26. Analysis and Interpretation of Footnote on Variable Interest Entities (VIEs) General Motors provides the following footnote in its 10-K report relating to its securitization of loans receivable:

December 31 (in millions)	Finance Receivables and Loans	
	2002	2001
Retail automotive	$ 92,890	$ 78,071
Residential mortgage	102,525	95,076
Total consumer	195,415	173,147
Wholesale	38,877	31,807
Commercial mortgage	18,356	16,503
Other automotive and commercial	22,994	25,885
Total commercial	80,227	74,195
Total managed portfolio	275,642	247,342
Securitized finance receivables and loans	(123,337)	(125,735)
Loans held for sale	(14,599)	(10,229)
Total finance receivables and loans	$ 137,706	$ 111,378

It also provides the following discussion relating to the potential effects of its consolidation of variable interest entities (VIEs):

> In January 2003, the FASB Issued *Interpretation No. 46,* "Consolidation of Variable Interest Entitles" (*FIN 46*), which requires the consolidation of certain entities considered to be variable interest entities (VIEs). An entity is considered to be a VIE when it has equity investors which lack the characteristics of a controlling financial interest, or its capital is insufficient to permit it to finance its activities without additional subordinated financial support. Consolidation of a VIE by an investor is required when it is determined that the investor will absorb a majority of the VIE's expected losses or residual returns if they occur. *FIN 46* provides certain exceptions to these rules, including qualifying SPEs subject to the requirements of *SFAS No. 140,* "Accounting for Transfers and Servicing of Financial Assets and Extinguishments of Liabilities." VIEs created after January 31, 2003 must be consolidated immediately, while VIEs that existed prior to February 1, 2003 must be consolidated as of July 1, 2003.
>
> GM may be required to consolidate certain VIEs (previously collectively referred to as SPEs) with which it does business. Management is currently reviewing existing VIEs that may require consolidation. However, it is reasonably possible that certain VIEs with assets totaling approximately $1.1 billion, established exclusively to facilitate GM's leasing activities related to the ACO business, may require consolidation. Should GM default on all of its obligations with respect to its involvement in these entities, GM's maximum exposure to loss would be approximately $1.1 billion.
>
> With respect to the FIO business, VIE structures are used to facilitate various activities of GMAC, including securitization of loans, mortgage funding, and other investing activities. Based on management's preliminary assessment, it is reasonably possible that VIEs with assets totaling approximately $17.5 billion may require consolidation. Management is considering restructuring alternatives to ensure the continued non-consolidation of such assets. In the absence of successful alternatives, the consolidation of such VIEs would have the effect of increasing both assets and liabilities in an amount equal to the assets of the VIEs. GM's exposure to loss related to these entities is approximately $3.2 billion.

Its *ACO* business lines refer to automotive, communications services and other. Its *FIO* businesses refer to financing and insurance operations.

a. What is the 2002 total portfolio of loans that GM has originated and currently services? What is the balance of the loan portfolio that is reported on GM's 2002 balance sheet? What activity accounts for the difference between these amounts?

b. Explain the aim of *FIN 46.* What is the estimated effect of this new standard on GM's balance sheet?

c. What action is GM taking in response to this new standard? Why do you think GM is taking this action?

■ PROBLEMS

P9-27. **Analysis, Interpretation and Capitalization of Leasing Disclosures**   The Abercrombie & Fitch 2002 10-K report contains the following footnote relating to its leasing activities. This is the only information it discloses relating to its leasing activity.

Abercrombie & Fitch (ANF)

> At February 1, 2003, the Company was committed to noncancelable leases with remaining terms of one to fourteen years. These commitments include store leases with initial terms ranging primarily from ten to fifteen years. A summary of minimum rent commitments under noncancelable leases follows (thousands):

2003	$120,313	2006	112,899
2004	121,316	2007	99,381
2005	118,695	Thereafter	316,724

Required

a. What is the balance of its lease assets and lease liabilities as reported on Abercrombie's balance sheet? How do you know?

      b.   Assuming that all of A&F's leases are classified as *operating,* what effect has this classification had on A&F's balance sheet? Over the life of the lease, what effect does this classification have on its net income?

      c.   Using a 10% discount rate, estimate the assets and liabilities that A&F fails to report as a result of its off-balance-sheet lease financing.

      d.   What financial ratios from ROE disaggregation (such as margins, turnover, and leverage) are affected and in what direction (increased or decreased) by its off-balance-sheet lease financing?

Best Buy (BBY)   **P9-28.**   **Analysis, Interpretation and Capitalization of Leasing Disclosures**   The Best Buy 10-K report has the following footnote related to its leasing activities. This is the only information it discloses relating to its leasing activity.

Future minimum lease obligations by year (not including percentage rentals) for all operating leases at March 2, 2002, were as follows ($ millions):

Fiscal Year	
2003	$ 472
2004	459
2005	417
2006	376
2007	361
Thereafter	2,698

Required

      a.   What is the balance of its lease assets and lease liabilities as reported on its balance sheet? How do you know?

      b.   Assuming that all of its leases are classified as operating, what effect has this classification had on its balance sheet? Over the life of the lease, what effect does this classification have on its net income?

      c.   Using a 10% discount rate, estimate the assets and liabilities that it fails to report as a result of its off-balance-sheet lease financing.

      d.   What financial ratios from ROE disaggregation (such as margins, turnover, and leverage) are affected and in what direction (increased or decreased) by its off-balance-sheet lease financing?

FedEx (FDX)   **P9-29.**   **Analysis, Interpretation and Capitalization of Leasing Disclosures**   FedEx reports total assets of $13,812 and total liabilities of $6,545 for 2002 ($ millions). Its 10-K report has the following footnote related to its leasing activities:

A summary of future minimum lease payments under capital leases and noncancellable operating leases (principally aircraft and facilities) with an initial or remaining term in excess of one year at May 31, 2002 is as follows:

In millions	Capital Leases	Operating Leases
2003	$ 12	$ 1,501
2004	12	1,235
2005	12	1,162
2006	12	1,053
2007	12	1,028
Thereafter	253	8,791
	313	$14,770
Less amount representing interest	(107)	
Present value of net minimum lease payments	$ 206	

Required

      a.   What is the balance of its lease assets and lease liabilities as reported on its balance sheet? Explain.

      b.   Impute the discount rate that FedEx is using to compute the present value of its capital leases (see Wal-Mart Business Insight box in the module for a description of the mechanics).

c. Using the discount rate imputed in part (*b*), estimate the amount of assets and liabilities that FedEx fails to report as a result of its off-balance-sheet lease financing. (*Hint:* If you cannot impute the interest rate in *b*, use 3.5% for this part.)

d. What financial ratios from ROE disaggregation (such as margins, turnover, and leverage) are affected and in what direction (increased or decreased) by its off-balance-sheet lease financing?

e. What portion of its total lease liabilities is reported on-balance-sheet and what is reported off-balance-sheet?

f. Based on your analysis, do you believe that FedEx's balance sheet adequately reports its aircraft and facilities assets and related obligations? Explain.

P9-30. Analysis and Interpretation of Pension Disclosures FedEx's 10-K report has the following disclosures related to its retirement plans: FedEx (FDX)

In millions	Pension Plans	
	2002	2001
Change in Projected Benefit Obligation		
Projected benefit obligation at beginning of year	$5,384	$4,494
Service cost	348	325
Interest cost	409	382
Actuarial loss (gain)	168	211
Benefits paid	(84)	(57)
Amendments, benefit enhancements and other	2	29
Projected benefit obligation at end of year	$6,227	$5,384
Accumulated Benefit Obligation	$5,097	$4,104
Change in Plan Assets		
Fair value of plan assets at beginning of year	$5,622	$5,727
Actual loss on plan assets	(191)	(142)
Company contributions	161	97
Benefits paid	(84)	(57)
Other	2	(3)
Fair value of plan assets at end of year	$5,510	$5,622
Funded Status of the Plans	$ (717)	$238
Unrecognized actuarial loss (gain)	823	(160)
Unamortized prior service cost	130	144
Unrecognized transition amount	(8)	(9)
Prepaid (accrued) benefit cost	$ 228	$213
Amounts Recognized in the Balance Sheet at May 31		
Prepaid benefit cost	$ 411	$365
Accrued benefit liability	(183)	(152)
Minimum pension liability	(19)	(20)
Accumulated other comprehensive income	5	—
Intangible asset	14	20
Prepaid (accrued) benefit cost	$ 228	$213

In millions	Pension Plans		
	2002	2001	2000
Service cost	$ 348	$ 325	$ 338
Interest cost	409	382	336
Expected return on plan assets	(621)	(624)	(546)
Net amortization and deferral	13	(23)	6
	$ 149	$ 60	$ 134

(Continued on next page)

(Continued from previous page)

Weighted-Average Actuarial Assumptions

	Pension Plans		
	2002	2001	2000
Discount rate	7.1%	7.7%	8.5%
Rate of increase in future compensation levels	3.3	4.0	5.0
Expected long-term rate of return on assets	10.9	10.9	10.9

Required

a. How much pension expense (revenue) does FedEx report in its 2002 income statement?

b. FedEx reports a $621 million expected return on plan assets as an offset to 2002 pension expense. Approximately, how is this amount computed? What is the actual gain or loss realized on its 2002 plan assets? What is the purpose of using this estimated amount instead of the actual gain or loss?

c. What factors affected its 2002 pension liability? What factors affected its 2002 plan assets?

d. What does the term *funded status* mean? What is the funded status of the 2002 FedEx retirement plans? What amount of asset or liability does FedEx report on its 2002 balance sheet relating to its retirement plans? What factors account for the difference between these two amounts?

e. FedEx reduced its discount rate from 7.7% to 7.1% in 2002. What effect(s) does this reduction have on its balance sheet and its income statement?

f. FedEx reduced its estimate of expected annual wage increases from 4% to 3.3% in 2002. What effect(s) does this reduction have on its financial statements? In general, does such a reduction increase or decrease income?

**Dow
Chemical
(DOW)**

P9-31.   Analysis and Interpretation of Pension Disclosures   Dow Chemical provides the following footnote disclosures in its 10-K report relating to its pension plans:

(In million)	Defined Benefit Pension Plans	
	2002	2001
Service cost	$ 219	$ 206
Interest cost	748	708
Expected return on plan assets	(1,105)	(1,072)
Amortization of transition obligation	—	—
Amortization of prior service cost (credit)	20	23
Amortization of unrecognized (gain) loss	(20)	(73)
Special termination/curtailment cost (credit)	(7)	113
Net periodic cost (credit)	$ (145)	$ (95)
Change in projected benefit obligation		
Benefit obligation at beginning of year	$11,341	$ 9,985
Service cost	219	206
Interest cost	748	708
Plan participant's contributions	8	11
Amendments	28	31
Actuarial changes in assumptions and experience	443	629
Acquisition/divestiture activity	5	190
Benefits, paid	(745)	(625)
Currency impact	76	93
Special termination/curtailment cost (credit)	(26)	113
Benefit obligation at end of year	$12,097	$11,341

(Continued on next page)

(Continued from previous page)

(In million)	Defined Benefit Pension Plans	
	2002	2001
Change in plan assets		
Market value of plan assets at beginning of year	$11,424	$12,435
Actual return on plan assets	(1,230)	(611)
Employer contributions	112	30
Plan participant's contributions	9	11
Acquisition/divestiture activity	4	158
Benefits paid	(741)	(599)
Special settlement paid	(17)	—
Market value of plan assets at end of year	$ 9,561	$11,424
Funded status and net amounts recognized		
Plan assets in excess of (less than) benefit obligation	$ (2,536)	$ 83
Unrecognized net transition obligation	2	5
Unrecognized prior service cost (credit)	132	123
Unrecognized net (gain) loss	2,796	(34)
Net amounts recognized in the consolidated balance sheets	$ 394	$ 177

Assumptions for Pension Plans	2002	2001
Weighted-average discount rate	6.75%	7.00%
Rate of increase in future compensation levels	5.00%	5.00%
Long-term rate of return on assets	9.25%	9.18%

Required

a. How much pension expense (revenue) does Dow Chemical report in its 2002 income statement?

b. Dow reports a $1,105 million expected return on plan assets as an offset to 2002 pension expense. Approximately, how is this amount computed? What is the actual gain or loss realized on its 2002 plan assets? What is the purpose of using this estimated amount instead of the actual gain or loss?

c. What factors affected its 2002 pension liability? What factors affected its 2002 plan assets?

d. What does the term *funded status* mean? What is the funded status of the 2002 Dow retirement plans? What amount of asset or liability does Dow report on its 2002 balance sheet relating to its retirement plans? What factors account for the difference between these two amounts?

e. Dow reduced its discount rate from 7% to 6.75% in 2002. What effect(s) does this reduction have on its balance sheet and its income statement?

f. Dow increased its estimate of expected returns on plan assets from 9.18% to 9.25% in 2002. What effect(s) does this increase have on its income statement? Explain.

10 Adjusting and Forecasting Financial Statements

PROCTER & GAMBLE

HEAD AND SHOULDERS ABOVE COMPETITORS

Procter & Gamble (P&G) has successfully reinvented itself . . . again. It has shed its image as the "lumbering giant" of its industry with new products and directed marketing. Its annual sales now exceed $50 billion, which far exceeds competitors such as Colgate-Palmolive and Kimberly-Clark. P&G has also focused on its higher margin products such as those in beauty care. This has improved its profit margin and provided much needed dollars for marketing activities. It advertising budget is up to nearly 11% of sales, which is nearly double the budget of some of its key competitors.

P&G's financial performance has been equally impressive. Its return on average equity (ROE) in 2004 was 38.7%, with RNOA comprising 52% of it. Although more financially leveraged than the average publicly traded company, there is little need for concern since P&G generates over $9 billion in operating cash flow, which is more than sufficient to cover its $2 billion in interest and principal payments on long-term debt. P&G also generates sufficient cash to allow it to pay dividends in excess of $2.5 billion annually to shareholders.

P&G's product stable is impressive. It consists of numerous well-recognized household brands—a partial listing follows by business segment:

- **Fabric and Home Care**—Tide, Downy, Joy, Cascade, Mr. Clean, Bounce, Swiffer, and Febreze
- **Beauty Care**—Head & Shoulders, Pantene, Olay, Clairol, Max Factor, Old Spice, and Ivory
- **Baby and Family Care**—Pampers, Charmin, Bounty, and Puffs
- **Health Care**—Crest, Vicks, Fixodent, PUR, and Pepto-Bismol
- **Snacks and Beverages**—Pringles and Folgers

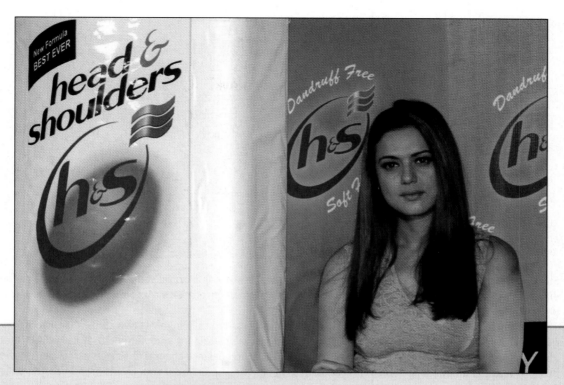

Sales of its products are distributed across each of these business segments as illustrated in the following chart:

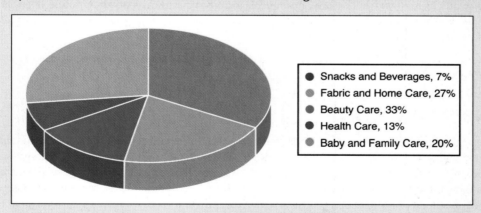

- Snacks and Beverages, 7%
- Fabric and Home Care, 27%
- Beauty Care, 33%
- Health Care, 13%
- Baby and Family Care, 20%

P&G's recent successes have coincided with new leadership. A.G. Lafley took the helm in 2000. His innovations and market savvy have consistently propelled P&G. *BusinessWeek* (2004) writes: "From its Swiffer mop to battery-powered Crest SpinBrush toothbrushes and Whitestrip tooth whiteners, P&G has simply done a better job than rivals . . . 'We are growing market share in 70% of our businesses,' says Clayton C. Daley Jr., P&G's chief financial officer. 'That doesn't happen unless you have strong innovation.' "

Since assuming the top job, Lafley has guided P&G to successive increases in sales, income, and cash flows. In turn, such increases have driven impressive gains in its stock price.

(Continued on next page)

(Continued from previous page)

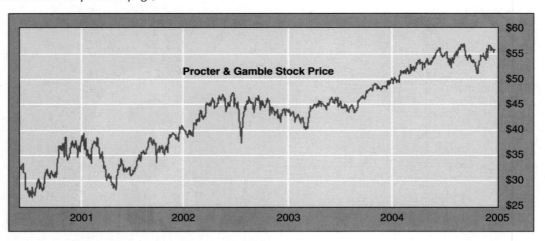

Stock price is driven by *forecasts* of financial performance. Historical financial statements are relevant to the extent that they provide information useful to forecast financial performance. Accordingly, considerable emphasis is placed on generating reliable forecasts.

This module explains the forecasting process. That process typically involves two steps: (1) Historical financial statements are adjusted, if needed, to yield an income statement and statement of cash flows that identifies core operating income and cash flows, and an adjusted balance sheet that reflects assets used in the business and the amounts for which the company is liable. (2) The financial statements are forecasted once any necessary adjustments are made.

The steady increase in P&G's stock price reflects increases in forecasts about its future financial performance and condition. Throughout this module, reflect on P&G's stock price graph and consider its relation to P&G's expected core income and cash flows.

Sources: *Procter & Gamble* 2004 & 2005 10-K Reports; *Procter & Gamble* 2004 Annual Report; *BusinessWeek,* 4 October 2004; *The Wall Street Journal,* January 2005.

■ INTRODUCTION

Forecasting financial performance is integral to a variety of business decisions ranging from investing to managing a company effectively. We might, for example, wish to value a company's common stock before purchasing its shares. To that end, we forecast free cash flows or residual operating income as inputs into one of the valuation models we discuss in Module 11. Or, we might be interested in evaluating the creditworthiness of a prospective borrower. In that case, we forecast cash flows to estimate the ability of the borrowing firm to repay its obligations. We might also be interested in evaluating alternative strategic plans for management decisions. In this case, our forecasts can be evaluated with respect to the creation of shareholder value.

The forecasting process begins with a retrospective analysis. That is, we analyze current and prior years' statements to be sure that they reflect our analysis of the financial condition and performance of the company. If we believe that they do not, we adjust those statements to better reflect our analysis inferences. Once we've adjusted the historical results, we are ready to forecast future results.

Why would we need to adjust historical results? The answer resides in the fact that financial statements prepared in conformity with GAAP do not always accurately reflect the "true" financial condition and performance of the company. This situation can arise for several reasons including the following:

- The income statement might include transitory items, such as an asset write-down or the accrual of expected restructuring costs.
- The balance sheet might include nonoperating assets and liabilities such as those from discontinued operations. Conversely, the balance sheet might exclude operating assets and liabilities such as those from operating leases or from investments accounted for using the equity method.

- The statement of cash flows might include operating cash inflows from excessive inventory reductions, from securitization of accounts receivable, or from tax benefits on the exercise of employee stock options.

$\$$

Cash Effect

These are just a few examples of how financial statements can be prepared in conformity with GAAP, but do not accurately reflect core operating activities of the company. Consequently, we want to adjust such financial statements before forecasting financial statements.

■ ADJUSTING FINANCIAL STATEMENTS

We begin with a discussion of the process by which financial statements are adjusted for purposes of forecasting—the *adjusting process* is also referred to as recasting or reformulating. To be sure, the adjusting process is not "black and white." It requires judgment and estimation. Our discussion of adjusting (and forecasting) financial statements is meant to introduce a reasonable and reliable, but not the only, process for these tasks.[1]

Adjusting the Income Statement

This section describes adjustments that are often made to the income statement for forecasting purposes. These adjustments generally fall into one of three categories:

1. **Separate core (persistent) and transitory items**—The aim of forecasting is to project financial results. Since transitory items are, by definition, nonrecurring, they are generally excluded from current operating results. Common transitory items include gains and losses from asset sales, the results of discontinued operations, and costs related to restructuring activities.
2. **Separate operating and nonoperating items**—Core operating activities have the most long-lasting (persistent) effects on future profitability and cash flows and, thus, are the primary value drivers for company stakeholders. It is important to separate core operating items from nonoperating items for effective profitability analysis.
3. **Include expenses that net income excludes**—We review the composition and level of operating expenses to determine their reasonableness. To the extent a company fails to recognize expenses, whether due to underaccrual of reserves or liabilities or due to reduced expenditures for key operating activities, reported income is overstated. Such unrecognized expenses are included in the adjusting process.

Exhibit 10.1 lists some typical adjustments. Exhibit 10.1 is not meant to be an exhaustive list, only an indication of the types of adjustments that are commonly made.

The first category in Exhibit 10.1 includes gains and losses from asset sales and asset write-downs, and the financial gains and losses from debt retirements and subsidiary stock sales. These items are transitory and should not be included when forecasting operating results. GAAP also help by identifying three types of items that it specifically highlights as transitory and then reports (net of tax) below income from continuing operations—those are discontinued operations, extraordinary items, and changes in accounting principles. These should likewise be excluded from the forecasting process. (Under a newly proposed standard, changes in accounting principles will be included in income from continuing operations with restatement of prior periods—see Module 4.) Finally, any other transitory items in current income are excluded. Common items include restructuring expenses, merger and acquisition costs, LIFO liquidation gains and losses, excessive liability accruals, and increases and decreases in tax expense (and, thus, net income) from changes in the deferred tax asset valuation account.

---

[1]It is important to separate the purposes of GAAP-based financial statements and the adjusting process of this module for purposes of forecasting. Specifically, GAAP-based statements serve more than just information for forecasting. For example, financial statements are key inputs in contracting between business parties. This means that historical results, including any transitory activities, must be reported to meet management's fiduciary responsibilities. On the other hand, forecasting wishes to purge itself of transitory activities and focus on those items that persist, with a special emphasis on persistent operating activities.

EXHIBIT 10.1 ■ Common Income Statement Adjustments

1. Separate core (persistent) and transitory items—examples of items to exclude:
   a. Gains and losses relating to
      (1) Asset sales on long-term assets and investments
      (2) Asset write-downs of long-term assets and inventories
      (3) Stock issuances by subsidiaries
      (4) Debt retirements
   b. Transitory items reported after income from continued operations
      (1) Discontinued operations
      (2) Extraordinary items
      (3) Changes in accounting principles
   c. Restructuring expenses
   d. Merger costs
   e. LIFO liquidation gains
   f. Liability accruals deemed excessive
   g. Gains and losses from changes in deferred tax valuation allowance

2. Separate operating and nonoperating items—examples:
   a. Treating interest revenue and expense, and investment gains and losses, as nonoperating
   b. Treating pension service cost as operating, and pension interest costs and expected returns as nonoperating
   c. Treating debt retirement gains and losses as nonoperating
   d. Treating income and losses from discontinued operations as nonoperating
   e. Treating short-term fluctuations in tax expense as nonoperating

3. Include expenses not reflected in net income—examples:
   a. Employee stock option expense
   b. Inadequate reserves for bad debts or asset impairment
   c. Reductions in R&D, advertising, and other discretionary expenses that were made to achieve short-term income targets

The second category focuses on separating operating and nonoperating components. The financial (nonoperating) income items commonly excluded are interest revenue and expense, the gains and losses from sales of investments, and pension interest costs and expected returns. Nonoperating components also include gains and losses on debt retirements and income or losses related to discontinued operations. Short-term gains and losses from temporary swings in the tax position are also commonly treated as nonoperating.

The third category of adjustments involves inclusion of expenses not included in current income per GAAP. These commonly include expenses relating to employee stock option plans, the inadequate reserve for uncollectible accounts receivable, and unrecognized asset impairment costs. Adjustments might also involve additional amounts for R&D, advertising, and other operating expenses that reflect discretionary reductions of operating activities to achieve short-term income targets.

BUSINESS INSIGHT   **What Is eBay's Income?**

How much income did eBay earn over the past five years? Albert Meyer, an accounting sleuth who runs 2nd Opinion Research says, "For the life of me, I wouldn't be able to tell." The main culprit is its stock options. eBay's reported income from 1999 through 2003 is $840 million. Under GAAP, this doesn't include its stock option costs of $827 million. If we subtract that cost, eBay has earned just $13 million in total for the past five years. Even that cost estimate only measures the value of options when granted. Alternatively, Meyer estimates that eBay employees pocketed $1.6 billion in option-based compensation over this five-year period. So, did the options cost $827 million or $1.6 billion? Consider that $1.6 billion is the cumulative figure eBay claimed as expense on its tax return. At $1.6 billion, eBay has *lost* $760 million for this five-year period. (*Fortune* May 31, 2004)

MANAGERIAL DECISION	You Are a Corporate Analyst

You are a corporate analyst working in the finance department for a company that is preparing its financial statements. You must make a decision regarding the format of its income statement. Specifically, should you subtotal to *pretax operating profit* and segregate nonoperating items? Or, should you subtotal to *pretax profit* and include operating and nonoperating items together? [Answer, p. 10-21]

Adjusting the Balance Sheet

The primary focus of balance sheet adjustments is to separate (exclude) nonoperating assets and liabilities that are reported on the balance sheet and to include operating assets and liabilities that are *not* reported on the balance sheet. These adjustments typically require use of footnote disclosures, including information for capitalizing assets and liabilities that are excluded by the company per GAAP.

Exhibit 10.2 lists several common balance sheet adjustments, but this listing is not meant to be exhaustive.

EXHIBIT 10.2 ■ Common Balance Sheet Adjustments

1. Separate nonoperating assets and liabilities—examples of items to exclude:
   a. Eliminate assets and liabilities from discontinued operations
   b. Write-downs on any assets, including goodwill, that is judged to be impaired

2. Include operating assets and liabilities not reflected in balance sheet—examples:
   a. Capitalize assets and liabilities from operating leases
   b. Consolidate off-balance-sheet investments
      (1) Equity method investments
      (2) Variable interest entities (VIEs)
   c. Accrue understated liabilities and assets

The first category in Exhibit 10.2 involves separating (excluding) nonoperating assets and liabilities on the balance sheet. Discontinued operations are segregated in the income statement (see Exhibit 10.1), and their assets and liabilities are commonly segregated, as well, in the balance sheet. Those assets and liabilities are excluded in the adjusting process since, by definition, neither those assets and liabilities, nor the sales and expenses of discontinued operations, remain in continuing operations. Other adjustments to the balance sheet include the write-down of impaired assets. Adjustments to reduce assets are difficult judgment calls, which benefit from information outside of the financial statements such as financial reports of competitors and analyst reports of the state of the industry so as to form an opinion about such potential asset impairments.

The second category focuses on including operating assets and liabilities not reported in the balance sheet per GAAP. One example is operating leases that are prevalent in several industries, including the retailing, franchising, and airline industries. Lease disclosures mandated under GAAP provide sufficient information for us to effectively capitalize these lease assets and liabilities for forecasting purposes (see Module 9). Investments that confer significant influence, but not control, and are reported using the equity method of accounting are another example of assets and liabilities not reported in the balance sheet per GAAP.[2] The equity method reports an investment balance equal to the percentage of the equity in the investee company that is owned, rather than the assets and liabilities of the investee company that would be recognized on-balance-sheet if the entity were consolidated. This means that many assets and liabilities are unreported. Unfortunately, usual footnote disclosures by companies with equity method investments are poor and insufficient to estimate the assets and liabilities (and risk) of the investee companies. To the extent that summary balance sheets and income statements are provided in the footnotes, the adjustment

---

[2]The equity method of accounting is used for investments in partnerships, joint ventures, and trusts in addition to minority interest in corporations.

process replaces the investment account with the assets and liabilities to which they relate using the consolidation mechanics discussed in Module 6.

Other adjustments to the balance sheet include the accrual of understated liabilities. Common accruals such as those relating to operating activities like warranties, premiums, and coupons are somewhat easier to assess and estimate from prior balance sheet data. Accruals for contingent liabilities such as environmental and litigation exposure are more difficult and require use of information outside of the financial statements.

RESEARCH INSIGHT   **Earnings Quality and Accounting Conservatism**

Accounting researchers commonly measure *earnings quality* in terms of sustainability, meaning that the income items persist in future periods. This is consistent with the definition of *core* income described in Module 3. Sustainability is important because core income items are better indicators of future earnings than are transitory items. One factor that affects earnings quality is accounting conservatism. Research finds that conservative accounting leads to transitory earnings changes when the levels of investment within the firm changes. Researchers have constructed a conservatism index to study the effect conservatism and growth have on earnings changes. The index is defined as the level of estimated reserves created by conservative accounting (such as LIFO versus FIFO, and expensing of R&D and advertising) divided by the level of net operating assets. Earnings quality is then a function of changes in the conservatism index for each firm, and it is a function of the difference between the firm-specific and industry-specific conservatism index. Poor earnings quality occurs when the firm grows its estimated reserves at a different rate than the growth of its net operating assets. A firm-specific conservatism index that substantially differs from that of the firm's industry is one sign of poor earnings quality. This is because profitability trends toward the industry mean. While the index is one indicator of firms with unsustainable earnings, market participants do not appear to fully consider the information contained in this index when determining stock prices.

Adjusting the Statement of Cash Flows

The focus of cash flow adjustments is threefold: (1) to adjust operating cash flows for any nonoperating (abnormal) items, (2) to adjust (exclude) transitory items from cash flows, and (3) to review the assignment of cash flows into their proper sections—investing, investing, and financing. These adjustments typically require use of the other financial statements, including footnote disclosures, and sometimes information from outside the financial statements.

Cash Effect

Exhibit 10.3 lists several common statement of cash flow adjustments, but this listing is not meant to be exhaustive.

EXHIBIT 10.3 ■ Common Statement of Cash Flow Adjustments

1. Adjust operating cash flows for nonoperating items—examples:
   a. Adjust discretionary costs (advertising, R&D, maintenance) to normal, expected levels
   b. Adjust current operating assets (receivables, inventory) to normal, expected levels
   c. Adjust current operating liabilities (payables, accruals) to normal, expected levels

2. Adjust cash flows for transitory items—examples:
   a. Separate (exclude) operating cash flows from tax benefits due to exercise of employee stock options

3. Review cash flows and reassign them, if necessary, to operating, investing, or financing sections—examples:
   a. Separate and reassign operating cash inflows from asset securitization to financing section
   b. Separate and reassign operating cash flows from discontinued operations to investing section

The first category in Exhibit 10.3 involves adjusting operating cash flows for nonoperating items. These nonoperating items commonly involve discretionary activities whose amounts are determined by management and are not in line with reasonable norms. To better understand, recall that operating cash flows increase with an increase in operating income and/or a decrease in net operating working capital (the latter occurs from either or both a decrease in current assets or an increase in current liabilities). Although higher operating cash flows are generally viewed favorably, it is necessary to understand the drivers of that increase to discern whether or not future cash flows are expected to exhibit similar behavior. Following are several common adjustments to operating cash flows for nonoperating items:

- **Cost decreases.** Transitory, abnormal reductions of necessary, expected operating costs related to discretionary expenditures on advertising, promotion, R&D, and maintenance. Such reductions increase income and operating cash flows, which usually yield short-term benefits at long-term costs.

- **Current asset decreases.** Transitory, abnormal reductions in current operating assets such as accounts receivable and inventory increase net cash flows from operations. Such reductions are generally desirable. However, if such reductions are the result of overly restrictive credit policies or result in inventories below what is necessary to conduct operations, then increased (short-term) operating cash flows likely arise from long-term costs as customers leave or face stock-outs causing the company's image to deteriorate.

- **Current liability increases.** Transitory, abnormal increases in current operating liabilities such as accounts payable and other accrued liabilities increase operating cash flows. After some point, however, the cash inflows from extending the payment of accounts payable or other liabilities come at the cost of supplier and creditor relations.

The second category involves adjusting cash flows for transitory items. One example is tax benefits from exercise of employee stock options, which are typically transitory. The IRS considers the cost of employee stock options a tax-deductible expense, even if unrecognized as an expense under GAAP. The persistence of this tax benefit, however, is predicated on increased stock prices. When the stock price falls below the option's exercise (strike) price, options are no longer exercised and the tax benefit ceases.

BUSINESS INSIGHT   What is eBay's Operating Cash Flow?

Steve Milunovich of Merrill Lynch believes that operating cash flow should exclude what companies spend to buy back stock to offset option-related dilution. This gets tricky in eBay's case because it, unlike many others, hasn't bought back any stock. This means that, even if you're a stockholder who never sold a share, you own less of eBay now than you did five years ago. It is estimated that had eBay bought back shares to enable stockholders to maintain their ownership stake rather than seeing it decline, the cash outflow would have been $1.2 billion—which is huge relative to eBay's five-year cumulative operating cash flow of $1.8 billion. (*Fortune* May 31, 2004)

The third category involves the proper categorization of cash flows into operating, investing, and financing sections. One example is cash inflows from asset securitizations, which are reported as operating cash flows per GAAP. However, companies commonly sell accounts receivable to a variable interest entity (see Module 9), which is categorized as an operating cash inflow in the year of sale, but is better viewed as a financing cash inflow (similar to borrowing against the receivables). Another example is cash flows from discontinued operations that should be reclassified from operating to investing.

BUSINESS INSIGHT   Tyco Buys Operating Cash Flow

Corporate management is aware of the market's focus on operating cash flow, which is a main driver of free cash flow and is used in many stock valuation models (see Module 11). In 2001, Tyco touted its free cash flows in a press release: *Free Cash Flow Reaches $1.7 Billion for the Fourth Quarter and $4.75 Billion for the Fiscal Year.* Said L. Dennis Kozlowski, chairman and CEO of Tyco, "Strong cash flow generation throughout all of our businesses funds further investment in these businesses and provides the means to opportunistically expand them as circumstances allow." Tyco eventually admitted to spending $830 million in 2001 to purchase roughly 800,000 individual customer contracts for its security-alarm business from a network of independent dealers. Cash outflows relating to this purchase were reported in the *investing* section of the statement of cash flows. However, fees paid by these new customers were reported in net income and immediately added to its *operating* cash flow. *The Wall Street Journal* (March 5, 2002) declared that Tyco effectively bought earnings and operating cash flow with its contract purchases.

■ MID-MODULE REVIEW ■

Following is the income statement ($ millions) of Time Warner, Inc.:

	2003	2002	2001
Revenues			
Subscriptions	$ 20,448	$ 18,959	$ 15,657
Advertising	6,182	6,299	6,869
Content	11,446	10,216	8,654
Other	1,489	1,840	2,327
Total revenues	39,565	37,314	33,507
Costs of revenues	(23,285)	(22,116)	(18,789)
Selling, general and administrative	(9,862)	(8,835)	(7,486)
Merger and restructuring costs	(109)	(327)	(214)
Amortization of intangible assets	(640)	(557)	(6,366)
Impairment of goodwill and other intangible assets	(318)	(44,039)	—
Net gain on disposal of assets	14	6	—
Operating income (loss)	5,365	(38,554)	652
Interest expense, net	(1,844)	(1,758)	(1,316)
Other income (expense), net	1,210	(2,447)	(3,458)
Minority interest income (expense)	(214)	(278)	46
Income (loss) before income taxes, discontinued operations and cumulative effect of accounting change	4,517	(43,037)	(4,076)
Income tax provision	(1,371)	(412)	(145)
Income (loss) before discontinued operations and cumulative effect of accounting change	3,146	(43,449)	(4,221)
Discontinued operations, net of tax	(495)	(1,012)	(713)
Income (loss) before cumulative effect of accounting change	2,651	(44,461)	(4,934)
Cumulative effect of accounting change	(12)	(54,235)	—
Net income (loss)	$ 2,639	$(98,696)	$ (4,934)

Identify and discuss any items that you believe should be considered in the adjusting process as we prepare to forecast Time Warner's earnings performance based on results for this three-year period.

Solution

Several items from its income statement should be considered when adjusting Time Warner's earnings for this period in anticipation of generating forecasts. Consider the following three categories of common income statement adjustments and potential Time Warner adjustments:

1. *Separate core (persistent) and transitory items*
   a. Its cost of revenues increases from 54.5% to 59% of sales over this period. We want more information regarding the causes of this trend. For example, has the cost of revenues been impacted by transitory items, like the write-off of inventory?
   b. Merger and restructuring costs, while they have recurred over this period, are usually transitory. Further, Time Warner is not a typical *roll-up company* (achieving growth via acquisitions). Thus, we treat these costs as nonrecurring and we want to know more about the details of these costs.
   c. Its impairment of goodwill and other intangibles is mainly related to its write-off of goodwill from the merger of Time Warner and AOL. This amount is now written off and is not recurring.
   d. Its net gain on disposal of assets, although a minor amount in this case, warrants attention. We must watch for recognition of gains and losses on asset sales, especially when the gain allows a company to achieve earnings targets or the loss is taken in a year of excessive income (or losses).
   e. Its income (loss) from discontinued operations is, by definition, eliminated from the income statement once the operations are disposed of.
   f. Its cumulative effect of accounting change is the cumulative adjustment following adoption of a new accounting rule. It is treated as nonrecurring.

2. *Separate operating and nonoperating items*
    a. Its SGA expenses increase from 22.3% to 24.9% of sales. Aside from the potential for out-of-control overhead, we are interested in knowing whether SG&A includes transitory and/or nonoperating items that would distort the underlying economic picture. Footnote disclosures are one source of information.
3. *Include expenses not reflected in net income*
    a. Its other income and expense item has fluctuated over the past three years, from a loss of $3,458 million to a gain of $1,210 million. The composition of this account is of great interest and we would search the footnotes for any insights. (This also fits under adjustment no. 1.)

■ FORECASTING FINANCIAL STATEMENTS

Common stock valuation models use forecasted financial information to compute estimates of stock price. Creditors also utilize forecasted financial information to evaluate the cash flows available to repay indebtedness. Knowledge of the forecasting process is, therefore, an important skill to master. In this section, we introduce the most common method to forecast the income statement, balance sheet, and statement of cash flows. It is important to forecast the income statement first, then the balance sheet, and then the statement of cash flows in that order since each succeeding statement uses forecast information from the previous forecasted statement(s). Our description, therefore, proceeds in that same order.

$ Cash Effect

We use **Procter & Gamble**'s fiscal 2004 financial statements for illustration. In practice, the forecasting process uses adjusted financial statements resulting from the adjusting process explained in the prior section. However, for ease in learning, we deliberately select P&G because it is generally free from needed adjustments. This allows us to focus on the forecasting mechanics.

Forecasting the Income Statement

Procter & Gamble's fiscal year income statement is shown in Exhibit 10.4.

EXHIBIT 10.4 ■ Procter & Gamble Income Statement

	Years Ended June 30		
Amounts in millions	**2004**	**2003**	**2002**
Net sales	$51,407	$43,377	$40,238
Cost of products sold	25,076	22,141	20,989
Selling, general and administrative expense	16,504	13,383	12,571
Operating income	9,827	7,853	6,678
Interest expense	629	561	603
Other nonoperating income, net	152	238	308
Earnings before income taxes	9,350	7,530	6,383
Income taxes	2,869	2,344	2,031
Net earnings	$ 6,481	$ 5,186	$ 4,352

Assuming that we have made all necessary adjustments (see prior section), we identify several important financial relations from the income statement information in Exhibit 10.4. These relations are identified and reported in Exhibit 10.5.[3]

---

[3]A key to financial statement forecasting is the sales forecast. Although there is no perfect method, the more information we can gather and assimilate, the more accurate the forecast will be. Use of the current sales growth rate is a simple, but often reasonable, sales forecast and is applied in this module and its assignments. Many other forecasting methods are available, with varying claims of success. For example, we could use a time series of sales and fit a trend line. We also could use other company, industry, and economic variables in a so-called multivariate forecast model in a desire to better predict sales. However, there is no guarantee that the costs of such forecasts are worth the benefits. Forecasting is an uncertain setting.

EXHIBIT 10.5 ■ Key Procter & Gamble Income Statement Relations

($ millions)	2004
Sales growth ([$51,407/$43,377] − 1)	18.5%
Cost of goods sold percentage ($25,076/$51,407)	48.8%
Gross profit margin (1 − 48.8%)	51.2%
Selling, general and administrative expense margin ($16,504/$51,407)	32.1%
Depreciation expense (per statement of cash flow)	$1,733
Net nonoperating expense ($629 − $152)	$ 477
Tax expense/Pretax income ($2,869/$9,350)	30.7%

We use these key income statement relations and measures to forecast future performance. In practice, we also review the MD&A section, footnotes, and nonfinancial information to assess whether these historical income statement relations are representative of core operating performance and, if not, adjust these income statement relations accordingly. Following are examples of how we can use nonfinancial information to enhance our income statement relations and measures:

Company Scenario	Forecasting Implications
McDonalds reports an 11% increase in 2003 sales; its MD&A reports that sales increased by 5% from a weakened $US	We might forecast a less than 11% sales growth if we do not expect the $US to further weaken or strengthen
Altria reports a $2.6 billion gain on sale of its Miller Brewing subsidiary	This is a transitory item and we do not want to forecast its recurrence; we also do not want to include any operating results from this discontinued subsidiary in our forecasting process
Hewlett-Packard reports a 28% increase in 2003 revenues, from $57 billion in 2002 to $73 billion in 2003; note that in May 2002 it acquired Compaq	Compaq's revenues impact HP's consolidated totals from the date of acquisition onward; footnotes reveal that 2002 revenues would have been $72 billion had Compaq been included for an entire year, meaning that we do not want to assume continuation of a 28% growth
Target reports a 2003 sales increase of 12%; most of this is from new store openings as comparable store growth is 4.4%	Growth via acquisition or construction requires capital outlays, and is different from *organic growth;* if we forecast continuation of a 12% growth, we also must forecast the required capital outlays
Boeing reports a 2003 goodwill impairment charge of $913 million	This is a transitory item that we should not forecast as it is nonrecurring (assuming remaining goodwill is not further impaired)

This module aims to illustrate forecasting mechanics given key financial statement relations as assumptions. In practice, these relations must be carefully reviewed and modified from reported levels if needed. This is the *art* of forecasting.

Using the income statement relations from Exhibit 10.5, the P&G forecasted income statement is shown in Exhibit 10.6. Net nonoperating expense is assumed constant as we do not forecast any changes to the investing and financing activities of the company (at this point).

EXHIBIT 10.6 ■ Procter & Gamble Forecasted Income Statement

($ millions)	2005 Est.
Net sales ($51,407 × 1.185)	**$60,917**
Cost of goods sold ($51,407 × 1.185 × 48.8%)	29,727
Gross profit ($60,917 × 51.2%)	31,190
Selling, general and administrative expense ($60,917 × 32.1%)	19,554
Operating income (subtotal)	11,635
Net nonoperating expense (unchanged)	477
Income before income taxes (subtotal)	11,158
Income taxes ($11,158 × 30.7%)	3,426
Net income (total)	**$ 7,733**

Forecasting the Balance Sheet

Forecasting the balance sheet requires information from our forecasted income statement as well as historical financial and nonfinancial information. It, therefore, is prepared *after* forecasting the income statement. P&G's historical balance sheet is reproduced in Exhibit 10.7.

EXHIBIT 10.7   ■   Procter & Gamble Balance Sheet

	June 30	
Amounts in millions	**2004**	**2003**
Assets		
Current Assets		
Cash and cash equivalents	$ 5,469	$ 5,912
Investment securities	423	300
Accounts receivable	4,062	3,038
Inventories		
Materials and supplies	1,191	1,095
Work in process	340	291
Finished goods	2,869	2,254
Total inventories	4,400	3,640
Deferred income taxes	958	843
Prepaid expenses and other receivables	1,803	1,487
Total current assets	17,115	15,220
Property, Plant, and Equipment		
Buildings	5,206	4,729
Machinery and equipment	19,456	18,222
Land	642	591
	25,304	23,542
Accumulated depreciation	(11,196)	(10,438)
Net property, plant, and equipment	14,108	13,104
Goodwill and Other Intangible Assets		
Goodwill	19,610	11,132
Trademarks and other intangible assets, net	4,290	2,375
Net Goodwill and Other Intangible Assets	23,900	13,507
Other Noncurrent Assets	1,925	1,875
Total Assets	$ 57,048	$ 43,706
Liabilities and Shareholders' Equity		
Current Liabilities		
Accounts payable	$ 3,617	$ 2,795
Accrued and other liabilities	7,689	5,512
Taxes payable	2,554	1,879
Debt due within one year	8,287	2,172
Total current liabilities	22,147	12,358
Long-Term Debt	12,554	11,475
Deferred income taxes	2,261	1,396
Other noncurrent liabilities	2,808	2,291
Total Liabilities	39,770	27,520
Shareholders' Equity		
Convertible Class A preferred stock, stated value $1 per share		
(600 shares authorized)	1,526	1,580
Common stock, stated value $1 per share		
(5,000 shares authorized; shares outstanding:		
2004—2,543.8, 2003—2,594.4)	2,544	2,594

(Continued on next page)

(Continued from previous page)

EXHIBIT 10.7 ■ Procter & Gamble Balance Sheet *(Continued)*

	June 30	
Amounts in millions	**2004**	**2003**
Liabilities and Shareholders' Equity *(Continued)*		
Shareholders' Equity *(Continued)*		
Additional paid-in capital	$ 2,425	$ 1,634
Reserve for ESOP debt retirement	(1,283)	(1,308)
Accumulated other comprehensive income	(1,545)	(2,006)
Retained earnings	13,611	13,692
Total shareholders' equity	17,278	16,186
Total liabilities and shareholders' equity	$ 57,048	$ 43,706

Forecasting of the balance sheet follows two general steps:

Cash Effect

1. Forecast each asset account (*other than cash*) and each liability and equity account
2. Compute the cash amount needed to balance the forecasted accounting equation (Assets = Liabilities + Equity)

To obtain forecasts of specific asset, liability, and equity accounts, several methods can be used such as:

- Assume no change in balance sheet amounts.
- Use detailed relations and predicted events; such as capital expenditures to sales and the depreciation expense to prior year gross PPE, and identify events such as scheduled payments of long-term debt and dividend policies drawn from information gleaned from MD&A and footnote disclosures.
- Use turnover rates and simple assumptions to forecast balance sheet amounts.

The first method is straightforward. The second method requires estimates and assumptions beyond the scope of this book. The third method is the one we use and, thus, requires some explanation. Recall the definition of a generic turnover rate *based on year-end account balances:*

Turnover Rate = Sales (or Cost of Goods Sold)/Account Balance at Year-End

Rearranging terms, we get the forecasted year-end balance as

$$\textbf{Forecasted Year-End Account Balance} = \frac{\textbf{Forecasted Sales (or Cost of Goods Sold)}}{\textbf{Estimated Turnover Rate}}$$

The reason for the use of year-end amounts in the denominator of the turnover rate estimate, while inconsistent with the turnover definition in Module 3, is because of the year-end forecast target. Namely, since we are estimating year-end account balances (and not the average balance), we must compute the turnover rate using year-end balances. The forecasted year-end balance is, thus, forecasted sales (or forecasted cost of goods sold, COGS) divided by the turnover rate estimated from prior year-end balances.

Assuming that we have made all necessary adjustments (see adjusting section), we identify and estimate several important turnover relations and other measures from information in the balance sheet and income statement. These relations and measures are identified and reported in Exhibit 10.8, and are used to forecast the balance sheet.

EXHIBIT 10.8 ■ Key P&G Relations using Income Statement and Balance Sheet Information

($ millions)	2004
Sales/Year-end accounts receivable ($51,407/$4,062)	12.66
Cost of goods sold/Year-end inventories ($25,076/$4,400)	5.70
Cost of goods sold/Year-end accounts payable ($25,076/$3,617)	6.93
Sales/Year-end accrued and tax liabilities ($51,407/[$7,689 + $2,554])	5.02
Capital expenditures/Sales ($2,024/$51,407)	3.9%
Cash dividends (per statement of cash flows in Exhibit 10.10)	$2,539
Current maturities of long-term debt (per footnotes)	$1,519

There is support for the relations and amounts in Exhibit 10.8. For example, accounts receivable and accrued liabilities are typically related to sales levels (because receivables are at selling prices and accruals typically include operating costs that relate to sales volume). Also, inventories and accounts payable are logically related to cost of goods sold (because inventories are at costs and payables typically relate to inventory volume). The amounts for capital expenditures and dividends are taken from the statement of cash flows (see Exhibit 10.10), and the current maturities of long-term debt is provided in the long-term debt footnote (not reproduced here).

Using the income statement and balance sheet relations from Exhibit 10.8, the P&G forecasted balance sheet is shown in Exhibit 10.9—detailed computations are shown in parentheses.

EXHIBIT 10.9 ■ Procter & Gamble Forecasted Balance Sheet

($ millions)	2005 Est.
Cash (total equity and liabilities less all other assets)	$ 9,501
Investment securities (no change assumed)	423
Accounts receivable ($60,917/12.66)	4,812
Inventories ($29,727/5.7)	5,215
Other current assets ($958 + $1,803, no change assumed)	2,761
Total current assets	22,712
Net property, plant, and equipment ($14,108 + [$60,917 × 3.9%] − $1,733)	14,751
Other noncurrent assets ($23,900 + $1,925, no change assumed)	25,825
Total assets (set equal to total liabilities and equity)	$63,288
Accounts payable ($29,727/6.93)	$ 4,290
Accrued and tax liabilities ($60,917/5.02)	12,135
Debt due within one year (no change assumed)	8,287
Total current liabilities	24,712
Long-term debt ($12,554 − $1,519; 2004 debt less current maturities)	11,035
Other long-term liabilities ($2,261 + $2,808, no change assumed)	5,069
Stock and additional paid-in capital ($1,526 + $2,544 + $2,425, no change assumed)	6,495
Retained earnings, AOCI, and ESOP reserve ([$13,611 + $(1,283) + $(1,545)] + $7,733 − $2,539)	15,977
Shareholders' equity	22,472
Total liabilities and equity	$63,288

The final step in forecasting the balance sheet is computing the cash balance, which equals total assets less all noncash assets. Since this is a residual amount, it can be unusually high, low, or even negative. The residual cash balance is an indicator of whether the company is accumulating too much or too little cash from its operating activities less its capital expenditures (note that we are holding financing activities constant at this point). The following table presents two alternative levels of cash and possible adjustments that we would consider at this point in the forecasting process:

$

Cash Effect

Residual Cash	Possible Adjustments to Forecasted Balance Sheet and Income Statement
Too low	• Liquidate marketable securities (then adjust forecasted investment income)
	• Raise cash by increasing long-term debt and/or equity (then adjust forecasted interest expense and/or expected dividends)
Too high	• Invest excess in marketable securities (then adjust investment income)
	• Repay debt or pay out to shareholders as treasury stock or dividends (then adjust forecasted interest expense and/or expected dividends)

What benchmark should we use to determine whether the resulting cash balance is too high or too low? This is a judgment call. Many use the historical cash balance as a percentage of total assets (for our company or the industry in general) as the benchmark. When determining the proper cash balance, we must take care to not inadvertently change the financial leverage of the company in this cash adjustment process. Financial leverage is an important consideration in both the analysis and forecasting of company financials (see Module 3 for a discussion). Accordingly, we must adjust the proportion of debt and equity affected to ensure that financial leverage is not inadvertently shifted.

To illustrate, the projected cash balance for P&G of $9,501 million is 15% of total assets. In 2004, PG's cash level was 10% of total assets. This suggests that P&G will accumulate excess cash in 2005 and will not require additional financing. We can take its excess cash, say $3,172 ($9,501 − [$63,288 × 10%]) and (1) invest it in securities, in which case we must adjust the forecast of investment returns, or (2) assume the P&G repays some of its debt and repurchases some of its stock in the proportion to maintain P&G's existing financial leverage ratio (which stood at 3.30, computed as $57,048/$17,278, at December 31, 2003).

Forecasting the Statement of Cash Flows

Procter & Gamble's fiscal year statement of cash flows is shown in Exhibit 10.10.

EXHIBIT 10.10 ■ Procter & Gamble Statement of Cash Flows

| | Years Ended June 30 | | |
Amounts in millions	2004	2003	2002
Operating Activities			
Net earnings	$ 6,481	$ 5,186	$ 4,352
Depreciation and amortization	1,733	1,703	1,693
Deferred income taxes	415	63	389
Change in accounts receivable	(159)	163	96
Change in inventories	56	(56)	159
Change in accounts payable, accrued and other liabilities	625	936	684
Change in other operating assets and liabilities	(88)	178	(98)
Other	299	527	467
Total operating activities	9,362	8,700	7,742
Investing Activities			
Capital expenditures	(2,024)	(1,482)	(1,679)
Proceeds from asset sales	230	143	227
Acquisitions	(7,476)	(61)	(5,471)
Change in investment securities	(121)	(107)	88
Total investing activities	(9,391)	(1,507)	(6,835)
Financing Activities			
Dividends to shareholders	(2,539)	(2,246)	(2,095)
Change in short-term debt	4,911	(2,052)	1,394
Additions to long-term debt	1,963	1,230	1,690
Reductions of long-term debt	(1,188)	(1,060)	(461)
Proceeds from the exercise of stock options	555	269	237
Treasury purchases	(4,070)	(1,236)	(568)
Total financing activities	(368)	(5,095)	197
Effect of Exchange Rate Changes on Cash and Cash Equivalents	(46)	387	17
Change in cash and cash equivalents	(443)	2,485	1,121
Cash and cash equivalents, beginning of year	$ 5,912	$ 3,427	$ 2,306
Cash and cash equivalents, end of year	$ 5,469	$ 5,912	$ 3,427

$

Cash Effect

The forecasted statement of cash flows is prepared using the forecasted income statement and forecasted balance sheet, the historical statement of cash flows is primarily used for reasonableness checks (outside of the information that was already used to forecast the income statement and balance sheet). We draw on the mechanics from preparation of the statement of cash flows, which are discussed in Module 2. Specifically, once we have forecasts of the balance sheet and income statement, we can compute the forecasted statement of cash flows just as we would its historical statement. The forecasted statement of cash flows for P&G, and its related computations, is in Exhibit 10.11.

EXHIBIT 10.11 ■ Procter & Gamble Forecasted Statement of Cash Flows

($ millions)	2005 Est.
Operating activities	
Net income	$ 7,733
Depreciation expense (per Exhibit 10.5)	1,733
Change in accounts receivable ($4,062 − $4,812)	(750)
Change in inventories ($4,400 − $5,215)	(815)
Change in other current assets (assume no change)	0
Change in accounts payable ($4,290 − $3,617)	673
Change in accrued and tax liabilities ($12,135 − [$7,689 + $2,554])	1,892
Net cash flow from operating activities (subtotal)	10,466
Investing activities	
Capital expenditures ($60,917 × 3.9%, per Exhibit 10.8)	(2,376)
Change in other noncurrent assets (assume no change)	0
Net cash flow from investing activities (subtotal)	(2,376)
Financing activities	
Change in current and long-term debt (per Exhibit 10.8)	(1,519)
Cash dividends to shareholders (per Exhibit 10.8)	(2,539)
Net cash flow from financing activities (subtotal)	(4,058)
Net change in cash (subtotal)	4,032
Cash, beginning of year (per Exhibit 10.10)	5,469
Cash, end of year (total)	$ 9,501

Reassessing the Forecasts

It is useful to reassess the set of forecasted financial statements for reasonableness in light of current economic and company conditions. This task is subjective and benefits from your knowledge of company, industry, and economic factors.

Many prepare "what-if" forecasted financial statements. Specifically, key assumptions are changed, such as the forecasted sales growth, and then forecasted financial statements are recomputed. These alternative forecasting scenarios give management a set of predicted outcomes under different assumptions of future economic conditions. Such forecasts can be useful for setting contingency plans and in identifying areas of vulnerability for future company performance and condition.

Forecasting Multiple Years

Many business decisions require forecasted financial statements for more than one year ahead. For example, managerial and capital budgeting, security valuation, and strategic analyses all benefit from reliable multiyear forecasts. Module 11 uses multiyear forecasts of financial results to estimate current stock price for investment purposes.

Although there are different methods to achieve multiyear forecasts, we apply a straightforward approach. To illustrate, using the forecasting assumptions underlying Exhibit 10.6, we can forecast P&G's 2006 sales as $72,187 million, computed as $60,917 million × 1.185. The remainder of the income statement can be forecasted from this sales level using the methodology discussed above for one-year-ahead forecasts. Similarly for the balance sheet, assuming a continuation of the current asset (and liability) turnover rates, we can forecast current assets and liabilities using the same methodology for one-year-ahead forecast. For example, 2006 accounts receivable are forecasted as $5,702 million, computed as $72,187/12.66.

Exhibit 10.12 illustrates two-year-ahead (2006) forecasting for P&G's income statement, balance sheet, and statement of cash flows—the 2005 forecasts are shown in the first column for reference purposes. The two-year-ahead forecast is prepared using the same forecast assumptions we employed previously. Any forecast assumptions (such as cost percentages and turnover rates) can be changed in future years if we feel it necessary. An example might be a reduction in expected sales growth if we feel that the market is becoming saturated or a reduction in the accounts receivable turnover rate if the economy is expected to slow. The process can then be replicated for any desired forecast horizon.

EXHIBIT 10.12   Procter & Gamble Two-Year-Ahead Forecasted Income Statement

2005 Est.	($ millions)	2006 Est.
$60,917	Net sales ($60,917 × 1.185)	$72,187
29,727	Cost of goods sold ($72,187 × 48.8%)	35,227
31,190	Gross profit ($72,187 × 51.2%)	36,960
19,554	Selling, general and administrative expense ($72,187 × 32.1%)	23,172
11,635	Operating income (subtotal)	13,788
477	Net nonoperating expense (unchanged)	477
11,158	Income before income taxes (subtotal)	13,311
3,426	Income taxes ($13,311 × 30.7%)	4,087
$7,733	Net income (total)	$ 9,224

Procter & Gamble Two-Year-Ahead Forecasted Balance Sheet

2005 Est.	($ millions)	2006 Est.
$ 9,501	Cash (total equity and liabilities less all other assets)	$14,768
423	Investment securities (no change assumed)	423
4,812	Accounts receivable ($72,187/12.66)	5,702
5,215	Inventories ($35,227/5.7)	6,180
2,761	Other current assets (no change assumed)	2,761
22,712	Total current assets	29,834
14,751	Net property, plant, and equipment ($14,751 + [$72,187 × 3.9%] − $1,733)	15,833
25,825	Other noncurrent assets (no change assumed)	25,825
$63,288	Total assets (equal to total liabilities and equity)	$71,492
$ 4,290	Accounts payable ($35,227/6.93)	$ 5,083
12,135	Accrued and tax liabilities ($72,187/5.02)	14,380
8,287	Debt due within one year (no change assumed)	8,287
24,712	Total current liabilities	27,750
11,035	Long-term debt ($11,035 − $1,518)	9,516
5,069	Other long-term liabilities (no change assumed)	5,069
6,495	Stock and additional paid-in capital (no change assumed)	6,495
15,977	Retained earnings, AOCI, and ESOP reserve ($15,977 + $9,224 − $2,539)	22,662
22,472	Shareholders' equity	29,157
$63,288	Total liabilities and equity	$71,492

Procter & Gamble Two-Year-Ahead Forecasted Statement of Cash Flows

2005 Est.	($ millions)	2006 Est.
	Operating activities	
$ 7,733	Net income	$ 9,224
1,733	Depreciation expense (same level assumed)	1,733
(750)	Change in accounts receivable ($4,812 − $5,702)	(890)
(815)	Change in inventories ($5,215 − $6,180)	(965)
0	Change in other current assets (assume no change)	0

(Continued on next page)

(Continued from previous page)

EXHIBIT 10.12 ■ Procter & Gamble Two-Year-Ahead Forecasted Statement of Cash Flows *(Continued)*

2005 Est.	($ millions)	2006 Est.
	Operating activities *(continued)*	
	Net income *(continued)*	
673	Change in accounts payable ($5,083 − $4,290)	$ 793
1,892	Change in accrued and tax liabilities ($14,380 − 12,135)	2,245
10,466	Net cash flow from operating activities (subtotal)	12,140
	Investing activities	
(2,376)	Capital expenditures ($72,187 × 3.9%)	(2,815)
0	Change in other noncurrent assets (assume no change).......................	0
(2,376)	Net cash flow from investing activities (subtotal)...........................	(2,815)
	Financing activities	
(1,519)	Change in current and long-term debt (assume same scheduled payment)	(1,519)
(2,539)	Cash dividends to shareholders (assume no change in level)	(2,539)
(4,058)	Net cash flow from financing activities (subtotal)............................	(4,058)
4,032	Net change in cash (subtotal)	5,267
5,469	Cash, beginning of year..	9,501
$ 9,501	Cash, end of year (total)	$14,768

The two-year-ahead forecasts in Exhibit 10.12 illustrate the technique used to forecast an additional year. To simplify exposition, we have not altered any of the forecast assumptions, and focus solely on the forecasting mechanics. However, we often do modify these assumptions. For example, we might wish to increase the forecasted depreciation expense due to the forecasted acquisition of $2,376 million of depreciable long-term operating assets in 2005, and to reduce the forecasted interest expense for 2006 in consideration of the repayment of $1,519 million of long-term debt. Also, we might want to forecast investment returns on the $3,172 million of excess cash generated in 2005. Alternatively, if the excess cash is forecasted to be used for debt repayment, we would want to incorporate that payment into our forecast of 2006 interest expense.

Parsimonious Method to Multiyear Forecasting

The forecasting process described in this module uses a considerable amount of available information to, presumably, increase forecast accuracy. We can simplify the process considerably using less information. Stock valuation models commonly use more parsimonious methods to compute multiyear forecasts. For example, in Module 11 we introduce two stock valuation models that use parsimonious methods. One model utilizes forecasted free cash flows and the other uses forecasted net operating profits after tax (NOPAT) and net operating assets (NOA)—see Module 3 for descriptions of the variables. Since free cash flows are equal to net operating profits after tax (NOPAT) less the change in net operating assets (NOA), we can accommodate both models with forecasts of NOPAT and NOA.

One approach is to forecast NOPAT and NOA using the methodology outlined in this Module. Alternatively, we can use a more parsimonious method that requires three crucial inputs:

1. Sales growth
2. Net operating profit margin (NOPM)—defined in Module 3 as NOPAT as a percent of sales
3. Net operating asset turnover (NOAT)—defined in Module 3 as sales divided by average NOA

To illustrate, we compute P&G's 2004 NOPAT as $6,812, from $9,827 × (1 − [$2,869/$9,350])[4], and its 2004 NOA as $37,696, from $57,048 − $423 − [$22,147 − $8,287] − $2,261 − $2,808. Assuming a sales growth of 18.5% per year, a NOPM of 13.25% ($6,812/$51,407), and a NOAT of 1.36 ($51,407/$37,696), we generate 2005 through 2008 forecasts of NOPAT and NOA in Exhibit 10.13—supporting computations are in parentheses.

---

[4]$2,869/$9,350 is the estimated average tax rate and, thus, [1 − $2,869/$9,350] is the after-tax rate.

EXHIBIT 10.13 ■ Procter & Gamble Multiyear Forecasts of NOPAT and NOA ($ millions)

	2004	2005 Est.	2006 Est.	2007 Est.	2008 Est.
Sales	$51,407	$60,917	$72,187	$85,542	$101,367
		($51,407 × 1.185)	($60,917 × 1.185)	($72,187 × 1.185)	($85,542 × 1.185)
NOPAT	$ 6,812	$ 8,072	$ 9,566	$11,335	$ 13,432
	($51,407 × 0.1325)	($60,917 × 0.1325)	($72,187 × 0.1325)	($85,542 × 0.1325)	($101,367 × 0.1325)
NOA	$37,696	$44,792	$53,079	$62,898	$ 74,534
		($60,917/1.36)	($72,187/1.36)	($85,542/1.36)	($101,367/1.36)

This forecasting process can be continued for any desired forecast horizon. Also, the forecast assumptions such as sales growth, NOPM, and NOAT can be varied by year, if desired. This alternative, parsimonious method is much simpler than the primary method illustrated in this module. However, its simplicity does forgo information that can impact forecast accuracy.

■ MODULE-END REVIEW ■

Following is financial statement information from **Kraft Foods, Inc.**

Income Statements		
($ 000s)	2003	2002
Net sales	$31,010	$29,723
Cost of goods sold	18,828	17,720
Gross profit	12,182	12,003
Marketing, administrative, research and amortization	6,209	5,716
Other expense (revenue)	(38)	173
Interest expense	665	847
Income before taxes	5,346	5,267
Income taxes	1,870	1,873
Net income	$ 3,476	$ 3,394

Balance Sheets		
($ 000s)	2003	2002
Cash	$ 514	$ 215
Receivables	3,369	3,116
Inventories	3,343	3,382
Other current assets	898	743
Total current assets	8,124	7,456
Property, plant, and equipment, gross	15,805	14,450
Less accumulated depreciation	5,650	4,891
Property, plant, and equipment, net	10,155	9,559
Prepaid pension assets	3,243	2,814
Intangible assets	36,879	36,420
Other assets	884	851
Total assets	$59,285	$57,100
Notes payable	553	220
Accounts payable	2,005	1,939

(Continued on next page)

(Continued from previous page)

Balance Sheets *(Continued)*		
($ 000s)	**2003**	**2002**
Current maturities of long-term debt	$ 775	$ 352
Accrued liabilities	3,534	3,400
Income taxes payable	451	363
Other current liabilities	543	895
Total current liabilities	7,861	7,169
Deferred income	7,750	7,317
Long-term debt	11,591	10,416
Other long-term liabilities	3,553	6,366
Total liabilities	30,755	31,268
Common stock and paid-in capital	23,704	23,655
Retained earnings	7,020	4,814
Treasury stock	402	170
Other equities	(1,792)	(2,467)
Shareholders' equity	28,530	25,832
Total liabilities and equity	$59,285	$57,100

Forecast the Kraft balance sheet and income statement for 2004 using the following additional information:

Key Financial Relations and Measures ($000s)	2003
Sales growth ($31,010/$29,723 − 1)	4.33%
Gross profit margin ($12,182/$31,010)	39.28%
Marketing, administrative and R&D expense incl. depreciation/Sales ($6,209/$31,010)	20.0%
Other expense/Sales ($38/$31,010)	0.124%
Interest expense	$ 665
Tax rate ($1,870/$5,346)	34.9%
Cash dividends (per statement of cash flows)	$1,089
Sales/Year-end accounts receivable ($31,010/$3,369)	9.205
COGS/Year-end inventories ($18,828/$3,343)	5.632
Depreciation expense	$ 813
COGS/Year-end accounts payable	9.391
Sales/Year-end accrued liabilities	8.775
Capital expenditures/Sales	0.035
Income taxes payable/Income taxes	0.242

Solution

Forecasted 2004 financial statements for Kraft Foods follow:

Forecasted Income Statement	
($ 000s)	**2004 Est.**
Net sales ($31,010 × 1.0433)	$32,353
Cost of goods sold ($31,010 × [1 − 39.28%])	19,643
Gross profit ($32,353 × 39.28%)	12,709
Marketing, administrative and R&D expense ($32,353 × 20.0%)	6,471
Other expense (revenue) ($32,353 × 0.124%)	40
Interest expense	665
Income before taxes	5,534
Income taxes ($5,534 × 34.9%)	1,932
Net income	$ 3,603

Forecasted Balance Sheet	
($ 000s)	**2004 Est.**
Cash (amount needed to yield total assets)	$ 1,898
Receivables ($32,353/9.205)	3,515
Inventories ($19,645/5.632)	3,488
Other current assets (assumed level unchanged)	898
Total current assets (subtotal)	9,799
Property, plant, and equipment ($15,805 + $32,353 × 0.035)	16,937
Less accumulated depreciation ($5,650 + $813)	6,463
Property, plant, and equipment, net (subtotal)	10,474
Deferred charges (assumed level unchanged)	3,243
Intangible assets (assumed level unchanged)	36,879
Deposits and other asset (assumed level unchanged)	884
Total assets (equals liabilities plus equity)	$61,279
Notes payable (assumed level unchanged)	$ 553
Accounts payable ($19,645/9.391)	2,092
Current maturities of long-term debt (assumed level unchanged)	775
Accrued liabilities ($32,353/8.775)	3,687
Income taxes payable ($1,932 × 0.242)	467
Other current liabilities (assumed level unchanged)	543
Total current liabilities (subtotal)	8,117
Deferred income (assumed level unchanged)	7,750
Long-term debt ($11,591 − $775)	10,816
Other long-term liabilities (assumed level unchanged)	3,553
Total liabilities (subtotal)	30,236
Common stock and paid-in capital (assumed level unchanged)	23,704
Retained earnings ($7,020 + $3,603 − $1,089)	9,534
Treasury stock (assumed level unchanged)	(402)
Other equities (assumed level unchanged)	(1,792)
Shareholders' equity (subtotal)	31,044
Total liabilities and equity (total)	$61,279

Note: To compute the residual cash balance, we initially assume no change in the capital accounts and the level of debt (other than repayment of $775 in current maturities of long-term debt). This yields a forecasted cash balance of $1,898, which is 3.10% of projected total assets. In 2003, Kraft reported cash at 0.87% of total assets. It appears, therefore, that the forecasting process suggests an accumulation of excess cash—that is, more cash than necessary to efficiently operate. One forecasting adjustment would be to assume either the investment of the excess cash in securities or the use of it to retire long-term debt and equity (in a manner to maintain the present leverage ratio).

GUIDANCE ANSWERS

MANAGERIAL DECISION   You Are a Corporate Analyst

GAAP allows considerable flexibility in the format of the income statement, as long as all of the required elements are present. Although combining operating and nonoperating items and subtotaling to pretax profit is common in practice, many companies subtotal to pretax operating profit, which segregates nonoperating items. The argument to break with tradition and subtotal to pretax operating profit rests on the concept of *transparency*. Transparency in financial reporting means that the financial statements are clearer to the reader. Many feel that greater transparency results in more trust and credibility by users of financial information. Since analysts are concerned with operating profits, your company might reap intangible benefits by being up-front in its presentation. Conversely, seeking to mask operating results, especially if misleading to outsiders, can damage management credibility.

■ DISCUSSION QUESTIONS

Q10-1. Describe the process of *adjusting* financial statements in preparation for forecasting them.

Q10-2. Identify three types of adjustments (for forecasting purposes) that relate to the income statement and provide two examples of each.

Q10-3. What is the objective of the adjusting process as it relates to forecasting of the balance sheet?

Q10-4. What are the main types of adjustments (for forecasting purposes) that relate to the statement of cash flows? Provide two examples of each.

Q10-5. Identify at least two applications that benefit from use of forecasted financial statements.

Q10-6. What procedures must normally take place before the forecasting process begins?

Q10-7. In addition to recent trends, what other types and sources of information can be brought to bear in the forecasting of sales?

Q10-8. Describe the rationale for use of year-end balances in the computation of turnover rates that are used to forecast selected balance sheet accounts.

Q10-9. Identify and describe the steps in forecasting the income statement.

Q10-10. Describe the two-step process of forecasting and adjusting the residual cash balance when forecasting the balance sheet.

■ MINI EXERCISES

M10-11. Forecasting an Income Statement   Abercrombie & Fitch reports the following income statement:

Abercrombie & Fitch (ANF)

(Thousands)	2003	2002
Net sales	$1,707,810	$1,595,757
Cost of goods sold, occupancy and buying costs	990,412	939,708
Gross income	717,398	656,049
General, administrative, and store operating expenses	385,764	343,432
Operating income	331,634	312,617
Net interest income	3,708	3,768
Income before income taxes	335,342	316,385
Provision for income taxes	130,240	121,450
Net Income	$ 205,102	$ 194,935

Forecast its 2004 income statement assuming the following income statement relations ($ 000s):

Net sales growth	7.02%
Gross income margin	42.0%
General, administrative and store operating expenses/Net sales	22.6%
Net interest income	$4,000
Provision for income taxes/Income before income taxes	38.8%

M10-12. Forecasting an Income Statement   Best Buy reports the following income statement:

Best Buy (BBY)

For the Fiscal Years Ended ($ in millions)	February 28, 2004	March 1, 2003	March 2, 2002
Revenue	$24,547	$20,946	$17,711
Cost of goods sold	18,350	15,710	13,941
Gross profit	6,197	5,236	3,770
Selling, general and administrative expenses	4,893	4,226	2,862
Operating income	1,304	1,010	908
Net interest (expense) income	(8)	4	18
Earnings from continuing operations before income tax expense . .	1,296	1,014	926
Income tax expense	496	392	356
Earnings from continuing operations	800	622	570

(Continued on next page)

(Continued from previous page)

For the Fiscal Years Ended ($ in millions)	February 28, 2004	March 1, 2003	March 2, 2002
Loss from discontinued operations, net of $17 and $119 tax	$ (29)	$ (441)	$ —
Loss on disposal of discontinued operations, net of $0 tax	(66)	—	—
Cumulative effect of change in accounting principle for goodwill, net of $24 tax	—	(40)	—
Cumulative effect of change in accounting principle for vendor allowances, net of $26 tax	—	(42)	—
Net earnings	$ 705	$ 99	$ 570

Forecast its fiscal year 2005 income statement assuming the following income statement relations (*Hint:* Do not project discontinued operations for 2005 as they are sold in 2004):

Revenue growth	17.19%
Gross profit margin	25.2%
Selling, general, and administrative expenses/Revenue	19.9%
Net interest (expense) income	$(8) mil.
Income tax expense/Earnings before income tax expense	38.3%

**General Mills
(GIS)**

M10-13. Forecasting an Income Statement   General Mills reports the following income statement:

In millions	May 30, 2004	May 25, 2003
Net sales	$11,070	$10,506
Costs and expenses		
Cost of sales	6,584	6,109
Selling, general and administrative	2,443	2,472
Net interest expense	508	547
Restructuring and other exit costs	26	62
Total costs and expenses	9,561	9,190
Earnings before taxes and earnings from joint ventures	1,509	1,316
Income taxes	528	460
Earnings from joint ventures, net of tax	74	61
Net earnings	$ 1,055	$ 917

Forecast its fiscal year 2005 income statement assuming the following income statement relations (*Note:* combine restructuring and exit costs with selling, general, and administrative for forecasting:

Net sales growth	5.4%
Gross profit margin	40.5%
Selling, general and administrative (incl. restructuring and exit costs)/Net sales	22.3%
Net interest expense	$508 mil.
Income taxes/Earnings before taxes and earnings from joint ventures	35.0%
Earnings from joint ventures, net of tax (assume no change)	$ 74 mil.

**Harley-Davidson
(HDI)**

M10-14. Analyzing, Forecasting, and Interpreting Working Capital   Harley-Davidson reports 2003 net operating working capital of $1,587 million and 2003 long-term operating assets of $1,854 million.

a.   Forecast its 2004 net operating working capital assuming forecasted sales of $5,227 million, net operating working capital turnover of 2.91 times, and long-term operating asset turnover of 2.49 times. (Both turnover rates use year-end balances.)

b.   Does it seem reasonable that its net operating working capital turnover is higher than its long-term operating asset turnover? Explain.

M10-15. Analyzing, Forecasting, and Interpreting Working Capital   Nike reports 2003 net operating working   Nike (NKE)
capital of $3,255 million and 2003 long-term operating assets of $1,961 million.
   a.   Forecast its 2004 net operating working capital assuming forecasted sales of $14,036 million,
        net operating working capital turnover of 3.76 times, and long-term operating asset turnover of
        6.25 times. (Both turnover rates use year-end balances.)
   b.   Does it seem reasonable that its operating working capital turnover is less than its long-term
        operating asset turnover? Explain.

M10-16. Interpreting and Adjusting Balance Sheet Forecasts for a Negative Cash Balance   Assume that your
initial forecast of a balance sheet yields a negative cash balance.
   a.   What does a forecasted negative cash balance imply?
   b.   Given a negative cash balance, what would be your next step in forecasting the balance sheet?
        Explain.

M10-17. Forecasting the Balance Sheet and Operating Cash Flows   Refer to the General Mills information in   General Mills
M10-13. General Mills reports the following current assets and current liabilities from its 2004 balance   (GIS)
sheet:

In millions	May 30, 2004
Cash	$ 751
Accounts receivable	1,010
Inventories	1,063
Other current assets	391
Total current assets	$3,215
Accounts payable	$1,145
Accrued liabilities	796
Notes payable	816
Total current liabilities	$2,757

Using your forecasted income statement from M10-13, and the following information on General Mills'
financial statement relations, forecast its:
   a.   Current asset and current liability sections of its balance sheet.
   b.   Net cash flow from operating activities section of its statement of cash flows.

Key Financial Relations ($ millions)	2004
Net sales/Year-end accounts receivable	10.96
Cost of sales/Year-end inventories	6.19
Cost of sales/Year-end accounts payable	5.75
Net sales/Year-end accrued liabilities	13.93
Depreciation expense (included in forecasted SGA expense in M10-13)	$399
Other current assets (including cash)	no change
Notes payable	no change

M10-18. Adjusting the Balance Sheet   Black & Decker Corporation (BDK) reports the following footnote to its   Black &
2003 10-K: Decker
     Corporation
     (BDK)

> **DISCONTINUED OPERATIONS** As of December 31, 2003, the Corporation met the require-
> ments to classify its European security hardware business as discontinued operations. The Euro-
> pean security hardware business, consisted of the NEMEF, Corbin, and DOM businesses. . . . In
> January 2004, the Corporation completed the sale of the NEMEF and Corbin businesses to Assa
> Abloy for an aggregate sales price of $80.0 million, subject to post-closing adjustments. Also, in
> January 2004, the Corporation signed an agreement with Assa Abloy to sell . . . DOM for $28.0
> million. The Corporation's sale of its European security hardware business in 2004 is expected to
> result in a net gain.

Assets of the European hardware business are reported on Black & Decker's balance sheet in separate asset categories titled "current assets of discontinued operations" and "long-term assets of discontinued operations." What balance sheet adjustment(s) might you consider in anticipation of your forecasting of its balance sheet?

■ EXERCISES

Wal-Mart (WMT)

E10-19.   Analyzing, Forecasting, and Interpreting both Income Statement and Balance Sheet   Following are the fiscal year income statement and balance sheet of **Wal-Mart:**

Income Statement ($ millions)	2004	2003
Net sales	$258,681	$231,577
Cost of goods sold	198,747	178,299
Gross profit	59,934	53,278
Operating, selling, general, and administrative expense	44,909	39,983
Operating profit	15,025	13,295
Interest expense	832	927
Income before taxes	14,193	12,368
Tax expense	5,118	4,357
Income from continuing operations	9,075	8,011
Minority interest expense	214	193
Discontinued operations	193	137
Net income	$ 9,054	$ 7,955

Balance Sheet ($ millions)	1/31/2004	1/31/2003
Cash	$ 5,199	$ 2,736
Receivables	1,254	1,569
Inventories	26,612	24,401
Other current assets	1,356	2,016
Total current assets	34,421	30,722
Property, plant, and equipment, gross	75,887	66,100
Accumulated depreciation	17,357	14,726
Property, plant, and equipment, net	58,530	51,374
Other noncurrent assets	11,961	12,712
Total assets	$104,912	$ 94,808
Accounts payable	$ 19,332	$ 16,829
Accrued liabilities	11,719	9,605
Short-term debt and current maturities of long-term debt	6,367	6,085
Total current liabilities	37,418	32,519
Long-term debt	20,099	19,597
Other long-term liabilities	2,288	1,869
Minority interest	1,484	1,362
Common stock and additional paid-in capital	2,566	2,394
Retained earnings and other comprehensive income	41,057	37,067
Shareholders' equity	43,623	39,461
Total liabilities and equity	$104,912	$ 94,808

a.   Forecast its fiscal 2005 income statement and fiscal 2005 year-end balance sheet using the following relations (assume all other accounts remain constant at January 2004 levels). Apply the same forecasting procedures illustrated in the module ($ millions).

Net sales growth	11.70%
Gross profit margin	23.2%
Operating and SGA expense (includes depreciation)/Net sales	17.4%
Depreciation expense/Prior year gross PPE*	5.8%
Interest expense/Short- and long-term debt and current maturities	3.2%
Tax expense/Pretax income	36.1%
Cash dividends	$1,569
Net sales/Year-end receivables	206.28
Cost of goods sold/Year-end inventories	7.47
Cost of goods sold/Year-end accounts payable	10.28
Net sales/Year-end accrued liabilities	22.07
Capital expenditures/Net sales	3.8%
Current maturities of long-term debt	$2,904

*Depreciation expense is included in SGA expense. This relation is provided as it is required to compute accumulated depreciation on the balance sheet.

(*Note:* Its discontinued operations were sold in 2004 and those assets do not appear in the January 2004 balance sheet; thus, do not forecast 2005 income for the discontinued.)

b. What does your forecasted cash balance from part *a* reveal to you about the forecasted financing needs of the company? Explain.

E10-20. Analyzing, Forecasting, and Interpreting both Income Statement and Balance Sheet Following are the fiscal year income statement and balance sheet of Abercrombie & Fitch:

Abercrombie & Fitch (ANF)

Income statement ($ millions)	2003	2002
Net sales	$1,708	$1,596
Cost of goods sold	991	940
Gross profit	717	656
General, administrative, and store operating expense	386	343
Operating profit	331	313
Net interest revenue	4	4
Income before taxes	335	317
Income taxes	130	122
Net income	$ 205	$ 195

Balance sheet ($ millions)	2003	2002
Cash	$ 511	$ 420
Marketable securities	10	10
Receivables	7	11
Inventories	171	143
Other current assets	54	45
Total current assets	753	629
Property, plant, and equipment, net	445	393
Other noncurrent assets	1	1
Total assets	$1,199	$1,023
Accounts payable	$ 91	$ 79
Accrued and other liabilities	189	166
Total current liabilities	280	245
Other long-term liabilities	48	28
Common stock and additional paid-in capital	140	144
Retained earnings	920	715
Treasury stock	(189)	(109)
Shareholders' equity	871	750
Total liabilities and equity	$1,199	$1,023

a. Forecast its fiscal 2004 income statement and balance sheet using the following relations (assume all other accounts remain constant at 2003 levels). Apply the same forecasting procedures illustrated in the module.

Net sales growth	7.02%
Gross profit margin	42.0%
GA and store expense (includes depreciation expense)/Net sales*	22.6%
Depreciation expense/Prior year net PPE*	17.0%
Tax expense/Pretax income	38.8%
Net sales/Year-end receivables	244.00
Cost of goods sold/Year-end inventories	5.80
Cost of goods sold/Year-end accounts payable	10.89
Net sales/Year-end accrued and other liabilities	9.04
Capital expenditures/Net sales	5.8%
Cash dividends	$0 mil.
Net interest revenue	$4 mil.

*Depreciation expense is included in GA and store expense. This relation is provided as it is required to compute accumulated depreciation on the balance sheet.

b. What does your forecasted cash balance from part *a* reveal to you about the forecasted financing needs of the company? Explain.

E10-21. Analyzing, Forecasting, and Interpreting both Income Statement and Balance Sheet   Following are the fiscal year income statement and balance sheet of Merck & Company:

Merck &
Company
(MRK)

Income Statement ($ millions)	2003	2002
Sales	$ 22,486	$ 21,446
Cost of goods sold	4,315	3,907
Gross profit	18,171	17,539
Marketing and administrative expense	6,395	5,652
Research and development expense	3,280	2,677
Other income	474	644
Operating profit	8,970	9,854
Interest expense (revenue)	(82)	202
Income before taxes	9,052	9,652
Income taxes expense	2,462	2,857
Income from continuing operations	6,590	6,795
Discontinued operations	241	355
Net income	$ 6,831	$ 7,150

Balance Sheet ($ millions)	2003	2002
Cash	$ 1,201	$ 2,243
Short-term investments	2,972	2,728
Accounts receivable	4,024	5,423
Inventories	2,555	2,964
Other current assets	776	1,028
Total current assets	11,528	14,386
Property, plant, and equipment, gross	21,294	20,984
Accumulated depreciation	7,125	6,788
Property, plant, and equipment, net	14,169	14,196
Long-term investments	7,941	7,255
Other long-term assets	6,950	11,724
Total assets	$ 40,588	$ 47,561

(Continued on next page)

(Continued from previous page)

Balance Sheet ($ millions)	2003	2002
Trade accounts payable	$ 735	$ 2,413
Accrued and other current liabilities	7,134	6,292
Notes payable	1,700	3,670
Total current liabilities	9,569	12,375
Long-term debt	5,096	4,879
Other long-term liabilities	6,430	7,178
Minority interest	3,915	4,928
Common stock and additional paid-in capital	6,987	6,974
Retained earnings and other comprehensive income	34,208	35,336
Treasury stock	(25,617)	(24,109)
Shareholders' equity	15,578	18,201
Total liabilities and equity	$ 40,588	$ 47,561

a.   Forecast its fiscal 2004 income statement and balance sheet using the following relations (assume all other accounts remain constant at 2003 levels). Apply the same forecasting procedures illustrated in the module ($ millions).

Sales growth	4.80%
Gross profit margin	80.8%
Marketing & admin. expense (includes depreciation expense)/Sales	28.4%
R&D expense/Sales	14.6%
Depreciation expense/Prior year gross PPE*	6.3%
Income taxes expense/Pretax income	27.2%
Cash dividends	$3,250
Current maturities of long-term debt	$310
Sales/Year-end accounts receivable	5.59
Cost of goods sold/Year-end inventories	1.69
Cost of goods sold/Year-end trade accounts payable	5.87
Sales/Year-end accrued and other liabilities	3.15
Capital expenditures/Sales	8.5%
Interest revenue	$ 82

*Depreciation expense is included in marketing and admin. expense. This relation is provided as it is required to compute accumulated depreciation on the balance sheet.

(*Note:* Its discontinued operations were sold in the past year and those assets do not appear in the fiscal year 2003 balance sheet; thus, do not forecast 2004 income for the discontinued operations.)

b.   What does your forecasted cash balance from part *a* reveal to you about the forecasted financing needs of the company? Explain.

E10-22.   Analyzing, Forecasting, and Interpreting Both Income Statement and Balance Sheet   Following are the fiscal year income statement and balance sheet of Nike, Inc.:

Nike, Inc.
(NKE)

Income Statement ($ millions)	2004	2003
Sales	$12,253	$10,697
Cost of goods sold	7,001	6,314
Gross profit	5,252	4,383
Selling, general, and administrative expense	3,777	3,232
Operating profit	1,475	1,151
Interest expense	25	29
Income before taxes	1,450	1,122
Income taxes expense	504	382
Net income	$ 946	$ 740

(Continued on next page)

(Continued from previous page)

Balance Sheet ($ millions)	2004	2003
Cash	$ 828	$ 634
Marketable securities	401	—
Accounts receivable	2,120	2,084
Inventories	1,634	1,515
Other current assets	529	554
Total current assets	5,512	4,787
Property, plant, and equipment, net	1,587	1,621
Other noncurrent assets	792	413
Total assets	$ 7,891	$ 6,821
Accounts payable	$ 764	$ 573
Accrued liabilities	1,092	1,167
Notes payable	153	281
Total current liabilities	2,009	2,021
Long-term debt	682	552
Other long-term liabilities	418	258
Common stock and paid-in capital	891	592
Retained earnings and other comprehensive income	3,891	3,398
Shareholders' equity	4,782	3,990
Total liabilities and equity	$ 7,891	$ 6,821

a.   Forecast its fiscal year 2005 income statement and balance sheet using the following relations (assume all other accounts remain constant at 2004 levels). Apply the same forecasting procedures illustrated in the module.

Sales growth	14.55%
Gross profit margin	42.9%
SGA expense (includes depreciation expense)/Sales	30.8%
Depreciation expense/Prior year PPE, net*	15.5%
Income taxes expense/Pretax income	34.8%
Sales/Year-end accounts receivable	5.78
Cost of goods sold/Year-end inventories	4.28
Cost of goods sold/Year-end accounts payable	9.16
Sales/Year-end accrued liabilities	11.22
Capital expenditures/Sales	1.7%
Current maturities of long-term debt	$ 6 mil.
Interest expense	$25 mil.

*Depreciation expense is included in SGA expense. This relation is provided as it is required to compute accumulated depreciation on the balance sheet.

b.   What does your forecasted cash balance from part *a* reveal to you about the forecasted financing needs of the company? Explain.

Toys 'R' US,
Inc. (TOY)

E10-23.   Analyzing, Forecasting, and Interpreting both Income Statement and Balance Sheet   Following are the fiscal year income statement and balance sheet of Toys 'R' US, Inc.:

Balance Sheet ($ millions)	2004	2003
Cash	$ 2,003	$ 1,083
Accounts receivable	146	202
Inventories	2,123	2,190
Other current assets	412	111
Total current assets	4,684	3,586
Property, plant, and equipment, net	4,572	4,743
Other noncurrent assets	962	1,068
Total assets	$10,218	$ 9,397
Accounts payable	$ 991	$ 896
Accrued and other liabilities	1,124	1,103
Debt due within one year	657	379
Total current liabilities	2,772	2,378
Long-term debt	2,349	2,139
Other long-term liabilities	866	837
Common stock and paid-in capital	446	457
Retained earnings and other comprehensive income	5,492	5,308
Treasury stock	(1,707)	(1,722)
Stockholders' equity	4,231	5,765
Total liabilities and equity	$10,218	$11,119

Income Statement ($ millions)	2004	2003
Sales	$11,566	$11,305
Cost of goods sold	7,849	7,799
Gross profit	3,717	3,506
SG&A, depreciation, and other expenses	3,455	3,035
Operating income	262	471
Interest expense	124	110
Income before taxes	138	361
Taxes expense	50	132
Net income	$ 88	$ 229

a. Forecast its fiscal year 2005 income statement and balance sheet using the following relations (assume all other accounts remain constant at 2004 levels). Apply the same forecasting procedures illustrated in the module ($ millions).

Sales growth	2.30%
Gross profit margin	32.1%
SGA, depreciation, and other expenses/Sales	29.9%
Depreciation expense*	$348
Interest expense	$142
Taxes expense/Pretax income	36.2%
Sales/Year-end accounts receivable	79.22
Cost of goods sold/Year-end inventories	3.70
Cost of goods sold/Year-end accounts payable	7.92
Sales/Year-end accrued and other liabilities	10.29
Capital expenditures/Sales	12.8%
Cash dividends	$ 0
Debt due within one year	$657

*Amount is required to compute accumulated depreciation on the balance sheet.

b. What does your forecasted cash balance from part *a* reveal to you about the forecasted financing needs of the company? Explain.

Toys 'R' US, Inc. (TOY)

E10-24. Forecasting the Statement of Cash Flows Refer to the Toys 'R' Us, Inc., financial information from Exercise 10-23. Prepare a forecast of its fiscal year 2005 statement of cash flows.

Walgreen Co. (WAG)

E10-25. Analyzing, Forecasting and Interpreting both Income Statement and Balance Sheet Following are the fiscal year income statement and balance sheet of Walgreen Co.:

Balance Sheet ($ millions)	2003	2002
Cash	$ 1,017	$ 450
Accounts receivable	1,018	955
Inventories	4,202	3,645
Other current assets	121	116
Total current assets	6,358	5,166
Property, plant, and equipment, net	4,940	4,591
Other noncurrent assets	108	121
Total assets	$11,406	$ 9,878
Accounts payable	$ 2,077	$ 1,836
Accrued and other liabilities	1,344	1,119
Total current liabilities	3,421	2,955
Other long-term liabilities	790	694
Common stock and paid-in capital	778	828
Retained earnings and other comprehensive income	6,418	5,402
Stockholders' equity	7,196	6,230
Total liabilities and equity	$11,407	$ 9,879

Income Statement ($ millions)	2003	2002
Sales	$32,505	$28,681
Cost of goods sold	23,706	21,076
Gross profit	8,799	7,605
SGA, depreciation, and other expenses	6,951	5,981
Operating income	1,848	1,624
Net interest revenue	40	13
Income before taxes	1,888	1,637
Taxes expense	713	618
Net income	$ 1,175	$ 1,019

a. Forecast its fiscal year 2004 income statement and balance sheet using the following relations (assume all other accounts remain constant at 2003 levels). Apply the same forecasting procedures illustrated in the module ($ millions).

Sales growth	13.30%
Gross profit margin	27.1%
SGA, depreciation, and other expenses/Sales	21.4%
Depreciation expense*	$346
Net interest revenue	$ 40
Taxes expense/Pretax income	37.8%
Sales/Year-end accounts receivable	31.93
Cost of goods sold/Year-end inventories	5.64
Cost of goods sold/Year-end accounts payable	11.41
Sales/Year-end accrued and other liabilities	24.19
Capital expenditures / sales	2.4%
Cash dividends	$152

*Amount is required to compute accumulated depreciation on the balance sheet.

b. What does your forecasted cash balance from part *a* reveal to you about the forecasted financing needs of the company? Explain.

E10-26. **Forecasting the Statement of Cash flows**   Refer to the Walgreen Co. financial information from Exercise 10-25. Prepare a forecast of its fiscal year 2004 statement of cash flows.

Walgreen Co. (WAG)

E10-27. **Adjusting the Balance Sheet for Operating Leases**   Midwest Air reports total net operating assets of $291.6 million, liabilities of $167.3 million, and equity of $124.3 in its 2003 10-K. Footnotes reveal the existence of operating leases that carry a present value of $357.5 million (see Module 9 for computations). (a) What balance sheet adjustment(s) might you consider relating to these operating leases in anticipation of forecasting its financial statements? (*Hint:* Consider the distinction between operating and nonoperating assets and liabilities.) (b) What income statement adjustment(s) might you consider? (*Hint:* Reflect on the operating and nonoperating distinction for lease-related expenses.)

Midwest Air (MEH)

E10-28. **Adjusting the Balance Sheet for Equity Method Investments**   SBC Communications Inc., reports its 60% investment in Cingular Wireless under the equity method of accounting (footnotes reveal that Cingular Wireless is a joint venture between SBC and Southwest Bell where SBC has significant influence, but not control), and it reports an investment balance of $5.1 billion on its 2003 balance sheet. Cingular has total assets of $25.5 billion, liabilities of $17 billion, and equity of $8.5 billion. SBC's investment balance is, thus, equal to its 60% interest in Cingular's equity ($8.5 billion × 60% = $5.1 billion). What adjustment(s) might you consider to SBC's balance sheet in anticipation of forecasting its financial statements? (*Hint:* Consider the distinction between operating and nonoperating assets and liabilities.) What risks might SBC face that are not revealed on the face of its balance sheet?

SBC Communications Inc. (SBC)

Cingular Wireless

■ PROBLEMS

P10-29. **Forecasting the Income Statement, Balance Sheet, and Statement of Cash Flows**   Following are fiscal year financial statements of Gap Inc.:

Gap Inc. (GPS)

($ In millions)	52 Weeks Ended Jan. 31, 2004	Percentage to Net Sales	52 Weeks Ended Feb. 1, 2003	Percentage to Net Sales
Net sales	$15,854	100.0%	$14,455	100.0%
Cost and expenses				
Cost of goods sold and occupancy expenses	9,886	62.4	9,542	66.0
Operating expenses	4,089	25.8	3,901	27.0
Interest expense	234	1.5	249	1.7
Interest income	(38)	(0.2)	(37)	(0.3)
Earnings before income taxes	1,683	10.6	800	5.5
Income taxes	653	4.1	323	2.2
Net earnings (loss)	$ 1,030	6.5%	$ 477	3.3%

($ In millions except par value)	Jan. 31, 2004	Feb. 1, 2003
Assets		
Current Assets		
Cash and equivalents	$ 2,261	$ 3,027
Short-term investments	1,073	313
Restricted cash	1,351	49
Cash and equivalents, short-term investments and restricted cash	4,685	3,389
Merchandise inventory	1,704	2,048
Other current assets	300	303
Total current assets	6,689	5,740
Property and Equipment		
Leasehold improvements	2,224	2,242
Furniture and equipment	3,591	3,439

(Continued on next page)

(Continued from previous page)

($ In millions except par value)	Jan. 31, 2004	Feb. 1, 2003
Assets *(Continued)*		
Property and Equipment *(Continued)*		
Land and buildings	$ 1,033	$ 943
Construction-in-progress	131	202
	6,979	6,826
Accumulated depreciation and amortization	(3,611)	(3,049)
Property and equipment, net	3,368	3,777
Other assets	286	385
Total assets	$10,343	$ 9,902
Liabilities and Shareholders' Equity		
Current Liabilities		
Current maturities of long-term debt	$ 283	$ 500
Accounts payable	1,178	1,159
Accrued expenses and other current liabilities	872	874
Income taxes payable	159	193
Total current liabilities	2,492	2,726
Long-Term Liabilities		
Long-term debt	1,107	1,516
Senior convertible notes	1,380	1,380
Lease incentives and other liabilities	581	621
Total long-term liabilities	3,068	3,517
Shareholders' Equity		
Common stock $.05 par value; Authorized 2,300,000,000 shares; issued 976,154,229 and 968,010,453 shares; outstanding 897,202,485 and 887,322,707 shares	49	48
Additional paid-in capital	732	638
Retained earnings	6,241	5,290
Accumulated other comprehensive earnings (loss)	31	(16)
Deferred compensation	(9)	(13)
Treasury stock, at cost	(2,261)	(2,288)
Total shareholders' equity	4,783	3,659
Total liabilities and shareholders' equity	$10,343	$ 9,902

($ In millions)	52 Weeks Ended Jan. 31, 2004	52 Weeks Ended Feb. 1, 2003	52 Weeks Ended Feb. 2, 2002
Cash Flows from Operating Activities			
Net earnings (loss)	$ 1,030	$ 477	$ (8)
Adjustments to reconcile net earnings (loss) to net cash provided by operating activities:			
Depreciation and amortization	664	693	732
Tax benefit from exercise of stock options and vesting of restricted stock	7	44	58
Deferred income taxes	103	6	(29)
Loss on disposal and other non-cash items affecting net earnings	70	117	64
Change in operating assets and liabilities:			
Merchandise inventory	385	(258)	122
Prepaid expenses and other	5	33	(13)
Accounts payable	(10)	(47)	134

(Continued on next page)

(Continued from previous page)

($ In millions)	52 Weeks Ended Jan. 31, 2004	52 Weeks Ended Feb. 1, 2003	52 Weeks Ended Feb. 2, 2002
Cash Flows from Operating Activities *(Continued)*			
Change in operating assets and liabilities *(continued)*:			
Accrued expenses	$ (79)	$ 129	$ 176
Deferred lease credits and other long-term liabilities	(4)	44	99
Net cash provided by operating activities	2,171	1,238	1,335
Cash Flows from Investing Activities			
Purchase of property and equipment	(272)	(303)	(957)
Proceeds from sale of property and equipment	1	9	—
Purchase of short-term investments	(1,202)	(472)	—
Maturities and sales of short-term investments	442	159	—
Acquisition of lease rights, net increase (decrease) of other assets	5	3	(11)
Net cash used for investing activities	(1,026)	(604)	(968)
Cash Flows from Financing Activities			
Net decrease in notes payable	—	(42)	(735)
Net issuance of long-term debt	—	—	1,194
Net issuance of senior convertible notes	—	1,346	—
Payments of long-term debt	(668)	—	(250)
Restricted cash	(1,303)	(20)	(15)
Issuance of common stock	111	153	139
Net purchase of treasury stock	—	—	(1)
Cash dividends paid	(79)	(78)	(76)
Net cash (used for) provided by financing activities	(1,939)	1,359	256
Effect of exchange rate fluctuations on cash . . .	28	27	(11)
Net (decrease) increase in cash and equivalents	(766)	2,020	612
Cash and equivalents at beginning of year	3,027	1,007	395
Cash and equivalents at end of year	$ 2,261	$3,027	$1,007

Required

Forecast its fiscal year 2005 income statement, balance sheet, and statement of cash flows applying the same forecasting procedures illustrated in the module ($ millions). Clearly identify all relations you estimate and assumptions made. What do your forecasts imply about the financing needs of Gap?

P10-30. **Forecasting the Income Statement, Balance Sheet, and Statement of Cash Flows**   Following are the fiscal year financial statements of **Target Corporation**:

Target Corporation (TGT)

(millions)	Year Ended		
	Jan. 31, 2004	Feb. 1, 2003	Feb. 2, 2002
Sales	$46,781	$42,722	$39,114
Net credit card revenues	1,382	1,195	712
Total revenues	48,163	43,917	39,826
Cost of sales	31,790	29,260	27,143

(Continued on next page)

(Continued from previous page)

(millions)	Year Ended		
	Jan. 31, 2004	Feb. 1, 2003	Feb. 2, 2002
Selling, general and administrative expense	$10,696	$ 9,416	$ 8,461
Credit card expense	838	765	463
Depreciation and amortization	1,320	1,212	1,079
Interest expense	559	588	473
Earnings before income taxes	2,960	2,676	2,207
Provision for income taxes	1,119	1,022	839
Net earnings	$ 1,841	$ 1,654	$ 1,368

(millions)	January 31, 2004	February 1, 2003
Assets		
Cash and cash equivalents	$ 716	$ 758
Accounts receivable, net	5,776	5,565
Inventory	5,343	4,760
Other	1,093	852
Total current assets	12,928	11,935
Property and equipment		
Land	3,629	3,236
Buildings and improvements	13,091	11,527
Fixtures and equipment	5,432	4,983
Construction-in-progress	995	1,190
Accumulated depreciation	(6,178)	(5,629)
Property and equipment, net	16,969	15,307
Other	1,495	1,361
Total assets	$31,392	$28,603
Liabilities and shareholders' investment		
Accounts payable	$ 5,448	$ 4,684
Accrued liabilities	1,618	1,545
Income taxes payable	382	319
Current portion of long-term debt and notes payable	866	975
Total current liabilities	8,314	7,523
Long-term debt	10,217	10,186
Deferred income taxes and other	1,796	1,451
Shareholders' investment		
Common stock*	76	76
Additional paid-in-capital	1,341	1,256
Retained earnings	9,645	8,107
Accumulated other comprehensive income	3	4
Total shareholders' investment	11,065	9,443
Total liabilities and shareholders' investment	$31,392	$28,603

Common Stock Authorized 6,000,000,000 shares, $.0833 pare value; 911,808,051 shares issued and outstanding at January 31, 2004; 909,801,560 shares issued and outstanding at February 1, 2003.

Preferred Stock Authorized 5,000,000 shares, $.01 par value; no shares were issued or outstanding at January 31, 2004 or February 1, 2003.

	Year Ended		
(millions)	Jan. 31, 2004	Feb. 1, 2003	Feb. 2, 2002
Operating activities			
Net earnings	$ 1,841	$ 1,654	$ 1,368
Reconciliation to cash flow			
Depreciation and amortization	1,320	1,212	1,079
Bad debt provision	532	460	230
Deferred tax provision	249	248	49
Loss on disposal of fixed assets, net	54	67	52
Other non-cash items affecting earnings	11	159	160
Changes in operating accounts providing (requiring) cash			
Accounts receivable	(744)	(2,194)	(1,193)
Inventory	(583)	(311)	(201)
Other current assets	(255)	15	(91)
Other assets	(196)	(174)	(178)
Accounts payable	764	524	584
Accrued liabilities	57	(21)	29
Income taxes payable	91	(79)	124
Other	19	30	—
Cash flow provided by operations	3,160	1,590	2,012
Investing activities			
Expenditures for property and equipment	(3,004)	(3,221)	(3,163)
Increase in receivable-backed securities	—	—	(174)
Proceeds from disposals of property and equipment	85	32	32
Other	—	—	(5)
Cash flow required for investing activities	(2,919)	(3,189)	(3,310)
Financing activities			
Decrease in notes payable, net	(100)	—	(808)
Additions to long-term debt	1,200	3,153	3,250
Reductions of long-term debt	(1,172)	(1,071)	(793)
Dividends paid	(237)	(218)	(203)
Repurchase of stock	—	(14)	(20)
Other	26	8	15
Cash flow (required for) provided by financing activities	(283)	1,858	1,441
Net (decrease) increase in cash and cash equivalents	(42)	259	143
Cash and cash equivalents at beginning of year	758	499	356
Cash and cash equivalents at end of year	$ 716	$ 758	$ 499

Required

Forecast its fiscal year 2005 income statement, balance sheet, and statement of cash flows applying the same forecasting procedures illustrated in the module. Clearly identify all relations you estimate and assumptions made. (*Note:* Target's long-term debt footnote reveals that its current maturities of long-term debt for fiscal 2005 are $857 million.) What do your forecasts imply about Target's financing needs for the upcoming year?

P10-31. Adjusting the Income Statement Prior to Forecasting   Following is the income statement of Tyco International, Ltd.:

Tyco International, Ltd. (TYC)

Year Ended September 30 (in millions)	2003	2002	2001
Revenue from product sales	$29,427.7	$28,741.8	$28,953.1
Service revenue	7,373.6	6,848.0	5,049.0
Net Revenues	36,801.3	35,589.8	34,002.1
Cost of product sales	19,740.2	19,495.1	18,319.7
Cost of services	4,151.7	3,570.2	2,615.9
Selling, general and administrative expenses	8,813.4	8,181.6	6,745.3
Restructuring and other (credits) charges, net	(74.3)	1,124.3	400.4
Charges for the impairment of long-lived assets	824.9	3,309.5	120.1
Goodwill impairment	278.4	1,343.7	—
Write off of purchased in-process research and development	—	17.8	184.3
Operating Income (Loss)	3,067.0	(1,452.4)	5,616.4
Interest income	107.2	117.3	128.3
Interest expense	(1,148.0)	(1,077.0)	(904.8)
Other (expense) income, net	(223.4)	(216.6)	250.3
Net gain on sale of common shares of a subsidiary	—	—	24.5
Income (Loss) from Continuing Operations before Income Taxes and Minority Interest	1,802.8	(2,628.7)	5,114.7
Income taxes	(764.5)	(208.1)	(1,172.3)
Minority interest	(3.6)	(1.4)	(47.5)
Income (Loss) from Continuing Operations	1,034.7	(2,838.2)	3,894.9
Income (loss) from discontinued operations of Tyco Capital (net of tax expense of $0, $316.1 million and $195.0 million for the years ended September 30, 2003, 2002 and 2001, respectively)	20.0	(6,282.5)	252.5
Loss on sale of Tyco Capital, net of $0 tax	—	(58.8)	—
Income (loss) before cumulative effect of accounting changes	1,054.7	(9,179.5)	4,147.4
Cumulative effect of accounting changes, net of tax benefit of $40.4 million and $351.9 million for the year ended September 30, 2003 and 2001, respectively	(75.1)	—	(683.4)
Net Income (Loss)	$ 979.6	$ (9,179.5)	$ 3,464.0

Required

Identify and explain any income statement line items over the past three years that you believe should be considered for potential adjustment in preparation for forecasting the income statement of Tyco.

P10-32. Adjusting the Income Statement Prior to Forecasting   Following is the 2003 income statement of **Xerox Corporation**:

Xerox
Corporation
(XRX)

Year ended December 31, (in millions, except per-share data)	2003	2002	2001
Revenues			
Sales	$ 6,970	$ 6,752	$ 7,443
Service, outsourcing and rentals	7,734	8,097	8,436
Finance income	997	1,000	1,129
Total revenues	15,701	15,849	17,008
Costs and Expenses			
Cost of sales	4,436	4,233	5,170
Cost of service, outsourcing and rentals	4,311	4,494	4,880
Equipment financing interest	362	401	457
Research and development expenses	868	917	997
Selling, administrative, and general expenses	4,249	4,437	4,728

(Continued on next page)

(Continued from previous page)

Year ended December 31, (in millions, except per-share data)	2003	2002	2001
Costs and Expenses *(Continued)*			
Restructuring and asset impairment charges	$ 176	$ 670	$ 715
Gain on sale of half of interest in Fuji Xerox	—	—	(773)
Gain on affiliate's sale of stock	(13)	—	(4)
Provision for litigation	239	—	—
Other expenses, net	637	593	510
Total costs and expenses	15,265	15,745	16,680
Income before Income Taxes, Equity Income, and Cumulative Effect of Change in Accounting Principle	436	104	328
Income taxes	134	4	473
Income (Loss) before Equity Income and Cumulative Effect of Change in Accounting Principle	302	100	(145)
Equity in net income of unconsolidated affiliates	58	54	53
Income (Loss) before Cumulative Effect of Change in Accounting Principle	360	154	(92)
Cumulative effect of change in accounting principle	—	(63)	(2)
Net Income (Loss)	360	91	(94)

Required

Identify and explain any income statement line items over the past 3 years that you believe should be considered for potential adjustment in preparation for forecasting the income statement of Xerox.

P10-33. Adjusting the Income Statement and Forecasting the Income Statement, Balance Sheet, and Statement of Cash Flows   Following is the income statement and balance sheet of **Bristol-Myers Squibb**:

Bristol-Myers Squibb (BMY)

Dollars in Millions	Year Ended December 31,		
	2003	Restated 2002	Restated 2001
Net Sales	$20,894	$18,106	$18,044
Cost of products sold	7,592	6,532	5,515
Marketing, selling and administrative	4,660	4,124	4,058
Advertising and product promotion	1,416	1,143	1,201
Research and development	2,279	2,206	2,157
Acquired in-process research and development	—	169	2,772
Provision for restructuring and other items	26	14	456
Litigation charges, net	199	659	77
Gain on sales of businesses/product lines	—	(30)	(475)
Asset impairment charge for investment in ImClone	—	379	—
Equity in net income from affiliates	(151)	(80)	(78)
Other expense, net	179	229	98
Total Expenses	16,200	15,345	15,781
Earnings from Continuing Operations Before Minority Interest and Income Taxes	4,694	2,761	2,263
Provision for income taxes	1,215	391	213
Minority interest, net of taxes	373	303	179
Earnings from Continuing Operations	3,106	2,067	1,871
Discontinued Operations			
Net earnings	—	32	226
Net gain on disposal	—	38	2,565
	—	70	2,791
Net Earnings	$ 3,106	$ 2,137	$ 4,662

Dollars in Millions	December 31,	
	2003	Restated **2002**
Assets		
Current Assets		
Cash and cash equivalents	$ 2,444	$ 2,367
Marketable securities	3,013	1,622
Receivables, net of allowances of $154 and $129	3,646	2,968
Inventories, including consignment inventory	1,601	1,608
Deferred income taxes, net of valuation allowances	864	1,013
Prepaid expenses	350	482
Total Current Assets	11,918	10,060
Property, plant and equipment, net	5,712	5,334
Goodwill	4,836	4,836
Other intangible assets, net	1,732	1,904
Deferred income taxes, net of valuation allowances	1,234	1,097
Other assets	2,039	1,791
Total Assets	$27,471	$25,022
Liabilities		
Current Liabilities		
Short-term borrowings	$ 127	$ 1,379
Accounts payable	1,893	1,551
Accrued expenses	2,967	2,537
Accrued rebates and returns	950	883
U.S. and foreign income taxes payable	707	525
Dividends payable	543	542
Accrued litigation liabilities	267	600
Deferred revenue on consigned inventory	76	470
Total Current Liabilities	7,530	8,487
Other liabilities	1,633	1,518
Long-term debt	8,522	6,261
Total Liabilities	17,685	16,266
Stockholders' Equity		
Preferred stock, $2 convertible series: Authorized 10 million shares; issued and outstanding 8,039 in 2003 and 8,308 in 2002, liquidation value of $50 per share	—	—
Common stock, par value of $.10 per share: Authorized 4.5 billion shares; 2,201,012,432 issued in 2003 and 2,200,823,544 in 2002	220	220
Capital in excess of par value of stock	2,477	2,491
Restricted stock	(55)	(52)
Other accumulated comprehensive loss	(855)	(904)
Retained earnings	19,439	18,503
	21,226	20,258
Less cost of treasury stock—261,029,539 common shares in 2003 and 263,994,580 in 2002	11,440	11,502
Total Stockholders' Equity	9,786	8,756
Total Liabilities and Stockholders' Equity	$27,471	$25,022

Required

a. Identify and explain any income statement line items over the past three years that you believe should be considered for potential adjustment in preparation for forecasting the income statement of Bristol-Myers Squibb.

b. Prepare an adjusted income statement for 2003 (for forecasting purposes).

c. Forecast its 2004 income statement, balance sheet, and statement of cash flows applying the same forecasting procedures illustrated in the module. Clearly identify all assumptions you make. (*Note:* Its long-term debt footnote reveals that its current maturities of long-term debt for 2004 are $13 million and is included in short-term borrowings; 2003 depreciation expense is $491 million; 2003 capital expenditures are $937 million; 2003 interest expense, included in other expense, is $212 million; and cash dividends are $2,169 million).

d. What do your forecasts imply about BMS's financing needs for 2004?

11 Analyzing and Valuing Equity Securities

CONSTRUCTING A WINNING STRATEGY

Pharmaceutical companies have long been the growth stocks of choice for many investors. Their income was steady and climbing, their stocks grew in value, and their growth appeared limitless as the population aged. Stakeholders pushed them to grow through acquisition of competitors, and encouraged them to further market existing drugs and pursue new product development. All looked rosy. The high profit margins from successful drug products fueled further expansion. Meanwhile, many pharmaceutical companies sold off their lower-growth business segments such as those manufacturing and distributing medical instruments and devices. Pfizer sold off its segments manufacturing surgical devices, heart valves, and orthopedic implants, while Eli Lilly sold off many of its medical device segments, including Guidant.

A few pharmaceutical companies bucked the trend to reorganize and consolidate. One of those was Johnson & Johnson (J&J). For example, in December 2004, Johnson & Johnson actually purchased, for $25 billion, the same Guidant that Eli Lilly had previously sold off. In contrast with the operating strategies of other pharmaceutical companies, and anticipating a gradual decline in pharmaceutical operating profits, J&J has been steadily increasing its investment in the medical devices and instruments segment of its business. That segment now accounts for 32% of J&J's operating profit, up from 25% in 2001 (J&J 2003 10-K). The recent acquisition of Guidant will further increase this share.

By contrast, and as expected, the pharmaceutical segment's proportion of J&J's operating profit has decreased from 62% to 55% in the past few years, while its proportion of J&J sales has remained constant at 46%. The following graphics using data from J&J's 10-K report reflect these trends:

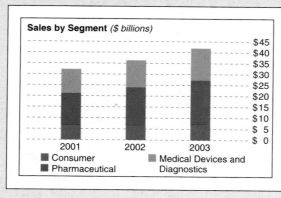

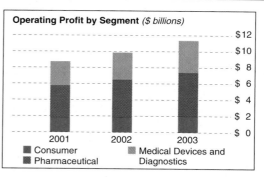

Getty Images/
Chris Hondros

J&J is currently riding high while many other pharmaceutical companies are struggling. Says Mason Tenaglia, a drug-industry consultant, J&J is "casting a broader net for innovation—it's not just blockbuster drugs. They've held their value or grown, and the pure pharma plays that everyone thought could grow forever are the companies that have lost their luster." (*TWSJ*, December 2004).

Supported by its more diversified operations and fueled by a steady increase in operating profits, J&J's stock price has climbed steadily since late 2003, as shown here:

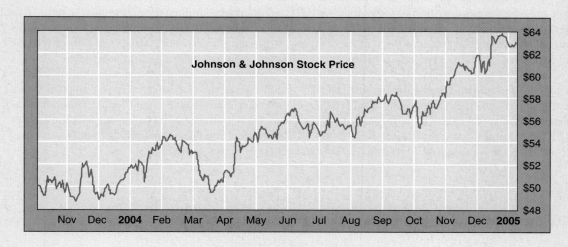

Despite the run-up in stock price, however, analysts remain bullish, continuing to rate the J&J stock a "BUY."

This raises several questions. What factors drive the J&J stock price? Why do analysts expect its price to continue to rise? How do accounting measures of performance and financial condition impact this price? This module provides insights and answers to these questions. It explains how we can use forecasts of operating profits and cash flows in pricing equity securities such as that of J&J's stock.

Sources: *Johnson & Johnson* 2004 and 2003 10-K Reports; *Johnson & Johnson* 2004 and 2003 Annual Reports; *The Wall Street Journal*, December 2004.

■ INTRODUCTION TO SECURITY VALUATION

This module focuses on determining the value of equity securities (we explain the valuation of debt securities in Module 7). We describe two approaches to valuing equity securities: the discounted free cash flow (DCF) and residual operating income (ROPI) models. We then conclude with a discussion of the management implications from an increased understanding of the factors that impact values of equity securities. It is important that we understand the determinants of equity value to make informed decisions from financial reports. Further, employees at all levels of an organization, whether public or private, should understand the factors that create shareholder value so that they can work effectively toward that objective. For many senior managers, stock value serves as a scorecard. Successful managers are those that better understand the factors determining that scorecard.

Equity Valuation Models

Module 7 explains that the value of a debt security is the present value of the interest and principal payments that the investor *expects* to receive from it. The valuation of equity securities is similar, and is also based on expectations. The main difference is the increased uncertainty surrounding the payments from equity securities.

There are several equity valuation models in use today. Each of them defines the value of an equity security in terms of the present value of future forecasted amounts. They differ primarily in terms of what is forecasted.

The basis of equity valuation is the premise that the value of an equity security is determined by the payments that the investor can expect to receive from an investment in that security. There are two types of payoffs from an equity investment: (1) dividends received during the holding period and (2) capital gains when the security is sold.[1] The value of an equity security is, then, based on the present value of expected dividend receipts plus the value of the security at the end of the forecasted holding period. This valuation mechanism is called the **dividend discount model,** and is appealing in its simplicity and its intuitive focus on dividend distribution. As a practical matter, however, it is not useful in valuation as many companies that have a positive stock price have never paid a dividend and are not expected to pay a dividend in the foreseeable future.

A more practical approach to valuing equity securities focuses, instead, on the company's operating and investing activities—that is, the *generation* (and use) of cash rather than the *distribution* of cash. This approach is called the **discounted cash flow (DCF)** model. The focus of the forecasting process for this model is the expected *free cash flows* of the company, which are defined as operating cash flows net of the expected new investment in long-term operating assets that are required to support the business.

A second practical approach to equity valuation also focuses on operating and investing activities. It is known as the **residual operating income (ROPI)** model. This model uses both net operating profits after tax (NOPAT) and the net operating assets (NOA) to determine equity value—see Module 3 for complete descriptions of these measures. This approach highlights the importance of return on net operating assets (RNOA), and the disaggregation of RNOA into NOPAT margin and NOA turnover, for equity valuation. We discuss the implications of this insight for managers later in this module.

■ DISCOUNTED CASH FLOW (DCF) MODEL

The discounted cash flow (DCF) model defines company value as follows:

> **Firm Value = Present Value of Expected Free Cash Flows to Firm**

The expected free cash flows to the firm do not include the cash flows from financing activities. Instead, the *free cash flows to the firm* (FCFF) are typically defined as net cash flows from operations ± net cash

---

[1] The future stock price is, itself, also assumed to be related to the expected dividends that the new investor expects to receive. As a result, the expected receipt of dividends is the sole driver of stock price under this type of valuation model.

flows from investing activities. That is, FCFF reflects increases and decreases in net operating working capital and in long-term operating assets.[2] Using the terminology of Module 3

FCFF = NOPAT − Increase in NOA

where
NOPAT = Net operating profit after tax
NOA = Net operating assets

Stated differently, free cash flows to the firm equal net operating profit that is not used to grow net operating assets.

Net operating profit after tax is normally positive and net cash flows from investments (increases) in net operating assets are normally negative. The sum of the two (positive or negative) represents the net cash flows available to financiers of the firm, both creditors and shareholders. Positive FCFF imply funds available for distribution to creditors and shareholders either in the form of debt repayments, dividends, or stock repurchases (treasury stock). Negative FCFF imply funds are required from creditors and shareholders in the form of new loans or equity investments to support its business activities.

The DCF valuation model requires forecasts of *all* future free cash flows; that is, free cash flows for the remainder of the company's life. Generating such forecasts is not realistic. Consequently, practicing analysts typically estimate FCFF over a horizon period, often 4 to 10 years, and then make simplifying assumptions about the behavior of those FCFFs subsequent to that horizon period.

Application of the DCF model to equity valuation involves five steps:

1. Forecast and discount FCFF for the **horizon period**.[3]
2. Forecast and discount FCFF for the post-horizon period, called **terminal period**.[4]
3. Sum the present values of the horizon and terminal periods to yield firm (enterprise) value.
4. Subtract net financial obligations (NFO) from firm value to yield firm equity value.
5. Divide firm equity value by the number of shares outstanding to yield stock value per share.

To illustrate, we apply DCF to our focus company, Johnson & Johnson. J&J's recent financial statements are reproduced in Appendix 11A. Forecasted financials for J&J (forecast horizon 2004–2007 and terminal period 2008) are in Exhibit 11.1. These forecasts are based on analysts' expectations regarding J&J's future operating results and balance sheet for the next four years.[5] The forecasts (in bold) are for sales, NOPAT, and NOA. These forecasts assume an annual 8% (analysts' consensus) sales growth during the horizon period, a terminal period sales growth of 2%, and a continuation of the current period's 17.24% net operating profit margin (NOPM) and its 1.57 net operating asset turnover (NOAT).[6,7]

---

[2]FCFF is sometimes approximated by net cash flows from operating activities less capital expenditures.

[3]When discounting FCFF, the appropriate discount rate (r) is the **weighted average cost of capital (WACC)**, where the weights are the relative percentages of debt (d) and equity (e) in the capital structure that are applied to the expected returns on debt (r_d) and equity (r_e), respectively: WACC = r_w = (r_d × % of debt) + (r_e × % of equity).

[4]For an assumed growth, g, the terminal period (T) present value of FCFF in perpetuity (beyond the horizon period) is given by, $\dfrac{FCFF_T}{r_w - g}$, where $FCFF_T$ is the free cash flow to the firm for the terminal period, r_w is WACC, and g is the assumed growth rate of those cash flows. The resulting amount is then discounted back to the present using the horizon period discount factor.

[5]We use a four-period horizon in the text and assignments to simplify the exposition and to reduce the computational burden. In practice, we perform the forecasting and valuation process using a spreadsheet, and the number of periods in the forecast horizon is increased to typically 7 to 9 periods.

[6]**NOPAT** equals revenues less operating expenses such as cost of goods sold, selling, general, and administrative expenses, and taxes; it excludes any interest revenue and interest expense and any gains or losses from financial investments. NOPAT reflects the operating side of the firm as opposed to nonoperating activities such as borrowing and security investment activities. **NOA** equals operating assets less operating liabilities. (See Module 3.)

[7]NOPAT and NOA are typically forecasted using the detailed forecasting procedures discussed in Module 10. This module uses the parsimonious method to multiyear forecasting (see Module 10) to focus attention on the valuation process.

EXHIBIT 11.1 ■ Application of Discounted Cash Flow Model

(In millions, except per share values and discount factors)	2003	Horizon Period				Terminal Period
		2004	2005	2006	2007	
Sales	$ 41,862	$45,211	$48,828	$52,734	$56,953	$58,092
NOPAT*	7,216	7,793	8,417	9,090	9,817	10,014
NOA*	26,733	28,872	31,181	33,676	36,370	37,097
Increase in NOA		2,139	2,309	2,495	2,694	727
FCFF (NOPAT − Increase in NOA)		5,654	6,108	6,595	7,123	9,287
Discount factor [1/(1 + r_w)^t]		0.94127	0.88598	0.83394	0.78496	
Present value of horizon FCFF		5,322	5,412	5,500	5,591	
Cum present value of horizon FCFF	21,825					
Present value of terminal FCFF	171,932					
Total firm value	193,757					
Less (plus) NFO†	(136)					
Firm equity value	$193,893					
Stock outstanding	2,968					
Stock value per share	$ 65.33					

*2003 computations: NOPAT = ($41,862 − $12,176 − $14,131 − $4,684 − $918 + $385) × (1-[$3,111/$10,308]) = $7,216; NOA = $48,263 − $4,146 − $84 − ($13,448 − $1,139) − $780 − $2,262 − $1,949 = $26,733

†NFO is negative when investments exceed borrowings (such as for J&J); in this case NFO is added, not subtracted (see footnote 10 for the NFO computation).

The bottom line of Exhibit 11.1 is the estimated J&J equity value of $193,893 million, or a per share stock value of $65.33. Present value computations use a 6.24% WACC(r_w) as the discount rate.[8] Specifically, we obtain this stock valuation as follows:

1. **Compute present value of horizon period FCFF.** The forecasted 2004 FCFF of $5,654 million is computed from the forecasted 2004 NOPAT less the forecasted increase in 2004 NOA. The present value of this $5,654 million as of 2003 is $5,322 million, computed as $5,654 million × 0.94127 (the present value factor for one year discounted at 6.24%).[9] Similarly, the present value of 2005 FCFF (2 years from the current date) is $5,412 million, computed as $6,108 million × 0.88598, and so on through 2007. The sum of these present values (*cumulative present value*) is $21,825 million.

2. **Compute present value of terminal period FCFF.** The present value of the terminal period FCFF is $171,932 million, computed as $\dfrac{\left(\dfrac{\$9,287 \text{ million}}{0.0624 - 0.02}\right)}{(1.0624)^4}$

---

[8]The weighted average cost of capital (WACC) for J&J is computed as follows:

a.   The cost of equity capital is given by the capital asset pricing model (CAPM): $r_e = r_f + \beta\,(r_m - r_f)$, where β is the beta of the stock (an estimate of its variability that is reported by several services such as Standard and Poors), r_f is the risk free rate (commonly assumed as the 10-year government bond rate), and r_m is the expected return to the entire market. The expression $(r_m - r_f)$ is the "spread" of equities over the risk free rate, often assumed to be around 5%. For J&J, given its beta of 0.476 and a 10-year treasury bond rate of 4.15% (r_f) as of January 2004, r_e is estimated as 6.53%, computed as 4.15% + (0.476 × 5%).

b.   The cost of debt capital is the 3.66% after-tax weighted average rate on J&J borrowings as disclosed in its footnotes (5.23% pretax rate × [1 − 30% effective tax rate of J&J]).

c.   WACC is the weighted average of the two returns. For J&J, 90% is weighted on equity and 10% on debt, which reflects the relative proportions of the two financing sources in J&J's capital structure: (90% × 6.53%) + (10% × 3.66%) = 6.24%.

[9]Horizon period discount factors follow: 1/(1.0624)¹ = 0.94127; 1/(1.0624)² = 0.88598; 1/(1.0624)³ = 0.83394; 1/(1.0624)⁴ = 0.78496.

3. **Compute firm equity value.** Sum present values from the horizon and terminal period FCFF to get firm (enterprise) value of $193,757 million. Subtract (add) the value of its net financial obligations (investments) of $(136) million to get firm equity value of $193,893.[10] Dividing firm equity value by the 2,968 million shares outstanding yields the estimated per share valuation of $65.33.

This valuation would be performed in early 2004 (when J&J's 10-K is released in mid-March 2004). J&J's stock closed at $51.66 at year-end 2003. Our valuation estimate of $65.33 indicates that its stock is undervalued. In January 2005 (roughly one year later) J&J stock traded at near $63 and analysts continued to recommend it as a BUY with a price target in the high $60s to low $70s per share.

Estimates of earnings and cash flows are key to security valuation. Following are earnings estimates, as of January 2005, for Johnson & Johnson by the forecasting firm I/B/E/S, a division of Thomson Financial™:

Period	Ending	Mean EPS	High EPS	Low EPS
Fiscal Year	Dec. 2005	3.40	3.43	3.30
Fiscal Year	Dec. 2006	3.72	3.81	3.57
Long-term growth (%)	—	11.0*	15.0	9.40

*Median instead of mean.

The mean (consensus) EPS estimate for 2005 (one year ahead) is $3.40 per share, with a high of $3.43 and a low of $3.30. For 2006, the mean (consensus) EPS estimate is $3.72, with a high of $3.81 and a low of $3.57. The estimated long-term growth rate for EPS (similar to our terminal year growth rate) ranges from 9.4% to 15%, with a mean (consensus) estimate of 11%. Since the terminal year valuation is such a large proportion of total firm valuation, especially for the DCF model, the variability in stock price estimates across analysts covering JNJ is due more to variation in estimates for long-term growth rates than to 1- and 2-year-ahead earnings forecasts.

MANAGERIAL DECISION   **You Are the Division Manager**

Assume that you are managing a division of a company that has a large investment in plant assets and sells its products on credit. Identify steps you can take to increase its cash flow. [Answer p. 11-15]

■ MID-MODULE REVIEW ■

Following are forecasts of **Procter & Gamble**'s sales, net operating profit after tax (NOPAT), and net operating assets (NOA)—these are taken from our forecasting process in Module 10 and now include a terminal year forecast:

(In millions)	2004	Horizon Period				Terminal Period
		2005	2006	2007	2008	
Sales	$51,407	$60,917	$72,187	$85,542	$101,367	$103,394
NOPAT	6,812	8,072	9,566	11,335	13,432	13,701
NOA	37,696	44,792	53,079	62,898	74,534	76,025

Drawing on these forecasts, compute P&G's free cash flows to the firm (FCFF) and an estimate of its stock value using the DCF model and assuming the following: discount rate (WACC) of 7.5%, shares outstanding of 2,543 million, and net financial obligations (NFO) of $20,841 million.

[10]J&J's net financial obligation (NFO) is equal to $(136), computed as its debt ($1,139 + $2,955) less its investments ($4,146 − $84). J&J is in a net investment position (more investments than debt) rather than a net debt position.

Solution

The following DCF results yield a P&G stock value estimate of $58.98 as of December 31, 2003. P&G's stock closed at a split-adjusted price of $49.94 on that date. This estimate suggests that P&G's stock is undervalued on that date. P&G stock traded at $55.08 one year later.

(In millions, except per share values and discount factors)	2004	Horizon Period				Terminal Period
		2005	2006	2007	2008	
Increase in NOA[a]		$ 7,096	$ 8,287	$ 9,819	$11,636	$ 1,491
FCFF (NOPAT − Increase in NOA)		976	1,279	1,516	1,796	12,210
Discount factor $[1/(1 + r_w)^t]$		0.93023	0.86533	0.80496	0.74880	
Present value of horizon FCFF		908	1,107	1,220	1,345	
Cum present value of horizon FCFF	$ 4,580					
Present value of terminal FCFF	166,236[b]					
Total firm value	170,816					
Less (plus) NFO	20,841					
Firm equity value	$149,975					
Stock outstanding	2,543					
Stock value per share	$ 58.98					

[a]NOA increases are viewed as a cash outflow.

[b]Computed as $\dfrac{\left(\dfrac{\$12{,}210 \text{ million}}{0.075 - 0.02}\right)}{(1.075)^4}$, where 7.5% is WACC and 2% is the long-term growth rate subsequent to the horizon period (used to estimate terminal period FCFF).

■ RESIDUAL OPERATING INCOME (ROPI) MODEL

The residual operating income (ROPI) model focuses on net operating profit after tax (NOPAT) and net operating assets (NOA). This means it uses key measures from both the income statement and balance sheet in determining firm value. The ROPI model defines firm value as the sum of two components:

Firm Value = NOA + Present Value of Expected ROPI

where

    NOA = Net operating assets
    ROPI = Residual operating income

Net operating assets (NOA) are the foundation of firm value under the ROPI model. The measure of NOA using the balance sheet is the outcome of accounting procedures, which are unlikely to fully and contemporaneously capture the true (or intrinsic) value of these assets.[11] However, the ROPI model adds an adjustment that corrects for the usual undervaluation (but sometimes overvaluation) of NOA. This amount is the present value of expected residual operating income and is defined as follows:

$$\text{ROPI} = \underbrace{\text{NOPAT} - (\text{NOA}_{Beg} \times r_w)}_{\text{Expected NOPAT}}$$

where

    NOA_{Beg} = Net operating assets at beginning (*Beg*) of period
    r_w = Weighted average cost of capital (WACC)

---

[11]For example, R&D and advertising are not fully and contemporaneously reflected on the balance sheet as assets though they likely produce future cash inflows. Likewise, internally generated goodwill is not fully reflected on the balance sheet as an asset. Also, companies can delay or accelerate the write-down of impaired assets and, thus, overstate their book values. Similarly, assets are generally not written up to reflect unrealized gains. These examples, and a host of others, can yield reported book values of NOA that differs from its market value.

The ROPI model's use of the balance sheet (NOA_{Beg}), in addition to the income statement (NOPAT), is informative because book values of net operating assets incorporate estimates (of varying relevance) of their future cash flows. Understanding this model also helps us reap the benefits from disaggregation of return on net operating assets (DuPont analysis) in Module 3. Finally, the ROPI model is the foundation for many internal and external performance evaluation and compensation systems marketed by management consulting and accounting services firms.[12]

Application of the ROPI model to equity valuation involves five steps:

1. Forecast and discount ROPI for the horizon period.[13]
2. Forecast and discount ROPI for the terminal period.[14]
3. Sum the present values of the horizon and terminal periods; then add this sum to current NOA to get firm (enterprise) value.
4. Subtract net financial obligations (NFO) from firm value to yield firm equity value.
5. Divide firm equity value by the number of shares outstanding to yield stock value per share.

To illustrate application of the ROPI model, we again use Johnson & Johnson. Forecasted financials for J&J (forecast horizon 2004–2007 and terminal period 2008) are in Exhibit 11.2. The forecasts (in bold) are for sales, NOPAT, and NOA, and are the same forecasts from the illustration of the DCF model.

EXHIBIT 11.2 ■ Application of Residual Operating Income Model

(In millions, except per share values and discount factors)	2003	Horizon Period				Terminal Period
		2004	2005	2006	2007	
Sales	$ 41,862	$45,211	$48,828	$52,734	$56,953	$58,092
NOPAT	7,216	7,793	8,417	9,090	9,817	10,014
NOA	26,733	28,872	31,181	33,676	36,370	37,097
ROPI (NOPAT − [$NOA_{Beg} \times r_w$])		6,125	6,615	7,144	7,716	7,745
Discount factor [$1/(1 + r_w)^t$]		0.94127	0.88598	0.83394	0.78496	
Present value of horizon ROPI		5,765	5,861	5,958	6,056	
Cum present value of horizon ROPI	23,641					
Present value of terminal ROPI	143,385					
NOA	26,733					
Total firm value	193,758					
Less (plus) NFO*	(136)					
Firm equity value	$193,894					
Stock outstanding	2,968					
Stock value per share	$ 65.33					

*NFO is negative when investments exceed borrowings (such as for J&J); in this case NFO is added, not subtracted.

The bottom line of Exhibit 11.2 is the estimated J&J equity value of $193,894 million, or a per share stock value of $65.33. As before, present value computations use a 6.24% WACC as the discount rate. Specifically, we obtain this stock valuation as follows:

1. **Compute present value of horizon period ROPI.** The forecasted 2004 ROPI of $6,125 million is computed from the forecasted 2004 NOPAT less the product of beginning period NOA and WACC.

---

[12]Examples are economic value added (EVA™) from Stern Stewart & Company, the economic profit model from McKinsey & Co., the cash flow return on investment (CFROI) from Holt Value Associates, the economic value management from KPMG, and the value builder from PricewaterhouseCoopers (PwC).

[13]The present value of expected ROPI uses the weighted average cost of capital (WACC) as its discount rate—same as with the DCF model.

[14]As with the DCF model, for an assumed growth, g, the present value of the perpetuity of ROPI beyond the horizon period is given by $\dfrac{ROPI_T}{r_w - g}$, where $ROPI_T$ is the residual operating income for the terminal period, r_w is WACC for the firm, and g is the assumed growth rate of ROPI following the horizon period. The resulting amount is then discounted back to the present at the horizon period discount factor.

The present value of this ROPI as of 2003 is $5,765 million, computed as $6,125 million $\times$ 0.94127 (the present value 1 year hence discounted at 6.24%). Similarly, the present value of 2005 ROPI (2 years hence) is $5,861 million, computed as $6,615 million $\times$ 0.88598, and so on through 2007. The sum of these present values (cumulative present value) is $23,641 million.

2. **Compute present value of terminal period ROPI.** The present value of the terminal period ROPI is $143,385 million, computed as $\dfrac{\left(\dfrac{\$7,745 \text{ million}}{0.0624 - 0.02}\right)}{(1.0624)^4}$

3. **Compute firm equity value.** We must sum the present values from the horizon period ($23,641 million) and terminal period ($143,385 million), plus NOA ($26,733 million), to get firm (enterprise) value of $193,758 million. Subtract (add) the value of its net financial obligations (investments) of $(136) million to get firm equity value of $193,894 (the $1 difference from the DCF value of $193,893 is from rounding). Dividing firm equity value by the 2,968 million shares outstanding yields the estimated per share valuation of $65.33.

J&J's stock closed at $51.66 at year-end 2003. The ROPI model estimate of $65.33 indicates that its stock is undervalued. In January 2005 (roughly one year later) J&J stock traded at near $63.

The ROPI model estimate is equal to that computed using the DCF model. This is the case so long as the firm is in a steady state, that is, NOPAT and NOA are growing at the same rate (for example, when RNOA is constant).

RESEARCH INSIGHT   **Power of NOPAT Forecasts**

Discounted cash flow (DCF) and residual operating income (ROPI) models yield identical estimates when the expected payoffs are forecasted for an infinite horizon. For practical reasons, we must use horizon period forecasts and a terminal period forecast. This truncation of the forecast horizon is a main cause of any difference in value estimates for these models. Importantly, research finds that forecasting (GAAP-based) NOPAT, rather than FCFF, yields more accurate estimates of firm value given a finite horizon.

■ MANAGERIAL INSIGHTS FROM THE ROPI MODEL

The ROPI model defines firm value as the sum of NOA and the present value of expected residual operating income as follows:

$$\text{Firm Value} = \text{NOA} + \text{Present Value of } \underbrace{[\text{NOPAT} - (\text{NOA}_{\text{Beg}} \times r_w)]}_{\text{ROPI}}$$

Increasing ROPI, therefore, increases firm value. This can be accomplished in two ways:

1. Decrease the NOA required to generate a given level of NOPAT
2. Increase NOPAT with the same level of NOA investment (improve profitability)

These are two very important observations. It means that achieving better performance requires effective management of *both* the income statement and balance sheet. Most operating managers are accustomed to working with income statements. Further, they are often evaluated on profitability measures, such as achieving desired levels of gross profit or efficiently managing operating expenses. The ROPI model focuses management attention on the balance sheet as well.

The two points above highlight two paths to increase ROPI and, accordingly, firm value. First, let's consider how management can reduce the level of NOA while maintaining a given level of NOPAT. Many managers begin by implementing procedures that reduce net operating working capital, such as:

- Reducing receivables through:
  - Better underwriting of credit quality
  - Better controls to identify delinquencies and automated payment notices
- Reducing inventories through:
  - Use of less costly components (of equal quality) and production with lower wage rates
  - Elimination of product features not valued by customers
  - Outsourcing to reduce product cost
  - Just-in-time deliveries of raw materials
  - Elimination of manufacturing bottlenecks to reduce work-in-process inventories
  - Producing to order rather than to estimated demand
- Increasing payables through:
  - Extending the payment of low or no-cost payables—so long as the relationship is not harmed

Management would next look at its net operating long-term assets for opportunities to reduce unnecessary net operating assets, such as the:

- Sale of unused and unnecessary assets
- Acquisition of production and administrative assets in partnership with other entities for greater throughput
- Acquisition of finished or semifinished goods from suppliers to reduce manufacturing assets

The second path to increase ROPI and, accordingly, firm value is to increase NOPAT with the same level of NOA investment. Management would look to strategies that maximize NOPAT, such as:

- Increasing gross profit dollars through:
  - Better pricing and mix of products sold
  - Reduction of raw material and labor cost without sacrificing product quality, perhaps by outsourcing, better design, or better manufacturing
  - Increase of throughput to minimize overhead costs per unit, provided inventory does not build up
- Reducing selling, general, and administrative expenses through:
  - Better management of personnel
  - Reduction of overhead
  - Use of derivatives to reduce commodity and interest costs
  - Minimization of tax burden

Management must pursue these actions with consideration of both short- and long-run implications for the company. The ROPI model helps managers assess company performance (income statement) relative to the net operating assets committed (balance sheet).

MANAGERIAL DECISION	**You Are the Operations Manager**

The residual operating income (ROPI) model highlights the importance of increasing NOPAT and reducing net operating assets, which are the two major components of the return on net operating assets (RNOA). What specific steps can you take to improve RNOA through improvement of its components: net operating profit margin and turnover of net operating assets? [Answer, p. 11-15]

■ ASSESSMENT OF VALUATION MODELS

Exhibit 11.3 provides a brief summary of the advantages and disadvantages of the DCF and ROPI models. No model dominates the other—and both are theoretically equivalent. Instead, professionals must pick and choose the model that performs best under the practical circumstances confronted.

EXHIBIT 11.3 ■ Advantages and Disadvantages of DCF and ROPI Valuation Models

Model	Advantages	Disadvantages	Performs Best

DCF	• Popular and widely accepted model
	
	• Cash flows are unaffected by accrual accounting
	
	• FCFF is intuitive
		• Cash investments in plant assets are treated as cash outflows, even when creating shareholder value
		• No recognition of value unless evidenced by cash flows
		• Computing FCFF can be difficult as operating cash flows are affected by
		  —Cutbacks on investments (receivables, inventories, plant assets); can yield short-run benefits at long-run costs
		  —Tax benefits of stock option exercise; but likely are transitory as they depend on maintenance of current stock price
		  —GAAP treats securitization as an operating cash flow when many view it as a financing activity
			• When the firm reports positive FCFF
			
			• When FCFF grows at a relatively constant rate

ROPI	• Focuses on value drivers such as profit margins and asset turnovers • Uses both balance sheet and income statement, including accrual accounting information • Reduces weight placed on terminal period value	• Financial statements do not reflect all company assets, especially for knowledge-based industries (for example, R&D assets and goodwill) • Requires some knowledge of accrual accounting	• When financial statements reflect all assets and liabilities; including items often reported off-balance-sheet

There are numerous other equity valuation models in practice. Many require forecasting, but several others do not. A quick review of selected models follows:

The **method of comparables** (often called *multiples*) **model** predicts equity valuation or stock value using price multiples. Price multiples are defined as stock price divided by some key financial statement number. That financial number varies across investors but is usually one of the following: net income, net sales, book value of equity, total assets, or cash flow. Companies are then compared with competitors on their price multiples to assign value.

The **net asset valuation model** draws on the financial reporting system to assign value. That is, equity is valued as reported assets less reported liabilities. Some investors adjust reported assets and liabilities for several perceived shortcomings in GAAP prior to computing net asset value. This method is also commonly applied by privately held companies.

The **dividend discount model** predicts that equity valuation or stock values equal the present value of expected cash dividends. This model is founded on the dividend discount formula and depends on the reliability of forecasted cash dividends.

There are additional models applied in practice that involve dividends, cash flows, research and development outlays, accounting rates of return, cash recovery rates, and real option models. Further, some practitioners, called *chartists* and *technicians,* chart price behavior over time and use it to predict equity value.

RESEARCH INSIGHT   Using Models to Identify Mispriced Stocks

Implementation of the ROPI model can include parameters to capture differences in growth opportunities, persistence of ROPI, and the conservatism in accounting measures. Research finds differences in how such factors, across firms and over time, affect ROPI and changes in NOA. This research also hints that investors do not understand the properties underlying these factors and, consequently, individual stocks are mispriced for short periods of time. Other research contends that the apparent mispricing is due to an omitted valuation variable related to riskiness of the firm.

■ MODULE-END REVIEW ■

Following are forecasts of Procter & Gamble's sales, net operating profit after tax (NOPAT), and net operating assets (NOA). These are taken from our forecasting process in Module 10 and now include a terminal year forecast:

(In millions)	2004	Horizon Period				Terminal Period
		2005	2006	2007	2008	
Sales	$51,407	$60,917	$72,187	$85,542	$101,367	$103,394
NOPAT	6,812	8,072	9,566	11,335	13,432	13,701
NOA	37,696	44,792	53,079	62,898	74,534	76,025

Drawing on these forecasts, compute P&G's residual operating income (ROPI) and an estimate of its stock value using the ROPI model. Assume the following: discount rate (WACC) of 7.5%, shares outstanding of 2,543 million, and net financial obligations (NFO) of $20,841 million.

Solution

Results from the ROPI model below yield a P&G stock value estimate of $58.98 as of December 31, 2003. P&G's stock closed at a split-adjusted price of $49.94 on that date. This estimate suggests that P&G's stock is undervalued on that date. P&G stock traded at $55.08 one year later as shown in the stock price chart below.

(In millions, except per share values and discount factors)	2004	Horizon Period				Terminal Period
		2005	2006	2007	2008	
ROPI (NOPAT − [NOA$_{Beg}$ × r_w])		$5,245	$6,206	$7,354	$8,715	$8,111
Discount factor [1/(1 + r_w)^t]		0.93023	0.86533	0.80496	0.74880	
Present value of horizon ROPI		4,879	5,370	5,920	6,526	
Cum present value of horizon ROPI	$ 22,695					
Present value of terminal ROPI	110,425[a]					
NOA	37,696					
Total firm value	170,816					
Less (plus) NFO	20,841					
Firm equity value	$149,975					
Stock outstanding	2,543					
Stock value per share	$ 58.98					

[a]Computed as $\dfrac{\left(\dfrac{\$8{,}111\text{ million}}{0.075 - 0.02}\right)}{(1.075)^4}$.

The P&G stock price chart, extending from year-end 2003 through early 2005, follows:

APPENDIX 11A

Johnson & Johnson Financial Statements

Income Statement

(Dollars in Millions)	2003	2002	2001
Sales to customers	$41,862	$36,298	$32,317
Cost of products sold	12,176	10,447	9,581
Gross profit	29,686	25,851	22,736
Selling, marketing and administrative expenses	14,131	12,216	11,260
Research expense	4,684	3,957	3,591
Purchased in-process research and development	918	189	105
Interest income	(177)	(256)	(456)
Interest expense, net of portion capitalized	207	160	153
Other (income) expense, net	(385)	294	185
	19,378	16,560	14,838
Earnings before provision for taxes on income	10,308	9,291	7,898
Provision for taxes on income	3,111	2,694	2,230
Net earnings	$ 7,197	$ 6,597	$ 5,668

Balance Sheet

At December 28, 2003 and December 29, 2002 (Dollars in Millions Except Share and Per Share Data)	2003	2002
Assets		
Current assets		
Cash and cash equivalents	$ 5,377	$ 2,894
Marketable securities	4,146	4,581
Accounts receivable trade, less allowances for doubtful accounts $192 (2002, $191)	6,574	5,399
Inventories	3,588	3,303
Deferred taxes on income	1,526	1,419
Prepaid expenses and other receivables	1,784	1,670
Total current assets	22,995	19,266
Marketable securities, non-current	84	121
Property, plant and equipment, net	9,846	8,710
Intangible assets, net	11,539	9,246
Deferred taxes on income	692	236
Other assets	3,107	2,977
Total assets	$48,263	$40,556
Liabilities and Shareholders' Equity		
Current liabilities		
Loans and notes payable	$ 1,139	$ 2,117
Accounts payable	4,966	3,621
Accrued liabilities	2,639	2,059
Accrued rebates, returns and promotions	2,308	1,761
Accrued salaries, wages and commissions	1,452	1,181
Accrued taxes on income	944	710
Total current liabilities	13,448	11,449

(Continued on next page)

(Continued from previous page)

Balance Sheet *(Continued)*

At December 28, 2003 and December 29, 2002 (Dollars in Millions Except Share and Per Share Data)	2003	2002
Liabilities and Shareholders' Equity *(Continued)*		
Long-term debt	$ 2,955	$ 2,022
Deferred tax liability	780	643
Employee related obligations	2,262	1,967
Other liabilities	1,949	1,778
Shareholders' equity		
Preferred stock—without par value (authorized and unissued 2,000,000 shares)	—	—
Common stock—par value $1.00 per share (authorized 4,320,000,000 shares; issued 3,119,842,000 shares)	3,120	3,120
Note receivable from employee stock ownership plan	(18)	(25)
Accumulated other comprehensive income	(590)	(842)
Retained earnings	30,503	26,571
	33,015	28,824
Less: common stock held in treasury, at cost (151,869,000 and 151,547,000)	6,146	6,127
Total shareholders' equity	26,869	22,697
Total liabilities and shareholders' equity	$48,263	$40,556

Statement of Cash Flows

(Dollars in Millions)	2003	2002	2001
Cash flows from operating activities			
Net earnings	$ 7,197	$ 6,597	$ 5,668
Adjustments to reconcile net earnings to cash flows			
Depreciation and amortization of property and intangibles	1,869	1,662	1,605
Purchased in-process research and development	918	189	105
Deferred tax provision	(720)	(74)	(106)
Accounts receivable reserves	6	(6)	99
Changes in assets and liabilities, net of effects from acquisition of businesses			
Increase in accounts receivable	(691)	(510)	(258)
Decrease (increase) in inventories	39	(109)	(167)
Increase in accounts payable and accrued liabilities	2,192	1,420	1,401
Increase in other current and non-current assets	(746)	(1,429)	(270)
Increase in other current and non-current liabilities	531	436	787
Net cash flows from operating activities	10,595	8,176	8,864
Cash flows from investing activities			
Additions to property, plant and equipment	(2,262)	(2,099)	(1,731)
Proceeds from the disposal of assets	335	156	163
Acquisition of businesses, net of cash acquired	(2,812)	(478)	(225)
Purchases of investments	(7,590)	(6,923)	(8,188)
Sales of investments	8,062	7,353	5,967
Other	(259)	(206)	(79)
Net cash used by investing activities	(4,526)	(2,197)	(4,093)
Cash flows from financing activities			
Dividends to shareholders	(2,746)	(2,381)	(2,047)
Repurchase of common stock	(1,183)	(6,538)	(2,570)
Proceeds from short-term debt	3,062	2,359	338

(Continued on next page)

(Continued from previous page)

Statement of Cash Flows *(Continued)*

(Dollars in Millions)	2003	2002	2001
Cash flows from financing activities *(Continued)*			
Retirement of short-term debt	$ (4,134)	$ (560)	$(1,109)
Proceeds from long-term debt	1,023	22	14
Retirement of long-term debt	(196)	(245)	(391)
Proceeds from the exercise of stock options	311	390	514
Net cash used by financing activities	(3,863)	(6,953)	(5,251)
Effect of exchange rate changes on cash and cash equivalents	277	110	(40)
Increase/(decrease) in cash and cash equivalents	2,483	(864)	(520)
Cash and cash equivalents, beginning of year	2,894	3,758	4,278
Cash and cash equivalents, end of year	$ 5,377	$ 2,894	$ 3,758

GUIDANCE ANSWERS

MANAGERIAL DECISION   You Are the Division Manager

Cash flow is increased with asset reductions. For example, receivables are reduced by the following:

- Encouraging up-front payments or progress billings on long-term contracts
- Increasing credit standards to remove slow-paying accounts before sales are made
- Monitoring account age and sending reminders to past due customers
- Selling accounts receivable to a financial institution or special purpose entity

As another example, plant assets are reduced by the following:

- Selling unused or excess plant assets
- Forming alliances with other companies for special purpose plant asset requirements
- Owning assets in a special purpose entity with other companies
- Selling production facilities to a contract manufacturer and purchasing the output

MANAGERIAL DECISION   You Are the Operations Manager

RNOA can be disaggregated into its two key drivers: NOPAT margin and net operating asset turnover. NOPAT margin can be increased by improving gross profit margins (better product pricing, lower cost manufacturing, etc.) and closely monitoring and controlling operating expenses. Net operating asset turnover can be increased by reducing net operating working capital (better monitoring of receivables, better management of inventories, extending payables, etc.) and making more effective use of plant assets (disposing of unused assets, forming corporate alliances to increase plant asset capacity, selling productive assets to contract producers and purchasing the output, etc). The ROPI model effectively focuses managers on the balance sheet *and* income statement.

■ DISCUSSION QUESTIONS

Q11-1. Explain how information contained in financial statements is useful in pricing securities. Are there some components of earnings that are more useful than others in this regard? What nonfinancial information might also be useful?

Q11-2. In general, what role do expectations play in pricing equity securities? What is the relation between security prices and expected returns (the discount rate, or WACC, in this case)?

Q11-3. What are free cash flows to the firm (FCFF) and how are they used in the pricing of equity securities?

Q11-4. Define the weighted average cost of capital.

Q11-5. Define net operating profit after tax (NOPAT).

Q11-6. Define net operating assets (NOA).

Q11-7. Define the concept of residual operating income. How is the concept of residual operating income used in pricing equity securities?

Q11-8. What insight does disaggregation of RNOA into profit margin and asset turnover provide for managing a company?

■ MINI EXERCISES

M11-9. Interpreting Earnings Announcement Effects on Stock Prices In a recent quarterly earnings announcement, Starbucks announced that its earnings had markedly increased (up 7 cents per share over the prior year) and were 1 cent higher than analyst expectations. Starbucks' stock "edged higher," according to *The Wall Street Journal,* but did not markedly increase. Why do you believe that Starbucks stock price did not markedly increase given the good news?

Starbucks
(SBUX)

M11-10. Computing Residual Operating Income (ROPI) 3M Company reports net operating profit after tax (NOPAT) of $2,491 million in 2003. Its net operating assets at the beginning of 2003 are $9,370 million. Assuming a 6.25% weighted average cost of capital (WACC), what is 3M's residual operating income for 2003? Show computations.

3M Company
(MMM)

M11-11. Computing Free Cash Flows to the Firm (FCFF) 3M Company reports net operating profit after tax (NOPAT) of $2,491 million in 2003. Its net operating assets at the beginning of 2003 are $9,370 million and are $10,822 million at the end of 2003. What are 3M's free cash flows to the firm (FCFF) for 2003? Show computations.

3M Company
(MMM)

M11-12. Computing, Analyzing and Interpreting Residual Operating Income (ROPI) In its 2003 fiscal year annual report, PepsiCo reports 2003 net operating income after tax (NOPAT) of $3,649.4 million. As of the beginning of fiscal year 2003 it reports net operating working capital of $716 million and net operating long-term assets of $11,349 million.

PepsiCo (PEP)

a. Did PepsiCo earn positive residual operating income (ROPI) in 2003 if its weighted average cost of capital (WACC) is 8.7%? Explain.

b. At what level of WACC would PepsiCo not report positive residual operating income for 2003? Explain.

■ EXERCISES

E11-13. Estimating Share Value using the DCF and ROPI Models Following are forecasts of Target Corporation's sales, net operating profit after tax (NOPAT), and net operating assets (NOA) as of January 31, 2004:

Target
Corporation
(TGT)

(In millions)	Reported 2004	Horizon Period				Terminal Period
		2005	2006	2007	2008	
Sales	$48,163	$52,979	$58,277	$64,105	$70,516	$72,631
NOPAT	2,189	2,408	2,649	2,914	3,205	3,301
NOA	22,148	24,363	26,799	29,479	32,427	33,400

Answer the following requirements assuming a discount rate (WACC) of 6.2%, shares outstanding of 911.8 million, and net financial obligations (NFO) of $11,083 million.

a. Estimate the value of a share of Target common stock using the (1) discounted cash flow (DCF) model and (2) residual operating income (ROPI) model as of January 31, 2004.

b. Target Corporation (TGT) stock closed at $37.96 on January 31, 2004. How does your valuation estimate compare with this closing price? What do you believe are some reasons for the difference? What investment position does it suggest you pursue?

E11-14. **Estimating Share Value using the DCF and ROPI Models**   Following are forecasts of Abercrombie & Fitch's sales, net operating profit after tax (NOPAT), and net operating assets (NOA) as of January 31, 2003:

| | Reported | Horizon Period | | | | Terminal |
(In millions)	2003	2004	2005	2006	2007	Period
Sales	$1,708	$1,879	$2,067	$2,274	$2,501	$2,551
NOPAT	203	223	246	270	297	303
NOA	861	947	1,042	1,146	1,261	1,286

Answer the following requirements assuming a discount rate (WACC) of 10.0%, common shares outstanding of 94.6 million, and net financial obligations (NFO) of $(10) million (negative NFO reflects net investments rather than net obligations).

a.   Estimate the value of a share of Abercrombie & Fitch common stock using the (1) discounted cash flow (DCF) model and (2) residual operating income (ROPI) model as of January 31, 2003.

b.   Abercrombie & Fitch (ANF) stock closed at $26.80 on January 31, 2003. How does your valuation estimate compare with this closing price? What do you believe are some reasons for the difference?

E11-15. **Estimating Share Value using the DCF and ROPI Models**   Following are forecasts of Albertson's sales, net operating profit after tax (NOPAT), and net operating assets (NOA) as of January 29, 2004:

| | Reported | Horizon Period | | | | Terminal |
(In millions)	2004	2005	2006	2007	2008	Period
Sales	$35,436	$36,499	$37,594	$38,722	$39,884	$40,682
NOPAT	809	833	858	884	911	929
NOA	10,705	11,026	11,357	11,698	12,049	12,290

Answer the following requirements assuming a discount rate (WACC) of 6.5%, common shares outstanding of 368.0 million, and net financial obligations (NFO) of $5,324 million.

a.   Estimate the value of a share of Albertson's common stock using the (1) discounted cash flow (DCF) model and (2) residual operating income (ROPI) model as of January 29, 2004.

b.   Albertson (ABS) stock closed at $24.14 on January 29, 2004. How does your valuation estimate compare with this closing price? What do you believe are some reasons for the difference?

E11-16. **Identifying and Computing Net Operating Assets (NOA) and Net Financial Obligations (NFO)**   Following is the balance sheet for 3M Company:

At December 31 (Dollars in millions)	2003	2002
Assets		
Current assets		
Cash and cash equivalents	$ 1,836	$ 618
Accounts receivable—net	2,714	2,527
Inventories	1,816	1,931
Other current assets	1,354	983
Total current assets	7,720	6,059
Investments	218	238
Property, plant and equipment—net	5,609	5,621
Goodwill	2,419	1,898
Intangible assets	274	269
Other assets	1,360	1,244
Total assets	$17,600	$15,329

(Continued on next page)

(Continued from previous page)

At December 31 (Dollars in millions)	2003	2002
Liabilities and Stockholders' Equity		
Current liabilities		
Short-term borrowings and current portion of long-term debt	$ 1,202	$ 1,237
Accounts payable	1,087	945
Accrued payroll	436	411
Accrued income taxes	880	518
Other current liabilities	1,477	1,346
Total current liabilities	5,082	4,457
Long-term debt	1,735	2,140
Other liabilities	2,898	2,739
Total liabilities	9,715	9,336
Stockholders' equity		
Common stock, par value $.01 per share	9	5
Shares outstanding—2003: 784,117,360		
Shares outstanding—2002: 780,391,362		
Capital in excess of par value	287	291
Retained earnings	14,010	12,748
Treasury stock	(4,641)	(4,767)
Unearned compensation	(226)	(258)
Accumulated other comprehensive income (loss)	(1,554)	(2,026)
Stockholders' equity—net	7,885	5,993
Total liabilities and stockholders' equity	$17,600	$15,329

a. Compute net operating assets (NOA) and net financial obligations (NFO) for 2003.
b. For 2003, show that: NOA = NFO + Stockholders' equity.

E11-17. **Identifying and Computing Net Operating Profit after Tax (NOPAT) and Net Financial Expense (NFE)** Following is the income statement for 3M Company:

3M Company
(MMM)

Year Ended December 31 (Millions)	2003	2002	2001
Net sales	$18,232	$16,332	$16,054
Operating expenses			
Cost of sales	9,285	8,496	8,749
Selling, general and administrative expenses	4,039	3,720	4,036
Research, development and related expenses	1,102	1,070	1,084
Other expense (income)	93	—	(88)
Total operating expenses	14,519	13,286	13,781
Operating income	3,713	3,046	2,273
Interest expense and income			
Interest expense	84	80	124
Interest income	(28)	(39)	(37)
Total	56	41	87
Income before income taxes and minority interest	3,657	3,005	2,186
Provision for income taxes	1,202	966	702
Minority interest	52	65	54
Net income	$ 2,403	$ 1,974	$ 1,430

a. Compute net operating profit after tax (NOPAT) and net financial expense (NFE) for 2003. (*Hint:* Other expense is an operating item for 3M.)

b. For 2003, show that: Net income = NOPAT − NFE.

3M Company
(MMM)

E11-18. Estimating Share Value Using the DCF and ROPI Models Following are forecasts of 3M Company's sales, net operating profit after tax (NOPAT), and net operating assets (NOA) as of December 31, 2003:

| | Reported | Horizon Period | | | | Terminal |
(In millions)	2003	2004	2005	2006	2007	Period
Sales	$18,232	$19,691	$21,266	$22,967	$24,804	$25,300
NOPAT	2,493	2,693	2,908	3,140	3,392	3,459
NOA	10,604	11,453	12,369	13,358	14,426	14,715

Answer the following requirements assuming a discount rate (WACC) of 5.75%, common shares outstanding of 784 million, and net financial obligations (NFO) of $2,719 million.

a. Estimate the value of a share of 3M's common stock using the (1) discounted cash flow (DCF) model and (2) residual operating income (ROPI) model as of December 31, 2003.

b. 3M (MMM) stock closed at $85.03 on December 31, 2003. How does your valuation estimate compare with this closing price? What do you believe are some reasons for the difference?

E11-19. Equivalence of Valuation Models and the Relevance of Earnings This module focused on two different valuation models: the discounted cash flow (DCF) model and the residual operating income (ROPI) model. We stressed that these two models are theoretically equivalent.

a. What is the *intuition* for why these models—which focus on either free cash flows to the firm or on residual operating income and net operating assets—are equivalent?

b. Some analysts focus on cash flows as they feel that companies manage earnings, which presumably makes earnings less relevant. Are earnings relevant? Explain.

E11-20. Applying and Interpreting Value Driver Components of RNOA The net operating profit margin and the asset turnover components of net operating assets are often termed *value drivers,* which refers to their positive influence on stock value by virtue of their role as components of return on net operating assets (RNOA).

a. Why are profit margins and asset turnover ratios viewed as influencing stock values?

b. Assuming that profit margins and asset turnover ratios are value drivers, what insight does this give us about managing companies if the goal is to create shareholder value?

■ PROBLEMS

FedEx
Corporation
(FDX)

P11-21. Forecasting and Valuation Using Discounted Cash Flow (DCF) and Residual Operating Income (ROPI) Models Following are the income statement and balance sheet for FedEx Corporation:

Income Statement

Years Ended May 31, (In millions)	2004	2003	2002
Revenues	**$24,710**	$22,487	$20,607
Operating Expenses			
Salaries and employee benefits	10,728	9,778	9,099
Purchased transportation	2,407	2,155	1,825
Rentals and landing fees	1,918	1,803	1,780
Depreciation and amortization	1,375	1,351	1,364
Fuel	1,481	1,349	1,100
Maintenance and repairs	1,523	1,398	1,240
Business realignment costs	435	—	—
Airline stabilization compensation	—	—	(119)
Other	3,403	3,182	2,997
	23,270	21,016	19,286

(Continued on next page)

(Continued from previous page)
Income Statement *(Continued)*

Years Ended May 31, (In millions)	2004	2003	2002
Operating Income	$ 1,440	$ 1,471	$ 1,321
Other Income (Expense)			
Interest expense	(136)	(124)	(144)
Interest income	20	6	5
Other, net	(5)	(15)	(22)
	(121)	(133)	(161)
Income Before Income Taxes	1,319	1,338	1,160
Provision for Income Taxes	481	508	435
Income Before Cumulative Effect of Change in Accounting Principle	838	830	725
Cumulative Effect of Change in Accounting for Goodwill, Net of Tax Benefit of $10	—	—	(15)
Net income	$ 838	$ 830	$ 710

Balance Sheet

May 31, (In millions)	2004	2003
Assets		
Current Assets		
Cash and cash equivalents	$ 1,046	$ 538
Receivables, less allowances of $151 and $149	3,027	2,627
Spare parts, supplies and fuel, less allowances of $124 and $101	249	228
Deferred income taxes	489	416
Prepaid expenses and other	159	132
Total current assets	4,970	3,941
Property and Equipment, at Cost		
Aircraft and related equipment	7,001	6,624
Package handling and ground support equipment and vehicles	5,296	5,013
Computer and electronic equipment	3,537	3,180
Other	4,477	4,200
	20,311	19,017
Less accumulated depreciation and amortization	11,274	10,317
Net property and equipment	9,037	8,700
Other Long-Term Assets		
Goodwill	2,802	1,063
Prepaid pension cost	1,127	1,269
Intangible and other assets	1,198	412
Total other long-term assets	5,127	2,744
Total Assets	$19,134	$15,385
Liabilities and Stockholders' Investment		
Current liabilities		
Current portion of long-term debt	$ 750	$ 308
Accrued salaries and employee benefits	1,062	724
Accounts payable	1,615	1,168
Accrued expenses	1,305	1,135
Total current liabilities	4,732	3,335
Long-Term Debt, Less Current Portion	2,837	1,709
Other Long-Term Liabilities		
Deferred income taxes	1,181	882

(Continued on next page)

(Continued from previous page)

Balance Sheet (Continued)

May 31, (In millions)	2004	2003
Liabilities and Stockholders' Investment (Continued)		
Pension, postretirement healthcare and other benefit obligations .... $	768	$ 657
Self-insurance accruals	591	536
Deferred lease obligations	503	466
Deferred gains, principally related to aircraft transactions	426	455
Other liabilities	60	57
Total other long-term liabilities	3,529	3,053
Common Stockholders' Investment		
Common stock, $0.10 par value; 800 million shares authorized; 300 million shares issued for 2004 and 299 million shares issued for 2003	30	30
Additional paid in capital	1,079	1,088
Retained earnings	7,001	6,250
Accumulated other comprehensive loss	(46)	(30)
	8,064	7,338
Less deferred compensation and treasury stock, at cost	28	50
Total common stockholders investment	8,036	7,288
Total liabilities and shareholders' investment	**$19,134**	**$15,385**

Required

a. Compute net operating assets (NOA) and net financial obligations (NFO) for fiscal year-end 2004. Show that: NOA = NFO + Stockholders' equity.

b. Compute net operating profit after tax (NOPAT) and net financial expense (NFE) for fiscal year 2004. Show that: Net income = NOPAT − NFE.

c. Forecast FedEx' sales, NOPAT, and NOA for fiscal years 2005 through 2008 using the following assumptions:

Sales growth	10%
Net operating profit margin (NOPM)	7%
Net operating asset turnover (NOAT)	2.13

Forecast the terminal period (2009) values assuming a 2% terminal year growth and using the NOPM and NOAT assumptions above.

d. Estimate the value of a share of FedEx common stock using the (1) discounted cash flow (DCF) model, and (2) residual operating income (ROPI) model as of May 31, 2004; assume a discount rate (WACC) of 6.9%, common shares outstanding of 784 million, and net financial obligations (NFO) of $2,937 million.

e. FedEx (FDX) stock closed at $73.58 on May 28, 2004 (the last closing price prior to May 31, 2004). How does your valuation estimate compare with this closing price? What do you believe are some reasons for the difference? What investment position is suggested from your results?

Harley-Davidson (HDI)

P11-22. Forecasting and Valuation Using Discounted Cash Flow (DCF) and Residual Operating Income (ROPI) Models   Following are the income statement and balance sheet for Harley-Davidson:

Income Statement

Years Ended December 31 (In thousands)	2003	2002	2001
Net revenue	$4,624,274	$4,090,970	$3,406,786
Cost of goods sold	2,958,708	2,673,129	2,253,815
Gross profit	1,665,566	1,417,841	1,152,971
Financial services income	279,459	211,500	181,545
Financial services expense	111,586	107,273	120,272
Operating income from financial services	167,873	104,227	61,273
Selling, administrative and engineering expense	684,175	639,366	551,743

(Continued on next page)

(Continued from previous page)
Income Statement *(Continued)*

Years Ended December 31 (In thousands)	2003	2002	2001
Income from operations	$1,149,264	$ 882,702	$ 662,501
Interest income, net	23,088	16,541	17,478
Other, net	(6,317)	(13,416)	(6,524)
Income before provision for income taxes	1,166,035	885,827	673,455
Provision for income taxes	405,107	305,610	235,709
Net income	$ 760,928	$ 580,217	$ 437,746

Balance Sheet

December 31 (In thousands)	2003	2002
Assets		
Current assets		
Cash and cash equivalents	$ 812,449	$ 280,928
Marketable securities	510,211	514,800
Accounts receivable, net	112,406	108,694
Current portion of finance receivables, net	1,001,990	855,771
Inventories	207,726	218,156
Deferred income taxes	51,156	41,430
Prepaid expenses & other current assets	33,189	46,807
Total current assets	2,729,127	2,066,586
Finance receivables, net	735,859	589,809
Property, plant, and equipment, net	1,046,310	1,032,596
Goodwill	53,678	49,930
Other assets	358,114	122,296
	$4,923,088	$3,861,217
Liabilities and Shareholders' Equity		
Current liabilities		
Accounts payable	$ 223,902	$ 226,977
Accrued expenses and other liabilities	407,566	380,496
Current portion of finance debt	324,305	382,579
Total current liabilities	955,773	990,052
Finance debt	670,000	380,000
Other long-term liabilities	86,337	123,353
Postretirement health care benefits	127,444	105,419
Deferred income taxes	125,842	29,478
Shareholders' equity		
Series A Junior participating preferred stock, none issued	—	—
Common stock, 326,489,291 and 325,298,404 shares issued in 2003 and 2002, respectively	3,266	3,254
Additional paid-in capital	419,455	386,284
Retained earnings	3,074,037	2,372,095
Accumulated other comprehensive income (loss)	47,174	(46,266)
	3,543,932	2,715,367
Less		
Treasury stock (24,978,798 and 22,636,295 shares in 2003 and 2002, respectively), at cost	(586,240)	(482,360)
Unearned compensation	—	(92)
Total shareholders' equity	2,957,692	2,232,915
	$4,923,088	$3,861,217

Required

a.   Compute net operating assets (NOA) and net financial obligations (NFO) for year-end 2003. Show that: NOA = NFO + Shareholders' equity. (*Hint:* Treat HDI's financial receivables as an operating item and finance debt as a nonoperating item.)

b.   Compute net operating profit after tax (NOPAT) and net financial expense (NFE) for 2003. Show that: Net income = NOPAT − NFE.

c.   Forecast Harley-Davidson's sales, NOPAT, and NOA for 2004 through 2007 using the following assumptions:

Sales growth	13%
Net operating profit margin (NOPM)	18%
Net operating asset turnover (NOAT)	1.34

Forecast the terminal period (2008) values assuming a 2% terminal year growth and using the NOPM and NOAT assumptions above.

d.   Estimate the value of a share of Harley-Davidson common stock using the (1) discounted cash flow (DCF) model and (2) residual operating income (ROPI) model as of December 31, 2003; assume a discount rate (WACC) of 8%, common shares outstanding of 301.5 million, and net financial obligations (NFO) of $484 million.

e.   Harley-Davidson (HDI) stock closed at $47.53 on December 31, 2003. How does your valuation estimate compare with this closing price? What do you believe are some reasons for the difference?

P11-23. **Forecasting and Valuation using Discounted Cash Flow (DCF) and Residual Operating Income (ROPI) Models**   Following are the income statement and balance sheet for **Abbott Laboratories (ABT)**:

Abbott
Laboratories
(ABT)

Income Statement

Year Ended December 31, (In thousands)	2003
Net sales	$19,680,561
Cost of products sold	9,473,416
Research and development	1,733,472
Acquired in-process research and development	100,240
Selling, general, and administrative	5,050,901
Total operating cost and expenses	16,358,029
Operating earnings	3,322,532
Net interest expense	146,123
(Income) from TAP Pharmaceutical Products Inc. joint venture	(580,950)
Net foreign exchange (gain) loss	55,298
Other (income) expense, net	(32,356)
Earnings before taxes	3,734,417
Taxes on earnings	981,184
Net earnings	$ 2,753,233

Balance Sheet

December 31, (In thousands)	2003
Assets	
Current assets	
Cash and cash equivalents	$ 995,124
Investment securities	291,297
Trade receivables, less allowances of $259,514	3,313,377
Inventories	
Finished products	1,467,441
Work in process	545,977
Materials	725,021
Total inventories	2,738,439

(Continued on next page)

(Continued from previous page)
Balance Sheet *(Continued)*

December 31, (In thousands)	2003
Deferred income taxes	$ 1,165,259
Other prepaid expenses and receivables	1,786,919
Total Current Assets	10,290,415
Investment securities	406,357
Property and equipment, at cost	
Land	356,757
Buildings	2,662,023
Equipment	9,479,044
Construction in progress	792,923
	13,290,747
Less: accumulated depreciation and amortization	7,008,941
Net property and equipment	6,281,806
Intangible assets, net of amortization	4,089,882
Goodwill	4,449,408
Deferred income taxes, investments in joint ventures and other assets	1,197,474
Total assets	$26,715,342

Liabilities and Shareholders' Investment

Current Liabilities

Short-term borrowings	$ 828,092
Trade accounts payable	1,754,367
Salaries, wages and commissions	625,525
Other accrued liabilities	2,180,098
Dividends payable	383,352
Income taxes payable	158,836
Current portion of long-term debt	1,709,265
Total Current Liabilities	7,639,535
Long-term debt	3,452,329
Post-employment obligations and other long-term liabilities	2,551,220
Shareholders' investment:	
Preferred shares, one dollar par, Authorized—1,000,000 shares, none issued	—
Common shares, without par value, Authorized—2,400,000,000 shares; Issued at stated capital amount—Shares: 1,580,247,227	3,034,054
Common shares held in treasury, at cost—Shares: 15,729,296	$ (229,696)
Unearned compensation—restricted stock awards	(56,336)
Earnings employed in the business	9,691,484
Accumulated other comprehensive income (loss)	632,752
Total shareholders' investment	13,072,258
Total liabilities and shareholders' investment	$26,715,342

Required

a. Compute net operating assets (NOA) and net financial obligations (NFO) for year-end 2003. Show that: NOA = NFO + Shareholders' Investment.

b. Compute net operating profit after tax (NOPAT) and net financial expense (NFE) for 2003. (*Hint:* Treat equity income from TAP Pharmaceutical Products, foreign exchange loss, and other income as operating items.) Show that: Net income = NOPAT − NFE.

c. Forecast Abbott Laboratories' sales, NOPAT, and NOA for 2004 through 2007 using the following assumptions:

Sales growth	11.30%
Net operating profit margin (NOPM)	14.53%
Net operating asset turnover (NOAT)	1.07

Forecast the terminal period (2008) values assuming a 2% terminal year growth and using the NOPM and NOAT assumptions above.

d. Estimate the value of a share of Abbott Laboratories' common stock using the (1) discounted cash flow (DCF) model, and (2) residual operating income (ROPI) model as of December 31, 2003; assume a discount rate (WACC) of 6%, common shares outstanding of 1,564.5 million, and net financial obligations (NFO) of $5,293 million.

e. Abbott Laboratories (ABT) stock closed at a split-adjusted price of $43.59 on December 31, 2003. How does your valuation estimate compare with this closing price? What do you believe are some reasons for the difference? What investment position is suggested from your results?

P11-24. **Forecasting and Valuation using Discounted Cash Flow (DCF) and Residual Operating Income (ROPI) Models**   Following are the 2003 income statement and balance sheet for PepsiCo (PEP):

PepsiCo (PEP)

Income Statement

(in millions)	2003	2002	2001
Net revenue	$26,971	$25,112	$23,512
Cost of sales	12,379	11,497	10,750
Selling, general and administrative expenses	9,460	8,958	8,574
Amortization of intangible assets	145	138	165
Merger-related costs	59	224	356
Impairment and restructuring charges	147	—	31
Operating profit	4,781	4,295	3,636
Bottling equity income	323	280	160
Interest expense	(163)	(178)	(219)
Interest income	51	36	67
Income before income taxes	4,992	4,433	3,644
Provision for income taxes	1,424	1,433	1,244
Net income	$ 3,568	$ 3,000	$ 2,400

Balance Sheet

(in millions except per share amounts)	2003	2002
Assets		
Current assets		
Cash and cash equivalents	$ 820	$ 1,638
Short-term investments, at cost	1,181	207
	2,001	1,845
Accounts and notes receivable, net	2,830	2,531
Inventories	1,412	1,342
Prepaid expenses and other current assets	687	695
Total current assets	6,930	6,413
Property, plant, and equipment, net	7,828	7,390
Amortizable intangible assets, net	718	801
Goodwill	3,796	3,631
Other nonamortizable intangible assets	869	787
Nonamortizable intangible assets	4,665	4,418
Investments in noncontrolled affiliates	2,920	2,611
Other assets	2,266	1,841
Total assets	$25,327	$23,474
Liabilities and Shareholders' Equity		
Current liabilities		
Short-term obligations	$ 591	$ 562
Accounts payable and other current liabilities	5,213	4,998
Income taxes payable	611	492
Total current liabilities	6,415	6,052

(Continued on next page)

(Continued from previous page)

Balance Sheet *(Continued)*

(in millions except per share amounts)	2003	2002
Long-term debt obligations	1,702	2,187
Other liabilities	4,075	4,226
Deferred income taxes	1,261	1,486
Total liabilities	13,453	13,951
Preferred stock, no par value	41	41
Repurchased preferred stock	(63)	(48)
Common shareholders' equity		
Common stock, par value 1⅔¢ per share (issued 1,782 shares)	30	30
Capital in excess of par value	548	207
Retained earnings	15,961	13,489
Accumulated other comprehensive loss	(1,267)	(1,672)
	15,272	12,054
Less: repurchased common stock, at cost (77 and 60 shares, respectively)	(3,376)	(2,524)
Total common shareholders' equity	11,896	9,530
Total liabilities and shareholders' equity	$25,327	$23,474

Required

a. Compute net operating assets (NOA) and net financial obligations (NFO) for year-end 2003. Show that: NOA = NFO + Stockholders' Equity.

b. Compute net operating profit after tax (NOPAT) and net financial expense (NFE) for 2003. (*Hint:* Treat bottling equity income as an operating item.) Show that: Net Income = NOPAT − NFE.

c. Forecast PepsiCo's sales, NOPAT, and NOA for 2004 through 2007 using the following assumptions:

Sales growth	7.40%
Net operating profit margin (NOPM)	13.53%
Net operating asset turnover (NOAT)	2.08

Forecast the terminal period (2008) values assuming a 2% terminal year growth and using the NOPM and NOAT assumptions above.

d. Estimate the value of a share of PepsiCo common stock using the (1) discounted cash flow (DCF) model, and (2) residual operating income (ROPI) model; assume a discount rate (WACC) of 6%, common shares outstanding of 1,705 million, and net financial obligations (NFO) of $1,112 million.

e. PepsiCo (PEP) stock closed at $46.62 on December 31, 2003. How does your valuation estimate compare with this closing price? What do you believe are some reasons for the difference?

MODULE

12 Constructing and Illustrating a Comprehensive Case

KIMBERLY-CLARK

REINVENTING A CONSUMER PRODUCTS COMPANY

The past decade has seen a shift in the universe for consumer products companies. Gone are numerous competitors. Many having been gobbled up in the industry's consolidation trend. Also gone is media control. Hundreds of different media outlets and venues compete for promotion space and scarce consumer time.

Fortune (2003) reports that in 1995 it took three TV commercials to reach 80% of 18- to 49-year-old women. Just five years later, it took 97 ads to reach the same group. "Short of being embroiled in a scandal," says ad agency Doremus in a newsletter, "it's almost impossible to get your name in enough channels to build substantial awareness."

Another development is in-store branding. Companies such as Costco with its Kirkland Signature brand on everything from candy to apparel, and Walgreen's with its low cost alternatives, threaten the powerhouse brands from Kimberly-Clark, Procter & Gamble, Colgate-Palmolive, and other consumer products companies. Fortune (2003) declares that the "retail universe has consolidated, and the media universe has shattered. As the mass media have de-massified into 1,000 bits—500 channels . . . In short, brand makers are losing their connection to the consumer."

When Thomas J. Falk assumed the top spot at the nation's largest disposable diaper producer in September 2002, he inherited some extra baggage with it: an identity crisis, a decades-long rivalry with consumer-products behemoth Procter & Gamble, and a group of investors short on patience from a series of earnings misses. (*The Wall Street Journal*, 2002)

In a move aimed at boosting its stock price and its return on equity, Kimberly-Clark announced in 2004 that it's considering a tax-free spin-off of its paper and pulp businesses. Under CEO Falk's leadership, the company has been moving steadily in improving its focus on its health and hygiene segments. Kimberly-Clark's plan would follow a similar move by rival Procter & Gamble. (*BusinessWeek*, 2004)

Kimberly-Clark has also moved to shore up its brand images across its immense product line. It currently is a $14 billion in sales company that manufactures such well-recognized brands as Huggies and Pull-Ups disposable diapers, Kotex and Lightdays feminine products, Kleenex facial tissue, Viva paper towels, and Scott bathroom tissue.

The rocky ride endured by Kimberly-Clark investors over the past few years is unlikely to subside—see the following stock price chart. Competition is fierce and well-armed. The pending purchase of Gillette by Procter & Gamble further muddies the future of the industry.

12-1

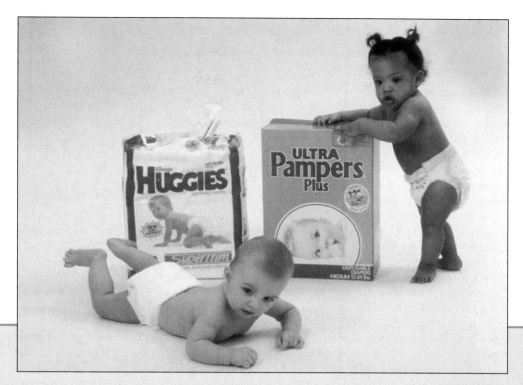

*Getty Images/
Henry Groskinsky*

On the positive side, Kimberly-Clark's earnings performance is consistent, and its financial position is solid. Further, Kimberly-Clark's RNOA for 2003 was 18%, and its financial leverage increased its RNOA to yield a robust 24% in return on equity. It also reported $16.8 billion in assets, nearly half of which is concentrated in plant, property, and equipment and another 16% in intangible assets.

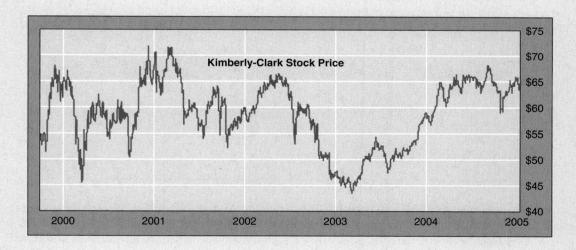

This module presents a financial accounting analysis and interpretation of Kimberly-Clark. It is intended to illustrate the key financial reporting topics we covered in the book. We begin with a detailed review of its financial statements and notes, followed by the forecasting of key accounts that are then used to value its common stock.

Sources: *Kimberly-Clark* 2004 Annual Report; *Kimberly-Clark* 2004 & 2003 10-K Reports; *BusinessWeek,* 2004; *The Wall Street Journal,* 2005; *Fortune,* 2003.

■ INTRODUCTION

Kimberly-Clark is one of the largest consumer products companies in the world. It is organized into three general business segments (percentages are for 2003):

- **Personal Care (37% of sales)**—manufactures and markets disposable diapers, training and youth pants and swim pants, feminine and incontinence care products, and others. Products in this segment are primarily for household use and are sold under a variety of brand names, including Huggies, Pull-Ups, Little Swimmers, GoodNites, Kotex, Lightdays, Depend, and Poise.

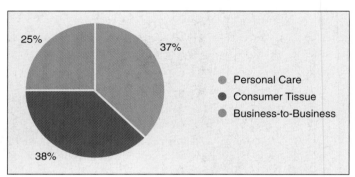

- **Consumer Tissue (38% of sales)**—manufactures and markets facial and bathroom tissue, paper towels and napkins for household use, wet wipes, and related products. Products in this segment are sold under the Kleenex, Scott, Cottonelle, Viva, Andrex, Scottex, Hakle, Page, Huggies, and other brand names.

- **Business-to-Business (25% of sales)**—manufactures and markets (1) facial and bathroom tissue, paper towels, wipes and napkins for away-from-home use; (2) health care products such as surgical gowns, drapes, infection control products, sterilization wraps, disposable face masks and exam gloves, respiratory products, and other disposable medical products; (3) printing, premium business and correspondence papers; (4) specialty and technical papers; and other products. Products in this segment are sold under the Kimberly-Clark, Kleenex, Scott, Kimwipes, WypAll, Surpass, Safeskin, Tecnol, Ballard and other brand names.

Approximately 62% of Kimberly-Clark's sales are in North America, 20% in Europe and 18% in Asia, Latin America, and other areas. Shown below are its U.S. market shares for key categories for each of the years 2001 through 2003:

Product Category	2003	2002	2001
Diapers	38%	40%	39%
Training, youth, and swim pants	68	73	79
Adult incontinence care	56	55	54
Facial tissue	53	54	53
Bathroom tissue	28	27	26
Paper towels	19	19	17

In addition, approximately 13% of Kimberly-Clark's sales are concentrated in Wal-Mart, primarily in the personal care and consumer tissue businesses (source: Kimberly-Clark 2003 10-K).

In its MD&A section of its 10-K, Kimberly-Clark describes its competitive environment as follows:

The Corporation experiences intense competition for sales of its principal products in its major markets, both domestically and internationally. The Corporation's products compete with widely advertised, well-known, branded products, as well as private label products, which are typically sold at lower prices. The Corporation has several major competitors in most of its markets, some of which are larger and more diversified than the Corporation. The principal methods and elements of competition include brand recognition and loyalty, product innovation, quality and performance, price, and marketing and distribution capabilities. Inherent risks in the Corporation's competitive strategy include uncertainties concerning trade and consumer acceptance, the effects of recent consolidations of retailers and distribution channels, and competitive reaction. Aggressive competitive reaction may lead to increased advertising and promotional spending by the Corporation in order to maintain market share. Increased competition with respect to pricing would reduce revenue and could have an adverse impact on the Corporation's financial results. In addition, the Corporation relies on the development and introduction of new or improved products as a means of achieving and/or maintaining category leadership. In order to maintain its competitive position, the Corporation must develop technology to support its products.

Beyond the competitive business risks described above, Kimberly-Clark faces fluctuating prices for its principle raw material of cellulose fiber, uncertain energy costs for its manufacturing operations, foreign currency translation risks, and risks resulting from fluctuating interest rates.

Given this background, we begin the accounting analysis of Kimberly-Clark with a discussion of its financial statements.

■ REVIEWING AND ANALYZING FINANCIAL STATEMENTS

This section reviews and analyzes the financial statements of Kimberly-Clark.

Income Statement Reporting and Analysis

Kimberly-Clark's income statement is reproduced in Exhibit 12.1. The remainder of this section provides a brief review and analysis for Kimberly-Clark's income statement line items.

EXHIBIT 12.1 ■ Kimberly-Clark Income Statement

KIMBERLY-CLARK CORPORATION AND SUBSIDIARIES Consolidated Income Statement			
	Year Ended December 31		
(Millions of dollars, except per share amounts)	2003	2002	2001
Net sales	$14,348.0	$13,566.3	$13,287.6
Cost of products sold	9,448.1	8,750.7	8,618.0
Gross profit	4,899.9	4,815.6	4,669.6
Marketing, research and general expenses	2,375.6	2,278.5	2,158.3
Goodwill amortization	—	—	89.4
Other (income) expense, net	111.9	73.3	83.7
Operating profit	2,412.4	2,463.8	2,338.2
Nonoperating expense	(105.5)	—	—
Interest income	18.0	15.7	17.8
Interest expense	(167.9)	(182.1)	(191.6)
Income before income taxes	2,157.0	2,297.4	2,164.4
Provision for income taxes	514.2	666.6	645.7
Income before equity interests	1,642.8	1,630.8	1,518.7
Share of net income of equity companies	107.0	113.3	154.4
Minority owners' share of subsidiaries' net income	(55.6)	(58.1)	(63.2)
Income before cumulative effect of accounting change	1,694.2	1,686.0	1,609.9
Cumulative effect of accounting change, net of income taxes	—	(11.4)	—
Net income	$ 1,694.2	$ 1,674.6	$ 1,609.9
Per share basis			
Basic			
Income before cumulative effect of accounting change	$ 3.34	$ 3.26	$ 3.04
Net income	$ 3.34	$ 3.24	$ 3.04
Diluted			
Income before cumulative effect of accounting change	$ 3.33	$ 3.24	$ 3.02
Net income	$ 3.33	$ 3.22	$ 3.02

Net Sales

Exhibit 12.1 reveals that its sales increased 5.76% in 2003 to $14,348 million ([$14,348.0 − $13,566.3] − 1), following a 2.1% sales increase in the prior year. In its MD&A report, K-C management attributes most of the 2003 increase (4% of the 5.76%) to favorable currency effects resulting from the weak $US as foreign currency denominated sales were translated into a higher $US equivalent. In addition, volume increases amounted to approximately 2% of this 5.76% increase. These two effects more than offset a reduction in Kimberly-Clark's product prices in its highly competitive markets (source: Kimberly-Clark 2003 10-K).

Kimberly-Clark describes its revenue recognition policy as follows:

Sales revenue for the Corporation and its reportable business segments is recognized at the time of product shipment or delivery, depending on when title passes, to unaffiliated customers, and when all of the following have occurred: a firm sales agreement is in place, pricing is fixed or determinable, and collection is reasonably assured. Sales are reported net of estimated returns, consumer and trade promotions, rebates and freight allowed.

Its revenue recognition conditions are taken directly from GAAP and SEC guidelines, which recognize revenues when "earned and realizable." For Kimberly-Clark, *earned* means when title to the goods passes to the customer, and *realizable* means an account receivable whose collection is reasonably assured.

Cost of Products Sold and Gross Profit

Kimberly-Clark's 2003 gross profit margin is 34.2% ($4,899.9/$14,348.0), which is almost a full percentage point below what it was in 2001 (35.1%). As a benchmark, Proctor & Gamble, the company's principle competitor, recently reported sales of $43.4 billion, three times the level of K-C, and a gross profit margin of 49%, up from 43.7% in 2001. This comparison highlights graphically the intense competition that K-C faces from its much larger rival.

Selling, General, and Administrative Costs

Kimberly-Clark's SGA expenses (which include marketing, research, maintenance, and other expenses) have remained steady at about 17.4% of sales. K-C reports 2003 net operating profit after taxes (NOPAT) of $1,945.2 million [$2,412.4 million × {1 − ($514.2 million/$2,157.0 million)} + $107 million] and a net operating profit margin (NOPM) of 13.6% ($1,945.2 million/$14,348 million) of sales.[1] P&G, by contrast, is able to use its higher gross profit margin to fund a higher level of advertising and other SGA expenditures. P&G's NOPM, however, is 12.5%. The difference in NOPM is primarily due to K-C's lower effective tax rate of 23.8% versus 31.1% for P&G.

Pension Costs. The SGA expenses of Kimberly-Clark include $168 million of pension expense. This is reported in the following table to its pension footnote disclosures:

Components of Net Periodic Benefit Cost

(Millions of dollars)	Pension Benefits			Other Benefits		
	Year Ended December 31					
	2003	2002	2001	2003	2002	2001
Service cost	$ 78.5	$ 69.7	$ 65.4	$16.8	$13.0	$12.0
Interest cost	291.4	275.1	266.8	49.9	50.5	48.2
Expected return on plan assets	(290.6)	(335.6)	(368.1)	—	—	—
Amortization of prior service cost	8.7	7.8	8.6	(1.6)	(2.1)	(2.1)
Amortization of transition amount	.1	(2.0)	(4.4)	—	—	—
Recognized net actuarial loss (gain)	74.6	14.5	4.5	2.0	(2.7)	(3.8)
Other	5.3	2.5	7.6	—	—	(.1)
Net periodic benefit cost (credit)	$ 168.0	$ 32.0	$ (19.6)	$67.1	$58.7	$54.2

---

[1] We include equity income (labeled as "share of net income of equity companies" in K-C's income statement) as operating because it relates to investments in paper-related companies and it, therefore, aligns with K-C's primary operating activities. This amount is reported by K-C net of tax, and therefore, no tax adjustment is necessary when computing NOPAT.

For 2003, the expected return on pension investments ($290.6 million) provides an offset to its pension service and interest costs ($78.5 million and $291.4 million, respectively). Footnotes reveal that its pension investments realized an *actual* return of $498.5 million in 2003 (from the pension footnote in its 10-K report). So, for 2003, use of the expected return results in an unrecognized *gain* that is deferred along with other unrecognized gains and losses that are not reported on the balance sheet.

Kimberly-Clark describes its determination of the expected return in its footnotes. It is instructive to review its rationale and, thus, that footnote follows:

> Consolidated pension expense for defined benefit pension plans was $168 million in 2003 compared with $32 million for 2002. Pension expense is calculated based upon a number of actuarial assumptions applied to each of the defined benefit plans. The weighted-average expected long-term rate of return on pension fund assets used to calculate pension expense was 8.42 percent in 2003 compared with 9.19 percent in 2002 and will be 8.32 percent in 2004. The expected long-term rate of return on pension fund assets was determined based on several factors, including input from our pension investment consultants and projected long-term returns of broad equity and bond indices. We also considered our U.S. plan's historical 10-year and 15-year compounded annual returns of 10.1 percent and 10.3 percent, respectively, which have been in excess of these broad equity and bond benchmark indices. We anticipate that on average the investment managers for each of the plans comprising the Principal Plans will generate annual long-term rates of return of at least 8.5 percent. Our expected long-term rate of return on the assets in the Principal Plans is based on an asset allocation assumption of about 70 percent with equity managers, with expected long-term rates of return of approximately 10 percent, and 30 percent with fixed income managers, with an expected long-term rate of return of about 6 percent. We regularly review our actual asset allocation and periodically rebalance our investments to our targeted allocation when considered appropriate. Also, when deemed appropriate, we execute hedging strategies using index options and futures to limit the downside exposure of certain investments by trading off upside potential above an acceptable level. We executed such hedging strategies in 2003, 2002 and 2001. No hedging instruments are currently in place beyond January 2004. We will continue to evaluate our long-term rate of return assumptions at least annually and will adjust them as necessary.

Other Income and Expense.   Kimberly-Clark's operating profit has benefited from elimination of goodwill amortization expense as mandated under GAAP since 2001 (see discussion below). However, it reports an increased level of $111.9 million for expenses classified as "other." Its footnotes reveal the following composition of this account:

> Other income (expense), net in 2003 included charges of $34 million consisting of $15.6 million for a legal judgment in Europe and $18.4 million for the costs associated with the redemption of $200 million of 7⅞% and $200 million of 7.0% debentures, and nearly $20 million for charges to write-off an investment in an historic restoration project and to record the cost of exiting a nonstrategic facility outside of North America. Also included were $25.1 million of operating losses related to the Corporation's participation in affordable housing and historic renovation projects, an increase of $8.0 million compared with 2002. Included in 2002 were $21 million of charges related to the settlement in December 2002 of securities and shareholder derivative litigation involving Safeskin Corporation ("Safeskin") and a charge of $26.5 million for the write-off of tax credits in Brazil. The litigation predated the Corporation's February 2000 acquisition of Safeskin. In addition, the Corporation recorded currency transaction losses in 2003 compared with gains in 2002.

$18.4 million of this expense relates to the cost of redeeming $200 million of debt. Under GAAP, this cost is treated as a SG&A expense (as opposed to "below the line," that is, after income from continuing operations) unless deemed to be both *unusual* and *infrequent*.

Transitory versus Persistent Classification

When examining operating profit we must look for any transitory items. Analysts typically treat gains and losses on debt redemption as both transitory (if nonrecurring) and nonoperating. In the footnote reproduced above, K-C reports expenses relating to a legal judgment, losses on debt redemption, and the write-off of an investment.[2] Each of these items is transitory, and the losses on debt redemption and the write-off of an investment are arguably nonoperating as well.

---

[2]The losses related to K-C's participation in affordable housing are recurring and, therefore, not transitory, but can be considered nonoperating.

Expenses relating to restructuring activities have become increasingly common in the past two decades. Kimberly-Clark pursued its own restructuring activities in 2001 and 2002 and recorded charges of $167 million and $44 million. Classification of these charges as transitory is a judgment call. As a practical matter, the 2001 charge would probably have been viewed as transitory at that time. However, its reoccurrence in 2002 increased the likelihood that the 2002 charge would not be viewed as transitory. Further, its 2003 operating results do not contain restructuring charges. Since the purpose of identifying transitory items is to exclude them when forecasting operating profit and cash flow, and since restructuring charges are absent in 2003, these charges are not an issue when forecasting for 2004 and beyond.

Kimberly-Clark's reported operating profit has improved slightly from $2,338.2 million in 2001 to $2,412.4 million in 2003. However, its relatively flat sales growth is a concern to analysts: Bill Steele, an analyst at **Banc of America Securities** in San Francisco says, "In 10 years of covering this sector, I've never had a company with flat sales growth three years in a row." He adds, "I just hope they give us something to look forward to." (*The Wall Street Journal,* 2002). However, its outlook for improved sales growth is less than certain.

Earnings per Share

Net income for Kimberly-Clark has only slightly increased from $1,609.9 million in 2001 to $1,694.2 million in 2003. Basic (diluted) earnings per share, however, has increased from $3.04 ($3.02) to $3.34 ($3.33). This increase reflects a reduction of the average number of common shares outstanding from 529.6 (533.2) million to 507.0 (508.6) million shares as a result of its share repurchase program (see the financing section in Exhibit 12.5). Following is Kimberly-Clark's computation of earnings per share from its footnotes:

Earnings Per Share A reconciliation of the average number of common shares outstanding used in the basic and diluted EPS computations follows:

(Millions)	Average Common Shares Outstanding		
	2003	**2002**	**2001**
Basic	**507.0**	517.2	529.6
Dilutive effect of stock options	**1.2**	2.5	3.4
Dilutive effect of deferred compensation plan shares	**0.4**	0.3	0.2
Diluted	**508.6**	520.0	533.2

Options outstanding that were not included in the computation of diluted EPS because their exercise price was greater than the average market price of the common shares are summarized below:

Description	2003	2002	2001
Average number of share equivalents (millions)	**20.5**	10.7	5.1
Weighted-average exercise price	**$60.19**	$65.89	$71.36
Expiration date of options	**2006 to 2013**	2006 to 2012	2006 to 2011
Options outstanding at year-end	**20.2**	11.4	5.8

The number of common shares outstanding as of December 31, 2003, 2002 and 2001 was 501.6 million, 510.8 million and 521.0 million, respectively.

Most of the difference between its basic and diluted earnings per share usually arises from the dilutive effects of employee stock options. For K-C, such effects were absent in 2003 as its stock options were *under water,* meaning that K-C's stock price was lower than the exercise price of the options. The stock options, therefore, are considered *antidilutive,* meaning that including them would increase EPS. Accordingly, they are excluded in the EPS computation, but remain potentially dilutive if K-C's stock price subsequently rises above the exercise price of the options. (Although not present for Kimberly-Clark, convertible debt and preferred shares are also potentially dilutive for many companies.)

Income Taxes

Kimberly-Clark's net income was positively affected by a reduction of its effective tax rate. K-C describes this tax effect in the following footnote:

The Corporation's effective income tax rate was 23.8 percent in 2003 compared with 29.0 percent in 2002. The lower effective tax rate was primarily due to the benefits from the synthetic fuel partnership.

We discuss this synthetic fuel partnership in our discussion of variable interest entities (VIEs) later in this Module. The reduction of K-C's effective tax rate is an important contributor to its after-tax profit and is the primary reason why its NOPAT margin is higher than that for P&G.

Stock Options Expense

Kimberly-Clark's net income has increased slightly as a result of the nonrecognition of stock options expense. K-C accounts for its employee stock options using the intrinsic-value method as allowed under GAAP. This method does not recognize expense relating to these options as Kimberly-Clark explains in the following footnote:

> ***Stock-Based Employee Compensation*** The Corporation's stock-based employee compensation plan is described in Note 11. The Corporation continues to account for stock-based compensation using the intrinsic-value method permitted by APB Opinion 25, *Accounting for Stock Issued to Employees.* No employee compensation for stock options has been charged to earnings because the exercise prices of all stock options granted under this plan have been equal to the market value of the Corporation's common stock at the date of grant. The following presents information about net income and earnings per share as if the Corporation had applied the fair value expense recognition requirements of Statement of Financial Accounting Standards ("SFAS") 123, *Accounting for Stock-Based Compensation,* to all employee stock options granted under the plan.

(Millions of dollars, except per share amounts)	Year Ended December 31		
	2003	**2002**	**2001**
Net income, as reported	**$1,694.2**	$1,674.6	$1,609.9
Less: Stock-based employee compensation determined under the fair value requirements of SFAS 123, net of income tax benefits	**55.6**	70.2	76.1
Pro forma net income	**$1,638.6**	$1,604.4	$1,533.8

Recognition of its stock options expense would have reduced net income by $55.6 million for 2003 and its earnings per share by 1 cent. Although not material in Kimberly-Clark's case, it is a substantial unrecognized expense for many companies, especially those in high-tech industries.

Common-Size Income Statement

It is useful for analysis purposes to compute common-size statements. Kimberly-Clark's common-size income statement covering its recent three years is shown in Exhibit 12.2.

EXHIBIT 12. 2 ■ Kimberly-Clark Common-Size Income Statement

(2003 computations in parentheses)	2003	2002	2001
Net sales	100.0%	100.0%	100.0%
Cost of products sold ($9,448.1 mil./$14,348.0 mil.)	65.8	64.5	64.9
Gross profit ($4,899.9 mil./$14,348.0 mil.)	34.2	35.5	35.1
Marketing, research, and general expense ($2,375.6 mil./$14,348.0 mil.)	16.6	16.8	16.2
Other (income) expense, net ($111.9 mil./$14,348.0 mil.)	0.8	0.5	1.3
Operating profit ($2,412.4 mil./$14,348.0 mil.)	16.8	18.2	17.6
Nonoperating expense ($105.5 mil./$14,348.0 mil.)	0.7	0.0	0.0
Interest expense, net ([$167.9 mil. − $18.0 mil.]/$14,348.0 mil.)	1.0	1.2	1.3
Income before income taxes ($2,157.0 mil./$14,348.0 mil.)	15.0	17.0	16.3
Provision for income taxes ($514.2 mil./$14,348.0 mil.)	3.6	4.9	4.9
Share of income of equity companies ($107.0 mil./$14,348.0 mil.)	0.7	0.8	1.2
Minority owners' share of subsidiaries income ($55.6 mil./$14,348.0 mil.)	0.4	0.4	0.5
Cumulative effect of accounting change, net of tax	0.0	(0.1)	0.0
Net income ($1,694.2 mil./$14,348.0 mil.)	11.8	12.3	12.1

The gross profit margin has declined in 2003 relative to both 2002 and 2001; specifically, from 35.1% in 2001 to 34.2% in 2003. This is disappointing and reflects the very competitive environment in which K-C operates. Companies typically offset a declining gross profit margin with reductions in SG&A expense. K-C has been unable to do that, however, as its SG&A expense in 2003 actually exceeds its 2001 level as a percentage of sales. Accordingly, 2003 income before taxes has declined by 1.3 percentage points relative to 2001. Further, income from equity companies (reported net of tax) has declined as a percentage of sales from 1.2% to 0.7% from 2001 to 2003. Yet, despite the 1.3 percentage point reduction in pretax profit, net income has declined by only three-tenths as a percent of sales, from 12.1% in 2001 to 11.8% in 2003. This is due to reduced tax expense as a percentage of taxable income.

Management Discussion and Analysis

The Management Discussion and Analysis section of a 10-K is usually informative for interpreting company financial statements and for additional insights into company operations. To illustrate, Kimberly-Clark provides the following analysis of its operating results in the MD&A section of its 2003 10-K:

> Consolidated operating profit decreased 2.1 percent due to higher promotional spending, increased fiber, distribution and energy costs, increased pension expense of approximately $140 million and a higher level of expenses in other income (expense), net that more than offset the benefits of cost reduction programs of about $190 million, favorable currency effects and increased sales volumes. Each of the three business segments incurred more than $40 million of the higher pension costs. Operating profit as a percentage of net sales decreased from 18.2 percent in 2002 to 16.8 percent in 2003.
>
> - Operating profit for personal care products increased 6.0 percent primarily because the benefits of cost reduction programs and favorable currency effects more than offset the lower net selling prices, lower sales volumes and higher raw materials and distribution costs. Although the competitive environment remained intense through product pricing and promotional activity, North America achieved strong fourth quarter results compared with the high level of incremental promotional spending in the year-ago quarter associated with diaper and training pant count changes at that time. North American operating profit for the full year increased because the aggressive cost reduction efforts more than offset lower net selling prices and the higher pension costs. Operating profit in Europe advanced as cost savings programs and favorable currency effects more than offset lower sales volumes. In Latin America, operating profit declined due to higher materials and fiber costs and unfavorable currency effects. Operating profit in Asia rose primarily due to higher sales volumes and favorable currency effects in Australia.
> - Operating profit for consumer tissue products decreased 8.4 percent because increased sales volumes and cost reductions were more than offset by higher fiber, distribution and energy costs, the higher pension costs and increased promotional spending. In each of the major regions—North America, Europe, Latin America and Asia—operating profit declined generally due to the same factors that affected the segment overall.
> - Operating profit for the business-to-business segment increased 1.9 percent as the benefits of cost savings programs, higher sales volumes and favorable currency effects more than offset lower net selling prices, higher fiber and other materials costs, higher distribution and energy expenses, and the increased pension costs. Operating profit for professional products rose in both North America and Europe primarily due to cost reductions and favorable currency effects. Operating profit for health care products increased because of higher sales volumes, cost savings and favorable currency effects, tempered by lower net selling prices. Operating profit for other businesses in the segment declined due to lower sales volumes and higher fiber costs.

Business Segments

Companies are required to disclose the composition of their operating profit by business segment. Segments are investment centers (those having both income statement and balance sheet data) that the company routinely evaluates at the chief executive level.

Kimberly-Clark's business segments are those outlined at the beginning of the module: personal care, consumer tissue, and business-to-business. Following are its disclosures, per GAAP, for each of its business segments:

Consolidated Operations by Business Segment

(Millions of dollars)	Personal Care	Consumer Tissue	Business-to-Business	Intersegment Sales	All Other	Consolidated Total
Net Sales						
2003	$5,257.5	$5,441.9	$3,800.8	$(152.2)	$ —	$14,348.0
2002	5,101.7	5,018.6	3,593.0	(147.0)	—	13,566.3
2001	5,156.6	4,747.9	3,544.6	(161.5)	—	13,287.6
Operating Profit						
2003	1,104.9	844.3	683.0	—	(219.8)	2,412.4
2002	1,042.7	921.7	670.0	—	(170.6)	2,463.8
2001	1,042.7	863.7	599.4	—	(167.6)	2,338.2
Depreciation						
2003	245.1	315.3	184.3	—	1.1	745.8
2002	242.7	287.1	176.0	—	0.8	706.6
2001	225.1	259.8	164.2	—	1.1	650.2
Assets						
2003	4,396.1	6,182.3	4,850.1	—	1,351.4	16,779.9
2002	4,065.8	5,281.4	4,768.6	—	1,523.8	15,639.6
2001	3,819.5	5,064.5	4,662.8	—	1,512.3	15,059.1
Capital Spending						
2003	294.2	416.8	145.7	—	20.9	877.6
2002	289.7	340.4	236.5	—	4.1	870.7
2001	381.0	419.6	260.4	—	38.5	1,099.5

Given these data, it is possible for us to perform a rudimentary return disaggregation analysis for each segment (and years 2002 and 2003). This analysis gives us insight into a company's dependence on any one or more segments. Following is a brief summary analysis of K-C's segment return disaggregation for 2003:

Segment ($ millions)	Net Sales	Operating Profit	Assets	Operating Profit Margin	Asset Turnover	Operating Profit Divided by Assets
Personal care	$5,257.5	$1,104.9	$4,396.1	21.0%	1.20	25.1%
Consumer tissue	5,441.9	844.3	6,182.3	15.5%	0.88	13.7%
Business-to-business	3,800.8	683.0	4,850.1	18.0%	0.78	14.1%

The intensely competitive consumer tissue market is evident in its low profit margin (15.5%) and low return on assets (13.7%). K-C relies to a greater extent on its personal care segment to generate income. Many analysts cite the pricing pressure in the consumer tissue segment as a negative factor in their valuations of K-C.

Balance Sheet Reporting and Analysis

Kimberly-Clark's balance sheet is reproduced in Exhibit 12.3.

EXHIBIT 12.3 ■ Kimberly-Clark Balance Sheet

KIMBERLY-CLARK CORPORATION AND SUBSIDIARIES
Consolidated Balance Sheet

(Millions of dollars)	December 31 2003	December 31 2002
Assets		
Current assets		
Cash and cash equivalents	$ 290.6	$ 494.5
Accounts receivable, net	1,955.1	2,005.9
Inventories	1,563.4	1,430.1
Deferred income taxes	281.4	191.3
Other current assets	347.6	205.9
Total current assets	4,438.1	4,327.7
Property		
Land	276.5	266.0
Buildings	2,272.4	2,042.9
Machinery and equipment	12,061.7	10,812.5
Construction in progress	568.9	442.6
	15,179.5	13,564.0
Less accumulated depreciation	6,916.1	5,944.6
Net property	8,263.4	7,619.4
Investments in equity companies	427.7	571.2
Goodwill	2,649.1	2,254.9
Other assets	1,001.6	866.4
	$16,779.9	$15,639.6
Liabilities and Stockholders' Equity		
Current liabilities		
Debt payable within one year	$ 864.3	$ 1,086.6
Trade accounts payable	857.9	844.5
Other payables	283.5	277.5
Accrued expenses	1,374.7	1,325.2
Accrued income taxes	367.2	404.3
Dividends payable	171.1	154.0
Total current liabilities	3,918.7	4,092.1
Long-term debt	2,733.7	2,844.0
Noncurrent employee benefit and other obligations	1,614.4	1,390.0
Deferred income taxes	880.6	854.2
Minority owners' interests in subsidiaries	298.3	255.5
Preferred securities of subsidiary	567.9	553.5
Stockholders' equity		
Preferred stock—no par value—authorized 20.0 million shares, none issued	—	—
Common stock—$1.25 par value—authorized 1.2 billion shares; issued 568.6 million shares at December 31, 2003 and 2002	710.8	710.8
Additional paid-in capital	406.9	419.0
Common stock held in treasury, at cost—67.0 million and 57.8 million shares at December 31, 2003 and 2002	(3,818.1)	(3,350.6)
Accumulated other comprehensive income (loss)	(1,565.4)	(2,157.7)
Retained earnings	11,059.2	10,054.0
Unearned compensation on restricted stock	(27.1)	(25.2)
Total stockholders' equity	6,766.3	5,650.3
	$16,779.9	$15,639.6

Kimberly-Clark reports total assets of $16,779.9 million in 2003. Its net working capital is relatively il-liquid as much of its current assets are tied up in accounts receivable and inventories, and its cash is only 1.7% ($290.6 mil./$16,779.9 mil.) of total assets at year-end 2003, down from 3.2% in 2002. It also re-ports no marketable securities that can serve as another source of liquidity if needed. The lack of liquidity is usually worrisome, but is not a serious concern in this case given Kimberly-Clark's moderate financial leverage and high free cash flow (see later discussion in this section).

Following is a brief review and analysis for each of Kimberly-Clark's balance sheet line items.

Accounts Receivable

Kimberly-Clark reports $1,955.1 million in net accounts receivable at year-end 2003. This represents 11.7% ($1,955.1 mil./$16,779.9 mil.) of total assets, down from 12.8% in the previous year. Footnotes re-veal the following additional information:

	December 31	
Summary of Accounts Receivable, net ($ millions)	2003	2002
Accounts Receivable		
From customers	$1,815.1	$1,711.3
Other	207.6	362.2
Less allowance for doubtful accounts and sales discounts	(67.6)	(67.6)
Total	$1,955.1	$2,005.9

Most accounts receivables are from customers. This means there are at least two issues we must consider:

1. **Magnitude**—Receivables are generally non-interest-bearing and, therefore, are a nonearning asset. Further, they must be financed at some cost. Accordingly, a company wants to optimize its level of investment in receivables—that is, keep them as low as possible subject to credit policies that meet industry demands.
2. **Collectibility**—Receivables represent unsecured loans to customers. We must, therefore, be cognizant of the creditworthiness of these borrowers. Receivables are reported at net realizable value, that is, net of the allowance for doubtful accounts. Kimberly-Clark reports an allowance of $67.6 million. In addition, the footnotes reveal its following history of its allowance versus its write-offs:

		Additions		Deductions	Balance
Description ($ millions)	Balance at Beginning of Period	Charged to Costs and Expenses	Other	Write-Offs and Reclassifications	at End of Period
December 31, 2003					
Allowances deducted from assets to which they apply					
Allowance for doubtful accounts	$48.4	$ 11.9	$6.5	$ 18.9	$47.9
Allowances for sales discounts	19.2	228.2	1.6	229.3	19.7

The allowance account is broken down into that relating to doubtful accounts and to sales discounts. Con-cerning the allowance for doubtful accounts, the company reported a balance of $48.4 million at the be-ginning of 2003, which is 2.3% of receivables [$48.4/($1,711.3 million + $362.2 million)]. During 2003 it increased this allowance account by $11.9 million. This is the amount of bad debt expense that is re-ported in the income statement. The company also increased the allowance by $6.5 million (see table above) as a result of currency translation effects and acquisitions. Write-offs and reclassifications of un-collectible accounts amounted to $18.9 million during the year, yielding a $47.9 balance at year-end, which is 2.4% of receivables [$47.9 million/($1,815.1 million + $207.6 million)]. It appears, therefore, that the company's receivables were adequately (but not excessively) reserved at year-end relative to the beginning of the year.

Following is Kimberly-Clark's explanation of its allowance policy:

Allowance for Doubtful Accounts We provide an allowance for doubtful accounts that represents our best estimate of the accounts receivable that will ultimately not be collected. We base our estimate on, among other things, historical collection experience, a review of the current aging status of customer receivables, and a review of specific information for those customers that are deemed to be higher risk. When we become aware of a customer whose continued operating success is questionable, we closely monitor collection of their receivable balance and may require the customer to prepay for current shipments. If a customer enters a bankruptcy action, we monitor the progress of that action to determine when and if an additional provision for non-collectibility is warranted. We evaluate the adequacy of the allowance for doubtful accounts on at least a quarterly basis. The allowance for doubtful accounts at December 31, 2003 and 2002 was $47.9 million and $48.4 million, respectively, and our write-off of uncollectible accounts was $15.5 million and $12.0 million in 2003 and 2002, respectively.

The allowance for doubtful accounts should always reflect the company's best estimate of the potential loss in its accounts receivable. This amount should not be overly conservative (which would understate profit), and it should not be inadequate (which would overstate profit). K-C's estimate of its potential losses results from its own (audited) review of the age of its receivables (older receivables are at greater risk of uncollectibility).

Inventories

Kimberly-Clark reports $1,563.4 million in inventories as of 2003. Footnote disclosures reveal the following inventory costing policy:

Inventories and Distribution Costs Most U.S. inventories are valued at the lower of cost, using the Last-In, First-Out (LIFO) method for financial reporting purposes, or market. The balance of the U.S. inventories and inventories of consolidated operations outside the U.S. are valued at the lower of cost. using either the First-In, First-Out (FIFO) or weighted-average cost methods, or market. Distribution costs are classified as cost of products sold.

Most of its U.S. inventories are reported on a LIFO basis. Some of its U.S. inventories, as well as those outside of the U.S., are valued at FIFO or weighted-average. The use of multiple inventory costing methods for different pools of inventories is common and acceptable under GAAP.

We are interested in the composition of inventories. Kimberly-Clark provides the following footnote disclosure to address this issue:

	December 31	
Summary of Inventories ($ millions)	2003	2002
Inventories by major class		
At the lower of cost on the FIFO method, weighted-average cost method or market		
Raw materials	$ 353.8	$ 323.2
Work in process	186.8	186.7
Finished goods	935.2	866.9
Supplies and other	238.1	210.7
	1,713.9	1,587.5
Excess of FIFO cost over LIFO cost	(150.5)	(157.4)
Total	$1,563.4	$1,430.1

Companies aim to optimize their investment in inventories as these represent a non-income-producing asset until sold. Inventories must also be financed, stored, moved, and insured at some cost. Kimberly-Clark reports $353.8 million of raw materials, which is 21% of the total $1,713.9 million inventories (see table above). Work-in-process inventories amount to another $186.8 million and supplies and other amount to $238.1 million. The bulk of its inventories, or $935.2 million (55% of total inventories), are in finished goods.

Kimberly-Clark reports that its total inventory cost *at FIFO* is $1,713.9 million. It then subtracts $150.5 million from this amount (the *LIFO reserve*) to yield its reported inventories of $1,563.4 million at LIFO. This means that Kimberly-Clark has realized a cumulative reduction in gross profit and pretax operating profit of $150.5 million. This has also reduced its pretax income, resulting in an approximate tax savings (and consequent increase in cash flow) of $52.675 million—this assumes a 35% tax rate, and is computed as $150.5 million $\times$ 35%. During 2003, its LIFO reserve actually *decreased* by $6.9 million, resulting in a $6.9 million *increase* in gross profit and pretax operating profit, and a $2.4 million ($6.9 million $\times$ 35%) reduction in cash flow from increased taxes, assuming a 35% tax rate.

Plant, Property, and Equipment

Net plant, property, and equipment (PPE), titled *net property* by Kimberly-Clark, is reported at $8,263.4 million at year-end 2003; it makes up 49% of total assets and is the largest single asset category. PPE is 46% depreciated assuming straight-line depreciation ($6,916.1 million/ $15,179.5 million) as of 2003. This suggests these assets are about the average age that we would expect assuming a regular replacement policy. Footnotes reveal a useful life range of 7 to 50 years for buildings and 2 to 40 years for machinery as follows:

> For financial reporting purposes, property, plant and equipment are stated at cost and are depreciated on the straight-line or units-of-production method. Buildings are depreciated over their estimated useful lives ranging from 7 to 50 years. Machinery and equipment are depreciated over their estimated useful lives ranging from 2 to 40 years. For income tax purposes, accelerated methods of depreciation are used. Purchases of computer software are capitalized. External costs and certain internal costs (including payroll and payroll-related costs of employees) directly associated with developing significant computer software applications for internal use are capitalized. Training and data conversion costs are expensed as incurred. Computer software costs are amortized on the straight-line method over the estimated useful life of the software but not in excess of five years.

Again assuming straight-line depreciation, Kimberly-Clark's 2003 depreciation expense of $745.8 million (reported in its statement of cash flows, Exhibit 12.5) reveals that its long-term depreciable assets, as a whole, are being depreciated over an average useful life of about 20 years, computed as $15,179.5 million $-$ $276.5 million of nondepreciable land and then divided by $745.8 million depreciation expense.

PPE is tested annually for impairment and written down to its net realizable value if deemed to be impaired. Following is Kimberly-Clark's discussion relating to its impairment testing:

> ***Property and Depreciation*** Estimating the useful lives of property, plant, and equipment requires the exercise of management judgment, and actual lives may differ from these estimates. Changes to these initial useful life estimates are made when appropriate. Property, plant, and equipment are tested for impairment in accordance with SFAS 144, *Accounting for the Impairment or Disposal of Long-Lived Assets,* whenever events or changes in circumstances indicate that the carrying amounts of such long-lived assets may not be recoverable from future net pretax cash flows. Impairment testing requires significant management judgment including estimating the future success of product lines, future sales volumes, growth rates for selling prices and costs, alternative uses for the assets and estimated proceeds from disposal of the assets. Impairment testing is conducted at the lowest level where cash flows can be measured and are independent of cash flows of other assets. An asset impairment would be indicated if the sum of the expected future net pretax cash flows from the use of the asset (undiscounted and without interest charges) is less than the carrying amount of the asset. An impairment loss would be measured based on the difference between the fair value of the asset and its carrying amount. We determine fair value based on an expected present value technique in which multiple cash flow scenarios that reflect a range of possible outcomes and a risk free rate of interest are used to estimate fair value.

The company did not report any impairment losses in the periods covered by its recent 10-K.

Investments in Equity Companies

K-C's equity investments are reported at $427.7 million at year-end 2003. This amount represents the book value of its investments in affiliated companies over which Kimberly-Clark can exert significant influence, but not control. Footnotes reveal inclusion of investments in the following companies:

> At December 31, 2003, the Corporation's equity companies and ownership interest were as follows: Kimberly-Clark Lever, Ltd. (India) (50%), Kimberly-Clark de Mexico S.A. de C.V. and subsidiaries (47.9%), Olayan Kimberly-Clark Arabia (49%), Olayan Kimberly-Clark (Bahrain) WLL (49%), PT Kimsari Paper Indonesia (50%) and Tecnosur S.A. (34%).

Consolidation is not required unless the affiliate is "controlled." Generally, control is presumed at an ownership level of more than 50%, which none of these companies are. Thus, these investments are accounted for using the equity method. This means that only the net equity owned of these companies is reported on the balance sheet. We further discuss these investments in the section on off-balance-sheet financing.

Goodwill

Kimberly-Clark reports $2,649.1 million of goodwill at year-end 2003. This amount represents the excess of the purchase price for acquired companies over their fair market value of the acquired tangible and identifiable intangible assets (net of liabilities assumed). GAAP dictates that goodwill is not amortized, but is annually tested for impairment.

For periods prior to 2001, GAAP required goodwill amortization. Accordingly, Kimberly-Clark last reported goodwill amortization in 2001 (see Exhibit 12.1). Since that time its annual net income has increased by approximately $89 million as a result of this mandated accounting change that eliminated goodwill amortization.

Other Assets

Kimberly-Clark reports $1,001.6 million as "other assets." There is no table detailing its composition, but footnotes reveal inclusion of the following: $10.5 million of long-term marketable securities, $191.9 million of acquired patents and trademarks that are being amortized, and $230.2 million of noncurrent deferred income tax assets. No information is given on the remaining $569 million of other assets, most likely because this amount represents several assets each of which is not determined to be "material" and, therefore, subject to disclosure.

Concerning the deferred income tax assets, Kimberly-Clark provides the following disclosure relating to its composition ($ millions):

Net noncurrent deferred income tax asset attributable to	
Accumulated depreciation	$ (15.2)
Income tax loss carryforwards	333.7
State tax credits	57.0
Pension and other postretirement benefits	28.5
Other	44.5
Valuation allowances	(218.3)
Net noncurrent deferred income tax asset included in other assets	$ 230.2

Most of this deferred tax asset (benefit) results from tax loss carryforwards. The IRS allows companies to carry forward losses to offset future taxable income, thereby reducing future tax expense. This benefit can only be realized if the company expects taxable income in the specific entity that generated the tax losses before those carryforwards expire. If the company deems it more likely than not that the carryforwards will *not* be realized, it is required to establish a valuation allowance for the unrealizable portion (this is similar to establishing an allowance for uncollectible accounts receivable). As of 2003, Kimberly-Clark has set up such a valuation allowance (of $218.3 million) which has reduced net income dollar-for-dollar. Following is its discussion relating to this allowance:

> Valuation allowances increased $7.3 million and $63.4 million in 2003 and 2002, respectively. Valuation allowances at the end of 2003 primarily relate to the potentially unusable portion of income tax loss carryforwards of $1,069.4 million, primarily in jurisdictions outside the United States. If not utilized against taxable income, $483.7 million of the loss carryforwards will expire from 2004 through 2023. The remaining $585.7 million has no expiration date.
>
> Realization of income tax loss carryforwards is dependent on generating sufficient taxable income prior to expiration of these carryforwards. Although realization is not assured, management believes it is more likely than not that all of the deferred tax assets, net of applicable valuation allowances, will be realized. The amount of the deferred tax assets considered realizable could be reduced or increased if estimates of future taxable income change during the carryforward period.

Current Liabilities

Kimberly-Clark reports current liabilities of $3,918.7 million at year-end 2003. Accrued liabilities make up the largest single amount at $1,374.7 million. Footnotes reveal that accrued liabilities constitute the following:

Summary of Accrued Expenses ($ millions)	December 31, 2003
Accrued advertising and promotion	$ 240.6
Accrued salaries and wages	374.1
Other	760.0
Total	$1,374.7

The "other" includes accrued benefit costs from the company's pension plans.

The remaining payables that make up current liabilities commonly arise from external transactions, such as trade accounts payable and taxes payable. These transactions are less prone to any management reporting bias. We must, however, determine any excessive "leaning on the trade" as a means to boost operating cash flow. K-C's trade accounts payable have decreased as a percentage of total liabilities and equity from 5.4% ($844.5 million/ $15,639.6 million) in 2002 to 5.1% ($857.9 million/ $16,779.9 million) in 2003. K-C does not exhibit any increased leaning on the trade as a means to boost its operating cash flow.

The possibility of management reporting bias is typically greater for accrued liabilities as they often are estimated (and difficult to audit), involve no external transaction, and can markedly impact reported balance sheet and income statement amounts. One of Kimberly-Clark's accrued liabilities involves promotions and rebates, which it estimates at $240.6 million as of 2003. Following is the description of its accrual policy in this area:

> **Promotion and Rebate Accruals** Among those factors affecting the accruals for promotions and rebates are estimates of the number of consumer coupons that will be redeemed, the type and number of activities within promotional programs between the Corporation and its trade customers and the quantity of products distributors have sold to specific customers. Generally, we base our estimates for consumer coupon costs on historical patterns of coupon redemption, influenced by judgments about current market conditions such as competitive activity in specific product categories. Estimates of trade promotion liabilities for promotional program costs incurred, but unpaid, are generally based on estimates of the quantity of customer sales, timing of promotional activities and forecasted costs for activities within the promotional programs. Settlement of these liabilities sometimes occurs in periods subsequent to the date of the promotion activity. Trade promotion programs include introductory marketing funds such as slotting fees, cooperative marketing programs, temporary price reductions, favorable end of aisle or in-store product displays and other activities conducted by the customers to promote the Corporation's products. Promotion accruals as of December 31, 2003 and 2002 were $222.0 million and $227.7 million, respectively. Rebate accruals as of December 31, 2003 and 2002 were $136.4 million and $159.5 million, respectively.

The company also reports accruals relating to its insurance risks, obsolete inventories, and environmental risks as described in the following footnote:

> **Retained Insurable Risks** We retain selected insurable risks, primarily related to property damage, workers compensation, and product, automobile and premises liability based upon historical loss patterns and management's judgment of cost effective risk retention. Accrued liabilities for incurred but not reported events, principally related to workers compensation and automobile liability, are based upon loss development factors provided to us by our external insurance brokers.

> **Excess and Obsolete Inventory** We require all excess, obsolete, damaged or off-quality inventories including raw materials, in-process, finished goods, and spare parts to be adequately reserved for or to be disposed of. Our process requires an ongoing tracking of the aging of inventories to be reviewed in conjunction with current marketing plans to ensure that any excess or obsolete inventories are identified on a timely basis. This process requires judgments be made about the salability of existing stock in relation to sales projections. The evaluation of the adequacy of provision for obsolete and excess inventories is performed on at least a quarterly basis. No provisions for future anticipated obsolescence, damage or off-quality inventories are made.

Environmental Expenditures Environmental expenditures related to current operations that qualify as property, plant, and equipment or which substantially increase the economic value or extend the useful life of an asset are capitalized, and all other such expenditures are expensed as incurred. Environmental expenditures that relate to an existing condition caused by past operations are expensed as incurred. Liabilities are recorded when environmental assessments and/or remedial efforts are probable and the costs can be reasonably estimated. Generally, the timing of these accruals coincides with completion of a feasibility study or a commitment to a formal plan of action. At environmental sites in which more than one potentially responsible party has been identified, a liability is recorded for the estimated allocable share of costs related to the Corporation's involvement with the site as well as an estimated allocable share of costs related to the involvement of insolvent or unidentified parties. At environmental sites in which the Corporation is the only responsible party, a liability for the total estimated costs of remediation is recorded. Liabilities for future expenditures for environmental remediation obligations are not discounted and do not reflect any anticipated recoveries from insurers.

K-C's accrued liabilities are 8.2% of total liabilities and equity ($1,374.7/$16,779.9) in 2003, compared with 8.5% ($1,325.2/$15,639.6) in 2002. The company provides a breakdown of these accruals over time in the following disclosure:

	December 31	
Summary of Accrued Expenses ($ millions)	**2003**	**2002**
Accrued advertising and promotion	$ 240.6	$ 245.7
Accrued salaries and wages	374.1	385.1
Other	760.0	694.4
Total	$1,374.7	$1,325.2

Neither accrued advertising and promotion nor accrued salaries and wages have changed appreciably from 2002 to 2003. A larger change of $65.6 million occurred in its "other" accrued expenses category. K-C does not provide specific numerical disclosures about this "other" category. Our information is limited to the general descriptions provided in the footnote prior to this numerical summary (for example, retained insurable risks, excess and obsolete inventory, and environmental expenditures). This category is one of the more common ones that management would use to bias the numbers if they were so inclined.

Additional insight can sometimes be gained from a comparison with peer companies. P&G, for example, reports accrued liabilities equal to 11.5% of total liabilities and equity (net of a liability accrual relating to an acquisition). The composition of its accruals is similar to K-C (advertising, promotion, and wages), but P&G's "other" category is markedly greater, which can lessen our concern with the observed increase in K-C's "other" category. Nevertheless, this is the category we must monitor for excessive increases as that would understate current income and provide a "reserve" to increase future income.

Long-Term Debt

Kimberly-Clark reports $2,733.7 million of long-term debt as of 2003. Footnotes reveal the following composition of debt:

Debt Long-term debt is composed of the following:

(Millions of dollars)	Weighted-Average Interest Rate	Maturities	December 31	
			2003	**2002**
Notes and debentures	5.87%	2004–2028	$2,342.9	$2,238.4
Industrial development revenue bonds	4.72%	2004–2037	381.3	427.1
Bank loans and other financings in various currencies	6.03%	2004–2025	194.9	202.8
Total long-term debt			2,919.1	2,868.3
Less current portion			185.4	24.3
Long-term portion			$2,733.7	$2,844.0

Most of its long-term financing is in the form of notes and debentures, $2,342.9 million in 2003, which mature over the next 25 years. GAAP requires disclosure of scheduled maturities for each of the 5 years subsequent to the balance sheet date. Kimberly-Clark's 5-year maturity schedule follows:

Scheduled maturities of long-term debt for the next five years are $185.4 million in 2004, $584.0 million in 2005, $15.4 million in 2006, $321.6 million in 2007 and $1.4 million in 2008.

Our concern with debt maturity dates is whether or not a company is able to repay it at the time demanded. Alternatively, a company can refinance the debt. If a company is unable or unwilling to repay or refinance its debt, it must approach creditors for a modification of debt terms for those issuances coming due. Creditors are usually willing to oblige with, of course, interest rate increases or imposition of additional debt covenants and restrictions. However, if waivers of default are not forthcoming, the company can ultimately face the prospect of bankruptcy. This prospect highlights the importance of these disclosures.

We have little concern about Kimberly-Clark's debt maturity schedule as the company has strong cash flows. Still, it is worth noting that Standard & Poor's (S&P) recently lowered K-C's debt rating from AA to AA−. This rating is still strong (described as lower "high grade" debt), but lower nonetheless. Following is Kimberly-Clark's explanation of this downgrade disclosed in its 2003 10-K:

In July 2003, Standard & Poor's ("S&P") revised the Corporation's credit rating for long-term debt from AA to AA−. Moody's Investor Service maintained its short- and long-term ratings but changed the Corporation's outlook to negative from stable, indicating that a ratings downgrade could be possible within the next 12 months. These changes were primarily based on the Corporation's business performance in the heightened competitive environment and because S&P changed the way in which it evaluates liabilities for pensions and other postretirement benefits. Management believes that these actions will not have a material adverse effect on the Corporation's access to credit or its borrowing costs since these credit ratings remain strong and are in the top eight percent of companies listed in S&P's ranking of the 500 largest companies. The Corporation's commercial paper continues to be rated in the top category.

Noncurrent Employee Benefit and Other Obligations

Kimberly-Clark reports $1,614.4 million of employee benefit and other obligations at year-end 2003 (disclosed in footnotes). Included in this amount is the company's net pension liability ($863.6 million from table below) plus an additional liability required by GAAP to recognize the underfunding of its pension plans ($818.1 million from its 10-K footnotes). K-C reports the following schedule relating to this pension obligation:

Funded status	
Benefit obligation in excess of plan assets	$(1,205.9)
Unrecognized net actuarial loss	1,634.4
Unrecognized transition amount	0.7
Unrecognized prior service cost (benefit)	51.6
Net amount recognized	$ 480.8
Amounts recognized in the balance sheet	
Prepaid benefit cost	$ 19.0
Accrued benefit cost	(863.6)
Intangible asset	56.1
Accumulated other comprehensive income	1,269.3
Net amount recognized	$ 480.8

The reported funded status of $(1,205.9) million means that its pension plans are underfunded by that amount. This is computed as the difference between the pension benefit obligation (PBO) of $5,233.8 million and the fair market value of the company's pension investments of $4,027.9 million—these amounts are reported in another pension footnote disclosure not reproduced here. The $1,205.9 million liability, however, is not reported on the balance sheet because of an $1,686.7 million ($1,634.4 million + $0.7 million + $51.6 million) offset due primarily to deferred actuarial loss. This actuarial loss arose from reduction of the discount rate used to compute the PBO from 6.62% in 2002 to 5.92% in 2003 (disclosed in K-C's footnotes). K-C describes its unrecognized actuarial loss in the following footnote to its 2003 10-K:

> We determine pension expense on the fair value of assets rather than a calculated value that averages gains and losses ("Calculated Value") over a period of years. Investment gains or losses represent the difference between the expected return calculated using the fair value of assets and the actual return based on the fair value of assets. We recognize the variance between actual and expected gains and losses on pension assets in pension expense more rapidly than we would if we used a Calculated Value for plan assets. As of December 31, 2003, the Principal Plans had cumulative unrecognized investment losses and other actuarial losses of approximately $1.6 billion. These unrecognized net losses may increase our future pension expense if not offset by (i) actual investment returns that exceed the assumed investment returns, or (ii) other factors, including reduced pension liabilities arising from higher discount rates used to calculate our pension obligations, or (iii) other actuarial gains, including whether such accumulated actuarial losses at each measurement date exceed the "corridor" determined under SFAS 87, *Employers' Accounting for Pensions.*

Reducing the discount rate increases the present value of K-C's pension liability (PBO). GAAP allows companies to accumulate these actuarial losses (gains), together with unexpected investment gains (losses), off-balance-sheet so long as the cumulative balance does not exceed prescribed limits. Since most of the unrecognized losses have arisen from a reduction in the discount (settlement) rate used to compute the present value of the pension obligation (PBO), it is useful to understand how the company determines this rate. Following is K-C's footnote relating to this issue:

> The discount (or settlement) rate that we utilize for determining the present value of future pension obligations generally has been based in the U.S. on the yield reported for the long-term AA-rated corporate bond indexes, converted to an equivalent one-year compound basis. From time-to-time, and most recently at December 31, 2002, we validated this practice by assembling a hypothetical portfolio of high-quality debt securities where the portfolio cash flows correspond to expected future benefit payments. We use similar techniques for establishing the discount rates for our non-U.S. Principal Plans. The weighted-average discount rate for the Principal Plans decreased to 5.97 percent at December 31, 2003 from 6.68 percent at December 31, 2002.

Companies are required under GAAP to provide investors with an indication of the sensitivity of their reported results to changes in assumed rates (that is, the expected return on plan investments and the discount rate used to compute PBO). Following is Kimberly-Clark's disclosure on these rates:

> If the expected long-term rate of return on assets for our Principal Plans was lowered by 0.25 percent, our annual pension expense would increase by approximately $9 million. If the discount rate assumptions for these same plans were reduced by 0.25 percent, our annual pension expense would increase by approximately $13 million and our December 31, 2003 minimum pension liability would increase by about $142 million.

The *bottom line* for the K-C pension analysis is the $480.8 million it reports on its balance sheet relating to its pension liability. This amount is reported under the following accounts: prepaid benefit cost ($19.0 million, an asset), accrued benefit cost ($863.6 million, a liability), an intangible asset ($56.1 million), and accumulated other comprehensive income ($1,269.3 million, a reduction of equity). Were it not for the GAAP requirement to report the additional minimum liability for severely underfunded plans, the company would have only reported the $480.8 million net pension liability referenced above. As it is, K-C is required to report an *additional* $818.1 million of pension liability on its balance sheet (included in the total reported amount of $1,614.4 million for employee benefits and other obligations).

Deferred Income Taxes

Kimberly-Clark reports a deferred tax liability of $880.6 million at year-end 2003. Footnote disclosures reveal this amount consists of the following components ($ millions):

Net noncurrent deferred income tax liability attributable to	
Accumulated depreciation	$(1,318.3)
Pension, postretirement and other employee benefits	531.5
Installment sales	(188.1)
Foreign tax credits and loss carryforwards	59.8
Prepaid royalties	27.2
Other	29.8
Valuation allowances	(22.5)
Net noncurrent deferred income tax liability	$ (880.6)

Most of the noncurrent deferred tax liability ($1,318.3 million) arises from use of straight-line depreciation for GAAP reporting and accelerated depreciation for tax reporting. As a result, tax depreciation expense is higher in the early years of the assets' lives. This will reverse in later years for individual assets, however, resulting in higher taxable income and tax liability. It is this expected tax liability that is reflected currently in the deferred tax account.

Although K-C will realize a reduction of depreciation expense for an individual asset, with the consequent increase in taxable income and tax liability, if new assets are added at a sufficient rate, the additional first-year depreciation on those assets will more than offset the reduction of depreciation expense on older assets, resulting in a long-term reduction of tax liability. That is, the deferred tax liability is unlikely to reverse in the aggregate. For this reason, many analysts treat the deferred tax liability as a "quasi-equity" account.

Still, while deferred taxes can be postponed, they cannot be eliminated. If the company's growth slows markedly, it will realize higher taxable income and tax liability. This is likely to occur when the company can least afford it. That is, when it is declining. We need to be mindful of the potential for a "real" tax liability (requiring cash payment) when companies begin to downsize.

Minority Owner's Interests in Subsidiaries

K-C's reports $298.3 million for the equity interests of minority shareholders in subsidiaries that have been acquired by Kimberly-Clark. Minority interests are shareholder claims against the net assets and cash flows of the company (after all senior claims are settled). Consequently, we treat minority interest as a component of stockholders' equity; even if not reported in that manner by the company.

Preferred Securities of Subsidiary

The preferred securities represent the sale of preferred stock by a subsidiary of Kimberly-Clark to outside interests. This account is treated like all other contributed capital accounts.

Stockholders' Equity

Kimberly-Clark reports the following statement of stockholders' equity for 2003:

(Dollars in millions, shares in thousands)	Common Stock Issued		Additional Paid-in Capital	Treasury Stock		Unearned Compensation on Restricted Stock	Retained Earnings	Accumulated Other Comprehensive Income (Loss)	Comprehensive Income
	Shares	Amount		Shares	Amount				
Balance at December 31, 2002	568,597	$710.8	$419.0	57,842	$(3,350.6)	$(25.2)	$10,054.0	$(2,157.7)	
Net income	—	—	—	—	—	—	1,694.2	—	$1,694.2
Other comprehensive income									
Unrealized translation	—	—	—	—	—	—	—	742.8	742.8
Minimum pension liability	—	—	—	—	—	—	—	(146.2)	(146.2)
Other	—	—	—	—	—	—	—	(4.3)	(4.3)
Total comprehensive income									$2,286.5
Options exercised and other awards	—	—	(18.0)	(988)	49.0	—	—	—	
Option and restricted share income tax benefits	—	—	7.4	—	—	—	—	—	
Shares repurchased	—	—	—	10,569	(537.1)	—	—	—	
Net issuance of restricted stock, less amortization	—	—	(1.5)	(415)	20.6	(1.9)	—	—	
Dividends declared	—	—	—	—	—	—	(689.0)	—	
Balance at December 31, 2003	568,597	$710.8	$406.9	67,008	$(3,818.1)	$(27.1)	$11,059.2	$(1,565.4)	

K-C has issued 568.597 million shares of its $1.25 par value common stock. The increase in the common stock account is, therefore, equal to $710.746 million (rounded to $710.8 million), computed as 568,597 million shares × $1.25. The additional paid-in capital (APIC) represents the excess of proceeds from stock issuance over par value. It also includes two other components for 2003: (1) the difference between the issue price of treasury stock and its original purchase cost is added or deducted from APIC; in this case deducted as the issue price is less than original cost, and (2) the tax benefits received by K-C relating to the value of stock options exercised by employees is reported as an increase in APIC; it is not reflected as a component of net income. Also, APIC is reduced by $1.5 million related to the issuance of restricted stock (see below).

Kimberly-Clark's stockholders' equity is reduced by a cumulative net amount of $3,818.1 million relating to repurchases of its common stock less the reissuance of those securities. These repurchases are the result of a stock purchase plan approved by K-C's board of directors and evidences K-C's conviction that its stock is undervalued by the marketplace. The repurchased shares are held in treasury and reduce stockholders' equity by the purchase price until such time they are reissued, perhaps to fund an acquisition or to compensate employees under a stock purchase or stock option plan (they can also be retired).

K-C compensates employees via restricted stock in addition to other forms of compensation. Under its restricted stock plan, eligible employees are issued stock, which is restricted as to sale until fully vested (owned). When issued, the market value of the restricted stock is treated as a reduction of stockholders' equity. As the employees gain ownership of the shares (vest), a portion of this account is transferred to the income statement as compensation expense. The consequent reduction in retained earnings offsets the reduction (and increase in equity) of the restricted stock account. Stockholders' equity is, therefore, unaffected in total, although its components change.

Retained earnings reflect an $1,694.2 million increase relating to net income and a $689.0 million decrease from declaration of dividends. Accumulated other comprehensive income (AOCI), which is often aggregated with retained earnings for analysis purposes, began 2003 with a balance of $(2,157.7) million; a reduction of stockholders' equity. During the period, this negative balance was reduced by $742.8 million relating to the increase in net assets of subsidiaries accounted for using currencies other than the $US. This increase in net asset value resulted from a weakened $US vis-à-vis other currencies in 2003. In addition, the AOCI account was reduced by $146.2 million relating to the recognition of a minimum pension liability and $4.3 million designated as "other." Finally, K-C's comprehensive income equals net income plus (minus) the components of other comprehensive income.

Common-Size Balance Sheet

Similar to our analysis of the income statement, it is useful to compute common-size balance sheets. Such statements can reveal changes or relations masked by other analyses. Kimberly-Clark's common-size balance sheet covering its recent two years is shown in Exhibit 12.4.

EXHIBIT 12.4   Kimberly-Clark Common-Size Balance Sheet

	2003 Computations ($ millions)	2003	2002
Cash and cash equivalents	$290.6/$16,779.9	1.73%	3.16%
Accounts receivable, net	$1,955.1/$16,779.9	11.65	12.83
Inventories	$1,563.4/$16,779.9	9.32	9.14
Deferred income taxes and other current assets	$629.0/$16,779.9	3.75	2.54
Total current assets	$4,438.1/$16,779.9	26.45	27.67
Property, gross	$15,179.5/$16,779.9	90.46	86.73
Less accumulated depreciation	$6,916.1/$16,779.9	41.22	38.01
Net property	$8,263.4/$16,779.9	49.25	48.72
Investments in equity companies	$427.7/$16,779.9	2.55	3.65
Goodwill	$2,649.1/$16,779.9	15.79	14.42
Other assets	$1,001.6/$16,779.9	5.97	5.54
Total assets		100.00	100.00
Debt payable within one year	$864.3/$16,779.9	5.15	6.95
Trade accounts payable	$857.9/$16,779.9	5.11	5.40
Accrued expenses	$1,374.7/$16,779.9	8.19	8.47

(Continued on next page)

(Continued from previous page)

EXHIBIT 12.4 ■ Kimberly-Clark Common-Size Balance Sheet *(Continued)*

	2003 Computations ($ millions)	2003	2002
Accrued income taxes	$367.2/$16,779.9	2.19%	2.59%
Dividends payable and other payables	$454.6/$16,779.9	2.71	2.76
Total current liabilities	$3,918.7/$16,779.9	23.35	26.16
Long-term debt	$2,733.7/$16,779.9	16.29	18.18
Noncurrent employee benefit and other	$1,614.4/$16,779.9	9.62	8.89
Deferred income taxes	$880.6/$16,779.9	5.25	5.46
Total long-term liabilities	$5,228.7/$16,779.9	31.16	27.07
Minority owners' interests in subsidiaries	$298.3/$16,779.9	1.78	1.63
Preferred securities of subsidiary	$567.9/$16,779.9	3.38	3.54
Common stock	$710.8/$16,779.9	4.24	4.54
Additional paid-in capital	$406.9/$16,779.9	2.42	2.68
Common stock held in treasury, at cost	$(3,818.1)/$16,779.9	(22.75)	(21.42)
Accumulated other comprehensive income (loss)*	$(1,592.5)/$16,779.9	(9.49)	(13.96)
Retained earnings	$11,059.2/$16,779.9	65.91	64.29
Total stockholders' equity†	$7,632.5/$16,779.9	45.49	36.13
Total liabilities and stockholders' equity		100.00	100.00

*Includes unearned compensation on restricted stock.

†Includes minority owners' interests and preferred securities.

K-C is somewhat less liquid in 2003 than in 2002 as evidenced by the reduction of cash to 1.73% of total assets in 2003 from 3.16% in 2002. (Later in the module the statement of cash flows reveals that this is primarily the result of reduced long-term debt.) The remaining assets and liabilities exhibit little variation from the prior year. There is a marked increase in retained earnings, from 64.29% of assets to 72.13%, but it is somewhat offset by the increase in treasury stock as K-C continues to draw on its operating cash flow to repurchase its common stock. At year-end 2003, stockholders provide 45.49% of its total capital, up from 36.13% in 2002.

Off-Balance-Sheet Reporting and Analysis

There are numerous assets and liabilities that do not appear on the balance sheet. Some are excluded because managers and accounting professionals only report what they can reliably measure. Others are excluded because of the rigidity of accounting standards combined with management incentives. Following are some areas we might consider in our evaluation and adjustment of the Kimberly-Clark balance sheet.

Internally Developed Intangible Assets

Many brands and their corresponding values are excluded from the balance sheet. For example, consider the brand "Kleenex." Many individuals actually refer to facial tissues as Kleenex—that is successful branding! So, is the Kleenex brand reported and valued on Kimberly-Clark's balance sheet? No. That brand value cannot be reliably measured and, hence, is not reported on K-C's balance sheet.

Likewise, other valuable assets are excluded from the balance sheet. Examples are the value of a competent management team, high employee morale, innovative production know-how, a superior supply chain, customer satisfaction, and a host of other assets.

R&D activities represent another set of internally generated intangible assets that are mostly excluded from the balance sheet. Footnotes reveal that Kimberly-Clark spends over $280 million (nearly 2% of sales) on R&D to remain competitive—and, this is for an admittedly non-high-tech company. Further, K-C reveals that it spends over $408 million (nearly 3% of sales) on advertising. Both R&D and advertising costs are expensed under GAAP. This means that they are not capitalized on the balance sheet such as with tangible assets. These unrecognized intangible assets often represent a substantial part of a company's market value.

Equity Method Investments

Kimberly-Clark reports investments in equity companies of $427.7 million at year-end 2003. These are unconsolidated affiliates over which K-C can exert significant influence (but not control) and, hence, are accounted for using the equity method. The amount reported on the balance sheet represents the initial cost of the investment, plus (minus) the percentage share of investee earnings and losses, and minus any cash dividends received. Consequently, the investment balance equals the percentage owned of the affiliates' stockholders' equity (plus any unamortized excess purchase price).

Footnotes reveal that, in sum, these K-C affiliates have total assets of $1,642.4 million, liabilities of $918.3 million, and stockholders' equity of $724.1 million. K-C's reported investment balance of $427.7 in the balance sheet does not reveal the extent of the investment (assets) required to manage these companies, nor the level of potential liability exposure. For instance, in the event of the failure of one of these affiliates, K-C might have to invest cash to support it rather than to let it fail. This is so because failure might affect K-C's ability to finance another such venture in the future.

These investments are reported at cost, not at market as are passive investments. This means that unrecognized gains and losses can be buried in such investments. For example, K-C footnotes reveal the following:

> Kimberly-Clark de Mexico, S.A. de C.V. is partially owned by the public and its stock is publicly traded in Mexico. At December 31, 2003, the Corporation's investment in this equity company was $374.8 million, and the estimated fair value of the investment was $1.5 billion based on the market price of publicly traded shares.

Thus, for at least one of its investments, there is an unrecognized gain of $1,125.2 million.

Operating Leases

Kimberly-Clark has executed a number of leases that are classified as "operating" for financial reporting purposes. As a result, neither the lease asset nor the lease obligation are reported on its balance sheet. For example, K-C reports the following disclosure relating to its operating leases:

> **Leases** The future minimum obligations under operating leases having a noncancelable term in excess of one year as of December 31, 2003, are as follows (Millions of dollars):

	Amount
Year Ending December 31	
2004	$ 67.5
2005	53.3
2006	37.6
2007	25.0
2008	17.8
Thereafter	47.8
Future minimum obligations	$249.0

These leases represent both an unreported asset and an unreported liability; both amounting to $186.8 million. This amount is computed as follows and assumes a 10% discount rate ($ millions):

Year	Operating Lease Payment	Discount Factor (i = 0.10)	Present Value
1	$67.5	0.90909	$ 61.4
2	53.3	0.82645	44.0
3	37.6	0.75131	28.2
4	25.0	0.68301	17.1
5	17.8	0.62092	11.1
		2.25816* × 0.62092	25.0†
>5	47.8		$186.8
Average life	$47.8/$17.8 = 2.6854 years		

*We compute the annuity factor for 2.6854 years as 2.25816 from the formula $\dfrac{1 - \dfrac{1}{(1 + .10)^{2.6854}}}{0.10}$.

†$17.8 × 2.25816 × 0.62092 = $25.0.

The classification of leases as operating for financial reporting purposes is a rigid application of accounting rules, which depends solely on the structure of the lease. A large amount of assets and liabilities is excluded from many companies' balance sheets because leases are structured as operating leases. For K-C, these excluded assets amount to $186.8 million. The valuation of K-C common stock (shown later) uses net operating assets (NOA) as one of its inputs. Our adjustment to the K-C balance sheet, then, would entail the addition of these assets to NOA and the inclusion of $186.8 million in *non*operating liabilities.

Pensions

Kimberly-Clark pension plan is markedly underfunded as described earlier in the module. Total pension obligations amount to $5,233.8 million and pension investments have a market value of $4,027.9 million at year-end 2003. Neither of these amounts appears on the balance sheet, but are reported in the footnotes. In fact, neither does the $1,205.9 million ($5,233.8 million − $4,027.9 million) shortfall as GAAP permits the deferment (nonrecognition) of $1,686.7 million of increased pension liabilities resulting from the reduction in the discount rate in 2003 and the consequent increase in the present value of the pension obligation. However, GAAP requires recognition of additional liabilities if the plans are sufficiently underfunded. For K-C's pension plan, such underfunding resulted in the recognition of an additional $818.1 million of pension liability on its balance sheet. This is reflected in long-term liabilities, with an offsetting amount (net of tax) in other comprehensive income (OCI).

Variable Interest Entities

Footnotes reveal that Kimberly-Clark has two categories of variable interest entities (VIEs). The first relates to two entities that the company established to securitize (sell) $617 million of notes receivable relating to asset sales. K-C sold the notes to these entities, which financed the purchase with debt sold to the capital markets. K-C maintains an equity interest in these entities, but their voting control rests with an independent party (bank) that provided credit guarantees for a fee. The bank is deemed to be the primary beneficiary for financial reporting purposes. As a result, K-C can continue to account for the investment under the equity method and is not required to consolidate the financial statements of the VIE.

The second entity is a synthetic fuel partnership in which it has a 49.5% interest. This entity provides significant tax benefits to K-C, amounting to $131.3 million in 2003 tax credits (from its 10-K footnote 12). Since K-C is the primary beneficiary of the partnership's cash flows, it is required to consolidate its financial statements as of March 2004. K-C asserts that consolidation will not have a material effect on its consolidated financial statements. As a result, it does not provide detailed disclosures of the financial statements of the VIE.

Derivatives

Kimberly-Clark is exposed to a number of market risks as outlined in the following footnote to its 2003 10-K:

> As a multinational enterprise, the Corporation is exposed to risks such as changes in foreign currency exchange rates, interest rates and commodity prices. A variety of practices are employed to manage these risks, including operating and financing activities and, where deemed appropriate, the use of derivative instruments. Derivative instruments are used only for risk management purposes and not for speculation or trading. All foreign currency derivative instruments are either exchange traded or are entered into with major financial institutions. The Corporation's credit exposure under these arrangements is limited to the fair value of the agreements with a positive fair value at the reporting date. Credit risk with respect to the counterparties is considered minimal in view of the financial strength of the counterparties.

The company hedges these risks in a number of ways, including forward, option, and swap contracts. This hedging process results in the transfer of risk from the company to another entity (called the counterparty), which assumes that risk for a fee.

The accounting for derivatives is summarized in an appendix to Module 6. In brief, the derivative contracts, and the assets or liabilities to which they relate, are reported on the balance sheet at fair market value. Any unrealized gains and losses are ultimately reflected in net income, although they can be accumulated in OCI for a short time. To the extent that a company's hedging activities are effective, the market values of the contracts and the assets or liabilities to which they relate are largely offsetting, as are the net gains or losses on the hedging activities. As a result, the effect of derivative activities is generally minimal on both income and equity.[3]

---

[3] It is generally only when companies use derivatives for speculative purposes that these investments significantly affect income and equity. The aim of the derivatives standard was to highlight these speculative activities.

Statement of Cash Flows Reporting and Analysis

The statement of cash flows for Kimberly-Clark is shown in Exhibit 12.5.

EXHIBIT 12.5   Kimberly-Clark Statement of Cash Flows

KIMBERLY-CLARK CORPORATION AND SUBSIDIARIES			
Consolidated Cash Flow Statement			
		Year Ended December 31	
(Millions of dollars)	**2003**	**2002**	**2001**
Operations			
Net income	$ 1,694.2	$ 1,674.6	$ 1,609.9
Cumulative effect of accounting change, net of income taxes	—	11.4	—
Depreciation	745.8	706.6	650.2
Goodwill amortization	—	—	89.4
Deferred income tax (benefit) provision	(53.0)	197.6	39.7
Net losses on asset dispositions	35.0	38.4	102.0
Equity companies' earnings in excess of dividends paid	(9.6)	(8.2)	(39.1)
Minority owners' share of subsidiaries' net income	55.6	58.1	63.2
Decrease (increase) in operating working capital	116.4	(197.6)	(232.6)
Postretirement benefits	(58.5)	(118.2)	(54.7)
Other	87.1	61.5	25.8
Cash provided by operations	2,613.0	2,424.2	2,253.8
Investing			
Capital spending	(877.6)	(870.7)	(1,099.5)
Acquisitions of businesses, net of cash acquired	(258.5)	(410.8)	(135.0)
Investments in marketable securities	(10.8)	(9.0)	(19.7)
Proceeds from sales of investments	29.4	44.9	33.1
Net increase in time deposits	(149.0)	(36.8)	(21.3)
Other	2.0	(11.7)	(5.1)
Cash used for investing	(1,264.5)	(1,294.1)	(1,247.5)
Financing			
Cash dividends paid	(671.9)	(612.7)	(590.1)
Net (decrease) increase in short-term debt	(424.2)	(423.9)	288.4
Proceeds from issuance of long-term debt	540.8	823.1	76.5
Repayments of long-term debt	(481.6)	(154.6)	(271.8)
Issuance of preferred securities of subsidiary	—	—	516.5
Proceeds from exercise of stock options	31.0	68.9	101.5
Acquisitions of common stock for the treasury	(549.7)	(680.7)	(891.5)
Other	(18.4)	(34.9)	(33.5)
Cash used for financing	(1,571.0)	(1,014.8)	(804.0)
Effect of exchange rate changes on cash and cash equivalents	18.6	14.7	(24.5)
(Decrease) increase in cash and cash equivalents	(203.9)	130.0	177.8
Cash and cash equivalents, beginning of year	494.5	364.5	186.7
Cash and cash equivalents, end of year	$ 290.6	$ 494.5	$ 364.5

In 2003, K-C generated $2,613.0 million of operating cash flow, primarily from income (net income plus the depreciation add-back amounts to $2,440 million). This amount is well in excess of K-C's capital expenditures and business acquisitions of $1,136.1 million ($877.6 million + $258.5 million). K-C has used this excess cash to pay dividends to shareholders ($671.9 million), repay debt ($424.2 million − $540.8 million + $481.6 million = $365 million), and repurchase stock ($549.7 million).

Kimberly-Clark offers the following commentary regarding its 2003 operating cash flow:

Cash Flow Commentary Cash provided by operations increased $188.8 million or 7.8 percent to a record $2.6 billion. The reported amounts of operating working capital are affected by changes in currency exchange rates. From a cash flow perspective, the Corporation invested less cash in operating working capital in 2003 primarily due to improved cash collections of trade accounts receivable in Europe, income tax refunds of prior year taxes and lower income tax payments.

Beyond the income component of operating cash flows, Kimberly-Clark also realized increased operating cash flows from reduced working capital investment and a lower tax rate. The increased operating cash flows helped K-C pursue several initiatives. Following are three initiatives that it highlights in its 10-K:

- Our strong cash flow permitted us to make cash contributions to our defined benefit pension trusts of about $185 million, and we plan to contribute an additional $100 million in 2004.
- We repurchased 10.4 million shares of our common stock under authorized share repurchase programs at a cost of $529 million.
- We increased our annual cash dividend 13 percent in 2003 and will increase it an additional 18 percent in 2004.

Kimberly-Clark also acknowledged the underfunded status of its pension plan and the need to devote additional cash flows to bolster pension assets. However, K-C cites the repurchase of shares as a priority. This, combined with increased dividend levels, will yield greater cash payments to its shareholders.

Overall, the cash flow picture for Kimberly-Clark is strong: operating cash flows are more than sufficient to cover capital expenditures and acquisitions, leaving excess cash that is being returned to the providers of capital (creditors and shareholders). The strength of its operating cash flows mitigates any concerns we might have regarding its relative lack of liquidity on the balance sheet.

Independent Audit Opinion

Kimberly-Clark is subject to various audit requirements. Its independent auditor is Deloitte & Touche LLP, which issued the following clean opinion on K-C's 2003 financial statements:

INDEPENDENT AUDITORS' REPORT

To the Board of Directors and Stockholders of Kimberly-Clark Corporation:

We have audited the accompanying consolidated balance sheets of Kimberly-Clark Corporation and Subsidiaries as of December 31, 2003 and 2002, and the related consolidated statements of income, stockholders' equity, and cash flows for each of the three years in the period ended December 31, 2003. Our audit also included the financial statement schedule listed in Item 15 (a) 2. These financial statements and the financial statement schedule are the responsibility of the Corporation's management. Our responsibility is to express an opinion on these financial statements and the financial statement schedule based on our audits.

We conducted our audits in accordance with auditing standards generally accepted in the United States of America. Those standards require that we plan and perform the audit to obtain reasonable assurance about whether the financial statements are free of material misstatement. An audit includes examining, on a test basis, evidence supporting the amounts and disclosures in the financial statements. An audit also includes assessing the accounting principles used and significant estimates made by management, as well as evaluating the overall financial statement presentation. We believe that our audits provide a reasonable basis for our opinion.

In our opinion, such consolidated financial statements present fairly, in all material respects, the financial position of Kimberly-Clark Corporation and Subsidiaries at December 31, 2003 and 2002, and the results of their operations and their cash flows for each of the three years in the period ended December 31, 2003, in conformity with accounting principles generally accepted in the United States of America. Also, in our opinion, the financial statement schedule, when considered in relation to the basic consolidated financial statements taken as a whole, presents fairly, in all material respects, the information set forth therein.

As discussed in Note 1 to the consolidated financial statements, effective January 1, 2002, the Corporation changed its method of accounting for customer coupons and its method of accounting for goodwill.

/s/ DELOITTE & TOUCHE LLP
Deloitte & Touche LLP
Dallas, Texas
February 11, 2004

Although this report is a routine disclosure, it should not be taken for granted. Exceptions to a clean audit report must be scrutinized. Also, any disagreements between management and the independent auditor must be documented in an SEC filing. If this occurs, it is a "red flag" that must be investigated. Management activities and reports that cannot meet usual audit standards raise serious concerns about integrity and credibility. At a minimum, the riskiness of investments and relationships with such a company markedly increases.

■ ASSESSING PROFITABILITY AND CREDITWORTHINESS

This section reports a profitability analysis of **Kimberly-Clark**. We begin with computations of several key measures that are used in ROE disaggregation, which is the overriding focus of this section. (These ratios are defined in Module 3, and a listing of the ratio acronyms and definitions is in the review section at the end of the book.)

K-C's 2003 net operating profit after-tax (NOPAT) is $1,945.2 million, computed as $2,412.4 million × [1 − ($514.2 million/$2,157.0 million)] + $107 million. Its 2003 net operating working capital (NOWC) is $1,383.7 million, computed as its $4,438.1 million in total current assets less $3,054.4 in net current liabilities (equal to its $3,918.7 million in current liabilities less its $864.3 million in current maturities of long-term debt). Its 2003 net operating long-term assets are $9,846.8 million, computed as net PPE plus investments in equity companies, goodwill, and other assets, and less its long-term operating liabilities such as pension obligations and deferred taxes: $8,263.4 million + $427.7 million + $2,649.1 million + $1,001.6 million − $1,614.4 million − $880.6 million. Thus, K-C's net operating assets (NOA) are $11,230.5 million, computed as $1,383.7 million + $9,846.8 million.

K-C's net financial obligation (NFO) is $3,598.0 million, computed as its current and long-term portion of its interest-bearing debt, or $864.3 million + $2,733.7 million. (Note: K-C does not report any financial assets; if present, they are subtracted from this amount to get NFO.) Its 2003 stockholders' equity is $7,632.5 million, computed as its reported amount of $6,766.3 million plus minority interest ($298.3 million) and preferred securities of subsidiary ($567.9 million). Thus, and as alternatively computed, K-C's net operating assets (NOA) of $11,230.5 million equal its net financial obligations (NFO) plus equity ($3,598.0 million + $7,632.5 million).

Level 1 Analysis—RNOA and Leverage

Our first step in profitability analysis is computation of ROE and, then, its disaggregation into return on net operating assets (RNOA) and leverage. Using the computations in the previous section, the 2003 (Level 1) disaggregation analysis of ROE for Kimberly-Clark follows:[4]

$$\text{ROE} = \text{RNOA} + (\text{FLEV} \times \text{Spread})$$
$$24.0\% = 18.0\% + (53.4\% \times 11.3\%)$$

where

ROE   = $1,694.2 mil./[($7,632.5 mil. + $6,459.3 mil.)/2]
RNOA = $1,945.2 mil. /[($11,230.5 mil. + $10,389.9 mil.) /2]
FLEV = [($3,598.0 mil. + $3,930.6 mil.)/2]/[($7,632.5 mil. + $6,459.3 mil.)/2]
Spread = RNOA − NFR[5] = 18.0% − 6.7%

RNOA comprises 75% (18%/24%) of K-C's ROE. Its financial leverage is 53.4%, which is slightly higher than the 40% median of all publicly traded companies, but it is not excessive. K-C successfully uses its leverage to increase its 18.0% RNOA to a 24% ROE; this is known as a positive borrowing spread. Kimberly-Clark has, therefore, capitalized on its favorable borrowing spread to increase its returns to shareholders.

---

[4]Many of these ratios require computation of averages, such as average assets. If we wanted to compute ratios for years prior to 2003, then we would obtain information from prior 10-Ks to compute the necessary averages for these ratios.

[5]NFR is 6.7%, computed as ($1,945.2 mil. − $1,694.2 mil.)/([$3,598.0 mil. + $3,930.6 mil.]/2).

Level 2 Analysis—Margin and Turnover

The next level analysis of ROE focuses on RNOA disaggregation. Kimberly-Clark's Level 2 analysis uses its net operating profit margin (NOPM) and its net operating asset turnover (NOAT) as follows:

RNOA = NOPAT/Average Net Operating Assets		= NOPAT/Sales	×	Sales/Average Net Operating Assets
		NOPM		**NOAT**
18.0%	=	**13.6%**	×	**1.33**

where
  NOPM = $1,945.2 million/$14,348.0 million
  NOAT = $14,348.0 million/([$11,230.5 million + $10,389.9 million]/2)

Kimberly-Clark's RNOA of 18% is comprised of a net operating profit margin of 13.6% and a net operating asset turnover of 1.33 times. In comparison, Procter and Gamble's 2003 RNOA is 18.7% with a NOPM of 12.5% and a NOAT of 1.50. K-C's reliance on NOPM for its RNOA is a potential risk factor given the intense competition in this industry and the consequent pressure on profit margins. To be competitive, K-C must increase its NOAT of 1.33 to at least be competitive with P&G's NOAT of 1.50.

Level 3 Analysis—Disaggregation of Margin and Turnover

This section focuses on Level 3 analysis, which is the disaggregation of profit margin and asset turnover to better understand the drivers of RNOA. Again, understanding the drivers of financial performance (RNOA) is key to predicting future company performance. Level 3 analysis of the drivers of operating profit margin and asset turnover for Kimberly-Clark follows:

Disaggregation of NOPM	
Gross profit margin (GPM) ($4,899.9 mil./$14,348.0 mil.)	34.2%
Operating expense margin (OEM) [($2,375.6 mil. + $111.9 mil)/$14,348.0 mil]	17.3%
Disaggregation of NOAT	
Accounts receivable turnover (ART) {$14,348.0 mil./[($1,955.1 mil. + $2,005.9 mil.)/2]}	7.24
Inventory turnover (INVT) {$9,448.1 mil./[($1,563.4 mil. + $1,430.1 mil.)/2]}	6.31
Long-term operating asset turnover (LTOAT) {$14,348.0 mil./[($8,263.4 mil. + $7,619.4 mil.)/2]}	1.81
Accounts payable turnover (APT) {$9,448.1 mil./[($857.9 mil. + $844.5 mil.)/2]}	11.10
Net operating working capital turnover (NOWCT) {$14,348.0 mil./[($1,383.7 mil. + $1,322.2 mil.)/2]} . .	10.60
Related turnover measures	
Average collection period [$1,955.1 mil./($14,348.0 mil./365)]	49.7 days
Average inventory days outstanding [$1,563.1 mil./($9,448.1 mil./365)]	60.4 days
Average payable days outstanding [$857.9 mil./($9,448.1 mil./365)]	33.1 days

First, let's look at the disaggregation of NOPM. K-C reports a gross profit margin of 34.3%. A schedule to its 2003 10-K indicates that this important measure has declined by 2 percentage points in the past four years—which is a significant decline. K-C provides the following explanation of this decline in its MD&A:

> **Competitive Environment** The Corporation experiences intense competition for sales of its principal products in its major markets, both domestically and internationally. The Corporation's products compete with widely advertised, well-known, branded products, as well as private label products, which are typically sold at lower prices. The Corporation has several major competitors in most of its markets, some of which are larger and more diversified than the Corporation.

Declines in gross profit margin are usually countered with reductions in operating expenses to maintain a company's operating profit margin. However, for K-C, it has not decreased its operating expenses to offset the decline in gross profit margin. Our analysis above showed that the stability in K-C's NOPM was driven primarily by K-C's decline in its effective tax rate from 29% in 2002 to 23.8% in 2003. This tax rate decline is mainly due to its synthetic fuel partnership. Although a laudable activity, we prefer to see cost reductions from improvements in operating activities; further, tax benefits are often transitory.

Next, let's look at the disaggregation of NOAT. K-C's receivables turnover rate of 7.24 times corresponds to an average collection period of 49.7 days, which is reasonable for normal credit terms. However, the more important issue here is asset productivity (turnover) instead of credit quality. This is because most of K-C's sales are to large retailers; for example, 13% of Kimberly-Clark's sales are to Wal-Mart.

Inventories turn over 6.31 times a year, resulting in an average inventory days outstanding of 60.4 days in 2003. Inventories are an important (and large) asset for companies like Kimberly-Clark. Improved turnover is always a goal so long as the company maintains sufficient inventories to meet market demand. For comparison, Procter and Gamble's average inventory days outstanding is 60.0 for the comparable period.

K-C's long-term operating assets are turning over 1.81 times a year, which is about average for publicly traded companies. However, K-C's LTOAT of 1.81 does not favorably compare with P&G's LTOAT of 3.28. P&G's level of goodwill is much greater than that for K-C. Thus, it is possible that P&G has acquired substantial manufacturing capacity via acquisition and that considerable PPE cost is in goodwill. In any case, the issue with respect to LTOAT is throughput, and K-C does not discuss this aspect of its business in its financial filings.

K-C's trade accounts payable turnover is 11.1, resulting in an average payable days outstanding of 33.1 days. Since payables represent a low cost source of financing, we would prefer to see its days payable lengthened so long as K-C is not endangering its relationships with suppliers. In comparison, P&G is able to use its bargaining power vis-à-vis suppliers to keep payables outstanding for over 41 days, on average.

Credit Analysis

Credit analysis is an important part of a complete company analysis. Following is a selected set of measures for 2003 that can help us gauge the relative credit standing of Kimberly-Clark:

Current ratio	1.13
Quick ratio	0.57
Total liabilities/Equity	0.64
Long-term debt/Equity	0.40
Earnings before interest and taxes/Interest expense	13.85
Net operating cash flows/Total liabilities	0.60

K-C's current and quick ratios are not particularly high, but both have increased over the past three years (not shown here). Further, these ratios do not imply any excess liquidity, and probably do not suggest any room for a further decrease in liquidity.

K-C's financial leverage, as reflected in both the liability-to-equity and long-term-debt-to-equity ratios, is slightly above the median for all publicly traded companies. Normally, this is cause for some concern. However, Kimberly-Clark has strong operating and free cash flows that mitigate this concern.

K-C's times interest earned ratio of 13.85 is quite healthy, indicating a sufficient buffer to protect creditors if a downturn in earnings occurs. It also has relatively little off-balance-sheet exposure. Thus, we do not have any serious concerns about K-C's ability to repay its maturing debt obligations.

Analysis Summary of Profitability and Creditworthiness

An increasingly competitive environment has resulted in a decreasing gross profit margin for Kimberly-Clark. It has not reduced its operating expenses sufficiently to offset this decline. However, it has been able to maintain its NOPAT as a result of a decline in its effective tax rate (which is less than persistent). Its operating working capital and long-term operating assets yield acceptable, although not stellar, turnover levels. K-C does not provide sufficient discussion to further assess the throughput performance of its operating assets. Finally, its leverage, although higher than average, is not of great concern given K-C's strong cash flows.

■ ADJUSTING AND FORECASTING FINANCIAL PERFORMANCE

The valuation of a share of K-C common stock requires forecasts of NOPAT and NOA over a forecast horizon period and a forecast terminal period. We can, of course, project individual income statement and balance sheet items using the methodology we discuss in Module 10. However, in this section, we employ the parsimonious method of forecasting NOPAT and NOA using only sales forecasts, profit margins, and asset turnover rates—described in a latter section of Module 10. We first discuss some possible adjustments to the financial statements that we can consider before commencing the forecasting process.

The two main targets of our parsimonious forecasting process are NOPAT and NOA. This means that we are primarily concerned with income statement and balance sheet adjustments that affect these two financial statements. Some adjustments we might consider for this purpose are shown in Exhibit 12.6 for Kimberly-Clark.

EXHIBIT 12.6 ■ Kimberly-Clark Adjustments for NOPAT and NOA

Adj.	($ millions)	
	Reported NOPAT	$ 1,945.2
1	Interest cost, expected return, and actuarial loss from pension plan	75.4
2	Legal judgment	15.6
3	Redemption of debentures	18.4
4	Write-off of investment	20.0
5	Affordable housing and historic renovation project	25.1
6	Unrecognized stock option expense	(55.6)
7	Rent expense on operating leases, net of depreciation	43.7
	Total adjustments, pretax	142.6
8	Provision for taxes (23.8% rate)	(33.9)
	Total adjustments, after-tax	108.7
	Adjusted NOPAT	$ 2,053.9
	Reported NOA	$11,230.5
9	Capitalization of operating leases	186.8
	Adjusted NOA	$11,417.3

Following is an explanation of the adjustments we make to NOPAT and NOA, which are coded by the number shown in the left column of Exhibit 12.6:

1. Pension expense is included in operating profit under GAAP. Many analysts consider the pension plan investment returns and the interest expense portion of the pension cost to be nonoperating. For K-C, the net pension investment cost is $75.4 million, computed as $291.4 million − $290.6 million + $74.6 million (which reflects interest cost less the expected return on plan assets less a net actuarial loss).
2. K-C experienced a $15.6 million legal judgment. This is reported as operating, but it is (expectantly) transitory.
3. Its loss from redemption of debentures (debt) is a financial (nonoperating) expense.
4. The write-off of an investment is a financial (nonoperating) expense.
5. K-C's costs for its investment in affordable housing are not transitory, but they are not operating either.
6. K-C reports its stock options under GAAP (*APB* 25), and as a result, no options expense is reported in its income statement. Footnotes report that this stock option expense is $55.6 million for 2003 and it is included for adjusting NOPAT.
7. K-C reports operating leases that are capitalized and used in the NOA adjustment below. Thus, the related expense of $68 million is added back, net of depreciation on the capitalized leased assets of $24.3 million ($186.8 million/7.6854 years), for a total of $43.7 million in adjusting NOPAT.
8. Total additional pretax operating profit is $142.6 million. Using K-C's effective tax rate of 23.8%, the net after-tax add-back to NOPAT is $108.7 million, resulting in an adjusted NOPAT of $2,053.9 million.

9. The lone NOA adjustment is for the present value of K-C's operating leases, $186.8 million. The adjusted NOA is $11,417.3 million. K-C's net financial obligations are, likewise, increased by the $186.8 million lease obligation from $3,598.0 million to $3,784.8 million.

These adjusted NOPAT and NOA amounts become the starting point for our forecasts that are used to estimate the value of K-C common stock. The simplified forecast process uses three inputs: sales growth, NOPAT margin, and NOA turnover. Our adjusted net operating profit margin (NOPM) is 14.31% ($2,053.9 million/$14,348 million) and the adjusted net operating asset turnover (NOAT) is 1.26 ($14,348 million/$11,417.3 million). (Note: For forecasting, turnover metrics use year-end figures; see Module 10.)

The sales growth forecast is complicated by the foreign currency exchange effects that we discussed earlier. K-C's sales increased by 5.76% in 2003, but 4% of this increase resulted from the weaker $US. The "real" increase was only about 1.76% in 2003. Also, our forecasts would be prepared around March 2004, after the 10-K was published. By then, K-C estimated that first quarter sales for 2004 increased approximately 10% year-over-year, with EPS increases in the 14% range (reflecting cost cutting and efficiency programs put in place in the prior two years). It is unknown how much of the 10% revenue increase in the first quarter of 2004 was due to a continued weakening of the $US. Accordingly, for our forecasts, we use a more conservative 5% sales increase—this forecast is somewhat conservative as it leans to the lower end of the range. We also use a NOPM of 14.31% and a NOAT of 1.26, both from 2003.

Exhibit 12.7 shows forecasts of Kimberly-Clark's sales, net operating profit after tax (NOPAT), and net operating assets (NOA)—these follow from our forecasting process explained in Module 10 and include the terminal year forecast assuming a terminal growth rate of 2%.

EXHIBIT 12.7 ■ Kimberly-Clark Forecasts of Sales, NOPAT, and NOA

(In millions)	Reported 2003	Horizon Period 2004	2005	2006	2007	Terminal Period
Sales	$14,348	$15,065	$15,819	$16,610	$17,440	$17,789
NOPAT	2,054	2,157	2,264	2,378	2,497	2,547
NOA	11,418	11,988	12,588	13,217	13,878	14,156

■ VALUING FIRM EQUITY AND STOCK VALUE

This section estimates the values of Kimberly-Clark's equity and common stock per share. Exhibit 12.8 shows the discounted cash flow (DCF) model results for this purpose. In addition to the forecast assumptions from the prior section, these results assume a discount (WACC) rate of 7.5%, a terminal growth rate of 2%, shares outstanding of 508 million, and net financial obligations (NFO) of $3,785 million.

EXHIBIT 12.8 ■ Kimberly-Clark Discounted Cash Flow (DCF) Valuation

(In millions, except per share values and discount factors)	2003	Horizon Period 2004	2005	2006	2007	Terminal Period
Increase in NOA		$ 571	$ 599	$ 629	$ 661	$ 278
FCFF (NOPAT − Increase in NOA)		1,586	1,665	1,748	1,836	2,269
Discount factor [$1/(1+r_w)^t$]		0.93023	0.86533	0.80496	0.74880	
Present value of horizon FCFF		1,475	1,441	1,407	1,375	
Cum. present value of horizon FCFF	$ 5,698					
Present value of terminal FCFF	30,890[a]					
Total firm value	36,588					
Less (plus) NFO	3,785					
Firm equity value	$32,803					
Stock outstanding	508					
Stock value per share	$64.57					

[a]Computed as $\dfrac{\left(\dfrac{\$2,269 \text{ million}}{0.075-0.02}\right)}{(1.075)^4}$.

Exhibit 12.9 reports estimates of the values of Kimberly-Clark's equity and common stock per share using the residual operating income (ROPI) model.

EXHIBIT 12.9 ■ Kimberly-Clark Residual Operating Income (ROPI) Valuation

(In millions, except per share values and discount factors)	2003	Horizon Period 2004	2005	2006	2007	Terminal Period
ROPI [NOPAT − (NOA$_{Beg}$ × r_w)]		$1,300	$1,365	$1,434	$1,505	$1,506
Discount factor [1/(1+ r_w)^t]		0.93023	0.86533	0.80496	0.74880	
Present value of horizon ROPI		1,210	1,181	1,154	1,127	
Cum. present value of horizon ROPI . . .	$ 4,672					
Present value of terminal ROPI[a]	20,498					
NOA	11,418					
Total firm value	36,588					
Less (plus) NFO	3,785					
Firm equity value	$32,803					
Stock outstanding	508					
Stock value per share	$64.57					

[a]Computed as $\frac{\left(\frac{\$1{,}506 \text{ million}}{0.075 - 0.02}\right)}{(1.075)^4}$.

Kimberly-Clark's equity value is estimated at $32,803 million as of December 2003, which is equivalent to a per share value estimate of $64.57. As expected, equity value estimates are identical for both models (because K-C is assumed to be in a steady state, that is, NOPAT and NOA growing at the same rate and, therefore, RNOA is constant).

The closing stock price on December 31, 2003, for Kimberly-Clark (KMB) was $59.09 per share. Our model's estimates, therefore, suggest that K-C stock is undervalued as of that date. As it turns out, this valuation proved prophetic as its stock price increased to the mid- to upper-$60s subsequent to that date as shown in the following graph:

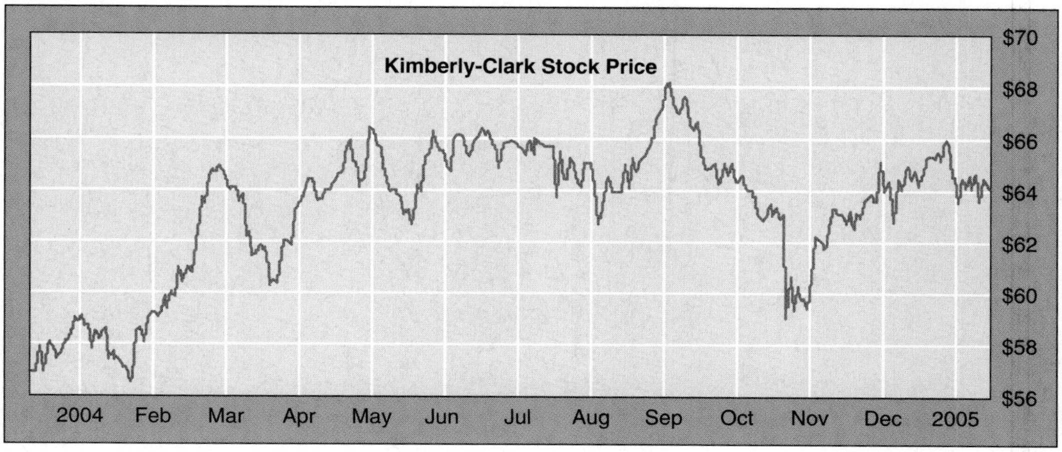

Overall, this module presented a financial accounting analysis and interpretation of Kimberly-Clark. It illustrated many of the key financial reporting topics covered in the book. We began with a detailed review of its financial statements and notes, followed by the forecasting of key accounts, and concluded with estimates of K-C's equity value.

Although no two companies are identical, the Kimberly-Clark case provided an opportunity for us to apply many of the procedures conveyed in the book (and course) in a comprehensive manner. With analyses of additional companies, we become more comfortable with and knowledgeable of variations in financial reporting, which enhances our analysis and business decision-making skills. As we discuss in Module 1, our analysis of a company must go beyond the accounting numbers to include competitor and economic factors, and we must appreciate that estimation and judgment are key ingredients in financial accounting. This comprehensive case, textbook, and course provide us with skills necessary to effectively use financial accounting and to advance our business and career opportunities.

A

Compound Interest Tables

TABLE 1 ■ Present Value of Single Amount

$p = 1/(1 + i)^t$

	Interest Rate											
Period	0.01	0.02	0.03	0.04	0.05	0.06	0.07	0.08	0.09	0.10	0.11	0.12
1	0.99010	0.98039	0.97087	0.96154	0.95238	0.94340	0.93458	0.92593	0.91743	0.90909	0.90090	0.89286
2	0.98030	0.96117	0.94260	0.92456	0.90703	0.89000	0.87344	0.85734	0.84168	0.82645	0.81162	0.79719
3	0.97059	0.94232	0.91514	0.88900	0.86384	0.83962	0.81630	0.79383	0.77218	0.75131	0.73119	0.71178
4	0.96098	0.92385	0.88849	0.85480	0.82270	0.79209	0.76290	0.73503	0.70843	0.68301	0.65873	0.63552
5	0.95147	0.90573	0.86261	0.82193	0.78353	0.74726	0.71299	0.68058	0.64993	0.62092	0.59345	0.56743
6	0.94205	0.88797	0.83748	0.79031	0.74622	0.70496	0.66634	0.63017	0.59627	0.56447	0.53464	0.50663
7	0.93272	0.87056	0.81309	0.75992	0.71068	0.66506	0.62275	0.58349	0.54703	0.51316	0.48166	0.45235
8	0.92348	0.85349	0.78941	0.73069	0.67684	0.62741	0.58201	0.54027	0.50187	0.46651	0.43393	0.40388
9	0.91434	0.83676	0.76642	0.70259	0.64461	0.59190	0.54393	0.50025	0.46043	0.42410	0.39092	0.36061
10	0.90529	0.82035	0.74409	0.67556	0.61391	0.55839	0.50835	0.46319	0.42241	0.38554	0.35218	0.32197
11	0.89632	0.80426	0.72242	0.64958	0.58468	0.52679	0.47509	0.42888	0.38753	0.35049	0.31728	0.28748
12	0.88745	0.78849	0.70138	0.62460	0.55684	0.49697	0.44401	0.39711	0.35553	0.31863	0.28584	0.25668
13	0.87866	0.77303	0.68095	0.60057	0.53032	0.46884	0.41496	0.36770	0.32618	0.28966	0.25751	0.22917
14	0.86996	0.75788	0.66112	0.57748	0.50507	0.44230	0.38782	0.34046	0.29925	0.26333	0.23199	0.20462
15	0.86135	0.74301	0.64186	0.55526	0.48102	0.41727	0.36245	0.31524	0.27454	0.23939	0.20900	0.18270
16	0.85282	0.72845	0.62317	0.53391	0.45811	0.39365	0.33873	0.29189	0.25187	0.21763	0.18829	0.16312
17	0.84438	0.71416	0.60502	0.51337	0.43630	0.37136	0.31657	0.27027	0.23107	0.19784	0.16963	0.14564
18	0.83602	0.70016	0.58739	0.49363	0.41552	0.35034	0.29586	0.25025	0.21199	0.17986	0.15282	0.13004
19	0.82774	0.68643	0.57029	0.47464	0.39573	0.33051	0.27651	0.23171	0.19449	0.16351	0.13768	0.11611
20	0.81954	0.67297	0.55368	0.45639	0.37689	0.31180	0.25842	0.21455	0.17843	0.14864	0.12403	0.10367
21	0.81143	0.65978	0.53755	0.43883	0.35894	0.29416	0.24151	0.19866	0.16370	0.13513	0.11174	0.09256
22	0.80340	0.64684	0.52189	0.42196	0.34185	0.27751	0.22571	0.18394	0.15018	0.12285	0.10067	0.08264
23	0.79544	0.63416	0.50669	0.40573	0.32557	0.26180	0.21095	0.17032	0.13778	0.11168	0.09069	0.07379
24	0.78757	0.62172	0.49193	0.39012	0.31007	0.24698	0.19715	0.15770	0.12640	0.10153	0.08170	0.06588
25	0.77977	0.60953	0.47761	0.37512	0.29530	0.23300	0.18425	0.14602	0.11597	0.09230	0.07361	0.05882
30	0.74192	0.55207	0.41199	0.30832	0.23138	0.17411	0.13137	0.09938	0.07537	0.05731	0.04368	0.03338
35	0.70591	0.50003	0.35538	0.25342	0.18129	0.13011	0.09366	0.06763	0.04899	0.03558	0.02592	0.01894
40	0.67165	0.45289	0.30656	0.20829	0.14205	0.09722	0.06678	0.04603	0.03184	0.02209	0.01538	0.01075

TABLE 2 ■ ~~Future Value of Single Amount~~ *Present Value of Ordinary Annuity* (handwritten)

$$p = \dfrac{1 - \dfrac{1}{(1+i)^t}}{i}$$ (handwritten)

	Interest Rate											
Period	0.01	0.02	0.03	0.04	0.05	0.06	0.07	0.08	0.09	0.10	0.11	0.12
1	0.99010	0.98039	0.97087	0.96154	0.95238	0.94340	0.93458	0.92593	0.91743	0.90909	0.90090	0.89286
2	1.97040	1.94156	1.91347	1.88609	1.85941	1.83339	1.80802	1.78326	1.75911	1.73554	1.71252	1.69005
3	2.94099	2.88388	2.82861	2.77509	2.72325	2.67301	2.62432	2.57710	2.53129	2.48685	2.44371	2.40183
4	3.90197	3.80773	3.71710	3.62990	3.54595	3.46511	3.38721	3.31213	3.23972	3.16987	3.10245	3.03735
5	4.85343	4.71346	4.57971	4.45182	4.32948	4.21236	4.10020	3.99271	3.88965	3.79079	3.69590	3.60478
6	5.79548	5.60143	5.41719	5.24214	5.07569	4.91732	4.76654	4.62288	4.48592	4.35526	4.23054	4.11141
7	6.72819	6.47199	6.23028	6.00205	5.78637	5.58238	5.38929	5.20637	5.03295	4.86842	4.71220	4.56376
8	7.65168	7.32548	7.01969	6.73274	6.46321	6.20979	5.97130	5.74664	5.53482	5.33493	5.14612	4.96764
9	8.56602	8.16224	7.78611	7.43533	7.10782	6.80169	6.51523	6.24689	5.99525	5.75902	5.53705	5.32825
10	9.47130	8.98259	8.53020	8.11090	7.72173	7.36009	7.02358	6.71008	6.41766	6.14457	5.88923	5.65022
11	10.36763	9.78685	9.25262	8.76048	8.30641	7.88687	7.49867	7.13896	6.80519	6.49506	6.20652	5.93770
12	11.25508	10.57534	9.95400	9.38507	8.86325	8.38384	7.94269	7.53608	7.16073	6.81369	6.49236	6.19437
13	12.13374	11.34837	10.63496	9.98565	9.39357	8.85268	8.35765	7.90378	7.48690	7.10336	6.74987	6.42355
14	13.00370	12.10625	11.29607	10.56312	9.89864	9.29498	8.74547	8.24424	7.78615	7.36669	6.98187	6.62817
15	13.86505	12.84926	11.93794	11.11839	10.37966	9.71225	9.10791	8.55948	8.06069	7.60608	7.19087	6.81086
16	14.71787	13.57771	12.56110	11.65230	10.83777	10.10590	9.44665	8.85137	8.31256	7.82371	7.37916	6.97399
17	15.56225	14.29187	13.16612	12.16567	11.27407	10.47726	9.76322	9.12164	8.54363	8.02155	7.54879	7.11963
18	16.39827	14.99203	13.75351	12.65930	11.68959	10.82760	10.05909	9.37189	8.75563	8.20141	7.70162	7.24967
19	17.22601	15.67846	14.32380	13.13394	12.08532	11.15812	10.33560	9.60360	8.95011	8.36492	7.83929	7.36578
20	18.04555	16.35143	14.87747	13.59033	12.46221	11.46992	10.59401	9.81815	9.12855	8.51356	7.96333	7.46944
21	18.85698	17.01121	15.41502	14.02916	12.82115	11.76408	10.83553	10.01680	9.29224	8.64869	8.07507	7.56200
22	19.66038	17.65805	15.93692	14.45112	13.16300	12.04158	11.06124	10.20074	9.44243	8.77154	8.17574	7.64465
23	20.45582	18.29220	16.44361	14.85684	13.48857	12.30338	11.27219	10.37106	9.58021	8.88322	8.26643	7.71843
24	21.24339	18.91393	16.93554	15.24696	13.79864	12.55036	11.46933	10.52876	9.70661	8.98474	8.34814	7.78432
25	22.02316	19.52346	17.41315	15.62208	14.09394	12.78336	11.65358	10.67478	9.82258	9.07704	8.42174	7.84314
30	25.80771	22.39646	19.60044	17.29203	15.37245	13.76483	12.40904	11.25778	10.27365	9.42691	8.69379	8.05518
35	29.40858	24.99862	21.48722	18.66461	16.37419	14.49825	12.94767	11.65457	10.56682	9.64416	8.85524	8.17550
40	32.83469	27.35548	23.11477	19.79277	17.15909	15.04630	13.33171	11.92461	10.75736	9.77905	8.95105	8.24378

Future Value of Single Amount

$$f = (1+i)^t$$
$$p = [1 - [1/(1+i)^t]]/i$$

TABLE 3 ▪ Present Value of Ordinary Annuity

Period	0.01	0.02	0.03	0.04	0.05	0.06	0.07	0.08	0.09	0.10	0.11	0.12
1	1.01000	1.02000	1.03000	1.04000	1.05000	1.06000	1.07000	1.08000	1.09000	1.10000	1.11000	1.12000
2	1.02010	1.04040	1.06090	1.08160	1.10250	1.12360	1.14490	1.16640	1.18810	1.21000	1.23210	1.25440
3	1.03030	1.06121	1.09273	1.12486	1.15763	1.19102	1.22504	1.25971	1.29503	1.33100	1.36763	1.40493
4	1.04060	1.08243	1.12551	1.16986	1.21551	1.26248	1.31080	1.36049	1.41158	1.46410	1.51807	1.57352
5	1.05101	1.10408	1.15927	1.21665	1.27628	1.33823	1.40255	1.46933	1.53862	1.61051	1.68506	1.76234
6	1.06152	1.12616	1.19405	1.26532	1.34010	1.41852	1.50073	1.58687	1.67710	1.77156	1.87041	1.97382
7	1.07214	1.14869	1.22987	1.31593	1.40710	1.50363	1.60578	1.71382	1.82804	1.94872	2.07616	2.21068
8	1.08286	1.17166	1.26677	1.36857	1.47746	1.59385	1.71819	1.85093	1.99256	2.14359	2.30454	2.47596
9	1.09369	1.19509	1.30477	1.42331	1.55133	1.68948	1.83846	1.99900	2.17189	2.35795	2.55804	2.77308
10	1.10462	1.21899	1.34392	1.48024	1.62889	1.79085	1.96715	2.15892	2.36736	2.59374	2.83942	3.10585
11	1.11567	1.24337	1.38423	1.53945	1.71034	1.89830	2.10485	2.33164	2.58043	2.85312	3.15176	3.47855
12	1.12683	1.26824	1.42576	1.60103	1.79586	2.01220	2.25219	2.51817	2.81266	3.13843	3.49845	3.89598
13	1.13809	1.29361	1.46853	1.66507	1.88565	2.13293	2.40985	2.71962	3.06580	3.45227	3.88328	4.36349
14	1.14947	1.31948	1.51259	1.73168	1.97993	2.26090	2.57853	2.93719	3.34173	3.79750	4.31044	4.88711
15	1.16097	1.34587	1.55797	1.80094	2.07893	2.39656	2.75903	3.17217	3.64248	4.17725	4.78459	5.47357
16	1.17258	1.37279	1.60471	1.87298	2.18287	2.54035	2.95216	3.42594	3.97031	4.59497	5.31089	6.13039
17	1.18430	1.40024	1.65285	1.94790	2.29202	2.69277	3.15882	3.70002	4.32763	5.05447	5.89509	6.86604
18	1.19615	1.42825	1.70243	2.02582	2.40662	2.85434	3.37993	3.99602	4.71712	5.55992	6.54355	7.68997
19	1.20811	1.45681	1.75351	2.10685	2.52695	3.02560	3.61653	4.31570	5.14166	6.11591	7.26334	8.61276
20	1.22019	1.48595	1.80611	2.19112	2.65330	3.20714	3.86968	4.66096	5.60441	6.72750	8.06231	9.64629
21	1.23239	1.51567	1.86029	2.27877	2.78596	3.39956	4.14056	5.03383	6.10881	7.40025	8.94917	10.80385
22	1.24472	1.54598	1.91610	2.36992	2.92526	3.60354	4.43040	5.43654	6.65860	8.14027	9.93357	12.10031
23	1.25716	1.57690	1.97359	2.46472	3.07152	3.81975	4.74053	5.87146	7.25787	8.95430	11.02627	13.55235
24	1.26973	1.60844	2.03279	2.56330	3.22510	4.04893	5.07237	6.34118	7.91108	9.84973	12.23916	15.17863
25	1.28243	1.64061	2.09378	2.66584	3.38635	4.29187	5.42743	6.84848	8.62308	10.83471	13.58546	17.00006
30	1.34785	1.81136	2.42726	3.24340	4.32194	5.74349	7.61226	10.06266	13.26768	17.44940	22.89230	29.95992
35	1.41660	1.99989	2.81386	3.94609	5.51602	7.68609	10.67658	14.78534	20.41397	28.10244	38.57485	52.79962
40	1.48886	2.20804	3.26204	4.80102	7.03999	10.28572	14.97446	21.72452	31.40942	45.25926	65.00087	93.05097

TABLE 4 ▪ Future Value of an Ordinary Annuity

$$f = [(1+i)^t - 1]/i$$

Period	0.01	0.02	0.03	0.04	0.05	0.06	0.07	0.08	0.09	0.10	0.11	0.12
1	1.00000	1.00000	1.00000	1.00000	1.00000	1.00000	1.00000	1.00000	1.00000	1.00000	1.00000	1.00000
2	2.01000	2.02000	2.03000	2.04000	2.05000	2.06000	2.07000	2.08000	2.09000	2.10000	2.11000	2.12000
3	3.03010	3.06040	3.09090	3.12160	3.15250	3.18360	3.21490	3.24640	3.27810	3.31000	3.34210	3.37440
4	4.06040	4.12161	4.18363	4.24646	4.31013	4.37462	4.43994	4.50611	4.57313	4.64100	4.70973	4.77933
5	5.10101	5.20404	5.30914	5.41632	5.52563	5.63709	5.75074	5.86660	5.98471	6.10510	6.22780	6.35285
6	6.15202	6.30812	6.46841	6.63298	6.80191	6.97532	7.15329	7.33593	7.52333	7.71561	7.91286	8.11519
7	7.21354	7.43428	7.66246	7.89829	8.14201	8.39384	8.65402	8.92280	9.20043	9.48717	9.78327	10.08901
8	8.28567	8.58297	8.89234	9.21423	9.54911	9.89747	10.25980	10.63663	11.02847	11.43589	11.85943	12.29969
9	9.36853	9.75463	10.15911	10.58280	11.02656	11.49132	11.97799	12.48756	13.02104	13.57948	14.16397	14.77566
10	10.46221	10.94972	11.46388	12.00611	12.57789	13.18079	13.81645	14.48656	15.19293	15.93742	16.72201	17.54874
11	11.56683	12.16872	12.80780	13.48635	14.20679	14.97164	15.78360	16.64549	17.56029	18.53117	19.56143	20.65458
12	12.68250	13.41209	14.19203	15.02581	15.91713	16.86994	17.88845	18.97713	20.14072	21.38428	22.71319	24.13313
13	13.80933	14.68033	15.61779	16.62684	17.71298	18.88214	20.14064	21.49530	22.95338	24.52271	26.21164	28.02911
14	14.94742	15.97394	17.08632	18.29191	19.59863	21.01507	22.55049	24.21492	26.01919	27.97498	30.09492	32.39260
15	16.09690	17.29342	18.59891	20.02359	21.57856	23.27597	25.12902	27.15211	29.36092	31.77248	34.40536	37.27971
16	17.25786	18.63929	20.15688	21.82453	23.65749	25.67253	27.88805	30.32428	33.00340	35.94973	39.18995	42.75328
17	18.43044	20.01207	21.76159	23.69751	25.84037	28.21288	30.84022	33.75023	36.97370	40.54470	44.50084	48.88367
18	19.61475	21.41231	23.41444	25.64541	28.13238	30.90565	33.99903	37.45024	41.30134	45.59917	50.39594	55.74971
19	20.81090	22.84056	25.11687	27.67123	30.53900	33.75999	37.37896	41.44626	46.01846	51.15909	56.93949	63.43968
20	22.01900	24.29737	26.87037	29.77808	33.06595	36.78559	40.99549	45.76196	51.16012	57.27500	64.20283	72.05244
21	23.23919	25.78332	28.67649	31.96920	35.71925	39.99273	44.86518	50.42292	56.76453	64.00250	72.26514	81.69874
22	24.47159	27.29898	30.53678	34.24797	38.50521	43.39229	49.00574	55.45676	62.87334	71.40275	81.21431	92.50258
23	25.71630	28.84496	32.45288	36.61789	41.43048	46.99583	53.43614	60.89330	69.53194	79.54302	91.14788	104.60289
24	26.97346	30.42186	34.42647	39.08260	44.50200	50.81558	58.17667	66.76476	76.78981	88.49733	102.17415	118.15524
25	28.24320	32.03030	36.45926	41.64591	47.72710	54.86451	63.24904	73.10594	84.70090	98.34706	114.41331	133.33387
30	34.78489	40.56808	47.57542	56.08494	66.43885	79.05819	94.46079	113.28321	136.30754	164.49402	199.02088	241.33268
35	41.66028	49.99448	60.46208	73.65222	90.32031	111.43478	138.23688	172.31680	215.71075	271.02437	341.58955	431.66350
40	48.88637	60.40198	75.40126	95.02552	120.79977	154.76197	199.63511	259.05652	337.88245	442.59256	581.82607	767.09142

GLOSSARY

A

accelerated cost recovery system (ACRS, MACRS) A system of accelerated depreciation for tax purposes introduced in 1981 (ACRS) and modified starting in 1987 (MACRS); it prescribes depreciation rates by asset classification for assets acquired after 1980

accelerated depreciation method Any depreciation method under which the amounts of depreciation expense taken in the early years of an asset's life are larger than the amounts expensed in the later years; includes the double-declining balance method

access control matrix A computerized file that lists the type of access that each computer user is entitled to have to each file and program in the computer system

account A record of the additions, deductions, and balances of individual assets, liabilities, permanent owners' equity, revenues, and expenses

accounting cycle A series of basic steps followed to process accounting information during a fiscal year

accounting entity An economic unit that has identifiable boundaries and that is the focus for the accumulation and reporting of financial information

accounting equation An expression of the equivalency of the economic resources and the claims upon those resources of a specific entity; often stated as Assets = Liabilities + Owners' Equity

accounting period The time period, typically one year (or quarter), to which periodic accounting reports are related

accounting system The structured collection of people, policies, procedures, equipment, files, and records that a company uses to collect, record, classify, process, store, report, and interpret financial data

accounting The process of measuring the economic activity of an entity in money terms and communicating the results to interested parties; the purpose is to provide financial information that is useful in making economic decisions

accounts payable turnover The ratio obtained by dividing cost of goods sold by average accounts payable

accounts receivable A current asset that is created by a sale on a credit basis; it represents the amount owed the company by the customer

accounts receivable aging method A procedure that uses an aging schedule to determine the year-end balance needed in the allowance for uncollectible accounts account

accounts receivable turnover Annual net sales divided by average accounts receivable (net)

accrual accounting Accounting procedures whereby revenues are recorded when they are earned and realized and expenses are recorded in the period in which they help to generate revenues

accruals Adjustments that reflect revenues earned but not received or recorded and expenses incurred but not paid or recorded

accrued expense An expense incurred but not yet paid; recognized with an adjusting entry

accrued revenue Revenue earned but not yet billed or received; recognized with an adjusting entry

accumulated depreciation The sum of all depreciation expense recorded to date; it is subtracted from the cost of the asset in order to derive the asset's net book value

adjusted trial balance A list of general ledger accounts and their balances taken after adjustments have been made

adjusting The process of adjusting the historical financial statements prior to the projection of future results; also called *recasting* and *reformulating*

adjusting entries Entries made at the end of an accounting period under accrual accounting to ensure the proper matching of expenses incurred with revenues earned for the period

aging schedule An analysis that shows how long customers' accounts receivable balances have remained unpaid

allowance for uncollectible accounts A contra asset account with a normal credit balance shown on the balance sheet as a deduction from accounts receivable to reflect the expected realizable amount of accounts receivable

allowance method An accounting procedure whereby the amount of uncollectible accounts expense is estimated and recorded in the period in which the related credit sales occur

Altman's Z-score A predictor of potential bankruptcy based on multiple ratios

amortization The periodic writing off of an account balance to expense; similar to depreciation and usually refers to the periodic writing off of an intangible asset

annuity A pattern of cash flows in which equal amounts are spaced equally over a number of periods

articles of incorporation A document prepared by persons organizing a corporation in the United States that sets forth the structure and purpose of the corporation and specifics regarding the stock to be issued

articulation The linkage of financial statements within and across time

asset turnover Net income divided by average total assets

asset write-downs Adjustment of carrying value of assets down to their current salable value

assets The economic resources of an entity that are owned, will provide future benefits and can be reliably measured

audit An examination of a company's financial statements by a firm of independent certified public accountants

audit report A report issued by independent auditors that includes the final version of the financial statements, accompanying notes, and the auditor's opinion on the financial statements

authorized stock The maximum number of shares in a class of stock that a corporation may issue

available-for-sale securities   Investments in securities that management intends to hold for capital gains and dividend income; although it may sell them if the price is right

average cash cycle   Average collection period + modified average inventory days outstanding − modified average payable days outstanding

average collection period   Determined by dividing accounts receivable by average daily sales, sometimes referred to as days sales outstanding or DSO

average inventory days outstanding (AIDO)   An indication of how long, on average, inventories are on the shelves, computed as inventory divided by average daily cost of goods sold

B

balance sheet   A financial statement showing an entity's assets, liabilities, and owners' equity at a specific date; sometimes called a statement of financial position

bearer   One of the terms that may be used to designate the payee on a promissory note; means the note is payable to whoever holds the note

bond   A long-term debt instrument that promises to pay interest periodically and a principal amount at maturity, usually issued by the borrower to a group of lenders; bonds may incorporate a wide variety of provisions relating to security for the debt involved, methods of paying the periodic interest, retirement provisions, and conversion options

book value per share   The dollar amount of net assets represented by one share of stock; computed by dividing the amount of stockholders' equity associated with a class of stock by the outstanding shares of that class of stock

book value   The dollar amount carried in the accounts for a particular item; the book value of a depreciable asset is derived by deducting the contra account accumulated depreciation from the cost of the depreciable asset

borrows at a discount   When the face amount of the note is reduced by a calculated cash discount to determine the cash proceeds

C

calendar year   A fiscal year that ends on December 31

call provision   A bond feature that allows the borrower to retire (call in) the bonds after a stated date

capital expenditures   Expenditures that increase the book value of long-term assets; sometimes abbreviated as *CAPEX*

capital lease   A lease that transfers to the lessee substantially all of the benefits and risks related to ownership of the property; the lessee records the leased property as an asset and establishes a liability for the lease obligation

capital markets   Financing sources, which are formalized when companies issue securities that are traded on organized exchanges; they are informal when companies are funded by private sources

capitalization   The recording of a cost as an asset on the balance sheet rather than as an expense on the income statement; these costs are transferred to expense as the asset is used up

capitalization of interest   A process that adds interest to an asset's initial cost if a period of time is required to prepare the asset for use

cash   An asset category representing the amount of a firm's available cash and funds on deposit at a bank in checking accounts and savings accounts

cash and cash equivalents   The sum of cash plus short-term, highly liquid investments such as treasury bills and money market funds; includes marketable securities maturing within 90 days of the financial statement date

cash discount   An amount that a purchaser of merchandise may deduct from the purchase price for paying within the discount period

cash-basis accounting   Accounting procedures whereby revenues are recorded when cash is received from operating activities and expenses are recorded when cash payments related to operating activities are made

cash (operating) cycle   The period of time from when cash is invested in inventories until inventory is sold and receivables are collected

certificate of deposit (CD)   An investment security available at financial institutions generally offering a fixed rate of return for a specified period of time

change in accounting estimate   Modification to a previous estimate of an uncertain future event, such as the useful life of a depreciable asset, uncollectible accounts receivable, and warranty expenses; applied currently and prospectively only

changes in accounting principles   Cumulative income or loss from changes in accounting methods (such as depreciation or inventory costing methods)

chart of accounts   A list of all the general ledger account titles and their numerical code

clean surplus accounting   Income that explains successive equity balances

closing procedures   A step in the accounting cycle in which the balances of all temporary accounts are transferred to the retained earnings account, leaving the temporary accounts with zero balances

commitments   A contractual arrangement by which both parties to the contract still have acts to perform

common stock   The basic ownership class of corporate capital stock, carrying the rights to vote, share in earnings, participate in future stock issues, and share in any liquidation proceeds after prior claims have been settled

common-size financial statement   A financial statement in which each item is presented as a percentage of a key figure such as sales or total assets

comparative financial statements   A form of horizontal analysis involving comparison of two or more periods' financial statements showing dollar and/or percentage changes

compensating balance   A minimum amount that a financial institution requires a firm to maintain in its account as part of a borrowing arrangement complex capital structure

comprehensive income   The total income reported by the company, including net profit and all other changes to stockholders' equity other than those arising from capital (stock) transactions; typical components of other comprehensive income (OCI) are unrealized gains (losses) on available-for-sale securities and derivatives, minimum pension liability adjustment, and foreign currency translation adjustments

conceptual framework A cohesive set of interrelated objectives and fundamentals for external financial reporting developed by the FASB

conservatism An accounting principle stating that judgmental determinations should tend toward understatement rather than overstatement of net assets and income

consistency An accounting principle stating that, unless otherwise disclosed, accounting reports should be prepared on a basis consistent with the preceding period

consolidated financial statements Financial statements reflecting a parent company and one or more subsidiary companies and/or a variable interest entity (VIE) and its primary beneficiary

contingency A possible future event; significant contingent liabilities must be disclosed in the notes to the financial statements

contingent liabilities A potential obligation, the eventual occurrence of which usually depends on some future event beyond the control of the firm; contingent liabilities may originate with such events as lawsuits, credit guarantees, and environmental damages

contra account An account related to, and deducted from, another account when financial statements are prepared or when book values are computed

contract rate The rate of interest stated on a bond certificate

contributed capital The net funding that a company receives from issuing and acquiring its equity shares

convertible bond A bond incorporating the holder's right to convert the bond to capital stock under prescribed terms

convertible securities Debt and equity securities that provide the holder with an option to convert those securities into other securities

copyright An exclusive right that protects an owner against the unauthorized reproduction of a specific written work or artwork

core income A company's income from its usual business activities that is expected to continue (persist) into the future

corporation A legal entity created by the granting of a charter from an appropriate governmental authority and owned by stockholders who have limited liability for corporate debt

cost of goods sold percentage The ratio of cost of goods sold divided by net sales

cost of goods sold The total cost of merchandise sold to customers during the accounting period

cost method An investment is reported at its historical cost, and any cash dividends and interest received are recognized in current income

cost principle An accounting principle stating that asset measures are based on the prices paid to acquire the assets

coupon bond A bond with coupons for interest payable to bearer attached to the bond for each interest period; whenever interest is due, the bondholder detaches a coupon and deposits it with his or her bank for collection

coupon (contract or stated) rate The coupon rate of interest is stated in the bond contract; it is used to compute the dollar amount of (semiannual) interest payments that are paid to bondholder during the life of the bond issue

covenants Contractual requirements put into loan or bond agreements by lenders

credit (entry) An entry on the right side (or in the credit column) of any account

credit card fee A fee charged retailers for credit card services provided by financial institutions; the fee is usually stated as a percentage of credit card sales

credit guarantee A guarantee of another company's debt by cosigning a note payable; a guarantor's contingent liability that is usually disclosed in a balance sheet footnote

credit memo A document prepared by a seller to inform the purchaser that the seller has reduced the amount owed by the purchaser due to a return or an allowance

credit period The maximum amount of time, usually stated in days, that the purchaser of merchandise has to pay the seller

credit terms The prescribed payment period for purchases on credit with discount specified for early payment

cumulative (preferred stock) A feature associated with preferred stock whereby any dividends in arrears must be paid before dividends may be paid on common stock

cumulative effect of a change in principle The cumulative effect on net income to the date of a change in accounting principle

cumulative translation adjustment The amount recorded in the equity section as necessary to balance the accounting equation when assets and liabilities of foreign subsidiaries are translated into $US at the rate of exchange prevailing at the statement date

current assets Cash and other assets that will be converted to cash or used up during the normal operating cycle of the business or one year, whichever is longer

current liabilities Obligations that will require within the coming year or operating cycle, whichever is longer, (1) the use of existing current assets or (2) the creation of other current liabilities

current rate method Method of translating foreign currency transactions under which balance sheet amounts are translated using exchange rates in effect at the period-end consolidation date and income statement amounts using the average exchange rate for the period

current ratio A firm's current assets divided by its current liabilities

D

days' sales in inventory Inventories divided by average cost of goods sold

debenture bond A bond that has no specific property pledged as security for the repayment of funds borrowed

debit (entry) An entry on the left side (or in the debit column) of any account

debt-to-equity ratio A firm's total liabilities divided by its total owners' equity

declining-balance method An accelerated depreciation method that allocates depreciation expense to each year by applying a constant percentage to the declining book value of the asset

default   The nonpayment of interest and principal and/or the failure to adhere to the various terms and conditions of the bond indenture

deferrals   Adjustments that allocate various assets and revenues received in advance to the proper accounting periods as expenses and revenues

deferred revenue   A liability representing revenues received in advance; also called *unearned revenue*

deferred tax liability   A liability representing the estimated future income taxes payable resulting from an existing temporary difference between an asset's book value and its tax basis

deferred tax valuation allowance   Reduction in a reported deferred tax asset to adjust for the amount that is not likely to be realized

defined benefit plan   A type of retirement plan under which the company promises to make periodic payments to the employee after retirement

defined contribution plan   A retirement plan under which the company makes cash contribution into an employee's account (usually with a third-party trustee like a bank) either solely or as a matching contribution

depletion   The allocation of the cost of natural resources to the units extracted and sold or, in the case of timberland, the board feet of timber cut

depreciation   The decline in economic potential (using up) of plant assets originating from wear, deterioration, and obsolescence

depreciation accounting   The process of allocating the cost of equipment, vehicles, and buildings (not land) to expense over the time period benefiting from their use

depreciation base   The acquisition cost of an asset less estimated salvage value

depreciation rate   An estimate of how the asset will be used up over its useful life—evenly over its useful life, more heavily in the early years, or in proportion to its actual usage

derivatives   Financial instruments such as futures, options, and swaps that are commonly used to hedge (mitigate) some external risk, such as commodity price risk, interest rate risk, or risks relating to foreign currency fluctuations

diluted earnings per share   The earnings per share computation taking into consideration the effects of dilutive securities

dilutive securities   Securities that can be exchanged for shares of common stock and, thereby, increase the number of common shares outstanding

discontinued operations   Net income or loss from business segments that are up for sale or have been sold in the current period

discount bond   A bond that is sold for less than its par (face) value

discount on notes payable   A contra account that is subtracted from the Notes Payable amount on the balance sheet; as the life of the note elapses, the discount is reduced and charged to interest expense

discount period   The maximum amount of time, usually stated in days, that the purchaser of merchandise has to pay the seller if the purchaser wants to claim the cash discount

discounting   The exchanging of notes receivable for cash at a financial institution at an amount that is less than the face value of the notes

discounted cash flow (DCF) model   The value of a security is equal to the present value of the expected free cash flows to the firm, discounted at the weighted average cost of capital (WACC)

dividends account   A temporary equity account used to accumulate owner dividends from the business

dividend discount model   The value of a security today is equal to the present value of that security's expected dividends, discounted at the weighted average cost of capital

dividend payout ratio   Annual dividends per share divided by the earnings per share

dividend yield   Annual dividends per share divided by the market price per share

double-entry accounting system   A method of accounting that recognizes the duality of a transaction such that the analysis results in a recording of equal amounts of debits and credits

E

earned   When referring to revenue, the seller's execution of its duties under the terms of the agreement, with the resultant passing of title to the buyer with no right of return or other contingencies

earned capital   The cumulative net income (losses) retained by the company (not paid out to shareholders as dividends)

earnings per share (EPS)   Net income less preferred stock dividends divided by the weighted average common shares outstanding for the period

earnings quality   The degree to which reported earnings represent how well the firm has performed from an economic standpoint

earnings smoothing   Earnings management with a goal to provide an earnings stream with less variability

economic profit   The number of inventory units sold multiplied by the difference between the sales price and the replacement cost of the inventories (approximated by the cost of the most recently purchased inventories)

economic value added (EVA)   Net operating profits after tax less a charge for the use of capital equal to beginning capital utilized in the business multiplied by the weighted average cost of capital (EVA = NOPAT − r_w × Net Operating Assets)

effective interest method   A method of amortizing bond premium or discount that results in a constant rate of interest each period and varying amounts of premium or discount amortized each period

effective interest rate   The rate determined by dividing the total discount amount by the cash proceeds on a note payable when the borrower borrowed at a discount

effective rate   The current rate of interest in the market for a bond or other debt instrument; when issued, a bond is priced to yield the market (effective) rate of interest at the date of issuance

efficient markets hypothesis   Capital markets are said to be efficient if at any given time, current equity (stock) prices reflect all relevant information that determines those equity prices

employee severance costs   Accrued (estimated) costs for termination of employees as part of a restructuring program

employee stock options   A form of compensation that grants a select group of employees the right to purchase a fixed number of company shares at a fixed price for a predetermined time period

equity carve out   A corporate divestiture of operating units

equity method   The prescribed method of accounting for investments in which the investor company has a significant influence over the investee company (usually taken to be ownership between 20-50% of the outstanding common stock of the investee company)

ethics   An area of inquiry dealing with the values, rules, and justifications that governs one's way of life

expenses   Decreases in owners' equity incurred by a firm in the process of earning revenues

extraordinary items   Revenues and expenses that are both *unusual* and *infrequent* and are, therefore, excluded from income from continuing operations

F

face amount   The principal amount of a bond or note to be repaid at maturity

factoring   Selling an account receivable to another company, typically a finance company or a financial institution, for less than its face value

financial accounting   The area of accounting activities dealing with the preparation of financial statements showing an entity's results of operations, financial position, and cash flows

Financial Accounting Standards Board (FASB)   The organization currently responsible for setting accounting standards for reporting financial information

financial assets   Normally consist of excess resources held for future expansion or unexpected needs; they are usually invested in the form of other companies' stock, corporate or government bonds, and real estate

financial leverage   The proportionate use of borrowed funds in the capital structure, computed as net financial obligations (NFO) divided by average equity

financial reporting objectives   A component of the conceptual framework that specifies that financial statements should provide information (1) useful for investment and credit decisions, (2) helpful in assessing an entity's ability to generate future cash flows, and (3) about an entity's resources, claims to those resources, and the effects of events causing changes in these items

financial statement elements   A part of the conceptual framework that identifies the significant components—such as assets, liabilities, owners' equity, revenues, and expenses—used to put financial statements together

financing activities   Methods that companies use to raise the funds to pay for resources such as land, buildings, and equipment

finished goods inventory   The dollar amount of inventory that has completed the production process and is awaiting sale

first-in, first-out (FIFO) method   One of the prescribed methods of inventory costing; FIFO assumes that the first costs incurred for the purchase or production of inventory are the first costs relieved from inventory when goods are sold

fiscal year   The annual accounting period used by a business firm

five forces of competitive intensity   Industry competition, bargaining power of buyers, bargaining power of suppliers, threat of substitution, threat of entry

fixed assets   An alternate label for long-term assets; may also be called property, plant, and equipment (PPE)

fixed costs   Costs that do not change with changes in sales volume (over a reasonable range)

forecast   The projection of financial results over the forecast horizon and terminal periods

foreign currency transaction   The $US equivalent of an asset or liability denominated in a foreign currency

foreign exchange gain or loss   The gain (loss) recognized in the income statement relating to the change in the $US equivalent of an asset or liability denominated in a foreign currency

franchise   Generally, an exclusive right to operate or sell a specific brand of products in a given geographic area

free cash flow   This excess cash flow (above that required to manage its growth and development) from which dividends can be paid; computed as NOPAT − Increase in NOA

full disclosure principle   An accounting principle stipulating the disclosure of all facts necessary to make financial statements useful to readers

fully diluted earnings per share   *See* diluted earnings per share

functional currency   The currency representing the primary currency in which a business unit conducts its operations

fundamental analysis   Uses financial information to predict future valuation and, hence, buy-sell stock strategies

funded status   The difference between the pension obligation and the fair market value of the pension investments

future value   The amount a specified investment (or series of investments) will be worth at a future date if invested at a given rate of compound interest

G

general journal   A journal with enough flexibility so that any type of business transaction can be recorded in it

general ledger   A grouping of all of an entity's accounts that are used to prepare the basic financial statements

generally accepted accounting principles (GAAP)   A set of standards and procedures that guide the preparation of financial statements

going concern concept   An accounting principle that assumes that, in the absence of evidence to the contrary, a business entity will have an indefinite life

goodwill   The value that derives from a firm's ability to earn more than a normal rate of return on the fair market value of its specific, identifiable net assets; computed as the residual of the purchase price less the fair market value of the net tangible and intangible assets acquired

gross margin   The difference between net sales and cost of goods sold: also called *gross profit*

gross profit on sales   The difference between net sales and cost of goods sold; also called *gross margin*

gross profit margin (GPM) (percentage)   The ratio of gross profit on sales divided by net sales

H

held-to-maturity securities The designation given to a portfolio of bond investments that are expected to be held until they mature

historical cost Original acquisition or issuance costs

holding company The parent company of a subsidiary

holding gain The increase in replacement cost since the inventories were acquired, which equals the number of units sold multiplied by the difference between the current replacement cost and the original acquisition cost

horizon period The forecast period for which detailed estimates are made, typically 5–10 years

horizontal analysis Analysis of a firm's financial statements that covers two or more years

I

impairment A reduction in value from that presently recorded

impairment loss A loss recognized on an impaired asset equal to the difference between its book value and current fair value

income statement A financial statement reporting an entity's revenues and expenses for a period of time

indirect method A presentation format for the statement of cash flows that refers to the operating section only; that section begins with net income and converts it to cash flows from operations

intangible assets A term applied to a group of long-term assets, including patents, copyrights, franchises, trademarks, and goodwill, that benefit an entity but do not have physical substance

interest cost (pensions) The increase in the pension obligation due to the accrual of an additional year of interest

internal auditing A company function that provides independent appraisals of the company's financial statements, its internal controls, and its operations

internal controls The measures undertaken by a company to ensure the reliability of its accounting data, protect its assets from theft or unauthorized use, make sure that employees are following the company's policies and procedures, and evaluate the performance of employees, departments, divisions, and the company as a whole

inventory carrying costs Costs of holding inventories, including warehousing, logistics, insurance, financing, and the risk of loss due to theft, damage, or technological or fashion change

inventory shrinkage The cost associated with an inventory shortage; the amount by which the perpetual inventory exceeds the physical inventory

inventory turnover Cost of goods sold divided by average inventory

investing activities The acquiring and disposing of resources (assets) that a company uses to acquire and sell its products and services

investing creditors Those who primarily finance investing activities

investment returns The increase in pension investments resulting from interest, dividends, and capital gains on the investment portfolio

invoice A document that the seller sends to the purchaser to request payment for items that the seller shipped to the purchaser

invoice price The price that a seller charges the purchaser for merchandise

IOU A slang term for a receivable

issued stock Shares of stock that have been sold and issued to stockholders; issued stock may be either outstanding or in the treasury

J

journal A tabular record in which business transactions are analyzed in debit and credit terms and recorded in chronological order

just-in-time (JIT) inventory philosophy Receive inventory from suppliers into the production process just at the point it is needed

L

land improvements Improvements with limited lives made to land sites, such as paved parking lots and driveways

last-in, first-out (LIFO) method One of the prescribed methods of inventory costing; LIFO assumes that the last costs incurred for the purchase or production of inventory are the first costs relieved form inventory when goods are sold

lease A contract between a lessor (owner) and lessee (tenant) for the rental of property

leasehold improvements Expenditures made by a lessee to alter or improve leased property

leasehold The rights transferred from the lessor to the lessee by a lease

lessee The party acquiring the right to the use of property by a lease

lessor The owner of property who transfers the right to use the property to another party by a lease

leveraging The use of borrowed funds in the capital structure of a firm; the expectation is that the funds will earn a return higher than the rate of interest on the borrowed funds

liabilities The obligations, or debts, that an entity must pay in money or services at some time in the future because of past transactions or events

LIFO conformity rule IRS requirement to cost inventories using LIFO for tax purposes if they are costed using LIFO for financial reporting purposes

LIFO liquidation The reduction in inventory quantities when LIFO costing is used; LIFO liquidation yields an increase in gross profit and income when prices are rising

LIFO reserve The difference between the cost of inventories using FIFO and the cost using LIFO

liquidation value per share The amount that would be received by a holder of a share of stock if the corporation liquidated

liquidity How much cash the company has, how much is expected, and how much can be raised on short notice

list price The suggested price or reference price of merchandise in a catalog or price list

long-term liabilities Debt obligations not due to be settled within the normal operating cycle or one year, whichever is longer

lower of cost or market (LCM)   GAAP requirement to write down the carrying amount of inventories on the balance sheet *if* the reported cost (using FIFO, for example) exceeds market value (determined by current replacement cost)

M

maker   The signer of a promissory note

management discussion and anaysis (MD&A)   The section of the 10-K report in which a company provides a detailed discussion of its business activities

managerial accounting   The accounting activities carried out by a firm's accounting staff primarily to furnish management with accounting data for decisions related to the firm's operations

manufacturers   Companies that convert raw materials and components into finished products through the application of skilled labor and machine operations

manufacturing costs   The costs of direct materials, direct labor, and manufacturing overhead incurred in the manufacture of a product

market method accounting   Securities are reported at current market values (marked-to-market) on the statement date

market (yield) rate   This is the interest rate that investors expect to earn on the investment in this debt security; this rate is used to price the bond issue

market value   The published price (as listed on a stock exchange) multiplied by the number of shares owned

market value per share   The current price at which shares of stock may be bought or sold

matching principle   An accounting guideline that states that income is determined by relating expenses, to the extent feasible, with revenues that have been recorded

materiality   An accounting guideline that states that transactions so insignificant that they would not affect a user's actions or perception of the company may be recorded in the most expedient manner

materials inventory   The physical component of inventory; the other components of manufactured inventory are labor costs and overhead costs

maturity date   The date on which a note or bond matures

measuring unit concept   An accounting guideline noting that the accounting unit of measure is the basic unit of money

merchandise inventory   A stock of products that a company buys from another company and makes available for sale to its customers

merchandising firm   A company that buys finished products, stores the products for varying periods of time, and then resells the products

method of comparables model   Equity valuation or stock values are predicted using price multiples, which are defined as stock price divided by some key financial statement number such as net income, net sales, book value of equity, total assets, or cash flow; companies are then compared with their competitors

minority interest   The equity claim of a shareholder owning less than a majority or controlling interest in the company

modified accelerated cost recovery system (MACRS)   See accelerated cost recovery system

N

natural resources   Assets occurring in a natural state, such as timber, petroleum, natural gas, coal, and other mineral deposits

net assets   The difference between an entity's assets and liabilities; net assets are equal to owners' equity

net asset based valuation model   Equity is valued as reported assets less reported liabilities

net book value (NBV)   The cost of the asset less accumulated depreciation; also called *carrying value*

net financial obligations (NFO)   net total of all financial (nonoperating) obligations less financial (nonoperating) assets

net income   The excess of a firm's revenues over its expenses

net loss   The excess of a firm's expenses over its revenues

net operating assets (NOA)   Current and long-term operating assets less current and long-term operating liabilities; or net operating working capital plus long-term net operating assets

net operating profit after tax (NOPAT)   Sales less operating expenses (including taxes)

net realizable value   The value at which an asset can be sold, net of any costs of disposition

net sales   The total revenue generated by a company through merchandise sales less the revenue given up through sales returns and allowances and sales discounts

net working capital   Current assets less current liabilities

nominal rate   The rate of interest stated on a bond certificate or other debt instrument

noncash investing and financing activities   Significant business activities during the period that do not impact cash inflows or cash outflows

noncurrent liabilities   Obligations not due to be paid within one year or the operating cycle, whichever is longer

nonoperating expenses   Expenses that relate to the company's financing activities and include interest income and interest expense, gains and losses on sales of securities, and income or loss on discontinued operations

no-par stock   Stock that does not have a par value

NOPAT   Net operating profit after tax

normal operating cycle   For a particular business, the average period of time between the use of cash in its typical operating activity and the subsequent collection of cash from customers

note receivable   A promissory note held by the note's payee

notes to financial statements   Footnotes in which companies discuss their accounting policies and estimates used in preparing the statements

not-sufficient-funds check   A check from an individual or company that had an insufficient cash balance in the bank when the holder of the check presented it to the bank for payment

O

objectivity principle   An accounting principle requiring that, whenever possible, accounting entries are based on objectively determined evidence

off-balance-sheet financing   The structuring of a financing arrangement so that no liability shows on the borrower's balance sheet

operating activities   Using resources to research, develop, produce, purchase, market, and distribute company products and services

operating asset turnover   The ratio obtained by dividing sales by average net operating assets

operating cash flow to capital expenditures ratio   A firm's net cash flow from operating activities divided by its annual capital expenditures

operating cash flow to current liabilities ratio   A firm's net cash flow from operating activities divided by its average current liabilities

operating creditors   Those who primarily finance operating activities

operating cycle   The time between paying cash for goods or employee services and receiving cash from customers

operating expense margin (OEM)   The ratio obtained by dividing any operating expense category by sales

operating expenses   The usual and customary costs that a company incurs to support its main business activities; these include cost of goods sold, selling expenses, depreciation expense, amortization expense, research and development expense, and taxes on operating profits

operating lease   A lease by which the lessor retains the usual risks and rewards of owning the property

operating profit margin   The ratio obtained by dividing NOPAT by sales

operational audit   An evaluation of activities, systems, and internal controls within a company to determine their efficiency, effectiveness, and economy

organization costs   Expenditures incurred in launching a business (usually a corporation), including attorney's fees and various fees paid to the state

outstanding checks   Checks issued by a firm that have not yet been presented to its bank for payment

outstanding stock   Shares of stock that are currently owned by stockholders (excludes treasury stock)

owners' equity   The interest of owners in the assets of an entity; equal to the difference between the entity's assets and liabilities

P

packing list   A document that lists the items of merchandise contained in a carton and the quantity of each item; the packing list is usually attached to the outside of the carton

paid-in capital   The amount of capital contributed to a corporation by various transactions; the primary source of paid-in capital is from the issuance of shares of stock

par (bonds)   Face value of the bond

par value (stock)   An amount specified in the corporate charter for each share of stock and imprinted on the face of each stock certificate, often determines the legal capital of the corporation

parent company   A company owning one or more subsidiary companies

parsimonious method to multiyear forecasting   Forecasting multiple years using only sales growth, net operating profit margin (NOPM), and the turnover of net operating assets (NOAT)

partnership   A voluntary association of two or more persons for the purpose of conducting a business

password   A string of characters that a computer user enters into a computer terminal to prove to the computer that the person using the computer is truly the person named in the user identification code

patent   An exclusive privilege granted for 20 years to an inventor that gives the patent holder the right to exclude others from making, using, or selling the invention

payee   The company or individual to whom a promissory note is made payable

payment approval form   A document that authorizes the payment of an invoice

pension plan   A plan to pay benefits to employees after they retire from the company; the plan may be a defined contribution plan or a defined benefit plan

percentage-of-completion method   Recognition of revenue by determining the costs incurred per the contract as compared to its total expected costs

percentage of net sales method   A procedure that determines the uncollectible accounts expense for the year by multiplying net credit sales by the estimated uncollectible percentage

period statement   A financial statement accumulating information for a specific period of time; examples are the income statement, the statement of owners' equity, and the statement of cash flows

permanent account   An account used to prepare the balance sheet; that is, asset, liability, and equity capital (capital stock and retained earnings) accounts; any balance in a permanent account at the end of an accounting period is carried forward to the next period

physical inventory   A year-end procedure that involves counting the quantity of each inventory item, determining the unit cost of each item, multiplying the unit cost times quantity, and summing the costs of all the items to determine the total inventory at cost

plant assets   Land, buildings, equipment, vehicles, furniture, and fixtures that a firm uses in its operations; sometimes referred to by the acronym PPE

pooling of interests method   A method of accounting for business combinations under which the acquired company is recorded on the acquirer's balance sheet at its book value, rather than market value; this method is no longer acceptable under GAAP for acquisitions occurring after 2001

position statement   A financial statement, such as the balance sheet, that presents information as of a particular date

post-closing trial balance   A list of general ledger accounts and their balances after closing entries have been recorded and posted

postdated check   A check from another person or company with a date that is later than the current date; a postdated check does not become cash until the date of the check

preemptive right   The right of a stockholder to maintain his or her proportionate interest in a corporation by having the right to purchase an appropriate share of any new stock issue

preferred stock   A class of corporate capital stock typically receiving priority over common stock in dividend payments and distribution of assets should the corporation be liquidated

premium bond　A bond that is sold for more than its par (face) value

present value　The current worth of amounts to be paid (or received) in the future; computed by discounting the future payments (or receipts) at a specified interest rate

price-earnings ratio　Current market price per common share divided by earnings per share

pro forma income　A computation of income that begins with the GAAP income from continuing operations (that excludes discontinued operations, extraordinary items and changes in accounting principle), but then excludes other transitory items (most notably, restructuring charges), and some additional items such as expenses arising from acquisitions (goodwill amortization and other acquisition costs), compensation expense in the form of stock options, and research and development expenditures; pro forma income is not GAAP

promissory note　A written promise to pay a certain sum of money on demand or at a determinable future time

purchase method　The prescribed method of accounting for business combinations; under the purchase method, assets and liabilities of the acquired company are recorded at fair market value, together with identifiable intangible assets; the balance is ascribed to goodwill

purchase order　A document that formally requests a supplier to sell and deliver specific quantities of particular items of merchandise at specified prices

purchase requisition　An internal document that requests that the purchasing department order particular items of merchandise

Q

qualitative characteristics of accounting information　The characteristics of accounting information that contribute to decision usefulness; the primary qualities are relevance and reliability

quarterly data　Selected quarterly financial information that is reported in annual reports to stockholders

quick ratio　Quick assets (that is, cash and cash equivalents, short-term investments, and current receivables) divided by current liabilities

R

realized (or realizable)　When referring to revenue, the receipt of an asset or satisfaction of a liability as a result of a transaction or event

recognition criteria　The criteria that must be met before a financial statement element may be recorded in the accounts; essentially, the item must meet the definition of an element and must be measurable

registered bond　A bond for which the issuer (or the trustee) maintains a record of owners and, at the appropriate times, mails out interest payments

relevance　A qualitative characteristic of accounting information; relevant information contributes to the predictive and evaluative decisions made by financial statement users

reliability　A qualitative characteristic of accounting information; reliable information contains no bias or error and faithfully portrays what it intends to represent

remeasurement　The computation of gain or loss in the translation of subsidiaries denominated in a foreign currency into $US when the temporal method is used

residual operating income　Net operating profits after tax (NOPAT) less the product of net operating assets (NOA) at the beginning of the period multiplied by the weighted average cost of capital (WACC)

residual net operating income (ROPI) model　An equity valuation approach that equates the firm's value to the sum of its net operating assets (NOA) and the present value of its residual operating income (ROPI)

retailers　Companies that buy products from wholesale distributors and sell the products to individual customers, the general public

retained earnings　Earned capital, the cumulative net income and loss, of the company (from its inception) that has not been paid to shareholders as dividends

retained earnings reconciliation　The reconciliation of retained earnings from the beginning to the end of the year; the change in retained earnings includes, at a minimum, the net income (loss) for the period and dividends paid, if any, but may include other components as well; also called *statement of retained earnings*

return　The amount earned on an investment; also called *yield*

return on assets　A financial ratio computed as net income divided by average total assets; sometimes referred to by the acronym ROA

return on common stockholders' equity　A financial ratio computed as net income less preferred stock dividends divided by average common stockholders' equity; sometimes referred to by the acronym ROCE

return on equity　The ultimate measure of performance from the shareholders' perspective; computed as net income divided by average equity; sometimes referred to by the acronym ROE

return on investment　The ratio obtained by dividing income by average investment; sometimes referred to by the acronym ROI

return on net operating assets (RNOA)　The ratio obtained by dividing NOPAT by average net operating assets

return on sales　The ratio obtained by dividing net income by net sales; sometimes referred to by the acronym ROS

revenue recognition principle　An accounting principle requiring that revenue be recognized when earned and realized (or realizable)

revenues　Increases in owners' equity a firm earns by providing goods or services for its customers

S

sale on account　A sale of merchandise made on a credit basis

salvage value　The expected net recovery when a plant asset is sold or removed from service; also called *residual value*

secured bond　A bond that pledges specific property as security for meeting the terms of the bond agreement

Securities and Exchange Commission (SEC)　The commission, created by the 1934 Securities Act, that has broad powers to regulate the issuance and trading of securities, and the financial reporting of companies issuing securities to the public

segments   Subdivisions of a firm for which supplemental financial information is disclosed

serial bond   A bond issue that staggers the bond maturity dates over a series of years

service cost (pensions)   The increase in the pension obligation due to employees working another year for the employer

significant influence   The ability of the investor to affect the financing or operating policies of the investee

sinking fund provision   A bond feature that requires the borrower to retire a portion of the bonds each year or, in some cases, to make payments each year to a trustee who is responsible for managing the resources needed to retire the bonds at maturity

solvency   The ability to meet obligations, especially to creditors

source document   Any written document or computer record evidencing an accounting transaction, such as a bank check or deposit slip, sales invoice, or cash register tape

special purpose entity   (*See* variable interest entity)

spin-off   A form of equity carve out in which divestiture is accomplished by distribution of a company's shares in a subsidiary to the company's shareholders who then own the shares in the subsidiary directly rather than through the parent company

split-off   A form of equity carve out in which divestiture is accomplished by the parent company's exchange of stock in the subsidiary in return for shares in the parent owned by its shareholders

spread   The difference between the net financial return (NFR) and the return on net operating activities (RNOA)

stated value   A nominal amount that may be assigned to each share of no-par stock and accounted for much as if it were a par value

statement of cash flows   A financial statement showing a firm's cash inflows and outflows for a specific period, classified into operating, investing, and financing categories

statement of equity   See statement of stockholders' equity

statement of financial position   A financial statement showing a firm's assets, liabilities, and owners' equity at a specific date; also called a balance sheet

statement of owners' equity   A financial statement presenting information on the events causing a change in owners' equity during a period; the statement presents the beginning balance, additions to, deductions from, and the ending balance of owners' equity for the period

statement of retained earnings   See retained earnings reconciliation

statement of stockholders' equity   The financial statement that reconciles all of the components of stockholders' equity

stock dividends   The payment of dividends in shares of stock

stock split   Additional shares of its own stock issued by a corporation to its current stockholders in proportion to their current ownership interests without changing the balances in the related stockholders' equity accounts; a formal stock split increases the number of shares outstanding and reduces proportionately the stock's per share par value

straight-line depreciation   A depreciation procedure that allocates uniform amounts of depreciation expense to each full period of a depreciable asset's useful life

subsequent events   Events occurring shortly after a fiscal year-end that will be reported as supplemental information to the financial statements of the year just ended

subsidiaries   Companies that are owned by the parent company

subsidiary ledger   A set of accounts or records that contains detailed information about the items included in the balance of one general ledger account

summary of significant accounting policies   A financial statement disclosure, usually the initial note to the statements, which identifies the major accounting policies and procedures used by the firm

sum-of-the-years'-digits method   An accelerated depreciation method that allocates depreciation expense to each year in a fractional proportion, the denominator of which is the sum of the years' digits in the useful life of the asset and the numerator of which is the remaining useful life of the asset at the beginning of the current depreciation period

T

T account   An abbreviated form of the formal account in the shape of a T; use is usually limited to illustrations of accounting techniques and analysis

temporary account   An account used to gather information for an accounting period; at the end of the period, the balance is transferred to a permanent owners' equity account; revenue, expense, and dividends accounts are temporary accounts

term loan   A long-term borrowing, evidenced by a note payable, which is contracted with a single lender

terminal period   The forecast period following the horizon period

times interest earned ratio   Income before interest expense and income taxes divided by interest expense

total compensation cost   The sum of gross pay, payroll taxes, and fringe benefits paid by the employer

trade credit   Inventories purchased on credit from other companies

trade discount   An amount, usually based on quantity of merchandise purchased, that the seller subtracts from the list price of merchandise to determine the invoice price

trade name   An exclusive and continuing right to use a certain term or name to identify a brand or family of products

trademark   An exclusive and continuing right to use a certain symbol to identify a brand or family of products

trading on the equity   The use of borrowed funds in the capital structure of a firm; the expectation is that the funds will earn a return higher than the rate of interest on the borrowed funds

trading securities   Investments in securities that management intends to actively trade (buy and sell) for trading profits as market prices fluctuate

transitory items   Transactions or events that are not likely to recur

translation adjustment   The change in the value of the net assets of a subsidiary whose assets and liabilities are denominated in a foreign currency

treasury stock   Shares of outstanding stock that have been acquired (and not retired) by the issuing corporation; treasury stock is recorded at cost and deducted from stockholders' equity in the balance sheet

trend percentages A comparison of the same financial item over two or more years stated as a percentage of a base-year amount

trial balance A list of the account titles in the general ledger, their respective debit or credit balances, and the totals of the debit and credit amounts

U

unadjusted trial balance A list of general ledger accounts and their balances taken before adjustments have been made

uncollectible accounts expense The expense stemming from the inability of a business to collect an amount previously recorded as a receivable; sometimes called *bad debts expense*; normally classified as a selling or administrative expense

unearned revenue A liability representing revenues received in advance; also called *deferred revenue*

units-of-production method A depreciation method that allocates depreciation expense to each operating period in proportion to the amount of the asset's expected total production capacity used each period

useful life The period of time an asset is used by an entity in its operating activities, running from date of acquisition to date of disposal (or removal from service)

V

variable costs Those costs that change in proportion to changes in sales volume

variable interest entity (VIE) Any form of business organization (such as corporation, partnership, trust) that is established by a sponsoring company and provides benefits to that company in the form of asset securitization or project financing; VIEs were formerly known as special purpose entities (SPEs)

vertical analysis Analysis of a firm's financial statements that focuses on the statements of a single year

voucher Another name for the payment approval form

W

warranties Guarantees against product defects for a designated period of time after sale

wasting assets Another name for natural resources; see natural resources

weighted average cost of capital (WACC) The discount rate where the weights are the relative percentages of debt and equity in the capital structure and are applied to the expected returns on debt and equity respectively

work in process inventory The cost of inventories that are in the manufacturing process and have not yet reached completion

working capital The difference between current assets and current liabilities

Z

z-score The outcome of the Altman Z-score bankruptcy prediction model

zero coupon bond A bond that offers no periodic interest payments but that is issued at a substantial discount from its face value

SUBJECT INDEX

COMPANY INDEX

VIGNETTE CITATIONS AND REFERENCES

Module 1

Berkshire Hathaway 2004, 2003, and 2002 Annual Reports and 10-K Reports

Module 2

The Walt Disney Company 2004 and 2001 Annual Reports and 10-K Reports

Mark Albright, "Mutiny at the Mouse," *St. Petersburg Times,* March 1, 2004

Laura M. Holson, "Disney Performance to Get Tough Scrutiny Quarterly Results under A Microscope," *The New York Times,* March 26, 2004

Frank Ahrens, "Disney's New Drama: Dissension; Angry Shareholders Turn Harsh Spotlight on CEO Eisner," *The Washington Post,* March 1, 2004

Bruce Orwall and Peter Grant, "Mouse Trap: Disney, Struggling to Regain Glory, Gets $48.7 Billion Bid from Comcast—Already on Defense, Eisner Faces Biggest Challenge of Nearly 20-Year Reign—Cable Giant's Huge Ambitions," *The Wall Street Journal,* February 12, 2004

"ABC, Inc.'," Hoover's, Inc., Hoover's Company Profiles, May 12, 2004

Bruce Orwall, "Disney to Close Go.Com `Portal,' Absorb Internet Tracking Stock," *The Wall Street Journal,* January 30, 2001

Jacqueline Doherty, "Wishing on a Star: There's Lots of Magic Left at Disney—With or without Its Chief Mouseketeer," Barron's, November 4, 2002

Module 3

3M Company 2004 and 2003 Annual Reports and 10-K Reports

Michael Arndt with Diane Brady, "3M's Rising Star; Jim Mcnerney Is Racking Up Quite a Record at 3M. Now, Can He Rev Up Its Innovation Machine?" *BusinessWeek,* April 12, 2004, 62, Number 3878

Jerry Useem, "[3M] + [General Electric] = ? ; Jim Mcnerney Thinks He Can Turn 3M from a Good Company into a Great One—With a Little Help from His Former Employer, General Electric," *Fortune,* August 12, 2002, 127, Vol. 146, Issue: 3

Simon London, "When Quality Is Not Quite Enough," *Financial Times* (FT.Com), July 14, 2002

Module 4

Cisco Systems, Inc. 2004, 2003, and 2001 10-K Reports

Cisco Systems, Inc. 2004, 2003, and 2001 Annual Reports

John Chambers: "We Never Lost Track," *BusinessWeek* online, November 24, 2003

"Chambers: Stock Options Inspire Innovation," *BusinessWeek* online, December 22, 2003.

Module 5

The Gillette Company 2003 and 2004 10-K Reports

The Gillette Company 2003 and 2004 Annual Reports

Charles Forelle, "Gillette's Profit and Sales Jump; Restructuring Starts To Pay Off," *The Wall Street Journal,* April 30, 2004

Charles Forelle, "Gillette Earnings Are Squeezed by Cost-Reduction Expenses," *The Wall Street Journal,* January 31, 2003

Module 6

Hewlett-Packard Company 2004, 2003, and 2002 Annual Reports and 10-K Reports

Pui-Wing Tam, "H-P Posts Big Loss Due to Compaq Purchase," *The Wall Street Journal,* August 28, 2002

Quentin Hardy, "We Did It; Carly Fiorina's Boast: HP Pulled Off a Complex Merger and Saved $3.5 Billion. Her Sales Pitch: We Can Work This Magic on Your Company," *Forbes,* August 11, 2003, 76, Volume 171 Issue 16

Stephen Manning, "Fiorina: Compaq Merger Was Critical for HP," *Associated Press Newswires,* October 10, 2003, 17:49

"Carly Fiorina, Up Close-How Shrewd Strategic Moves in Grueling Proxy Battle Let H-P Chief Take Control," *The Wall Street Journal,* January 13, 2003.

San Jose Mercury News, Calif.," Hewlett-Packard's Compaq Purchase Proves Beneficial," KRTBN Knight-Ridder Tribune Business News: *San Jose Mercury News,* April 13, 2003

Module 7

Verizon Communications, Inc. 2003 and 2004 Annual Reports and 10-K Reports

Julie Creswell, "Ivan Seidenberg, CEO of Verizon, Vows to Overpower the Cable Guys by Plowing Billions into a '90s-Style Broadband Buildout. But Will He Really? Or Is the Most Powerful Man in Telecom Pulling a Megabluff?" *Fortune,* May 31, 2004

Steve Rosenbush, Tom Lowry, Roger O. Crockett, and Brian Grow, "Verizon: Take That, Cable; It Seeks to Reclaim Lost Ground with a Gutsy Plunge into Pay-TV Services," *BusinessWeek,* May 24, 2004, 81, Number 3884

Steve Rosenbush, "Verizon's Mega-Makeover Its Network Upgrade May Create a New Industry Standard," *BusinessWeek,* March 31, 2003, 68, Number 3826

"Verizon's Daring Vision," *BusinessWeek,* August 4, 2003, 112, Number 3844

Almar Latour, "Verizon Revenue Increases 3.9%—Wireless Business Surges, But Profit Plunges on Costs of Huge Employee Buyout," *The Wall Street Journal,* April 28, 2004, B5

Scott Moritz, "'Tough Spot for Verizon on Debt Front," Thestreet.Com, 10/25/2002 02:55 PM EDT

Module 8

Pfizer, Inc. 2003 and 2004 Annual Reports and 10-K Reports

Bill Alpert, "Drug War: Who Wins and Loses in the Brawl over Cholesterol-Lowering Medications," *Barron's,* June 14, 2004, 21

Andrew Bary, "Buying Time Again: Corporate Earnings Are Running Ahead of Stocks; How High Can the S&P 500 Go This Year?," *Barron's,* May 31, 2004, 17

Allison Fass, "Make War, Not Love; Pfizer's Shrinking Viagra Sales," *Forbes,* May 10, 2004, 56, Volume 173, Issue 10

John Carey and Michael Arndt, "Making Pills the Smart Way; Drugmakers Are Revamping Factories to Save Money and Avoid Production Mishaps," *BusinessWeek,* May 3, 2004, 102, Number 3881

Matthew Herper and Robert Langreth, "The Immortal Pill; Pfizer's Plans for Lipitor's Successor," *Forbes,* April 26, 2004, 50, Volume 173, Issue 9

Jeffrey E. Garten, "The Right Remedy for Pricey Drugs," *BusinessWeek,* April 12, 2004, 28, Number 3878

Scott Hensley, "Pfizer's Earnings Dropped by Half in First Quarter," *The Wall Street Journal,* April 21, 2004

Module 9

Midwest Air Group, Inc. 2003 and 2004 10-K Reports

Midwest Air Group, Inc. 2003 and 2004 Annual Reports

"Business Brief—Midwest Express Holding Inc.: Unions Agree to Concessions in Bid to Avert Reorganization," *The Wall Street Journal,* July 14, 2003, B2

Module 10

The Procter & Gamble Company 2003 and 2004 10-K Reports

The Procter & Gamble Company 2003 and 2004 Annual Reports

Robert Berner, Nanette Byrnes, and Wendy Zellner, "P&G Has Rivals in a Wringer; Colgate and Unilever Are Hurting As It Rolls Out Creative Products and Marketing," *BusinessWeek,* October 4, 2004, 74, Volume 3902.

Bethany McLean, "Weighing eBay's Options How profitable is eBay? Hard to say. And that could be a problem, "Fortune, 31 May 2004

Mark Maremont, "Cash Flow', a Highly Touted Measure of Strength, Is Open to Interpretation," *The Wall Street Journal,* March 5, 2002

Module 11

Johnson & Johnson 2003 and 2004 Annual Reports and 10-K Reports

Gregory Zuckerman and Scott Hensley, "Drug-Stock Ills Are Hard to Cure," *The Wall Street Journal,* December 21, 2004, C1

Scott Hensley and Thomas M. Burton, "Johnson & Johnson—Guidant Deal Constructs a Cardiac Powerhouse," *The Wall Street Journal,* December 17, 2004, B5

Scott Hensley, "A Takeover of Guidant Won't Fix Pharmaceutical Problems at J&J," *The Wall Street Journal,* December 13, 2004, A3

Module 12

Kimberly-Clark 2003 and 2004 Annual Reports and 10-K Reports

Allison Fass, "Diaper Rash; Kimberly-Clark," *Forbes,* April 26, 2004, Volume 173, Issue 9

Edited By Monica Roman, "Paper Cuts at Kimberly?" *BusinessWeek,* March 8, 2004, 41, Number 3873

Matthew Boyle, "Brand Killers; Store Brands Aren't for Losers Anymore. In Fact, They're Downright Sizzling and That Scares the Soap Out of the Folks Who Bring Us Tide and Minute Maid and Alpo and . . . ," *Fortune,* August 11, 2003, 88

Aliya Sternstein, "Paper Chase; Procter & Gamble," *Forbes,* March 17, 2003, 40, Volume 171, Issue 06

Matthew Boyle, "Dueling Diapers; Think Big Companies Can't Innovate? Look How Kimberly-Clark and P&G Are Fighting Over Disposable Training Pants," *Fortune,* February 17, 2003, 115, Vol. 147, Issue: 3

Robert Levering, Milton Moskowitz, Ann Harrington and Christopher Tkaczyk, "100 Best Companies to Work For," *Fortune,* January 20, 2003, 127, Vol. 147, Issue: 1

"Business Brief-Kimberly—Clark Corp.: Net Climbs 8.9%, As Cost Cuts Offset Rising Materials Prices," *The Wall Street Journal,* July 23, 2004

"Consumer Products Brief—Kimberly-Clark Corp.: First-Quarter Profit Rose 15% on Weak Dollar, U.S. Sales," *The Wall Street Journal,* April 23, 2004, A10

Sarah Ellison, "Kimberly-Clark Raises Profit Target," *The Wall Street Journal,* April 13, 2004, B3

Sarah Ellison, "Kimberly-Clark To Reorganize; High-Ranking Official To Retire—Split between Developing and Developed Markets Is Planned for Businesses," *The Wall Street Journal,* January 20, 2004, A3

"Consumer Products Brief—Kimberly-Clark Corp.: Argentine Plant to Get Upgrade with Investment of $12 Million," *The Wall Street Journal,* December 29, 2003, C3

Sarah Ellison, "Kimberly-Clark Slashes Outlook for Second Time," *The Wall Street Journal,* December 12, 2002, B7

Sarah Ellison," Kimberly-Clark: Paper Tiger?—CEO Falk to Give Forecast Amid Multiple Challenges, Rivalries," *The Wall Street Journal,* December 11, 2002, B3

ROE = Net Income/Average Equity

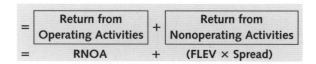

RNOA = NOPAT/Average NOA

where

NOPAT is net operating profit after tax

NOA is net operating assets

Net Operating Assets (NOA) = Net Financial Obligations (NFO) + Stockholders' Equity

NOPAT = (Sales − Operating Expenses) × [1 − (Tax Expense/Pretax Income)]

Ratio	Definition
ROE: return on equity	Net Income/Average Equity
RNOA: return on net operating assets	NOPAT/Average NOA
NOPAT: net operating profit after tax	Sales and other operating revenues less operating expenses such as cost of sales, taxes, selling, general, and administrative; it excludes nonoperating revenues and expenses such as those from financial assets and liabilities
NOA: net operating assets	Current and long-term operating assets less current and long-term operating liabilities; it excludes investments in securities, short- and long-term interest-bearing debt, and capitalized lease obligations
FLEV: financial leverage	Average NFO/Average Equity
NFO: net financial obligations	Financial (nonoperating) obligations less financial (nonoperating) assets
Spread	RNOA − NFR
NFR: net financial rate	NFE/Average NFO
NFE: net financial expense	NOPAT − Net income; it includes interest expense less revenues from nonoperating assets, net of tax

Distinguishing Operating and Nonoperating Assets and Liabilities

Typical GAAP Balance Sheet [Nonoperating (Financial) Items Highlighted]	
Current assets	**Current liabilities**
Cash and cash equivalents	Short-term notes and interest payable
Short-term investments	Accounts payable
Accounts receivable	Accrued liabilities
Inventories	Deferred income tax liabilities
Prepaid expenses	Current maturities of long-term debt
Deferred income tax assets	
	Long-term liabilities
Long-term assets	Bonds and notes payable
Long-term investments in securities	Capitalized lease obligations
Property, plant & equipment, net	Pension and other postretirement liabilities
Natural resources	Deferred income tax liabilities
Equity method investments	
Intangible assets	**Minority interest**
Deferred income tax assets	
Capitalized lease assets	
Other long-term assets	**Total stockholders' equity**

Simplified Operating and Nonoperating Balance Sheet

	Assets	Liabilities
Net Operating Assets (NOA) . . . . (Assets − Liabilities)	Current Operating Assets Long-Term Operating Assets	Current Operating Liabilities Long-Term Operating Liabilities
Net Financial Obligations (NFO) . . . . . (Liabilities − Assets)	Financial Assets (Nonoperating)	Financial Obligations (Nonoperating)
		Equity
Equity (NOA-NFO)		Stockholders' Equity
	Total Assets	Total Liabilities and Equity

Distinguishing Operating, Nonoperating, Core, and Transitory Income

	Core	Transitory
Operating	Sales; cost of goods sold; selling, general and administrative expenses; research and advertising expenses; income taxes	Gains and losses on sales of operating assets; operating asset write-downs; nonrecurring restructuring accruals
Nonoperating	Interest revenues and expenses; dividend revenues; hedging gains and losses	Debt retirement gains and losses; gains and losses on discontinued operations

$$\text{RNOA} = \text{NOPAT/Average Net Operating Assets} = \underbrace{\text{NOPAT/Sales}}_{\textbf{Margin}} \times \underbrace{\text{Sales/Average Net Operating Assets}}_{\textbf{Turnover}}$$

Net Operating Profit Margin Analysis

Gross Profit Margin (GPM) = Gross Profit/Sales
Operating Expense Margin (OEM) = Operating Expenses/Sales

Net Operating Asset Turnover Analysis

Net Operating Asset Turnover (NOAT) = Sales/Average Net Operating Assets
Accounts Receiable Turnover (ART) = Sales/Average Accounts Receivable
Average Collection Period = Accounts Receivable/Average Daily Sales
Inventory Turnover (INVT) = Cost of Goods Sold/Average Inventory
Average Inventory Days Outstanding = Inventory/Average Daily Cost of Goods Sold
Long-Term Operating Asset Turnover (LTOAT) = Sales/Average Long-Term Operating Assets
Accounts Payable Turnover (APT) = Cost of Goods Sold/Average Accounts Payable
Net Operating Working Capital Turnover (NOWCT) = Net Sales/Average Net Operating Working Capital

Average Cash Cycle = Average Collection Period +	Modified Average Inventory Days Outstanding	−	Modified Average Payable Days Outstanding

Liquidity and Solvency Analysis

Current Ratio = Current Assets/Current Liabilities
Quick Ratio = (Cash + Marketable Securities + Accounts Receivables)/Current Liabilities
Debt-to-Equity = Total Liabilities/Stockholders' Equity
Long-Term Debt-to-Equity = Long-Term Debt/Stockholders' Equity

Times Interest Earned = Earnings before Interest and Taxes/Interest Expense

Operating Cash Flow to Liabilities = Net Cash Flow from Operations/Total Liabilities

Common Size Analysis

Common-Size Percent (%) = (Analysis Period Amount/Base Period Amount) × 100

Module 4

Revenue recognition criterias: Revenue must be (1) **realized or realizable**, and (2) **earned**

Balance Sheet Effects of Euro Strengthening versus the Dollar

Currency	Assets	=	Liabilities	+	Equity
$US weakens	Increase	=	Increase	+	Increase
$US strengthens	Decrease	=	Decrease	+	Decrease

Tax Expense = Taxes Paid ± Changes in Deferred Tax Assets and Liabilities

Gain or Loss on Asset Sale = Asset Sale Proceeds − Asset Book Value

Income Items Categorized by Core versus Transitory and Operating versus Nonoperating

	Core	Transitory
Operating	• Revenues • Cost of goods sold • Selling, general and administrative expense • Footnoted employee stock option expense • Severance cost portion of pension expense • Gains and losses from hedging of foreign currencies and commodities	• Restructuring costs (unless recurring) • Asset write-downs • Goodwill impairment expense • Gains and losses from asset sales • Merger and acquisition expense, including purchased research and development expense • Litigation settlements and insurance proceeds • Extraordinary items tied to operations
Nonoperating	• Interest revenue and expense • Dividend revenue • Interest, expected return, and amortization portions of pension expense • Unrealized gains and losses from income on investments categorized as trading securities • Gains and losses from hedging related to interest costs	• Gains and losses on sales of investments, excluding "trading securities" • Income and losses on discontinued operations and gains and losses on disposal of discontinued operations • Extraordinary items not tied to operations (gains and losses on early debt retirement)

Module 5

Reconciliation of Allowance for Uncollectible Accounts

Beginning allowance for uncollectible accounts
Add: Provision for uncollectible accounts
Less: Write-offs of accounts receivable
_____
Ending allowance for uncollectible accounts

Accounts receivable (gross)
Less: Allowance for uncollectible accounts
_____
Accounts receivable (net)

Cost of Goods Sold Computation

> Beginning inventory (prior period balance sheet)
> + Inventory purchases and/or production
> ---
> Cost of goods available for sale
> − Ending inventory (current period balance sheet)
> ---
> Cost of goods sold (current income statement)

Components of Depreciation Expense Computation:
1. **Useful life.** Period of time over which the asset is expected to generate cash inflows
2. **Salvage value.** Expected disposal amount for the asset at the end of its useful life
3. **Depreciation rate.** An estimate of how the asset will be used up over its useful life

Depreciation Expense = Depreciation Base × Depreciation Rate

Straight-line Depreciation

Depreciation Base	Depreciation Rate
Cost − Salvage value	1/Estimated useful life

Double-Declining Balance Depreciation

Depreciation Base	Depreciation Rate
Net Book Value = Cost − Accumulated Depreciation	2 × SL rate

Module 6

Intercorporate Investment Diagram

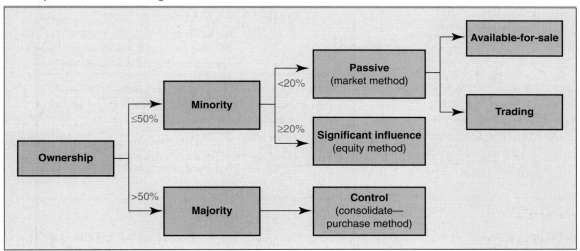

Investment Type, Accounting Treatment, and Financial Statement Effects

	Accounting	Balance Sheet Effects	Income Statement Effects	Cash Flow Effects
Passive	Market method	Investment account is reported at current market value	Dividends and capital gains affect income Interim changes in market value may or may not affect income depending on classification	Dividend and sale proceeds are cash inflows Purchases are cash outflows
Significant influence	Equity method	Investment account equals percent owned of investee company's equity*	Dividends reduce investment account Investor reports income equal to percent owned of investee income Capital gains are income	Dividend and sale proceeds are cash inflows Purchases are cash outflows
Control	Consolidation	Balance sheets of investor and investee are combined	Income statements of investor and investee are combined (and sale of investee yields capital gain or loss)	Cash flows of investor and investee are combined (and sale/purchase of investee yields cash inflow/outflow)

*Investments are often acquired at purchase prices in excess of book value (on average, market prices are 1.5 times book value for public companies). In this case the investment account exceeds the proportionate ownership of the investee's equity. We discuss this later in the module.

Accounting Treatment for Available-for-Sale and for Trading Investments

Investment Classification	Reporting of Market Value Changes	Reporting Dividends Received and Gains and Losses on Sale
Available-for-Sale (AFS)	Market value changes bypass the income statement and are reported directly in *other comprehensive income* (OCI) of equity	Reported as *other income* in income statement
Trading (T)	Market value changes are reported in the income statement as unrealized gains or losses; impacts equity via retained earnings	Same as above

Equity Method Accounting Summarized as follows:
- Investments are initially recorded at their purchase cost.
- Dividends received are treated as a recovery of the investment and, thus, reduce the investment balance (dividends are *not* reported as income as with passive investments).
- The investor reports income equal to its percentage share of the reported income of the investee; the investment account is increased by that income or decreased by its share of any loss.
- The investment is *not* reported at market value as passive market investments are.

Module 7

Coupon (contract or stated) rate   The coupon rate of interest is stated in the bond contract. It is used to compute the dollar amount of (semiannual) interest payments that are paid to bondholders during the life of the bond issue.

Market (yield) rate   This is the interest rate that investors expect to earn on the investment for this debt security. This rate is used to price the bond issue.

Market value of bond = percent value of interest payments plus present value of principle payment(s)

Coupon Rate, Market Rate, and Bond Pricing

Coupon rate > market rate	→	Bond sells at a **premium** (above face amount)
Coupon rate = market rate	→	Bond sells at **par** (at face amount)
Coupon rate < market rate	→	Bond sells at a **discount** (below face amount)

Cash interest paid		Cash interest paid
+ Amortization of discount	or	− Amortization of premium
Bond interest expense		Bond interest expense

Gain or Loss on Bond Repurchase = Bonds Payable, Net − Repurchase Payment

Module 8

Components of Stockholders' Equity:
*   Contributed capital: common stock, preferred stock, additional paid-in capital, treasury stock, minority interest
*   Earned capital: retained earnings, accumulated other comprehensive income (AOCI)

Stock Issuance:
*   Common stock is increased by number of shares issued × par value
*   Additional paid-in capital is increased for the balance of the issue price

Treasury Stock:
*   Record at purchase cost
*   When reissued, treasury stock is reduced by the cost of the shares reissued and the balance is reflected as an increase in additional paid-in capital

Dividends and Splits:
*   Cash: reduce retained earnings by the cash dividends paid
*   Stock (small): reduce retained earnings by the market value of the shared distributed and increase common stock and additional paid-in capital by the market value of the shares issued
*   Stock (large): reduce retained earnings by the par value of the shares issued and increase common stock by the same amount (no increase in additional paid-in capital)
*   Split: no accounting entry (adjust number of shares outstanding and their par value, if any)

Components of Comprehensive Income:
*   Currency translation adjustment
*   Unrealized gains and losses on available-for-sale securities
*   Minimum pension liability adjustment
*   Unrealized gains and losses on certain derivatives

Module 9

Financial Statement Effects of Lease Methods for the Lessee

Lease Type	Assets	Liabilities	Expenses	Cash Flows
Capital	Lease asset reported	Lease liability reported	Depreciation and interest	Same—per lease contract
Operating	Lease asset not reported	Lease liability not reported	Rent expense	

Financial Statement Effects of Defined Benefit Plans

Balance Sheet				Income Statement	
Cash + Noncash Assets	=	Liabilities	+	Contributed Capital + Retained Earnings	Revenues — Expenses
		Pension Obligation			— Service Cost
					Interest Cost
		− Pension Investments			Investment Returns
		Net Pension Liability			Net Pension Cost

	Beginning balance of pension obligation
+	Service cost
+	Interest cost
−	Benefits paid to retirees
=	**Ending balance of pension obligation**

	Beginning balance of pension investment account
+	Actual returns on invested assets
+	Company contributions to pension plan assets
−	Benefits paid to retirees
=	**Ending balance of pension investment account**

Funded status = Fair market value of pension investments − Pension obligation

Pension Liability Recognized on Balance Sheet

	Funded status at end of year
±	Unrecognized net actuarial loss
±	Unrecognized prior service cost
=	**Accrued benefit liability**

Pension Expense Recognized on Income Statement

	Service cost
+	Interest cost
−	Expected return on pension plan investments
±	Amortization of deferred losses (gains)
=	**Pension expense**

Module 10

Common Income Statement Adjustments

---

1. Separate core (persistent) and transitory items—examples:
   a. Gains and losses relating to
      (1) Asset sales on long-term assets and investments
      (2) Asset write-downs of long-term assets and inventories
      (3) Stock issuances by subsidiaries
      (4) Debt retirements
   b. Transitory items reported after income from continued operations
      (1) Discontinued operations
      (2) Extraordinary items
      (3) Changes in accounting principles
   c. Restructuring expenses
   d. Merger costs
   e. LIFO liquidation gains
   f. Liability accruals deemed excessive
   g. Gains and losses from changes in deferred tax valuation allowance

2. Separate operating and nonoperating items—examples:
   a. Treating interest revenue and expense, and investment gains and losses, as nonoperating
   b. Treating pension service cost as operating, and pension interest costs and expected returns as nonoperating
   c. Treating debt retirement gains and losses as nonoperating
   d. Treating income and losses from discontinued operations as nonoperating
   e. Treating short-term fluctuations in tax expense as nonoperating

3. Include expenses not reflected in net income—examples:
   a. Employee stock option expense
   b. Inadequate reserves for bad debts or asset impairment
   c. Reductions in R&D, advertising, and other discretionary expenses that were made to achieve short-term income targets

---

Common Balance Sheet Adjustments

---

1. Separate nonoperating assets and liabilities—examples:
   a. Eliminate assets and liabilities from discontinued operations
   b. Write-down impaired assets and/or goodwill

2. Include operating assets and liabilities not reflected in balance sheet—examples:
   a. Capitalize assets and liabilities from operating leases
   b. Consolidate off-balance-sheet investments
      (1) Equity method investments
      (2) Variable interest entities (VIEs)
   c. Accrue understated liabilities and assets

Common Statement of Cash Flow Adjustments

1. Adjust operating cash flows for nonoperating items—examples:
    a. Adjust discretionary costs (advertising, R&D, maintenance) to normal, expected levels
    b. Adjust current operating assets (receivables, inventory) to normal, expected levels
    c. Adjust current operating liabilities (payables, accruals) to normal, expected levels

2. Adjust cash flows for transitory items—examples:
    a. Separate (exclude) operating cash flows from tax benefits due to exercise of employee stock options

3. Review assignment of cash flows and reassign them, if necessary, to operating, investing, or financing sections—examples:
    a. Separate and reassign operating cash inflows from asset securitization to financing section
    b. Separate and reassign operating cash flows from discontinued operations to investing section

Forecasting Using Turnover Rates

$$\text{Forecasted Year-End Account Balance} = \frac{\text{Forecasted Sales (or COGS)}}{\text{Estimated Turnover Rate}}$$

Module 11

Discounted Cash Flow (DCF) Model

$$\text{Firm Value} = \text{Present Value of Expected Free Cash Flows to Firm}$$

$$\text{FCFF} = \text{NOPAT} - \text{Increase in NOA}$$

where
    NOPAT = Net operating profit after tax
    NOA = Net operating assets

Residual Operating Income (ROPI) Model

$$\text{Firm Value} = \text{NOA} + \text{Present Value of Expected ROPI}$$

where
    NOA = Net operating assets
    ROPI = Residual operating income

$$\text{ROPI} = \text{NOPAT} - \underbrace{(\text{NOA}_{\text{Beg}} \times r_w)}_{\text{Expected NOPAT}}$$

where
    NOA_{Beg} = Net operating assets at beginning (*Beg*) of period
    r_w = Weighted average cost of capital (WACC)